Citrix® Access Suite 4 Advanced Concepts: The Official Guide, Second Edition

Citrix® Access Suite 4 Advanced Concepts: The Official Guide, Second Edition

STEVE **KAPLAN**
ANDY **JONES**

McGraw-Hill/Osborne

New York   Chicago   San Francisco
Lisbon   London   Madrid   Mexico City   Milan
New Delhi   San Juan   Seoul   Singapore   Sydney   Toronto

The McGraw-Hill Companies

McGraw-Hill/Osborne
2100 Powell Street, 10th Floor
Emeryville, California 94608
U.S.A.

To arrange bulk purchase discounts for sales promotions, premiums, or fund-raisers, please contact **McGraw-Hill**/Osborne at the above address.

Citrix® Access Suite 4 Advanced Concepts: The Official Guide, Second Edition

This book provides a summary of information regarding advanced concepts of the Citrix Access Suite. To further your knowledge, Citrix offers a full curriculum of structured educational opportunities, including instructor-led training through Citrix Authorized Learning Centers, eLearning, and Citrix Certification exams.

For in-depth training on the Citrix Access Suite, or to prepare to earn your Citrix Certified Administrator (CCA), Citrix Certified Enterprise Administrator (CCEA), or Citrix Certified Integration Architect (CCIA), we recommend that you visit www.citrix.com/edu.

34567890 CUS CUS 019876

ISBN 0-07-226293-1

Acquisitions Editor
Wendy Rinaldi
Project Editor
Mark Karmendy
Acquisitions Coordinator
Alex McDonald
Technical Editor
Jennifer Lang
Copy Editor
Marcia Baker
Proofreader
Susie Elkind

Indexer
Claire Splan
Composition
International Typesetting
and Composition
Illustration
International Typesetting
and Composition
Cover Design
Pattie Lee

This book was composed with Adobe® InDesign®.

I would like to thank my wife and children for allowing me the time and occasionally aiding in helping me focus on this project. I would also like to thank my sister Donna Jean and her husband Stan for cutting a check that changed the course of my life. Thanks guys, I owe you more than you know! Lastly, I would be remiss if I didn't thank Steve, Wendy, Jennifer, Alex, Mark, Ali, and all the rest of the Citrix and McGraw-Hill teams for helping to make this book a reality.

—Andy Jones

ABOUT THE AUTHORS

Steve Kaplan is president of AccessFlow and also runs By The Bell, an ROI consulting firm dedicated to helping organizations assess the value of implementing enterprise access platforms. Kaplan is co-author of *Citrix Access Suite for Windows Server 2003: The Official Guide* (McGraw-Hill/Osborne), and also co-authored the first two editions. He has written dozens of articles on subjects such as security, disaster recovery, and the effect of regulatory compliance on IT, and has spoken across the globe at events such as Citrix 2005 Asia Pacific iForum, 2005 Continuity Insights Management Conference, and 2005 VMworld. Kaplan has held positions on the advisory boards of several industry manufactures including Microsoft, and he is a Microsoft MVP (Most Valuable Professional) for Terminal Server. Kaplan holds a BS in Business Administration from U.C. Berkeley and an MBA from Northwestern's J.L. Kellogg Graduate School of Management.

Anthony "Andy" Jones (CCIA, CCEA, CCI, MCSE+I, MCT, MCIW) is an industry expert in Access Infrastructure and technologies surrounding and supporting the solution. He is currently an Area Service Director for MTM Technologies, the premier Citrix Platinum reseller in North America, where he manages the professional services group for the Ohio Valley. He provides comprehensive solutions focused on Citrix and Microsoft technologies for clients ranging from 50 to 50,000 users, focusing mainly on architecting and deploying Access Infrastructure solutions for enterprise customers. One of Andy's primary focuses is in developing best practices, processes and methodologies surrounding Access Infrastructure that take into consideration and integrate with virtually every part of a customer's infrastructure. He holds a BA and an MA in Communications from Morehead State University. Andy has co-authored *Deploying Citrix MetaFrame Presentation Server 3.0 with Windows Server 2003 Terminal Services* (Syngress). He also actively contributes articles to the community site www.msterminalservices.org. Andy is currently based in Cincinnati, OH, where he lives with his wife and children. He enjoys flying when his schedule permits!

AT A GLANCE

CONTENTS

Part I

An Introduction to Citrix Access Suite

Part II

Access Suite: Administration, Maintenance, and Troubleshooting

FOREWORD

What is access? Access is a means to an end—the means of closing the gap that separates ideas, understanding, knowledge, insight, and action. Access facilitates, access informs, access empowers, and access has the ability to transform the way we work, live, play and learn. From the telegraph to radio to television and the Internet, technological evolution over the past 100 years has focused on advancing access to create a wireless, always-connected world without borders. In today's information economy, access is more relevant than ever. Access creates opportunities for businesses and individuals to communicate and collaborate in ways that drive economic growth and improve the quality of our lives. Access means the ability to communicate wherever, whenever, and on any device—a quick glance at e-mail on a smartphone while rounding the golf course, secure connectivity to vital corporate data from a laptop in a hotel room, real-time patient updates while toting a tablet PC from the operating room to the recovery room. Boundless and easy information access transforms work from just being a place to an activity and is the engine driving the successful 21st century enterprise.

In today's global business climate, competitive advantage pivots on how well companies offer their employees access to information. Since Citrix's founding in 1989 its vision has been clear—to simplify information access to allow people to do their jobs more effectively and productively. A well-thought-out access strategy extends beyond tactical implementations and must relate to the organization as a whole as well as to individual needs for information and collaboration. Increasingly, this information—whether financial data, personal identity information, customer transaction history, credit card numbers, or private healthcare records—resides in applications.

This is where Citrix comes in. Citrix's core objective is to offer the most comprehensive platform for delivering applications—whether client/server applications, web applications, or desktop applications—through the best access experience. Citrix does this by securely offering a full range of access methods—virtualization of client/server applications, optimization of web applications, and in the near future by streaming desktop applications. In this way, the Citrix Access Platform can bring information to you everywhere that critical business decisions are being made, whether at headquarters, customer sites, airports, hotels, and even taxis.

This book is designed to help you plan, deploy, and administer the Citrix Access Suite 4, the most complete solution for meeting the needs of on-demand access and helping your enterprise to run more cost-efficiently and grow faster. By providing secure, easy, and instant access to information anytime from anywhere, using any device, your employees and customers can realize the full potential of an on-demand enterprise. The Access Suite 4 represents the most comprehensive access platform available today to enable flexible, mobile, and secure access to even the most widely dispersed enterprises. Nearly 50 million people and more than 160,000 organizations around the world currently rely on this market-proven access philosophy to drive their business forward and sustain competitive advantage.

Products comprising the suite include the industry-standard for application virtualization, Citrix Presentation Server 4; the fastest-growing enterprise single sign-on (ESSO) solution, Citrix Password Manager 4; and a market-leading SSL VPN, the Citrix Access Gateway.

Citrix Presentation Server 4 has extended the capabilities of the suite with new features that improve resource usage, facilitate better mobile device integration, yield faster printing, and offer greater application support. The new Citrix Password Manager 4 features upgrades that streamline management and deployment, improve enterprise security and regulatory compliance, and power superior user productivity. The Citrix Access Gateway, an SSL VPN, offers unprecedented information control capabilities with Advanced Access Control. This software option, unique to Citrix, increases granular control over how information is accessed, allowing administrators to set policies to allow or deny viewing, editing, printing, and saving documents depending on the user's identity, device, location, and connection. All products in the suite extend access to more devices and users, and are also supported on all 64-bit computing environments. Moreover, Citrix has entered a new market with its Citrix NetScaler systems, which improve user experiences with corporate applications and Citrix Access Suite products. Citrix NetScaler speeds up access to web applications, supports more users on the same infrastructure, and scales to optimize some of the world's most popular web sites.

The authors of this book, Steve Kaplan and Andy Jones, have had something to do with this success. They come from two companies that are founding members of a select group of Platinum-level Citrix Solution Advisors. They have contributed to our success and the increasing adoption of the Citrix vision of access infrastructure and the access platform for the on-demand enterprise with both how-to information and hands-on implementation. In a combination of cutting-edge ideas and market-tested experience, the authors present the very latest on our portfolio of integrated solutions, along with best practices based on years of setting up hundreds of Citrix environments for customers of all sizes. I am grateful to them for their expertise and proud to contribute this foreword. I am also very proud of the Citrix Product Development Team for researching, validating, and documenting the contents of this book.

While access infrastructure for the on-demand enterprise simplifies the complexity of information systems, successful implementation requires careful planning and skillful administration. That's what this book is all about, and anyone looking to deliver the best access experience to work more productively and run their IT departments at lower cost will benefit from reading it.

—By Russ Naples, Vice President of Product Development
for the Access Management Group for Citrix

ACKNOWLEDGMENTS

We would like to thank the following departments within Citrix Systems, Inc., for their contribution to the content of the book:

- ▼ Product Development
- ■ Technical Communication
- ■ Consulting Services
- ■ Technical Support
- ▲ System Engineering

Also a special thanks to all of the Test Engineers within Product Development for researching, validating, and documenting the content for this book. Additionally, Jennifer Lang, Software Test Engineer and Ali Shahheidari, Senior Manager, Product Development, worked many tireless days and weekends writing, coordinating all the Citrix resources, and ensuring content accuracy.

In addition to Citrix's help, Tim Reeser and Alan Wood of 3TSystems contributed through their efforts on the first edition.

INTRODUCTION

This edition of the *Advanced Concepts Guide* expands and updates the first edition to focus on Citrix Access Suite 4. As with the first edition, this book represents our efforts to assist Citrix in turning their internal documents into a comprehensive book encompassing best practices and recommendations for the Citrix Access Suite.

How This Book Differs from *Citrix Access Suite for Windows Server 2003: The Official Guide*

McGraw-Hill/Osborne's companion book is written for two audiences: business decision makers who evaluate enterprise IT options, and the IT administrators responsible for implementing and maintaining access infrastructure. It covers both the technical and business requirements of implementing a Citrix access platform capable of accommodating thousands of users running their desktop applications from central datacenters. Topics such as Windows Terminal Server 2003, project and organizational management, and various third-party add-on applications are all discussed at length.

This guide is strictly a technical book focused on the planning, configuration, administration, and troubleshooting of the Citrix Access Suite. It provides in-depth analyses of the three Citrix Access Suite components: Citrix Presentation Server, Citrix Access Gateway, and Citrix Password Manager. This book is written for experienced IT administrators who want to improve their Citrix environments by incorporating best practices.

How This Book Is Organized

The book is divided into three main parts. Part I covers the concepts, planning, and configuration of the Citrix Access Suite. It is designed to assist in the pre-deployment of the different Citrix Access Suite components. It contains best practices and explanations of methods used by Citrix engineers in the planning and configuration of these components within different types of environments. Part I also includes a chapter covering security issues and guideline concerns in a Citrix Access Suite environment, with a focus on security related to the Citrix Access Suite itself.

Part II presents best practices for the administration, maintenance, and troubleshooting of the Citrix Access Suite. It is designed to assist in the daily administration and maintenance of Citrix Access Suite products. Part II is targeted to administrators who need to fine-tune their systems as well as troubleshoot issues that arise within the Citrix environment.

Part III comprises the appendices. Appendix A details error messages, including Independent Management Architecture (IMA) error codes, IMA subsystem tracing, Citrix Presentation Server console error codes, Resource Manager billing error codes, and event log warning and error messages intended to help in troubleshooting and resolving problems with Citrix Presentation Server. Appendix B is a table showing all registered Citrix ports. Appendix C outlines the various files, locations, and registry entries that are added to a system when Citrix Presentation Server Client for 32-bit Windows (Program Neighborhood Client), Web Client, and Program Neighborhood Agent are installed onto a client machine. Appendix D shows the Citrix *e*Labs hardware used for the test cases discussed in this book. Finally, Appendix E describes the Citrix Access Suite performance characteristics on 64-bit architecture and offers a discussion of the performance and scalability improvements you may realize when using Citrix Presentation Server 4.0 for Microsoft Windows Server 2003 x64 Edition.

We also include Note, Tip, Important, and Caution elements to supply additional detail to the text. A Note is meant to provide information when the general flow of the discussion is concentrating on a different area or is not as detailed as the Note itself. A Tip is a specific way to do or implement something being discussed. An Important is a specific piece of information that is emphasized in order to catch the reader's attention. A Caution is meant to alert the reader to watch out for a potential problem.

When registry entries are discussed, we have abbreviated the keys to save space. For example, HKEY_LOCAL_MACHINE is abbreviated throughout the text to HKLM.

Throughout the book, we include appropriate references to further documentation that can be accessed from http://support.citrix.com.

Contacting the Authors

We welcome your feedback and will incorporate appropriate suggestions into further releases of the book. You can contact Andy Jones at ajones@mtm.com and Steve Kaplan at skaplan@accessflow.com.

PART I

An Introduction to Citrix Access Suite

CHAPTER 1

Introduction to Citrix Access Suite and Components

"On-demand access" is becoming a commonplace term in the Information Technology (IT) vernacular. *On-demand access* gives users access to the information required to build business by providing easy, secure, and instant access to enterprise information and applications from anywhere, using any device or connection.

In addition to providing this ubiquitous access, on-demand access utilizes an effective access infrastructure strategy, which both simplifies IT complexity and strengthens administrative control. Access is more efficient, secure, and cost-effective. The Citrix Access Suite offers organizations the easiest and most cost-effective way to provide a single, secure point of access to enterprise applications and information on-demand. The suite ensures a consistent user experience anywhere, on any device or connection, while allowing IT staffs to centrally deliver, manage, monitor, and control enterprise resources.

This chapter introduces the Citrix Access Suite and the products of which it is comprised: Citrix Presentation Server, Citrix Access Gateway, and Citrix Password Manager. It also introduces Citrix NetScaler, which, while not part of the Access Suite, is often simultaneously deployed to enhance the users' access experience by maximizing the performance of their organization's web applications.

THE CITRIX ACCESS SUITE

The *Citrix Access Suite* is an integrated infrastructure for delivering applications and information resources as IT services to any user, regardless of device, connection, or location. Each product component of the Citrix Access Suite—Citrix Presentation Server, Citrix Access Gateway, and Citrix Password Manager—adds to the technology portfolio to solve myriad access challenges for an organization. All the products work together seamlessly to provide a secure, single point of access to enterprise applications and information on-demand, while ensuring a consistent user experience anywhere, anytime, using any device, over any connection.

While the following is not a comprehensive list, it contains some of the benefits provided by the Citrix Access Suite component products:

▼   **Citrix Presentation Server**   Lowers the cost of IT and greatly improves scalability, adaptability, and predictability through Application Centralization. Citrix Presentation Server 4.0 includes Citrix Conferencing Manager. Conferencing Manager provides intuitive application conferencing to eliminate the geographical distance between team members, thus increasing the productivity of meetings and enabling easy collaboration.

■   **Citrix Access Gateway**   Provides a secure, always-on, single point-of-access to all applications and protocols. The Advanced Access Control option manages both what can be accessed and what actions are permitted based on the user's role, location, and Advanced End-Point Analysis. *Advanced End-Point Analysis* automatically reconfigures the level of access as users roam among devices, locations, and connections.

▲ **Citrix Password Manager**   Lowers help desk costs, improves security, and simplifies user experience by providing password security and enterprise Single Sign On access to any application or information resource delivered through the Citrix Access Suite.

Citrix Presentation Server Editions

Citrix Presentation Server enables application virtualization using a centralized and secure architecture. Presentation Server enables IT to centrally deploy and manage applications, while providing secure access to these resources for users anywhere, on any device, and on any network.

Citrix Presentation Server 4.0 is available in three different editions: Standard, Advanced, and Enterprise.

Citrix Presentation Server, Standard Edition

Citrix Presentation Server, Standard Edition is the standard version for standalone point solution implementations with one server and with 1 to 15 concurrent users. Standard Edition feature highlights include the Web Interface for Citrix Presentation Server, user shadowing, the Secure Gateway, Universal Print Driver, client time-zone support, Novell NDS support, client device support, and Citrix Presentation Server Client support. Although more than one server can be used with the Standard Edition, this is rare because applications cannot be load-balanced across servers. Any application publishing must be done separately on each server with different names.

Citrix Presentation Server, Advanced Edition

Citrix Presentation Server, Advanced Edition, is the advanced version that includes all the Standard Edition features with the addition of Load Management. This upgrade is designed for use in farms with 2 to 20 servers and 15 to 1,000 concurrent users.

Citrix Presentation Server, Enterprise Edition

Citrix Presentation Server, Enterprise Edition, contains all the features included with the Advanced Edition, as well as additional features required for enterprise management. These extended features include Resource Manager, Installation Manager, a plug-in for Microsoft Operations Manager, and Network Manager. Enterprise Edition is designed for 20 or more servers.

Table 1-1 is a comparative matrix of the three different editions and enumerates the feature support available with each edition.

	Citrix Presentation Server 4.0, Standard Edition	Citrix Presentation Server 4.0, Advanced Edition	Citrix Presentation Server 4.0, Enterprise Edition
ENABLING THE GLOBAL ON-DEMAND ENTERPRISE			
Enhanced Connection Policies	x	x	x
Management Console for the Citrix Access Suite	x	x	x
Delegated Administration	x	x	x
Increased Large Server Farm Support	x	x	x
Custom Dashboard Views with Active Content			x
Report Center			x
Zone Preference and Failover			x
SMOOTHROAMING: Increasing Productivity Through Reliable Mobile Access			
Dynamic Display Reconfiguration	x	x	x
Workspace Control		x	x
Session Reliability		x	x
IMPROVING APPLICATION PERFORMANCE			
SpeedScreen Acceleration: Images	x	x	x
SpeedScreen Acceleration: Audio and Video	x	x	x
SpeedScreen Acceleration: Macromedia Flash	x	x	x
Web Interface Enhancements	x	x	x
Improved User Login Screens	x	x	x
Microsoft Remote Desktop Client (RDC) Support	x	x	x
Bidirectional Audio		x	x

Table 1-1. Citrix Presentation Server Feature Grid

	Citrix Presentation Server 4.0, Standard Edition	Citrix Presentation Server 4.0, Advanced Edition	Citrix Presentation Server 4.0, Enterprise Edition
PROVIDING A SECURE PLATFORM FOR REGULATORY COMPLIANCE			
FIPS-140	x	x	x
Section 508	x	x	x
ON-DEMAND LICENSING			
Citrix Access Suite Licensing	x	x	x
ADVANCED SHADOWING			
Cross-server Shadowing	x	x	x
Many-to-One Shadowing	x	x	x
One-to-Many Shadowing	x	x	x
Shadowing Indicator	x	x	x
Shadowing Taskbar	x	x	x
APPLICATION MANAGEMENT			
Anonymous User Support	x	x	x
Application Publishing	x	x	x
Content Publish	x	x	x
Program Neighborhood	x	x	x
TCP-based Browsing	x	x	x
APPLICATION PACKAGING AND DELIVERY			
Centrally Install and Uninstall Applications			x
Create Logical Server Groups			x
Customizable Project Details			x
Delivery Verification			x
Distribute Service Packs, Updates, and Files			x
MSI Support			x

Table 1-1.   Citrix Presentation Server Feature Grid (*Continued*)

	Citrix Presentation Server 4.0, Standard Edition	Citrix Presentation Server 4.0, Advanced Edition	Citrix Presentation Server 4.0, Enterprise Edition
Package Applications, Files, and Service Packs			x
Package Inventory			x
Packager Rollback			x
Schedule Package Delivery			x
Server Reboot Support			x
Support for the Unattended Installs			x
CENTRALIZED ADMINISTRATION			
Active Directory Support	x	x	x
Novell NDS Support	x	x	x
User Policies	x	x	x
Administrator Toolbar	x	x	x
Centralized Data Store	x	x	x
Citrix Administrative Accounts	x	x	x
Presentation Server Console	x	x	x
Citrix Web Console	x	x	x
Connection Control		x	x
CPU Prioritization		x	x
Windows Installer Support	x	x	x
CENTRALIZED LICENSE MANAGEMENT			
Centralized License Activation	x	x	x
Enterprise-wide License Pooling	x	x	x
Plug-and-Play Licensing	x	x	x
CLIENT MANAGEMENT			
Auto-client Update	x	x	x
Business Recovery	x	x	x

Table 1-1. Citrix Presentation Server Feature Grid (*Continued*)

	Citrix Presentation Server 4.0, Standard Edition	Citrix Presentation Server 4.0, Advanced Edition	Citrix Presentation Server 4.0, Enterprise Edition
ReadyConnect	x	x	x
Web-based Client Installation	x	x	x
NETWORK MANAGEMENT			
Monitor and Manage from Third-party Management Consoles			x
SNMP Monitoring Agent			x
PRINTER MANAGEMENT			
Citrix Universel Print Driver	x	x	x
Printer Auto-creation Log	x	x	x
Printer Driver Access Control	x	x	x
Printer Driver Replication	x	x	x
Printing Bandwidth Control	x	x	x
RESOURCE-BASED LOAD-BALANCING			
Instant Load-balancing Feedback		x	x
Load-balancing Reconnect Support		x	x
Schedule Application Availability		x	x
Specify Client IP Range		x	x
SCALABILITY			
Enterprise-class Scalability	x	x	x
Cross-subnet Administration	x	x	x
SYSTEM MONITORING AND ANALYSIS			
Application Monitoring			x
Customized Reporting			x
Summary Database and Reporting			x
Perform System Capacity Planning			x
Real-time Graphing and Alerting			x

Table 1-1.   Citrix Presentation Server Feature Grid (*Continued*)

	Citrix Presentation Server 4.0, Standard Edition	Citrix Presentation Server 4.0, Advanced Edition	Citrix Presentation Server 4.0, Enterprise Edition
Server Farm Monitoring			x
Track User Access to Applications			x
User-definable Metrics			x
Watcher Window			x
ICA Session Monitoring			x
WEB APPLICATION ACCESS			
Web Interface	x	x	x
Application Filtering and Caching	x	x	x
Support for Citrix Secure Access Manager	x	x	x
Enterprise Services			x
ACCESS TO LOCAL SYSTEM RESOURCES			
Auto-printer Creation	x	x	x
Automatic Drive Redirection	x	x	x
Client Drive Mapping	x	x	x
Clipboard Redirection	x	x	x
COM Port Redirection	x	x	x
PERFORMANCE			
Instant Mouse-click Feedback	x	x	x
Persistent Bitmap Caching	x	x	x
Priority Packet Tagging	x	x	x
SpeedScreen 3	x	x	x
Text-entry Prediction	x	x	x
SEAMLESS USER EXPERIENCE			
High-/True-color Depth and Resolution	x	x	x
16-bit Audio Support	x	x	x
Application Save Position	x	x	x

Table 1-1. Citrix Presentation Server Feature Grid (*Continued*)

	Citrix Presentation Server 4.0, Standard Edition	Citrix Presentation Server 4.0, Advanced Edition	Citrix Presentation Server 4.0, Enterprise Edition
Auto-client Reconnect	x	x	x
Client Printer Management Utility	x	x	x
Client Time Zone Support	x	x	x
Server-to-Client Content Redirection	x	x	x
Client-to-Server Content Redirection		x	x
Multimonitor Support	x	x	x
Panning and Scaling	x	x	x
Pass-Thru Authentication	x	x	x
Roaming User Reconnect	x	x	x
Seamless Windows	x	x	x
Win16 Multisession Support	x	x	x
UNIVERSAL CONNECTIVITY			
Universal Client Access	x	x	x
Support for Direct Asynch Dial-up	x	x	x
Support for TCP/IP, IPX, SPX, and NetBios	x	x	x
USER COLLABORATION			
Support for Citrix Conferencing Manager	x	x	x
SECURITY			
Secure Gateway	x	x	x
Delegated Administration	x	x	x
SSL 128-bit Encryption	x	x	x
TLS Encryption	x	x	x
Smart Card Support	x	x	x
SecureICA 128-bit Encryption	x	x	x
SOCKS 4 & 5 Support	x	x	x
Ticketing	x	x	x

Table 1-1.   Citrix Presentation Server Feature Grid (*Continued*)

Citrix Conferencing Manager

Presentations and conferencing have evolved from one-way presentation broadcasts and web conferencing to full collaboration and application conferencing. The trend toward "virtual" teams that work together from remote locations and different time zones is expanding because such teams can reduce overhead costs, drive new business, and optimize productivity.

The lack of information and communication systems' flexibility are often obstacles to enabling the on-demand enterprise because remote people cannot securely connect to the business information they need. *Citrix Conferencing Manager* remedies this by adding intuitive application conferencing to Citrix Presentation Server, helping to increase the productivity of meetings and enabling easy collaboration from different geographic locations.

Citrix Conferencing Manager integrates three components: a Microsoft Exchange/ Outlook calendar form; a Citrix Conferencing Manager interface that initiates, cancels, and manages the users and applications of the conferences; and Citrix Presentation Server's session shadowing features. These three components form an intuitive interface by which users create and join a collaborative conference session among multiple people. Teams can share application sessions, work together on documents of all kinds, and conduct online training, regardless of the location of individual team members, the access devices, or network connections they're using.

CITRIX ACCESS GATEWAY

Citrix Access Gateway is a universal SSL VPN appliance that provides a secure, single point-of-access to all applications and protocols. Access Gateway is deployed in an organization's DMZ, and secures all traffic with standards-based SSL. Remote users connect via a web-downloaded and -updated client, enjoying a rich, desk-like experience. Access Gateway combines deliver both an extremely secure, yet easy to deploy and use, access solution.

Citrix Access Gateway makes any enterprise resource available through a single point of access, securely delivered over the Internet using the best features of IPSec and SSL VPNs to standards-based security—without the need to configure client-side software. IT administrators simply enable network resources to be presented through Citrix Access Gateway, and then configure access control based on each user's business requirements.

Advanced Access Control

Advanced Access Control is a software option that increases control over how information is accessed and which actions the user can perform, such as print, save, launch, and view.

SmartAccess

The *SmartAccess* feature of Advanced Access Control delivers advanced policy-based control of Presentation Server applications and individual features, such as print and save.

SmoothRoaming

The *SmoothRoaming* component of Advanced Access Control enables users to move seamlessly between access scenarios and devices, automatically adapting access to the configuration policy settings.

CITRIX PASSWORD MANAGER

Managing passwords can be problematic. Users tend to forget multiple passwords, select easily guessed words for passwords, or store passwords in insecure places. These problems affect employee productivity, increase support costs, and even threaten system security. *Citrix Password Manager* provides password security and Single Sign On access to Windows-, web-, proprietary-, and host-based applications running in the Citrix environment. Citrix Password Manager drives down the costs and confusion in managing multiple passwords, while improving network security. Users authenticate once and Citrix Password Manager does the rest, monitoring all password-related events and automating end-user tasks, including logon and password changes. Citrix Password Manager simplifies computing for the end user, who has just one secure password to log on everywhere. This, in turn, helps to reduce the cost of supporting password problems and frees IT staff for more strategic projects.

> **NOTE** One large financial institution we worked with used to have 20.4% of its help desk calls related to password issues (this is about 5 percentage points below the average). After mandating that users implement complex passwords, the ratio of help-desk related password calls fell by half. Why? Two reasons. Some users simply gave up trying to access certain applications. The primary reason, though, was virtually everyone compromised authentication security by keeping a list of their passwords (usually in their upper-right desk drawer or on a sticky note attached to their monitors). Implementing Citrix Password Manager enabled them to virtually eliminate password-related help-desk requests, while significantly improving security.

Citrix Password Manager is comprised of three components:

▼ **Citrix Password Manager agent**   A 32-bit agent that runs on Citrix Presentation Servers or on a local client workstation. The agent acts as an intermediary between users and the applications that require authentication.

■ **Citrix Password Manager Console**   A centralized management tool to configure the central credential store and control the settings and features available to the agent.

▲ **Central Credential Store**   The central location where copies of users' credential records and agent settings files are stored. The central credential store is implemented using a shared folder (file synchronization) or Microsoft Active Directory. The agent synchronizes its local store with the central store, enabling users to access and maintain their credentials from any workstation.

Once a user has logged in and authenticated to a directory service, the agent intercepts any future password requests with a query, asking if the user would like the password manager to manage this password. If the user answers yes, then the password information is stored in the agent's local store and handed back to the client workstation when the workstation queries for that password again. Depending on configurations in Citrix Password Manager Console, the agent's local store can synchronize this new information with a central credential store.

Citrix Password Manager enhances security by centralizing security policies, providing an encrypted file for each user's credentials, and allowing IT administrators to automatically generate passwords that are more difficult to crack. They can also change the passwords more frequently.

CITRIX NETSCALER

NetScaler is a network appliance that optimizes the delivery of mission-critical web applications. NetScaler has a TCP stack built from the ground up that delivers unparalleled performance. It is a reliable integrated platform for load balancing, caching, compression, SSL acceleration, and security. NetScaler puts a great deal of high-performance function into a small integrated package, which is easy both to install and manage.

Load Balancer

NetScaler's base function is a load balancer. Administrators configure their DNS server, so their domain resolves to a virtual server (vserver) IP address owned by the NetScaler. Web-browser Hypertext Transfer Protocol Secure (HTTPS) requests arriving at the NetScaler-owned vserver address are decrypted, if necessary, and buffered until a complete, well-formed request is available. This request is examined as a potential attack. The validated requests are then sent to a service on a real server.

NetScaler monitors the health and load-on services. These monitors—as well as rules based on cookies, URLs, or user-agent—can determine which service is selected. NetScaler can also rate limit services and prioritize the resulting request queues. In addition, where needed, various persistence options ensure that sessions started with a service will continue with that particular service.

In addition to load balancing local pools of servers, the Global Server Load Balancing feature enables load balancing across sites.

Application Accelerator

Integrated with the load-balancing functions previously described, NetScaler has several ways of improving response time and scalability. These include SSL offload, compression, caching, and protocol optimizations.

Secure Sockets Layer (SSL)

A Secure Sockets Layer (SSL) GET can take up to 40 times the CPU that an unencrypted GET takes. Offloading all the extra work associated with SSL can give back large amounts of capacity to servers.

Compression

Compression helps clients who must use wide area networks (WANs) to reach their servers. By reducing the number of packets that need to be transmitted across a narrow bandwidth, long latency, or error prone links these clients see better response time. Reducing bandwidth demand can also save IT organizations money spent on increasing bandwidth. NetScaler does HTTP object compression, TCP compression, and differential compression. This last feature reduces transmitted data by divisors of up to 40 by sending only differences from previously sent data.

Caching

NetScaler *caching* can reduce the load on the entire server infrastructure. Data provided by the NetScaler cache does not need processing by a web server, app server, or data base server. NetScaler can do RFC-compliant caching. These are conservative rules that assure no client ever gets stale data. NetScaler also provides a *dynamic caching* feature that lets a customer who knows the application and the way the enterprise uses the application to aggressively exploit this knowledge to improve performance. Dynamic caching enables the customer to set rules for cacheability that go beyond RFC compliance to allow caching of frequently accessed data that, while technically dynamic, is infrequently changed.

Protocol Optimizations

NetScaler protocol optimizations, such as *Keep-alive* and *FastRamp,* reduce the need for extra waits for unproductive protocol packets to travel over the WAN. *Request Switching* greatly reduces the number of connections a server must manage. *TCP Buffering* can reduce them even more.

Security

NetScaler has many ways of detecting attacks and protecting the continuous operation of applications. Many forms of attack are partial requests that tie up memory resources waiting for the completion of the requests. Because servers only see complete and vetted requests, these attacks end at the NetScaler. NetScaler can filter for malicious content.

Perl Scripts

If someone writes a Perl script to issue valid get requests against a site, NetScaler can protect the site's operation. It does this by recognizing that such an attack is under way and challenging clients to execute a JavaScript program. Unless the attacker has provided a JavaScript interpreter along with his attack script, he is unable to respond correctly. Correct responders get cookies that entitle their request to go to the head of the line. The *script kiddies*, or would-be hackers, must languish in the tail of the queue.

SSL VPN

NetScaler provides a high-capacity SSL VPN that supports web, Client/Server, File-system access and terminal access. It supports common two-factor authentication schemes, such as SecureID and Secure Computing. NetScaler can authenticate via an internal or external LDAP server, as well as external Radius, TACACS+ servers. NetScaler controls access to specific applications by administrator-defined policies that can check all relevant security factors. These include execution of policy-driven client checks.

CHAPTER 2

Server Configuration Design and Recommendations

This chapter covers general recommendations for server hardware and operating system (OS) configurations you should consider before deploying Citrix Presentation Server for Windows.

HARDWARE CONFIGURATIONS

In multiprocessor configurations, Citrix recommends a RAID (Redundant Array of Independent Disks) setup. Hard disks are the most common type of hardware failure. Taking steps to alleviate the impact of a hard disk failure is typically addressed with a RAID 1 (mirroring) configuration based on cost considerations. See the *MetaFrame Presentation Server Administrator's Guide* for more information regarding available RAID configurations. If RAID is not an option, a fast SCSI 2, 3, Ultra 160, or Ultra 320 drive is recommended. Faster hard disks are inherently more responsive and may eliminate or curtail disk bottlenecks.

For quad and eight-way servers, use a solid state disk or install at least two disk controllers: one for OS disk usage and the other to store applications and temporary files. Isolate the OS as much as possible, with no applications installed on its disk controller. Distribute hard-drive access loads as evenly as possible across the disk controllers.

NOTE In general, Citrix has found that two-processor deployments provide not only overall efficiency, but also a generally lower total cost of ownership. However, each environment varies in terms of situation, supportability, applications, and the like, so the decision relating to the number of processors should be based on specific requirements. For results of Citrix eLabs's testing, see the section "Effects of Varying the Number of CPUs and Hyper-Threading on Presentation Servers."

The sizes of the partitions and hard drives are dependent on both the number of users connecting to the Presentation Server and the applications being used on the server. Microsoft Internet Explorer, Microsoft Office, and other applications can cause user profile directory sizes to increase to hundreds of megabytes. Large numbers of user profiles can use gigabytes of disk space on the server. You must have enough disk space for these profiles on the server and retain a sufficient amount of space for temporary files used by the OS to maintain system stability.

NOTE Roaming profiles and permanent user data should be stored on a centralized file server, System Area Network (SAN), or network-attached storage (NAS) that can adequately support the environment. In addition, this storage medium should be logically located near the Presentation Servers so that the minimal router hops are required and login times are not unnecessarily increased.

Improve Logon Performance—Enabling Disk Write Caching

An improvement may occur in simultaneous logon performance if disk write caching is enabled on the server's RAID controller, if available. This section contains the results of tests performed in the Citrix *e*Labs to measure the effect of enabling disk write caching.

> **Misconception**   "Heavy usage of the data store causes logons to be slow."
>
> **Actual**   The logon process is not dependent on the data store. Logons are dependent on dynamic information and, thus, are handled by a data collector in the farm.

HP DL360 G3 Battery Back Write Cache Login Test

The following tests were performed in the Citrix *e*Labs in collaboration with Hewlett Packard (HP) to compile performance measurements of user logon time on HP DL360 G3 servers running Citrix MetaFrame XP Presentation Server FR3, with and without a Smart Array 5i Controller Battery Backed Write Cache (BBWC) Enabler Option Kit. The results of these tests, although dated, are still easily applicable today and demonstrate the vast performance gains from write cache-capable disk controllers.

Test Setup

Hardware   The HP DL360 G3 consisted of the following configuration:

- ▼ Dual Intel Xeon 2.8GHz processors
- ■ 533 MHz FSB
- ■ 4GB RAM
- ▲ Single 36GB SCSI drive

Session logon performance was compared using results obtained with and without the BBWC unit installed in the server under test.

Software   Test server configuration:

- ▼ Citrix MetaFrame XPe Presentation Server Feature Release 3
- ▲ Windows 2003

Automation utility configured on 25 client servers.

Test Methodology

User Logon Time—Progressive Load (no BBWC)

1. Configure the automation utility to launch 3 user sessions on each server.
2. Tests run on progressive groups of 5, 10, 15, 20, and 25 servers.
    - ▼ Logon time measured
    - ▲ Disk, Processor, and Memory utilization measured

User Logon Time—Progressive Load (BBWC Installed)

1. Install BBWC (wait 3 hours for full battery charge).
2. Configure the automation utility to launch 3 user sessions per client server.
3. Tests run on progressive groups of 5, 10, 15, 20, and 25 servers.
   ▼ Logon time measured
   ▲ Disk, Processor, and Memory utilization measured

Performance Results

Results were measured utilizing user logon times and PerfMon counters. Three test runs were measured for each indicator and an average of the three runs is reported:

Client Servers	Sessions/Server	Total Client Logons	No BBWC	BBWC
5	3	15	16 s	13 s
10	3	30	25 s	16 s
15	3	45	43 s	38 s
20	3	60	57 s	51 s
25	3	75	80 s	60 s

Performance Counters

The following sections and figures outline the system performance results that contrast the systems with Write-Caching Enabled and Disabled.

System Performance Without BBWC—20 Servers The PerfMon graph in Figure 2-1 is illustrative of typical system performance for two iterations of user logon tests without a BBWC unit. Note the PhysicalDisk object, %Disk Time counter averages 20.74%.

System Performance—BBWC Installed—20 Servers The PerfMon graph in Figure 2-2 is illustrative of typical system performance for two iterations of user logon tests with a BBWC unit installed. Note that the PhysicalDisk object %Disk Time counter average decreased from 20.74% to 3.047%. All other counters remain essentially unchanged.

Further information regarding HP BBWC performance improvements in a Server Based Computing environment can be found on the HP web site: http://h71019.www7 .hp.com/ActiveAnswers/Render/1,1027,6461-6-100-225-1,00.htm

Effects of Varying the Number of CPUs and Hyper-Threading on Presentation Servers

The number of users that a Presentation Server can support depends on several factors including:

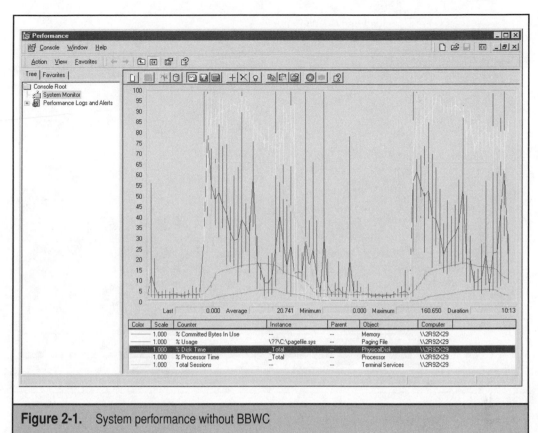

Figure 2-1.   System performance without BBWC

▼   The server's hardware specifications

■   The applications used (because of the applications' central processing unit (CPU) and memory requirements)

■   The amount of user input being processed by the applications

▲   What is considered as maximum desired resource usage on the server (for example, 90% CPU usage or 80% memory usage)?

This section discusses the increase in user capacity when more CPUs are added, as well as the effect of Hyper-Threading in the processor. First, the Citrix benchmarking test for user capacity, known as ICAMark, is described.

Citrix ICAMark

Citrix ICAMark is an internal tool that is based on the Citrix Server Test Kit (CSTK) and used by Citrix Engineering for benchmarking purposes to quantify the optimal number of simulated client sessions that can be connected to a Presentation Server with acceptable

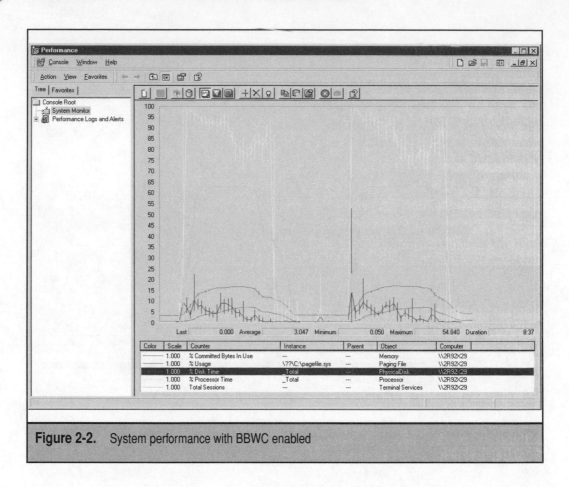

Figure 2-2. System performance with BBWC enabled

performance. Extending the number of concurrent simulated users beyond the optimal results causes a decrease in performance and may impact end user experience.

The test simulates users constantly typing and performing actions in Microsoft Excel, Microsoft Access, and Microsoft PowerPoint. Other applications can utilize more or less memory and CPU than Microsoft Office and, therefore, could produce different results. Note also that the simulated users in this test are constantly typing into these applications and may be considered more "rigorous" than normal users.

In this test, a step size "number of users" is defined as 5. During the course of the test, after the first 5 users are logged in, ICAMark launches simulated user scripts on all 5 sessions. Each script opens Microsoft Excel and simulates the creation of a spreadsheet, including calculations and charts. Once the Excel phase is complete, Excel is closed and Microsoft Access is opened. The script then simulates the creation of an Access database, including a table, query, and form with data manipulation. Once the Access phase is complete, a Microsoft PowerPoint presentation is created of 6 slides, including spell checking, font changes, and slide copies and deletions.

Based on how long the scripts take to complete, an ICAMark score is calculated. For this test, a score of *80* has been determined as the optimal load for a server. This means the server has enough additional CPU and memory resources to handle spikes in performance. When the test iteration score drops below 80, additional users added to the server consume more resources, producing lower test scores and slower performance.

Number of CPUs Effect on User Capacity

The benchmark test was performed with the following:
Server:

- ▼ Dell PowerEdge 6650
- ■ Quad Processor—3.0 GHz Xeon with 512KB L2 and 4MB L3 Cache
- ■ Hyper-Threading is enabled
- ■ 5x 73GB U320 15K RPM HDD with Dell PERC 4/DC Raid Controller
- ■ 16GB RAM
- ■ 16GB Page File
- ■ Presentation Server 4.0
- ■ Microsoft Windows Server 2003
- ▲ Microsoft Office XP Professional

Clients:

- ▼ Pentium3 800 MHz w/256KB Cache
- ■ 256MB RAM
- ■ Citrix ICA Program Neighborhood Client version 9.00.32649
- ▲ Microsoft Windows 2000 Service Pack 4

Tests were performed by keeping the hardware static and disabling processors on the server.

Results were collected on the following configurations:

- ▼ Dell 6650 with 1 processor enabled
- ■ Dell 6650 with 2 processors enabled
- ▲ Dell 6650 with 4 processors enabled

The following results were collected. Please view Figure 2-3 for the effects of multiple CPUs on User Capacity.

# of CPUs	# of Simulated Users	% Performance Increase
1	101 ± 1	N. A.
2	184 ± 1	82%
4	230 ± 1	25%

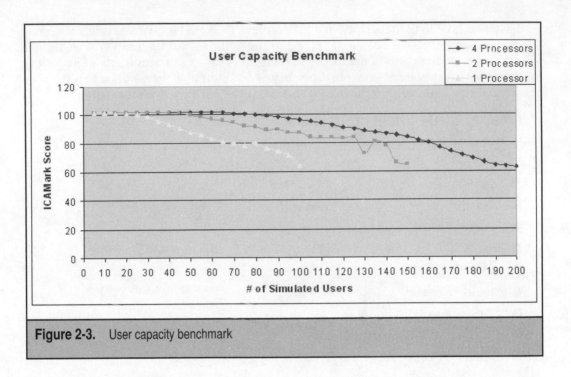

Figure 2-3. User capacity benchmark

The results conclude that the performance of the Dell PowerEdge 6650 with 4 processors enabled and 230 concurrent simulated users, is equivalent to the performance of 2 processors enabled with 184 concurrent simulated users, which is equivalent to the performance of 1 processor enabled with 101 concurrent simulated users.

Moving from a single to a dual processor system equates to an 82% increase in performance, while moving from a dual to a quad processor system equates to only a 25% increase in performance. In other words, as CPUs are added to the server, the increase in performance of the OS becomes less. As in this scenario, server scalability is not linear with the number of processors, and it drops off sharply between 2 and 4 processors.

All tests were run on Windows Server 2003 32-bit. A 32-bit OS is limited by the amount of kernel memory available. This limitation is illustrated in the graph above by the 4 processor scenario, which cannot reach the ICAMark score of 80.

NOTE When sizing Presentation Servers, the number of actual users per server varies based on the applications deployed.

The Affect of Hyper-Threading on User Capacity

Hyper-Threading technology enables a single physical processor to appear as two logical processors. Intel introduced this technology in the Pentium 4 line of processors. *Hyper-Threading* allows multithreaded programs to take advantage of extra execution units on the processor, resulting in as much as a 30% performance increase to some applications.

Performance Analysis of Blades vs. Standalone Servers

As datacenters grow larger to support thousands of users, datacenter space becomes increasingly expensive. Space, power, and HVAC all come at a price, prompting many organizations to look for ways to reduce the number of servers and the amount of rack space associated with housing the servers. To this end, Dell, HP, IBM, and others have developed blade servers that support higher density than previous form factors. This density provides a tremendous savings in rack space and datacenter space, but there is a decrease in the number of users supported on a blade because the current genre of blade servers generally support slower processors, less memory, and slower hard disks. Using the Single Server Scalability test, designed to quantify the maximum number of client sessions that can be connected to a Presentation Server with acceptable performance, the following table shows the number of users supported by a blade server versus a stand-alone server.

Server	Dell PowerEdge 1655MC	Dell PowerEdge 1650
Results (Simulated Users)	99 ± 1	108 ± 1

Results

With the variables defined in this test scenario, the results of the Single Server Scalability test conclude that the performance of the Dell PowerEdge 1655MC servicing 99 concurrent users is equivalent to the performance of the Dell PowerEdge 1650 servicing 108 concurrent users with the variables defined in this test scenario. Extending the number of concurrent users beyond the recommendation in this test environment would result in decreased performance and impact the end user experience on the Presentation Server. When sizing Presentation Servers, the number of actual users per server varies based on the applications deployed.

OPERATING SYSTEM CONFIGURATIONS

All partitions, especially the system partition, must be in NT File System (NTFS) format to allow security configuration, better performance, and fault tolerance. NTFS also saves disk space usage because NTFS partitions have much smaller and constant cluster sizes; minimum size is 4KB. File allocation table (FAT) partitions require much larger cluster sizes as the size of the partition increases, with the minimum being 32KB. More space is wasted on FAT partitions because the file system requires an amount of physical disk space equal to the cluster size of the partition used to store a file, even if the file is smaller than the cluster size. For more information about cluster sizes of FAT and NTFS partitions, see Microsoft Knowledge Base article 140365 or related information.

If possible, install only one network protocol on the server. This practice frees up system resources and reduces network traffic. If multiple protocols are needed, set the bind order so the most commonly used protocol is first.

When working with Terminal Services on Windows 2000 Server, increase the registry size to accommodate the additional user profile and applications settings that are stored in the registry. On a single-processor server, you need to reserve at least 40MB for the registry, while you need to reserve at least 100MB on quad and eight-way servers. In Microsoft Windows Server 2003, the Registry Size Limit functionality has been removed. Therefore, there are no longer any limits on the total amount of space that may be consumed by registry data (hives) in paged pool memory or in disk space. Views of the registry files are now mapped in the computer cache address space. Therefore, regardless of the size of the hive, it is not charged for more than 4 megabytes (MB) of space.

Performance can be also be increased by properly tuning the pagefile. For more information about the pagefile, see Microsoft Knowledge Base article 197379.

Service Packs and Updates

Microsoft, Citrix, and most hardware manufacturers provide patches, service packs, hotfixes, or other updates intended to ensure optimum performance, security, and stability of the systems. It is critical not only to keep up-to-date, but also to regression test all updates prior to installing them in a production environment.

NOTE   Before installing Presentation Server, please review the online Preinstallation Update Bulletin. The Preinstallation Update Bulletin offers late-breaking information and links to critical updates to server OSs and to Citrix installation files. A link to the bulletin is available on the Installation Checklist accessed through the autorun feature of the installation CDs.

Windows Service Packs

Service packs and hotfixes should be applied uniformly across all servers in the server farm. By ensuring this level of uniformity, consistency is assured and troubleshooting time is reduced.

Presentation Servers use Microsoft Jet drivers extensively. The Microsoft Jet Database Engine is used by the local host cache on every Presentation Server. It is also used when Resource Management is installed. Citrix recommends installing Microsoft service packs for the Microsoft Jet Database Engine. Older versions contain memory leaks that appear as IMA service memory leaks. Apply these service packs and patches before installing Presentation Server on the servers. See Microsoft Knowledge Base article 239114 or related materials for more information.

The amount of memory consumed by the IMA service can be reduced by changing the maximum buffer size for the Microsoft Jet 4.0 database engine.

To change max buffer size:

1. Run regedt32 for Windows 2000 or regedit for Windows Server 2003.

2. Locate the registry entry:

   `HKEY_LOCAL_MACHINE\SOFTWARE\Microsoft\Jet\4.0\Engines\Jet 4.0`

3. Double-click the value MaxBufferSize in the right pane.

4.   In the DWORD Editor dialog box, enter 0×200 in the Data box. Accept the default radix, Hex, in the Radix box. This sets MaxBufferSize to 512KB.

5.   Click OK.

CAUTION   Using Registry Editor incorrectly can cause serious problems that can require you to reinstall the OS. Citrix cannot guarantee that problems resulting from incorrect use of Registry Editor can be solved. Use Registry Editor at your own risk. Make sure you back up the registry before you edit it.

The IMA service consumes less memory if you change the value from 0 to 512KB.

NOTE   Installing a new MDAC or Microsoft Jet Database Engine service pack may reset MaxBuffer-Size to its default setting. Be sure to check this setting after applying any MDAC or Jet updates.

TEAMING NETWORK INTERFACE CARD CONFIGURATIONS

In all cases, the network interface cards (NICs) and switch ports should each be manually configured to support full duplex and the highest speed available on both devices because autosensing does not always result in an optimal or compatible configuration. If the speed or duplex settings are configured incorrectly, frames will likely be dropped and/or errors will occur, resulting in significantly degraded performance.

Many new servers are procured with two installed NIC ports. These NICs may be configured as follows, as listed in the order of Citrix's recommendation:

▼   Utilize both NICs and team via switch-assisted load balancing within the same subnet if connecting to different blades within a large Layer 3 switch

■   Utilize both NICs and team via adaptive load balancing within the same subnet if connecting to different blades within a large Layer 3 switch

■   Utilize both NICs and configure for failover onto two separate switches

■   Utilize one NIC and disable the second

▲   Utilize both NICs and multihome to two different subnets

Historically, most organizations have only used one NIC in each server. However, if two NIC and switch ports are available, these can be teamed, configured for failover, or multihomed. Of these two options—NIC teaming—is considered a Citrix Best Practice when the switch ports are located on different blades within a large Layer 3 switch (for example, Cisco 6500 series) because this enables both failover and redundancy, in addition to higher throughput. Although the Layer 3 switch does represent a single point of failure in this case, the availability of most large Layer 3 switches is in the 99.999% range and represents a minimal failure rate. More commonly, an individual blade may fail. If a large Layer 3 switch that supports teaming across blades is unavailable, then a failover configuration is the best option. While multihoming is a supported practice starting with MetaFrame XP Service Pack 1, NIC teaming is considered the better option in nearly all situations. Multihoming is often configured incorrectly, and security holes could be opened because access control lists configured on the router are bypassed.

If insufficient switch ports or other business decisions make it impossible to team the NICs and switch ports of all Presentation Servers and related servers, it is best to apply this recommendation to the following servers:

▼ Data store

■ Web Interface server(s)

■ Secure Gateway server(s)

■ Secure Ticket Authority server(s)

■ Secure Access Manager server(s)

▲ Zone data collector(s)

The following teaming NIC configurations have been tested on Presentation Servers and on a SQL server as the data store. In all cases, Citrix recommends teaming NICs using the MAC address, not the IP address. Because the MAC address is at a more basic and lower layer, as well as not subject to modification unless the burned-in address (BIA) is modified, this is a more basic and stable configuration. The switch vendor's recommended practice for manually configuring teaming or aggregating of the switch ports should be followed.

Network Fault Tolerance (Failover)

This failover option provides the safety of an additional backup link between the server and the switch. If the primary adapter fails, the secondary adapter takes over with minor interruption in server operations. When tested in Citrix eLabs, failover caused an interruption of less than 0.5 seconds and did not provide any noticeable impact on existing ICA sessions. There is no performance gain with this setting, but fault tolerance is improved.

Transmit Load Balancing (Formerly Adaptive Load Balancing)

This option creates a team of adapters to increase transmission throughput and ensure that all network users experience similar response times. All adapters must be linked to the same network switch. As adapters are added to the server, they are grouped in teams to provide a single virtual adapter with increased transmission bandwidth. For example, a transmit load balancing team containing two Fast Ethernet adapters configured for full-duplex operation provides an aggregate maximum transmit rate of 200 Mbps and a 100 Mbps receive rate, resulting in a total bandwidth of 300 Mbps. One adapter is configured for transmit and receive, while the others are configured for transmit only.

Adapter teams configured for transmit load balancing provide the benefit of network fault tolerance because, if the primary adapter that supports both transmit and receive fails, another adapter then supports this functionality.

Switch-assisted Load Balancing (Formerly Fast EtherChannel)

Unlike transmit load balancing, you can configure Fast Ether Channel (FEC) to increase both transmitting and receiving channels between the server and switch. For example, an FEC team containing two Fast Ethernet adapters configured for full-duplex operation provides an aggregate maximum transmit rate of 200 Mbps and an aggregate maximum receive rate of 200 Mbps, resulting in a total bandwidth of 400 Mbps. All adapters are configured for transmit and receive, with the load spread roughly equal.

FEC works only with FEC-enabled switches. The FEC software continuously analyzes load on each adapter and balances network traffic across the adapters as needed. Adapter teams configured for FEC not only provide additional throughput and redundancy, but also provide the benefits of Network Fault Tolerance (NFT). The switch ports should also be manually configured to support this configuration, so autosensed aggregation does not occur. For more information, please see Citrix Knowledge Base article CTX434260 and/or contact your hardware vendor.

MULTIHOMING PRESENTATION SERVERS

MetaFrame XP Service Pack 1 or later provides support for multihomed servers. The following section provides the details necessary for implementing Presentation Server on a server operating with two or more NICs.

Multihoming is commonly used to connect a Presentation Server directly to a database server located in another subnet. This may be advantageous where access to the remote subnet requires crossing several routers that have high latency or other bottlenecks. However, such can create security holes because the normal access medium, for example, the router, is bypassed, as well as its security configuration. Multihoming should be carefully considered and security implications should be reviewed.

For example, in the diagram shown in Figure 2-4, if multihoming is not configured properly on the Presentation Servers, external users may gain access to the SQL and Oracle database servers by means of the Presentation Servers, bypassing the router security that has been carefully configured.

CAUTION Multihoming is frequently not configured properly. The steps described in the following section must be followed exactly as specified for multihoming to function correctly and be supported.

In any event, all NICs should be manually configured to support full duplex and the maximum speed of the associated switch port, which is generally 100 Mbps. The switch port should be hard coded for this same configuration.

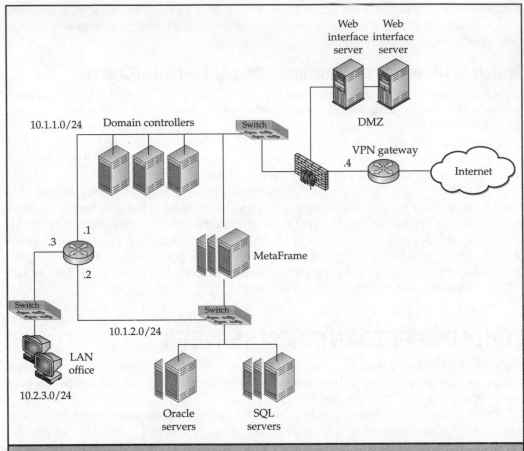

Figure 2-4. Sample environment with multihoming to connect servers to data collectors on different subnets

Presentation Server multihoming could be used to provide access to two network segments with no direct route to each. However, each network will utilize the same Citrix resources making the addition of another server farm redundant. Another application of multi-homing a Presentation Server would be to separate a network configured as the main corporate backbone dedicated to server-to-server traffic from a second subnet dedicated to ICA Client-to-MetaFrame server traffic. The latter configuration is illustrated in the following figure and is the subject of the remaining example provided in this section.

The recommendation is that multihomed Presentation Servers should not be configured to operate as a router (TCP/IP Forwarding). In addition, Presentation Server relies on a properly configured local routing table for accurate operation. Because Windows servers automatically build their routing tables, some care must be taken when configuring the network card binding order and default gateway.

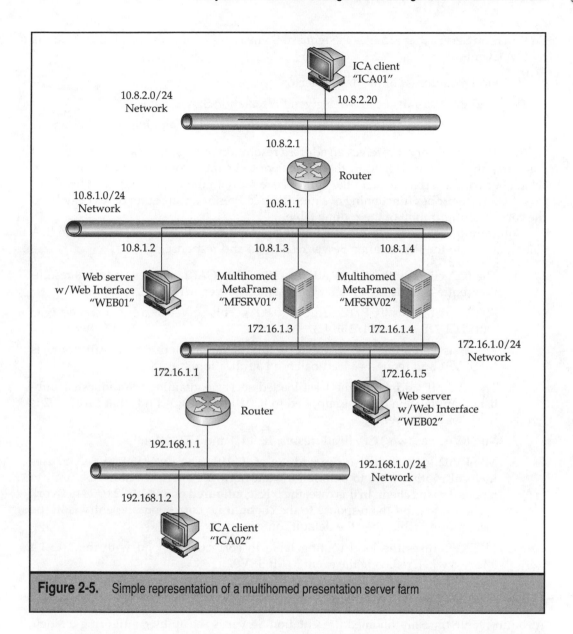

Figure 2-5.   Simple representation of a multihomed presentation server farm

Figure 2-5 illustrates two multihomed Presentation Servers, each with a connection to the 10.8.1.0/24 and 172.16.1.0/24 subnets. Neither server is configured to route between its two network interfaces.

ICA Clients requesting a server name or published application get a TCP/IP address to a Presentation Server that contains them. This address is resolved and returned by the

Presentation Server that receives the request. Some types of address resolution requests by ICA Clients are

▼ Find the address of the data collector

■ Find the TCP/IP address of a given Presentation Server name

▲ Find the TCP/IP address of the least-loaded server for a published application

A Presentation Server receives an address resolution request from an ICA Client and compares the TCP/IP address of the ICA Client to its local routing table to determine which network interface to send the appropriate reply to the requesting ICA client. For this reason, the proper functioning of a multihomed Presentation Server relies heavily on the correct configuration of the routing table.

Continuing with our example, the following steps describe the process from an ICA Client request to the Presentation Server resolution and response.

1. The ICA client with TCP/IP address 10.8.2.20, ICA01, sends an address resolution request to the MetaFrame Presentation Server, MFSRV01.

2. MFSRV01 has the TCP/IP address 10.8.1.3. This server also has a second NIC with TCP/IP address 172.16.1.3.

3. ICA01 is configured with MFSRV01 as its service location. ICA01 contacts MFSRV01 and requests a load-balanced application.

4. The TCP/IP address of the least-loaded server containing the requested published application must be supplied to ICA01. MFSRV01 finds that MFSRV02 is the least-loaded server.

5. MFSRV02 has two TCP/IP addresses, 10.8.1.4 and 172.16.1.4.

6. MFSRV02 looks at the source address of ICA01. The Presentation Server uses its local routing table to determine what network interface should be used to respond to the client. In this case, the NIC configured on the 10.8.2.0/24 network is chosen to send the response to the client. If no corresponding entry is in the local routing table, then the default route is used.

7. MFSRV01 uses the local routing table to correctly respond with the 10.8.1.4 address when referring the client to MFSRV02.

Configuring the Routing Table

A routing table on a multihomed Presentation Server is set up by configuring a single default gateway and the addition of static routes.

Configuring a Default Gateway

Windows servers automatically build their routing tables by default. For this reason, some care must be taken in the construction of the routing table to allow a multihomed Presentation Server to operate properly. While Windows servers build multiple default gateways, the network binding order of the NICs in the server determine which default gateway should be utilized. Using our example illustrated previously, we selected the 10.8.1.1 address as our default gateway. The network card operating on the 10.8.1.0/24 network must be moved to the top of the network binding order.

To configure the network binding order:

For Windows 2000

1. Open Start | Settings | Control Panel | Network and Dial-up Connections.

2. Select Advanced | Advanced Settings.

3. Under the section "Connections," place the NIC to operate as your default gateway first in the list.

For Windows Server 2003

1. Open Start | Control Panel | Network Connections.

2. Select Advanced | Advanced Settings.

3. Under the section "Connections," place the NIC to operate as your default gateway first in the list.

In certain environments, the configuration of the network binding order may not be sufficient for proper Presentation Server functionality.

An example would be a Presentation Server with two connections to the Internet, where each provides ICA connectivity for a diverse range of IP subnets. The Presentation Server only uses the Default Gateway of the first NIC in its network binding order, referenced as Network 1. If the Presentation Server were to receive a request from a Client on Network 2 of its second NIC, which is not the Default Gateway, and there was no routing table entry for Network 2 in the local routing table of the Presentation Server, then the response to the client request would be sent through Network 1. This likely would cause the request to fail.

Or, you can remove the additional default gateway configurations from each additional NIC on the server. This is done through the server's TCP/IP configuration. Using servers MFSRV01 and MFSRV02 from the previous illustration, we select 10.8.1.1 as our default gateway for both servers, and so remove the default gateway setting from the NICs operating on the 172.16.1.0/24 network.

Running the command line utility IPCONFIG on MFSRV01 shows the following:

```
Windows IP Configuration

Ethernet adapter Local Area Connection #1:

        Connection-specific DNS Suffix   . :
        IP Address. . . . . . . . . . . . : 10.8.1.3
        Subnet Mask . . . . . . . . . . . : 255.255.255.0
        Default Gateway . . . . . . . . . : 10.8.1.1
```

```
Ethernet adapter Local Area Connection #2:

        Connection-specific DNS Suffix  . :
        IP Address. . . . . . . . . . . : 172.16.1.3
        Subnet Mask . . . . . . . . . . : 255.255.255.0
        Default Gateway . . . . . . . . :
```

Running IPCONFIG on MFSRV02 shows:

```
Windows IP Configuration

Ethernet adapter Local Area Connection #1:

        Connection-specific DNS Suffix  . :
        IP Address. . . . . . . . . . . : 10.8.1.4
        Subnet Mask . . . . . . . . . . : 255.255.255.0
        Default Gateway . . . . . . . . : 10.8.1.1

Ethernet adapter Local Area Connection #2:

        Connection-specific DNS Suffix  . :
        IP Address. . . . . . . . . . . : 172.16.1.4
        Subnet Mask . . . . . . . . . . : 255.255.255.0
        Default Gateway . . . . . . . . :
```

Adding Static Routes

Defining static, persistent routes is the best way to avoid potential routing conflicts and, depending on your network configuration, this may be the only way to provide ICA connectivity to a multihomed Presentation Server. Refer to the previous illustration.

Executing the **ROUTE PRINT** command from the command prompt on the routing table on MFSRV01 shows the following:

```
===============================================================================
Interface List
0x1 .......................... MS TCP Loopback interface
0x2 ...00 a0 c9 2b f8 dc ...... Intel 8255x-based Integrated Fast Ethernet
0x3 ...00 c0 0d 01 12 f5 ...... Intel(R) PRO Adapter
===============================================================================
===============================================================================
Active Routes:
Network Destination        Netmask          Gateway       Interface Metric
        0.0.0.0          0.0.0.0         10.8.1.1        10.8.1.3       1
       10.8.1.0    255.255.255.0         10.8.1.3        10.8.1.3       1
       10.8.1.3  255.255.255.255        127.0.0.1       127.0.0.1       1
  10.255.255.255  255.255.255.255         10.8.1.3        10.8.1.3       1
      127.0.0.0        255.0.0.0        127.0.0.1       127.0.0.1       1
     172.16.1.0    255.255.255.0       172.16.1.3      172.16.1.3       1
```

```
      172.16.1.3   255.255.255.255        127.0.0.1        127.0.0.1       1
    172.16.1.255   255.255.255.255      172.16.1.3       172.16.1.3       1
       224.0.0.0         224.0.0.0        10.8.1.3         10.8.1.3       1
       224.0.0.0         224.0.0.0      172.16.1.3       172.16.1.3       1
 255.255.255.255   255.255.255.255        10.8.1.3         10.8.1.3       1
Default Gateway:                10.8.1.1
=========================================================================
Persistent Routes:
None
```

Currently, MFSRV01 is configured with a default gateway using the router at 10.8.1.1. Note, the second client, ICA02, is located on the 192.168.1.0/24 network, which is accessed via the router at 172.16.1.1. For MFSRV01 to have network connectivity and to avoid using the default gateway when responding to requests from ICA02, a static route must be defined for the 192.168.1.0/24 network:

```
ROUTE -p ADD 192.168.1.0 MASK 255.255.255.0 172.16.1.1
```

Executing ROUTE PRINT from a command prompt on MFSRV01 now shows the following:

```
===================================================
Interface List
0x1 ......................... MS TCP Loopback interface
0x2 ...00 a0 c9 2b f8 dc ...... Intel 8255x-based Integrated Fast Ethernet
0x3 ...00 c0 0d 01 12 f5 ...... Intel(R) PRO Adapter
=========================================================================
=========================================================================
Active Routes:
Network Destination        Netmask          Gateway        Interface  Metric
        0.0.0.0           0.0.0.0         10.8.1.1         10.8.1.3       1
       10.8.1.0     255.255.255.0         10.8.1.3         10.8.1.3       1
       10.8.1.3   255.255.255.255        127.0.0.1        127.0.0.1       1
 10.255.255.255   255.255.255.255         10.8.1.3         10.8.1.3       1
      127.0.0.0         255.0.0.0        127.0.0.1        127.0.0.1       1
     172.16.1.0     255.255.255.0       172.16.1.3       172.16.1.3       1
     172.16.1.3   255.255.255.255        127.0.0.1        127.0.0.1       1
   172.16.1.255   255.255.255.255       172.16.1.3       172.16.1.3       1
    192.168.1.0     255.255.255.0       172.16.1.1       172.16.1.3       1
      224.0.0.0         224.0.0.0         10.8.1.3         10.8.1.3       1
      224.0.0.0         224.0.0.0       172.16.1.3       172.16.1.3       1
255.255.255.255   255.255.255.255         10.8.1.3         10.8.1.3       1
Default Gateway:               10.8.1.1
=========================================================================
Persistent Routes:
  Network Address          Netmask  Gateway Address  Metric
     192.168.1.0     255.255.255.0      172.16.1.1       1
```

MFSRV02 is handled the same way. When the static routes are set up, both ICA Clients can ping both Presentation Servers' TCP/IP addresses and the servers can ping the clients.

Each Presentation Server can now correctly resolve the network interface to which either ICA Client is connecting. The TCP/IP addresses that the ICA01 client can receive are 10.8.1.3 and 10.8.1.4. The TCP/IP addresses that the ICA02 client can receive are 172.16.1.3 and 172.16.1.4.

CHAPTER 3

Independent Management Architecture

This chapter discusses Citrix Presentation Server architecture topics that must be addressed in the planning and pilot phases before deploying Presentation Server in the enterprise. The concepts you learn about in this section include zones, the server farm's data store, the local host cache, and bandwidth requirements for Independent Management Architecture (IMA) communication in the server farm.

IMA COMPONENTS

Citrix's IMA contains four components: the IMA data store, zone data collectors, local host caches, and the IMA protocol. The *IMA data store* is responsible for keeping information about generally static farm settings, such as published applications, load-balancing parameters, printer options, and security. Farm information that changes regularly, such as the number of connected users or which member servers are currently online, is maintained in an in-memory database on each data collector. Each zone in a farm has its own zone data collector (ZDC), which is responsible for maintaining the operating information for that zone. Data collectors gather their information through communication with the servers in their zone, and then communicate their zone's information to the data collectors in the other zones in the farm. Each server maintains a local database containing a subset of the information in the data store, this local database is referred to as the local host cache. The *IMA protocol* is responsible for communications between Presentation Servers, and to communicate between servers and the Presentation Server Console.

UNDERSTANDING ZONES

In a Presentation Server farm, a *zone* is a grouping of Presentation Servers that share a common data collector (a Presentation Server that receives information from all the servers in the zone). Zones in a farm serve two purposes: to collect data from member servers in a hierarchical structure and to efficiently distribute changes to all servers in the farm.

All member servers must belong to a zone. By default, the zone name is the subnet ID on which the member server resides. A zone in a Presentation Server farm elects a zone data Collector (ZDC) for the zone if a new server joins the zone, a member server restarts, or the current ZDC becomes unavailable.

The trade-off of adding more zones is the open link (and, thus, the bandwidth required) to maintain updates between each ZDC, so all updated data can be propagated throughout the farm. During a zone update, the member server updates the ZDC with the requests and the changed data.

Sizing Zones and Data Collectors

ZDCs are used to keep information within a server farm up-to-date between member servers and other ZDCs. Every server farm has at least one zone set up by default. The challenge is to design the right number of zones in a farm, so each ZDC does not get overloaded with traffic from its member servers while, at the same time, limiting the amount of additional load on the ZDCs and bandwidth required by multiple zones. The inter-zone traffic should be both minimized and balanced between ZDCs.

The number of zones needed by a farm is dependent on the topology of the site in which the farm is being deployed, the number of users connecting to the farm, the number of simultaneous user logons, the number of published applications with load evaluators attached, and the length of time the average user stays logged on to a session (a single daily session or repeated short sessions), and it should be kept to a minimum. The fewer zones a farm has, the more it will scale. The reason is this: every time a dynamic event occurs—such as a logon, a logoff, or a disconnect—an update is sent to the ZDC. The ZDC must then forward the update to all other ZDCs in the farm. This consumes both bandwidth and CPU processing because the other ZDCs must keep up with the events in other zones, as well as in their own.

Zones should not always be based on subnets. Zones can scale beyond 500 servers, unless other environmental conditions warrant limiting their size. Suppose, for example, a company has a Presentation Server farm containing 1000 servers distributed between two distinct data centers, which each host 500 servers. In this case, it would be more desirable to create two separate zones of 500 member servers each. In another scenario, this company plans to expand operations to a small, remote site in another location that would house 10 Presentation Servers in the same farm. In this case, it would be optimal for the servers in the new location to join one of the original site's zones. The reason is based on the number of events that would flow across the wide area network (WAN). If the new site was placed in its own zone, the data collector for the new zone would receive replicated events from all the other data collectors in the farm. The number of events (logons, logoffs, and so forth) coming from the other zones would be in the tens of thousands. On the other hand, the number of events generated by the new zone would be in the hundreds. It is optimal not to have to replicate the data collector traffic if this is unnecessary. Therefore, by consolidating the new site into the one of the original zones, the only traffic flowing across the WAN link would be events sent from the new site's member servers to the original site's ZDC.

ZDC Hardware Configuration

Because the data collectors store all dynamic information in memory, it is important that the ZDC has sufficient RAM to store all the records. For a farm consisting of 1,000 servers and 10,000 users, the data collector consumes approximately 200MB of memory. Memory usage can vary, based on the number of published applications and users in the farm. The CPU plays an important role in determining the number of resolutions the data collector can process in conjunction with managing dynamic information. In general, a fast dual processor server with 1GB of memory makes a good ZDC.

It is important that all data collectors in the farm are sized to accommodate the largest zone. Because data collectors must manage the global state of the farm, they require the same processing capability of the other data collectors in the farm, regardless of the size of their particular zone. Likewise, if the data collector needs to be dedicated for one zone, all data collectors in the farm should be dedicated for their own zones.

Traffic from a Member Server to a ZDC

During a zone update, the member server updates the data collector with the requests and the changed data. To approximate the number of bytes sent from a single server to the ZDC during a complete update, use the following formula.

Citrix Presentation Server 4.0: Bytes = 5600 + (200*Con) + (100*$Discon$) + (300*$Apps$)

where,

Con = Number of connected sessions

$Discon$ = Number of disconnected sessions

$Apps$ = Number of published applications in the farm

During a zone update, the member server updates the data collector with the requests and the changed data. This amount of traffic is represented by the previous formula. In turn, a small amount of traffic is then sent from the data collector to the member server. This traffic accounts for approximately one-half of the data sent from the member server to the data collector, so for full bandwidth utilization, multiply the number of bytes from the previous formula by 1.5. To approximate the amount of traffic destined for the data collector, multiply the number of bytes from the previous formula by the number of member servers in the zone.

NOTE These numbers are an approximation from data gathered in the Citrix eLabs; actual results may vary.

A *full zone transfer*, the transmission of all a zone's information, occurs when a ZDC comes online (for example, reboots or new ZDC added) or a new ZDC is elected because of ZDC failure detection. To approximate the amount of data sent between two data collectors during a full zone transfer, use the following formula:

Citrix Presentation Server 4.0: Bytes = 13000 + (300*Con) + (300*$Discon$) + (500*$Apps$)

where,

Con = Number of connected sessions

$Discon$ = Number of disconnected sessions

$Apps$ = Number of published applications in the farm

During a zone update, approximately the same amount of data is transmitted between data collectors, so for full bandwidth utilization, be sure to double the bytes from the previous formula. To approximate the amount of traffic across all data collector links, multiply the number of bytes obtained from the previous formula by the number of data collectors minus 1 in the farm.

Traffic Between Zones

Each ZDC has a connection open to all other data collectors in the farm. This connection is used to immediately relay any changes reported by member servers within its own zone to the data collectors of all other zones. Thus, all data collectors are aware of the session information, and for MetaFrame Presentation Server XP with Feature Release 3 and earlier, the server load for every server in the farm. Presentation Server 4.0 by default has load sharing between zones disabled. The formula for interzone connections is $N *$ $(N–1)/2$, where N is the number of zones in the farm.

Configure Data Collectors in Large Zones

The data collector maintains all load and session information for every server in its zone. By default, a single zone supports 512 member servers in MetaFrame Presentation Server XP with Feature Release 3 and above. If a zone contains more than 512 servers, each ZDC and potential ZDC must have a new registry setting. This new setting controls how many open connections to member servers a data collector can have at one time. Set the registry value higher than the number of servers in the zone to prevent the data collector from constantly destroying and re-creating connections to stay within the limit. This value is configurable by adding the following value to the registry in hex:

```
HKEY_LOCAL_MACHINE\SOFTWARE\Citrix\IMA\Runtime\MaxHostAddress CacheEntries
(DWORD)

Value: 0x200 (default 512 entries)
```

NOTE   If you do not have more than 512 servers in a zone, increasing this value does not increase the performance of a zone.

Number of Servers in a Zone

A common misconception is that no more than 100 servers should be placed within a zone. The problem with designing too many zones in a large datacenter deployment is this: the presence of multiple zones in a single data center can cause performance of the farm to decrease. This decrease is because ZDCs must keep up with all the information contained within all other ZDCs in the farm. Each time an event occurs, the ZDC must forward this information to all other ZDCs in the farm. This increases the network consumption and the CPU load on the ZDC as it needs to handle sending and receiving updates for all the events in the farm.

TIP   As a starting point, place 300 servers into a single zone, and then monitor the CPU utilization on the ZDC.

Data Collector Scalability in Large Farms

In large farms (800+ servers) containing more than one zone, where the data collectors are heavily utilized performing logon resolutions, a condition could arise causing the data collectors to become overloaded and stop performing resolutions for a short period of time. This state is caused when all the worker threads on each data collector are processing IMA maintenance items, such as IMA pings, gateway updates, load updates, and so forth. While performing resolutions, these resolutions require the processing of events at the remote data collector and the remote data collector has no worker threads available to deliver the event.

The following registry setting increases IMA processing bandwidth by increasing the amount of worker threads available to the data collector, and it shortens the timeout of stale events. Each ZDC and all potential ZDCs must have a new registry setting. These keys need to be created and, as always, use caution when modifying the registry.

```
HKEY_LOCAL_MACHINE\SOFTWARE\Citrix\IMA
WorkQueueThreadCount (DWORD)
Value: 0x00000080 (hex)
EventTimeout (DWORD)
Value: 0x000007d0 (hex)
HKEY_LOCAL_MACHINE\SOFTWARE\Citrix\IMA\RUNTIME
GatewayValidationInterval (DWORD)
Value: 0x00007530 (hex)
```

NOTE This condition only occurs if there are multiple zones and each data collector is processing upwards of 40 resolutions per second. Setting these registry keys does not improve performance if this condition is not experienced.

FUNCTION OF THE DATA STORE IN A CITRIX PRESENTATION SERVER FARM

The data store provides a repository of persistent farm information for all servers to reference. The data store retains information that does not change frequently, including the following:

▼ Published application configurations
■ Server configurations
■ MetaFrame Administrator accounts
■ Trust relationships
▲ Printer configurations

CAUTION Always maintain a backup of the data store database. If you do not have a backup from which to restore, you must re-create the farm if the database is lost. You cannot re-create the database from an existing farm.

Database Format

With the exception of indexes, all information in the data store is in binary format. No meaningful queries can be executed directly against the data store. Neither Citrix administrators nor users should directly query or change information in the data store. Use only IMA-based tools, such as the Presentation Server Console, to access the information in the data store.

CAUTION Never directly edit any data in the data store database with IBM DB2, Microsoft SQL Server, or Oracle tools. Directly editing the data with one of these tools corrupts the farm database and causes the farm to become unstable or completely unusable.

Data Store Activity

All servers in the farm query the data store during startup, if it is available. The following registry setting determines if IMA requires a connection to the data store to start:

```
HKEY_LOCAL_MACHINE\SOFTWARE\Citrix\IMA\Runtime\
PSRequired (DWORD)
Value: 0 or 1
```

If the value is 0, IMA can start without a connection to the data store. If the value is 1, IMA requires a connection to the data store to start. After the first time the IMA service starts successfully, the value is set to 0.

The Local Host Cache and the Data Store Polling Interval

For MetaFrame Presentation Server 3.0 and later, it is unnecessary to change the polling interval, even for large farms. Polling queries were optimized in such a way that the amount of information read from the data store during an update is negligible. High amounts of data store activity should not be seen during normal MetaFrame Presentation Server 3.0 farm operations.

A subset of the information from the data store is stored locally on each Presentation Server; this local copy of data is referred to as the Local Host Cache (LHC). The IMA service attempts to synchronize the LHC with the data store every time the IMA service is started. Every 30 minutes, IMA also queries the data store to determine if any changes were made since the LHC was last updated. The first LHC polling cycle starts at a random time between x and $2x$, where x is the LHC polling interval. By default, because the LHC polling interval is 30 minutes, the first cycle starts anywhere between 30 minutes to 60 minutes after the IMA starts. The subsequent polling cycles start at 30 minute intervals (there is no randomness). If changes were made since the last query, the servers request the changes and update their LHC. By default, the data store query interval is 30 minutes. However, the query interval is configurable through the following registry key with the value set in hex:

```
HKEY_LOCAL_MACHINE\SOFTWARE\Citrix\IMA\
DCNChangePollingInterval (DWORD)
Value: 0x1B7740 (default 1,800,000 milliseconds)
```

The IMA service needs to be restarted for the data-store polling interval change to take effect.

Prior to MetaFrame Presentation Server 3.0, with a small number of servers in a farm, 30-minute queries are not noticeable. As the farm grows in size, more servers are querying the data store and the response time may increase. This is especially an issue with farms prior to MetaFrame Presentation Server XP with Feature Release 3. In large farms, an incorrectly sized data store can consume all of its processing time just responding to the periodic polling queries. If the data store is experiencing high CPU usage when there should not be reads or writes to the data store, it is possible that the data store is not powerful enough to handle a query interval of 30 minutes. To determine that the data store query interval is causing the high CPU usage on the data store, the query interval can be set to a large number for testing purposes. If the CPU usage returns to normal with a large query interval, then the data store query interval is probably the cause of the high CPU usage and it needs to be adjusted by trial and error.

To troubleshoot, set the polling interval to 60 minutes, and then restart all the servers in the farm. If the data store is still experiencing constantly high CPU usage, the polling interval should be increased further. However, if the CPU usage returns to normal, a smaller value should be tested.

Ordinarily, when a change is made to the farm, that change is sent to all the servers in the farm. But it is possible that some servers could miss an update because of network problems. In a worst-case scenario, any changes to a server would not get propagated to that server until the next data store polling interval. Because the query interval is a backup method to guarantee synchronization if a server missed an event, it should not be set to abnormally high values. Also, the polling interval does not have to be uniformly applied across all servers. Consider leaving the default polling interval on the data collectors, but increase it on the member servers. For example, if a data store takes 10 seconds to respond to a single polling query, then theoretically that database server could support up to 180 farm servers (6 servers a minute * 30-minute polling interval) in the default configuration before it falls behind in servicing incoming requests. If the polling interval on all farm servers were set to 60 minutes, that same database server could respond to 360 farm servers before the requests would overlap.

NOTE When zone changes are made, such as zone membership or properties of a zone, the servers affected should be rebooted to force the data store update and speed the synchronization process. Because of optimizations in the way the LHC pulls data from the data store in MetaFrame Presentation Server 3.0 and later, normal farm operation should not cause data store CPU spikes.

Data Store and License Server Connectivity

The following section addresses the dependencies between Presentation Server and connectivity to the Data Store or the license server.

 NOTE Effective August 19, 2004, the license server grace period was increased from four days (96 hours) to 30 days. If you obtained your license file before August 19th, 2004, you must reallocate your license files to take advantage of the 30-day grace period. See Citrix knowledgebase article CTX104782 for more information.

Data Store Connectivity

In MetaFrame XP with Feature Release 3 and earlier versions, if a farm member server is unable to contact the data store for more than 96 consecutive hours, licensing stops functioning on the member server and connections are disabled. Connections to Presentation Server 3.0 and later are not dependant on connectivity to the Data Store. After installation, the Presentation Server makes an initial connection to the Data Store to identify the License Server. Provided the Presentation Server is able to connect to the License Server, or is within the grace period following a loss of connectivity to the License Server, a loss of connectivity to the Data Store does not affect user logins. Although user connections are no longer dependent on a server's ability to connect to the data store, if the farm's member servers are unable to connect to the Data Store, you will be unable to use the Presentation Server Console or make changes to the farm, such as adding, removing, or modifying the properties of published applications.

License Server Connectivity

User connections to Presentation Server 3.0 and later are dependent on connectivity to the License Server. If a farm member server loses connectivity to the License Server, the member server enters into a grace period. During this grace period, logins are not affected, but once the grace period expires, only one administrator logon is granted and all other connections are denied.

Misconception "Data collectors are the only servers that communicate with the data store."

Actual IMA on all the servers must be initialized with the same settings, regardless of the role of the server. Also, when the Presentation Server Console is opened, it connects to a specified Presentation Server. This server's IMA service performs all reads and writes to the data store for the Presentation Server Console. Most changes made through the Presentation Server Console are written to the data store.

CITRIX PRESENTATION SERVER COMMUNICATION BANDWIDTH REQUIREMENTS

The Citrix eLabs used a Microsoft SQL 2000 data store to determine bandwidth requirements for normal communication in a MetaFrame Presentation Server environment. This information can be used to determine potential bandwidth requirements for WAN-based farms.

CAUTION   The following results may not hold true for all situations. Recommendations vary based on how much bandwidth is used by other network applications.

Bandwidth of Server to Data Store Communication

The amount of data (in kilobytes) read from the data store during the startup of a Presentation Server is approximated by the following formula:

Citrix Presentation Server 4.0: KB Read = 436 + 3.15*($Srvs$ -1)

where,

$Srvs$ = Number of servers in the farm

$Apps$ = Number of published applications in the farm

The amount of data read from the data store can require higher bandwidth as the farm size increases and certain actions are executed, especially when several servers are started simultaneously. Most network traffic consists of reads from the database. In the case of high latency or low-bandwidth links, Citrix recommends that the data store be replicated across the link(s) (using the built-in replication tools of the database vendor chosen for your data store—Microsoft SQL, Oracle, or IBM DB2). A replicated data store allows all reads to occur on the network local to the Presentation Server, resulting in improved farm performance.

If performance across the WAN is an issue, and having a replicated database at each site is cost-prohibitive, analyze the WAN links for alternative solutions. The IMA service start time ranges from a few seconds to several minutes. When the amount of data requested from the data store by the IMA service is greater than the size of the pipe between WAN segments, IMA waits for all the data, resulting in a longer startup time.

NOTE   A third-party solution can be used to dedicate a certain size pipe for exclusive use by database traffic to avoid network flooding in WAN environments.

When the IMA service takes a long time to start after a restart, an error can display on the console of the server stating that the IMA service could not be started. The event log can have a message stating that the IMA service hung on starting. These errors are benign. The IMA service starts properly after the requests to the data store are serviced.

Event	Data Transmitted (approximate)
Connect	1.15KB
Disconnect	0.92KB
Reconnect	1.1KB
Logoff	0.66KB

Table 3-1.   Citrix Presentation Server 4.0 Sharing Load Information

Bandwidth of Data Collector Communication

To maintain consistent information between zones, data collectors must relay information to all other data collectors in a farm. The tables on the following pages illustrate the impact to network traffic.

Tables 3-1 and 3-2 list the amount of data transmitted for session-based events.

Each time these events occur, the member server sends data to the zone's data collector, which sends data to all other data collectors in the farm.

Table 3-3 lists the amount of data sent by one data collector to another when operations are performed by the Presentation Server Console on servers that reside in different zones.

Limit the use of zones to avoid the cost associated with the replication of zone data.

Application Publishing Bandwidth

The bandwidth consumed when you publish an application varies, depending on the number of servers in the server farm. In general, the amount of bandwidth consumed

Event	Data Transmitted (approximate)
Connect	0.87KB
Disconnect	0.50KB
Reconnect	0.80KB
Logoff	0.36KB

Table 3-2.   Citrix Presentation Server 4.0 *not* Sharing Load Information

Event	Data Transmitted (approximate)
Presentation Server Console server query	.61KB
Application publishing	3.78KB
Changing a ZDC	12.3KB

Table 3-3. Citrix Presentation Server 4.0

increases 466 bytes for every additional server in the server farm. Starting a new server generates the most amount of traffic to the other data collectors. Starting a new server generates about 5.6KB worth of traffic to the data collector in a default configuration.

NOTE You can use a third-party solution to dedicate a pipe for IMA traffic, which uses port 2512 by default, to avoid flooding the network in WAN environments.

Application of IMA Bandwidth Formulas

When a Presentation Server is booted, it must initialize the IMA Service during startup and it must also register with the data collector for the zone in which it resides. Figure 3-1 shows the steps for an initial boot of a Citrix Presentation Server Farm.

NOTE License communication is not included in this slide.

Communication occurs in the following sequence of events:

1. The IMA Service establishes a connection to the data store for the farm. The IMA Service then downloads the information it needs to initialize. It also makes sure the data contained in its local host cache is current.

2. After The IMA Service is initialized, the member server registers with the data collector for the zone. This is a function of the number of published applications the server is contributing to.

3. The data collector needs to relay all of the updated information written by the member servers in the zone to *all* other data collectors in the farm to keep them in sync with each other. The data collector-to-data collector updates are a function of the amount of information updated by the member server. The data collectors only replicate the delta, or items that have changed; they do not replicate all their tables every time an update is sent.

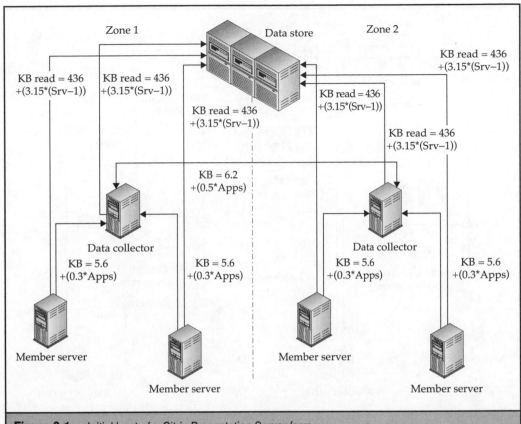

Zone 1

Data store

Zone 2

KB read = 436
+(3.15*(Srv−1))

KB read = 436
+(3.15*(Srv−1))

KB read = 436
+(3.15*(Srv−1))

KB read = 436
+(3.15*(Srv−1))

KB read = 436
+(3.15*(Srv−1))

KB read = 436
+(3.15*(Srv−1))

KB = 6.2
+(0.5*Apps)

Data collector

Data collector

KB = 5.6
+(0.3*Apps)

KB = 5.6
+(0.3*Apps)

KB = 5.6
+(0.3*Apps)

KB = 5.6
+(0.3*Apps)

Member server

Member server

Member server

Member server

Figure 3-1. Initial boot of a Citrix Presentation Server farm

NOTE In the example in Figure 3-2, there are only two zones, so the data collector must only replicate the updates it receives from the member servers once to the other data collector. If there were 3 zones, the data collector would have to replicate the same information twice. This causes higher bandwidth consumption and places a higher load on the data collectors in the farm.

Idle Farm Communication

IMA must use a small amount of overhead, even if the farm is idle. Figure 3-2 shows the communication that must take place on a farm after it is initialized. This communication has 3 primary components: an IMA coherency check between the member server's local host cache and the data store, an IMA Ping by the ZDC to the member servers in its zone, and an IMA Ping to the other ZDCs in the farm.

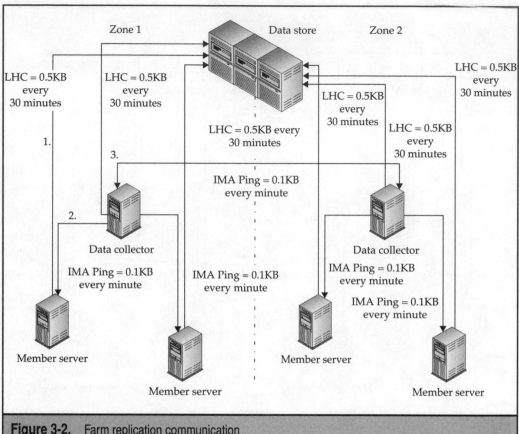

Figure 3-2. Farm replication communication

IMA Coherency Check

Every 30 minutes, IMA performs a coherency check between the member server's LHC and the data store. If neither has changed, this operation only consumes about 500 bytes of bandwidth. If the check determines that something has changed, the member server searches through the various contexts within the data store to determine what has changed to update the information in the LHC.

IMAPing to Member Servers

To make sure the Presentation Servers in its zone are functional and able to contribute to published applications, the data collector sends an IMAPing to each of the member servers in its zone, if it has not received an update from the member server within the last 60 seconds. The data collector also asks the member server for its server load if it has not received a load update within the past 5 minutes.

IMAPing to Other ZDCs

Finally, the data collectors perform an IMAPing to the other data collectors in the farm to ensure they are still data collectors, and to ensure they are still operational if they have not received an update in the last 60 seconds.

Event-based Communication

Most IMA traffic is a result of the generation of events. Figure 3-3 shows an example of a client logon event.

Most IMA traffic is a result of the generation of events. When a client connects, disconnects, logs off, and so forth, the member server must update information with the data collector in its zone. The data collector in turn must replicate this information to all the other data collectors in the farm. When "Load Share information across zones" is disabled, event-based communication is reduced by approximately 300 bytes. Figure 3-3 shows an example of a client logon event.

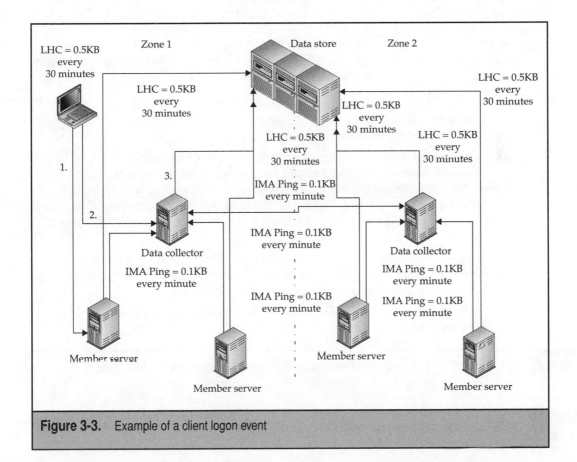

Figure 3-3.   Example of a client logon event

1. The client requests the data collector to resolve the published application to the IP address of the least-loaded servers in the farm.

2. The client then connects to the least-loaded server returned by the data collector.

3. The member server then updates its information to the data collector for its zone.

4. The data collector then forwards this information to all the other data collectors in the farm.

NOTE Notice in the client logon event example shown in Figure 3-3, the data store has no communication. Connections are independent of the data store and can occur when the data store is unavailable. Connection performance is not affected by a busy data store.

New Data Collector Election

When a communication failure occurs between a member server and the data collector for its zone or between data collectors, the election process is initiated. This is true whether network problems prevent communications to the network, whether the existing data collector for the zone is shut down gracefully, or whether it has an unplanned failure for some reason (that is, if a RAID controller fails, causing the server to blue screen). Figure 3-4 shows an example of this communication:

1. The existing data collector for Zone 1 has an unplanned failure, that is, a RAID controller fails causing the server to blue screen. If the server is shutdown gracefully, it triggers the election process before going down.

2. The servers in the zone recognizes the data collector has gone down and starts the election process. In this example, the backup data collector is elected as the new data collector for the zone. Please note, the "backup" data collector contains no replica information but, instead, is referring to the best practice of assigning election priorities to control which server is to become elected as the new data collector.

3. The member servers in the zone then send all their information to the new data collector for the zone. This information is a function of the number each server has of sessions, disconnected sessions, and applications.

4. In turn, the new data collector replicates this information to all other data collectors in the farm.

IMPORTANT The data collector election process is not dependent on the data store.

NOTE If the data collector goes down, sessions connected to other servers in the farm are unaffected.

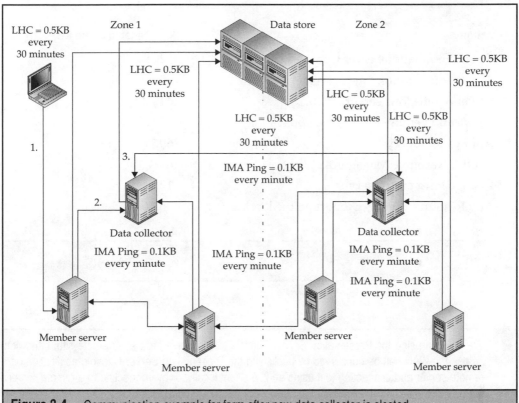

Figure 3-4. Communication example for farm after new data collector is elected

Citrix Presentation Server Console Communication Bandwidth

When the Presentation Server Console is launched, it gathers information from several different sources. It pulls static information, such as the server list, from the data store, dynamic data session information from the data collector, and Resource Manager-specific information from the farm metric server.

Misconception "If a data collector goes down, there is a single point of failure."

Actual The data collector election process is triggered automatically without administrative intervention. Existing, as well as incoming users, are unaffected by the election process, as a new data collector is elected almost instantaneously. Data collector elections are not dependent on the data store.

Action	Data Transmitted (in KB)
Open Presentation Server Console	462.49
Server enumeration (one server)	0
Server details (one server)	244.72
Application enumeration (one application)	7.62
Application query	150.11
Publish Resource Manager Application	60.3
Change farm metric server	17.9
Any Resource Manager report on the local server	5.46

Table 3-4.   Citrix Presentation Server 4.0

TIP   When using the Presentation Server Console to monitor a farm at a remote site, bandwidth across the WAN can be conserved by publishing the Presentation Server Console application on a remote server and connecting to it using an ICA Client locally, or by connecting to a remote server's console and executing the Presentation Server Console (in an effort to reduce the number of published applications).

Table 3-4 illustrates bandwidth consumption to the data store when the following actions are performed using the Presentation Server Console.

Local Host Cache Change Events

When configuration changes are modified in the Presentation Server Console, the changes are propagated across the farm using directory change notification broadcasts. These broadcasts take place when a change is made that is under 64KB in size. In Presentation Server 3.0 and earlier, the broadcast would occur if the change was under 10KB in size. These broadcasts help to minimize WAN traffic and alleviate contention on the data store. The propagation of the change notification is not guaranteed. If a server misses a change notification, it picks up the change the next time it does a local host cache coherency check.

NOTE   Almost all IMA changes are under 64KB in size.

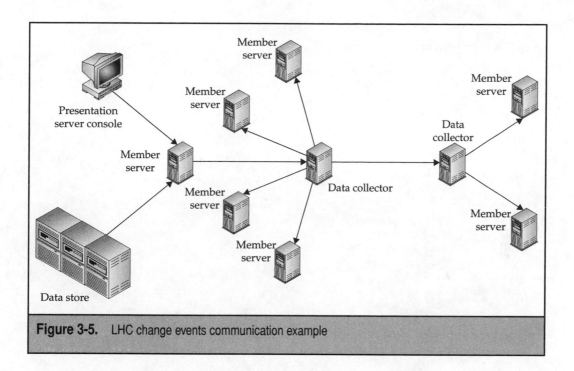

Figure 3-5.   LHC change events communication example

Figure 3-5 shows a communications example of LHC change events.

1. The administrator makes a change in the Presentation Server Console affecting all the servers in the farm.

2. The server the Presentation Server Console is connected to updates its LHC and writes the change to the data store.

3. The member server then forwards the change to the data collector for the zone in which it resides. The data collector updates its LHC.

4. The data collector, in turn, forwards the change to all the member servers in its zone and all other data collectors in the farm. All servers update their LHCs with the change.

5. The data collectors in the other zones, in turn, forward the update to all the member servers in their zones, and they subsequently update their LHCs.

CHAPTER 4

Data Store Design and Recommendations

DATA STORE CPU GUIDELINES

When selecting the hardware to host the data store, consider the following variables:

▼ Number of objects in the farm, including servers, applications, and so forth.

■ Frequency of events, such as adding/removing servers.

▲ Maximum number of servers starting the IMA service simultaneously.

Because each of these questions has a bearing on the type of hardware used to host the data store, the individual issues are discussed in the following sections.

Objects in the Data Store

To properly select the hardware to host a data store, a general understanding about the objects stored in the data store would be beneficial. Nearly every item displayed in the Citrix Presentation Server Console represents one or more entries in the data store, as shown in Table 4-1.

Some objects, such as applications and servers, create multiple entries in the data store. As the number of entries in the data store grows, the time required for IMA to search and retrieve the entries also grows.

As servers are added to the farm, the data store needs to service more requests. Plan the data store hardware platform based on the total number of servers that will eventually be in the farm.

The Size of Data Store Objects

When you create an object in the Presentation Server Console, such as publishing an application or adding a MetaFrame Administrator, you create a record for that object in the data store database. In the following table, Citrix *e*Labs has attempted to calculate the estimated size of objects' records as created in a data store utilizing a SQL 2000, service pack 3 database. Please note that the measurements shown in Table 4-2 should only be considered as guidelines because the sizes of an object's entries in the data store depend on many factors, such as the name of an object and its configurations.

Applications	Administrators	Folders	Installation Manager Groups
Installation Manager Packages	Servers	Load Evaluators	Printers
Printers Drivers	Policies	Resource Manager Metrics	Isolation Environment

Table 4-1. Typical Objects in the Data Store

Database Object	Size (Bytes)
Publish an application (Wordpad.exe, application name "Wordpad")	12064
Create an application isolation environment object (AIE1)	16468
Insert an application into an application isolation environment object (aiesetup aie1 rp505enu.exe)	4378
Publish an application into an application isolation environment (Acrobat5 and AIE 1)	10602
Create a blank policy named "policy one"	8694
Configure all rules and assign policy to domain users group	1018
Create a Resource Manager application named "notepad" configured for one server	7555
Import a Network Printer Server with one printer	2172
Add one printer—"HP laserJet 8100 PS"	4108
Add Resource Manager Metric for one server (Citrix MetaFrame Presentation Server/Data Store bytes written/sec)	3324
Add one Domain Administrator as a MetaFrame Administrator	1743
Add one User group as a MetaFrame Administrator	1763
Configure Installation Manager Properties (account, path)	1632
Add a package	24069
Create a package group named "Group1" that contains one package	4405
Create a server group for Installation Manager (Server Group 1) with one server	1133
Add a Server Folder named "Server Folder" with permissions copied	1187
Add an Application folder named "App folder"	1189
Create a load evaluator with one evaluation rule (server user load)	1812
Join a server to the farm	74320

Table 4-2.   Data Store Object/Action and Typical Size (in Bytes)

Data Store Hardware Guidelines

As with any client-server database application, the CPU power and speed of the database server can improve the response time of an application. Presentation Server is no different. In a Presentation Server environment, the following events are improved by increasing the processing power of the data store:

▼ Starting the IMA service on multiple servers simultaneously

■ Installing a server into the farm

▲ Removing a server from the farm

The response time of other farm events, such as starting the IMA service on a single server, re-creating the local host cache, or replication of printer drivers to all farm servers, is more related to the farm size, rather than on the response time of the data store.

Testing shows that adding processors to the data store can dramatically improve response time when multiple simultaneous queries are being executed. If the environment has large groups of servers coming online frequently, the additional processors can service the requests faster.

However, with serial events, such as installing or removing a farm server, the additional processors show lower performance gains. To improve the processing time for these types of events, increase the processor speed of the data store hardware platform.

Data Store Network Optimizations

You can configure the data store in several different ways to increase the performance and throughput of the database server. In large farms with powerful database servers, the network can become the performance bottleneck when reading information from the data store during startup. This is particularly true when the database server hosts various resource-intensive databases. As with the Presentation Servers, Citrix recommends that you use a teaming NIC solution, such as switch-assisted load balancing, to improve the available bandwidth of the server hosting the data store. To find out if the network is the bottleneck, monitor the CPU usage on the data store. If the CPU utilization is not at 100% while the IMA service is starting, and it is still in the process of starting, the network can be the bottleneck. If the CPU utilization is at or near 100%, it is likely that additional processor(s) may be needed.

Data store connectivity testing was performed in the Citrix *e*Labs on a 100 Mbps switched LAN. This testing was also repeated in a Gigabit Ethernet environment. Two NICs that were teamed via switch-assisted load balancing, that is, 400 Mbps throughput, provided ample throughput without the additional cost associated with gigabit NICs, cables, and switch ports. However, in large environments, gigabit connectivity may be beneficial.

Data Store Guidelines

The general guidelines for choosing a data store are listed in Table 4-3 and are also found in the *MetaFrame Presentation Server Administrator's Guide*.

The following are general recommendations for the server farm's data store:

▼ Microsoft Access and Microsoft SQL Desktop Engine (MSDE) are suitable for all small and many medium-sized environments

▲ Microsoft SQL Server, Oracle, and IBM DB2 are suitable for any size environment and are especially recommended for all large and enterprise environments

The following is a list of things to consider when choosing a data store for a farm:

▼ Microsoft Access and MSDE are best used for centralized farms.

■ Microsoft Access and MSDE support only indirect mode for all servers other than the host server and, therefore, have slower performance than a direct mode data store in large farm implementations.

■ Database replication is not supported with Microsoft Access.

■ For MSDE replication information, please visit www.microsoft.com/sql/techinfo/development/2000/msde2000.asp.

■ Use databases that support replication when deploying large farms across a WAN. You can obtain considerable performance advantage by distributing the load over multiple database servers.

▲ In the Citrix *e*Labs, Microsoft SQL Server, Oracle, and IBM DB2 perform similarly with large farms. Oracle Real Application Clusters (RAC) includes the added advantage of load balancing incoming requests between the servers.

	Small	Medium	Large	Enterprise
Servers	1–50	25–100	50–100	100 or more
Named users	<150	<3000	<5000	>3000
Applications	<100	<100	<500	<2000

Table 4-3.   Data Store Selection Guidelines

Using Replicated Data Store Databases

Having a single data store is recommended where appropriate, but in some situations, a replicated data store can improve farm performance. This section covers the concerns and situations that arise from using replicated database technology.

High-latency WAN Concerns

High-latency links without the use of replicated databases can create situations where the data store is locked for extended periods of time when performing maintenance from remote sites. This means the IMA service may start after extended periods of time and some normal operations may fail when performed from the remote site.

TIP Performing farm maintenance using the Presentation Server Console from a remote site that has high latency is not recommended. For better performance, run the console as a published application.

In a high-latency situation:

▼ Data store writes take longer to complete and, for a period of time, block all additional writes from local or remote sites.

▲ Data store reads will probably not adversely affect local connections, but the remote site can experience slower performance.

Replicated Database Issues

Using replicated databases to speed performance may be justified. The farm servers perform many more reads from the data store than writes to the data store. Most reads occur during startup, when each server populates its local host cache.

In a LAN environment, using replicated databases can speed the startup time of the IMA service and improve the responsiveness of the servers in large farms.

In a WAN environment, the configuration of the data store is important. Because Presentation Server is read-intensive, place replicas of the data store at sites where a considerable number of servers reside. This practice minimizes reads across the WAN link. Limit the use of replicated databases to situations where the remote site has enough Presentation Servers to justify the cost of placing a replicated copy of the database at the site.

TIP Database replication consumes bandwidth. The database server software configuration, not Presentation Server, controls the frequency of database updates.

THE DATA STORE REQUIREMENTS

Table 4-4 lists the versions and releases of third-party databases tested during the development of Presentation Server. While this list is not the end-all list of supported databases, it does represent those that have been tested.

Databases	Versions	Platform
Microsoft Access Jet Engine 4.x	4.x up to SP8	Windows
Microsoft SQL Server Desktop Engine (MSDE)	8.00.760 up to MSDE 2000 Release A	Windows
Microsoft SQL Server	7.0 SP2 or later, 2000 up to SP3A	Windows
Oracle	7 (7.3.4)	Windows
	8 (8.0.6)	
	8i (8.1.5, 8.1.6, 8.1.7)	Windows /UNIX
	9i (9.0.1)	Windows
	9i R2	Windows/Solaris
	10g (10.1.0.2.0)	Windows
IBM DB2 UDB	7.2 (FixPac 5 or later),	Windows
	8.1 (FixPac 4)	Windows

Table 4-4.   List of Tested and Supported Third-party Databases

The following table denotes the supported and tested ODBC Client Database versions. Updates to the third-party ODBC clients occur frequently; please use Table 4-5 as a guideline. Citrix recommends updating to the latest available ODBC client version for the particular database being used prior to the installation of Presentation Server.

CAUTION   Oracle client 8.1.5 is not supported. This client must be upgraded to 8.1.55 prior to the installation of MetaFrame XP 1.0 or higher.

IMPORTANT   The 8.1.7 and 8.1.7.2 native Oracle clients require a registry modification prior to the installation of MetaFrame XP 1.0. This does not apply to later versions. The Citrix Knowledge Base Article CTX949726 refers to this issue. Please see the Citrix Support Knowledge Base on the Web at http://support.citrix.oom/ for more information.

Additional considerations for Microsoft Access, Microsoft SQL Server, Oracle, and IBM DB2 as data stores for Presentation Server are listed in the following. Although Presentation Server uses ODBC for connectivity, other ODBC compliant databases are not supported with Presentation Server.

Client Databases	Driver Versions
SQL 7.0 Enterprise for NT MDAC 2.5	3.70.0820
SQL 7.0 Enterprise for NT MDAC 2.5 SP1	3.70.0821
SQL 2000 Enterprise for NT MDAC 2.5 SP2	3.70.0961
SQL 2000 Enterprise for NT MDAC 2.6 SP1	2000.80.380.0
SQL 2000 Enterprise for NT MDAC 2.7	2000.81.7713.00
SQL 2000 Enterprise for NT MDAC 2.7 SP1	2000.81.9030.04
SQL 2000 Enterprise for NT MDAC 2.8	2000.85.1022.00
Oracle 7.3.4 for NT	2.50.0301
Oracle 8.0.6 for NT	8.0.6.00
Oracle 8.1.55 for NT	8.01.55.00
Oracle 8.1.6 for NT	8.1.6.00
Oracle 8.1.6 for NT and UNIX/Solaris	8.1.6.00
Oracle 8.1.7.2 for NT	8.1.7.2.00
Oracle 9.0.1 for NT	9.00.11.00
Oracle 9i R2 for NT and UNIX/Solaris	9.2.0.1.0
Oracle 9i R2 for NT	9.2.0.1.0
Oracle 10g for NT	10.01.00.02
IBM DB2 UDB 7.2, FixPak 5 for NT	7.01.00.55
IBM DB2 UDB 7.2, FixPak 7 for NT	7.01.00.65
IBM DB2 UDB 8.1, FixPak 4 for NT	8.01.04.341

Table 4-5. Tested and Supported MDAC, Oracle, and DB2 Clients

Using Microsoft Access

All servers connect indirectly and maintain connections to the host server.

▼ By default, the server that hosts the database is also its zone's data collector.

■ Tuning the Jet Database Engine with registry settings can improve performance for large farms. Consult the Microsoft documentation about performance tuning for the Jet Database Engine. Back up both the registry and the Mf20.mdb file before changing the tuning parameters.

■ Use dsmaint backup to perform an online backup of the data store. This can be scripted easily in a batch file.

▲ Back up the data store before using the Presentation Server Console to change the data store. Scheduling a daily backup is sufficient in most cases.

Using Microsoft SQL Server

The practices outlined in this section suggest the best practices for using Microsoft SQL Server as the data store. This is not intended as a substitute for the Microsoft SQL Server documentation. Read all of the Microsoft SQL Server documentation prior to installing Microsoft SQL Server. These instructions do not refer to Microsoft SQL Server Desktop Engine (MSDE). See the Administrator's Guide for information about using MSDE as the data store.

Server Configuration

▼ When using Microsoft SQL Server in a replicated environment, be sure to use the same user account on each Microsoft SQL Server for the data store.

■ Each Presentation Server farm requires a dedicated database. However, multiple databases can run on a single Microsoft SQL Server. Do not install the Presentation Server farm in a database that is shared with any other client/server applications.

■ On both SQL 7 and SQL 2000, follow Microsoft recommendations for configuring database and transaction logs for recovery.

■ Whenever a change is made using the Presentation Server Console, back up the database. Scheduling a daily backup is sufficient in most cases.

▲ Disable Hyper-Threading. Tests have shown an increase in performance in administrative actions (IMA start time, Presentation Server Console) when Hyper-Threading is disabled on the SQL server acting as the farm data store. The decrease in performance with Hyper-Threading enabled is caused when two or more threads do the same type of action (I/O, calculations, and so forth) on the same physical processor. Please note, this recommendation applies to the data store only and Presentation Servers do realize a benefit from Hyper-Threading but, as always, this depends on the types of applications published on those servers. Refer to your server vendor for specific details on disabling Hyper-Threading.

NOTE Previous recommendations stated that if installing more than 256 servers into a farm configured to use a Microsoft SQL Server data store, the number of worker threads available for the database must be equal to or greater than the number of servers in the server farm. This statement has been found to be incorrect. The current recommendation is to leave the default setting of 255 worker threads for up to and greater than 1,000 servers in a farm. For more information regarding SQL Server configuration settings, see Microsoft Knowledge Base article 319942.

SQL TempDB Considerations

When using SQL server as a data store, Presentation Server operations can cause the tempdb to grow larger than its default size. Although the tempdb database's *Autogrow* feature is set by default in SQL Server 7.0 and 2000, the automatic growth of the tempdb can result in performance degradation. Citrix recommends that you permanently set the tempdb to a reasonable size initially.

The tempdb database is re-created every time SQL Server starts. By default, the tempdb has a data file of 8.0MB and log file of 0.5MB. By having the tempdb file set to the "typical" size when SQL Server is restarted (and when it is re-created from scratch to the size you set), you can eliminate the overhead from the tempdb growing.

Citrix recommends the following regarding the usage of tempDB in a Presentation Farm:

▼ Permanently change the tempdb database file's initialization size. Set the tempdb data file size according to the size of your farm. Citrix recommends reserving 0.75MB to 1.25MB of space in a tempdb data file for each Presentation Server in the farm. For example, in a 100-server farm, Citrix recommends permanently setting the tempdb data file size from 75MB to 125MB and the tempdb log file size to half the data file size. You can accomplish this by using the Enterprise Manager or ALTER DATABSE … MODIFY FILE command. Even after the SQL server restarts, the tempdb keeps the size you set.

■ Set the auto growth increment of the tempdb in terms of file size, rather than percentage. For farm sizes less than 100 servers, set the increment to 50MB for the data file and 25MB for the log file. For a farm size larger than 100 servers, set the increment to 100MB for the data file and 50MB for the log file.

■ If possible, put the tempdb on its own physical disk, preferably a RAID 0 Array or other disk subsystem.

■ In SQL server 7.0, make sure the truncate log on checkpoint database option is set for the tempdb. When this database option is set, the tempdb log will be truncated each time the checkpoint process is run. To truncate the transaction log on SQL 2000, create a maintenance plan or follow the next recommendation.

■ In SQL Server 2000, make sure the Recovery mode of the tempdb is set to simple. Under this Recovery mode, the tempdb log file automatically truncates when a SQL server check point event occurs.

▲ If the tempdb transaction log file grows too large before the checkpoint process occurs, you can issue a BACKUP LOG tempdb WITH TRUNCATE_ONLY to manually truncate the tempdb transaction log.

NOTE If the tempdb data file has been expended and/or used all the disk space, certain Presentation Server operations will fail. You can add more data files to the tempdb using either SQL Server enterprise manager or the ALTER DATABASE … ADD FILE command line to add more files to the tempdb. The recommendation is to use the previous methods to add more files to the tempdb at installation to prevent the tempdb from being used up.

Using Oracle

The practices outlined in this section are suggested implementations for the Oracle data store. They are not intended to be a substitute for the Oracle documentation. Read all of the Oracle documentation prior to installing Oracle. Guidelines given here can be used on Oracle7, Oracle8, Oracle8*i*, Oracle 9*i*, and Oracle 10*g*, except as noted otherwise.

Client Configuration

If you use the Oracle 8.1.7 client to access the data store, you must take several steps to ensure proper operation with Presentation Server. The Oracle 8.1.7.0 driver installs a security feature, called NT Security (NTS) that uses Windows NT credentials to authenticate to the Oracle server. Because the IMA service is configured to use the System account to access the data store, IMA fails to connect to the Oracle server when the NTS feature is enabled. If this happens, IMA reports error code 2147483649.

NOTE The following steps are not required with the Oracle 8.1.6 client because it does not use NTS.

For the Presentation Server installation to recognize that the Oracle 8.1.7.*x* client is installed, do the following:

1. Install the Oracle 8.1.6.*x* client and upgrade to 8.1.7.*x*.
2. Run the Net8 Assistant.
3. Navigate to Configuration | Local | Profile.
4. Select Oracle Advanced Security.
5. Select the Authentication tab.
6. Remove NTS from the Selected Methods list if it is present.
7. Install MetaFrame Presentation Server.

If you use dsmaint to migrate from an Access data store to an Oracle 8.1.7 data store, the IMA service fails to start because the Oracle 8.1.7.0 driver alters the logon authentication method. To avoid this problem, when migrating from Microsoft Access to Oracle 8.1.7, disable the Oracle NTS feature.

To Disable the Oracle NTS Feature

1. Run the Net8 Assistant.
2. Navigate to Configuration | Local | Profile.
3. Select Oracle Advanced Security.
4. Select the Authentication tab.
5. Remove NTS from the Selected Methods list if it is present.

Failover   Oracle enables administrators to maintain a standby database for quick disaster recovery. A *standby database* maintains a copy of the production database in a permanent state of recovery. If a disaster occurs in the production database, you can open the standby database with a minimum amount of recovery.

Important items concerning Oracle failover:

▼ With Oracle8*i*, the management of standby databases is fully automatic.

■ The standby database must run on the same version of the kernel that is on the production system.

■ Standby databases only fail one way. They cannot fail back.

■ If a database fails, use dsmaint config to reconfigure the Presentation Servers to point to the standby database.

▲ Citrix recommends the use of a standby database for Presentation Server farms. See the Oracle documentation for instructions about setting up a standby database.

For MetaFrame Presentation Server 3.0 and Later   To reduce the load on a single Oracle database server, use Oracle Synchronous Multi-Master Replication to distribute the database load over multiple Oracle Database Servers. Install and distribute the farm servers evenly across these databases.

Presentation Server requires data coherency across multiple databases. Therefore, Synchronous Multi-Master Replication is required for writes to the multiple databases.

Using Oracle as a distributed database solution requires the following:

▼ All participating databases must be running Oracle Enterprise Versions.

■ All clients (Presentation Server direct servers) must be SQL*Net Version 2 or Net8.

■ Install the farm database first on the master definition site, and then configure the Multi-Master Replication.

▲ Replicate all the table objects contained in the data store user's schema and any indexes that are used for performance purposes. Do not replicate the index created automatically by the Oracle server while creating Primary Key Constraint and Unique Constraint.

Citrix recommends that you consult the Oracle documentation when setting up replication.

▼ The documentation for Oracle8*i* is at the following web address:

http://www.oracle.com/technology/documentation/oracle8i.html

■ The documentation for Oracle9*i* is at the following web address:

http://www.oracle.com/technology/documentation/oracle9i.html

▲ The documentation for Oracle10*g* is at the following web address:

http://www.oracle.com/technology/documentation/database10g.html

Using IBM DB2

Citrix Presentation Server 4.0 supports IBM DB2 Universal Database Enterprise Edition Version 7.2 for Windows 2000 with FixPak 5 or greater, as well as Version 8.1 for Windows 2000 with FixPak 4 or greater.

Install the IBM DB2 run-time client and apply the latest FixPak on each Presentation Server that will directly access the database server.

If you have multiple Presentation Server farms, create a separate database/tablespace for each farm's data store. Restart the system after you install the IBM DB2 run-time client and the FixPak, and before you install Presentation Server. In some cases, you may also need to restart the system after you install the run-time client and before you install the FixPak. See the IBM DB2 documentation for more information.

> **IMPORTANT** Presentation Server uses the data type of binary large object (BLOB) to store information in an IBM DB2 database. IBM DB2 does not support the use of BLOB data types in an updatable replication scenario. Therefore, if your server farm needs to have updatable replicas, use Microsoft SQL Server or Oracle for the farm's data store, instead of IBM DB2.

Depending on the size of your server farm, you may need to modify the following options in IBM DB2 Control Center:

- ▼ **appheapsz, app_ctl_heap_sz, maxlocks** You may need to modify these options if you have a large server farm (50 or more servers) that is relatively active.

- ■ **Maxappls** This setting must be greater than the number of servers in the farm, or the servers will fail to connect (the default is 40).

- ■ **avg_appls** This setting should be equal to the number of servers in the farm.

- ▲ **logfilsiz, logprimary, logsecond** You may need to adjust these settings upwards if you move the farm from another database.

Citrix recommends using a separate database with a dedicated tablespace for the Presentation Server farm's data store.

REPLICATING A SQL SERVER 2000 DATABASE

This section outlines the steps necessary to replicate with SQL Server 2000. To replicate an SQL Server 2000 database, use SQL Enterprise Manager. Begin by creating a new database on the SQL server to be used as the source for all replicas you create. Be sure that the account you use to create the database has db_owner permissions and is the same one you use on the replicated database.

Before setting up replication, ensure the following:

▼ Ideally, the Windows installations should be clean, fresh (from CD) installations instead of images. If images of Windows are used, make sure they do not come from the same image, but from different ones for each server. If your Windows installations come from the same image, then replication will not work.

■ Do not mix Windows 2000 with Windows 2003. The Distributed Transaction Co-ordinator service operates differently in Windows 2003 than it does in Windows 2000. If you mix the operating systems (OSs), replication will fail.

■ For Windows 2003 Server verify that both Publisher and Subscriber SQL servers are in the same domain. If they are not, please review Microsoft Article 817064.

▲ Install SQL Server on the servers designated for the data stores

Verify that the Microsoft Distributed Transaction Coordinator is installed on the servers designated for the data stores.

Setting Up the SQL Server Data Store for Distribution

Perform these steps for both servers:

1. From the Start menu, start the Services Manager.

2. From Services Manager, set up the same domain log on account for the following services (the local system account does not work):

   ▼ SQLServerAgent

   ■ MSSQLServer

   ▲ MSDTC (Distributed Transaction Coordinator on Windows 2000)

NOTE   If you are configuring SQL replication on a Windows 2003 server, verify the MSDTC service is using the Network Services security account (this account uses a blank password).

The following describes the general tasks to successfully replicate a SQL Server database. Each task is explained in more detail in the following sections.

1. Establish the distributor server.

2. Set the distributor properties.

3. Publish the source database.

4. Push the published database out to subscribers.

Step 1—Establish the Distributor Server

Complete the following steps to define the server that will act as the distributor.

MS SQL 2000 servers acting as Publisher, Distributor, and Subscriber need to be in the same NT/AD domain and the SQL services should be started under the same account.

1. Open Enterprise Manager on the server on which the source database is located.

2. Right-click the Replication folder and select Configure Publishing | Subscribers | Distribution Wizard.

3. On the Select Distributor page, select the current server to act as the distributor.

4. Keep the default Snapshot folder.

5. On the Customize the Configuration page, choose the option No, use the following default settings.

6. Click Finish.

Step 2—Set the Distributor Properties

Complete the following steps to set the distributor properties.

1. Right-click the Replication Monitor folder and choose Distributor Properties.

2. On the Publication Databases tab, check the Trans box next to the database you want to replicate, as shown in Figure 4-1.

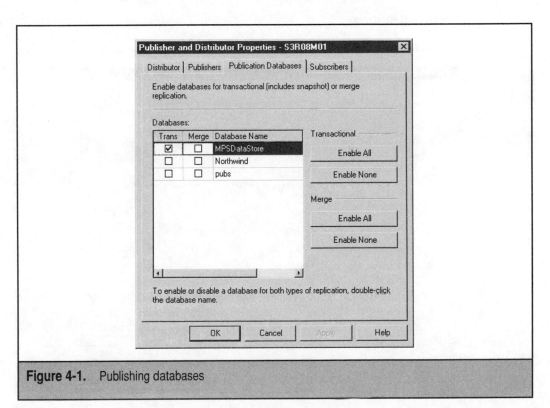

Figure 4-1. Publishing databases

Step 3—Publish the Source Database

Complete the following steps to publish the database that you want to replicate.

1. Right-click the database name and go to New | Publication to start the Create Publication wizard.

2. Click Show advanced options in this wizard, and then click Next.

3. On the Choose Publication Database screen, select the database you want to replicate, and then click Next.

4. On the Select Publication Type page, choose Transactional publication.

5. On the Updatable Subscriptions page, select the Immediate updating option, as shown in Figure 4-2.

6. On the Specify Subscriber Types page, select the Servers running SQL Server 2000 option.

On the Specify Articles page, shown in Figure 4-3, select both Show and Publish for the tables object type on the left side of the page. Do not publish stored procedures to the replicated databases.

1. Click Next on the Article Issues page.

2. Name the publication.

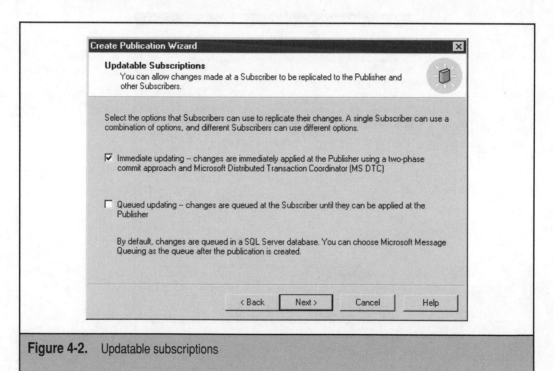

Figure 4-2. Updatable subscriptions

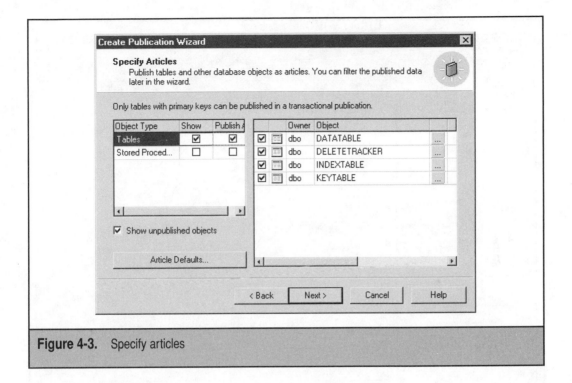

Figure 4-3.   Specify articles

3. On the Customize the Properties of the Publication page, choose No, create the publication as specified.

4. Click Finish to complete the wizard. The publication is displayed in the Publications folder, as shown in Figure 4-4.

Step 4—Push the Published Database to Subscribers

Complete the following steps to push the publication to subscribers.

1. Right-click the published database in the Publications folder and choose Push new subscription to start the Push Subscription Wizard.

2. Click Show advanced options in this wizard, and then click Next.

3. On the Choose Subscribers page, select the subscribers for the published database.

4. On the next page, choose the destination database to which you want to replicate the source database.

5. On the Set Distribution Agent Location page, choose to run the agent at the distributor.

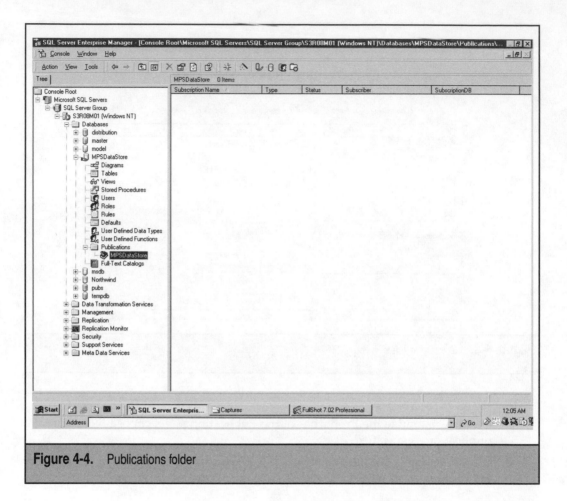

Figure 4-4.   Publications folder

6. Set the Distribution Agent Schedule to continuously.

7. On the Initialize Subscription page, shown in Figure 4-5, choose Yes, initialize the schema and data and select the option to Start the Snapshot Agent.

8. On the Updatable Subscriptions page, select the Immediate updating option.

9. On the Start Required Services page, displayed in Figure 4-6, the services that must be running are listed. Verify that the applicable required services are running on the distributor server.

10. Click Finish on the next screen to complete the wizard.

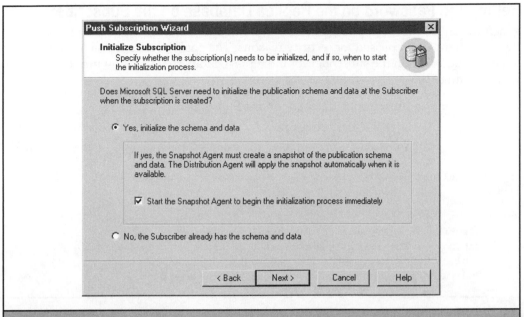

Figure 4-5.   Initialize subscription

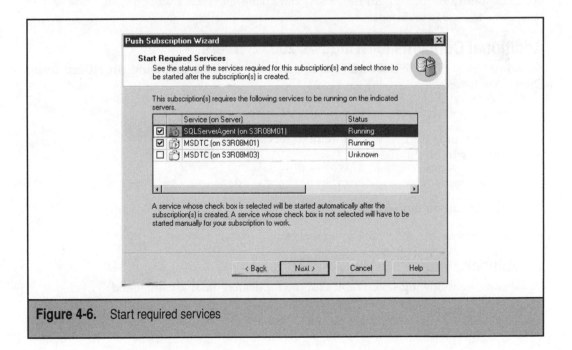

Figure 4-6.   Start required services

Setting the Password on the Replica Database on the Subscriber

When the subscription (replica) database is created on the Subscriber, the password for the sa account is not passed for security reasons. The password for the sa account needs to be manually set on the subscriber for the replica database. The following steps are one way to change the password for the sa account:

1. Select the subscription database on the Subscriber.
2. Select Tools | SQL Query Analyzer.
3. In the SQL Query Analyzer window, type and run the following stored procedure:

```
sp_link_publication '<Distributor>', '<Database>', '<Publication>', 0, 'SA',
'<Pwd>'
```

```
Where:
     Distributor = The name of the distributor server
     Database = The name of the published database on the distributor
     Publication = The name of the publication that is to be linked
     Pwd = The password for the SA account on the distributor
```

NOTE In some scenarios, the previous stored procedure did not work. If you are experiencing this, try using the following stored procedure instead:

```
sp_link_publication 'publisher', 'database', 'publication', 0, 'sa',
'password', 'distributor'
```

Additional Concerns for Windows 2003 Servers

As a final step on both Subscriber and Publisher, run the following procedure using Query Analyzer:

```
exec sp_serveroption 'myServer', 'data access', 'true'
```

where myServer is the name of the remote server.

Example run on Publisher:

```
exec sp_serveroption 'SubscriberServer', 'data access', 'true'
```

Example run on Subscriber:

```
exec sp_serveroption 'PublisherServer', 'data access', 'true'
```

Troubleshooting

Make sure the following seven tables on the replicated database are listed:

▼ DATATABLE

■ INDEXTABLE

- KEYTABLE
- MSreplication_objects
- MSreplication_subscriptions
- MSsubscription_agents
- ▲ MSsubscription_properties

If all tables are not listed, delete the replication setup and begin again. The dtproperties table appears if you used the Database Diagram Wizard in Enterprise Manager.

If you are installing Presentation Server for the first time, select the server hosting the replicated database when prompted.

If you have a server in the server farm that you want to connect to the new database, create a new DSN file on the Presentation Server and point it to the replicated SQL Server database. You can then use the dsmaint config command to point the IMA Service to the new database.

Multisubscriber Replication

Special consideration must be taken when configuring a multisubscriber model (one publisher and two or more subscribers) for the Presentation Server database.

By default, Microsoft SQL Server leaves foreign-key referential-integrity constraints intact at the subscriber databases. Presentation Server uses a two-phase commit between the subscriber and the publisher, so these relationships are not necessary because integrity is maintained at the master/publisher. After a subscriber commits a transaction at the master/publisher, the publisher pushes the changes out to all remaining subscribers. However, the referential integrity constraints on the remaining subscribers prevent the transactions from completing correctly.

When this occurs, you see errors similar to the following:

```
"DELETE statement conflicted with COLUMN REFERENCE constraint
'FK__DATATABLE__nodei__35BCFE0A'. The conflict occurred in database
'CTXIMA', table 'DATATABLE', column 'nodeid'. The row was not found at
the Subscriber when applying the replicated command."
```

To prevent the foreign key relationships from blocking the replicated transaction, perform the following steps on all of the subscriber servers, as well as the distribution server.

1. In Enterprise Manager, select the MetaFrame Presentation Server database.
2. Click on Tables.
3. Right-click DATATABLE in right pane and select Design Table from the Context menu.
4. Click the Manage Relationships button.
5. Verify the Enforce Relationship for Replication check box is marked for the relationship that starts with FK__DATATABLE__nodei.

6. Save the changes to the DATATABLE.

7. Repeat steps 3 through 6 for INDEXTABLE and the foreign key relationship that starts with FK__INDEXTABL__nodei.

8. Verify the foreign key relationships under KEYTABLE do not have the Enforce relationship for replication box checked.

9. Repeat steps 1 through 8 at each subscriber database.

Promoting a Subscriber to a Publisher

Microsoft SQL Server 2000 has no predefined procedure for promoting a subscriber to a publisher. The recommended method is to stop all replication between the old publisher and all the subscribers, and then reestablish subscriptions between the new publisher and the remaining subscribers. These steps also work if the desire is simply to break replication and use the old subscriber as a Master, instead of a replica.

After discontinuing all replication activities for the Presentation Server database, perform the following steps on the promoted subscriber *before* reestablishing replication with the former subscribers.

1. Reestablish the autoincrementing functionality of the KEYTABLE *nodeid* field.

   a. In Enterprise Manager, select the MetaFrame Presentation Server database.

   b. Click on Tables.

   c. Right-click KEYTABLE in the right pane and select Design Table from the Context menu.

   d. Select the *nodeid* field.

   e. From the Columns tab on the bottom panel:

      1) Delete any default value.

      2) Set Identity to a value of Yes.

      3) Set Identity Seed to a value of 1.

      4) Set Identity Increment to a value of 1.

   f. Save the changes made to the KEYTABLE.

2. Reestablish the autoincrementing functionality of the DATATABLE *dummyid* field.

   a. In Enterprise Manager, select the MetaFrame Presentation Server database.

   b. Click on Tables.

   c. Right-click DATATABLE in the right pane and select Design Table from the Context menu.

   d. Select the *dummyid* field.

   e. From the Columns tab on the bottom panel:

      1) Delete any default value.

      2) Set Identity to a value of Yes.

      3) Set Identity Seed to a value of 1.

      4) Set Identity Increment to a value of 1.

   f. Save the changes made to the DATATABLE.

3. Reestablish the autoincrementing functionality of the INDEXTABLE *dummyid* field.

   a. In Enterprise Manager, select the MetaFrame Presentation Server database.

   b. Click on Tables.

   c. Right-click DATATABLE in the right pane and select Design Table from the Context menu.

   d. Select the *dummyid* field.

   e. From the Columns tab on the bottom panel:

      1) Delete any default value.

      2) Set Identity to a value of Yes.

      3) Set Identity Seed to a value of 1.

      4) Set Identity Increment to a value of 1.

   f. Save the changes made to the DATATABLE.

4. Reestablish the enforcement of Foreign Key Relationships if in a Multisubscriber scenario.

   a. In Enterprise Manager, select the MetaFrame Presentation Server database.

   b. Click on Tables.

   c. Right-click DATATABLE in the right pane and select Design Table from the Context menu.

   d. Click the Manage Relationships button.

   e. Verify the Enforce Relationship for Replication check box is marked for the relationship that starts with FK__DATATABLE__nodei.

   f. Save the changes to the DATATABLE.

   g. Repeat steps c through f for INDEXTABLE and the foreign key relationship that starts with FK__INDEXTABLE__nodci.

After completing the previous steps, reboot all the SQL servers and the promoted subscriber should be a functional master. The remaining subscribers, if any, may have replication reestablished. At this point, the old publisher/master is no longer functional in that role. If replication is to be reestablished with the old publisher, it must be configured as a subscriber.

Oracle Replication on Oracle 9i and 10g

Oracle replication involves two types: Basic and Advanced. *Basic replication* provides an elementary means to replicate data between databases. Basic replication is always one-way. *Advanced replication* is only available in the Enterprise edition of Oracle and provides more complex replication solutions, such as:

▼ Updatable Materialized Views

■ Writeable Materialized Views

■ Multi-Master replication

▲ Procedural replication

Citrix Presentation Server requires and supports only the Oracle Advanced Replication feature. In particular, Presentation Server supports Synchronous Multi-Master Replication. Oracle Synchronous Multi-Master Replication can be set up using Oracle Enterprise Manager or Replication Management API. Citrix recommends using the Replication Management API to set up the Oracle Synchronous Multi-Master Replication.

All the databases involved in the Oracle Synchronous Multi-Master Replications are called *master sites*. For the purpose of this illustration of using the Replication Management API to set up the Synchronous Multi-Master Replication, two databases are used: one is called east.citrix.com and the other is called west.citrix.com. In this example, objects are replicated from east.citrix.com to west.citrix.com.

The general steps for setting up the Oracle Synchronous Multi-Master Replication in Oracle database versions 9*i* and 10*g* are the following:

▼ Configure the initialization parameters

■ Set Up master sites

■ Create necessary schemas on both master sites

■ Create master group

▲ Start replication

Step 1: Configuring the Initialization Parameter

For Oracle replication to work, certain Oracle server initialization parameters must be set. Table 4-6 gives a list of initialization parameters that must be configured for the Oracle Synchronous Multi-Master Replication to work. These parameters must be configured on all the databases involved in the Synchronous Multi-Master Replication.

These parameters need to be set up at both master sites that participated in the Synchronous Multi-Master Replications. You can use the Oracle Server Enterprise Manager to change these parameters, or you can use the ALTER SYSTEM command to change these parameters. After you change the initialization parameter, you need to restart your Oracle server to have the initialization parameter to take effect.

Parameter Name	Default Value	Recommended Value
Global_names	FALSE	It is required to set global_names to TRUE in each database to be involved in multi-master replication.
Job_queue_processes	0	This parameter must be set to the value of at least one. Citrix recommends 3 + 1 per additional master site.
Open_links	4	*Open_links* defines the number of concurrent database links that are required to a given database. This parameter needs to be configured for an initial setting of 4 + 2 additional links for each master site.
Processes	Derived from the value of the parameter parallel_max_servers	Add at least 12 to the current value.
Shared_pool_size	OS-dependent	Add 80 *M* for Multi-Master Replication.

Table 4-6.   Oracle Initialization Parameters

Step 2: Setting Up Master Sites

Before you set up the master sites, configure your network and Oracle Net so both databases can communicate with each other. The following section illustrates how to set up master sites using Oracle Management API.

Complete the following steps to set up the East.citrix.com master site.

1. Connect as SYSTEM at a master site at East.citrix.com.

   CONNECT SYS/citrix@east.citrix.com as sysdba

2. Create the replication administrator at east.citrix.com.

The replication administrator must be granted the necessary privileges to create and manage a replication environment. The replication administrator must be created at each database that participates in the replication environment.

```
CREATE USER repadmin IDENTIFIED BY repadmin;
```

3. Grant privileges to the replication administrator at east.citrix.com.

```
BEGIN
DBMS_REPCAT_ADMIN.GRANT_ADMIN_ANY_SCHEMA (
      username => 'repadmin');
END;
/


GRANT COMMENT ANY TABLE TO repadmin;
GRANT LOCK ANY TABLE TO repadmin;
```

The following statement gives repadmin the capability to connect to the Replication Management tool if later on you want to monitor the Multi-Master Replication using Replication Management tool.

```
GRANT SELECT ANY DICTIONARY TO repadmin;
```

4. Register the propagator at east.citrix.com.

The propagator is responsible for propagating the deferred transaction queue to other master sites.

```
BEGIN
DBMS_DEFER_SYS.REGISTER_PROPAGATOR (
      username => 'repadmin');
END;
/
```

5. Register the receiver at east.citrix.com.

The receiver receives the propagated deferred transactions sent by the propagator from other master sites.

```
BEGIN
DBMS_REPCAT_ADMIN.REGISTER_USER_REPGROUP (
      username => 'repadmin',
      privilege_type => 'receiver',
      list_of_gnames => NULL);
END;
/
```

6. Schedule purge at master site east.citrix.com.

To keep the size of the deferred transaction queue in check, you should purge successfully completed deferred transactions. The SCHEDULE_PURGE procedure automates the purge process for you. You must execute this procedure as the replication administrator.

```
CONNECT repadmin/repadmin@east.citrix.com

BEGIN
DBMS_DEFER_SYS.SCHEDULE_PURGE (
     next_date => SYSDATE,
     interval => 'SYSDATE + 1/24',
     delay_seconds => 0);
END;
/
```

Complete the following steps to set up the west.citrix.com master site.

1. Connect as SYSTEM at a master site at West.citrix.com.

   ```
   CONNECT sys/citrix@west.citrix.com as sysdba
   ```

2. Create the replication administrator at west.citrix.com.

   The replication administrator must be granted the necessary privileges to create and manage a replication environment. The replication administrator must be created at each database that participates in the replication environment.

   ```
   Create user REPADMIN identified by REPADMIN;
   ```

3. Grant privileges to the replication administrator at west.citrix.com.

   ```
   BEGIN
   DBMS_REPCAT_ADMIN.GRANT_ADMIN_ANY_SCHEMA (
        username => 'repadmin');
   END;
   /


   GRANT COMMENT ANY TABLE TO repadmin;
   GRANT LOCK ANY TABLE TO repadmin;
   ```

   The following statement gives repadmin capability to connect to the Replication Management tool, and then grant SELECT ANY DICTIONARY to repadmin:

   ```
   GRANT SELECT ANY DICTIONARY TO repadmin;
   ```

4. Register the propagator at west.citrix.com.

   The propagator is responsible for propagating the deferred transaction queue to other master sites.

   ```
   BEGIN
   DBMS_DEFER_SYS.REGISTER_PROPAGATOR (
        username => 'repadmin');
   END;
   /
   ```

5. Register the receiver at west.citrix.com.

   The receiver receives the propagated deferred transactions sent by the propagator from other master sites.

```
BEGIN
DBMS_REPCAT_ADMIN.REGISTER_USER_REPGROUP (
        username => 'repadmin',
        privilege_type => 'receiver',
        list_of_gnames => NULL);
END;
/
```

6. Schedule purge at master site west.citrix.com.

   To keep the size of the deferred transaction queue in check, you should purge successfully completed deferred transactions. The SCHEDULE_PURGE procedure automates the purge process for you. You must execute this procedure as the replication administrator.

```
CONNECT repadmin/repadmin@west.citrix.com

BEGIN
DBMS_DEFER_SYS.SCHEDULE_PURGE (
        next_date => SYSDATE,
        interval => 'SYSDATE + 1/24',
        delay_seconds => 0);
END;
/
```

Complete the following steps to create database links between the master sites.

1. Create database links between master sites.

   The database links provide the necessary distributed mechanisms to allow the different replication sites to replicate data among themselves. Before you create any private database links, you must create the public database links that each private database link will use. You then must create a database link between all replication administrators at each of the master sites that you have set up.

```
CONNECT sys/citrix@east.citrix.com as sysdba
CREATE PUBLIC DATABASE LINK west.citrix.com USING 'west.citrix.com';

CONNECT repadmin/repadmin@east.citrix.com
CREATE DATABASE LINK west.citrix.com CONNECT TO repadmin IDENTIFIED BY
repadmin;
```

```
CONNECT sys/citrix@west.citrix.com as sysdba
CREATE PUBLIC DATABASE LINK east.citrix.com USING 'east.citrix.com';

CONNECT repadmin/repadmin@west.citrix.com
CREATE DATABASE LINK east.citrix.com CONNECT TO repadmin IDENTIFIED BY
repadmin;
```

Step 3: Creating Necessary Schemas on Both Master Sites

Before you create the master group, make sure you have the tablespaces and users created on both master sites. The user names, that is, schema names, should be identical on both databases participating in Oracle Synchronous Multi-Master Replication. Citrix also recommends creating identical tablespaces name on both databases for easy management. If you already installed Presentation Server using one of your Oracle databases as the data store, you just need to create the tablespace and user on the other database, which will be used as the second master site.

If you have not yet installed any Presentation Servers, at least one Presentation Server must be installed using the east.citrix.com database as its data store. Refer to the Presentation Server Administrator's Guide for instructions to install Presentation Server using Oracle 9*i* or Oracle 10*g* as the data store.

Step 4: Creating a Master Group

In this example, you create the CPS_REP master group and replicate the objects that are used by Presentation Server. The schema used by the Presentation Server is called MPS. Complete the following steps to create the CPS_REP master group.

1. Create the master group.

   Use the CREATE_MASTER_REPGROUP procedure to define a new master group. When you add an object to your master group or perform other replication administrative tasks, you reference the master group name defined during this step. This step must be completed by the replication administrator.

   ```
   CONNECT repadmin/repadmin@east.citrix.com

   BEGIN
      DBMS_REPCAT.CREATE_MASTER_REPGROUP(
         gname => 'CPS_REP',
         qualifier => '',
         group_comment => '');
   END;
   /
   ```

2. Add objects to the master group.

    First, use the CREATE_MASTER_REPOBJECT procedure to add the database
    tables used by the Citrix Presentation Server to the master group.

```
BEGIN
    DBMS_REPCAT.CREATE_MASTER_REPOBJECT(
        gname => 'CPS_REP',
        type => 'TABLE',
        oname => 'deletetracker',
        sname => 'MPS',
        copy_rows => TRUE,
        use_existing_object => TRUE);
END;
/
BEGIN
    DBMS_REPCAT.CREATE_MASTER_REPOBJECT(
        gname => 'CPS_REP',
        type => 'TABLE',
        oname => 'indextable',
        sname => 'MPS',
        copy_rows => TRUE,
        use_existing_object => TRUE);
END;
/
BEGIN
    DBMS_REPCAT.CREATE_MASTER_REPOBJECT(
        gname => 'CPS_REP',
        type => 'TABLE',
        oname => 'keytable',
        sname => 'MPS',
        copy_rows => TRUE,
        use_existing_object => TRUE);
END;
/
BEGIN
    DBMS_REPCAT.CREATE_MASTER_REPOBJECT(
        gname => 'CPS_REP',
        type => 'TABLE',
        oname => 'seqtab',
        sname => 'MPS',
        copy_rows => TRUE,
        use_existing_object => TRUE);
END;
/
```

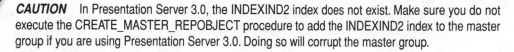

CAUTION   In Presentation Server 3.0, the INDEXIND2 index does not exist. Make sure you do not execute the CREATE_MASTER_REPOBJECT procedure to add the INDEXIND2 index to the master group if you are using Presentation Server 3.0. Doing so will corrupt the master group.

3. Add the following index to the master group.

```
BEGIN
    DBMS_REPCAT.CREATE_MASTER_REPOBJECT(
        gname => 'CPS_REP',
        type => 'INDEX',
        oname => 'indexind',
        sname => 'MPS',
        copy_rows => TRUE,
        use_existing_object => TRUE);
END;
/
BEGIN
    DBMS_REPCAT.CREATE_MASTER_REPOBJECT(
        gname => 'CPS_REP',
        type => 'INDEX',
        oname => 'indexind2',
        sname => 'MPS',
        copy_rows => TRUE,
        use_existing_object => TRUE);
END;
/
BEGIN
    DBMS_REPCAT.CREATE_MASTER_REPOBJECT(
        gname => 'CPS_REP',
        type => 'INDEX',
        oname => 'readbycontextid',
        sname => 'MPS',
        copy_rows => TRUE,
        use_existing_object => TRUE);
END;
/
BEGIN
    DBMS_REPCAT.CREATE_MASTER_REPOBJECT(
        gname => 'CPS_REP',
        type => 'INDEX',
        oname => 'readbyname',
        sname => 'MPS',
        copy_rows => TRUE,
        use_existing_object => TRUE);
END;
/
```

```
BEGIN
  DBMS_REPCAT.CREATE_MASTER_REPOBJECT(
    gname => 'CPS_REP',
    type => 'INDEX',
    oname => 'readbyuid',
    sname => 'MPS',
    copy_rows => TRUE,
    use_existing_object => TRUE);
END;
/
```

4. Add additional master sites.

    After you define your master group at the master definition site (the site where the master group was created becomes the master definition site by default), you can define the other sites that will participate in the replication environment. The use_existing_objects parameter in the ADD_MASTER_DATABASE procedure is set to FALSE because the schema used by Citrix Presentation Server does not exist at the other master site, west.citrix.com.

```
BEGIN
DBMS_REPCAT.ADD_MASTER_DATABASE (
    gname => 'CPS_REP',
    master => 'west.citrix.com',
    use_existing_objects => FALSE,
    copy_rows => TRUE,
    propagation_mode => 'SYNCHRONOUS');
END;
/
```

    You should wait until west.citrix.com appears in the DBA_REPSITES view before continuing. Execute the following SELECT statement in another SQL*Plus session to make sure that west.citrix.com. has appeared:

```
SELECT DBLINK FROM DBA_REPSITES WHERE GNAME = 'CPS_REP';
```

5. Generate replication support.

```
BEGIN
  DBMS_REPCAT.GENERATE_REPLICATION_SUPPORT(
    sname => 'MPS',
    oname => 'deletetracker',
    type => 'TABLE',
    min_communication => TRUE,
    generate_80_compatible => FALSE);
END;
/
```

```
BEGIN
   DBMS_REPCAT.GENERATE_REPLICATION_SUPPORT(
      sname => 'MPS',
      oname => 'indextable',
      type => 'TABLE',
      min_communication => TRUE,
      generate_80_compatible => FALSE);
END;
/
BEGIN
   DBMS_REPCAT.GENERATE_REPLICATION_SUPPORT(
      sname => 'MPS',
      oname => 'keytable',
      type => 'TABLE',
      min_communication => TRUE,
      generate_80_compatible => FALSE);
END;
/
BEGIN
   DBMS_REPCAT.GENERATE_REPLICATION_SUPPORT(
      sname => 'MPS',
      oname => 'seqtab',
      type => 'TABLE',
      min_communication => TRUE,
      generate_80_compatible => FALSE);
END;
/
```

Step 5: Starting Replication

After creating your master group, adding replication objects, generating replication support, and adding additional master databases, you need to start replication activity.

Before resuming replication activity, verification of replication support for objects must be verified for all four tables. Execute the following SELECT statement against DBA_REPOBEJCT view to verify that the value Generation_Status column is shown as Generated for the four tables:

```
SELECT ONAME, GENERATION_STATUS FROM DBA_REPOBJECT WHERE GNAME = 'CPS_REP' AND
TYPE='TABLE';
```

You also need to make sure that the DBA_REPCATLOG view is empty before resuming master activity. Execute the following SELECT statement to monitor your DBA_REPCATLOG view:

```
SELECT COUNT(*) FROM DBA_REPCATLOG WHERE GNAME = 'CPS_REP';
```

You can use the RESUME_MASTER_ACTIVITY procedure to "turn on" replication for the specified master group.

```
BEGIN
DBMS_REPCAT.RESUME_MASTER_ACTIVITY (
     gname => 'CPS_REP');
END;
/
```

IMPLEMENTING THE DATA STORE IN A STORAGE AREA NETWORK

Storage Area Network (SAN) is a dedicated high-speed network. It is separate and distinct from the local area network (LAN) that provides shared storage through an external disk storage pool. The SAN is a back-end network that carries only I/O traffic between servers and a disk storage pool, while the front-end network—the LAN—carries e-mail, file, print, and web traffic.

Fibre Channel Technology

Some early SCSI implementations have a distance limitation of six feet and can support only seven devices. These implementations use a parallel bus with multiple lines running in parallel.

Although some SAN configurations utilize this implementation, the most commonly used SCSI technology for SAN implementations is Fibre Channel (FC). *FC* is the standard for bidirectional communications implementing serial SCSI through a single cable connecting servers, storage systems, workstations, hubs, and switches. It features high-performance, serial-interconnections.

FC has the following capabilities:

▼ Bidirectional data transfer rates up to 200 Mbps

■ Support for up to 126 devices on a single host adapter

▲ Communications up to 20km (approximately 12 miles)

FC implementations can use either of the following networking technologies:

▼ **Fibre Channel Arbitrated Loop (FC-AL)** FC-AL networks use shared media technology similar to Fibre Distributed Data Interface (FDDI) or Token Ring. Each network node has one or more ports that allow external communication; FC-AL creates logical point-to-point connections between ports.

▲ **Fibre Channel Fabric (FC-SW)** Fabric networks use switched network technology, similar to switched Ethernet. A fabric switch divides messages into packets containing data and a destination address, and then transmits the packets individually to the receiving node, which reassembles the message. Fabric switches can cascade, allowing a SAN to support thousands of nodes.

Hardware Components

SANs typically include the following hardware components:

▼ **Host I/O Bus** The current I/O bus standard is Peripheral Component Interface (PCI). Older standards include Industry Standard Architecture (ISA) and Extended Industry Standard Architecture (EISA).

■ **Host Bus Adapter** The host bus adapter (HBA) is the interface from the server to the host I/O bus. The HBA is similar in function to a network interface card (NIC), but it is more complex. HBA functions include the following:

    ▼ Converting signals passed between the LAN and the SAN's serial SCSI.

    ■ Initializing the server onto a FC-AL network or providing a Fabric network logon.

    ▲ Scanning the FC-AL or Fabric network, and then attempting to initialize all connected devices in the same way that parallel SCSI scans for logical devices at system startup.

■ **Cabling** FC cables include lines for transmitting and for receiving. Because of the shape, you cannot install them incorrectly.

■ **SAN networking equipment** Many similarities exist between a SAN and other networks, such as a LAN. The basic network components are the same: hubs, switches, bridges, and routers.

▲ **Storage devices and subsystems** A *storage subsystem* is a collection of devices that share a power distribution, packaging, or management system, such as tape libraries or RAID disk drives.

SAN Tape Backup Support

SANs provide easy, on-the-fly tape backup strategies. Tape backups are much quicker and consume fewer resources, because all of the disk access occurs on the SAN's fiber network, and not on the LAN. This allows the data store to be backed up easily even while it is in use.

Cluster Failover Support

The data store is an integral part of the Presentation Server farm architecture. In large enterprise environments, it is important to have the database available all the time. For maximum availability, the data store should be in a clustered database environment with a SAN backbone.

Hardware redundancy allows the SAN to recover from most component failures. Additional software, such as Oracle 9*i* Real Application Cluster or SQL Server 2000 utilizing Microsoft Clustering Services (MSCS), allows for the failover in a catastrophic software failure and in Oracle's case, performance improvements.

> **NOTE** Software such as Compaq's SANWorks is required to manage database clusters in certain hardware configurations.

MSCS provides the capability to failover the Presentation Server farm data store to a functioning server in the event of a catastrophic server failure. MSCS is available on Windows 2000 Advanced Server and DataCenter, plus Windows Server 2003 Enterprise and DataCenter editions.

MSCS monitors the health of standard applications and services, and automatically recovers mission-critical data and applications from many common types of failures. A graphical management console enables you to monitor the status of all resources in the cluster and to manage workloads accordingly. In addition, Windows 2000 Server and Windows Server 2003 integrate middleware and load-balancing services that distribute network traffic evenly across the clustered servers.

Redundancy and recovery can be built into each major component of the data store. Deploying the following technologies can eliminate single points-of-failure from the data store:

▼ Microsoft Cluster Service

■ Redundant hardware

▲ Software monitoring and management tools.

The basic SAN configuration in Figure 4-7 shows each clustered server with dual HBAs cabled to separate FC-AL switches. A system with this redundancy can continue running when any component in this configuration fails.

SAN architecture is, by definition, reliable. It provides redundant systems in all aspects of the configuration with multiple paths to the network. Windows 2000 Advanced Server allows two nodes to be clustered. Windows 2000 Data Center allows four clustered nodes.

If a software or hardware failure occurs on the owner of the cluster node, the Presentation Servers lose their IMA connection to the database. When the servers sense that the connection has been dropped, the farm goes into a two-minute wait period. The servers then attempt to reconnect to the database. If IMA cannot immediately reconnect to the data store, it retries, indefinitely, every two minutes. The Presentation Servers automatically reconnect to the database, which has the same IP address, once it fails over to the other node of the cluster.

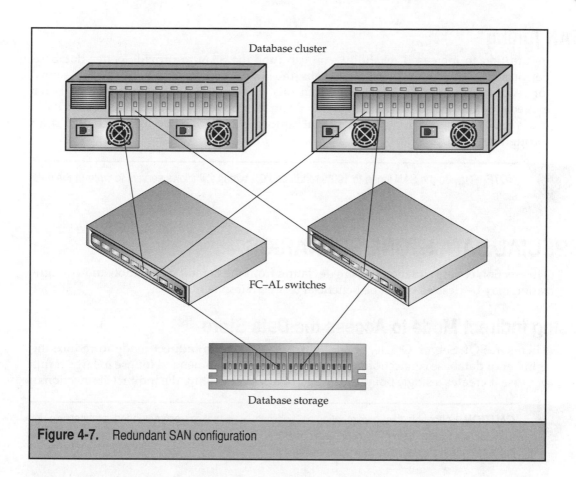

Figure 4-7. Redundant SAN configuration

SQL Clustering

SQL clustering does not mean that both databases are active and load balanced. With SQL clustering, the only supported clustering method allows one server to handle all the requests, while the other server simply stands by waiting for the other machine to fail. This is referred to as *Active/Passive Clustering*.

NOTE   For increased security, when installing Presentation Servers in a farm using a clustered SQL server, Windows NT authentication should be used for connecting IMA to the database.

Oracle Clustering

Oracle Real Application Cluster (RAC) does allow true active-active clustering. As database requests are sent via ODBC, they are load balanced between the nodes of the cluster. This configuration provides both fault tolerance and increased performance.

SAN Tuning

In addition to increased reliability, you can tune the SAN to provide better database performance. In testing at the Citrix *e*Labs, the data store is mainly used as a repository for reading configuration information. In this configuration, the number of reads far exceeds the number of writes. The Array Controller on the SAN can be tuned for 100% reads and 0% writes. This allows optimal performance for data access to the data store through the SAN.

NOTE   Having the SAN tuned to 100% reads and 0% writes still allows servers to write to the data store.

SPECIAL DATA STORE SCENARIOS

This section covers situations where deviating from the default installation and configuration may be desired or can be beneficial to an environment.

Using Indirect Mode to Access the Data Store

Microsoft SQL Server, Oracle, or IBM DB2 can be used in indirect mode to reduce the number of database connections. This practice is not recommended for use in large farms because it creates a single point of failure at the server hosting the indirect connections.

CAUTION   Although this configuration is possible, it is not a recommended architecture for a MetaFrame farm. Using Microsoft SQL Server, Oracle, or IBM DB2 in indirect mode creates a bottleneck and can cause performance issues.

To prevent a single point of failure for the entire farm, install a core set of direct servers, and then point groups of member servers to each of the core direct servers. This process provides better performance than sharing a single server for all queries.

Using a Presentation Server in indirect mode does not reduce the number of queries made to the third-party database. Instead, it channels them through a single ODBC connection.

To use indirect mode with a third-party database:

1. Install the first server into the server farm in direct mode and configure it to properly point to the third-party database.

2. You can install subsequent servers in indirect mode by specifying the direct server from step 1.

3. When prompted for the account permissions, specify the user name and password of the MetaFrame administrator created in step 1.

Dedicating a Host Server in an Indirect Mode Server Farm

When an Access or MSDE data store resides on a Presentation Server, the data store has only one direct server connection. The other servers in this indirect mode server farm access the data store through this host server. The host server, acting as a single point of access, can potentially be a performance bottleneck. The host server can have further demands on its resources if it is also handling ICA connections.

When the host server has a full user load, the following problems can occur:

▼ Delays when using the Presentation Server Console to configure applications

■ Longer Presentation Server Console refresh times

▲ Longer IMA start times for member servers because the data store server is splitting processor time between users and the IMA service

For these reasons, configure the host server to have a lighter user load than the other member servers of the server farm. The exact tuning of this is dependent on the applications being used and the usual load on the servers.

Make user load on the host server one-half to two-thirds of the load on member servers. If using load balancing, tune the parameters so the host server is sent less user traffic than the other servers. If servers are restarted often, you must factor in longer start times. In larger Presentation Server environments running in indirect mode, dedicating the host server to handle data store requests exclusively can be necessary.

NOTE   If the same server is used as the zone data collector, the recommendations for dedicating a server as a zone data collector take precedence over the recommendations in this section. However, better performance can be achieved by utilizing separate machines for the data collector and direct server in a large farm.

CAUTION   Although it is possible to configure multiple Presentation Servers to connect directly to a single MSDE database, Citrix does not recommend this configuration because it is not supported by MSDE. MSDE allows only five connections per installed instance of MSDE. A Presentation Server may use multiple connections to the MSDE instance. Therefore, if more than one Presentation Server attempts to connect to the MSDE database at the same time, the connections may be denied, resulting in intermittent failures. Because of this, Citrix recommends that you configure the first server installed to the MSDE database using direct access and configure all other servers for indirect access.

CHAPTER 5

Citrix Presentation Server 4.0 Deployment

This section contains deployment recommendations for Citrix Presentation Server. Citrix recommends installing Presentation Server on a Windows 2000 or Windows 2003 Member Server, not a Domain Controller. The server must have Terminal Server installed in Application mode. In fact, Service Pack 2005.04 for MetaFrame Presentation Server 3.0 and Presentation Server 4.0 cannot be installed on a Domain Controller. See Citrix Knowledgebase article CTX106529 for more details.

Domain Controllers replicate the Active Directory database and other data, as well as provide user authentication, and, thus, have heavy network and processing requirements. More importantly, the security holes that may be opened by allowing users to access applications loaded onto a Domain Controller should be carefully considered.

Additionally, the servers with Presentation Server installed should not provide any additional services, such as DHCP, DNS, and WINS. These services not only require additional server resources that reduce user performance, but also utilize network resources to respond to frequent client requests and updates. All available server resources should be available to support Presentation Server and associated applications.

Presentation Server setup is compiled into a Windows Installer installation package. Windows Installer is a component of Windows 2000 and 2003 that manages the installation and removal of applications. Windows Installer applies a set of centrally defined setup rules during the installation process that define the configuration of the application. For more information about Windows Installer technology and the Windows Installer Service, see the Windows 2000 online Help or the Microsoft web site. For more information about working with the Presentation Server's Windows Installer package, see the *MetaFrame Presentation Server Administrator's Guide.*

IMPORTANT   When upgrading a farm using Microsoft Access as the data store, always upgrade the host server first. Otherwise, installation will fail. For additional important considerations during upgrade installations, see the *MetaFrame Presentation Server Administrator's Guide.*

UPDATES FOR CITRIX PRESENTATION SERVER

The updates for Presentation Server 4.0 are summarized in the Installation Checklist and the Preinstallation Update Bulletin.

Installation Checklist

After inserting the installation CD and before installing the product, Citrix recommends reading the Installation Checklist. The Installation Checklist can be viewed by selecting View installation checklist on the Presentation Server Setup window that appears after inserting your CD. It outlines, among other items:

1. Downloading and installing critical updates before you install the product
2. Meeting system requirements

3. Installing and configuring the Citrix Access Suite licensing

4. Remapping server drive letters

5. Installing Presentation Server

6. Downloading and installing critical updates after you install the product

The focus of this section is on installing the required Preinstallation Updates, and the Critical Installation and Postinstallation Updates—items 1 and 6, respectively—which may be required to properly install or run the product.

Preinstallation Update Bulletin

The Preinstallation Update Bulletin for MetaFrame Presentation Server 3.0 and the Citrix Access Suite 4.0 Preinstallation Update Bulletin offer late-breaking information and links to critical updates to server operating systems (OSs) and to Citrix installation files. These updates may be required to install or run the product and should be applied prior to installation. Information regarding the required updates can be found on the Preinstallation Update Bulletin. A link to the bulletin is available on the Installation Checklist. The bulletin is divided into three sections, which the following describes.

Preinstallation Updates

Follow the instructions in step 1 of the bulletin to download and install the updates to Microsoft OS components required to install or run the product. Links to both the Microsoft Knowledge Base articles and a patch for download are provided. Read the Knowledge Base articles for detailed descriptions of the updates.

Installation Updates

Follow the instructions in step 2 of the bulletin to download and apply critical updates to Citrix installation packages. After downloading and executing the update package, the Critical Update Wizard can guide you through the process of applying the update to the Citrix components. The *Critical Update Wizard* creates a modified administrative image of the original CD-ROM of Presentation Server 4.0 for Windows on your hard drive. You need to use the modified administrative image containing the critical installation updates instead of the original CD-ROM to install Presentation Server.

Postinstallation Updates and the Critical Updates Web Page

Follow the instructions in step 3 of the bulletin to download and install critical post-installation Hotfixes. The instructions in step 3 of the bulletin direct you to the Critical Updates web page, where the Hotfixes can be downloaded. The Critical Updates web page should be visited frequently, on an ongoing basis, to determine if any critical Hotfixes have been released by Citrix.

REMAPPING SERVER DRIVES

If you intend to change the server's drive letters to enable users to retain their original drive letters on client devices, do so before installing Presentation Server or prior to upgrading to Presentation Server. If you change server drive letters after installing or upgrading, you must do so before you install any applications. To change the server's drive letters, you can use the Presentation Server CD's Autorun feature, selecting the Remap Drives option from the Product Installations Screen.

> *IMPORTANT*   If you are upgrading from an earlier release, the Remap Drives option is not available from Autorun. Your existing drive mapping is preserved for the upgrade. To modify the existing drive mapping, run the DriveRemap utility (DriveRemap.exe) located in the root folder of the Presentation Server CD. Typically, you should *never* remap the drives as part of an upgrade.

When running driveremap.exe with no parameters, the drive letter choices in the pull-down list may be grayed out. This happens because some aspect of being able to remap the existing drive letters cannot be done.

Some reasons for this are

▼   Noncontiguous drive letters, for example, *C, D, X*. The mapped drive letters are spread over the interval [a...z] and no reasonable interval shifting can be performed. Shifting *C* to *M* is a shift of ten. Drive letter *X* would not be able to shift ten letters and wrap around the alphabet. Even Network Drives are taken into account. To work around this, change the drive letters to *C:*, *D:*, *E:*, and then rerun the utility.

■   At the command prompt, if you silently remap to a letter that is *in use*, such as a mapped network drive, nothing will happen. The process just returns to the prompt. To see if mappings take place, launch Windows Explorer.

▲   Presentation Server drive remapping is not supported on Windows 2000 or Windows 2003 Dynamic Disks.

For more detailed information, please refer to Citrix Knowledgebase article CTX950520.

> *NOTE*   Driveremap.exe does not remap hidden (administrative) shares listed in the registry. For example, if you install Trend ServerProtect on Windows Server 2003 and view the registry value: HKEY_LOCAL_MACHINE\SOFTWARE\TrendMicro\ServerProtect\CurrentVersion\ UncHomeDirectory, the value will be similar to: \\%computername%\c$\Program Files\Trend\SProtect. If you remap the server drive at this point, the previous registry value is not modified.

MANUAL INSTALLATION/UPGRADE TO METAFRAME PRESENTATION SERVER

NOTE You can install or upgrade in silent mode, using msiexec /i MPS.msi /qn. If you are using unattended installation or command line parameters to install Presentation Server, a log file (msi.log) is automatically created in the %systemroot% directory.

To Install or Upgrade to Presentation Server 3.0 or 4.0

1. Start Autorun from the Presentation Server CD, a network share point or a mapped network drive containing all the files from the CD image.

2. Click Product installations, and then select Install Presentation Server and its components.

3. Accept the License Agreement and click Next.

4. Select the components to be installed and click Next.

5. Choose the option to install a Citrix License Server or choose to install Citrix license server at another time and click Next.

NOTE To be functional, Presentation Server 3.0 and 4.0 require connectivity to a Citrix License Server. The License Server can be installed in the environment before or after Presentation Server is installed. The name of the Citrix License Server can be provided either during an installation or after installation in the Presentation Server Console.

NOTE Installation automatically detects a previous install of Presentation Server and the version. If a previous version is found, setup then asks if you want to upgrade.

NOTE If you install Presentation Server directly by mps.msi for a silent or unattended install, you need to make sure all the prerequisite components are installed. Run Autorun.exe from the installation CD and select the option View installation checklist. You can print a copy of the checklist for easy reference.

Upgrading to Citrix Presentation Server 4.0

In addition to the information located in the Administrator's Guide and *Readme for MetaFrame Presentation Server, Version 4.0*, the following lists some considerations to be aware of when upgrading to Presentation Server 4.0.

Upgrading Presentation Server Versions Prior to MetaFrame XP, Feature Release 3 to 4.0

You cannot upgrade servers running MetaFrame 1.0, MetaFrame 1.8, or versions of MetaFrame XP prior to Feature Release 3 directly to Presentation Server 4.0. These versions can be upgraded to MetaFrame XP, Feature Release 3, and then upgraded to 4.0. Refer to the Administrator's Guide for more details.

Consider the following when upgrading to MetaFrame Presentation Server 3.0:

▼ If MetaFrame 1.8 for Windows 2000 was installed with remapped drives, the COM + Catalog may have been damaged. To determine if the server is in this state, go to Start | Programs | Administrative Tools | Component Services. In the Console Root, go to Component Services | Computers | My Computer | COM+ Applications. If it is damaged, use the drvremap utility located on the MetaFrame 1.8 for Windows 2000, Feature Release 1, or MetaFrame 1.8 for Windows 2000 Service Pack 3 CDs. Use these steps:

  1. subst C: M:/

  2. drvremap /drive:M /remap /com

  3. subst C: /d

  4. Restart the server.

■ Refer to Citrix Online Knowledge Base article CTX240747 for more information.

■ After an upgrade from MetaFrame 1.8 for Windows 2000 to MetaFrame Presentation Server 3.0, the system cannot be downgraded.

▲ SSL settings are intentionally not migrated for security reasons. When upgrading to Presentation Server, reconfigure SSL manually. For more information about configuring SSL, see the SSL Relay utility's online help.

If upgrading a server that does not have Installation Manager and Resource Manager installed, these components will not be installed during the upgrade. To install these components, verify that an Enterprise edition license is loaded in the Citrix License Server, and install these components using the Add/Remove Programs applet in the Control Panel.

Additional Considerations

▼ Presentation Server 4.0 introduces a new policy, the session printers policy, which replaces previous methods of managing network printer settings. This new policy cannot be used to manage the network printer settings of previous versions of Presentation Server. Citrix only recommends maintaining a farm containing mixed versions of Presentation Server for minimal periods of transition. If you have a farm with multiple versions of Presentation Server, use the previous version of the Presentation Server Console to manage network printer settings for previous versions of Presentation Server in your farm.

▲   If you are upgrading Conferencing Manager, please note that a direct upgrade from Conferencing Manager 2.0 to version 4.0 is not supported. Refer to the *Administrator's Guide for Citrix MetaFrame Conferencing Manager Version 4.0* for more details.

Downgrading from Citrix Presentation Server 4.0

Presentation Server 4.0 is a platform upgrade. Once you install Presentation Server 4.0, you cannot rollback to previously installed versions of Presentation Server.

RAPID DEPLOYMENT OF CITRIX PRESENTATION SERVER

Having a means of quickly building or rebuilding a Presentation Server ensures that users are impacted for the minimum period of time if an unplanned failure were to occur. Optimally, an automated process provides the fastest and most efficient means of building or rebuilding a server. This section covers practices regarding rapid deployment of Presentation Server in the enterprise environment, including server cloning, unattended installations, and simultaneous installations. For further information regarding unattended installations, refer to the *MetaFrame Presentation Server Administrator's Guide*.

Blades in a Citrix Presentation Server Environment

The introduction of blade servers has been an ideal fit for Presentation Server. With server sprawl and increasing data center costs, the most-asked question has been shifting from "How many users can I get on a box?" to "How many users can I get per square foot?" Blade servers in the 2P market are traditionally twice as dense as 1U dual servers (pizza boxes). This means 84 servers can now be placed into a single 42U Rack.

Blade servers have been introduced by most of the major server hardware vendors. They offer a wide range of options, depending on the vendor, from SAN connectivity to storage blades to unique imaging solutions.

Blades and Imaging

Most blade servers ship with some form of imaging software. Each of these imaging solutions offers image capture and deployment to servers. A base image can be installed on a single machine, which is stored on the image server and can then be deployed to all other like servers in your data center.

You can image the base OS, and then have the imaging software perform an unattended install of Presentation Server using an answer file or you can image the system with Presentation Server already installed.

For more information about using the HP Rapid Deployment Pack to deploy Presentation Server, see the HP whitepaper "Using HP ProLiant Essentials Rapid Deployment Pack 1.51 to deploy Citrix MetaFrame Presentation Server on HP ProLiant servers."

NOTE   If the Presentation Server is to have remapped drives, then running drive remap after the imaging process is complete is best because of incompatibilities with some third-party imaging solutions.

Scripting Configuration After Imaging

If a cloned version of Presentation Server is deployed, a few steps must first be performed to allow the Presentation Server to function properly.

Most imaging software suites enable the administrator to define scripts to be run on the server after imaging completes. MetaFrame Feature Release 3 and later includes a utility called Apputil. *Apputil* is a command-line utility that adds a server to the Configured Servers list of a published application. If the application does not exist on the server, then Apputil can also be used to deploy the application using an Installation Manager package.

With this utility, the administrator can script various different configurations of a Presentation Server installation, depending on the application silo in which it resides. Once the machine has finished imaging, the script executes and the Installation Manager package is deployed to the server.

For more information regarding this utility, please refer to the *MetaFrame Presentation Server Administrator's Guide.*

The MFCOM SDK also allows for the scripting of other configuration options through most kinds of scripting languages. Through the MFCOM SDK, new applications can be published; the data collector preference level can be set, load-evaluators applied, and so forth. This allows Presentation Server configuration tweaks to be applied on the fly as well. Please refer to the MFCOM SDK documentation for scripting usage.

Rip and Replace

In the event of a hardware failure, blades present the opportunity simply to pull out the one experiencing the failure and to replace it with a new server blade. Presentation Server can then be imaged back down to the new blade. If the blade server assumes the same name, then it continues to function in the capacity as the previous Presentation Server that had the same name.

NOTE   For servers that were previously hosting an indirect data store, the data store needs to be migrated using the dsmaint command. Refer to the *MetaFrame Presentation Server Administrator's Guide* for instructions.

Server Cloning

A few manual steps are required for cloning Presentation Servers. These steps vary, depending on the type of data store used for the farm, and are described in the following sections. Presentation Server is compatible with server cloning, but cloning software can contain issues that cause the OS or its add-ons to function incorrectly after being cloned. When using server cloning, it is important to clone one server and test its operation before deploying the rest of the farm.

CAUTION Do not attempt to image a server with an SSL certificate installed because SSL certificates are unique to the hardware.

Precloning Considerations

Zone settings are not retained when cloning a server. When the IMA service on the cloned server starts for the first time, the Presentation Server joins the default zone. The name of the default zone is the ID of the subnet on which the cloned server resides. When deploying images to servers on multiple subnets, assign zone information for each server after the imaging process completes.

Prior to changing the Security ID (SID) on the machine used to access the Presentation Server Console, add one of the following as a Citrix Administrator with read-write privileges:

▼ A domain administrator

■ The Local Administrators group

▲ A local administrator from a machine where the SID is not being changed

CAUTION   Do not attempt to use drive image software to restore an image of a Presentation Server with remapped drives. Remapped drives partially revert to the original configuration on the deployed server, rendering the server unusable. Servers with remapped drives may be duplicated using a hardware solution, such as Compaq Smart Array controllers with RAID1 drive mirroring. Also, some drive imaging software, such as Symantec Ghost, provides configuration settings to *preserve* the remapped drives, letters, and signatures. Consult your drive imaging software's documentation to determine if it supports these features.

You must do the following before re-imaging a server that is already a member of a Presentation Server farm.

To prepare a server in a Citrix Presentation Server Farm for re-imaging:

1. From the Presentation Server Console, remove the list of servers configured to host any applications.

2. Remove the server from the server farm by uninstalling Presentation Server.

3. If the server entry still exists in the Presentation Server Console server list, right-click and manually remove the server name from the server list.

4. Apply the system image and add the server to the server farm.

IMPORTANT   If a server is not removed from a Presentation Server farm before a new system image is applied to it, performance problems can result. The Presentation Server Console can display invalid data if the server is added back to the same server farm. This is because the old server's host record in the data store is applied to the newly imaged server.

If cloning is not an option, such as when configuring with remapped drives, consider creating custom unattended installation scripts for both the OS and applications, including Presentation Server.

Rapid Deployment with Microsoft Access or MSDE

Manually install the first server in the new Presentation Server farm that will host the data store. You can image the second server in the farm for the deployment of additional servers.

To image a server for rapid deployment with Access or MSDE:

1. Follow all necessary steps from the *MetaFrame Presentation Server Administrator's Guide* to install the first Presentation Server into the farm.

2. Install a second server into the farm with an indirect connection to the data store created on the first server.

3. With the second server successfully installed and restarted, log on to the console of the second server as a local or domain administrator.

4. On the second server, delete the Wfcname.ini file, if it exists, from the root drive of the server.

5. Stop the IMA service using the Services Control Panel. Set the startup type to Manual.

6. If the Enterprise edition components are installed, see the "Cloning on Presentation Server, Enterprise Edition System" section.

7. Take the image of the second server, and then restart the second server.

8. Deploy the image obtained in step 7.

IMPORTANT   It is important that some type of SID generation utility be executed when deploying Windows 2000 or Windows 2003 images.

To set up the server and verify that it is added:

1. Set the SID of the server with the SID generator of choice.

2. Rename the new server with a unique name.

3. Manually start the IMA service and set the service to start automatically.

4. Verify that the server was successfully added to the farm by executing qfarm at the command prompt. The newly imaged server appears in the list of servers.

5. Modify the following registry values:

    ▼ HKEY_LOCAL_MACHINE\SOFTWARE\Citrix\IMA

    change value ServerHost to [*newservername*]

    ▲ HKEY_CLASSES_ROOT\AppID\{BBBF5400-E091-11D8-AD76-005056C00008}

    (Note: This subkey may be alphanumerically different—you may need to search for Ctx_SmaUser to find the correct sub key.)

    change value RunAs to [*newservername*]\Ctx_SmaUser

6. Reboot the server.

Rapid Deployment with Microsoft SQL Server, Oracle, or IBM DB2   When using Microsoft SQL Server, Oracle, or IBM DB2 for the server farm data store, you can image the first server in the farm and use it to deploy all other servers.

To image a server for rapid deployment with SQL Server, Oracle, or IBM DB2:

1. Follow the steps from the *MetaFrame Presentation Server Administrator's Guide* for installing the first Presentation Server into the farm.

2. When the server is successfully restarted, log on to the console as a local or domain administrator.

3. Delete the Wfcname.ini file, if it exists, from the root drive of the server.

4. Save the changes to the DSN file.

5. Stop the IMA service and set the startup option to Manual.

6. If the Enterprise edition components are installed, see the "Cloning on Presentation Server, Enterprise Edition System" section.

7. Take the image of the server, and then restart the server.

8. Deploy the image obtained.

IMPORTANT   It is important that some type of SID generation utility be executed when deploying Windows 2000 and Windows 2003.

To set up the server and verify that it is added:

1. Set the Security ID of the server with the SID generator of choice.

2. Rename the new server with a unique name.

3. Manually start the IMA service and set the service to start automatically.

4. Verify that the server was successfully added to the farm by executing qfarm at a command prompt on any server in the farm. The newly imaged server appears in the list of servers.

Cloning on Presentation Server, Enterprise Edition Systems   If Resource Manager is installed, re-create the RMLocalDatabase prior to making an image of the server.

To re-create the RMLocalDatabase:

1. Delete %Program Files%\Citrix\Citrix Resource Manager\LocalDB\ RMLocalDatabase.*.

2. The next time the IMA service is started, it will re-create the database.

Simultaneous Installations

Citrix recommends that no more than 30 servers be simultaneously installed if you are using a high-powered server for your data store (that is, a current generation dual CPU database server or above). For older database servers, no more than 10 servers should be installed at the same time. During installation, servers must write configurations to the same indexes in the data store. The more servers installed at once, the greater the probability of creating deadlocks on the database server.

IMPORTANT   Deadlocks occur when one server times out while waiting to write to a piece of data that is locked by another server. In this event, the IMA service simply retries after a short interval.

When installing servers to a new zone, it is recommended that you initially install a single server into the new zone. Presentation Server sets the first server in a zone as the Most Preferred data collector. This avoids problems with new servers in the zone becoming the zone data collector during installation. After installation is completed, the data collector election preference can be changed using the Presentation Server Console.

INSTALLATION OF ADMINISTRATIVE TOOLS

This section covers installation scenarios for the Presentation Server Console.

To Skip Installation of the Citrix Presentation Server Console

Use the following command to skip the installation of the Presentation Server Console during Presentation Server installation:

       msiexec /i *mps.msi* **CTX_ADDLOCAL=all REINSTALL=CTX_MF_CMC**

NOTE   CTX_MF_CMC must be in uppercase.

To Install or Upgrade the Presentation Server Console on Standalone Servers

1. Run Autorun from the Presentation Server CD.
2. Select Product installations and updates.
3. Select Install management consoles.
4. Accept the license agreement and click Next | Next to select Presentation Server Console.
5. Follow the dialog boxes to finish the installation of the Presentation Server Console.

NOTE   If the Sun JRE 1_5_0_02 is installed prior to installing the Presentation Server 4.0 Console, logins to the console may fail. When JRE 1.5 is already present, the JRE 1.4.2_06 installer doesn't add a registry key that is needed by the console. This is resolved by manually adding one key and one value to the registry:

1. Create the following registry key:

   HKEY_LOCAL_MACHINE\Software\JavaSoft\Java Runtime Environment\1.4

2. Create a string value "JavaHome".

3. Locate the following key in the registry:

   HKEY_LOCAL_MACHINE\Software\JavaSoft\Java Runtime Environment\ 1.4.2_06

4. Copy the data from the "JavaHome" value in that key to the "JavaHome" value in the key you created.

To Install the Access Suite Console on Standalone Servers

1. Run Autorun from the Presentation Server CD.

2. Select Product installations and updates.

3. Select Install management consoles.

4. Accept the license agreement and click Next | Next to select Access Suite Console.

5. Follow the dialog boxes to finish the installation of the Access Suite Console.

PROGRAM NEIGHBORHOOD AGENT AS A PASS-THROUGH CLIENT

You can choose to install Program Neighborhood Agent to be used as a pass-through client on the Presentation Server during Presentation Server setup. This gives users the ability to connect to the server desktop and use the functionality of the Program Neighborhood Agent.

To install the Program Neighborhood Agent, click the Program Neighborhood Agent component during the component selection of the Presentation Server install, and select "Will be installed on local hard drive".

▼ If you install the Program Neighborhood Agent, you are prompted later during setup to enter the URL of the server running Web Interface. This server hosts the Program Neighborhood Agent configuration file. By default, Presentation Server attempts to resolve the localhost as a server running the web interface.

■ If you are upgrading from a previous release of Presentation Server, you will not be given an opportunity to set up the Program Neighborhood Agent as a Pass-Through Client.

▲ If you performed a fresh install and did not choose to install the Program Neighborhood Agent or you performed an upgrade, you can install the Program Neighborhood Agent after the Presentation Server setup process.

> *NOTE*   By default, Program Neighborhood Agent is not selected to be installed during a Presentation Server installation.

Installation of Program Neighborhood Agent as a Pass-through Client

This section describes how to install the Program Neighborhood Agent and use it as a Pass-Through Client on a Presentation Server if the Program Neighborhood Agent was not a selected component during the initial Presentation Server installation.

1. Launch Add/Remove Programs in the Control Panel.
2. Select Change on Citrix MetaFrame Presentation Server for Windows entry name.
3. Select to Modify the Windows Installer packages installed on the system and click Next.
4. Select the Program Neighborhood Agent component, select "Will be installed on local hard drive", and then click Next.
5. Enter the server URL for the Web Interface Server or leave as localhost if Web Interface is installed on the same computer as MetaFrame Presentation Server.
6. Select whether or not to enable Pass Through Authentication and click Next.
7. Verify the component changes and click Finish.

DEPLOYMENT OF THE PRESENTATION SERVER CLIENT FOR 32-BIT WINDOWS

This section outlines best practices, recommendations, and advanced scenarios when dealing with the various Presentation Server Clients for 32-bit Windows and Presentation Server. Please refer to the respective client administrative guides for additional information.

Dynamic Client Name vs. Machine Name

Dynamic Client Name is a feature that is included in client versions 7.00 and later. Prior versions of the client only reported the client name that was statically configured during the installation of the client and stored in the *wfcname.ini*. If the Dynamic Client Name feature is not enabled, the client name that is reported to the Presentation Server when connecting to a session is stored in the following registry key:

```
HKLM\Software\Citrix\ICA Client\ClientName
```

When the Dynamic Client Name feature is enabled, the Presentation Server client calls the Windows function GetComputerName, which gets the computer's NetBIOS name and is then reported to the Presentation Server.

The `ClientName` registry value should not be present when the Dynamic Client Name feature is enabled. Dynamic Client Name is initially enabled or disabled during the install process. In the Program Neighborhood client, this can be changed after install by opening Program Neighborhood and setting the Dynamic Client Name check box under Tools | ICA Settings | General. In all other Presentation Server Clients, including Program Neighborhood Agent, you can enable or disable this feature by deleting or creating the `ClientName` registry value in:

```
HKLM\Software\Citrix\ICA Client
```

These changes should take effect on all new connections.

NOTE   Earlier releases of the ICA clients (prior to version 7.00) stored the client name in the file C:\wfcname.ini.

CAB-based Client Packages

Three different CAB packages are available with Presentation Server 4.0:

▼ **Wfica.cab**   The full Program Neighborhood client packaged in CAB format (4,331,039 bytes).

■ **Wficat.cab**   The "thick" web client packaged in CAB format (2,425,783 bytes).

▲ **Wficac.cab**   The "Zero Footprint" web client packaged in CAB format (1,507,442 bytes). This is the new "zero install" client that customers requested.

There are several benefits to the thin (Active-X) web clients (wficat.cab and wficac .cab), such as:

▼ The user doesn't initiate the install. The Internet browser (Internet Explorer or Netscape Navigator) initiates the install on a need-to-download-and-install basis.

■ The CAB file package install is fast as it is limited in size.

▲ The CAB file is expanded into a scratch directory, leaving no or little footprint on the target desktop. Changes made to the locked down desktop are none or minimal (registration of ActiveX ICA control).

Along with the benefits, there are trade-offs to be made to keep the thin web package small and efficient. Because a smaller footprint means a reduction in size of the client package, certain features from the full-fledged Program Neighborhood or Program Neighborhood Agent are unavailable for the two smaller sized CAB-based client packages wficat.cab and wficac.cab.

Supported Features

Wficat.cab   The following features are supported by the wficat.cab install:

Client engine, Thinwire, Client drive mapping, Licensing, Connection Center, Runtime Manager, Auto-client reconnection, Zero Latency, Font Manager, Client Audio Mapping, Client Printer Mapping, Universal Printer Driver, Client COM port mapping, Netscape plug-in, Protocol Driver (128 bit), Protocol driver (old compression), Smartcard support, Active X control, ICA Client Object, SSL support, Auto-client update, Name Resolver (TCP/IP), Name Resolver (HTTP), INI files, Support DLLs, TCP/IP protocol support., Bi-directional Audio, Session Reliability, Dynamic Session Resizing, and login look and feel.

Wficac.cab   The following features are supported by the wficac.cab install:

Client engine, Thinwire, Client drive mapping, Licensing, Connection Center, Runtime Manager, Auto-client reconnection, Client Printer Mapping, Smartcard support, Active X control, ICA Client Object, SSL support, Name Resolver (TCP/IP), Name Resolver (HTTP), INI files, Support DLLs, TCP/IP protocol support, Session Reliability, Dynamic Session Resizing, and login look and feel.

Features *Not* Supported

Wfica.cab   Wfica.cab is the full Program Neighborhood client and all features supported in the Program Neighborhood full-client install are supported by the wfica.cab install.

Wficat.cab   SpeedScreen Multimedia Acceleration is not supported.

Wficac.cab   The following features are not supported: Zero Latency, Font manager, Client Audio Mapping, Universal Printer Driver, Client COM port mapping, Netscape Plug-in, Protocol Driver (128 bit), Protocol Driver (old compression), Auto Client update, SpeedScreen Multimedia Acceleration, and Bi-directional audio.

Wficac.cab Considerations

Listed in the following are some of the known issues and considerations regarding the new cab file Wficac.cab, coupled with any known workarounds.

Upgrade Considerations:

1. If one version of the client is already installed on the target machine by any of these methods:

   ▼ Full Program Neighborhood client using Installshield (ICA32.exe)

   ■ Full Program Neighborhood MSI (ica32pkg.msi) install

   ■ Program Neighborhood Agent using Installshield (ICA32a.exe)

- ■ Program Neighborhood Agent MSI (ica32pkg.msi) install
- ▲ Thin web client (wficac.cab) install package

NOTE The same version CAB-based web client package will not be downloaded and installed by the Internet Explorer browser.

2. For the same version of web client installed on a target machine installed via the thin (wficac.cab) CAB file, users will be unable to install the web client via thick (wficat.cab) CAB file if a need arises to use more features. The reason for this is the version numbers on the CAB files remain the same and Internet Explorer will not download and explode the thick (wficat.cab) CAB-based client.

TIP First, the user must uninstall the thin (wficac.cab) CAB-based web client via the Add-Remove applet in the Control Panel, and then visit a web page that points them to the location to download the thick version (wficat.cab) of the web client.

3. If a lower version of the full web client is installed on the target machine and the user visits a web page that points them to a higher version CAB-based web client, Internet Explorer always prompts the user to download and install the latest web client. This leads to multiple client installations on the target machine.

TIP Uninstall the previously installed web client, and then visit the web page pointing to a higher version CAB-based client.

NOTE By installing a smaller-sized CAB client, even if it is a higher version, some features will be lost due to the streamlining of the client.

Limitations/Constraints of WficaC.cab

- ▼ Any user wanting to use the CAB-based ActiveX Win32 web client needs permissions to download an ActiveX control via Internet Explorer. An appropriate level of permissions to be able to create subkeys under HKEY_CLASSES_ROOT registry hive is necessary for the user to correctly register the ActiveX control and to register the .ICA file type extension to support launching of ICA connections outside the browser.
- ■ Internet Explorer 4.0 and above is the only supported browser for these versions of the CAB-based client.
- ▲ Only a limited number of client features, as previously noted, are available in the thin version (wficac.cab) of the CAB-based Win32 ActiveX based client.

DEPLOYING AND PUBLISHING OF PROGRAM NEIGHBORHOOD AGENT OR PROGRAM NEIGHBORHOOD CLIENT WINDOWS INSTALLER PACKAGES USING ACTIVE DIRECTORY

Active Directory can be used to publish or assign the Presentation Server Client for 32-bit Windows. This section describes how to publish or assign an application for a group of users or computers using Active Directory. The Microsoft definition of "publish" is to make an application available to a user for installation through Add-Remove Programs or to prompt the installation by launching a file associated with the application. If the MSI package is "assigned" to a user, whenever the user logs into a workstation the Windows Installer service will "advertise" the set of applications listed in the Active Directory Organizational Unit for that particular user. Advertising means the class IDs, extensions, and shortcuts are installed for the user, so when the user double-clicks on a file with an associated extension, or double-clicks on the advertised shortcut, the application is then fully installed for that user. For more information regarding assigning and publishing applications to users and computers using Active directory group policies, please refer to the Windows online documentation.

Requirements

1. Program Neighborhood Agent (Version 7.00.13547 or greater)
2. Program Neighborhood Client (Version 7.00.13547 or greater)
3. Web Client (Version 8.*x* or greater)
4. Windows Installer Service. The Windows Installer Service (Instmsi.exe) is present by default on computers running the Windows 2000 OS. If the client device is running Windows NT 4.0 or Windows 9*x*, you must install Windows Installer Version 2.0 or higher.

To Deploy the Presentation Server Client MSI Package on a Computer or Set of Computers

1. Start with a clean client machine with no Presentation Server client installed on it.

2. Join an ADS domain. Joining the ADS domain enables you to assign or publish a Windows Installer application for computers and users in that domain or an organizational unit within the ADS domain.

NOTE On a machine that belongs to the ADS domain, launch the Microsoft Management Console (MMC) and load the Active Directory Users and Computers snap-in or go to Start | Programs | Administrative Tools | Active Directory Users and Computers.

3. For this example, create a new Organizational Unit (OU) called MSI test, and a new user called MSIuser. Go to the Computers group and find the machine you added to the ADS Domain. Right-click on the machine and select Move. Select the MSI Test folder and click OK. Follow the same steps to add the new user from the Users group to the new OU folder.

NOTE The previous step is necessary to test a contained number of users and computers. In the next step, we edit the Group Policy of that container. This way, any changes made to the Group Policy do not affect the rest of the ADS domain.

4. Right-click on the MSI test OU and go to Properties. Select the Group Policy tab and create a new Group Policy Objects Link called Presentation Server Client Install.

NOTE Highlight the Presentation Server Client Install policy and click Edit. Under Computer Configuration | Software Settings | Software Installation, right-click Software Installation and select New | Package.

5. Browse to a network share containing the Ica32pkg.msi, select the MSI package, and set the deployment method to Assigned. This step is to ensure that all environment settings are present for the Automated Install for the Presentation Server Client. Once you click OK, Software Installation should display a software package assignment for deployment.

NOTE If you use a hidden share, for example, \\Servername\c$\temp\, users will receive a pop-up window asking for the path of ICA32PKG.msi when they launch Program Neighborhood after it has been deployed to the client machines. The client machines must have access to read from the share; otherwise, Windows won't be able to deploy the installation. This is "as designed" behavior of an Active Directory.

6. Restart the client machine. As the client restarts, ADS Group Policy automatically installs the Presentation Server client on the computer. On the Windows Startup dialog status box, a message should be displayed that the Citrix Presentation Server client is being installed by Remote Managed Apps. This message appears before the login dialog box appears.

7. Log on to the client machine and verify the client is installed.

NOTE For Windows XP Professional OSs, the machine has to be rebooted twice before the ADS Group Policy automatically installs the Presentation Server client on the computer. However, if the Active Directory is a Windows 2003 Active Directory, you can avoid the second reboot after creating the policy by going to a command line on the client machine and typing **gpupdate /force.** This command prompts you to reboot, but it is only necessary to reboot the Windows XP Professional OS once.

To Uninstall the Citrix Presentation Server Client MSI Package from Computers via Active Directory

1. On a machine that belongs to the ADS domain, launch the MMC and load the Active Directory Users and Computers snap-in or go to Start | Programs | Administrative Tools | Active Directory Users and Computers.

2. Right-click the MSI Test OU folder and select Properties. Select the Group Policy tab and edit the ICA Client Install policy. Under Computer Configuration | Software Settings | Software Installation, right-click on the Presentation Server Client Package and select All Tasks | Remove. Make sure Immediately Uninstall… is checked, and then click OK.

3. Restart the client machine. As the system restarts, ADS Group Policy automatically uninstalls the Presentation Server client from the computer. On the Windows Startup dialog status box, a message should be displayed that the Citrix Presentation Server client is being removed by Remote Managed Apps. This message appears before the login dialog box appears.

4. Log on to the client machine and verify that the Presentation Server Client was completely removed from the client machine.

To Publish the Citrix Presentation Server Client MSI Package to a User or Group of Users in an ADS Domain

1. On a machine that belongs to the ADS domain, launch the MMC and load the Active Directory Users and Computers snap-in or go to Start | Programs | Administrative Tools | Active Directory Users and Computers.

2. If you have not already created a new test OU for previous client installations, create a new OU called MSI test, and a new user called MSIuser.

3. Under the Users folder, right-click MSIuser and select Move. Select the MSI Test OU folder and click OK.

4. Right-click the MSI Test OU and select Properties. Go to the Group Policy tab and highlight the Presentation Server Client Install policy and click Edit. If you do not already have a Presentation Server Client Install policy from a previous example, create a new Group Policy Objects Link named Presentation Server Client Install.

5. Under User Configuration | Software Settings | Software Installation, right-click Software Installation and select New | Package. Browse to a network share containing the ica32pkg.msi, select the MSI package, and set the deployment method to Published. Once you click OK, Software Installation should display a software package assignment for deployment.

NOTE If you use a hidden share, for example, \\Servername\c$\temp\, users receive a pop-up window asking for the path of ICA32PKG.msi when they launch Program Neighborhood after it has been deployed to the client machines. The client machines must have access to read from the share; otherwise, Windows won't be able to deploy the installation. This is "as designed" behavior of an Active Directory.

6. Close all management windows and restart the client.

7. Log on to the client machine as MSIuser.

8. Go to Add/Remove Programs and click on Add New Programs. Verify that Citrix Presentation Server Client is included in the list and is ready to be added. Click on Add and verify that the Presentation Server Client is successfully installed.

NOTE When using the Published method to make the Presentation Server client MSI package available to users for installation, the user can also initiate installation of the Presentation Server client by opening a file with the .ica extension.

Additional Notes   The Presentation Server client MSI package can also be made available to users using the assigned deployment method. If you assign a package to users, the Presentation Server client is not installed automatically for the user on login, but only the class IDs, extensions, and shortcuts are installed. When the user double-clicks on a file with an .ica extension or double-clicks on the shortcut, the client is then fully installed for that user.

If you answer Yes to the option "Would you like to enable and automatically use your local user name and password for MetaFrame sessions from this client?", at least one reboot is required following the installation of the client.

To Unpublish Citrix Presentation Server Client MSI Package to a User or Group of Users in an ADS Domain

1. Log on to the client machine as MSIuser. Go to Add/Remove Programs and Remove Presentation Server Client.

2. Go to Add/Remove Programs and click on Add New Programs. Verify that Citrix Presentation Server Client is still listed and is ready to be added. Even though the client has been uninstalled, the MSI package is still available for install due to the group policy. The client can also be uninstalled from the client machine automatically with the following steps.

3. On a machine that belongs to the ADS domain, launch the MMC and load the Active Directory Users and Computers snap-in or go to Start | Programs | Administrative Tools | Active Directory Users and Computers.

4. Right-click the MSI Test OU and select Properties. Go to the Group Policy tab and highlight the Presentation Server Client Install policy and click Edit.

5. Under User Configuration | Software Settings | Software Installation, right-click on the Presentation Server Client Package and select All Tasks | Remove. Make sure that Immediately Uninstall … is checked and click OK.

6. Reboot client machine and log in as MSIuser. ADS Group Policy automatically removes the Presentation Server Client from the Add New Programs list as the MSIuser logs in. Go to Add/Remove Programs and verify that Presentation Server Client is not published in the available list under Add New Programs.

NOTE   The same previous steps can be used to deploy, uninstall, publish, and unpublish the Program Neighborhood Agent Client and the Web Client (Ica32pkg.msi) using Active Directory.

Troubleshooting

Publishing the Program Neighborhood Agent, Program Neighborhood Client, and the Web Client MSI Packages to users is not supported on Windows 2000 Servers or on Windows 2003 servers. The only available method of using Active Directory to deploy Citrix ICA clients to Windows 2000 Servers or to Windows 2003 Servers is to assign the package to a computer or to a group of computers.

To enable logging for a Presentation Server client MSI package install, you can add an entry to the group policy for Windows Installer logging.

1. On a machine that belongs to the ADS domain, launch the MMC and load the Active Directory Users and Computers snap-in or go to Start | Programs | Administrative Tools | Active Directory Users and Computers.

NOTE   This is a per-machine setting. If you are deploying clients to users, only you will need an OU that contains target computers.

2. Right-click the OU containing the target computers and select Properties.

3. Go to the Group Policy tab and highlight the Presentation Server Client Install policy and click Edit. If you created a separate OU for your target servers, create a new policy for the OU. Within the properties of the policy, go to Computer Configuration | Administrative Templates | Windows Components | Windows Installer | Logging.

4. Choose Enabled and select the type of logging desired from the list of available options.

5. Enter **voicewarmup** to enable all possible logging. The log file is created in %systemroot%\Temp\msi*.log. Use the creation dates to differentiate log files.

Citrix Presentation Server Client Deployment on the Compaq iPaq

The Presentation Server Client is supported on Compaq iPaq devices. This device can be used as a client as well as a server farm management tool for high density Presentation Servers.

The client version should be Presentation Server Client for WinCE ARM version 7.*x* or later.

> **TIP** The Presentation Server Client supports input from both the iPaq keyboard and character recognizer and transcriber within a session.

IPaq Configuration

Configure the following settings in the Presentation Server Client for better performance with cellular digital packet data (CDPD) or code division multiple access (CDMA) connections:

- ▼ Disable sound
- ■ Select Enable Palette Device
- ■ Limit session color depth to 256 colors
- ■ Set the encryption level to Basic
- ▲ Avoid accessing the client drives in the session, if possible

To run the Presentation Server Console in an ICA session, set the ICA settings as follows:

- ▼ Window Size: Absolute (in pixels), 640×480. The ICA Client can dynamically zoom the session window.
- ■ Window Color: 256
- ▲ Data Compression: On

Deploying a Citrix Presentation Server Farm Using Oracle Real Application Clusters

For MetaFrame XP for Windows with Feature Release 3, Citrix *e*Labs configured an Oracle Real Application Cluster (RAC) environment using an EMC² Celerra Network Enterprise Server for the shared disk subsystem. The configuration tested used the Oracle Cluster File System (CFS) on Oracle servers running Microsoft Windows 2000 SP3.

When using an Oracle RAC configuration, all Oracle server nodes actively process requests against the same back-end database. Running with a RAC configuration provides the following benefits:

- ▼ All nodes can run using the same Oracle Home executable files. Using shared executables guarantees that all nodes are using the same version and decreases upgrade time.

- All nodes can simultaneously access the same data, providing multiple front-end servers to access the data. This provides exceptional performance gains with read-intensive database operations.

- Requests are automatically load-balanced across active nodes.

▲ New requests to a failed server are automatically routed to a surviving node.

In addition to the fault-tolerance benefits, using a RAC cluster for the Presentation Server data store provided improved response time for the IMA Service on startup and during read-intensive operations, such as LHC updates.

Tested Environment

Two Cluster Servers with the following configuration:

▼ Compaq ProLiant 1850R Dual P3 600 MHz

- 1GB RAM

- 16GB SCSI Local Disk

- Emulex LightPulse 9000 host bus adapter (HBA) connected via fiber-optic cable directly to the EMC^2 Celerra

▲ 1 100MB Compaq NIC used for both normal and cluster communication

1 EMC^2 Celerra Enterprise Network Server with the following configuration:

▼ 51GB partition available to the cluster servers

- Arbitrated Loop SAN configuration

▲ Dedicated Fiber Adapter (FA) ports for access by the Emulex HBA cards

Obtaining the Oracle CFS Software

The software for the Oracle Real Application Clusters—Cluster File System for Windows NT/2000—can be downloaded from this following location:

http://otn.oracle.com/software/products/oracle9i/htdocs/winsoft.html.

Included in the download are files updated from the software provided on the Oracle 9iR2 CD media and the installation instructions in a file named *ocfs_relnotes.pdf*.

The *ocfs_relnotes* file contains pertinent information on setting up the CFS environment. Failure to follow the guidelines explained in this document may result in a failed Oracle RAC install. Before beginning an install, read this document in its entirety. This document is also available for download at:

http://otn.oracle.com/docs/products/oracle9i/doc_library/ocfs_relnotes.htm.

The instructions that follow are brief descriptions of the steps outlined in the *ocfs_relnotes* document. For a more complete explanation of the steps, please refer to that document.

Process Overview

A.   Configure the physical connection to the shared disk subsystem.

B.   Configure the shared disks on Windows 2000.

C.   Install Oracle Cluster File System (CFS).

D.   Install Oracle 9*i*R2.

E.   Patch the Oracle RAC files.

F.   Reconfigure the Oracle listeners.

G.   Create the database using the Database Configuration Assistant (DBCA).

H.   Create a TNSNAMES.ORA file for the cluster configuration.

 I.   Install Presentation Server.

A. Configure the physical connection to the shared disk subsystem.

1.   Create a metavolume of the appropriate size to host both the Oracle Home files (8GB) and the Oracle data files. The MetaFrame database will reside in the Oracle data files partition, so verify that the space created is appropriate. For MetaFrame sizing guidelines, refer to the *MetaFrame Presentation Server Administrator's Guide*.

2.   Using dedicated FA ports on the EMC² Celerra server map, connect the newly created metavolume to each FA port to be used by the Oracle servers.

3.   Install the HBA cards into the Oracle servers and connect them to the EMC² Celerra server.

4.   Verify that the Oracle servers can see the EMC² Celerra shared disk using the HBA.

B. Configure the shared disks on Windows 2000.

When configuring Windows 2000 to view the shared disks, adhere to the following guidelines:

▼   Do not allow Windows 2000 to write a disk signature on the drive

■   Do not assign drive letters to the Windows 2000 partitions

▲   Do not format the Windows 2000 partitions

1.   Log into the Oracle Server as an administrator.

2.   Launch Computer Management and create a new partition to hold the Oracle server files.

a. From within Computer Management, select the Disk Management Folder.

b. Right-click on the EMC2 disk and choose Create Partition from the Context menu. This launches the Create Partition Wizard.

c. Select Next.

     d. Select Extended Partition.

     e. Set "Amount of disk space to use" and click Next.

     f. Click Finish.

  3. Create a logical drive inside the partition to hold the Oracle Home files.

     a. Right-click on the new partition and choose Create Logical Drive.

     b. Click Next.

     c. Set "Amount of disk space to use" to 8GB for the Oracle Home files and click Next.

     d. Choose the "Do not assign a drive letter or drive path" radio button, and then click Next.

     e. Choose "Do not format this partition".

     f. Click Finish.

  4. Create a logical drive inside the partition to hold the Oracle data files.

     a. Right-click on the new partition and choose Create Logical Drive.

     b. Click Next.

     c. Set "Amount of disk space to use" to 8GB for the Oracle Home files and click Next.

     d. Choose "Do not assign a drive letter or drive path" radio button, and then click Next.

     e. Choose "Do not format this partition".

     f. Click Finish.

  5. Repeat steps 3 and 4 for all Oracle servers in the cluster.

  6. Verify TCP/IP and shared disk connectivity between all Oracle Servers.

C. Install Oracle Cluster File System (CFS).

When installing the Oracle CFS, adhere to the following guidelines:

▼ Do not run the executables from the Oracle 9*i* CD media, use the executables provided with download.

▲ The Oracle cluster name should be a derivative of the Oracle server machine names. For instance, if the Oracle server machine names are OCLUSTER1 and OCLUSTER2, then the cluster name should be OCLUSTER.

  1. Start the \preinstall_rac\clustersetup\clustersetup.exe program to create the cluster nodes. This starts the Oracle Cluster Setup Wizard. Complete this *before* installing the Oracle 9*i* server.

  2. Choose Create Cluster.

3. Select the appropriate network interconnect type and configure for the environment.

4. Enter the cluster name.

5. Choose "CFS for Oracle Home and Datafiles".

6. Configure CFS for Oracle Home and set it to the 8GB logical drive created earlier.

7. Configure CFS for Datafiles and set it to the data logical drive created earlier.

8. Complete the wizard.

9. Start the \install\win32\setup.exe program to install the OraCFS file system on the cluster nodes.

10. Select the 8GB logical drive for Oracle Home files.

At this point, the drive letters assigned to the shared disk should be visible from all cluster nodes. In addition, several new services should now be visible in the Services Control Panel applet.

D. Install Oracle 9*i* R2.

When installing Oracle 9*i* R2, do not select a preinstalled database. Before installing a database, certain files must be patched for RAC to work properly. Selecting a preinstalled database causes the DBCA Wizard to start and automatically create a database before the RAC components are successfully patched.

1. From the Oracle9*i* CD, start the setup.exe program to install database server software.

2. On the node selection page, select all the Oracle servers to be included in this cluster.

3. Navigate to the \stage\products.jar directory on the CD to select the appropriate products file.

4. Set the Oracle Home name.

5. In the path field, select the 8GB logical drive path you created earlier for the Oracle Home files.

6. On the next page, select Enterprise Edition.

7. On the Database Type page, select custom so the DBCA wizard does not autocreate a database at the end of install.

8. Complete the remainder of the Installation Wizard.

9. Complete the Network Configuration Assistant. Click Yes to ignore the warning message. This is a known issue with cluster servers.

10. The Database Configuration Assistant starts. Click Cancel to quit out of this wizard. CFS patches must be applied before running this wizard.

11. End the installation.

12. If Enterprise Manager starts, click Cancel to close it.

E. Patch the Oracle RAC files.

1. Navigate to the \patch folder from the downloaded file.
2. On each node, perform the patch procedures indicated in the srvm.txt file.
3. On each node, perform the patch procedures indicated in the dbca.txt file.

F. Reconfigure the Oracle listeners.

1. Stop the Oracle | OracleHome | TNSListener service from the Windows Services Control Panel applet.
2. Change the startup type to Disabled.
3. Open a command prompt window and run the command: **lsnrctl start listener_ <nodename>**. For example: **lsnrctl start listener_ocluster1**.
4. Repeat steps 1 through 3 on each node in the cluster.

G. Create the database using the Database Configuration Assistant (DBCA).

1. Create an oradata directory on the root of the data file's logical drive.
2. Open a command prompt window and run the DBCA from the command prompt specifying the file location created in the previous step 1. For example, **dbca–datafileDestination P:\oradata**.
3. Choose Create Database and click Next.
4. Select the nodes to create the database on.
5. When complete, restart all Oracle servers.
6. Refer to the *MetaFrame Presentation Server Administrator's Guide* for steps to correctly configure an Oracle database for a MetaFrame Presentation Server farm.

H. Create a TNSNAMES.ORA file for the cluster configuration.

1. Add an entry to the TNSNAMES.ORA file for the cluster configuration.
2. Include each Oracle server in the cluster in the address list.

```
OCLUSTER.TEST.COM =
  (DESCRIPTION =
    (ADDRESS_LIST =
      (ADDRESS = (PROTOCOL = TCP)(HOST = ocluster1.test.com)(PORT = 1521))
      (ADDRESS = (PROTOCOL = TCP)(HOST = ocluster2.test.com)(PORT = 1521))
    )
    (CONNECT_DATA =
      (SERVICE_NAME = ocluster.test.com)
    )
  )
```

3. Use TNSPING to verify that all nodes of the cluster are reachable.

I. Install Presentation Server.

1. Copy the TNSNAMES.ORA file to the \network\admin folder of the Oracle client.

2. Start the Presentation Server install.

3. Specify Use a Third-Party Database and select Oracle.

4. Specify the cluster service name for the Service Name field.

5. Specify the user name/password configured in the previous step G.

6. Complete the rest of the wizard using the guidelines for Presentation Server databases, as outlined in the *MetaFrame Presentation Server Administrator's Guide*.

CHAPTER 6

Novell Directory Services Integration

Citrix Presentation Server supports NDS (Novell Directory Services) authentication to Presentation Server, published applications, and published content. This section explains how to use NDS with Presentation Server, Web Interface, and the Presentation Server Client for 32-bit Windows (version 6.20 and later).

This section assumes familiarity with NDS and related Novell products. See the Novell web site at http://www.novell.com for more information about the Novell products referred to in this document.

Prior to Feature Release 1, MetaFrame XP 1.0 offered limited support for NDS users through the BUILTIN group. In *MetaFrame XP*, you select the BUILTIN group to specify dynamic local users managed by Novell's ZENworks for Desktops when you publish applications and assign users to network printers.

While use of the BUILTIN group is supported in Presentation Server for backward compatibility, Citrix recommends enabling NDS support in Presentation Server. Presentation Server allows tighter integration between Presentation Server and NDS trees, and it allows NDS users to take advantage of more features. NDS support in MetaFrame XP with Feature Release 3 requires a Feature Release 1 or later license to be added to the farm and at least one server with Feature Release 3 enabled. Presentation Server 3.0 and higher does not require any additional licenses beyond the basic licensing to enable NDS support.

IMPLEMENTING NDS SUPPORT IN CITRIX PRESENTATION SERVER

Citrix Presentation Server can now publish applications, desktops, and content for users managed by NDS or Directory Services in Windows 2000 and Windows NT. However, using Presentation Server in a network environment that employs multiple directory services requires careful planning.

Read the following sections carefully before installing Presentation Server in an NDS environment.

Planning Your Deployment of Citrix Presentation Server for NDS Support

Using Citrix Presentation Server in an NDS environment requires the following tasks in the order they are listed. Each task is explained in detail in this document.

1. Decide which servers will host applications and content published for NDS users when Presentation Server is installed.

2. Install the Novell Client for Windows NT/2000, version 4.81 or later, on those servers.

3. Install Citrix Presentation Server:

   ▼ Activate the required MetaFrame XP and Feature Release 3 licenses.

   ▲ Set the MetaFrame XP server Feature Release level to Feature Release 3.

NOTE The previous licensing steps are *not* required for Presentation Server 3 and 4.

4. Enable the Dynamic Local User policy in ZENworks for Desktops or make sure the same user accounts and passwords exist in both NDS and NT4 or ADS domains. You may also enable the SyncedDomainName key in each Presentation Server with NDS Integration. This will not require the ZENworks DLU Component requirement.

   ▼ Open the Registry Editor on the Citrix Presentation Server.

   ■ Go to HKEY_LOCAL_MACHINE\SOFTWARE\Citrix and add a new key called NDS.

   ■ On the new key, add a new SZ subkey called SyncedDomainName.

   ▲ Set the value to the NetBIOS name of the domain you want to synch the user names with. It is not required to restart the server or IMA service; users can now sync the NetWare users with those of the NT/ADS domain. Both users still need to exist on the NetWare tree and the NT/ADS domain.

5. Enable NDS support in the Citrix Presentation Server farm.

   ▼ Assign Citrix administrator privileges to NDS objects.

   ■ Log on to the Presentation Server Console with NDS credentials.

   ▲ Publish applications, desktops, or content for NDS users on Presentation Servers to which only NDS users will connect.

6. If you are using Web Interface, enable NDS support for the Web Interface in the Access Suite Console.

7. Instruct end users how to connect to published applications and content using their NDS credentials. If you are deploying the Program Neighborhood Agent, enable NDS support in the Program Neighborhood Agent.

The sections that follow outline the procedures required to use Citrix Presentation Server in an NDS environment.

Farm Layout and System Requirements

Using Citrix Presentation Server in a network environment that employs multiple directory services requires careful planning. While the Citrix Presentation Server farm can contain servers in Windows NT or Windows 2000/2003 domains and servers enabled for

NDS, Citrix Presentation Servers running the Novell Client and that use Dynamic Local User functionality should be members of a workgroup, and not members of a domain. The Dynamic Local User feature of Novell ZENworks for Desktops must be used in this configuration.

To implement Presentation Server in an NDS environment, designate application servers to host applications and content published only for NDS users. These servers must run version 4.81 or later of the Novell Client for Windows NT/2000 and MetaFrame XP, Feature Release 3 or later. Figure 6-1 illustrates the required layout of a Citrix Presentation Server farm supporting NDS.

The following software must be installed for Citrix Presentation Server to successfully access NDS:

On the NDS server (a server supporting NDS authentication and responding to NDS queries from clients):

▼ NDS eDirectory 8.5 for Windows or for Novell NetWare 5 with Support Pack 6 or later, or for Novell NetWare 5.1 with Support Pack 2 or later, or Netware 6 and later.

On Citrix Presentation Servers:

▼ Novell Client for Windows NT/2000, version 4.81 or later

▲ MetaFrame XP for Windows, Feature Release 3 or later

If using ZENworks Dynamic Local User function to gain access to Windows, you must install Novell ZENworks for Desktops 3 or later.

If you are not using ZENworks to gain access to Windows, you must have accounts with the same user name and password that exist in both NDS and NT4 or ADS domains.

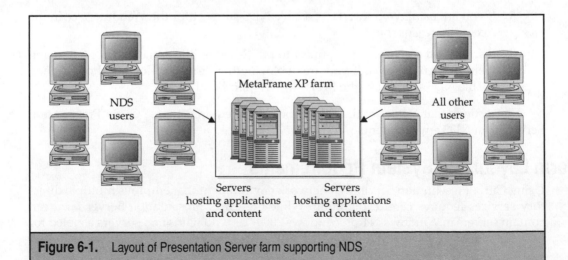

Figure 6-1. Layout of Presentation Server farm supporting NDS

To synchronize domains, perform either of the following:

▼ Manually synchronize accounts

▲ Use third-party software, such as Novell's Account Manager 2.1 for NT or DirXML, that can automatically synchronize accounts between NDS and NT domains

IMPORTANT Internet Protocol (IP) is the only supported protocol for correct interaction between Citrix Presentation Server NDS and ZENworks for Desktops.

Installing Required Software

Citrix recommends installing the Novell Client and related service packs on a server before installing Citrix Presentation Server. If the server is already running Presentation Server, see the section "Installing the Novell Client on a Server with Presentation Server."

Installing the Novell Client on a Server Without Citrix Presentation Server

Complete the following tasks prior to installing Presentation Server.

1. Install and configure the Novell Client for Windows NT/2000, version 4.81 or later.

NOTE If you choose to use ZENworks DLU, it may be necessary to perform a custom installation of the Novell Client and add the Workstation Manager component. Some clients do not install this component when performing a typical install.

2. Restart the server.

3. Verify that you can log on to NDS.

If you cannot log on to NDS, you may need to add a Directory Agent (DA) location to the Novell Client. A DA is needed when the NDS server is located on a different subnet. If a DA does not exist, make sure the NDS server and the Presentation Server are part of the same subnet.

1. To optimize logon and browsing response times, change the order of the network providers using the following steps:

   a. Right-click the My Network Places icon on the server's desktop.

   b. Choose Properties from the shortcut menu. The Network and Dial-up Connections window appears.

   c. Choose Advanced Settings on the Advanced menu. The Advanced Settings dialog box appears.

d. On the Provider Order tab, adjust the order of the network providers so that Microsoft Windows Network is above NetWare Services.

e. Click OK to close the Advanced Settings dialog box.

2. To optimize logon time, add the Windows fonts directory located in %SYSTEM-ROOT% to the system-path environment variable.

3. To suppress a Citrix Presentation Server setup program error message that says the FileSysChange parameter is invalid, complete the following steps:

a. Open the System.ini file located in %SYSTEMROOT%.

b. In the [386Enh] section of System.ini, set the following value:

```
FileSysChange=off
```

c. Save and close System.ini.

NOTE The appearance of this error message causes unattended setup of Citrix Presentation Server to fail. Make sure the FileSysChange parameter is set to Off before running an unattended installation.

4. Install Presentation Server 3/4 or MetaFrame XP with Feature Release 3. Be sure to activate the appropriate licenses and, if necessary, set the Feature Release level of the server to Feature Release 3.

If MetaFrame XP FR3 fails to install, complete the following steps:

1. Uninstall the Novell Client from the server.

2. Install MetaFrame XP FR3, and then install the Novell Client by following the instructions in the section "Installing the Novell Client on a Server with Presentation Server."

If the system is working properly, skip to the section "Configuring ZENworks for Desktops Settings for Presentation Server Support."

Installing the Novell Client on a Server with Presentation Server

If Presentation Server is already installed on the server before you install the Novell Client, you must change the Windows registry on the server before *and* after you install the Novell Client. If the Novell Client being installed is 4.9 or later, the following steps are unnecessary because the 4.9 client detects GINA chaining and respects such chaining with Citrix.

NOTE If the Presentation Server has the IPX protocol installed along with the Novell Client, the FR3 installation may fail with a wowexec error message. To work around this issue, disable the NWLINK protocol on all adapters in the server. After FR3 is installed, reenable NWLink.

If Presentation Server is already installed on the server, complete the following tasks.

1. Run regedt32.

2. Edit the following registry key:

   `HKEY_LOCAL_MACHINE\SOFTWARE\Microsoft\WindowsNT\CurrentVersion\Winlogon`

3. Double-click the GinaDLL entry located in the right-hand pane. In the String Editor window that pops up, replace the value Ctxgina.dll with the value Msgina.dll.

4. Install and configure the Novell Client for Windows NT/2000, Version 4.81 or later.

5. Do not restart when prompted by the Novell Client setup program.

6. Edit the registry entry for GinaDLL, as in step 2. In the String Editor window that appears, replace the value nwgina.dll with the value Ctxgina.dll.

7. With the key path for Winlogon still selected, choose Add Value on the Edit menu.

8. Type **CTXGINADLL** in the Add Value dialog box. The data type is REG_SZ.

9. Enter **Nwgina.dll** in the String Editor window to assign this value to the new CTXGINADLL entry.

10. Restart the server.

On Presentation Servers, Ctxgina.dll is loaded by Winlogon.exe to process the autologon information transmitted by ICA clients. Ctxgina.dll can process autologon credentials in excess of 20 characters. For example, if Ctxgina.dll is not loaded, autologon user names greater than 20 characters are truncated to 20 characters by Termsrv.exe. When Ctxgina.dll acquires the user's autologon credentials, they are passed in their entirety to the installed Gina.dll file to complete the authentication process. In most cases, the installed GINA is Msgina.dll. When the Novell Client is installed, the GINA is Nwgina.dll. The previous steps are required to ensure that CTXGINA is installed on the Presentation Server. CTXGINA is required for logging on automatically with user names that exceed 20 characters. If the Novell Client being installed is 4.9 or later, the previous steps are unnecessary because the 4.9 client detects GINA chaining and respects such chaining with Citrix.

NOTE If the Novell Client is upgraded after the installation of Presentation Server, the GINA values are overwritten and it is necessary to reconfigure the registry with the previous steps.

1. To optimize logon and browsing response times, change the order of the network providers using the following steps:

   a. Right-click the My Network Places icon on the server's desktop.

   b. Choose Properties from the shortcut menu that appears. The Network and Dial-up Connections window appears.

c. Choose Advanced Settings on the Advanced menu. The Advanced Settings dialog box appears.

d. On the Provider Order tab, adjust the order of the network providers, so Microsoft Windows Network is above NetWare Services.

e. Click OK to close the Advanced Settings dialog box.

2. To optimize logon time, add the Windows fonts directory located in `%systemroot%` to the system-path environment variable.

The system is now ready to set up the Windows account authentication to be used to access Windows 2000/2003 servers.

Windows Account Authentication

When a NetWare Client is running on a Windows NT or Windows 2000 Server, users are required to have two accounts: one for authentication to NDS and one to gain access to Windows.

Two different approaches can give Windows access to users. The first option uses Novell's Dynamic Local User functionality, available in Novell's ZENworks for Desktop Product (this is the only supported method in FR1).

The second option is by having the same user name and password in both NDS and NT or ADS domains for each user (this support is available for MetaFrame XP FR2 and higher). This allows integration of Presentation Server and NDS without the use of Novell's ZENworks.

If using Presentation Server with NDS integration using ZENworks, continue in the following section with "Configuring ZENworks for Desktops Settings for Presentation Server Support."

If using Presentation Server with NDS integration without ZENworks, skip to the "Configuring NDS Support in Citrix Presentation Server Without ZENworks" section.

Configuring ZENworks for Desktops Settings for Presentation Server Support

When a Novell Client is running on a Windows NT or Windows 2000/2003 Server, users are normally required to enter separate credentials to log on to Windows and NDS. Enabling the Dynamic Local User policy in ZENworks for Desktops eliminates this need.

The following section explains how to configure the Container Package and User Package in ZENworks for Desktops to eliminate the need to specify two sets of credentials when connecting to a Citrix Presentation Server. Configure the Container Package to specify which users (by container) should have the Dynamic Local User policy applied to them. Configure the User Package to specify how the Dynamic Local User policy is applied to those users.

NOTE   These settings are configured on the NDS server through ConsoleOne.

Configuring the ZENworks for Desktops Container Package

The Container Package searches for policies located within the tree, and then applies them to users who are associated with a particular container. Follow the next example to create a Container Package that searches only the local container for policies applied to users within that container. This sample configuration is useful for small companies.

Perform the following steps for containers that hold user objects that require the Dynamic Local User policy:

1. Select a container that holds user objects.

2. On the New Object menu, choose Policy Package | Container Package.

3. Choose Define Additional Properties and click Finish.

4. On the Policies tab, enable the search policy.

5. In the search policies up to field, choose Object Container to search only the container in which the search policy resides.

   The other choices are

   ▼ **Root (default)**   Searches the local container and any container in the direct path to the root of the tree. This is not recommended for medium-to-large trees.

   ■ **Partition**   Searches the local container and any container up to the root of the partition. This method works well for large environments, but you need to locate the partition boundaries.

   ▲ **Selected Container**   Searches the container between the current container and the root of the tree you select.

6. Leave the search level at the default setting of 0.

7. Click Apply, and then Close.

8. Click the Associations tab.

9. Choose Add and browse to the container that holds the Container Package you just created.

10. Click OK, and then Close.

Configuring the ZENworks for Desktops User Package

The User Package in ZENworks for Desktops enables Dynamic Local User functionality for users who are associated with that particular package. Follow the next example to create a User Package that enables the Dynamic Local User functionality.

IMPORTANT   If the Container Package, the User Policy Package, and the user are not located in the same container, the User Policy Package that contains the DLU settings will not be applied to the user.

1. Choose the Organizational Unit that holds the Container Package from the previous section.

2. On the New Object menu, choose Policy Package | User Package.

3. Near the end of the wizard, choose Define Additional Properties, and then click Finish.

4. Choose WinNT-2000 on the Policies tab.

5. Choose Enable Dynamic Local User, and then choose Properties.

6. Choose Dynamic Local User at the top of the page.

7. Choose Manage Existing NT Account (if any). This changes the password and other items to match for a seamless integration.

NOTE   Novell recommends that you create a separate Dynamic Local User policy for users who have the user name Administrator if the local administrator account has not been renamed.

8. Choose Use NetWare Credential. This creates a local Microsoft user who has the same name and password as the NDS user. If this is not enabled, the Dynamic Local User feature creates a random user name and password, resulting in a loss of Presentation Server functionality.

9. Do not enable Volatile User unless you have large profiles and want to conserve disk space.

10. On the Not Member of tab, choose User | Add. Select the users or groups to which the policy will apply. This gives them rights to log on and run Presentation Server applications.

11. Click Apply, and then OK two times to finish the policy.

12. If the Citrix Presentation Server is a Windows 2003 server, make sure you add a Custom Group to the Policy. The Custom Group name should be Remote Desktop Users; this is the group that is granted Log On Locally to log in remotely through Terminal Services.

Configuring NDS Support in Citrix Presentation Server Without ZENworks

In a environment with a Novell Client running on a Windows NT or Windows 2000 Server, users are required to enter separate credentials to log on to Windows and NDS. Using synchronized accounts between NDS and NT4 or ADS domains eliminates this need. MetaFrame XP FR2 and later add support for this type of configuration.

To enable NDS support in Presentation Server without ZENworks, set the following registry key on all the servers that have the Novell Client installed, but are not using ZWFD DLU functionality. Set the Value to the NT or ADS downlevel domain name containing the user accounts that match the accounts in NDS.

1. Run regedt32.
2. Edit the registry key:

   `HKEY_LOCAL_MACHINE\SOFTWARE\Citrix`
3. With the key path for Citrix still selected, choose New Key on the Edit menu.
4. Rename the newly created key to NDS.
5. Highlight the new NDS key.
6. With the NDS still selected, choose New String Value on the Edit menu.
7. Type **SyncedDomainName** in the String Value dialog box.
8. Enter the name of the domain that has the same user accounts as NDS in the String Editor window to assign this value to the new SyncedDomainName entry.

NOTE   When this registry key is set, ctxgina.dll replaces the NDS tree name passed from the client to the server with the String placed in SyncedDomainName. Ctxgina.dll then passes the credentials on to nwgina.dll. This allows the passed-on user name and password to authenticate to NDS, and then the domain specified in the SyncedDomainName.

Enabling NDS Support in the Citrix Presentation Server Farm

By default, a Citrix Presentation Server farm supports only Microsoft Windows users. Follow the next steps to specify the preferred NDS tree for the farm. Presentation Server supports only one NDS tree in each farm.

1. Log on to the Presentation Server Console and connect to a Presentation Server configured for NDS support.
2. Right-click the farm node in the left pane of the console and choose Properties.
3. Click the MetaFrame Settings tab in the Properties dialog box.
4. Specify the tree name in the NDS Preferred Tree field, and then click OK. To disable NDS support for the farm, erase the value in the NDS Preferred Tree field, and then click OK.

Assigning Citrix Administrator Privileges to NDS Objects

Follow the next steps to assign Citrix administrator privileges to objects in an NDS tree, such as country, organization, organization unit, group, user, or alias.

1. Log on to the Presentation Server Console.
2. Right click the MetaFrame Administrators node in the left-hand pane and choose Add Citrix Administrator from the menu that appears.
3. In the Add Citrix Administrator dialog box, open the NDS tree. Objects in the NDS tree represent container and leaf objects.

4. When prompted to log on to the tree, enter the distinguished name and password of an NDS user.

5. Select the Show Users option to display user and alias objects in this hierarchy.

6. Double-click to open container objects. Select the objects to be granted MetaFrame administrator privileges. Add at least one NDS user account that has read-and-write privileges.

NOTE   While it is possible to grant a MetaFrame administrator access to a context, users within the context or in contexts that are children of the granted context will also be MetaFrame administrators. This is not recommended because of the difficulty in managing permissions granted to contexts.

7. Click Add. Choose View Only, Full Administration, or Custom privileges.

8. Click Finish to close the Add Citrix Administrator dialog box.

CHAPTER 7

Advanced Access
Control

This chapter focuses mainly on compatibility with previous implementations of Advanced Access Control, namely Secure Access Manager, and Access Gateway Enterprise. Also, content around security of split tunneling and split DNS is considered.

SPLIT TUNNELING IN CITRIX ACCESS GATEWAY

Split tunneling is the name of a feature provided by Citrix Access Gateway that allows a client device to maintain connectivity to both the local network and a remote network over the VPN link at the same time. For a client, a tunnel is *split* when some of the network traffic it generates is sent to the VPN server and other traffic is sent directly to the local network without passing through the VPN server.

Examples and Use Cases

Company *A* acquires company *B*, and users in company *A* want to access resources in company *B* via Access Gateway, and at the same time, access the resources in their own company. This can be accomplished by enabling split tunneling on the Access Gateway servers in company *B*. This way, once users have established a VPN connection to company *B*, they can access both local network resources (in company *A*) and those of company *B*.

Another example is that of home users with a home office network. These users might want to use their local network printer to print a corporate document while they are connected via VPN into their corporate network. Split tunneling enables users to do that. Figures 7-1 and 7-2 illustrate this idea.

Because traffic destined for noncorporate networks does not go to the VPN server, enabling split tunneling also helps reduce the load on the VPN server and frees up bandwidth.

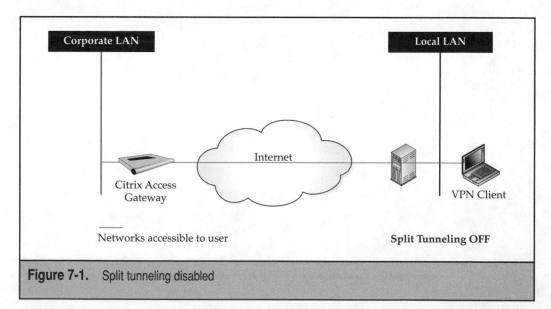

Figure 7-1. Split tunneling disabled

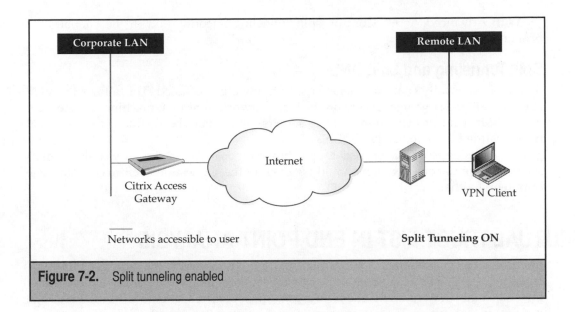

Figure 7-2.   Split tunneling enabled

This raises a logical question. Why would an administrator ever want to turn off split tunneling? The downside to using split tunneling is security.

With a split tunnel, a malicious user or viral process with network access to the client device may be able to use the client device as an entry point to the corporate network, because it has connectivity to the corporate network via its VPN tunnel. For example, say a user has a wireless network at home and the shared permissions of the home network are set up incorrectly. If their neighbor hacks into that network, the neighbor might be able to use the split tunnel set up to access the corporate network. Another downside of split tunneling is this: it forces the administrator to be aware of (and manually enter) all the corporate subnets in the Accessible Networks user interface (UI). As new subnets are added, the Accessible Networks list requires updating.

Configuration

In Access Gateway 4.2, split tunneling is configured under the Global Cluster Policies tab. When turned on, a set of accessible subnets should also be specified. These consist of those networks for which traffic is captured by the VPN Client and sent to the remote network. For example, if 10.0.0.0/255.0.0.0 is configured as an accessible network, any traffic for an IP address of the form 10.x.x.x will *not* be placed on the local network. It will either be sent to the remote network via the VPN or dropped altogether if the user's permissions do not allow them to access the particular remote IP address. In other words, if the user tries to reach IP 10.2.3.4 and such an IP does not exist on the remote network, but it does exist on the local network, then only an attempt is made to send the packet to the remote network, which means the packet is never ultimately delivered to the destination.

With Advanced Access Control, split tunneling is configured in the Global VPN properties node.

Split Tunneling and Split DNS

Split DNS is usually enabled whenever split tunneling is enabled. This allows the VPN client to fall back to name servers on the local network to resolve machines on the local network, instead of using remote DNS servers, which may be unable to resolve local fully qualified domain names (FQDNs).

The decision to enable or disable split tunneling is a classic case of usability versus security. Careful consideration should be given to these questions before choosing one option or another.

MUTUAL TRUST LIST IN END POINT ANALYSIS

End Point Analysis clients download scan packages from servers that end users have decided to trust. The first time an end user visits a logon point on a server that is configured for End Point Analysis scans, the user is asked whether he wants to trust scan package code from that server. The end user may choose to trust to download packages from a server just once or always to trust that server.

Administrators may also configure End Point Analysis clients to use packages that have already been downloaded from a set of trusted servers. This might be useful in the case where the external users are served by a distinct logon point host in the DMZ, but internal connections go through another Advanced Access Control server. A mobile laptop user could connect to both external and internal logon points in such a scenario, and it might be preferable simply to reuse previously downloaded scan packages from one or other servers. The list of such servers is called the *mutual trust list*.

The mutual trust list is controlled via an option in the web.config file in a logon point's physical directory. The list members are specified in the key "MutualTrustList" and consist of a series of server names separated by spaces. For the "mutual" trust mechanism to work, the web.config files for the logon points on all the servers in the list should be modified.

Here's an example of how this might work. Let's say the administrator wants users who login to serverA to trust packages already downloaded from serverB. In the web .config file for one of the logon points on serverA, SampleLogonPoint for instance, the administrator adds the following:

```
<add key="MutualTrustList" value="serverB"/>
```

Similarly, for a logon point on serverB the administrator changes the web.config to reference serverA:

```
<add key="MutualTrustList" value="serverA"/>
```

Now, when a user logs in to serverA/SampleLogonPoint, his End Point Analysis client records that serverB is trusted. Next time the user logs in to serverB, he may download scan packages that were not downloaded during his initial visit to serverA. Each time scan package files are downloaded, they are saved to a cache on the endpoint machine. The cache is organized by logon server origin. The mutual trust list for serverB includes serverA and that information is also saved by the End Point Analysis client. When the user returns to a logon point on serverA, and if a new End Point Analysis scan package is configured to run for that logon point, which contains a file already downloaded from serverB, then the scan package file is not downloaded from serverA. Instead, it is used from the cached copy for serverB on the endpoint machine.

LEGACY CDA COMPATIBILITY

This chart represents all the CDAs included in Secure Access Manager 2.0, 2.0 SP1, and 2.2. Each CDA was tested inside Access Gateway Enterprise 4.0 and Advanced Access Control 4.2 to verify functionality. See Table 7-1. You can find details on the "fail" items in the section "Workarounds and Possible Solutions."

Workarounds and Possible Solutions

Following are the CDAs marked as "fail" in the previous table. This list details the workaround or upgrade that resolves the issue.

▼ **Adapter v1.1.0 for Microsoft SharePoint** There is no replacement for this CDA. Use the Website Viewer 4.0 CDA instead.

■ **Adapter v1.1.0 for Stellent** There is no replacement for this CDA. Use the Website Viewer 4.0 CDA instead.

■ **Adapter v1.0.1 for Microsoft Outlook Web Access** There is no replacement for this CDA. Use the Website Viewer 4.0 CDA instead.

■ **Alert Broadcast Manager CDA v1.0.1** This CDA has been replaced with Alert Broadcast Manager 4.0.

■ **Alert Broadcaster CDA v1.0.1** This CDA has been replaced with Alert Broadcaster CDA 4.0.

■ **Interactive Poll CDA v1.0.1** This CDA has been replaced with Interactive Poll CDA 4.0.

■ **Message Center CDA v1.0.0** This CDA has been replaced with Message Center CDA 4.0.

■ **Web Search CDA v1.0.1** This CDA has been replaced with Search CDA 4.0.

■ **Website Viewer CDA v2.0.1** This CDA has been replaced with Website Viewer CDA 4.0.

▲ **Website Viewer CDA v2.1.0** This CDA has been replaced with Website Viewer CDA 4.0.

CDA Name	Version	IE 6.0	Netscape 7.2	Safari
Account Summary CDA v1.0.1 for Documentum	1.0.1	Pass	Pass	Pass
Adapter v1.1.0 for Microsoft SharePoint	1.1.0	Fail	Fail	Fail
Adapter v1.1.0 for Stellent	1.1.0	Fail	Fail	Fail
Advanced Search CDA v1.0.1 for Documentum	1.0.1	Pass	Pass	Pass
My Account CDA v1.0.1 for Documentum	1.0.1	Pass	Pass	Pass
Adapter v1.0.0 for Windows NetMeeting	1.0.0	Pass	Pass	Pass
Adapter v1.0.1 for Lotus iNotes	1.0.1	Pass	Pass	Pass
Adapter v1.0.1 for Microsoft Outlook Web Access	1.0.1	Fail	Fail	Fail
Alert Broadcast Manager CDA v1.0.1	1.0.1	Fail	Fail	Fail
Alert Broadcaster CDA v1.0.1	1.0.1	Fail	Fail	Fail
Database Viewer CDA v1.0.1	1.0.1	Pass	Pass	Pass
Events CDA v1.0.1 for eRoom	1.0.1	Pass	Pass	Pass
Interactive Poll CDA v1.0.1	1.0.1	Fail	Fail	Fail
Internal Search CDA v1.0.1	1.0.1	Pass	Pass	Pass
Message Center CDA v1.0.0	1.0.0	Fail	Fail	Fail
Personal CDA v1.0.1 for eRoom	1.0.1	Pass	Pass	Pass
Personnel Locator CDA v1.0.1	1.0.1	Pass	Pass	Pass
Search CDA v1.0.1 for eRoom	1.0.1	Pass	Pass	Pass
Shared Documents CDA v1.0.0	1.0.0	Pass	Pass	Pass
Shared Documents CDA v2.1.0	2.1.0	Pass	Pass	Pass
Web Favorites CDA v1.0.1	1.0.1	Pass	Pass	Pass
Web Favorites CDA v2.1.0	2.1.0	Pass	Pass	Pass
Web Search CDA v1.0.1	1.0.1	Fail	Fail	Fail
Website Viewer CDA v2.0.1	2.0.1	Fail	Fail	Fail
Website Viewer CDA v2.1.0	2.1.0	Fail	Fail	Fail
World Clock CDA v1.0.1	1.0.1	Pass	Pass	Pass

Table 7-1. Legacy CDA Interoperability

HTML PREVIEW

By default, The Advanced Access Control server is configured to support the HTML rendering of Microsoft Word, Excel, Visio, and PowerPoint documents, as well as Adobe Acrobat files.

For HTML rendering to occur, Microsoft Office products must be installed on at least one of the Advanced Access Control servers in the farm. Additionally, if the administrator wants to have .PDF document types rendered in HTML, the administrator must also install pdftohtml.exe version 0.36. This executable can be obtained from sourceforge at http://pdftohtml.sourceforge.net/.

The executable should be installed in the c:\program files\Citrix\Access Gateway\ PDF folder for Advanced Access Control and in the c:\program files\Citrix\Access Gateway Enterprise\PDF folder for Access Gateway Enterprise. If the administrator wants to place the executable for PDF conversions outside of the previous install path, a registry key should be modified, so Advanced Access Control knows where to find the executable and can activate this type of HTML rendering.

The registry key is located at:

```
HKLM\software\citrix\msam\activationservice\enginemanager\previewengine
ValueName: PDFConverter
ValueType: string
Default Value(for Advanced Access Control): <installpath>\Citrix\Access
Gateway\PDF\pdftohtml.exe
Default Value(for Access Gateway Enterprise): <installpath>\Citrix\
Access Gateway Enterprise\PDF\pdftohtml.exe
```

For HTML rendered PDF files to illustrate embedded images, the administrator must also install GhostScript version 8.14 or later. Access Gateway Enterprise and Advanced Access Control were both tested on version 8.14. GhostScript can be downloaded from http://www.ghostscript.com/. After installing the application, the administrator must add the path to the bin directory where the Ghostscript executable is located to the server's environment variables PATH. (A reboot of the server may be necessary at this point.)

Adding Other File Types to Be Associated and Rendered Through Existing Rendering Handlers

This section details how to add other file types for rendering by external handlers.

Supported File Type for Each Handler

When a handler is loaded (determined by the handler list and if the required component exists), it reports the file type list that can be supported. The handler reads the file type list from registry and, if such a file type list doesn't exist in the registry, a default list is returned.

Table 7-2 indicates what is set by default. The registry keys do not exist by default and need to be created to associate additional file types with handlers.

Key Name	ROOT\EngineManager\PreviewEngine\caps	
Value Name	MSWORDHANDLER	– word
	MSVISIOHANDLER	– visio
	MSPPTHANDLER	– power point
	PDFHANDLER	– pdf
	MSEXCELHANDLER	– excel
Value Type	String	
Installation Value	None	
Default Value	ExcelHandler	":.xls:.csv:.dbf:.dif: .slk:.wql:.xlt:"
	PDFHandler	":.pdf:"
	PowerPntHandler	":.ppt:.pot:.pps:"
	VisioHandler	":.vsd:.vss:.vst:"
	WordHandler	":.doc:.ans:.mcw:.rtf:"

Table 7-2. Default File Type Handlers

NOTE The registry key values must begin and end with a colon.

Step-by-step Instructions to Modifying an Existing Handler

(The following sample will cause .txt file types to have the preview option available in the choice page and to be rendered as HTML for previewing. This is only an example.)

1. Create registry key "caps" under

   `HKLM\software\citrix\msam\activationservice\enginemanager\previewengine`

2. Under

   `HKLM\software\citrix\msam\activationservice\enginemanager\previewengine\caps`

   add the value:

   ▼ Value Name: MSWORDHANDLER

   ▲ Value Type: String

   Values: ":.doc:.ans:.mcw:.rtf:.txt:" (Remove the quotation marks when you add the values.)

3. Stop/Start the services via the server config console:
    ▼ Citrix Activation Host Service
    ▲ Citrix Activation Engine Service

4. In the files shares tab of the Navigation UI, click on a .txt file and notice Preview is available in the choice page. Select the option and view the text file as rendered HTML.

Controlling Cache Behavior

Cache is used by the engine manager service to boost performance. The default settings should work well in most cases. The only key the administrator should modify for this is CacheSize, which, by default, is set to 10000. If drive space becomes an issue, this number should be lowered. The setting should never be less than 2.

In simple terms, the number 10000 refers to the number of folders that appear in C:\Program Files\Citrix\Access Gateway\ActivationCache before the items begin to overwrite. The order for replacing items is based on the oldest and least used. So, if the first cached item created is used everyday, it will not be overwritten.

CacheSize

To control the maximum count of cache items, reference this table for possible CacheSize values:

Key Name	ROOT\EngineManager
Value Name	CacheSize
Value Type	DWORD
Installation Value	None
Default Value	10000

ADVANCED ACCESS CONTROL CDA SDK CONFIGURATION WIZARD GENERATION FEATURE

The Content Delivery Agent (CDA) software development kit (SDK) shipped with Access Gateway Enterprise 4.0 and Advanced Access Control 4.2 enables you to generate a Configuration Wizard for your CDA, while you develop your CDA. This contrasts with previous versions of the CDA SDKs CDAPad (for script CDAs) did not offer any support for creating Configuration Wizards. The previous version of the .NET CDA SDK only let you specify the configuration parameters for your CDA—the Configuration Wizard dialogs got rendered dynamically when the administrator configured the CDA in the Access Suite Console. You, as the CDA developer, had no control over the look and feel of the controls in the Configuration Wizard dialogs or the validation logic for the values entered for the configuration parameters.

The Access Gateway Enterprise CDA SDK enables you to generate a Configuration Wizard by using the Create CDA Configuration Wizard dialog. For .NET CDAs, this dialog generates a Configuration Wizard for configuring the CDA in the Access Suite Console, and a corresponding personalization .aspx page for end-user personalization of the configurable parameters in the Access Center page. For script CDAs, this dialog generates only the Configuration Wizard because your script CDA handles the CDA personalization by the end user in its "personalize" action.

Support for Multiple Configuration Wizards

Once you create a Configuration Wizard (and a personalization page for .NET CDAs), you can edit the generated code to change the look and feel of the user interface and add more validation logic. You cannot use the SDK to add more configuration parameters to an existing Configuration Wizard. While you could edit the generated Configuration Wizard code to add the additional controls and logic, you may find it easier to generate another Configuration Wizard with just the additional configuration parameters. Then, you can copy-and-paste the generated Configuration Wizard code (and personalization page for .NET CDAs) into your original Configuration Wizard. For this reason, the SDK enables you to generate multiple Configuration Wizards for your CDA. The SDK also lets you experiment with multiple Configuration Wizards for your CDA, finally settling on one as the one to be used to configure the CDA when you package the CDA for deployment to the Access Gateway Enterprise server farm.

In addition to the generated Configuration Wizards, the CDA SDK supports using your own Configuration Wizard, packaged into a Microsoft Installer file (.msi). Using an .msi-based Configuration Wizard applies to both .NET CDAs and script CDAs, although it is most useful when editing an existing script CDA from a .cab file, and the .cab file for the CDA already contains the .msi-based Configuration Wizard.

Finally, you can use the SDK to generate a Configuration Wizard for a CDA that has an .msi-based Configuration Wizard, and then switch back and forth between the one—.msi-based or generated—that is to act as the Configuration Wizard. You use the "Use the Configuration Wizard Installer instead of the generated Configuration Wizard" check box in the Project tab of the CDA Properties dialog to control which Configuration Wizard acts as the Configuration Wizard for the CDA.

Configuration Wizards Project

The first time you generate a Configuration Wizard, using the Create CDA Configuration Wizard dialog, the SDK creates a C# or VB.NET project in the same solution as your CDA project to contain the dialog and user controls for the Configuration Wizard. The SDK adds any subsequently generated Configuration Wizards to the same Configuration Wizard project. For .NET CDAs, the SDK decides between C# and VB.NET, based on the wizard you chose when you created the .NET CDA (a C# CDA application or a VB.NET CDA application). For script CDAs, you control the language of the generated Configuration Wizards in the Language Preference group box of one of the dialogs when you first created the script CDA project.

For .NET CDAs, the dialog and user controls for the Configuration Wizard reside in a folder, whose name matches the name of the generated personalization .aspx page. For script CDAs, you control the name of the folder when you add the CDA Configuration Wizard item to your CDA project.

In addition to the separate folder for each generated Configuration Wizard, the Configuration Wizard project contains two files: AdvancedConfiguration (.vb or .cs) and IGroupOfParameters (.vb or .cs). The AdvancedConfiguration class contains the Configure method, which implements the ISequoiaAdvCDAConfig interface.

Managing Multiple Generated Configuration Wizards

When you add a Configuration Wizard to your CDA using the Create CDA Configuration Wizard dialog, the dialog enables you to specify whether the new Configuration Wizard you generate will act as the Configuration Wizard (replacing the existing generated Configuration Wizard, if any) or whether the existing generated Configuration Wizard will continue to act as the Configuration Wizard. You specify this using the two right-most toggle buttons in the toolbar of the dialog.

Editing Generated Configuration Wizard

Create CDA Configuration Wizard GUI, each group corresponds to one dialog that the Access Suite console presents to the administrator. Put related configuration parameters in the same group.

For each CDA configuration parameter that you add to a group, you can set the properties of the parameter in the properties page of the dialog. For example, for a Numeric Text Parameter, you can set the minimum and maximum valid values for the parameter.

The Configuration Wizard (and the personalization page for .NET CDAs) use the property values of the configuration parameters during the configuration in the Access Suite console (and personalization in the Access Center for the .NET CDAs). If you forget to set some configuration parameter property in the Create CDA Configuration Wizard dialog, you can set the property values after the SDK generates the Configuration Wizard.

For the personalization page for .NET CDAs, click the control that corresponds to the configuration parameter. You see the same properties the wizard displayed in the properties page portion of the dialog, in the properties page of the Visual Studio .NET IDE.

To set the configuration parameter property in the generated Configuration Wizard, you need to edit the generated source code:

▼ Find the UserControl file in the Configuration Wizard project that corresponds to the group containing the parameter whose properties you want to change. The UserControls all reside in the folder for the Configuration Wizard and have sequentially numbered file names GroupControl1, GroupControl2, and so forth.

- Edit the code for that group control and find the InitializeParameterGroup() method.

▲ In this method, you see a section of code that assigns the property values, configured in the Create CDA Configuration Wizard dialog, to an object that represents the CDA configuration parameter in the Configuration Wizard at run time. The name of the object starts with an underscore, followed by the name of the parameter in all uppercase. In the previous example, this name is _PERCENTAGE. You set the run-time property values for the configuration parameter by changing these assignment statements:

```
// PERCENTAGE Parameter
this._PERCENTAGE.ID = "PERCENTAGE";
this._PERCENTAGE.CenterConfigurable = true;
this._PERCENTAGE.InstanceConfigurable = true;
this._PERCENTAGE.UserConfigurable = true;
this._PERCENTAGE.DisplayName = this.displayNamePERCENTAGE.Text;
this._PERCENTAGE.Instructions = "Enter the percent of the total";
this._PERCENTAGE.ShowUseDefaultCheckbox = this.useDefaultPERCENTAGE.Visible;
this._PERCENTAGE.ShowUserCustomizableCheckbox =
this.userCustomizablePERCENTAGE.Visible;
this._PERCENTAGE.Value = this.textBoxPERCENTAGE.Text;
this._PERCENTAGE.MinimumValue = "0";
this._PERCENTAGE.MaximumValue = "100";
```

You can also add validation logic to the generated Configuration Wizard and personalization page. For example, if you want to use a date as a configuration parameter, you would use a TextBox Parameter in the Configuration Wizard, but the TextBox Parameter accepts any string as valid input. You need to add the code to ensure that the administrator (and the end user in the .NET CDA case) enters a valid date in the TextBox for that parameter. Note, for .NET CDAs, if the parameter can be configured in the Access Suite Console and in the user settings (personalization page), you need to add the validation logic to both the generated Configuration Wizard and the generated personalization page.

Selecting Among Multiple Generated Configuration Wizards

If you generate multiple Configuration Wizards for your CDA, experimenting with different sets of configuration parameters, you may want to switch among your Configuration Wizards, selecting which one will act as the Configuration Wizard for the CDA.

For .NET CDAs, the SDK associates each Configuration Wizard with the personalization page the Configuration Wizard was generated with (remember, the Create CDA Configuration Wizard dialog generates the personalization page, as well as the Configuration Wizard for .NET CDAs). The SDK lets you interactively select the personalization page to act as the user settings page for the CDA. When you select the personalization page for the CDA, the SDK automatically selects the corresponding Configuration Wizard to act as the Configuration Wizard for the CDA.

The SDK gives you two ways of selecting the personalization page for your CDA:

▼ To select the .aspx page in the Solution Explorer, right-click the .aspx file and select Set As Personalization Page from the menu.

▲ In the CDA Properties dialog, select the personalization page from the Combo Box in the Customization tab.

For script CDAs, the SDK does not offer a UI-driven way of specifying the Configuration Wizard. You specify the Configuration Wizard by editing the using (or Imports) statement in the `AdvancedConfiguration` file:

```
using CitrixCDA135Config.Editing.Personalization2;
```

Change the previous statement to refer to the namespace used by the dialog and user controls generated for the Configuration Wizard you want to use.

MAKING ICA FILE MODIFICATIONS IN ADVANCED ACCESS CONTROL 4.2

In Advanced Access Control 4.2, ICA file modifications are made by updating two files: ICAFile.xslt and UserPreferences.xslt.

The ICAFile.xslt file is similar to the template.ica file used in Web Interface. This file enables you to make global changes to the parameters generated in an ICA file. ICAFile .xslt is located under \Program Files\Citrix\Access Gateway\Bin\Binders. Any changes to this file should be made on all servers running the Citrix Resource Aggregation Service. After changes are made, the Citrix Resource Aggregation Service must be restarted for the changes to take effect.

A number of sample modifications are shown next.

Proxy Configuration

Several proxy configurations can be configured by modifying the ICAFile.xslt. This allows your ICA client to connect to a Citrix Presentation Server through an HTTP or SOCKS proxy server.

```
ProxyType=[VALUES: None, Auto, Socks(Detect Version), SocksV4, SocksV5, Tunnel, Script]
ProxyHost=[Proxy Address:Proxy Port]
ProxyBypassList=
ProxyAutoConfigURL=[http path to AutoConfig or PAC file]
ProxyUsername=[Proxy/SOCKSv5 Username]
ProxyPassword=[Proxy/SOCKSv5 Password]
ProxyTimeout=[Time in seconds the client waits for initial response from proxy server]
ProxyUseFQDN=True
```

Auto Client Reconnect

If you want to disable Auto Client Reconnect globally, add the following line:

```
TransportReconnectEnabled=Off
```

Root Certificate for the Java Client

You can use the ICAFile.xslt to specify a root certificate to be used by the Java ICA client when making ICA connections through Access Gateway. This keeps you from having to package the certificate in a cab or jar file. To do this, add the following line:

```
SSLNoCACerts=1
SSLCACert0=cert_name.cer
```

If it is a multiple certificate (chain certificate), you need to modify the following:

```
SSLNoCAcerts=<no. of certs>
SSLCACert0=<sslcert1.cer>
SSLCACert1=<sslcert2.cer>
```

The root certificate must be copied to the Java Client directory on the web server.

Remapping Hot Keys

To remap the hot keys, insert the hotkey parameters in the WFClient section of the Icafile.xslt file:

```
ClientName=<xsl:value-of select="ica:ClientName" />
Hotkey1Char=F1
Hotkey1Shift=Shift
Hotkey2Char=F3
Hotkey2Shift=Shift
Hotkey3Char=F2
Hotkey3Shift=Shift
Hotkey4Char=F1
Hotkey4Shift=Ctrl
Hotkey5Char=F2
Hotkey5Shift=Ctrl
Hotkey6Char=F2
Hotkey6Shift=Alt
Hotkey7Char=plus
Hotkey7Shift=Alt
Hotkey8Char=minus
Hotkey8Shift=Alt
Hotkey9Char=F3
```

```
HotKey10Shift=Ctrl
Hotkey10Char=F5
HotKey9Shift=Ctrl
Hotkey11Char=plus
Hotkey11Shift=Ctrl
BrowserRetry=1
BrowserTimeout=20000
HttpBrowserAddress=!
<xsl:apply-templates select="ica:CSGEnabled"/>
```

These are the default hot-key parameters. You can disable them by setting the value to "none" or if any keys affect your application, you can change them to reflect a key that does not conflict with your application.

Customizing Application Launch

The UserPreferences.xslt file can be used to modify launch parameters for specific applications. The UserPreferences.xslt file is located under \Program Files\Citrix\Access Gateway\Bin\Binders. One of the most common modifications is window size. The following shows two example modifications. One sets applications to a percent of the screen size and the other sets a specific window size.

```
<!--
    This template will set the window type to "Percent" for the named application. For
all other applications the above semantics for applying user preferences are preserved
    -->
    <xsl:template match="ica:WindowType">
        <xsl:choose>
            <xsl:when test="/ica:ICABinding[ica:ApplicationName='Notepad']">
                <xsl:copy>
                    <ica:Percent>100</ica:Percent>
                </xsl:copy>
            </xsl:when>
            <xsl:when test="/ica:ICABinding[ica:ApplicationName='Solitaire']">
                <xsl:copy>
                    <ica:Percent>50</ica:Percent>
                </xsl:copy>
            </xsl:when>
            <xsl:otherwise>
                <xsl:call-template name="replace.context.element">
                    <xsl:with-param name="replacement"
select="$Transform/Arguments/ica.UserPreferences/ica:ApplicationSettings/ica:
WindowType"/>
                    <xsl:with-param name="allowed"
select="$Transform/Arguments/ApplicationSettingsControl/@WindowType"/>
                </xsl:call-template>
            </xsl:otherwise>
        </xsl:choose>
    </xsl:template>
```

This example shows how to set an application to a specific window size:

```
<xsl:when test="/ica:ICABinding[ica:ApplicationName='APP01']">
<xsl:copy>
    <ica:Pixels>
        <ica:Width>800</ica:Width>
        <ica:Height>600</ica:Height>
    </ica:Pixels>
    </xsl:copy>
</xsl:when>
```

MANUALLY CHANGE LOGON AGENT AND SERVER CONFIG WEB SITES

The following procedure describes the steps to manually change the location of web sites on an Advanced Access Control server.

Step 1: Remove Logon Point Deployments

1. Run the Logon Agent Configuration utility (Start | Programs | Citrix | Logon Agent | Logon Agent Configuration).

2. Select the Configured Logon Points and remember all whose status is set to "The folder is deployed to the Web site."

3. Remove all deployed Logon Points.

4. Close.

Step 2: Remove Access Center and Server Deployment

1. Run the Access Suite Console (Start | Programs | Citrix | Management Consoles | Access Suite Console).

2. Select the Servers node to reconfigure (Console Root | MetaFrame Access Suite Console | Suite Components | Access Gateway Enterprise | <Farm Name> | Servers).

3. Select task Manage Server Roles.

4. Uncheck the Web Server Role for selected server(s).

   If only a single web server is deployed in a farm, the console does not let you remove the only remaining web server. In this case, your options are

   ▼ Temporarily set another server in the farm as a web server. This can be removed after changing the web site for the current web server.

▲   Temporarily remove the server from the farm and add it back into the farm.

    a.   Select Server.

    b.   Run task "Remove server."

    c.   Add the server back into the farm using the Server Configuration utility on the web server. (Start | Programs | Citrix | Management Consoles | Access Suite Console).

       i.   Select Server Farm Information.

      ii.   Set the "Access server farm name:" to the name of the farm.

     iii.   The server should now be added back to the farm with no roles configured.

5.   Wait for the Deployment Service to delete all AC directories from Internet Information Server (IIS). Event viewer will display an event with Source: CtxMsamDeployment and Description: Unintializing Web server.

6.   Select Server.

7.   Run task "Remove server."

Step 3: Delete Remaining IIS Deployments

1.   Run "Internet Information Services (IIS) Manager."

2.   Delete the following Virtual Directories from IIS:

▼   CitrixAuthService

■   CitrixEPAService

■   CitrixFEI

■   CitrixLogonPoint

■   CitrixSessionInit

▲   WebSiteViewerRoot

3.   Delete the physical files for IIS deployments for the following Virtual Directories (do not delete the physical files for WebSiteViewerRoot). Make sure to back up any custom configurations before deleting files.

▼   CitrixAuthService

■   CitrixEPAService

■   CitrixFEI

■   CitrixLogonPoint

▲   CitrixSessionInit

Step 4: Make Registry Modifications

1. Run regedit.exe or other registry editing tool.
2. Select the registry key: HKLM\Software\Citrix\Msam.
3. Modify the DWORD value of ServerConfigured to "0."
4. Modify the DWORD value of WebServicesConfigured to "0."

Step 5: Redeploy Server

1. Run "Server Configuration" (Start | Programs | Citrix | Access Gateway Enterprise | Server Configuration).
2. Select "Join an existing access server farm."
3. Enter all configuration information, including the new web site for deployment.

Step 6: Re-Create Entry for Web Site Viewer

1. Run "Internet Information Services (IIS) Manager."
2. Select the deployed web site.
3. Create a Virtual Directory (Action | New | VirtualDirectory).
4. Set "Description" = Website Viewer ActiveX Control Virtual Directory. Click Next.
5. Set the Path for the Virtual directory to: %CommonFiles%\Citrix\CDAs\WebsiteViewerRoot.
6. Check allow permissions for:
   ▼ Read
   ▲ Run scripts (such as ASP)

Step 7: Redeploy Logon Points

1. Run Logon Agent Configuration utility (Start | Programs | Citrix | Logon Agent | Logon Agent Configuration).
2. Select the logon points tab.
3. For each logon point originally deployed on the selected server, select the logon point and click the Deploy button.

THIRD-PARTY FILES IN END POINT ANALYSIS (EPA)

Third-party vendors can implement End Point Analysis (EPA) scan packages for Access Gateway with the Advanced Access Control option. Doing so gives customers even more choices to use in the Advanced Access Control policies for configuring filters to grant users access to network resources.

Sometimes vendors ask how they can package additional files in the scan package cabinet (.CAB) files. Typically, their implementations require additional data or executable files that perform the examination of the endpoint, and then send the results back to the scan package and the End Point Analysis policy system. These files may need to be updated on a frequent basis if they include a signature database of viruses or something similar.

Currently, the EPA scan package format does not provide a means to specify additional files beyond the dispatcher (server-side) and client-side modules. This section presents an alternative approach of storing the additional files in the logon point, and then using the vendor's client-side module to download them using an HTTP-style GET.

Caveats

The vendor's client-side module needs to know the URL of the logon point to request the additional files it needs. Two potential problems arise immediately: how to inform the client-side module of this URL, which may be different depending on whether a logon point is accessed internally to the network or externally through Access Gateway; and how to make the additional files visible through Access Gateway.

When a logon point is configured to work with Access Gateway, a copy of certain registered files is made to a cache on Access Gateway. This cache consists of files whose content are static. This performance optimization means that new or updated third-party files copied to the virtual directory of a logon point on an Advanced Access Control server are not automatically replicated to the cache on the Access Gateway. At present, the only way to re-cache the files after a logon point has been configured with Access Gateway is to do so manually in the Advanced Access Control console.

Solution

Allow administrators to enter the URLs to logon points as EPA scan rule parameters, so logon points can be accessed both internally and externally by client-side modules. Leverage the static content caching feature of Access Gateway to make the ICS files visible externally. Third-party scan package implementers should store their additional files in the logon point directory, instead of in a separate vendor virtual directory. They should register these files with the Advanced Access Control logon agent service. Any time updates are made to these files, have the administrator refresh the Access Gateway cache for that logon point.

1. Create a scan package with client-side and dispatcher modules as usual in Visual Studio using the End Point Analysis Package Wizard.
2. Add a parameter for the logon point URL to the scan package properties.
   a. Open the scan package solution file in Visual Studio.
   b. Navigate to the solution node in the solution explorer pane.
   c. Right-click on the node and choose Edit Endpoint Analysis Package Properties.
   d. Choose the Parameters tab and add a parameter for the URL the administrator will enter for this scan package.

3. Add a call to a client method and pass the logon point URL as an argument. In the dispatcher, add code similar to this:

```
CComBSTR objectName(L"http://.../ZLTest.cab/1.0/downloadable/ClientDownload.dll");
CComBSTR methodName(L"DownloadableEntryPoint");
CComPtr<IEPAExpression> exp = NULL;
pEnvironment->CreateExpression(objectName, methodName, &exp);

CComBSTR URL(L"");
pParameters->get_Value(CComBSTR(L"LogonPointURL"),&URL.m_str);

exp->AddArgument(URL);

pEnvironment->SetEnquiry(MyIdentifier, exp);
```

4. Create another executable the administrator can run to copy the additional files needed by the scan package to the logon point. Register them with the logon agent service. To register the ICS files with the logon agent service, open the web.config file for the CitrixLogonAgentService web service. Add file extensions of the additional files to the StaticFileExtensions key.

Configuring a Test Environment

1. Add internal/external logon points.

2. In the Advanced Access Control console, navigate to the Logon Points node and choose the task "Create logon point."

3. Input a name for the logon point, for example, InternalLogonPoint. Then, choose the default values for the rest of the wizard. You see a message that the logon point files have not yet been deployed, that is, created on the Advanced Access Control server. Ignore that message for now.

4. Go back and choose "Create logon point" again, but this time, name the logon point ExternalLogonPoint and, once more, take all the defaults in the wizard.

5. Execute the Server Configuration option in Start | All Programs | Citrix | Access Gateway. Choose Configured Logon Points on the left. Highlight InternalLogonPoint and choose Deploy. Do the same for ExternalLogonPoint. At this point, verify that virtual directories for both the logon points have been set up in IIS on the Advanced Access Control server.

6. Import the ICS scan package into the Advanced Access Control console.

7. In the Advanced Access Control console, navigate to the Endpoint Analysis | Miscellaneous node. Choose the "Import scan package" task and import the .CAB file for your scan package.

Add Scan Package Rules for Internal/External Logon Points

1. In the Advanced Access Control console, select the node for the scan package that you just imported.

2. Choose the "Create scan" task.

3. Pick a name for the scan.

4. On the Select Conditions page, choose Logon Point.

5. On the Define Rule page, name the rule InternalLogonPoint Rule.

6. On the Configure Conditions page, select all the operating systems (OSs).

7. On the second Configure Conditions page, select InternalLogonPoint.

8. On the Define Property To Verify page, enter the URL to your AAC logon point virtual directory.

9. In the Advanced Access Control console, select the newly created scan package scan node and choose the "Create rule" task. Run through the same steps as before, but this time, call the rule ExternalLogonPoint Rule. In the second Configure Conditions page, select ExternalLogonPoint and, in the Define Property To Verify page, enter the URL to the AG server logon point virtual directory.

Testing the Internal Logon Point

1. Copy the additional package-related files to the internal logon point virtual directory and register the file extensions with the logon agent service.

2. Log on to Advanced Access Control/InternalLogonPoint and verify the EPA scan package functions as expected.

Testing the External Logon Point

1. Expose the external logon point through the Access Gateway administration tool.

2. Copy the additional package-related files to the external logon point exposed through Access Gateway.

3. In the Advanced Access Control console, select the ExternalLogonPoint logon point node and choose the "Refresh logon page information" task. This caches the additional files to the Access Gateway server.

4. Log on to Access Gateway/ExternalLogonPoint and verify the EPA scan package functions as expected.

CHAPTER 8

Password Manager

In this chapter, we explore Password Manager deployment scenarios, including Installation Manager, Active Directory Group Policy, and other techniques. We also look at several other administrator-related tasks, such as selecting a synchronization solution, performance charateristics, and scalability of Password Manager.

DEPLOYMENT MODELS AND SCENARIOS

This section details the most common deployment methods for Citrix Password Manager in various scenarios. The methods detailed are the Presentation Server Installation Management feature, Active Directory Group Policy Objects, and standard file sharing.

Citrix Presentation Server and Installation Management

You must install the Password Manager Agent on all Presentation Server systems hosting applications that require authentication. The enterprise version of Presentation Server has a feature called *Installation Manager,* which allows for efficient deployment of MSI-based installs across a Presentation Server farm. The following lists how to quickly deploy Password Manager to your Presentation Server farm.

NOTE   Installation Manager deploys the agent MSI in silent mode, so no user interaction is needed for deployment on remote servers.

1. Create the Agent Installation Image MSI file, as detailed in the *Password Manager Administrator's Guide.*

2. Save or copy this MSI to a network share that will be accessible to all the servers in your farm.

3. Open the Presentation Server Console.

4. If Installation Manager was not previously configured with a network account, right-click the Installation Manager node. Select Properties, and then enter a valid administrator account, which has Read access to the previous share and Write access to all the servers to which you want to deploy the package.

5. Right-click the Packages node and select "add package."

6. Browse to the location of your saved, previously created, installation-image MSI file.

7. Follow the Installation Manager prompts to deploy the package to all desired servers in the Server Farm (see the *MetaFrame Presentation Server Administrator's Guide* for details).

Active Directory Group Policy Objects

Group Policy is a feature available in an Active Directory Domain, which can be used to install software on systems within the domain. Detailed information on how to use Group Policy Objects can be found on the Microsoft web site. If your server farm is in a pure Active Directory environment, you can use a Group Policy to deploy the Password Manager Agent.

1. Create the desired installation image MSI file, as detailed in the *Password Manager Administrator's Guide.*

2. Save or copy this MSI to a network share that will be accessible to all the servers to which you want to deploy.

3. Create a Group Policy Object for the groups of computers or users to which you want to deploy the agent (search the Microsoft knowledgebase for articles on how to use group policy objects—you have many to choose from, depending on your particular environment).

File Share Deployment

In smaller environments or in certain situations, deployment by file share may be desirable.

1. Copy the agent MSI file from the Password Manager install CD (or your installation image MSI file) to a file share location, which is accessible to the machines on which you will deploy.

2. Make sure MSI 3.0—the Microsoft Installer Service—is already present on your machine.

3. Run the following command:

```
Msiexec /i <path_to_MSI_file_and_its_filename>
```

If you want to suppress rebooting after the install, use the following:

```
Msiexec reboot=suppress /i <path_to_MSI_file_and_its_filename>
```

UNDERSTANDING THE LICENSE BEHAVIOR OF CITRIX PASSWORD MANAGER 4.0 AND LATER ON THE CITRIX LICENSING SERVER

Citrix Password Manager requires a license server to distribute and track licenses, as compared to the manual process seen in MetaFrame Password Manager 2.5. A proper understanding of the technical details of this process enables the administrator to troubleshoot errors quickly and efficiently. This article compares the licensing operation of Password Manager to that of Presentation Server. It also explores the check-out and check-in process of licenses on the Password Manager server.

Licensing Differences Between Citrix Password Manager and Citrix Presentation Server's Licensing Operation

The Password Manager licensing operation is similar to the licensing operation used by Presentation Server. However, their modes of operation have differences:

▼ *Continuous TCP connection is not used.* Unlike Presentation Server, Password Manager does not maintain a TCP connection to the license server. TCP connections are established and broken for every individual operation.

■ *Heartbeat information is not exchanged between Agent and license server.* If the communication path between the agent and license server is broken, the agent does not realize the license server is unreachable until it tries to check out, renew, or check in a license.

▲ *Client software uses a different Macrovision API.* The Password Manager Agent uses the Linger API, which is different from the one used by Presentation Server. The check-in and check-out behavior is also different. If you are trying to interpret the debug log entries on the license server for troubleshooting purposes, you may find that Password Manager log entries are hard to understand at first glance. Check-in and check-out behavior (and how to interpret the resulting log entries) is explained in the next section.

Startup, Check-out, Check-in, Renewal, and Behavior

Password Manager Agents require a license server to check out and check in licenses. Password Manager does not function without the presence of a license server. The agent makes a request to the server to check out a license to permit it to operate. After a license is checked out, only that agent can use the license for the duration of the Disconnected Mode Period, or until the agent checks in the license. One important piece of information to keep in mind is this: the agent can only check out licenses and the server can only check in licenses. This process will become clearer with the review of the Check-out, Renewal, and Check-in behavior in the debug log file, found at C:\Program Files\Citrix\ Licensing\LS\ lmgrd_debug.log.

NOTE For a more in-depth look into licensing, see the Licensing_Guide.pdf in the documentation folder of the Password Manager CD.

Startup Process

Whenever the agent starts up, it checks out a *start-up license,* which delivers generic operating parameters to the agent.

```
21:00:50 (CITRIX) TCP_NODELAY enabled
21:00:50 (CITRIX) OUT: "CITRIX" USER15@GENE-VM-2K3  [ec26edf8]
<-Agent checked out start-up license
21:00:50 (CITRIX) IN: "CITRIX" USER15@GENE-VM-2K3  [ec26edf8]
<-Agent checked in start-up license
21:00:50 (CITRIX) OUT: "MPM_ADV_RC" USER15@GENE-VM-2K3  [ec26edf8]
21:01:05 (CITRIX) OUT: "MPM_ADV_RC" USER15@GENE-VM-2K3  [ec26edf8]
21:01:05 (CITRIX) IN: "MPM_ADV_RC" USER15@GENE-VM-2K3  [ec26edf8]
21:01:40 (CITRIX) IN: "MPM_ADV_RC" USER15@GENE-VM-2K3  [ec26edf8]
```

The agent checks out a start-up license, and then immediately checks it back in again.

The start-up license does not use the Linger API. The OUT: entry represents the license being checked out and the IN: entry represents the license being checked in.

Check-out Process

The agent only performs one type of operation with the license server: check-out. In the following example, a Password Manager Agent is started (and receives a license), and is then shut down (and returns the license). Here is what the debug log on the license server shows:

```
21:00:50 (CITRIX) TCP_NODELAY enabled
21:00:50 (CITRIX) OUT: "CITRIX" USER15@GENE-VM-2K3  [ec26edf8]
21:00:50 (CITRIX) IN: "CITRIX" USER15@GENE-VM-2K3  [ec26edf8]
21:00:50 (CITRIX) OUT: "MPM_ADV_RC" USER15@GENE-VM-2K3  [ec26edf8]
<- Agent has checked out a license
21:01:05 (CITRIX) OUT: "MPM_ADV_RC" USER15@GENE-VM-2K3  [ec26edf8]
<- Agent has checked out the license with linger time = 1 second
(Agent intends to return the license)
21:01:05 (CITRIX) IN: "MPM_ADV_RC" USER15@GENE-VM-2K3  [ec26edf8]
21:01:40 (CITRIX) IN: "MPM_ADV_RC" USER15@GENE-VM-2K3  [ec26edf8]
```

The agent has started and has checked out a license. Here, the agent keeps the licenses, depending on the licensing mode set by the administrator.

NOTE All OUT: log entries accompany a request from the agent. If you are using a network monitor, you should see communication between the agent and license server at all times OUT: entries occur.

Check-in Process

To explain the check-in process, see the following debug log entries.

```
21:00:50 (CITRIX) TCP_NODELAY enabled
21:00:50 (CITRIX) OUT: "CITRIX" USER15@GENE-VM-2K3  [ec26edf8]
21:00:50 (CITRIX) IN: "CITRIX" USER15@GENE-VM-2K3  [ec26edf8]
21:00:50 (CITRIX) OUT: "MPM_ADV_RC" USER15@GENE-VM-2K3  [ec26edf8]
21:01:05 (CITRIX) OUT: "MPM_ADV_RC" USER15@GENE-VM-2K3  [ec26edf8]
21:01:05 (CITRIX) IN: "MPM_ADV_RC" USER15@GENE-VM-2K3  [ec26edf8]
<- License server has checked in a license for [ec26edf8].
21:01:40 (CITRIX) IN: "MPM_ADV_RC" USER15@GENE-VM-2K3  [ec26edf8]
<- Linger timer expires, and License server finally checks in the
"last" license for [ec26edf8].
```

This log entry is the result of the agent shutting down and returning the license.

Because the agent can perform check-out operations only, the agent needs to check out the same license a second time for only one second, causing the license server to check it back in. This is done by the agent setting a check-out parameter called a linger period to one second, which tells the license server how long to keep the license checked out. At the end of the linger period, the server automatically checks in the license.

Therefore, to return a license, the agent checks *out* a license with a linger time of 1 second. This, in turn, causes the license server to check in the license a second later.

```
21:01:05 (CITRIX) IN: "MPM_ADV_RC" USER15@GENE-VM-2K3  [ec26edf8]
```

This is the first of two **IN:** entries that occur. Note, this entry occurs at exactly the same time as the previous **OUT:** entry. That's because, from the license server's point of view, the previous **IN:** entry results in **two instances of** the same licenses [ec26edf8] being checked out. The license server tries to keep only one instance of a license checked out at all times, so it corrects this situation by performing a check-in.

Now, only one instance of license with identifier [ec26edf8] is checked out. To fully release the license, another check-in must occur (see the next section).

NOTE   Only the license server performs check-ins. Any IN: log entry results from the license server's actions, not from a request from the agent. If you are using a network monitor, you should not expect to see communication between the agent and license server at times that IN: entries occur.

```
21:01:40 (CITRIX) IN: "MPM_ADV_RC" USER15@GENE-VM-2K3  [ec26edf8]
```

Once the Linger timer expires for a particular license, the license is not checked in immediately. Instead, it must wait for a thread of the license server process to wake up and check it in. This thread wakes up every minute, and it may take up to a minute to execute. So it may take up to just under 2 minutes for a license to, once again, be available for check-out.

In the previous example, a license was checked in at 21:01:05 with a linger time of 1 second. Its linger time should have expired at 21:01:06. Finally, at 21:01:40, the license server returned the license to the system. Now, no more licenses are checked out with identifier [ec26edf8].

Renewal Process

While an agent is running, it periodically tries to renew its license. There is no renew operation; rather, the agent only attempts to check out the license again using the same linger time.

For example, consider the scenario of a Named User license with a linger time of 21 days. Every six hours, the agent tries to check out a license with a linger time of 21 days.

By having a proper understanding of the technical details of the differences in licensing among the Citrix products and knowledge of the licensing debug log, an administrator can have a valuable tool for troubleshooting. When using the log file, an administrator can see the licensing process to assist in tracking down issues.

NOTE The log file is cleared by restarting the licensing service. To set up the log file to retain the past information, please see the Licensing_Guide.pdf.

IMPORTING METAFRAME PASSWORD MANAGER 2.5 APPLICATION DEFINITIONS INTO CITRIX PASSWORD MANAGER 4.0

To facilitate the migration of MetaFrame Password Manager 2.5 to Citrix Password Manager 4.0, Password Manager offers the capability to import application definitions stored in INI or XLM format. This section discusses the procedure to import MetaFrame Password Manager 2.5 application definitions into Citrix Password Manager 4.0. This procedure is unnecessary when migrating to Citrix Password Manager 4.1—the migration is automatic.

NOTE If these applications already reside on your Password Manager 2.5 central store deployments, performing an upgrade of your central store automatically imports the application definitions into Password Manager 4.0. For further information on upgrading the central store, refer to the *Password Manager Administrator's Guide.*

Step 1: Converting .ini Files to .xml

The Password Manager 4.0 Console only accepts application templates in .xml format. If you have Password Manager 2.5 application definitions in INI format, perform the following steps to convert these INI files to XML format:

1. Launch the Password Manager 2.5 Console.
2. Import the INI file(s) that contain your application definitions.
3. Choose File | Save As and save the file as an XML.

Step 2: Editing the .xml File

1. Using an XML editor, such as Notepad, open the XML file that contains your application definitions.
2. For each application definition instance in the file, find the flag **isTemplate="false"**.
3. Modify the flag, so it is set to **isTemplate="true"**.
4. Save the XML file.

Step 3: Importing into the Password Manager 4.0 Console

1. Launch the Password Manager 4.0 Console.
2. Click the Application Definitions node and choose the task "Manage templates."
3. Choose Import Template.
4. Browse to the XML file you created and modified, and then import it.
5. Your files are now imported as application templates. To create application definitions from them, click the template and choose Create Application Definition.

IDENTITY VERIFICATION QUESTION WITH CITRIX PASSWORD MANAGER

In Citrix Password Manager 4.1, the Multiple-Question Authentication and Identity Verification Question were replaced with Question-Based Authentication. For more information about Question-Based Authentication, please reference "Question-Based Authentication" on page 92 of *Password Manager Administrator's Guide*.

Overview

The *Identity Verification Question*'s primary function is to work as a secondary form of authentication to the agent. The user question is created the first time a user creates their profile.

The first part of the profile setup procedure is where the user is prompted to enter their Windows domain credentials. After successfully authenticating their user credentials, the user is prompted to answer the Identity Verification Question. Whichever Identity Verification Question the user answers (custom created or default) will be the one permanently linked with their data.

Whenever the user's Windows domain password is changed, the Password Manager Agent asks the Identity Verification Question (to identify the user) and the user needs to provide the answer they originally entered during the initial profile setup. In this situation, the user's password storage database is opened and the new Windows domain password will be updated.

Because the Identity Verification Question is stored in the First-Time-User list and it is encrypted, the Identity Verification Question also serves to protect the user's password database from the administrator, who could easily change a user's Windows domain password, but would not know the user's answer to the Identity Verification Question.

Issues

▼ Each question has its own globally unique identifier (GUID), so if the administrator modifies the Identity Verification Question, the GUID does not change and the user can open their database by answering the modified question with their old answer. In some cases, this can be misleading and the text of the question should not be modified if users have already answered the question. Please refer to the example in the *Password Manager Administrator's Guide*.

■ The answer is stored in the user's database with the Question GUID. Once the Identity Verification Question has been answered, the answer can neither be modified nor can the user switch to a different Identity Verification Question and provide a different answer.

■ Currently, if the administrator creates a custom Identity Verification Question, and then later deletes the FTUlist.ini file from the synchronization point, any users that answered any Identity Verification Question from that file will be unable to unlock their password storage database when their password is changed.

■ The default question cannot be edited or deleted.

■ On the console, when an administrator creates a custom Identity Verification Question, it cannot be deleted, only disabled. Unfortunately, it still can be overwritten from another console, or deleted manually from the file system or Active Directory tree.

▲ If the administrator wants to delete a user profile, they need to delete all the data from the following points.

   ▼ HKCU\Software\Citrix\MetaFrame Password Manager

   ■ The folder from C:\Documents and Settings\<username>\ApplicationData\Citrix\MetaFrame Password Manager

   ▲ The data from the user's folder under the People folder on the File Synchronization (for file synchronization) or delete the SSOConfig objects from under the user's object in the Active Directory (for Active Directory synchronization).

Additional Notes

Administrators can use extended characters when creating custom Identity Verification Questions. Users also can use extended characters when answering their Identity Verification Question.

DISABLING THE DEFAULT IDENTITY VERIFICATION QUESTION FOR CITRIX PASSWORD MANAGER 4.0

When a user begins using Password Manager for the first time, they may be required to define secondary credentials by selecting an identity verification question (also referred to as a user question in previous versions of Password Manager) and providing an answer to this question. The combination of question and answer is known as the identity verification phrase.

In Citrix Password Manager 4.0, end users can choose from console defined questions or the default question. Since the default question does not provide the user with any clue as to what the answer might have been, some administrators see this as a source of confusion. Disabling this question will allow administrators to further customize the user experience by controlling the set of questions that the user can choose from.

Administrators must be careful with this option as it may prevent existing users from authenticating to the agent. When a user is challenged to answer their identity verification question and their chosen question is no longer defined or no longer available, they will be unable to authenticate themselves to Password Manager. Because of this, it is important to disable this default question before users begin using the agent. This will ensure that you are not disabling an existing user's identity verification question. If the administrator disables the default question without creating or enabling any custom questions, the User configuration cannot get created. Password Manager users must belong to a User configuration.

Disable the Default Identity Verification Question

From the Access Suite Console, choose User Configuration | *your chosen configuration* | Edit User configuration | Identity Verification method. Deselect the checkbox for Include 'What is your Identity Verification phrase?' in the list of questions presented to the users.

FORCING USERS TO COMPLETE THE FIRST-TIME-USE WIZARD

When users first launch the Citrix Password Manager Agent, they are presented with a First-Time-Use Wizard. Users are prompted to choose an identity verification question and supply an answer to configure. This information is stored, and Password Manager loads and is ready for use. Until the information in the First-Time-Use Wizard is completed successfully, the agent will not start.

At the First-Time-Use screen, it is also possible to click the *x* at the top right-hand corner of the window to cancel the configuration screen all together. Many administrators have found that users are closing the screen and not leveraging the use of Password Manager to store credential data.

Because a console is configurable, a central-store enforced setting is not currently available to enforce First-Time-Use Wizard completion, an agent-side registry entry can be manually pushed to force users to complete this screen and begin using Password Manager.

Configuration

On user workstations with the Password Manager Agent installed, the following registry key can be created to enforce completion of the First-Time-Use Wizard:

- ▼ **Path** HKLM\Software\Citrix\Metaframe Password Manager\Extensions\ SetupManager
- ■ **Key** ForceFTU
- ■ **Type** Dword
- ▲ **Value** 0/1

By default, when the registry key is created, it is set to 0, that is, disabled. Set the value to 1 to enable the setting.

HOT DESKTOP HOST EMULATORS SUPPORT

The following is the list of host emulators supported in the Hot Desktop Environment:

Host Emulator	Version	Executable Name
Attachmate MyExtra!	7.11	extra.exe
IBM Personal Communicator	5.6	pcsfe.exe
NetManage Rumba	7	rumbawsf.exe
Nexus	4.6	nmt.exe
WRQ Reflections IBM	10.*x*	R8win.exe
ZephyrPC	2002–621	Passport.exe
Ericom PowerTerm Pro	8.8	ptpro.exe
Hummingbird emulator	10	hostex32.exe

To configure supported emulators:

1. Create a host-based application definition (see the *Password Manager Administrator's Guide* for details) and add this definition to the desired application group of a user's configuration.

2. Enable support for host emulators from the Password Manager Administrative Console.

   a. Edit user configuration.

   b. Select the Application Support tab on the left pane.

   c. Select enable support for terminal emulators' check box.

3. Edit the Process.xml file to launch the defined host emulator as a Hot Desktop User.

NOTE For details about Process.xml, refer to the *Password Manager Administrator's Guide* and "Configuring and Managing a Hot Desktop Environment" in Chapter 15 of this book.

As an example, to launch NetManage Rumba as a Hot Desktop User, you need to edit the ShellExecute entry in the process.xml file:

```
<shellexecute_processes>
    <process>
        <name> rumbawsf.exe</name>
    </process>
</shellexecute_processes>
```

NOTE Executable file names for supported host emulators are located in the third column of the previous table.

IMPLEMENTING PER USER FILE SYNCHRONIZATION

In Citrix Password Manager, the agent acts as an intermediary between users and applications that require authentication. You can set up Password Manager to synchronize with either a shared folder or Microsoft Active Directory. When configuring Password Manager to synchronize with a shared folder, you can:

▼ Create multiple sets of user credentials for an agent and store them centrally.

■ Define a shared folder to synchronize information between the Password Manager Console and agent.

▲ Define individual file synchronizations for individual users.

Configuring Synchronization Points

From a command prompt, access the /Tools directory on the Password Manager CD and type the following:

```
CtxFileSyncPrep /path:<pathname> /share:<sharename>
```

Run this tool for each individual synchronization point you are going to deploy.

```
Tools>ctxfilesyncprep /path:c:\%username% /share: %username%
```

Once the previous command is run, the shared folder and people folder are created with appropriate sharing and security permissions. Your shared folders are now ready to be used for synchronization.

Confirm the following before configuring per user file synchronization:

▼ Each synchronization point has been created using the CtxFileSyncPrepTool.

■ Each client workstation has the Password Manager Agent installed.

▲ Each Password Manager Agent has been configured to use File Synchronization. In the console, configure a synchronizer of type NTFS File Share, but do not configure a synchronization point and push this registry file to the agent.

The main purpose for configuring the client workstation with a synchronizer of type NTFS File Share with no synchronization point is to preserve the hierarchy of precedence. If a synchronization point defined in the registry file is pushed out to agent workstations, this will populate the field:

```
HKLM\Software\Citrix\MetaFrame Password
Manager\Extensions\SyncManager\Syncs\%SyncName%\Server1\Server1
```

If a value exists under HKLM under Server1, then the agents are automatically directed to this synchronization point without checking HKCU for a server entry.

Configuring Per User File Synchronization

1. Log in to the user workstation as the user being configured to use a specific synchronization point.

2. As each user, enter the user's corresponding share as a Registry String Value in the Windows registry hive:

   ```
   HKCU\Software\Citrix\MetaFrame Password Manager\Extensions
   ```

3. Create a new key called *SyncManager*.

4. Under the *SyncManager* key, create another key called *Syncs*.

5. Under the *Syncs* key, create a new string value called *Server1*.

6. For the *Server1* string, set the Value Data to the full UNC path for the user's corresponding file share.

7. Restart the agent.

8. Configure the agent and confirm that agent settings correspond to the sync point.

9. Repeat these steps for each user who requires an individually configured file-synchronization point.

INTEGRATING CITRIX PASSWORD MANAGER WITH A DISTRIBUTED FILE SYSTEM

A Citrix Password Manager File synchronization point can be implemented using Windows 2000 or Windows 2003 distributed file system (DFS). The capabilities to distribute the work load across multiple servers and to provide fault tolerance are some of the reasons to consider using DFS as an alternative to a single synchronization point. The following explains the steps to configure DFS for use with Password Manager.

Step 1: Create a Domain Distributed File System (DFS) Root

The first step to integrate Password Manager with distributed file system (DFS) is to create a Domain DFS root. Creating a Domain DFS root is not needed if your Windows Deployment already has one Domain DFS root in place. If this is the case, skip to step 2, "Prepare the Shares for Citrix Password Manager."

1. Open the mmc snap-in for the Distributed File System, typically located in Start | Programs | Administrative Tools | Distributed File System.

2. Right-click the DFS icon and select the option New DFS root.

3. Click Next.

4. Select "Create a domain DFS root."

5. Click Next.

6. Select the host domain of the DFS root.

7. Click Next.

8. Select the name of the host server for this DFS root.

9. Click Next.

10. Either use an existing share on the server or create a new share to host the DFS tree.

11. Click Next.

12. Type a name for the DFS root.

13. Click Finish.

Step 2: Prepare the Shares for Citrix Password Manager

After creating a Domain DFS root, the shares hosting the file synchronization point should be created in the designated servers. The ctxfilesyncprep utility is used to create the directory c:\citrixsync on the C:\ drive and shares it as \\%servername%\citrixsync$, assigning the proper permissions.

1. On two or more Windows 2000/2003 Servers, open a command console.
2. Insert the Password Manager Distribution CD.
3. Type **CD x:**, where *x* is the letter of your CD-ROM, and then press ENTER.
4. Type **CD x:\Tools**, and then press ENTER.
5. Type **ctxfilesyncprep.exe**, and then press ENTER.

Step 3: Create the DFS Link

The third step of the process is creating a DFS link to host the first of the shares created in the previous step. The share name used for the DFS Link is citrixsync$.

1. Open the mmc snap-in for the DFS, typically located in Start | Programs | Administrative Tools | Distributed File System.
2. Right-click the new DFS root and select New DFS Link.
3. In the Link Name Field, write **citrixsync$**.
4. In the Shared Folder, insert the UNC Location (%server1name%\citrixsync$) of the first server hosting the synchronization point.
5. Press OK.

Step 4: Add the Replicas

To have a redundant, fault-tolerant solution, replicas should be added to the synchronization point. The replicas are the additional server shares we created on the other servers.

1. Open the mmc snap-in for the DFS, typically located in Start | Programs | Administrative Tools | Distributed File System.
2. Right-click the DFS link created in step 3 and select New Replica.
3. In the Send user to this shared folder field, insert the UNC location (%server2name%\citrixsync$) of the server hosting the other synchronization point prepared in step 2.
4. Change Replication Policy from Manual Replication to Automatic Replication.
5. Press OK.
6. On the following screen, highlight the first server and Enable Replication.

7. Highlight the second server and Enable Replication.

8. Press OK.

9. Repeat steps 2 through 8 for each of the servers.

Step 5: Connecting to the Share from the Console

Connecting to the DFS Shared Folder and configuring Password Manager exporting the configuration to the synchronization point is the final task of the procedure. To successfully connect, the agents and the console must be part of the domain where the DFS was created.

1. Deploy the Password Manager Console on a workstation that is part of the same Active Directory Domain.

2. Logon with a user that has administrative rights to the active directory domain and select Directory | Connect To | Shared Folder.

3. The Shared folder name is \\activedirectorydomainname\DFS\citrixsync$.

Step 6: Distributed File System Replication (FRS)

Replica Synchronization is managed by the File Replication Service (FRS). FRS operates on Windows Active Directory Domain Controllers and Member Servers. It is a multi-threaded, multimaster replication engine that replicates system policies, login scripts, fault-tolerant DFS root, and child node replicas.

In Active Directory deployments, the Knowledge Consistency Checker (KCC) is responsible for building NTDS connection objects to form a well-connected topology between domain controllers in the domain and the forest.

RepAdmin.exe is a utility available in the support.cab archive of the Windows 2000 Servers' installation CD. It can be used to check if replication is taking place using the default intervals for intersite replication: once every three hours between domain controllers in different sites (the minimum is 15 minutes).

FRS replicates whole files in sequential order according to when files are closed, so the entire file will be replicated, even if you change only a single byte in the file.

Changes for intersite replication are set using a three-second aging cache, so only the last iteration of a file that is constantly modified is sent to the replica members.

Five minutes is the maximum replication value for servers hosting replicas, but this can even be seconds if the server is not overwhelmed.

The following articles can be useful for administrators to set up and tune the FRS: "Description of the FRS Replication Protocol, Notification, and Schedule for DFS Content" http://support.microsoft.com/default.aspx?scid=kb;en-us;220938&Product=win2000 "FRS Builds Full-Mesh Replication Topology for Replicated DFS ROOT and Child Replicas" http://support.microsoft.com/default.aspx?scid=kb;en-us;224512&Product=win2000

LIMIT THE NUMBER OF DAYS TO KEEP TRACK OF DELETED CREDENTIALS

The "Limit the number of days to keep track of deleted credentials" setting (previously DaysBeforeDelete) is important because it allows the agent to remember what credentials have been deleted. This setting remembers the credentials for the specified amount of time, so the user has the opportunity to synchronize all the Password Manager Agents on the other machines. The "Delete user's data folder and registry keys when the agent is shut down" setting (previously "Delete on Shutdown") does not affect this because the data is stored in the MMF file, and then synchronized to your synchronization point as the agent is shutting down. Here is an example of what could happen if the agent deleted the credentials without remembering:

1. The user runs the Password Manager Agent on ComputerA (the user's desktop PC).
2. The user adds credentials for ApplicationA.
3. ApplicationA's credential is stored in the local MMF and synchronized to the central credential store.
4. The user then runs the agent on ComputerB (for example, the user's laptop PC).
5. The Password Manager Agent gets synchronized and ApplicationA gets stored in the local MMF on ComputerB.
6. The user decides to delete ApplicationA's credential, and it is removed from the local MMF and the central credential store.
7. Later that day, the user logs back on to ComputerA.
8. The agent on ComputerA synchronizes with the central credential store, which still has ApplicationA's credential stored in its local MMF. It does not see this credential in the central credential store, however, so it adds the ApplicationA credential back.

If users only work on one machine, then the user's local MMF file is stored only on that machine. In theory, the Days Before Delete setting could be set to 0 without any issues in a single-machine scenario. If the scenario is different, however, and the user roams to different machines, has a laptop and a desktop, or uses multiple servers in a Presentation Server farm, then you should set this value to something higher than 0 (the default is 30 days).

In summary, with "Limit the number of days to keep track of deleted credentials" set to 0, the Password Manager Agents would conflict with each other by deleting and re-adding credentials.

USING CITRIX PASSWORD MANAGER WITH CITRIX SECURE ACCESS MANAGER 2.0

The following are special considerations when using Citrix Password Manager with Citrix Secure Access Manager:

▼ Password Manager does not autorecognize most of the Secure Access Manager's access center CDAs or the login CDA. The administrator must create web application definitions for the CDAs to work with Password Manager. Certain CDAs use Windows authentication and are exceptions to this rule (for example, Lotus Notes, Exchange, and Sharepoint) and no further configuration at the administration console is required.

■ With Secure Access Manager 2.0, if an administrator defines a web application definition for the Login CDA, and then pushes this out to the agents, whenever an agent machine logs out from an Secure Access Manager site, the user automatically gets logged back into Secure Access Manager. The end user should either close their browser or the administrator should not define the Login CDA. To correct this problem, the administrator can install Secure Access Manager 2.0 SP1 or later on their Secure Access Manager servers.

■ Every CDA on each Secure Access Manager page that the end user wants to have under the control of Password Manager must be individually defined as individual web application definitions within the Password Manager Administration Console.

■ Secure Access Manager administrators can move CDAs around in a page and Password Manager can recognize them with no adverse effects. However, CDAs added to a page, or copied or moved from one page to another (or one folder to another) require the creation of a new web application definition. Exporting and importing a portal does not require new web application definitions.

■ Password Manager logs in to Secure Access Manager CDAs on a given page serially. In the event that the end user has many CDAs requiring passwords, several page re-draws will ensue.

■ If the Password Manager administrator wants the product to handle the login of a CDA, he needs to disable the autologin feature in the given CDAs ACW.

■ It is advisable to define the Submit button when generating Secure Access Manager web application definitions.

▲ CDAs modified through CDA pad, and then redeployed to Secure Access Manager, require the creation of a new web application definition.

USING PROFILES (ROAMING, MANDATORY, AND HYBRID) WITH CITRIX PASSWORD MANAGER

This section discusses best practices concerning user profile issues with Citrix Password Manager. Specifically, Local, Roaming, Mandatory, and Hybrid are discussed here.

Local User Profiles

Local User Profiles are stored on the local server to which the user has logged on. Password Manager saves registry information in the `HKCU\Software\Citrix\MetaFrame Password Manager` hive of the User Registry located at:

`%SystemDrive%\Documents and Settings\%username%\NTUSER.DAT`.

Password Manager also saves files in:

`%SystemDrive%\Documents and Settings\%username%\Application Data\Citrix\ MetaFrame Password Manager`.

IMPORTANT   It is *critical* that Password Manager has Full Control Access to the following files:

File Name	Description
%username%.mmf	User's credential information file with pointers to aelist.ini file.
entlist.ini	Application definition file created at enterprise level in the synchronization point or Active Directory.
aelist.ini	Application definition file created by merging user's local application definition file (applist.ini) and the enterprise application definitions (entlist.ini).

Roaming User Profiles

Roaming user profiles are saved in a network share and synchronized to a local server copy each time the user logs on. Characteristics of a successful roaming profile deployment include high-speed network connectivity, such as a SAN system area network (SAN) or Network-Attached Storage (NAS). Other common deployments include clustering solutions where the profiles are stored on high-availability servers.

Currently, two issues affect roaming and mandatory profile deployments:

▼   A single roaming profile can only be used with one file synchronization point. When multiple synchronization points are used, data in the MMF file may get corrupted.

▲ When roaming profiles are used with multiple concurrent sessions, they share the same backend Memory Mapped File. The end result is this: all active sessions share some common session data, such as retry lock counters, last used data counters, and event log entries.

Mandatory User Profile/Hybrid Profile

Mandatory user profiles are by definition user read-only profiles. Password Manager needs write permission to the profile directory under Application Data. With mandatory profiles, a user may make changes, but the changes are not saved back to the profile at logoff. For Password Manager to work correctly in a mandatory profiles environment, the Application Data Folder must be redirected.

With Password Manager, the registry changes are written each time the user logs on and credential information is synchronized with the synchronization point, but the changes are not saved back to the profile.

Beginning with Windows 2000, Microsoft provides a mechanism for redirecting the Application Data folder, but using Windows NT4 domains requires login scripts capable of modifying the location of the Application Data folder. This can be achieved by using tools like Kix or VBScript to define a writeable location for the Application Data user folder.

An example using Kix to redirect the Application Data folder during user logon follows.

IMPORTANT   The following sample script is for informational purposes only and should not be used in your environment without previous testing.

```
$LogonServer = "%LOGONSERVER%"
$HKCU = "HKEY_CURRENT_USER"
$ShellFolders_Key    =
"$HKCU\Software\Microsoft\Windows\CurrentVersion\Explorer\Shell Folders"
$UserShellFolders_Key =
"$HKCU\Software\Microsoft\Windows\CurrentVersion\Explorer\User Shell Folders"

$UserProfFolder = "$LogonServer\profiles\@userID"
$UserAppData = "$LogonServer\profiles\@userID\Application Data"
$UserDesktop = "$LogonServer\profiles\@userID\Desktop"
$UserFavorites = "$LogonServer\profiles\@userID\Favorites"
$UserPersonal = "X:\My Documents"
$UserRecent = "$LogonServer\profiles\@userID\Recent"


if (exist("$UserAppData") = 0)
    shell '%ComSpec% /c md "$UserAppData"'
endif
if (exist("$UserDesktop") = 0)
    shell '%ComSpec% /c md "$UserDesktop"'
endif
```

```
if (exist("$UserRecent") = 0)
    shell '%ComSpec% /c md "$UserRecent"'
endif
if (exist("$UserFavorites") = 0)
    shell '%ComSpec% /c md "$UserFavorites"'
endif
```

The hybrid user profile is another solution for the mandatory profile issue. When the user logs on, the mandatory profile loads, and a custom application loads and unloads user registry hives based on applications available to the user. The user, as in a mandatory profile scenario, can modify those portions of registry during the session. The big difference from the pure mandatory profile is that changes get saved when the user logs off and they get reloaded when the user logs in again.

When the hybrid profile is used, the following registry keys must be imported and exported as part of the logon and logoff process:

```
HKEY_CURRENT_USER\Software\Citrix\MetaFrame Password
```

Folder Redirection

Folder redirection is a new feature of Windows 2000 and Windows 2003 operating systems (OSs), and is implemented using Group Policy Objects and Active Directory. Folder redirection uses Group Policies to define a location for folders that are part of the user profile.

Four folders may be redirected using folder redirection:

▼ My Documents

■ Application Data

■ Desktop

▲ Start Menu

Two modes of redirection can be configured using Group Policies: basic redirection and advanced redirection. Both types of redirection are supported with Password Manager. In Windows 2000, the share where application data is stored should be referenced using the user name variable, for example, \\servername\sharename\%username%.

Folder redirection is global for the user and it affects all the user's applications, therefore, all applications that use the Application Data folder need to support it.

The following Microsoft articles may be useful in learning more about folder redirection:

"HOW TO: Dynamically Create Secure Redirected Folders By Using Folder Redirections" http://support.microsoft.com/?kbid=274443

"Folder Redirection Feature in Windows"
    http://support.microsoft.com/?kbid=232692

"Enabling the Administrator to Have Access to Redirected Folders"
    http://support.microsoft.com/?kbid=288991

Best Practices for Folder Redirection

▼ Use Application Data folder redirection when possible. This practice improves network performance, eliminating the need to copy that data each time a user logs on.

▲ When troubleshooting Password Manager Agent, always verify that the user logged on has Full Control permission on their Application Data folder.

USING REDIRECTED APPLICATION DATA FOLDERS AND CITRIX PASSWORD MANAGER

Many environments utilize the Microsoft Windows Group Policy that enables the redirection of users' Application Data directories to a separate network resource (file server, DFS, and so forth). If Citrix Password Manager is deployed in an environment where a user's Application Data is redirected, be aware that some considerations exist,

In each user's Application Data directory, several files are used by Password Manager. Some or all of these files are created when a user goes through their "First Time Use" of Password Manager. Here is a basic description of what the files are used for:

▼ **Applist.ini**   Holds the available applications for which the user does not currently have definitions.

■ **Entlist.ini**   Has all the user application definitions.

■ **Aelist.ini**   A combination of Applist & Entlist. The agent uses this file when working with application definitions.

■ **UserName.mmf**   Holds all the admin override data along with the credentials for each application the user has defined.

■ **Ftulist.ini**   The applications available for configuration during the user's First Time Use experience.

▲ **License.ini**   Holds the user's license information.

If a Group Policy is enforced that redirects the Application Data directory of each user to a separate network resource, then each of the files previously listed is moved from the local profile. The file the user interacts with the most is *UserName*.mmf. The Memory Mapped File (MMF) allocates an address space and links it to a file located on the physical disk. This allows for the file to be accessed like a block of memory. Using redirected application data directories may impact the performance of Password Manager. The following are recommended practices when redirecting the Application Data directories of users:

▼ Do not use "delete on shutdown" in conjunction with redirected Application Data folders. The "delete on shutdown" option in the Password Manager Console controls whether the user's registry keys and Application Data folder (including encrypted credentials) are deleted when the agent is shut down. Using this option requires a user to re-create each of the files previously listed (from the data located on the synchronization point) each time the agent is started up again. This can cause a significant delay when using redirected Application Data folders.

▲ Do not use aggressive synchronization in conjunction with redirected Application Data folders. The aggressive synchronization option in the Password Manager Console controls whether the agent synchronizes user configuration information whenever a user launches a recognized application or Logon Manager. Using aggressive synchronization by itself can degrade performance on both the client and server. If using this option in conjunction with redirected Application Data, folders can cause even slower response times. For specific numbers on using redirected Application Data folders and aggressive synchronization, see the Agent Response Time section of the Citrix Password Manager Performance and Scalability article in the Advanced Concepts Guide.

BEST PRACTICES WITH CITRIX PASSWORD MANAGER AND THE NOVELL CLIENT

The following section is a collection of best practice recommendations to follow when integrating Citrix Password Manager and the Novell client.

Install the Latest Service Packs

The recommended environment should include installing the latest service packs for the Netware OS and applying the latest service packs for ZENworks. Reapply the manufacturer's latest NIC drivers (Novell recommends this always be done as Support Packs are prone to overwrite NIC drivers).

Novell Client Settings to Enhance Overall Performance

In certain situations with slow responsiveness to Presentation Servers with the Novell client, there are Novell client settings to enhance overall performance. Citrix has tested with the following client32 settings with improved results:

▼ LIP Start Size set to 512 or try turning off LIP

■ Net Status Busy Timeout = 1

▲ Burst Mode = on

The recommendation is that the Novell client not be configured with more than two Directory Agents as this lengthens the network query time.

Server Side Settings

On the server side, these settings may also be helpful:

▼ Set Maximum Concurrent Disk Cache Writes = 300

▲ Set Maximum Concurrent Directory Cache Writes = 100

Error: "NMAS.DLL could not initialize cryptographic services or cryptographic services are not available. (-1497)"

Occasionally, a Windows 2000 or Windows 2003 server with the Novell 4.9 sp1 client may display a NMASS error after locking the desktop's console. The following error may be displayed when unlocking the console: "Error: NMAS.DLL could not initialize cryptographic services or cryptographic services are not available. (-1497)." A work-around for this error is to disable the NMAS Authentication after the install or remove the NMAS Client using Add/Remove Programs.

CITRIX PASSWORD MANAGER AND ENTRUST INTEGRATION

Citrix Password Manager and Entrust PKI can be successfully integrated deploying Entrust Authority in a Windows 2000 Active Directory Domain and leveraging Microsoft LDAP implementation with Entrust Certificates. Once the Entrust Authority has been deployed, and the Entrust client packaged and configured on a per-user base, Password Manager can be integrated into the environment. The following versions were used during the testing: Entrust Software Versions 6.01 for the Authority Server and 6.1 SP1 for the Entrust Client Entelligence—Desktop Solutions. The following section guides you through the required steps.

Modify the AD Schema for Entrust

1. On the Domain Controller that holds the Schema Master role, log on with a user who is part of the Domain Administration and Schema Administration Groups, and extend the schema.

2. Insert the Entrust/PKI CD in the CD-ROM drive, navigate to the \Utilities folder, and run entadconfig.exe to start the Entrust Active Directory Configuration Wizard.

3. Select Entrust/Authority check box.

4. Select Configure the Active Directory Schema.

5. Create a CA Entry for Entrust/Authority and give it a name.

6. Publish the CA Certificate in the Certification Authorities Container.

7. Create a New Domain Account or use an existing one.

8. Grant access for Entrust Authority to existing users.

9. Execute the changes and save the log.

Certification Authority Deployment

1. The first step is the deployment of the Informix Database, needed to create the Entrust/Authority Database.

2. The server used for Entrust should be different from the Active Directory Domain Controller for Security Reasons.

3. The Certification Authority is installed after the Informix Database.

4. The Certification Authority requires licensing information, such as Serial Number, Enterprise User Limit, and Enterprise Licensing Code.

5. The following screen asks for Directory Node and Port. The Using Microsoft Active Directory Check Box should be selected.

6. The following screen requires the fully qualified name of the Domain Controller.

7. Next, the Certification Authority requires a distinguished name that may be customized, if required by the deployment scenario.

8. Confirm the CA Name.

9. The Directory Attributes dialog box should be left as LDAP Version 3 with the default transfer mode dimmed.

10. Enter the CA Name, using the same name specified when configuring AD and use the same password.

11. On the Advanced Directory Attributes, enter the First Officer DN.

12. Verify directory information.

13. After a short wait, the ENTDVT Log file dialog box appears and shows Directory Verification completed successfully.

14. The current User's Windows Login Password is needed to start Entrust Services. This is the login and the password for the Entrust/Authority Service to start when logging in to Entrust/Authority Master Control.

15. Select Yes for the Microsoft Crypto-API-enabled application Interoperability Setup window.

16. On the Entrust Authority Port Configuration, review the default data and make sure the node name is the one of the server running the Entrust Authority.

17. In the Cryptographic Information Dialog Box, choose the required parameters for the deployment.

18. Select a lifetime for the CA and complete the CA Configuration.

Certification Authority Initialization

The Entrust/PKI Authority must be initialized before it can be used.

During the Initialization Process, the three Master Users and The First Officer should be present.

1. In the Entrust/Authority Master Control Window, choose Log In.
2. A dialog box appears, stating the initialization will take a few minutes.
3. After an Initial Password Entry Dialog Box appears, each of the three users and the First Officer must privately choose, type, and verify their passwords.
4. The next screen communicates that the installation was successful.
5. Logon with one of the Master Users or First Officer Accounts and start the Entrust/Authority Service.

Client Configuration

1. On the Authority Server, start the Authority/RA Console Administration Program and Enumerate the Users in the Active Directory Domain.
2. Open the Properties Page of the User you want to add to Entrust and Add it.
3. Note the Reference Number and the Authorization Code.
4. On a workstation, deploy the Entelligence Desktop Designer and create a deployment package. Deploy the package to the client workstation and change the entrust.ini initialization file to point to the correct Authority and Directory Server.
5. Log on to the client with the user you added to Entrust Authority.
6. Create a new Entrust User Profile. Specify the Reference Number and the authorization code.
7. Assign the user a password and log on to Entrust.

Citrix Password Manager Agent Deployment

Deploy the agent and create a new application definition with the console for the Entrust Logon.

1. Open the Access Suite Console.
2. Select Applications Definitions Node.
3. Select Create Application Definition.
4. Select Create New and set the application type to Windows.
5. Select Start Wizard.

6. Enter Entrust Login as name.

7. Select Add Form.

8. On the form Identifiers, push the Select button.

9. Select Logon.

10. Right-click the Entrust Icon and select Log In to Entrust.

11. Refresh the Form Wizard and select Entrust Login Form.

12. Define UserID as Combo Box, Password, and OK button.

13. Confirm the default values.

14. Save the application definition.

15. Add the application definition to the user configuration.

16. When a new user needs to log on to Entrust, they should right-click the Citrix Password Manager Icon and select Logon Using Citrix Password Manager.

NOTE   The Logon Screen provided by Entrust is not detected automatically by MetaFrame Password Manager. This happens because Entrust doesn't use standard calls to the OS and the agent is unable to detect the Login Screen Window.

CITRIX PASSWORD MANAGER 4.1 SCALABILITY AND PERFORMANCE

This chapter covers the performance and scalability characteristics of Citrix Password Manager running with Citrix Presentation Server. All testing was done on Presentation Servers using Windows 2000 Server or Windows 2003 Server.

Number of Users Per Citrix Presentation Server

Installing Citrix Password Manager on a Citrix Presentation Server can affect the capacity of the server. Capacity is normally discussed in terms of the effective number of users the server can support.

When installed on a Presentation Server, an instance of Password Manager runs for each client session. For each Password Manager instance, the following processes may be running:

▼ **ssoshell.exe**   Primary agent process, which also handles windows applications

■ **ssobho.exe**   Process, which handles web applications

▲ **ssomho.exe**   Process, which handles mainframe host emulators

In addition, when synchronizing data with the synchronization point, an additional temporary ssoshell.exe process is spawned. This process disappears when the synchronization is complete. All these processes consume server resources that can impact the effective number of users per server.

Single Server Scalability Test

The Single Server Scalability test is designed to quantify—for benchmarking purposes—the optimal number of simulated client sessions that can be connected to a Citrix Presentation Server with acceptable performance. Extending the number of concurrent simulated users beyond the acceptable performance recommendation has a result of decreased performance and impacts end-user experience. The test is made up of three parts: logon, application launch, and sustained user. Password Manager only includes the application launch and sustained user tests. The logon phase of the test was designed to use local users with no passwords. The Password Manager testing requires the users are part of a domain and have passwords. With these types of users, gathering accurate results is difficult due to the variables experienced when a user logs in to a domain. A score is generated based on the amount of time it takes each user to complete the test script. Please note, the simulated users in this test are constantly typing into these applications and may be considered more "rigorous" than normal users. See Figures 8-1 through 8-4, and Tables 8-1 through 8-4.

A baseline test was first run using Citrix Presentation Server without Password Manager. The simulation script simulated user credentials being typed for the password-protected app. The test was then rerun with Password Manager installed on the Citrix Presentation Server. The simulation script was modified to allow Password Manager to provide credentials when needed. During the test, mainframe host support was not enabled, therefore, the ssomho.exe process was not running on the Citrix Presentation Server.

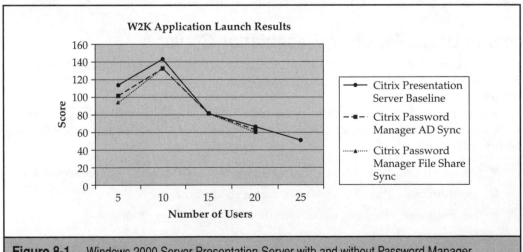

Figure 8-1.   Windows 2000 Server Presentation Server with and without Password Manager

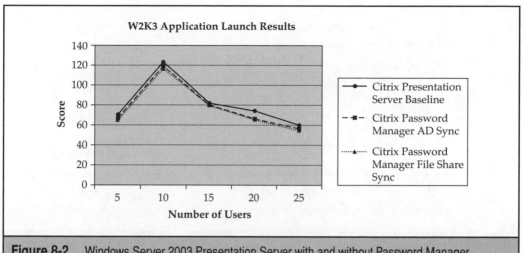

Figure 8-2. Windows Server 2003 Presentation Server with and without Password Manager

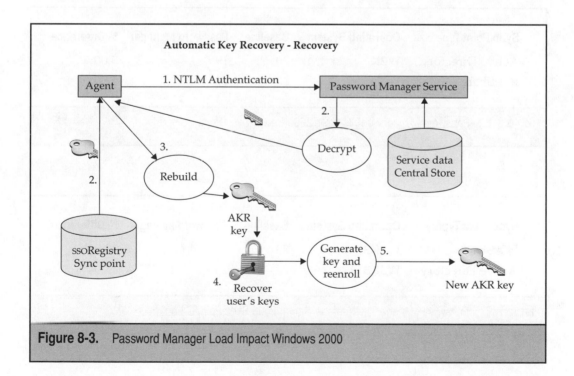

Figure 8-3. Password Manager Load Impact Windows 2000

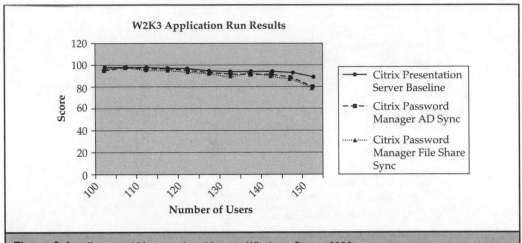

Figure 8-4. Password Manager Load Impact Windows Server 2003

Sync Point Type	Operating System	Baseline	Password Manager	% Difference
Active Directory	W2K	20	19	5.00%
File Share	W2K	20	19	5.00%

Table 8-1. Password Manager on Windows 2000 Server Sync Point Comparison

Sync Point Type	Operating System	Baseline	Password Manager	% Difference
File Share	W2K3	23	20	13.04%
Active Directory	W2K3	23	20	13.04%

Table 8-2. Password Manager on Windows Server 2003 Sync Point Comparison

Sync Point Type	Operating System	Baseline	Password Manager	% Difference
File Share	W2K3	93	85	8.60%
Active Directory	W2K3	93	85	8.60%

Table 8-3.   Password Manager Load Impact Windows 2000

The easiest way to determine the server's degradation point is to look at the score column in the test results. For the Application Launch test, a score of 65 was determined as the fail point. For the Application Run test, a score of 90 was determined as the fail point. This means the server has enough additional CPU and memory resources to handle spikes in performance and provide a consistent user experience. When the test iteration score drops below the fail points, additional users added to the server consume more resources. This produces lower test scores and slower performance.

On this specific hardware with a specific test (Windows Server 2003, application launch, Active Directory Synchronization), extrapolating the results allows for 139 simulated users to be concurrently and constantly running Microsoft Office applications and Citrix Password Manager without significant performance degradation. This is compared to 150 users without Password Manager installed on the server, a 7.33% decrease in the total number of users. This decrease is attributed to additional memory resources required by the Citrix Password Manager Agent.

Server Hardware Configuration:

▼   IBM x-Series 335

■   Dual Xeon 2.4 GHz Processors with 512KB L2 Cache

■   34GB Ultra 320 SCSI

■   3GB RAM

▲   4GB Page File

Sync Point Type	Operating System	Baseline	Password Manager	% Difference
File Share	W2K3	150	139	7.33%
Active Directory	W2K3	150	139	7.33%

Table 8-4.   Password Manager Load Impact Windows Server 2003

Client Hardware Configuration

▼ Compaq Proliant 800

■ Dual 500 MHz PIII Processors with 256KB L2 Cache

■ 8GB SCSI HDD

■ 512MB RAM

▲ 1GB Page File

Citrix Presentation Server Software Configuration

▼ Windows 2000 Server w/Service Pack 4 or Windows 2003 Server w/Service Pack 1

■ Citrix Presentation Server 4.0

■ Citrix Password Manager 4.1

▲ Microsoft Office XP—Excel, Access, & PowerPoint

Client Software Configuration

▼ Windows 2000 Server w/Service Pack 4

■ Citrix ICA Program Neighborhood Version 9.00.32649

▲ 15 ICA sessions exist on each machine

Citrix Password Manager Memory Usage

Table 8-5 shows the average memory usage observed for each Password Manager process running in a Citrix Presentation Server client session. These measurements were taken while the processes were idle, but had previously responded to credential requests. These numbers can be used to estimate the amount of additional memory needed for Password Manager.

Process	Private Bytes Windows 2000	Private Bytes Windows 2003
SSOShell.exe	5.18MB	5.47MB
SSOBHO.exe	2.82MB	2.46 MB
SSOMHO.exe	2.09MB	2.94MB

Table 8-5.   Password Manager Memory Usage Based on Operating System

Credential Synchronization Using NTFS File Share

This section discusses the scalability and performance characteristics related to using an NTFS File Share for password synchronization. These include

▼ Disk space utilization of the file share server

■ Network bandwidth utilization between Password Manager Agents and the file share server

▲ Citrix Password Manager Agent response times

 NOTE Citrix Presentation session login time was not significantly impacted by the Password Manager Agent.

The following test bed was used for this phase of testing:

File Server Hardware Configuration:

▼ IBM x-Series 335

■ Dual Xeon 2.4 GHz Processors with 512KB L2 Cache

■ 34GB Ultra 320 SCSI

■ 1GB RAM

▲ 3GB Page File

Citrix Presentation Server Hardware Configuration:

▼ IBM x-Series 335

■ Dual Xeon 2.4 GHz Processors with 512KB L2 Cache

■ 34GB Ultra 320 SCSI

■ 1GB RAM

▲ 3GB Page File

Client Hardware Configuration:

▼ IBM x-Series 335

■ Dual Xeon 2.4 GHz Processors with 512KB L2 Cache

■ 34GB Ultra 320 SCSI

■ 1GB RAM

▲ 3GB Page File

File Server Software Configuration:

▼ Windows 2000 w/Service Pack 4 or Windows 2003 w/Service Pack 1

Citrix Presentation Server Software Configuration

▼ Windows 2000 Server w/Service Pack 4 or Windows 2003 Server w/Service Pack 1

■ Citrix Presentation Server 4.0

■ Citrix Password Manager 4.1

▲ Microsoft Office XP—Excel, Access, & PowerPoint

Client Software Configuration

▼ Windows 2003 Server w/Service Pack 1

■ Citrix ICA Program Neighborhood Version 9.00.32649

▲ 30 ICA sessions exist on each machine

Disk Space Utilization of the File Share Server

With *file share synchronization*, the file share includes a separate directory for each user. Within each user's directory, credential information is stored for each application defined for use with Password Manager. Table 8-6 shows the disk space utilized for a single user with different Password Manager options configured.

With these measurements, the amount of disk space required on a file share server can be calculated with the following formula:

```
Disk Space required = (# of users) *  (FTU Configuration + (# of defined apps *
[User Defined or Provisioned apps]))
```

For example (using Windows 2003 as a Citrix Presentation Server), 1,000 users who are using Previous Password as their key recovery method, with 20 applications defined via provisioning for each user would require:

▼ Disk Space required = (1,000) * (4.88 + (20 * 0.95))

▲ Disk Space required = 23,880KB or 24MB

Network Bandwidth Utilization Between Citrix Password Manager Agents, the File Share Credential Store, and the Citrix Password Manager Server

Different events, such as logging on or changing a password, can trigger synchronization among the Password Manager Agent, the central store, or the Password Manager Service. These synchronizations put traffic on the network. The amount of network traffic can differ, depending on some of the following factors:

▼ Number of application definitions per user

■ Whether or not aggressive synchronization is enabled

▲ Frequency of synchronization events

Disk Utilization Measurement	Disk Usage with No Applications Defined	Disk Usage Per Application
FTU w/Previous Password	4.88KB	0.7KB
FTU w/Previous Password & Provisioning	14.6KB	0.95KB
Disk Usage prior to FTU (only Provisioning Commands)	14.4KB	0.95KB
FTU w/AKR	5.34KB	0.7KB
FTU w/AKR & Provisioning	15.0KB	0.95KB
FTU w/SSPR	7.61KB	0.7KB
FTU w/SSPR & Provisioning	17.3KB	0.95KB
FTU w/AKR & SSPR	8.07KB	0.7KB
FTU w/AKR & SSPR & Provisioning	17.7KB	0.95KB

Table 8-6. Disk Utilization of File Share Server Sync Point

Network Monitor was used to measure the amount of data in kilobytes passed among the file share credential store, the Password Manager Agent, and the Password Manager Server for various synchronization events. Each measurement was taken multiple times to obtain the average value for each event. The users were configured with ten defined applications divided between win32 applications and web applications. Important to note is that more or less application definitions could produce different results. See Table 8-7.

The following list details the various network traffic events that occur for Password Manager Managed Applications using a file sync option. These points correlate to data in Tables 8-6 and 8-7.

▼ **FTU** This is the first-time user-configuration event that takes place when a user logs in for the first time and configures Password Manager.

■ **Password Reset** This event happens when a user starts the Self Service Password Reset feature.

■ **Key Recovery** This event occurs after a user's password has been changed by either the domain administrator or the user. Password Manager updates the security keys, so the user can access their credentials.

▲ **Password Reset/Key Recovery** During this process, the user invokes the self-service password reset feature and changes their password. The user then logs in and automatic key recovery takes place.

File Share Credential Store			
Event	Agent/Sync Point	Agent/Service	Service/ Sync Point
FTU w/no applications defined	120.9KB	N/A	N/A
FTU w/10 applications provisioned	242.5KB	27.9KB	181.3KB
FTU (SSPR enabled) w/no applications defined	124.6KB	26.3KB	221.4KB
FTU (SSPR enabled) w/10 applications provisioned	255.7KB	52.8KB	385.3KB
Password Reset	N/A	49.5KB	446.4KB
Account Unlock	N/A	43.9KB	477.5KB
FTU (AKR enabled) w/no applications defined	148.8KB	17.4KB	186.4KB
FTU (AKR enabled) w/10 applications provisioned	280.0KB	43.8KB	341.7KB
Key Recovery	134.6KB	16.7KB	21.9KB
FTU (AKR & SSPR enabled) w/no applications defined	124.5KB	42.2KB	393.7KB
FTU (AKR & SSPR enabled) w/10 applications provisioned	246.8KB	68.6KB	567.6KB
Post FTU Logon (with no configuration changes)	61KB	N/A	N/A

Table 8-7.   Network Traffic for Several Password Manager-Managed Applications

NOTE   In an environment where aggressive synchronization is enabled, every time an application is launched, a synchronization event takes place. This is comparable to a user using the refresh feature in Logon Manager. Performing synchronizations across a WAN link could cause a bottleneck between the synchronization point and Password Manager Agents.

Citrix Password Manager Agent Response Time

The time it takes for Password Manager to recognize a password-protected application and provide its credentials can vary, depending on the user's environment and Password Manager configuration. Some factors that may affect response time are

▼ Network bandwidth availability

■ Use of redirected application data folders vs. local Windows profiles

■ Whether or not aggressive synchronization is enabled

■ Citrix Presentation Server resource availability

■ Whether agent synchronization is installed

▲ Network latency between the synchronization point and the Password Manager Agent

The following table lists agent response times with varying client configurations. All testing was done using a custom Win32 application, a custom web page, Scanpak Aviva Terminal Emulator, a custom Java application, and a custom Java applet running in an ICA session on a Citrix Presentation Server 4.0. For each configuration, the time between the application loading and the credentials being fully submitted by Password Manager is indicated.

NOTE Response times for Win32, Web, Java, and Java applet credential requests were gathered using an automated test tool.

Response times for Terminal Emulator applications were gathered using a stop watch (times may not be accurate due to human error). Mainframe Host polling time was set to 700 milliseconds, which may add to response time. The average response times for Windows 2000 Server and Windows Server 2003 can be seen in Tables 8-8 and 8-9.

Credential Synchronization Using Microsoft Active Directory

This section discusses the performance and scalability characteristics of using Microsoft Active Directory for credential synchronization. These include

▼ Active Directory replication network traffic

■ Network bandwidth utilization between Password Manager Agents and AD Domain Controllers

■ Active Directory domain controller CPU utilization

▲ Citrix Password Manager Agent response times

In all Active Directory testing, the Citrix Presentation Servers and the AD synchronization point were in different domains, but in the same forest. The two trusted domains had External nontransitive trust relationships. Citrix Presentation Server session login time was not significantly impacted by the Password Manager Agent.

Agent Response Time with File Share Synchronization Over a LAN	Results Windows 2000				
	Windows App	Web App	Terminal Emulator App	Java App	Java Applet
Single user operating on a Citrix Presentation Server with synchronization not installed & local Windows profile	0.03 sec	0.79 sec	2.16 sec	0.65 sec	0.55 sec
Single user operating on a Citrix Presentation Server with synchronization not installed & Redirected App-Data folders	0.34 sec	1.1 sec	2.88 sec	0.96 sec	0.89 sec
Single user operating on a Citrix Presentation Server with aggressive synchronization & local Windows profile	0.06 sec	1.83 sec	2.7 sec	0.67 sec	0.47 sec
Single user operating on a Citrix Presentation Server with aggressive synchronization & Redirected App-Data folders	1.07 sec	1.43 sec	3.8 sec	1.67 sec	1.48 sec
User operating on a Citrix Presentation Server that is at 65% CPU utilization with synchronization not installed & local profile	0.03 sec	0.84 sec	2.38 sec	0.65 sec	0.49 sec
User operating on a Citrix Presentation Server that is at 65% CPU utilization with synchronization not installed & Redirected App-data folders	0.41 sec	1.17 sec	2.9 sec	1.06 sec	0.95 sec
User operating on a Citrix Presentation Server that is at 65% CPU utilization with aggressive synchronization & local profile	0.06 sec	0.88 sec	2.7 sec	0.69 sec	0.7 sec
User operating on a Citrix Presentation Server that is at 65% CPU utilization with aggressive synchronization & Redirected App-data folders	1.15 sec	1.56 sec	4 sec	1.79 sec	1.64 sec

Table 8-8.   Average Response Time for File Share Sync over LAN Windows 2000 Server

Agent Response Time with File Share Synchronization Over a LAN	Results Windows 2003				
	Windows App	Web App	Terminal Emulator App	Java App	Java Applet
Single user operating on a Citrix Presentation Server with synchronization not installed & local Windows profile	0.03 sec	0.39 sec	2.38 sec	0.68 sec	0.91 sec
Single user operating on a Citrix Presentation Server with synchronization not installed & Redirected App-Data folders	0.28 sec	0.61 sec	2.63 sec	0.88 sec	1.2 sec
Single user operating on a Citrix Presentation Server with aggressive synchronization & local Windows profile	0.07 sec	0.87 sec	2.82 sec	0.66 sec	0.63 sec
Single user operating on a Citrix Presentation Server with aggressive synchronization & Redirected App-Data folders	1.02 sec	1.45 sec	3.69 sec	1.64 sec	1.57 sec
User operating on a Citrix Presentation Server that is at 65% CPU utilization with synchronization not installed & local profile	0.03 sec	0.53 sec	2.32 sec	0.66 sec	0.54 sec
User operating on a Citrix Presentation Server that is at 65% CPU utilization with synchronization not installed & Redirected App-data folders	0.38 sec	0.8 sec	2.79 sec	0.95 sec	0.91 sec
User operating on a Citrix Presentation Server that is at 65% CPU utilization with aggressive synchronization & local profile	0.07 sec	0.65 sec	2.87 sec	0.73 sec	0.61 sec
User operating on a Citrix Presentation Server that is at 65% CPU utilization with aggressive synchronization & Redirected App-data folders	1.16 sec	1.55 sec	4.23 sec	1.82 sec	1.69 sec

Table 8-9.   Average Response Time for File Share Sync over LAN Windows Server 2003

The following test bed was used for this phase of testing:

Active Directory Server Configuration:

- ▼ Dell PowerEdge 2650
- ■ Dual Xeon 2.4 GHz Processors with 512KB L2 Cache
- ■ GB SCSI HDD
- ■ 1GB RAM
- ▲ 4GB Page File

Citrix Presentation Server Hardware Configuration:

- ▼ IBM x-Series 335
- ■ Dual Xeon 2.4 GHz Processors with 512KB L2 Cache
- ■ 34GB Ultra 320 SCSI
- ■ 1GB RAM
- ▲ 3GB Page File

Client Hardware Configuration:

- ▼ IBM x-Series 335
- ■ Dual Xeon 2.4 GHz Processors with 512KB L2 Cache
- ■ 34GB Ultra 320 SCSI
- ■ 1GB RAM
- ▲ 3GB Page File

Citrix Presentation Server Software Configuration

- ▼ Windows 2000 Server w/Service Pack 4 or Windows 2003 Server w/Service Pack 1
- ■ Citrix Presentation Server 4.0
- ■ Citrix Password Manager 4.1
- ▲ Microsoft Office XP—Excel, Access, & PowerPoint

Client Software Configuration

- ▼ Windows 2003 Server w/Service Pack 1
- ■ Citrix ICA Program Neighborhood Version 9.00.32649
- ▲ 30 ICA sessions exist on each machine

Active Directory Server Software Configuration

- ▼ Windows 2003 Server w/Service Pack 1

Disk Space Utilization of the Active Directory Domain Controller Server

When Active Directory is used as a central data store, user configuration and credential information is stored in the Active Directory database. The file that makes up this database is labeled NTDS.dit. Active Directory allocates space for this file in 2MB blocks of disk space. Table 8-10 shows the average disk space utilized for a single user.

With these measurements, the amount of disk space required on a file share server can be calculated with the following formula:

```
Disk Space required = (# of users) * (FTU Configuration + (# of defined apps *
[User Defined or Provisioned apps]))
```

For example (using Windows 2003 as a Citrix Presentation Server), 1,000 users who are using Previous Password as their key recovery method, with 20 applications defined via provisioning for each user would require:

▼   Disk Space required = (1,000) * (4.88 + (20 * 0.95))

▲   Disk Space required = 23,880KB or 24MB

Disk Utilization Measurement	Disk Usage with No Applications Defined	Disk Usage Per Application
FTU w/Previous Password	4.88KB	0.7KB
FTU w/Previous Password & Provisioning	14.6KB	0.95KB
Disk Usage prior to FTU (only Provisioning Commands)	14.4KB	0.95KB
FTU w/AKR	5.34KB	0.7KB
FTU w/AKR & Provisioning	15.0KB	0.95KB
FTU w/SSPR	7.61KB	0.7KB
FTU w/SSPR & Provisioning	17.3KB	0.95 KB
FTU w/AKR & SSPR	8.07 KB	0.7KB
FTU w/AKR & SSPR & Provisioning	17.7KB	0.95KB

Table 8-10.   Average Disk Space per User for Active Directory Sync Option

Network Bandwidth Utilization Among Password Manager Agents, Active Directory Domain Controllers, and Password Manager Servers

Different events, such as logging on or changing a password, can trigger synchronization among the Password Manager Agent, the Active Directory, and the Password Manager Server. These synchronizations place traffic on the network. The amount of network traffic between an agent and an Active Directory domain controller can vary, depending on some of the following factors:

▼ Number of application definitions per user

■ Whether or not aggressive synchronization is enabled

▲ Frequency of synchronization events

Network Monitor was used to measure the amount of data passed among an Active Directory Domain controller, the Password Manager Agent, and Password Manager Server for various synchronization events. Each measurement was taken multiple times to obtain the average value for each event. The users were set up with ten defined applications (seven Windows-based applications and three web-based applications). Important to note is that more or less application definitions could produce different results. A second note, the logon measurements include the amount of bandwidth that takes place during a login without Password Manager. In our test environment, the average amount of bandwidth for a user who logs in for the first time was 150.1KB. Each subsequent login averaged approximately 130.1KB. See Table 8-11.

The following list details the various network traffic events that occur for Password Manager Managed Applications using an Active Directory sync option. These points correlate with data in Table 8-11.

▼ **FTU**   This is the first-time user configuration event that takes place when a user logs in for the first time and configures Password Manager.

■ **Password Reset**   This event happens when a user starts the Self-Service Password Reset feature.

■ **Key Recovery**   This event occurs after a user's password has been changed by either the domain administrator or the user. Password Manager updates the security keys, so the user can access their credentials.

▲ **Password Reset/Key Recovery**   During this process, the user invokes the self-service password reset feature and changes their password. The user then logs in and automatic key recovery takes place.

NOTE   In an environment where aggressive synchronization is enabled, every time an application is launched, a synchronization event takes place. This is comparable to a user using the refresh feature.

Active Directory Credential Store

Event	Agent/Sync Point	Agent/Service	Service/Sync Point
FTU w/no applications defined	471.9KB	N/A	N/A
FTU w/10 applications provisioned	839.9KB	27.9KB	158.5KB
FTU (SSPR enabled) w/no applications defined	134.5KB	26.3KB	291.4KB
FTU (SSPR enabled) w/10 applications provisioned	184.6KB	52.8KB	454.6KB
Password Reset	N/A	51.4KB	614.1KB
Account Unlock	N/A	43.9KB	622.0KB
FTU (AKR enabled) w/no applications defined	574.9KB	17.3KB	277.1KB
FTU (AKR enabled) w/10 applications provisioned	912.3KB	43.8KB	426.3KB
Key Recovery	108.6KB	16.7KB	37.8KB
FTU (AKR & SSPR enabled) w/no applications defined	139.1KB	42.2KB	561.7KB
FTU (AKR & SSPR enabled) w/10 applications provisioned	181.9KB	68.7KB	714.2KB
Post FTU Logon (with no configuration changes)	61KB	N/A	N/A

Table 8-11.   Network Bandwidth Usage for Password Manager Managed Applications with Active Directory Sync Option

Agent Response Time

The time it takes for Password Manager to recognize a password-protected application and provide its credentials can vary depending on the user's environment and Password Manager configuration. Some factors that may affect response time are

▼ Network bandwidth availability

■ Use of Redirected application data folders vs. local Windows profiles

■ Whether aggressive synchronization is enabled or not

- ■ Citrix Presentation Server resource availability
- ■ Whether agent synchronization is installed
- ▲ Network latency between the synchronization point and the Password Manager Agent

Tables 8-12 and 8-13 list agent response times with varying client configurations. All testing was done using a custom Win32 application, a custom web page, Scanpak Aviva Terminal Emulator, a custom Java application, and a custom Java applet running in an ICA session on a Citrix Presentation Server 4.0. For each configuration, the time between the application loading and the credentials being fully submitted by Password Manager is indicated.

NOTE   Response times for Win32, Web, Java, and Java applet credential requests were gathered using an automated test tool. Response times for Terminal Emulator applications were gathered using a stop watch (times may not be accurate due to human error). Mainframe Host polling time was set to 700 milliseconds, which may add to response time.

DETERMINING WHICH FILE SHARE SYNCHRONIZATION POINT THE CITRIX PASSWORD MANAGER 4.*X* AGENT WILL USE AS THE CENTRAL CREDENTIAL STORE

The *Citrix Password Manager 4.x agent* uses a defined logical search order to determine which synchronization point it should use. The agent attempts to locate a synchronization point (for example, HKCU, MMF, and so forth) from numerous places. This process differs slightly between servers with Presentation Server installed and those without it installed. Figures 8-5 and 8-6 outline how the agent locates a synchronization point and how it accepts a synchronization point for use.

NOTE   The MetaFrame Password Manager Policy, "Central Credential Store," is only applied at the initialization of each session for which it has been applied.

INCREASING THE DETECTION TIME OF APPLICATIONS WITHOUT WINDOW TITLES

Currently, a defined application with no window title takes a minimum of three seconds to be detected. This is because of the way Citrix Password Manager handles the detection of applications with no window title.

Agent Response Time with Active Directory Synchronization Over a LAN	Results Windows 2000				
	Windows App	Web App	Terminal Emulator App	Java App	Java Applet
Single user operating on a Citrix Presentation Server with synchronization not installed & local Windows profile	0.03 sec	0.77 sec	2.32 sec	0.65 sec	0.54 sec
Single user operating on a Citrix Presentation Server with synchronization not installed & Redirected App-Data folders	0.39 sec	1.21 sec	2.78 sec	1 sec	0.98 sec
Single user operating on a Citrix Presentation Server with aggressive synchronization & local Windows profile	0.05 sec	0.81 sec	2.89 sec	0.66 sec	0.5 sec
Single user operating on a Citrix Presentation Server with aggressive synchronization & Redirected App-Data folders	1.06 sec	1.58 sec	3.82 sec	1.65 sec	1.39 sec
User operating on a Citrix Presentation Server that is at 65% CPU utilization with synchronization not installed & local profile	0.03 sec	0.8 sec	2.36 sec	0.66 sec	0.53 sec
User operating on a Citrix Presentation Server that is at 65% CPU utilization with synchronization not installed & Redirected App-data folders	0.44 sec	1.34 sec	2.68 sec	1.08 sec	0.96 sec
User operating on a Citrix Presentation Server that is at 65% CPU utilization with aggressive synchronization & local profile	0.06 sec	0.88 sec	2.73 sec	0.69 sec	0.6 sec
User operating on a Citrix Presentation Server that is at 65% CPU utilization with aggressive synchronization & Redirected App-data folders	1.16 sec	1.74 sec	3.66 sec	1.79 sec	1.65 sec

Table 8-12.   Average Response Time for Active Directory Sync over LAN Windows 2000 Server

Agent Response Time with Active Directory Synchronization Over a LAN	Results Windows 2003				
	Windows App	Web App	Terminal Emulator App	Java App	Java Applet
Single user operating on a Citrix Presentation Server with synchronization not installed & local Windows profile	0.03 sec	0.39 sec	2.33 sec	0.63 sec	0.86 sec
Single user operating on a Citrix Presentation Server with synchronization not installed & Redirected App-Data folders	0.32 sec	0.61 sec	2.57 sec	0.92 sec	1.29 sec
Single user operating on a Citrix Presentation Server with aggressive synchronization & local Windows profile	0.06 sec	0.87 sec	2.91 sec	0.65 sec	0.59 sec
Single user operating on a Citrix Presentation Server with aggressive synchronization & Redirected App-Data folders	1.03 sec	1.45 sec	3.66 sec	1.6 sec	1.57 sec
User operating on a Citrix Presentation Server that is at 65% CPU utilization with synchronization not installed & local profile	0.03 sec	0.53 sec	2.31 sec	0.66 sec	0.57 sec
User operating on a Citrix Presentation Server that is at 65% CPU utilization with synchronization not installed & Redirected App-data folders	0.47 sec	0.8 sec	2.74 sec	0.97 sec	0.95 sec
User operating on a Citrix Presentation Server that is at 65% CPU utilization with aggressive synchronization & local profile	0.07 sec	0.65 sec	2.83 sec	0.68 sec	0.58 sec
User operating on a Citrix Presentation Server that is at 65% CPU utilization with aggressive synchronization & Redirected App-data folders	1.26 sec	1.55 sec	3.93 sec	1.74 sec	1.72 sec

Table 8-13.   Average Response Time for Active Directory Sync over LAN Windows 2003 Server

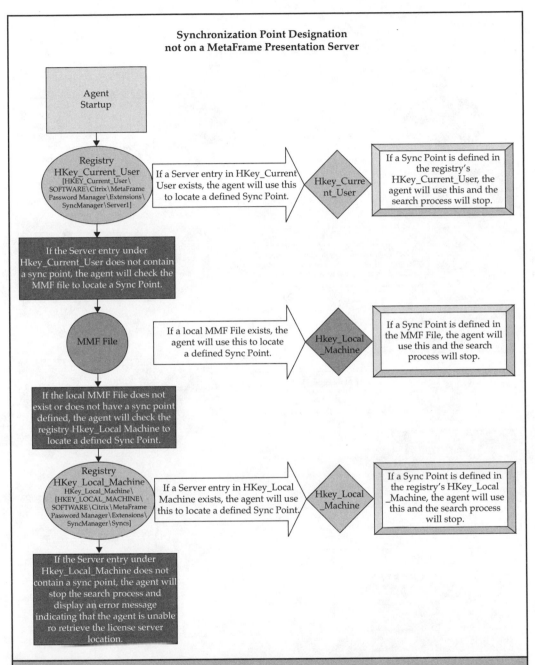

**Synchronization Point Designation
not on a MetaFrame Presentation Server**

Agent Startup

Registry HKey_Current_User
[HKEY_Current_User\
SOFTWARE\Citrix\MetaFrame
Password Manager\Extensions\
SyncManager\Server1]

If a Server entry in HKey_Current User exists, the agent will use this to locate a defined Sync Point.

Hkey_Current_User

If a Sync Point is defined in the registry's HKey_Current_User, the agent will use this and the search process will stop.

If the Server entry under Hkey_Current_User does not contain a sync point, the agent will check the MMF file to locate a Sync Point.

MMF File

If a local MMF File exists, the agent will use this to locate a defined Sync Point.

Hkey_Local_Machine

If a Sync Point is defined in the MMF File, the agent will use this and the search process will stop.

If the local MMF File does not exist or does not have a sync point defined, the agent will check the registry Hkey_Local Machine to locate a defined Sync Point.

Registry HKey_Local_Machine
HKey_Local_Machine\
[HKEY_LOCAL_MACHINE\
SOFTWARE\Citrix\MetaFrame
Password Manager\Extensions\
SyncManager\Syncs]

If a Server entry in HKey_Local Machine exists, the agent will use this to locate a defined Sync Point.

Hkey_Local_Machine

If a Sync Point is defined in the registry's HKey_Local_Machine, the agent will use this and the search process will stop.

If the Server entry under Hkey_Local_Machine does not contain a sync point, the agent will stop the search process and display an error message indicating that the agent is unable ro retrieve the license server location.

Figure 8-5.   Synchronization Point Designation *not* on Presentation Server

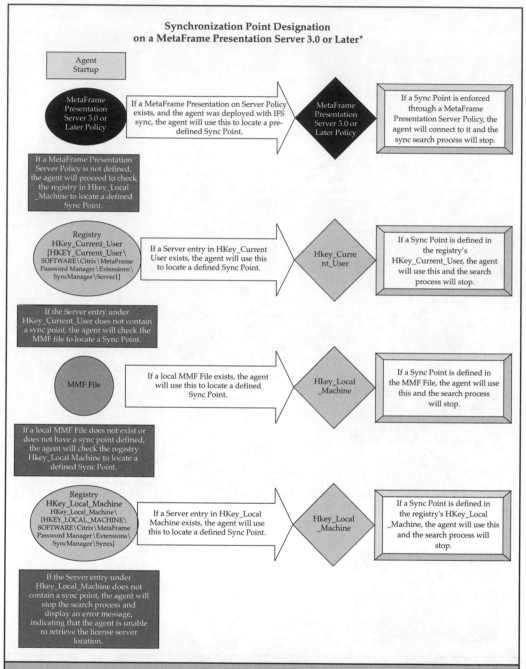

Figure 8-6.   Synchronization Point Designation on Presentation Server 3.0 or higher

When the agent detects a window with no title, the agent assumes the window is not initialized completely. The agent then reposts the window detection event every one-half second, up to six times, before determining the window has no window title. It then proceeds to process window detection. This means any defined application with no window title takes at least three seconds to be detected.

A registry setting can be created on the agent workstation to decrease the detection time of such applications. The value allows the repost detection time to be adjusted, based on the value in this setting. With this setting configured, the agent then reposts the application detection event, up to the number specified in this registry value. For example, if the administrator prefers to shorten discovery time to 2 seconds, he should set this registry value to 4 (2 seconds/0.5 second event repost interval). If the administrator prefers to lengthen the discovery time to 5 seconds, the setting should be configured to a value to 10. The default value of this registry value is 6, or 3 seconds.

To shorten the amount of time the Citrix Password Manager takes to detect an application without a window title, the following registry key can be created on the agent workstation:

```
Path:      HKLM\SOFTWARE\CITRIX\Metaframe Password Manager\Shell
Key:       EmptyTitleMaxRepostTime
Type:      Dword
Value:     0/1
```

By default, when the registry key is created, it is set to 0 (disabled). To enable the setting, the value must be set to 1.

NOTE   This setting should only be customized when configured Windows applications include those with empty window titles. The agent code uses this registry if it is set in a range between 1 and 20. Otherwise, the agent uses the default value of 6.

CHAPTER 9

Conferencing Manager

The following section describes considerations for integrating Citrix Conferencing Manager, such as Conferencing Manager architecture, sizing your Conferencing Manager servers, guest user considerations, and users who are members of 200 or more Active Directory groups.

NOTE If you are upgrading Conferencing Manager, please note that a direct upgrade from Conferencing Manager 2.0 to version 4.0 is not supported. Refer to the Administrator's Guide for Citrix MetaFrame Conferencing Manager Version 4.0 for more details.

CITRIX CONFERENCING MANAGER ARCHITECTURE AND SCALABILITY

To properly deploy Conferencing Manager into your existing Presentation Server environment, you must understand the core components in terms of how they interact and communicate with each other. Conferencing Manager is broken into five components and each of the components is necessary to start, join, leave, and end meetings.

▼ **Conferencing Manager User Interface (CMCM) Client**

  ○ Conferencing Manager User Interface (CMCM) client is a published application in the Presentation Server farm. It can be load balanced like any published application to gain performance improvements. The main function of the CMCM client is to allow conference participants access to the conference room.

■ **Conference Organizer**

  ○ The main function of the *Conference Organizer* is to maintain meeting information for all meeting servers in the farm. This information consists of created meetings, when meetings have started and on what servers, and the attendee lists of those meetings. This information is stored in the registry on the Conference Organizer server. The Conference Organizer also is responsible for loadbalancing meetings across your available meeting servers. Only one instance of Conference Organizer is allowed per server farm. It can be installed on a standalone server without Presentation Server installed, but it must be installed in the same domain where Conference Room and the CMCM client are installed.

■ **Conference Room**

  ○ Conference Room is installed as a hidden published application and can be load balanced like any other published application. Conference Room is invisible to the user, but it is automatically launched via Conference Manger User Interface when a meeting is started or joined. It is the component that provides the actual shadowing session in which the users collaborate during a conference. Note, this published application should not be renamed; otherwise, conferences cannot be started.

■ **Conference Room Manager**

○ Conference Room Manager maintains meeting information on a single server. It monitors the attendees and licensing information for the server, and it is responsible for meeting operations, such as start, join, leave, and end meetings. Conference Room Manager communicates information with the Conference Organizer service, such as when a meeting has started and the attendees who are currently in the meeting.

▲ **External Conference Service**

○ External Conference Service provides communication to the Conference Organizer from outside a firewall using the HTTP protocol. Requirements are that External Web Service is running on the same server on Conference Organizer and that Microsoft .NET 1.1 is installed.

Citrix Conferencing Manager Communications

When deploying Conferencing Manager into your Presentation Server environment, understanding how Conferencing Manager communicates with its various components is important. This is especially important when deploying over a wide area network (WAN). This section describes which Conferencing Manager components communicate with each other, the protocols they use, and the amount of bandwidth consumed.

It is important to know that when Conferencing Manager is idle—this means no meetings are in progress, and no users are creating and/or joining meetings—no bandwidth is overhead. Figure 9-1 displays the actions that happen when a user launches the Conferencing Manager Client.

1. When a user launches the Conferencing Manager Client, it communicates using RPC with the Conference Organizer service. This is to retrieve a list of available meetings the user can join. The amount of bandwidth used during this action is (KB = 11.9 + (1.5 * # of meetings).

2. The client then communicates to the Exchange server only if there is a valid Outlook profile. This also uses RPC and the amount of bandwidth can be represented by (KB = 2.9 + (24.7 * # of meetings).

3. The client communicates with the configured Citrix XML service to retrieve their list of available published applications on the Presentation Server farm. This communication uses the HTTP protocol and the bandwidth is calculated using the following formula (KB = 12.4 + (0.3 * # of meetings).

4. A user connects to a Presentation Server farm and launches the Conferencing Manager user-interface published application. This communication uses the ICA protocol and is optimized for WAN connections. When the interface is initialized, the communication shown in Figure 9-2 begins.

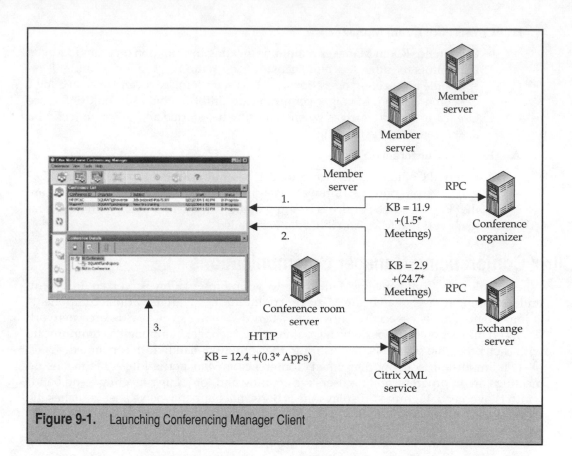

Figure 9-1.   Launching Conferencing Manager Client

1. When the user decides to create a meeting, the Citrix Conferencing Manager UI contacts the Conference Organizer and receives an ICA file directing them to the least-loaded meeting server. When the ICA file is launched they create a session on the meeting server and launch the CRoom application.

2. When CRoom initializes, the CRoom Manager communicates to the License Server and checks out a license for the meeting host. The bandwidth utilized for a license checkout is 1.3KB per license and uses the TCP protocol.

3. The CRoom Manager then communicates to the Conference Organizer that the meeting has started. The meeting is now ready for attendees to join.

4. A user connects to a Presentation Server farm and launches the Conferencing Manager user interface published application. This communication uses the ICA protocol and is optimized for WAN connections. When the interface is initialized, the communication shown in Figure 9-3 begins. The user decides to join a meeting displayed in the user interface.

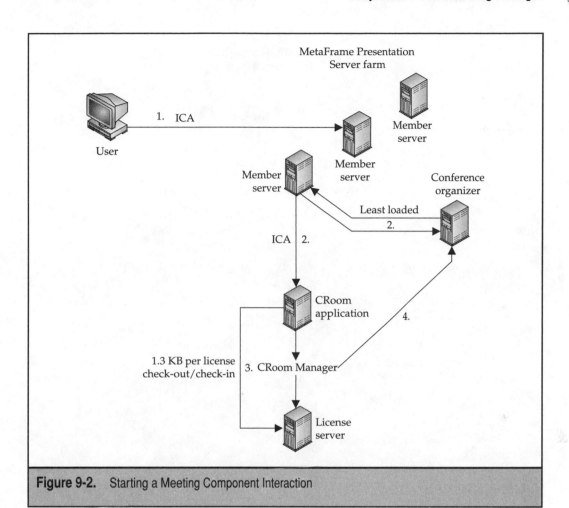

Figure 9-2.   Starting a Meeting Component Interaction

1. When the user decides to join a meeting, the Conferencing Manager UI contacts the Conference Organizer and receives an ICA file directing them to the meeting server where the conference is hosted. When the ICA file is launched, they create a session on the meeting server and launch the CRoom application. The CRoom Manager then communicates to the License Server and checks out a license for the meeting attendee.

2. After the license acquisition, CRoom shadows the host session and the attendee joins the meeting.

3. The CRoom Manager then communicates to the Conference Organizer that the current attendee has changed.

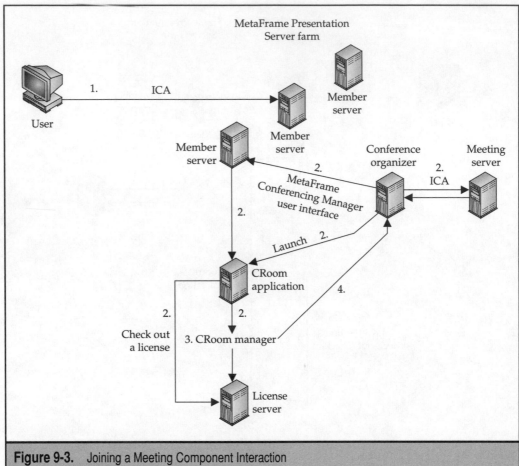

Figure 9-3. Joining a Meeting Component Interaction

Sizing Citrix Conferencing Manager 4.0 Servers

The number of users that a server can support depends on several factors, including:

▼ The Conferencing Manager server's hardware specifications (processor, memory, disk, and available network bandwidth)

■ The applications that are being run (because of the applications' CPU and memory requirements)

■ The amount of user input and graphics being processed and displayed by the applications

▲ The maximum desired resource usage on the server, for example, 90% CPU usage or 80% memory usage

This topic discusses how to size a Conference Manager Server, where memory becomes the first performance bottleneck. Also, note that applications which place a heavy load on the processor or consume large amounts of network bandwidth decrease the number of attendees able to join a meeting with acceptable performance. *Acceptable performance* can be described as session latency or how long it takes for all attendees to receive screen updates from the host session. The following scenario describes how to size a Conferencing Manager server, where all the Conferencing Manager components are located on the same server.

The components are

▼ Citrix Presentation Server 4.0

■ Citrix XML Service

■ Conference Organizer Service

■ Conference Room Manager Service

■ Conference Room Published Application

▲ Conferencing Manager 4.0 User Interface

The following formula is used to determine the user capacity for a particular server.

$$\text{\# of Users} = \frac{\text{Host Values} = ((\text{TotalMemory (DesiredThreshold)}) - (\text{SessionMemory} + \text{CRoom} + \text{MCM\_UI} + \text{Apps} + \text{OSOverhead})}{\text{Attendees Values} = (\text{SessionMemory} + \text{CRoom} + \text{MCM\_UI} + \text{CShadow})}$$

▼ **TotalMemory**   The amount of memory available on the server (Physical and Virtual)

■ **DesiredThreshold**   Maximum memory utilization desired

■ **SessionMemory**   Memory cost of all the components required for an ICA session (Winlogon.exe, WFShell.exe, Csrss.exe, and SSonSvr.exe). This is the same for both the Host and Attendee sessions. The variable SessionMemory in the numerator refers to the organizer's session memory and the variable SessionMemory in the denominator refers to the attendee's session memory.

■ **Apps**   Memory cost for applications inside a meeting (Microsoft PowerPoint)

■ **OSOverhead**   Memory cost of the operating system (OS) and related services

■ **MCM_UI**   Memory cost of the Citrix MetaFrame Conferencing Manager Client

■ **CRoom**   Memory cost of the Conference Room Published Application

▲ **CShadow**   Memory cost of the CShadow.exe process (Attendee Only)

Single Server Example

A Windows Server 2003 Enterprise, with 4GB of physical memory, plus 2GB of virtual memory, has 6GB TotalMemory. The DesiredThreshold is 80% utilization. The session memory usage is 9.7MB—this includes all the processes associated with an ICA session. The size of the Citrix Conference Manager UI depends on the number of published applications and meetings the user has rights to and is around 24MB. The PowerPoint application used within the meeting is 10MB and the OSOverhead is 700MB. The denominator portion of the equation is the attendee's memory usage, which is 54.1MB. This includes all the processes associated with an ICA session, MCM_UI, CRoom, and CShadow. Please see Figure 9-4.

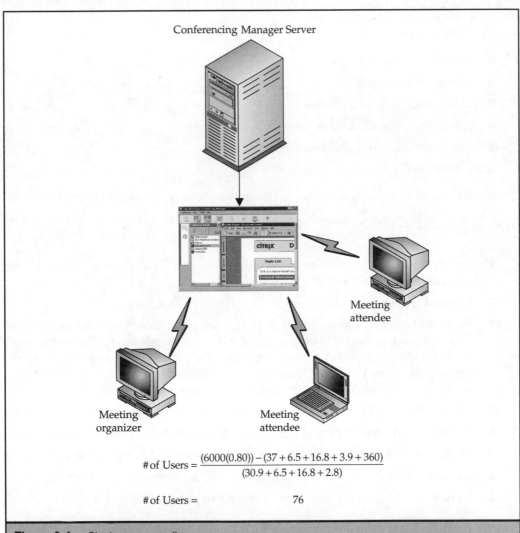

$$\# \text{of Users} = \frac{(6000(0.80)) - (37 + 6.5 + 16.8 + 3.9 + 360)}{(30.9 + 6.5 + 16.8 + 2.8)}$$

$$\# \text{of Users} = \qquad\qquad 76$$

Figure 9-4. Single server scaling

Multiple Server Example

Offloading the Citrix Conference Manager UI and applications to other Presentation Servers reduces overall memory utilization. The example in Figure 9-5 load balances the Citrix Conference Manager UI and meeting applications to other MetaFrame servers. This reduces the memory for each attendee by 17MB and the organizer by 21MB.

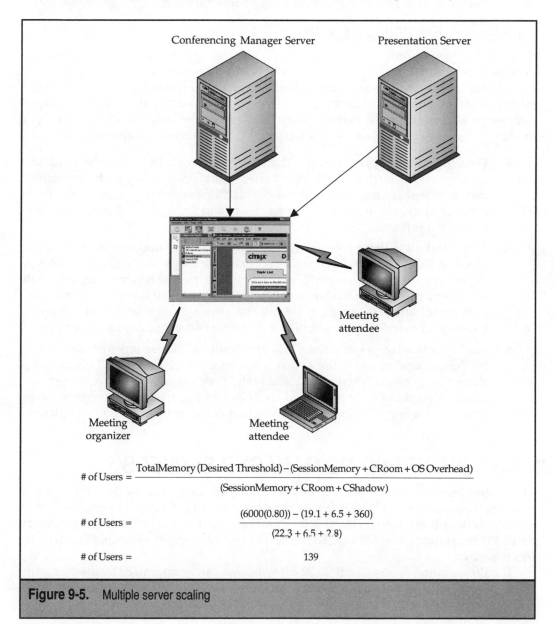

$$\text{\# of Users} = \frac{\text{TotalMemory (Desired Threshold)} - (\text{SessionMemory} + \text{CRoom} + \text{OS Overhead})}{(\text{SessionMemory} + \text{CRoom} + \text{CShadow})}$$

$$\text{\# of Users} = \frac{(6000(0.80)) - (19.1 + 6.5 + 360)}{(22.3 + 6.5 + 2.8)}$$

$$\text{\# of Users} = 139$$

Figure 9-5. Multiple server scaling

In the multiserver example, we hit a limit of 176 users. This formula is accurate up to a certain number of users when based on memory alone. Other considerations, such as OS limitations and latency, prevent scaling this high. Testing in Citrix *e*Labs show that a server of this size can adequately support between 90 and 100 users in a multiserver setup. This also depends on the type of applications in use. This is why it is important to size your servers according to your environment before placing them into production.

User Experience Within a Meeting

When sizing your Conferencing Manager servers, using the memory formula is not enough to determine an accurate value for how many users a server can support. The types of applications in a meeting must also be taken into account. Different applications exhibit different amounts of latency, depending on how much of the screen is changed with every action. *Latency* is defined in this scenario as the time for all attendees in a meeting to receive screen changes. The following lists three types of applications:

▼ **Documents and Spreadsheets**   These types of application, by design, update small portions of the screen. When users collaborate using such application, they notice small amounts of latency, which is sometimes unnoticeable. These types of meeting can support the most users and the upper end of the memory-formula spectrum.

■ **Presentations**   These types of application, by design, update the entire screen when slides are changed. When users collaborate they notice a degree of latency, depending on the actions performed. Changing the text has little impact, while adding pictures and transitions is more intensive. These types of meeting support the middle of the memory-formula spectrum. Typical latency on a meeting viewing a PowerPoint presentation with 60 users is about 2 seconds per slide.

▲ **Highly intensive graphic and CAD applications**   These types of application, by design, update the entire screen when changes occur and include complex shapes and colors. When users collaborate, they notice a degree of latency, depending on the actions performed. such as moving and resizing objects. These types of meeting will support the lower end of the memory formula spectrum.

TUNING CONFERENCING MANAGER SERVERS

The largest increase in performance is seen when the Conferencing Manager UI and available applications are load balanced across the servers in your Presentation Server farm. This distributes the workload across multiple servers, thus reducing the memory and CPU consumption on the Conference server and allowing more users to participate in a meeting.

The Presentation Server Client for 32-bit Windows can be optimized by disabling any unneeded virtual channels when creating or joining a meeting. An example would be if audio and printing are not needed in a conference, the administrator would disable these virtual channels for users connecting to that particular server. These virtual channels would not be initialized during logon, saving some memory and CPU resources.

On the conference server, for maximum-user capacity, all unneeded Windows services should be disabled. Examples would be IIS, Alerter, or the Spooler service, if printing is not needed. It is important that any unnecessary processes that exist in every session are disabled. For example, if Microsoft Office is published on the server, processes such as Find Fast, Help Assistant, and the automatic spelling checker should be disabled for each user.

Users Are Members of 200 or More Active Directory Groups

When a user attempts to start a conference, the user cannot see all their published applications or the following error message may appear:

"An error occurred while processing your request. You do not currently have access to any published applications. If you continue to receive this message, contact your MetaFrame Administrator."

A possible cause for this issue is if the user is a member of 200 or more Active Directory Groups.

To enable users to see their published applications, create the following values in the registry:

```
HKEY_LOCAL_MACHINE\SOFTWARE\Citrix\XML Service
Name: MaxRequestSize
Type: DWORD
Data: 0032000

HKEY_LOCAL_MACHINE\SYSTEM\CurrentControlSet\Services\CtxHttp
Name: MaximumIncoming
Type: DWORD
Data: 0032000
```

You can increase the data value to a larger number if the user is a member of more than 200 groups. If the user is a member of more than 200 Active Directory groups, increase the data value by intervals of 4000 until the error message disappears.

UNINSTALLING CONFERENCING MANAGER

The following section addresses considerations and various methods of uninstalling Conferencing Manager.

NOTE Uninstall Conferencing Manager before uninstalling Citrix Presentation Server.

For an Unattended Uninstall

For an unattended uninstall of Conferencing Manager, run the following from a command line:

```
msiexec /x /q CMCM.msi CTX_ADDLOCAL=CMCM,CR,CO,ECS"
```

Where CMCM.msi is the path and name of the Windows Installer package used to install Conferencing Manager.

To Uninstall Using Active Directory Services

An Active Directory Services uninstall is straightforward: check the box for Uninstall the package when the computer is removed out of the scope of the group policy.

To Uninstall Using Installation Manager

Nothing additional needs to be specified; just select Uninstall the package.

TROUBLESHOOTING CONFERENCE MANAGER

This section illustrates some common issues surrounding troubleshooting Conference Manager. Topics discussed include deleted/renamed or missing Citrix Conference Room published application, failures to start the conference room, and issues with the Outlook add-in.

How to Repair the Citrix Conference Room Component If the Published Application "Citrix Conference Room" Is Deleted or Renamed

During the installation of the Citrix Conference Room, a published application is automatically created with the name Citrix Conference Room. This published application is hidden from the browse list of published applications, but it is necessary for the Citrix Conferencing Manager to work properly. If the published application Citrix Conference Room is renamed or deleted for any reason, the Conferencing Manager will no longer work. If the published application is deleted or renamed and someone attempts to create a conference, they may receive the following error message: "An error occurred while processing your request. Try again. If you continue to receive this message, contact your MetaFrame XP Administrator." You may also see the following event in the server's application event log:

```
Event Type: Error
Event Source: Citrix MetaFrame Conferencing Manager
Event Category: None
```

```
Event ID: 1541
Date: 5/5/2003
Time: 2:29:42 PM
User: N/A
Computer: CTXMF3SRV
Description:
The Citrix XML Service returned error code unspecified.
```

To resolve this issue, perform a repair installation of the Citrix Conferencing Manager. The repair can be accomplished through the following steps:

1. Navigate to Start | Settings | Control Panel | Add/Remove Programs.

2. Highlight the program Citrix MetaFrame Conferencing Manager and select Change.

3. On the screen titled Citrix MetaFrame Conferencing Manager Setup—Application Maintenance, select the radio button next to Repair, and then select Next.

4. On the next screen, MetaFrame XP Administrator Credentials, select either Use my current credentials if the current user is a Citrix Administrator or Use my MetaFrame XP administrator credentials, if it is necessary to specify another Citrix Administrator's credentials.

5. Enter the appropriate credentials, and then select Next.

6. Once you are certain all options have been correctly configured, select Next on the Ready to Repair the Application screen.

7. When the repair installation has completed, select Finish.

Error: "Citrix Conference Room" Failed to Start

When initiating a meeting you may receive the following error message: "Citrix Conference Room failed to start. The Citrix server is unable to process your request to start this published application at this time. Please try again later. If the problem persists, contact your administrator." This error can occur if the initial published application specified for the meeting and the Conference Room is published on a separate server. To avoid this message, you can increase the amount of time Conference Room waits before starting the specified initial published application by creating the following registry value:

```
HKEY_LOCAL_MACHINE\ Software\ Citrix\ CMCM
Value: ConferenceDelay (REG_DWORD) :< number in milliseconds>
```

Initially, configure the delay time to be 5000 (5 seconds). Increase or decrease this value to avoid the error message and minimize the delay. Adding or modifying this registry value does not require a reboot.

Error When Running InstallAddIn.cmd to Install the Outlook Add-In DLL

When using InstallAddIn.cmd to manually install CMCMOL.dll on a client machine, you may see the following messages during the execution of the file:

```
C:\>xcopy /y /f CMCMOL.dll "C:\Program Files\Citrix\CMCM\Outlook"
File not found - CMCMOL.dll
0 File(s) copied

C:\>xcopy /y /f Resources*.txt "C:\Program Files\Citrix\CMCM\Outlook"
File not found - Resources*.txt
0 File(s) copied
```

After executing the file and launching Outlook, you may also notice that you do not see the MetaFrame Conference button on the Outlook Menu bar. It may be necessary at the command prompt to change directory locations to the directory that contains InstallAddIn.cmd and its supporting files before running the file. By default, these files are located in the Outlook folder on the Citrix Conferencing Manager CD-ROM.

CHAPTER 10

Security Issues and Guidelines

This chapter covers various security concerns in a Citrix Access Suite environment. The following guidelines help secure the Access Suite from both server and client perspectives.

SECURING CITRIX PRESENTATION SERVERS

The following section discusses security precautions to consider on all Citrix Access Suite servers.

Control Physical Access

Restrict physical access to servers to those individuals who are involved with administering the server environment.

Use NT File System (NTFS) Partitions

For maximum security, install Presentation Server only on NTFS-formatted disk partitions. Installing on NTFS partitions ensures that the local Access databases are secured, because the folder %Program Files%\Citrix\Independent Management Architecture is marked so only SYSTEM and the local Administrators group have Full Control. Do not change these access control lists (ACLs).

Control Connection Access

For increased control of access to the Terminal Server listeners, use the Citrix Connection Configuration utility (Mfcfg.exe) to remove the "Everyone" group from the Permissions list of each of the listeners and specify only the user groups that require access.

NOTE On Windows Server 2003, it is no longer necessary to remove the "Everyone" group from the Permissions lists of the listeners.

Configuring the Simple Network Management Protocol (SNMP) Service

If you use Network Manager for Citrix Presentation Server or other Simple Network Management Protocol (SNMP) management software for monitoring the server only (not remote management), Citrix recommends the privileges be read-only. If no SNMP consoles are used, remove the SNMP service from the server.

NOTE You must give Read Create permissions to the SNMP service for administrative tasks, such as Logoff and Disconnect through Network Manager.

You can configure the SNMP community and designated management consoles to prevent unauthorized access. Configure SNMP agents to accept traps from known SNMP consoles only. For more information about correctly configuring the SNMP agent, see the Windows Online Help file.

Microsoft has released security bulletins for SNMP security risks on Windows 2000 servers that do not have Service Pack 2 or higher installed (MS00-096, MS02-006).

TIP   Block incoming SNMP traffic from the Internet by using a firewall that prevents passage of traffic on UDP ports 161 and 162.

Configuring Presentation Server Administrator Accounts

Limit Presentation Administrator accounts to users who are members of the Windows network Administrators group. This group is presumed to be well-controlled and its users to have administrative access to network resources, including print servers.

To lessen the risk of compromising the domain administrator account, use a global group of limited user accounts to administer Presentation Servers.

To configure administrator accounts using a global group:

1. In the domain where you manage user accounts, create a domain global group named CPSAdmins.

2. Add the user accounts of people who need Presentation Server Administrator privileges to the CPSAdmins global group.

3. Add the CPSAdmins global group to each Presentation Server's local Administrators group.

4. In the Presentation Server Console, add the CPSAdmins global group to the list of MetaFrame Administrators.

5. When a new user account requires Presentation Administrator privileges, add the account to the CPSAdmins global group.

When setting up CPSAdmins in an Active Directory domain, use a domain local group for farms within a single Active Directory domain or a universal group for farms that span a forest.

SECURITY CONSIDERATIONS FOR THE DATA STORE

This section outlines Citrix recommendations, which vary, for security on the data store, depending on the database used for the data store.

In general, users who access Presentation Servers do not require, and should not be granted, any access to the data store.

With direct mode access, all farm servers share a single user account and password for accessing the data store. Select a password that is not easily guessed. Keep the user name and password secure, and give it to Presentation Server Administrators for installation only.

If the user account for direct mode access to the database is changed at a later time, the IMA service will fail to start on all Presentation Servers configured with that account. To reconfigure the IMA service password, use the dsmaint config command on each affected server. For information about the dsmaint config command, please see the *MetaFrame Presentation Server Administrator's Guide*.

The following discusses additional recommendations for each data store platform.

Microsoft Access

For an Access data store, the default user name is "citrix" and the password is "citrix." If users have access to the data store server, change the password using dsmaint config and keep the information in a safe place.

 IMPORTANT Ensure you create a backup of your data store before using dsmaint config to change the password on your data store.

Microsoft SQL Desktop Edition, Service Pack 3 (MSDE)

Windows NT authentication is supported for the MSDE database. For security reasons, Microsoft SQL Server authentication is not supported. For further information, please consult Microsoft documentation. The user name and password are typically the local System Administrator (SA) account. If users have access to the data store server, change the password using **dsmaint config** and keep the information in a safe place.

Microsoft SQL Server

The user account used to access the data store on Microsoft SQL Server has public and db_owner roles on the server and database. SA account credentials are not needed for data store access. Do not use an SAr account because of the inherent security risk.

If the Microsoft SQL Server is configured for mixed mode security (you can use either Microsoft SQL Server authentication or Windows NT authentication), it is useful to create a Microsoft SQL Server user for the sole purpose of accessing the data store. Because the Microsoft SQL Server user account would access the data store only, no risk occurs of compromising a Windows domain if the user's password is compromised.

For tighter security, after the initial installation of the database with db_owner permission, you can change the user account's permission to db_reader and db_writer.

 IMPORTANT Changing the user account's permission from db_owner might cause installation problems with future service packs or feature releases. Always change the account permission back to db_owner before installing a service pack or feature release.

Oracle

If the data store is hosted on Oracle, give the Oracle user account used for the Presentation Server farm only "connect" and "resource" permissions. SA (system or sys) account permissions are not needed for data store access.

IBM DB2

If the data store is hosted on IBM DB2, give the DB2 user account used for the Presentation Server farm the following permissions:

▼ connect database

■ create tables

■ register functions to execute to database manager's process

▲ create schemas implicity

SA (DB2Admin) account permissions are not needed for data store access.

SECURING YOUR NETWORK AGAINST DENIAL OF SERVICE (DoS) ATTACKS

Denial of service (DoS) attacks saturate networks and servers with useless calls for information. Attackers use multiple sites to make distributed attacks on one or more networks, servers, or web sites. Servers subjected to this sort of jamming either crash or become too busy to be of use when a network becomes flooded. Not only is it compromised for communication, but it also becomes unavailable as a tool for tracing the attacks.

CAUTION Always observe precautions to protect the security and integrity of the registry on Presentation Servers. For information about backing up the registry and other precautions, refer to Microsoft documentation. Editing registry settings, other than those discussed in this document, can corrupt your server configuration and is not supported by Citrix.

Microsoft makes recommendations for taking steps and fixing registry settings to make your networks and servers less prone to network DoS attacks. These are found on the Microsoft web site. Perform a keyword search using "Security Considerations for Network Attacks" to see this information. This page suggests changes to the following registry settings to help secure your network against DoS attacks:

▼ SynAttackProtect

■ TcpMaxHalfOpen

■ TcpMaxHalfRetried

- Enable PMTUDiscovery
- NoNameReleaseOnDemand
- EnableDeadGWDetect
- KeepAliveTime
- PerformRouterDiscovery
- ▲ EnableICMPRedirects

SECURING THE PRESENTATION SERVER CONSOLE

The *Presentation Server Console* is a Java application that can be run on Presentation Servers, as well as on other servers and workstations. To prevent packet capturing, however, execute the Presentation Server Console only on Presentation Servers or in environments where packet sniffing cannot occur.

To run the Management Console on a remote server:

1. Make a secure ICA Client connection to a Presentation Server.
2. Launch the Presentation Server Console in the ICA session.
3. In the Log On To Citrix Farm dialog box, select the server on which the ICA session is running.

Ensure that only Citrix administrators have access to the Presentation Server Console. You can set NTFS permissions, so nonadministrators do not have Execute permission for the Presentation Server Console executable (**Ctxload.exe**).

SECURE CLIENT COMMUNICATION

Depending on the Presentation Server environment, several features included with Presentation Server allow further secure communications between clients and Presentation Servers.

Presentation Server includes support for ICA encryption, which uses RSA's RC5 encryption, between Presentation Servers and clients. Support for open standards technology was added with the release of MetaFrame XP, Feature Release 1. Feature Release 1 added Citrix SSL Relay, which uses standard Secure Sockets Layer (SSL) encryption between MetaFrame XP servers and clients.

MetaFrame XPe and later versions of Presentation Server include the Secure Gateway. Secure Gateway provides an SSL/TLS Internet gateway between Presentation Servers and clients located on the Internet.

For more information about setting encryption, see the *Secure Gateway for Windows Administrator's Guide,* the *MetaFrame Presentation Server Administrator's Guide,* and the *Administrator's Guides* for the Presentation Server Client.

SMART CARD DEPLOYMENT

Smart card logon is a strong form of authentication because it uses cryptographically based identification and proof-of-possession when authenticating a user to a domain. Malicious users who obtain someone's password can use the password to assume that person's identity on the network. Many users choose passwords they can remember easily, which make passwords inherently weak and open to dictionary attack.

In the case of smart cards, that same malicious person would have to obtain the user's smart card and personal identification number (PIN) to impersonate the user. This combination is obviously more difficult to attack because an additional layer of information is needed to impersonate a user. A further benefit is this: smart cards lock after a PIN is entered incorrectly a small number of times in a row (for example, three times). This makes a dictionary attack against a smart card extremely difficult.

Enabling Smart Card Support

The following is a list of the minimum requirements to support smart card use:

▼   PC/SC software

■   Cryptographic Service Provider (CSP) software

▲   Smart card reader software drivers

Installing a Smart Card Reader

Smart card readers generally come with instructions on how to connect any necessary cables and software. The following steps can assist you in this process, but the process may differ, depending on the type of card reader and vendor. Additional information is available by referencing the following Microsoft support article: http://www.microsoft .com/technet/prodtechnol/windows2000serv/howto/smrtcard.mspx#EDAA.

To connect a smart card reader:

1.   Shut down and turn off your computer.

2.   Attach the reader to an available serial port or universal serial bus (USB) port.

NOTE   Some vendors require a USB reader be inserted during the Smart Card Reader Device Driver installation. Reference the reader's documentation to determine the correct method.

If your serial reader has a supplementary PS/2 cable/connector, attach your keyboard or mouse connector to it, and plug it into your computer's keyboard or mouse port. Many new smart card readers take power from the keyboard or mouse ports because it is not always provided by RS-232 ports and it is both expensive and cumbersome to require a separate power supply.

3.   Boot your machine and log on as a user with administrative privileges.

Installing a Smart Card Reader Device Driver   If the smart card reader has been detected and installed, the Welcome to Windows logon screen will acknowledge this. If not, then your smart card reader is not a plug and play device. If your smart card reader is not a plug and play device, media that contains the appropriate device driver from the vendor of the smart card reader is required.

Configuring a Certificate Authority (CA)

A certificate authority (CA) is a service that issues the certificates needed to run a public key infrastructure. The CA could be an external commercial CA or it could be a CA run by your company. The certificates enable a user to log on using a smart card, send encrypted e-mail, code-sign documents, and more. Because a CA is an important trust point in an organization, most organizations have their own CA.

Microsoft Windows 2000 provides two types of CAs: an enterprise CA or a stand-alone CA. Which CA type is used is determined by which policy modules are selected during installation. Within these classes are two types of CAs: a *root* or a *subordinate*. Typically, you should install an *enterprise CA* if you are issuing certificates to users or computers inside an organization that is part of a Windows 2000 domain. You should install a *stand-alone CA* if you are issuing certificates to users or computers outside a Windows 2000 domain. An enterprise CA requires all users requesting certificates have an entry in the Windows 2000 Server Active Directory services, whereas a stand-alone CA does not. Also, an enterprise CA can issue certificates used to log on to a Windows 2000-based domain, and a stand-alone CA cannot. Additional information is available by referencing Microsoft knowledgebase support article 231881 (http://support.microsoft .com/default.aspx?scid=kb;EN-US;231881).

NOTE   The configuration steps may vary slightly between Windows 2000 and Windows 2003.

To configure a Certificate Authority:

1. Click Start | Settings | Control Panel.

2. Double-click Add/Remove Programs.

3. Click Add/Remove Windows Components to start the Windows Components Wizard.

4. Select the Certificate Services check box and click Next.

5. If you intend to use the web components of the Certificate Services, ensure that the IIS check box is selected.

6. The wizard prompts you to specify the type of CA you want to install. Set up attempts to guess which option is selected to make installation simpler.

▼ If no Active Directory is detected, the two enterprise options are disabled.

■ If an Active Directory is detected, the "Enterprise root CA" option is selected if no CAs are already registered in the Active Directory.

▲ If CAs are registered in the Active Directory, the "Enterprise subordinate CA" option is selected.

7. If you are issuing certificates to entities in your organization or if you need to have seamless integration with the Active Directory or to enable smart card log-on, select an Enterprise CA. Select one of the following:

   ▼ **Enterprise root CA**   This is if you do not have any CAs in your directory or if you need a second enterprise root CA. The root CA is registered in the directory, and all computers in your enterprise using that directory automatically trust the root CA. A good security practice is to limit the root CA to issuing certificates to subordinate CAs only or to issuing only a few special purpose certificates. This means you want to install an enterprise subordinate after you finish installing the root. However, you can choose only the root CA.

   ▲ **Enterprise subordinate CA**   This is if you have already installed an enterprise root CA. Typically, you will have multiple enterprise-subordinate CAs. Each of these CAs either serves different communities of users or provides different types of certificates. If more than one subordinate exists, it is possible to revoke the subordinate's certificate in case of a disaster and not have to reissue all certificates in the organization.

8. If you are issuing certificates to entities outside your enterprise, and you do not want to use Active Directory or other Windows 2000 public key infrastructure (PKI) features, then you want a stand-alone CA. Select one of the following:

   ▼ **Stand-alone CA**   This is if you do not already have a stand-alone CA or if you need a second root for a purpose different than the first.

   ▲ **Stand-alone subordinate CA**   This is if this CA is a member of an existing CA hierarchy. The parent CA in the hierarchy can be a stand-alone CA, an enterprise CA, or an external commercial CA.

9. If you need to change the default cryptographic settings, select the Advanced Options check box. (Select Advanced Options only if you know how to change cryptographic settings.) Click Next.

10. If you selected Advanced Options, the wizard prompts you to specify the cryptographic service provider to use. (If you did not select Advanced Options, proceed to step 11.)

11. In this dialog box, you can change the cryptographic settings, such as the CSP, hash algorithm, and other advanced options. In general, you do not need to modify the default settings. Users who need to modify these settings must be familiar with cryptography, Certificate Server, and the CAPI 2.0 architecture.

12. The list of CSPs varies, depending on the software and hardware installed on the server. The key length specifies the length of the public and private key pair. A value of Default in this box generates a key pair whose default length is determined by the selected provider. Microsoft recommends you use a long key length, such as 1024 or 2048, for a root CA or an enterprise CA. (Note: a long key length is computationally more expensive and may not be accepted by all hardware devices. For example, some smart cards may not accept certificates issued by a CA that has a 4096 bit key, due to space limitations on the card.)

13. The "Use existing keys" option enables you to use keys generated previously or to reuse keys from a previously installed CA. When installing a CA, you should almost never reuse keys. The exception to this is when you are restoring a CA after a catastrophic failure. Then, you import a set of existing keys and install a new CA that uses those keys. In addition, if you are restoring a CA after a failure, you must select the "Use the associated certificate" check box. This ensures the new CA has a certificate identical to the old CA. If you do not check this box, a new certificate is generated that makes the new CA different from the old CA.

NOTE   The private key is always stored locally on the server, except in the case where a cryptographic hardware device is used. In such a case, the private key is stored in the device. The public key is placed in the certificate and, in the case of an enterprise CA, the certificate is published in Active Directory.

14. The wizard prompts you to supply identifying information appropriate for your site and organization.

15. Note, the CA name (or common name) is critical because it is used to identify the CA object created in the Directory. The Valid For time can only be set for a root CA. Set the root CA Valid For time to a reasonable value: the actual duration is a tradeoff between security and administrative overhead. Remember, each time a root certificate expires, an administrator has to update all trust relationships and administrative steps need to be taken to move the CA to a new certificate. A time period of two or more years is usually sufficient. When you finish entering the information, click Next.

16. A dialog box defines the locations of the certificate database, configuration information, and the location where the certificate revocation list (CRL) is stored. The Enterprise CA always stores its information, including the CRL, in the directory. The recommendation is that you select the Shared Folder check box. This option specifies the location of a folder where configuration information for the CA will be stored. You should make this folder a UNC path and have all your CAs point to the same folder. Then, the administration tools can use this folder for determining CA configuration if the Active Directory is unavailable. If you have an Active Directory, this folder is optional. If you do not have an Active Directory, this folder is required.

If you are installing a CA in the same location as a previously installed CA, the "Preserve existing certificate database" option is enabled. Check this option if you want your new CA to use this database. Otherwise, the database will be deleted.

When you have specified the storage locations for your information, click Next.

17. If IIS is running, a message prompts you to stop the service. Click OK to stop IIS. You must stop IIS to install the web components. If you do not have IIS installed, you will not see this message.

18. If you are installing a subordinate CA, the wizard next prompts you for information about how you will request the certificate.

19. Click Browse to locate an online CA, or select "Save the request to a file" if you will be making a request destined for a commercial CA or a CA that is inaccessible from the network. (If you create a file, you must take the file to a CA for processing. The CA provides you with a certificate, which you install using the MMC snap-in.) Click Next.

20. If you saved a certificate request to a file, a dialog box called Microsoft Certificate Services displays. Click OK to finish the installation, and then click Finish to close the wizard.

Smart Card Certificate Enrollment

A domain user cannot enroll for a smart card logon (authentication) or smart card user (authentication plus e-mail) certificate unless an SA has granted the user access rights to the Certificate Template stored in Active Directory. This is done because enrollment for a smart card certificate must be a controlled procedure in the same manner that employee badges are controlled for identification and physical access purposes. The recommended method for enrolling users for smart card-based certificates and keys is through the enroll-on-behalf-of station that is integrated with Certificate Services.

When an Enterprise CA is installed, the installation includes the enroll-on-behalf-of station. This station lets an administrator act on behalf of a specific user to request and install a smart card logon or smart card user certificate onto the user's smart card. The enrollment station does not provide any card-personalization functions, such as creating a file structure or setting of the personal identification number (PIN), because those are card-specific functions and can only be performed using specialized software provided by the smart card manufacturer. Additional information is available by referencing Microsoft knowledgebase support article 257480 (http://support.microsoft.com/default .aspx?scid=kb;en-us;257480).

For an administrator to enroll for a smart card logon or smart card user certificate on behalf of a specific user:

1. Launch Microsoft Internet Explorer.

2. To connect to a CA, type **http://machine-name/certsrv** into the **Address** field of Microsoft Internet Explorer (IE) (where machine-name is replaced with the name of the computer running the issuing Certification Authority).

3. The Microsoft Certificate Services Welcome page appears. Copy the URL address of this page, and then click Tools | Internet Options. Select the Security tab, click Trusted Sites, and then click the Sites button. The Trusted Sites window will display - paste the URL in the "Add this web site to the zone:" section and uncheck the check box at the bottom "Requires server verification (HTTPS) for all sites in this zone." Once you have done this, click OK to close the Trusted Sites window, and then click OK again to close the Internet Options windows.

NOTE If this step is not taken, you will receive an error message saying the browser was unable to load an ActiveX control.

4. Select "Request a certificate," and then click Next.

5. The Choose Request Type page appears. Select "Advanced request," and then click Next.

6. The Advanced Certificate Requests page appears. Select "Request a certificate for a smart card on behalf of another user" using the Smart Card Enrollment Station, and click Next.

7. The first time you use the Smart Card Enrollment Station, a digitally signed Microsoft ActiveX control is downloaded from the CA server to the enrollment station computer. To use the enrollment station, select Yes in the Security Warning dialog box to install the control.

8. The Smart Card Enrollment Station page appears. On this page, you must complete the following before submitting a certificate request on behalf of another user:

   ▼ Select either the Smart Card Logon or Smart Card User Certificate Template.

   ■ Select a Certification Authority.

   ■ Select a Cryptographic Service Provider.

   ■ Select an Administrator Signing Certificate.

   ■ Select the User To Enroll.

   ▲ Complete the first three items by selecting each item from the drop-down list boxes on the Smart Card Enrollment Station page.

9. After selecting the Certificate Template, Certification Authority, and Cryptographic Service Provider select the Administrator Signing Certificate by clicking Select Certificate. A dialog box appears showing a list of certificates that can be used. Choose only one certificate from the list (if more than one certificate is displayed), and then click OK. Optionally, you can view the certificate by clicking View Certificate. Clicking Cancel results in no certificate being selected.

10. Select the user who is being enrolled for the certificate. Click Select User. Click OK to complete.

11. You are now ready to submit the certificate request. Click Enroll.

12. If the target smart card is not already in the smart card reader, a dialog box appears, prompting you to insert the requested smart card. Once the card is inserted into the smart card reader, click the Retry button.

13. As part of the certificate enrollment procedure, the request must be digitally signed by the private key that corresponds to the public key included in the certificate request. Because the private key is stored on the smart card, the digital signature requires the signer of the request to authenticate the card to ensure the signer is the owner of the smart card (and, by extension, of the private key). Type in the PIN for the card, and then click OK.

Also, the user can change his or her PIN by clicking Change. This opens a new dialog box, where the user can input a new alphanumeric PIN. Changing the PIN requires that the user provide the old PIN first to prove ownership of the card. If the CA successfully processes the certificate request, the Smart Card Enrollment Station page informs you the enrollment is complete and the smart card is ready. You can either view the certificate by clicking View Certificate or specify a new user by clicking New User.

Smart Card Removal Options

You can enable two options for smart card removal. The first option locks the computer when a smart card is removed. The second option logs you off the workstation when you remove a smart card. Additional information is available by referencing Microsoft knowledgebase support article 227873 (http://support.microsoft.com/default .aspx?scid=kb;en-us;227873).

To enable either of these options, set the data value of the ScRemoveOption value in the following registry key:

```
HKEY_LOCAL_MACHINE\SOFTWARE\Microsoft\Windows NT\CurrentVersion\Winlogon
Value: ScRemoveOption (REG_SZ)

Setting:

0 - No action
1 - Lock workstation
2 - Force logoff
```

Miscellaneous

▼ Default readers and cards supported by Microsoft are listed in the registry under: HKEY_LOCAL_MACHINE\software\Microsoft\Cryptography\Calais

■ Windows 2000, Windows XP, and Windows Server 2003 have native support for some smart card readers. To check if the reader is supported by default, attach the reader to the client, and let the OS detect and install the drivers. After a restart of the system, if there is not an option to log on using the Smart Card, the vendor's software drivers need to be installed. Also Windows 2000 Server, Windows XP, and Windows 2003 Server have default CSPs installed for many Schlumberger and GemPlus smart cards.

■ The default PIN for Gemplus GemSAFE (identified by the oval shape of its metal contact) is **1234**.

■ The default PIN for Schlumberger Cryptoflex (identified by the square shape of its metal contact) is **00000000**.

■ If a Domain Controller is unavailable, smart card logon fails, even if the user has previously logged on to the computer using a smart card. If the Domain Controller is available, but does not have a valid CRL for the issuing CA, then the logon fails. The error message in each of the previous cases is the same: *The system could not log you on. Your credentials could not be verified.*

▲ Insert the smart card into the smart card reader and enter your PIN. Unlock works the same way as a smart card logon.

AGENT SECURITY FOR CITRIX PASSWORD MANAGER

This section focuses on security concerns for the Citrix Password Manager Agent, otherwise known as the *client side installation*.

MMF File

The *Username.MMF file* is a binary file that stores the following Agent information:

▼ Agent settings

■ Application Credentials

■ Application Credentials that have been deleted from Logon Manager

■ Excluded web sites

▲ Transmit information

The MMF file can be found at the following location within the Window's user profile:

▼ **Windows 2000, Windows 2003, and Windows XP**

Documents and Settings\%Username%\Application Data\Citrix\MetaFrame Password Manager

■ **Windows 2000 and Windows XP—Hot Desktop**

Documents and Settings\All Users\Application Data\Citrix\MetaFrame Password Manager\%Username%

▲ **Windows NT 4**

\%SystemRoot%\Profiles\%Username%\ApplicationData\Citrix\MetaFrame Password Manager

The permissions for the MMF file are

▼ Administrators—Full Control

■ System Account—Full Control

▲ The user—Full Control

The Agent updates the synchronization point with the information stored in the MMF file, and vice versa, if Admin/Application overrides are pushed from the Console to the synchronization point. If the MMF file is deleted from the user's Windows profile, the Agent utilizes the user data cached at the synchronization point to re-create the file. The latest information is always available at the synchronization point because the file cannot be deleted while the Agent is running and the Agent synchronizes during shutdown.

However, the previous scenario will not be true if the Agent is unable to synchronize for prolonged periods of time, for example, the Agent is off the network or synchronization cannot be established. For this reason, the recommendation is that a user make frequent backups of the file to avoid loss of data. If the user's system were to have a drive failure, the credentials that were added while offline cannot be recovered. Any attempts to manually re-create the file result in the Agent not storing new credentials and behaving erratically.

Method of Encryption

The Agent uses Triple-DES (Data Encryption Standard) for encryption and the end result can be verified in the following location:

```
HKEY_CURRENT_USER\Software\Citrix\MetaFrame Password Manager\Shell\CSP
The value should be 6464 (Hex) or 25700 (Decimal)
```

Delete User's Data Folder and Registry Keys When the Agent Is Shut Down (Previously Delete on Shutdown) as a Security Mechanism

Delete user's data folder and registry keys when the agent is shut down (previously DeleteOn-Shutdown) can be used by an administrator to make the Agent more secure. When enabled, *Delete user's data folder and registry keys when the agent is shut down* removes specific files and registry keys from a user's profile and from HKEY_CURRENT_USER.

Enabling *Delete user's data folder and registry keys when the agent is shut down* should be considered when a high number of users use the same computer or when physical security concerns exist.

Location of Files

The following illustrates the various paths and registry keys, based on the client operating system, that will have content removed when using *Delete user's data folder and registry keys when the agent is shut down.*

▼ **Windows 2000, Windows XP Pro, and Windows 2003**

Documents and Settings\%Username%\Application Data\Citrix\MetaFrame Password Manager

■ **Windows 2000 and Windows XP Pro—Hot Desktop**

Documents and Settings\All Users\Application Data\Citrix\MetaFrame Password Manager\%Username%

▲ **Windows NT 4.0**

%SystemRoot%\Profiles\%Username%\Application Data\Citrix\MetaFrame Password Manager

Files removed by the Agent during shutdown from the user's profile:

▼ **AEList.ini**   Consists of merged applist.ini and entlist.ini files. Agents use aelist .ini to identify and respond to credential and password change requests initiated by applications.

■ **ENTList.ini**   Contains the application definitions for Windows, Web, and Host applications.

■ **Username.MMF**   The local storage file used by the Agent.

■ **Lock Folder**   The folder contains a lock file that tracks changes done to the MMF file.

■ **FTUList.ini**   This file contains the Administrator-created questions and Bulk-Add information.

▲ **Registry.MMF**   This file contains the registry information normally found at HKEY_CURRENT_USER\Software\Citrix\MetaFrame Password Manager. This file is only present on a Hot Desktop-enabled workstation.

Registry keys removed by the Agent during shutdown from HKEY_CURRENT_USER: HKEY_CURRENT_USER\Software\Citrix\MetaFrame Password Manager

NOTE   This is not the case when working with a Hot Desktop-enabled workstation.

Using Console Settings to Secure the Agent

Additional settings can be used to secure the Agent against a walk-away scenario or when using sensitive applications.

▼   *Force User To Re-Authenticate before Submitting Application Credentials* is an application specific setting that instructs the Agent to verify the user. When enabled, the user is required to re-authenticate with the Agent prior to the Agent submitting credentials to an application. This setting can be used to prevent a third party from using an authenticated Agent's configured credentials. This setting could be used if users have access to confidential applications, such as payroll.

▲   *Time Between Agent Re-Authentication Requests* determines how long the user remains authenticated with the Agent. By default, the timer is set to eight hours, however, it can be set to a shorter length of time. Doing so forces the user to re-authenticate frequently and makes it more difficult for a third party to access stored credentials. This setting can be found under the Basic Agent Interaction section of the User Configuration.

The Windows Screensaver functionality is monitored by the Agent and is used to trigger a lock-down event. Depending on how the screensaver options are set, the Agent will behave differently during the lock-down process.

▼   *Windows Screensaver with Password Protected option enabled.* When the screensaver activates, the workstation is placed in a lock-down mode. Unlocking the workstation also unlocks the Agent because the Agent's GINA monitors the unlocking of the workstation and passes the same credentials to the Agent.

▲   *Windows Screensaver with Password Protected option disabled.* When the screensaver activates, the Agent continues to run, but it does not provide credentials to any applications that might run in the background. Any input from the user disables the screensaver and allows the Agent, once again, to provide credentials without requiring the user to re-authenticate.

CONFIGURING CITRIX PASSWORD MANAGER ADMINISTRATIVE ACCESS WITHOUT BEING A DOMAIN ADMINISTRATOR

This section discusses the process for delegating administration of a Citrix Password Manager central store to a group or user account that is not a domain administrator. By default, Password Manager installation assumes the Password Manager Administrator is also a domain administrator. When that assumption is not true, this information can be used as a guide to set up the necessary permissions for the Password Manager Administrator account to operate as a delegate.

The reader is assumed to have created a Password Manager Administrator account or Password Manager Administrators group that contains the user accounts with administrative permissions. That user or group is granted permissions to configure, maintain, and manage a Password Manager deployment. Because groups allow for easier management, the Password Manager Administrator user or group is collectively referred to as the Password Manager Administrators group throughout the remainder of this section.

Configuring Access to the Central Store

The central store repository is divided into two areas: the synchronization area and the administrative data area. The *synchronization area* is a location the agents contact to obtain agent settings and also store their encrypted credentials. By default, the *synchronization location* is secured so only Password Manager Administrators and the individual user can access the data. The *administrative data area* is a central location where the console stores the administrative configurations used to create the agent settings for the users, including application definitions, password policies, identity verification, and so forth. By default, the administrative data location is secured to allow only Password Manager Administrators access to the folder.

The set of delegation steps depend on where your central store resides. The following describes the configuration and setup for both types of central store hosts (NTFS file share or Microsoft Active Directory).

NTFS File Share

The configuration for access to the Central Store when using a NTFS File Share is detailed here.

Storage Structure   With a file share host, up to three folders are used to store the different areas of the central store repository. These folders are found in the root of the central store share. The synchronization location is kept in a folder called People in the root of the central store share. Under the *People folder*, each user has their own folder with appropriate permissions for reading and writing their credential data. The administrators have permissions to add and remove agent settings from the individual user's folders.

The administrative data are kept in a folder called CentralStoreRoot in the root of the central store share. By default, only administrators have permissions to read and write data within the CentralStoreRoot folder.

The domain hierarchy data are kept in a folder named using the NetBIOS name of the domain. This folder is only present when using NT or Active Directory domains for primary authentication with the file share and contains the user configuration settings when they are assigned to organizational units or individual users. The folder contains subfolders that are named using the Security ID (SID) of the Organizational Unit (OU) or user to which the settings should be applied. By default, only administrators have permissions to read and write data within the domain folder. Users have read permissions for this folder, so they can locate the settings that apply to them.

Depending on the type of file share host, the types of permissions granted will be different.

By default, no permissions are allowed to propagate from root share to the child folders CentralStoreRoot and People. However, permissions assigned at the root folder are allowed to propagate to the domain folder. The *CTXFILESYNCPREP tool* automatically grants Full Control to the local Administrators group for both the CentralStoreRoot and People subfolders, and it removes all permissions for Authenticated Users. No other folders are created by CTXFILESYNCPREP.

The Password Manager agent is responsible for creating all the subfolders inside the People folder and, on creation, sets the permissions of the folder to Modify for the Creator/Owner and enables inheritable permissions to propagate from the parent folder.

All remaining folders in the central store repository are created by the Password Manager Console during use, as necessary. The console creates the CentralStoreRoot/ AdminConsole folder during discovery and, if an NT or AD Domain is used, it creates a folder in the root of the central store share. The console automatically grants the current user Modify permissions for every folder created and leaves the propagation flag for inheritance enabled.

Delegation Setup   Although Local and Domain Administrators are configured by the Citrix prep tools to have write access to the appropriate folders, any additional accounts need to have permissions explicitly granted to them. For the most part, granting the permissions at the appropriate level allows access to the Password Manager Administrator account. To grant permissions, follow these steps:

1. Run CTXFILESYNCPREP to create the root share and the two subfolders People and CentralStoreRoot. If the folders are already created, proceed to the next step.

2. Grant the Password Manager Administrator account Full Control of the root share folder and both the subfolders inside the shared folder (CentralStoreRoot and People).

3. Log in as a Password Manager Administrator and launch the console. This causes all subsequent folders and objects to be created with the appropriate Password Manager Administrator permissions automatically.

4. Verify the appropriate permissions are added to the AdminConsole folder.

Further Delegation   You may want to further delegate or control permissions by individually modifying the permissions on the appropriate folders within the file folder hierarchy. Please be aware that the access permissions do not take effect until the user logs off and logs back on again, and then relaunches the console. In addition, each time the Password Manager Administrator's permissions change, the Password Manager Administrator should rerun discovery to refresh the object cache and display only objects to which the user has access. If the Password Manager Administrator chooses not to run discovery, the access permissions are still enforced, because the Password Manager Console verifies permissions before each read or write from the console.

Active Directory

The configuration for access to the Central Store when using Active Directory is detailed here.

Schema Preparation   The schema preparation tool, CTXSCHEMAPREP.EXE, must still be run by a member of the Schema Administrators group for the target forest. The *CTXSCHEMAPREP.EXE tool* adds several classes and attributes to the forest schema, allowing Password Manager to store user configuration data and encrypted credential information as objects inside Active Directory.

Domain Preparation   The domain preparation tool, *CTXDOMAINPREP.EXE,* must still be run by a member of the Domain Administrators group for the target domain.

When run without specifying a location, CTXDOMAINPREP affects the entire domain. However, if necessary, the tool can be run on a per OU basis. To only prepare an individual OU, provide the relative distinguished name of the OU on the command line following the executable name. For example, to apply the permissions to the Users container, use the following command:

```
CTXDOMAINPREP CN=Users
```

Note the full distinguished name (CN=Users,DC=Example,DC=com) is not used because the tool automatically appends the distinguished name for the domain. If you run this command for more than one OU within the domain, you may receive a message indicating a previous installation was found. This is normal behavior, as the tool expects to create the Central Store location each time it is executed.

Storage Structure   With an Active Directory host for the central store repository, the synchronization and domain hierarchy data are stored in the individual containers for users and organizational units. The administrative data is stored in an application data partition found under the domain root and can be viewed using ADSI Edit (available from www.microsoft.com), by opening the appropriate domain and navigating down the following containers: Program Data, Citrix, MetaFrame Password Manager, CentralStoreRoot.

For Password Manager Administrator access, the administrator needs the appropriate permissions to the following containers:

▼ CN=CentralStoreRoot,CN=MetaFrame Password Manager,CN=Citrix,CN= Program Data

■ OU containers to be managed

▲ User containers to be managed

By default, "Allow inheritable permissions from parent to propagate to this object" is set for all objects in the Program Data, MetaFrame Password Manager, and CentralStoreRoot containers. Therefore, any permissions delegated at the root of the Program Data container flow down to the CentralStoreRoot container.

The CTXDOMAINPREP tool assigns Full Control to the Domain Administrators group and SYSTEM account, as well as restricting Authenticated Users to Read and allowing the SELF account to create and delete Citrix SSO objects. For more information on the exact permissions assigned, see the *Password Manager Administrator's Guide*.

> **NOTE** By design, the Domain Administrator account has "Allow inheritable permissions from parent to propagate to this object" disabled. This setting prevents the domain administrator from using Automatic Key recovery and Self-service Password Reset functionality.

Delegation Setup All administrators accessing the central store need the same set of permissions. In an environment with multiple administrators, the recommended method is to create a Password Manager Administrators group with permissions for the central store. After creating the Password Manager Administrators group, assign the necessary central store permissions by following these steps:

1. Using ADSI Edit, navigate to the Citrix | Program Data | MetaFrame Password Manager | CentralStoreRoot container.

2. Right-click and choose Properties from the Context menu.

3. Select the Security tab.

4. Click Advanced.

5. Click Add and enter the Password Manager Administrators group in the Name field

6. Set the Apply Onto field to "This object and all child objects."

7. Select the Allow check box for each of the following permissions:

   ▼ List Contents
   ■ Read All Properties
   ■ Write All Properties
   ■ Delete
   ■ Delete Subtree
   ■ All Validated Writes
   ■ Create Container Objects
   ▲ Delete Container Objects

8. Click OK to close the Permission Entry dialog box.

9. Click OK to close the Permission Entry dialog box.

10. Click OK to close the Access Control Setting dialog box.

11. Click OK to close the CentralStoreRoot properties dialog box.

12. Add all user accounts that need to administer Password Manager to the Password Manager Administrators group.

Delegated Permissions For each user account that will be a Password Manager Administrator, you must delegate control of the domain, OUs, or user accounts the Password Manager Administrators will manage. Remember, if the user account will manage all user accounts or domain-level settings, they need to have control delegated at the root of the domain. To delegate permissions for a user or group account, follow these steps:

1. Using ADSI Edit, navigate to the OU or domain object for the delegated permissions.

2. Right-click the OU or domain name (for domain-level permissions) and select Properties.

3. Select the Security tab.

4. Click Advanced.

5. Click Add and enter the Password Manager Administrator's account in the Name field that will have administrator permissions for this OU or domain, and then click OK.

6. Set the Apply Onto field to "This object and all child objects."

7. Select the Allow check box for each of the following permissions:
   ▼   Create citrix-SSOConfig Objects
   ■   Delete citrix-SSOConfig Objects
   ■   Create citrix-SSOLicense Class Objects
   ▲   Delete citrix-SSOLicense Class Objects

8. Click OK.

9. Click Add and enter the Password Manager Administrator's account in the Name field that will have administrator permissions for this OU or domain, and then click OK.

10. Set the Apply Onto field to "User objects."

11. Select the Allow check box for Full Control.

12. Click OK.

13. To grant Full Control for the Citrix objects, repeat steps 9 through 12, changing the Apply Onto field from "User objects" to each of the following object types:
   ▼   citrix-SSOConfig objects
   ■   citrix-SSOLicenseClass objects
   ▲   citrix-SSOSecret objects

14. Click OK to close the Access Control Setting dialog box.

15. Click OK to close the OU Properties dialog box.

NOTE The Active Directory Users & Computers MMC Snap-in does not provide access to all the Citrix class objects. The previous steps need to be completed using ADSI Edit. Also, in testing, it was discovered that the Delegate Control Wizard may not properly assign the correct permissions, so using ADSI Edit is recommended.

Further Delegation Further delegation can be accomplished by granting granular access to the individual objects within the central store and the individual OUs, as necessary. When modifying permissions, remember the administrators should run discovery to obtain the latest list of objects in the central store, along with their associated permissions.

Running the Console

Launching the console as the Password Manager Administrator's account for the first time causes all objects to inherit the permissions from the original CentralStoreRoot folder. When running the console with a delegated administrator, remember the current user must have access to all the locations and containers where an object is stored or the update will fail. This means delegated administrators cannot update global objects (such as the Identity Verification Question) unless they have access to all the user accounts and OUs where the global object is used.

CAUTION The Citrix Password Manager console only checks permissions on the CentralStore object before performing the delete. If the administrative user does not have permissions to delete user objects in the OU, the object is left in the OU and removed from the central store.

Using the ADT As a Password Manager Administrator

The console automatically uses the credentials of the logged-in user for access to Active Directory. The same permissions for the full Access Suite Console are also required when accessing the Central Data Store through the ADT. If an application definition is used in deployed Application groups, the Password Manager Administrator needs permissions to write objects to those containers where the application definition is being used.

Configuration of the Password Manager Service

Depending on the modules installed in the Citrix Password Manager Service, you may need to complete different delegation steps. The following discusses each of the modules and the associated changes.

Data Integrity

When using the Citrix Password Manager Service, you need to grant access to the Password Manager Administrators group to authenticate to the service if the optional Data

Integrity Assurance feature is enabled. To grant access for the Password Manager Administrators to sign data settings, complete the following steps:

1. Launch Notepad.

2. Open the httpd.conf file found at %ProgramFiles%\Common Files\Citrix\ XTE\conf.

3. Locate the XML section titled <Files AuthenticatedWS.asmx>.

4. Add another require group statement below the Domain Administrators statement specifying the domain name and the name of the Password Manager Administrators group: require group "*DOMAINNAME* Password Manager Administrators."

5. Save and close the httpd.conf file.

CAUTION The ServiceConfigurationTool.exe automatically replaces the httpd.conf file each time it is used to make changes to the service configuration. Manually complete the previous steps after using the Service Configuration tool to make changes to the Password Manager service.

Automatic Key Recovery

If the deployment includes using the Password Manager Service for Automatic Key Recovery, you need to configure a data proxy account that has access to the central store and all the OUs that contain the Password Manager User accounts. Adding the data proxy account to the Password Manager Administrators group grants access to the central store. You then need to delegate control to the data proxy account at the appropriate domain-level, OU-level, or shared folder resource by completing the steps in the delegation section for appropriate central store type.

In the file share environment, the data proxy account should have the following permissions:

▼ Configure the data proxy account to be a regular Domain User.

▲ Give the user Full Control permissions to the central store as follows:

  ▼ For the CitrixSync$ folder (root), give Full Control for Share permissions to this user.

  ■ For the CitrixSync folder (root), give Full Control for NTFS permissions to this user.

  ■ For the CentralStoreRoot, give Full Control for NTFS permissions to this user.

  ■ For the <Domain Name> folder, this inherits Full Control from the Parent folder, so no changes are needed here.

  ▲ For the People folder, give Full Control for NTFS permissions to this user.

In the Active Directory environment, the data proxy account is granted the appropriate permissions by completing the steps outlined in the previous section "Delegated Permissions" for the data proxy account.

Self-Service Password Reset

If the deployment includes using the Password Manager Service for Self-Service Password Reset, you need to configure a data proxy account that has access to the central store and all the OUs that contain the Password Manager user accounts.

Adding the data proxy account to the Password Manager Administrators group grants access to the central store. You then need to delegate control to the data proxy account at the appropriate domain-level, OU-level, or shared folder resource by completing the steps in the delegation section for appropriate central store type.

In the file share environment, the data proxy account should be a member of the Local Administrator's group on the server hosting the file share. In the Active Directory environment, the data proxy account is granted the appropriate permissions by completing the previously outlined steps in the section "Delegated Permissions" for the data proxy account.

Password Reset Account

For most deployments, the data proxy account have Full Control of user objects and can be used as the Password Reset account. However, if a separate, more restricted account is desired, the following steps may be followed to grant the minimum necessary permissions to the Password Reset Account in Active Directory.

1. Using ADSI Edit, navigate to the OU or domain object for the delegated permissions. (The domain object is recommended for password reset.)

2. Right-click on the OU or domain name (for domain-level permissions) and select Properties.

3. Select the Security tab.

4. Click Advanced.

5. Click Add. Enter the Password Reset account in the Name, and then click OK.

6. Set the Apply Onto field to "User objects."

7. Select the Allow check box for the following permissions:

   ▼ Reset Password

   ■ Read PwdLastSet

   ■ Write PwdLastSet

   ■ Read Lockout Time

   ▲ Write Lockout Time

8. Click OK to close the Permissions dialog box.

9. Click OK to close the Access Control Setting dialog box.

10. Click OK to close the OU Properties dialog box.

Use the ServiceConfigurationTool executable to modify the Password Reset account. Remember, if Data Integrity Assurance is enabled, the httpd.conf file needs to be modified again to add the Password Manager Administrators group. When complete, restart the Citrix XTE Service.

Citrix Password Manager Support for Strong Authentication

Table 10-1 shows the smart cards tested with Citrix Password Manager 4.0 and Citrix Password Manager 4.1.

Vendor	Products	Form Factor	Tested in 4.0	Tested in 4.0 w/ Hot Desktop	Tested in 4.1	Tested in 4.1 w/ Hot Desktop
ActivCard Gold for DOD / CAC - PKI v3.0	Axalto/ Schlumberger Card Readers: *Reflex 72 *Reader Reflex USB	Smartcard	✓			
ActivClient— DOD/CAC PKI v5.0	ActivCard— 64K V1 Readers: *ActivCard Reader V2.0	Smartcard	✓	✓		
ActivCard 5.4	ActivCard— 64K V1 Readers: *ActivCard Reader V2.0	Smartcard			✓	✓
Alladin	eToken	USB-based tokens	✓			
Axalto/ Schlumberger	CyberFlex Version 2 Card Axalto/ Schlumberger Readers: *Reflex 72 Reader *Reflex USB	Smartcard	✓	✓	✓	✓

Table 10-1.   Tested Smart Card Solutions or Password Manager 4.0 and 4.1

Vendor	Products	Form Factor	Tested in 4.0	Tested in 4.0 w/ Hot Desktop	Tested in 4.1	Tested in 4.1 w/ Hot Desktop
Ensure Technologies	XyLoc Enterprise 3.x XyLoc MD 3.x Xyloc XC-2	Proximity	✓	•	✓	•
Ensure Technologies	XyLoc Solo 7.x	Proximity	✓	•		
Gemplus	GemSAFE Logon Card (8K,16K,32K) Readers: *Gemplus Serial GemPC 410 *GemPC 430 USB *GemPC USB-SL	Smartcard	✓	✓	✓	✓
PassGo	Defender v5	hardware and software tokens		X		X
Precise100MC	Biometric Fingerprint/Smart Card Reader	Biometric	✓	X		X
RSA	RSA SecureID for Windows 5.X RSA SecureID for Windows 6.X	Token	✓	X	✓	X
Saflink	SafLink/Safe Solution Enterprise SafRemote Authenticator	Biometric	✓	X	✓	X
Secure Computing	SafeWord for Citrix MetaFrame 2.0	Token	✓	X	✓	X

Legend: ✓ = Tested by Citrix - X = Known Issues - • = Requires Vendor Modification

Table 10-1 Tested Smart Card Solutions or Password Manager 4.0 and 4.1 (*Continued*)

BROWSER SECURITY CONSIDERATIONS FOR ADVANCED ACCESS CONTROL

Certain custom web browser security settings can prevent users from accessing Advanced Access Control. Therefore, follow these guidelines to ensure users can access the appropriate servers within your network.

For users to properly access corporate resources through Advanced Access Control, the following browser security settings must be enabled:

▼ **Cookies** Advanced Access Control uses per-session cookies that are not stored on disk. Therefore, third parties cannot access the cookies. Disallowing per-session cookies prevents connections to Advanced Access Control. Users cannot log on to Advanced Access Control because logging on requires a session cookie.

■ **File download** Disabling "File download" prevents the downloading of files from the corporate network, the launching of any seamless ICA session, and access to internal web servers outside the access server farm.

■ **Scripting** Disabling active scripting makes Advanced Access Control inaccessible. Disabling Java applet scripting prevents users from launching published applications with the client for Java.

■ Change the security settings only for zones that contain resources accessed through Advanced Access Control. If you fully trust the sites on your company's intranet, you can set the Local Intranet zone security level to Low. If you do not fully trust the sites on your intranet, keep the Local Intranet zone set to Medium-Low or Medium.

■ Several browser security settings required to access Advanced Access Control servers are disabled under the High security setting. Therefore, the security level for the Local Intranet zone is set to High.

■ If you not only want to keep the default security settings, but also customize individual security settings of your Advanced Access Control servers, you can configure each server in the access server farm as a "trusted site."

▲ Configuring servers as trusted sites lets you customize their security settings without affecting the Internet and Local Intranet settings.

IMPORTANT   If your access server farm requires SSL, make sure SSL is required for all sites in the Trusted Site zone.

Customizing Browser Security Settings

Table 10-2 lists additional IE browser security settings required for those deployment scenarios requiring client software. Most of these settings are available from the Security tab of the Internet Options dialog box.

Deployment Scenario	Require Settings
Endpoint Analysis Client	Run ActiveX controls and plug-ins (Enable) Script ActiveX controls marked safe for scripting (Enable) File download (Enable)
Live Edit Client	Run ActiveX controls and plug-ins (Enable) Script ActiveX controls marked safe for scripting (Enable) File download (Enable)
Website Viewer CDA (ActiveX mode)	Run ActiveX controls and plug-ins (Enable)
Web Client	Run ActiveX controls and plug-ins (Enable) Script ActiveX controls marked safe for scripting (Enable) File download (Enable) Do not save encrypted pages to disk (Disable)
Client for Java	Java Permissions (High safety or Custom) If you select Custom, set the following options: Run Unsigned Content (Run in sandbox) Run Signed Content (Prompt or Enable) Do not save encrypted pages to disk (Disable) All Additional Signed Permissions must also be set to Prompt or Enable

Table 10-2. Internet Explorer Browser Required Settings for Specific Deployment Scenarios

PART II

Access Suite: Administration, Maintenance, and Troubleshooting

CHAPTER 11

Application Publishing and Deployment

Citrix Presentation Server 4.0 provides access flexibility by enabling users to utilize published applications and content redirection within Program Neighborhood, Program Neighborhood Agent, and within a web browser. Handling application publishing according to the environment and adopting appropriate techniques can simplify maintenance and improve performance. This chapter contains recommendations for publishing application packages [Microsoft System Installer file (MSI) or Installation Manager's application deployment format (ADF)] with Installation Manager, as well as for the application deployment considerations with Installation Manager. This chapter also covers working with both Content Redirection and enhanced content and publishing in the Web Interface for Presentation Server 4.0.

PUBLISHING APPLICATIONS

This section contains recommendations for publishing packages (MSI) with Installation Manager, environments of thousands of objects, and content redirection.

MSI Considerations with Installation Manager

The following section outlines MSI considerations during deployment of Applications using Installation Management.

When applying more than one transform file for the same MSI, each installs different components, but applies them to the same MSI package. The selected components from the transforms do not get deployed, even though the installation job reports success.

Recording MSP (Microsoft Patch) packages is unnecessary. You can browse through Installation Manager and add the *.msp file.

You may uninstall a MSP package from the target server, but you cannot uninstall the patch from the server it was deployed to. If you need to apply another patch to the application installed on the target server, uninstall the application on the target server first, and then deploy the application and patch again.

CAUTION   When installing many MSI packages with or without Installation Manager, a memory leak may be detected in msiexec.exe. To avoid this issue, install the latest Windows 2000 service pack delivered by Microsoft.

Force Reinstall Option

When a package is scheduled to deploy to a target server, Installation Manager detects if the package is already installed. If the application is detected, Installation Manager aborts the new installation and returns an Already Installed status. If you need to over-write an existing installation, set the Force Reinstall option from the properties screen of the already installed package. This new installation can be used to fix any previously damaged installations or overwrite the existing application of the same version, with changes.

NOTE   After you Force Reinstall a package, the previous package cannot be used to uninstall the application from the target server. Uninstall can only proceed from the newly installed package.

After you Force Reinstall the same package, the Installed Packages tab of the target server reports two records for the same package.

Installation Manager Interoperability

Installation Manager, which ships with Citrix Presentation Server, supports packages made using Installation Manager 2.3 shipped with MetaFrame XP Server Feature Release 3, Installation Manager 2.2 shipped with MetaFrame XP Server Feature Release 2, and Installation Manager 2.1 shipped with MetaFrame XP Server Feature Release 1. However, some applications may cause issues with this compatibility. Because of this, Citrix recommends that you re-create the packages using the latest version of Installation Manager. Packages created with earlier versions may have been packaged on servers that did not have the operating system (OS) and other updates your Presentation Server farm contains. When recording a package, the source server should have a similar configuration to that of the target servers.

Interaction with Load Manager and Application Publishing

Use the Application Publishing Wizard to add the Installation Manager package to the farm through the Installation Manager node of the Presentation Server Console. The wizard lets you automatically install, publish, and load balance the applications. Additionally, the command line utility apputil can be used to add and remove servers from these published packages via scripting, further automating the application installation process. If you use Installation Manager without the wizard, applications are not automatically published or load balanced. For more information about apputil, please see the *MetaFrame Presentation Server Administrator's Guide*.

NOTE   Packages created by earlier versions of Installation Manager may not allow access to this feature.

Uninstall Behavior

By default, a deployed package can only be uninstalled from the original package.
    You cannot directly uninstall an ADF package that has a status of Already installed. Instead, perform another full installation using the Force Reinstall option, which can be used to uninstall the same package. The application can also be uninstalled from target servers locally, without Installation Manager using Add/Remove Programs.

NOTE   If you uninstall from the Already Installed package, the target server will not detect the uninstall and will still report that the MSI package is installed.

Publishing in Domains with Thousands of Objects

Citrix Presentation Server was tested in domains with over 10,000 objects in a single directory services container. A directory services or domain environment that contains a large number of objects, such as Novell Directory Service or Microsoft Active Directory Service, has factors to be considered. Recommendations for this type of environment are

▼   Use groups to categorize and easily assign permissions to large numbers of users. An application published to one group of 1,000 users requires Presentation Server to validate only one object for all 1,000 users. That same application published to 1,000 individual user accounts requires Independent Management Architecture (IMA) to validate 1,000 objects.

■   Publish applications with less than 1,000 users or group objects. This practice decreases the application publishing time, because all user and group accounts must be verified. Publishing an application with 10,000 objects may take up to 41 minutes to complete. Although the Presentation Server Console may time out after 5 minutes, IMA continues to publish the application in the background.

▲   Use the Add List of Names button, instead of scrolling to locate a user when the user's container holds thousands of objects.

Working with the Content Redirection Feature

This section concerns the various scenarios surrounding Content Redirection. Client-to-Server, Server-to-Client, and Server-to-Server are discussed.

Redirecting Content from Client to Server

When you configure Content Redirection from client to server, users running the Program Neighborhood Agent open all files of the associated type encountered in locally running applications with applications published on the Citrix Presentation Server. You must use the Web Interface to enable users to connect to published applications with the Program Neighborhood Agent.

NOTE   Content Redirection from client to server is available only with Citrix Presentation Server Advanced and Enterprise editions.

The *Program Neighborhood Agent* gets updated properties for published applications from the server running the Web Interface. When you publish an application and associate it with file types, the application's file type association is changed to reference the published application in the client device's Windows registry.

If you have users who run applications such as e-mail programs locally, you can use Presentation Server's content redirection capability in conjunction with the Program

Neighborhood Agent to redirect application launching from client device to Presentation Server. When users double-click attachments encountered in an e-mail application running locally, the attachment opens in an application published on the Presentation Server, associated with the corresponding file type, and assigned to the user.

> **IMPORTANT** You must enable client drive mapping to use this feature. You can enable client drive mapping for the entire server farm, for specific servers, or for specific users with user policies. For more information about user policies, see the *MetaFrame Presentation Server Administrator's Guide.*

If you do not want this to occur for *any* Program Neighborhood Agent users, do not associate the published application with any file types. If you do not want this to occur for *specific* Program Neighborhood Agent users, do not assign those users to the published application associated with the file type.

Follow the next procedure to configure Content Redirection from client to server.

1. Determine which of your users connect to published applications using the Program Neighborhood Agent. Content Redirection from client to server applies only to those users connecting with the Program Neighborhood Agent.

2. Verify that client drive mapping is enabled. You can enable client drive mapping for a specific connection using Citrix Connection Configuration or for specific users by creating user policies.

3. Publish applications you want the Program Neighborhood Agent users to open on the Presentation Server.

4. When you publish the application, associate it with file types on the last page of the Application Publishing Wizard.

Redirecting Content from Server to Client

When you enable Content Redirection from server to client, embedded URLs are intercepted on the Citrix Presentation Server and sent to the Citrix Access Client using the ICA Control virtual channel. The user's locally installed browser is used to play the URL. Users cannot disable this feature.

For example, users may frequently access web and multimedia URLs they encounter when running an e-mail program published on a Presentation Server. If you do not enable Content Redirection from server to client, users open these URLs with web browsers or multimedia players present on Presentation Servers.

To free servers from processing these types of requests, you can redirect application launching for supported URLs from the Presentation Server to the local client device.

> **NOTE** If the client device fails to connect to a URL, the URL is redirected back to the server.

The following URL types are opened locally on Windows 32-bit and Linux Presentation Server Clients when this type of content redirection is enabled:

▼ HTTP (Hypertext Transfer Protocol)

■ HTTPS (Secure Hypertext Transfer Protocol)

■ RTSP (Real Player and QuickTime)

■ RTSPU (Real Player and QuickTime)

■ PNM (Legacy Real Player)

▲ MMS (Microsoft's Media Format)

NOTE   If Content Redirection from server to client is not working for some of the HTTPS links, verify that the client device has an appropriate certificate installed. If the appropriate certificate is not installed, the HTTP ping from the client device to the URL fails and the URL is redirected back to the server. Content Redirection from server to client requires Internet Explorer Version 5.5 with Service Pack 2 on systems running Windows 98 or newer.

Follow the next procedures to enable Content Redirection from server to client.

1. Determine if you want Content Redirection from server to client to apply for the entire server farm, for specific Presentation Servers, or for specific users only.

2. To apply the behavior to the entire server farm, select the farm in the Presentation Server Console, and then click Properties. Select MetaFrame Settings in the left pane of the farm's Properties page. Select the option Enable Content Redirection from server to client.

3. To apply the behavior to a specific server, select the server in the Servers node in the Presentation Server Console, and then click Properties. Select MetaFrame Settings in the left pane of the server's Properties page. Select the option Enable Content Redirection from server to client.

4. To apply the behavior to specific users, create a user policy and enable the rule Content Redirection from Server to Client. Assign the policy only to those users you want to open supported URL file types on client devices. For more information about user policies, see the *MetaFrame Presentation Server Administrator's Guide*.

CHAPTER 12

Advanced Multimedia, CPU and Memory Optimization, and Virtual IP Addressing

Citrix Presentation Server 4.0 provides significant enhancements to access infrastructure by dramatically improving the speed and subsequent usefulness of multimedia applications. The software also, for the first time, enables TWAIN redirection in addition to many new features around Virtual IP addressing, PDA synching, CPU and Memory management tools, and multiple monitor support improvements, to name a few. This chapter covers the optimization of SpeedScreen Browser Acceleration, both with Internet Explorer (IE) and with the Presentation Server Client, including all the previously mentioned improvements.

OPTIMIZING SPEEDSCREEN BROWSER ACCELERATION

This section addresses SpeedScreen Browser Acceleration with Internet Explorer. We will review minimum browser requirements, Presentation Server Client requirements, and a few registry optimizations.

SpeedScreen Browser Acceleration and Internet Explorer

SpeedScreen Browser Acceleration improves the responsiveness of HTML pages when using Microsoft Outlook, Outlook Express, and IE 5.5 or higher as published applications. With SpeedScreen Browser Acceleration enabled, version 7.0 or later of the Presentation Server Clients for Win32, and a Presentation Server connection with a color depth of High Color (16 bit) or greater, the user can scroll the pages, and use the Back and Stop buttons immediately while image files download in the background. The following sections provide methods for the MetaFrame Administrator to further optimize the user's experience by controlling the default behavior of SpeedScreen Browser Acceleration through the use of registry value modifications and ICA file settings.

Play Animations in Web Page

When this feature is enabled, animated GIF images are rendered as animations and Speed-Screen Browser support for GIF images is disabled. Citrix recommends disabling "Play Animations in web pages." When this feature is disabled, SpeedScreen Browser Acceleration support for GIF images is enabled. The secondary benefit is a further bandwidth reduction due to the absence of animations, which consume significant bandwidth.

Citrix Presentation Server, by default, disables the "Play animations in web pages" option for all users on the server. The feature is disabled when the user logs in for the first time following the installation of Presentation Server. If a user subsequently enables the setting, it will not be modified again unless the Administrator changes specific values in the registry. For information about the necessary registry changes, see the following section "Advanced Configuration Information."

This feature can be accessed by opening IE and selecting Tools | Internet Options | Advanced or by navigating to Internet Options under the Control Panel.

Value Name	Default Value (if not present)	Description
DisablePlayAnimations	1	Disables "Play animations in web pages" in IE.

Table 12-1. Registry Values for SpeedScreen Settings in Internet Explorer

Advanced Configuration Information

MetaFrame Presentation Server disables the IE feature "Play animations in web pages" the first time a user logs in following the installation of MetaFrame Presentation Server. This feature is only disabled following the first login.

The disabling of this feature is controlled through a registry entry. The registry value is contained in the registry key HKCU\Software\Citrix. The registry value is defined in Table 12-1.

If this value is not present in the registry at login or is set to 1, the IE option is automatically disabled for the user. If the value is set to 0, the server does not attempt to disable the feature in the user's session at login, whether or not the feature is currently enabled or disabled in the user's profile.

Administrators may find this information useful when designing logoff scripts. Always having this option disabled at login may be useful, in which case a logoff script can be used to set the registry value to 1.

Configuring SpeedScreen Browser Acceleration on the Presentation Server Client

There is no Program Neighborhood UI control for SpeedScreen Browser Acceleration. SpeedScreen Browser Acceleration settings must be configured in the ICA files. The preferred configuration method is through Web Interface. By default, SpeedScreen Browser Acceleration is enabled on the client for all connections. Note, if either the server or the client has SpeedScreen Browser Acceleration configured to be OFF, then it will be disabled for that connection.

This section of the document describes the ICA file parameters that can be used to configure SpeedScreen Browser Acceleration. It is divided into two sections: Basic and Advanced settings. Typically, administrators only need to use the Basic settings.

Basic SpeedScreen Browser Acceleration ICA File Settings

The following examples illustrate the basic settings for SpeedScreen Browser Acceleration. These settings would be edited or added to a standard ICA file.

SpeedScreenBA

▼ **Usage**   SpeedScreenBA=[ON | OFF]

▲ **Description**   Setting **SpeedScreenBA=On** enables SpeedScreen Browser Acceleration for a connection. Note, the server settings may override this setting. Disabling SpeedScreen Browser Acceleration on the server causes this setting to be ignored for a connection. Setting **SpeedScreenBA=Off** disables SpeedScreen Browser Acceleration for a connection. This is disabled even if the server setting specifies that SpeedScreen Browser Acceleration is to be enabled.

SpeedScreenBACompressionEnabled

▼ **Usage**   SpeedScreenBACompressionEnabled=[ON | OFF]

▲ **Description**   Setting **SpeedScreenBACompressionEnabled=On** enables SpeedScreen Browser Acceleration JPEG image compression for a connection. Note, the server settings may override this setting. If the server has disabled JPEG Image compression, then the server setting overrides the client setting. Setting **SpeedScreenBACompressionEnabled=Off** disables SpeedScreen Browser Acceleration JPEG compression for a connection. This is disabled even if the server setting specifies that JPEG compression is to be enabled.

Advanced SpeedScreen ICA File Settings

Administrators may utilize the advanced cache file and compression settings of Speed-Screen to optimize SpeedScreen Browser Acceleration for slow connections, servers with limited memory or drive space, or servers with an overabundance of memory or drive space. Usage within the ICA File is as follows:

SpeedScreenBACompressedCacheSize=value

SpeedScreenBADecompressedCacheSize=value

SpeedScreenBAMaximumCompressionLevel=value

SpeedScreenBACompressedCacheSize

▼ **Usage**   SpeedScreenBACompressedCacheSize=*value*

▲ **Description**   SpeedScreen uses a compressed cache to store JPEG and GIF data sent from the Presentation Server. By caching this data on the client, pages that are revisited will display faster because the server does not retransmit the cached images to the client. The size of the cache determines how long images remain inside the cache and also, generally, the number of images that can fit into the cache. When the cache is filled, images previously added to the cache are removed. The least recently used image is deleted from the cache first. Initially, the cache is empty, and does not consume memory. As images are added to the cache, the cache grows to accommodate the images. If an image exceeds the maximum compressed cache size, it is not displayed through SpeedScreen.

The *value* parameter is the maximum memory consumption SpeedScreen uses to store JPEG and GIF image data, measured in KB. The default value for this parameter is 16384KB (16MB). Administrators can use this setting either to limit the maximum memory consumption of the client or to allow higher maximum memory consumption when this is required.

Increasing the memory consumption may provide some benefit on slow connections, where the transmission time for images is high. If images remain on the client for longer, then the probability that a retransmit of an image will need to occur is reduced.

SpeedScreenBADecompressedCacheSize

▼   **Usage**   SpeedScreenBADecompressedCacheSize=*value*

▲   **Description**   SpeedScreen stores the bitmap representations of JPEG and GIF images in a decompressed cache. Using a decompressed cache means the JPEG and GIF images do not need to be decompressed each time they are drawn. Using a decompressed cache provides a significant performance boost when a page is scrolled because a scroll operation results in a number of drawing operations on the same image.

When an image needs to be drawn, it is decompressed and added to the decompressed cache. Images remain in the decompressed cache until more space is required in the cache. Images are deleted from the decompressed cache when the operation of adding a new image could exceed the maximum decompressed cache size. Images can be added and removed from the decompressed cache any number of times while the image is in the compressed cache.

The maximum size of the decompressed cache size determines the maximum dimensions of an image that can be displayed through SpeedScreen. JPEG images require 24bpp (bits per pixel), while GIF images require 8bpp. A larger decompressed cache size allows images with a larger dimension to be displayed. Reducing the size of the decompressed cache reduces the maximum image dimensions that can be displayed.

Images that exceed the maximum decompressed cache size when decompressed are not downloaded to the client at all and are displayed in Legacy mode.

SpeedScreenBAMaximumCompressionLevel

▼   **Usage**   SpeedScreenBAMaximumCompressionLevel=*value*

▲   **Description**   The `SpeedScreenBAMaximumCompressionLevel` ICA file parameter defines the maximum SpeedScreen compression level for a connection. The valid values for this parameter are

0   Low Compression

1   Medium Compression

2   High Compression

The default value for this parameter is 2 (High compression).

As previously explained, SpeedScreen JPEG Image Recompression performs a lossy compression on the JPEG images transferred to the client. A higher compression level results in reduced bandwidth consumption, but has the most significant impact on image quality.

The lower of the two compression levels specified on the client and the server is used as the maximum compression level for a connection. Thus, if the client specifies medium compression and the server high, then the maximum compression level used for the connection will be medium compression.

This parameter is ignored if either the client or server indicates that compression is not enabled for a connection.

SPEEDSCREEN BROWSER ACCELERATION LIMITATIONS AND KNOWN ISSUES

This section outlines the known issues and limitations of SpeedScreen Browser Acceleration.

No Support for Transparent GIF Images

SpeedScreen Browser Acceleration does not support transparent GIF images. Transparent GIF images are rendered in Legacy mode.

Images Resized in HTML

The HTML that describes a web page can also specify the width and the height that an image may use. This may be different from the actual width and height of the image. In this case, IE grows or shrinks the image, as required to fit it into the size specified in the HTML.

SpeedScreen Browser Acceleration does not support images that are resized using this technique. Images that are resized in HTML are drawn in Legacy mode.

This feature is not the same as the Automatic Image Resizing feature available in IE. *Automatic Image Resizing* refers to the scaling of an image that is larger than the browser display area, so it fits into the display area of the browser.

MEDIA FORMATS SUPPORTED BY SPEEDSCREEN MULTIMEDIA ACCELERATION

This section describes the range of multimedia playback support for SpeedScreen Multimedia Acceleration. The following table lists a few of the Media Types that were tested successfully using Windows Media Player 6.4/8.0/9.0 and Real One Player. In general, SpeedScreen Multimedia Acceleration supports all Media Types that can be decoded by a DirectShow-based codec, regardless of File Format. SpeedScreen Multimedia Acceleration is supported when connecting to Windows 2000 and Windows 2003 servers, from Windows 9x, Windows 2000, and Windows XP clients.

NOTE Media Type differs from the File Format. Some examples of File Formats are AVI, MPEG, MPG, ASF, WMV, WMA, and MP3.

These File Formats can encapsulate various Media Types, such as those listed in Table 12-2. For example, a single AVI file could contain a DIVX Video stream and an AC3 Digital Audio Stream, and it would need both the DIVX and AC3 DirectShow codecs for proper playback.

Media Type (Media Encoding Format)	File Format (File Extension)	Media Player 6.4/8.0/9.0	RealOne Player	QuickTime	DirectShow Based Media Players
DIVX Video	AVI, MPEG,	√	√	X	√
XVID Video	MPG, ASF	√	√	X	√
Microsoft Video 1		√	√	X	√
MPEG-1 Video		√	√	X	√
MPEG-4 Video		√	√	X	√
Indeo Interactive Video		√	√	X	√
MPEG-1 Audio		√	√	X	√
AC3 Audio		√	√	X	√
Fraunhofer MPEG Layer-3 Codec		√	√	X	√
MP3	MP3	√*	X	X	X
WMA	WMA	√*	X	X	X
WMV	WMV	X	X	X	X
Real Media	RM	X	X	X	X
Quick Time	MOV	X	X	X	X

√ Supported through SpeedScreen Multimedia Acceleration
X Not supported through SpeedScreen Multimedia Acceleration
* Support through SpeedScreen Multimedia Acceleration only when playing through Windows Media Player 9.0. Data is transferred in uncompressed format.

Table 12-2. File Formats Supported by SpeedScreen Multimedia Acceleration

NOTE Table 12-2 only describes some of the more popular Media Types and File Formats. As previously stated, in general, SpeedScreen Multimedia Acceleration supports all Media Types that can be decoded by a DirectShow based codec, regardless of File Format.

Best Practices

▼ The recommendation is always to upgrade the client devices to use the latest version of Microsoft's DirectX software.

■ Another recommendation is to keep the server's version of Microsoft Windows Media Player upgraded to the latest version/update.

■ When publishing audio applications, it is advisable to disable the Windows Logon sound event. This is because the Citrix Audio Driver can only be opened by one process at a time, and the published application's attempt to open the Citrix Audio Driver could fail because the Windows logon event has exclusive access to the device until the sound has finished playing.

▲ Because QuickTime is not supported by SpeedScreen Multimedia Acceleration, it should be configured to use WaveOut instead of DirectSound. This is because Microsoft's DirectSound emulation for Terminal Server is not as efficient as the Citrix audio implementation and is, therefore, prone to poor performance and degraded audio quality.

SPEEDSCREEN MULTIMEDIA ACCELERATION INI FILE OPTIONS

The following examples illustrate the basic settings for SpeedScreen Multimedia Acceleration.

SpeedScreenMMAVideoEnabled

▼ **Default Value** TRUE

▲ **Description** Enable/Disable video playback through SpeedScreen Multimedia Acceleration.

SpeedScreenMMAAudioEnabled

▼ **Default Value** TRUE

▲ **Description** Enable/Disable audio playback through SpeedScreen Multimedia Acceleration.

SpeedScreenMMASecondsToBuffer

▼ **Default Value**   10

▲ **Description**   Approximate amount of seconds of buffer in the client. Values range from 1–10. Server and client both have this value set, and the connection IS set up with the smaller of the values (that is, server sets 5 seconds, client sets 4 seconds, and then the connection is set up with a 4-second buffer).

SpeedScreenMMAMaximumBufferSize

▼ **Default Value**   30240

▲ **Description**   Maximum size in KB of the media queue that the client can create. This is per stream, so the client could create a 30240KB queue for Audio and 30240 Queue for Video.

SpeedScreenMMAMinBufferThreshHold

▼ **Default Value**   10

▲ **Description**   Percent value with a range of 5–15. When the data in the media queue reaches this value, then the client will request a burst from the server to replenish its media queue.

SpeedScreenMMAMaxBufferThreshHold

▼ **Default Value**   90

▲ **Description**   Percent value with a range of 85–95. When the data in the media queue reaches this value, then the client will request the server stop sending data until the level of data in the queue levels off.

SpeedScreenMMAPlaybackPercent

▼ **Default Value**   35

▲ **Description**   Percent value with a range of 25–45. This is the percent of the media queue that needs to be filled before playback on the client end begins.

RECORDING SOUND IN A CITRIX PRESENTATION SERVER SESSION

One of the new features of MetaFrame Presentation Server 3.0 is the capability to record sound inside an ICA session. This feature was continued with Citrix Presentation Server 4.0. One of the primary uses for this is for professionals to be able to dictate a recording in one session, and then have that data transcribed at a later date. This feature requires a MetaFrame Presentation Server 3.0 or later and an 8.0 client or higher.

This process is usually facilitated by third-party software vendors, such as WinScribe, with its Internet Author and Internet Typist software. Usually, software like this is used in conjunction with Philips SpeechMike devices or similar hardware.

Also, note that playback can take advantage of the new SpeedScreen Multimedia Acceleration when playing MP3 or other such audio. In this case, Presentation Server doesn't play the data and send WAV data out to the client but, instead, it streams the compressed codec data to the client, and enables the client to decompress and play the data.

The settings that control SpeedScreen Multimedia Acceleration are totally separate from the settings that control the recording of audio. A user could use SpeedScreen Multimedia Acceleration for playback and optimize their settings for recording without degrading playback quality.

Setting Up for Recording Audio

The following section discusses the configuration required on both Presentation Server and Client in order to utilize the audio recording features.

Configuring the Server

By default, Presentation Server doesn't need any configuration to work. This lets you record audio using a standard microphone. However, to use the Philips SpeechMike devices, the drivers must be installed on all servers that are to have sessions that will record audio. The recommendation is that the Philips drivers be installed before installing Presentation Server.

Additionally, if using WinScribe's software, the Internet Author and/or the Internet Typist programs need to be installed on the servers. Please refer to the WinScribe documentation for any setup instructions.

Published desktops or published recording applications should be configured to use legacy audio. The client connection's ICA Settings Audio Quality should be set to medium or high. Medium is the default and should be satisfactory for most applications. If the Philips SpeechMagic Speech Recognition server is used in conjunction with WinScribe's software, high-quality audio is required for accurate speech-to-text translation. This is because high-quality audio does not use lossy compression on the recorded audio, which can interfere with the accuracy of the speech-recognition algorithms.

Policies can also be used to control audio recordings. Please see the policy documentation in the Administrator's Guide for more configuration information.

Configuring the Client

The client must have an audio playback device, such as a soundcard and an audio recording device, such as a microphone. The Philips SpeechMike devices often serve both purposes. Audio needs to be enabled in the Program Neighborhood, Program Neighborhood

Agent, or Web Interface clients, depending on which is used. (The feature works with all of them.) Ensure that either desktop sessions or published audio-recording applications are properly configured to allow sound in the client settings. For most uses, medium-audio quality is the recommended setting.

Ensure that the audio-security settings, available from the connection center or via a session's system menu, are configured to allow the recording of audio. These settings work in the same manner as the preexisting file security dialogs.

Using the Philips SpeechMike

Using a Philips SpeechMike should be a relatively straightforward process. Ensure that the drivers for the device are installed correctly on both the client and server. Make sure the recorder works correctly on the local client. Do this by loading the recorder utility that comes with the drivers. Ensure that audio records and plays back locally.

Presentation Server supports using the SpeechMike controls and Foot pedal devices, as well. Before attempting to use them in a session, however, test them locally once again in the Philips recording utility. If everything is working fine locally on a client device, then you should have no problems using the same devices inside an ICA Session.

SpeechMike controls may also have to be enabled inside the applications. This is currently true for Internet Author and Typist. Please see the specific application documentation for details. Additionally, Citrix testing has experienced issues with configured USB foot pedals in Internet Author and Typist. The recommendation is this: if using these devices, the settings for them should be left at the default setting or at none.

CLIENT AUDIO MAPPING VIRTUAL DRIVER

This section describes the Client Audio Mapping Virtual Driver configuration settings and the best practices when changing these settings in the Module.ini file.

NumCommandBuffers = 64

- ▼ **Description**   This setting defines how many commands can be buffered going from server to client.

- ■ **Maximum Limit**   65000. It is unadvisable to increase this value higher than 64 commands for the best performance of the server and client.

- ▲ **Minimum Limit**   0. If this value is set to 0, the performance of the server and client are affected. The client slows down or may not respond to the commands sent by the server. Having the proper buffers defined is necessary because, after executing a command sent by the server, the client looks in the buffer for the next command. Also, if no buffers are in the commands sent to the client, the server might not be stored on the client and executed. The best practice is to set it to 64.

NumDataBuffers = 24

▼ **Description** The maximum number of buffers that are dynamically allocated. This is only for 9.x Presentation Server clients for 32-bit Windows. For previous versions of the client connecting to Presentation Server 4.0, this setting defines how many Data Buffers are available on the client to store the sound data sent by the server to the client.

■ **Maximum Limit** 65000. It is unadvisable to set this value to the maximum, as this might lead to memory hogging on the client and could, eventually, result in the degraded performance of the client. The best practice is to set the NumDataBuffers value to 32 for the best performance of the server and the client.

▲ **Minimum Limit** 0. By setting this value to 0, no Data Buffers are available on the client, the sound data being sent from the server to the client is not stored, and eventually will not play. The best practice is to set this value to 32. These 32 buffers are defined to store a maximum of 2048 bytes of sound data.

MaxDataBufferSize = 2048

▼ **Description** This setting defines the size of the Data Buffer. It also defines how many bytes of sound data can be sent to the client from the server.

■ **Maximum Limit** 2048 bytes. Out of 2048 bytes, 10 bytes is reserved for the sound packet header, while the remainder is the actual sound that gets played on the client.

▲ **Minimum Limit** 1000 bytes. The best practice is to set it to 2048 bytes for the best sound performance on the client.

CommandAckThresh = 1

▼ **Description** This setting defines that the client will wait for one command to be sent by the server before it sends an acknowledgment to the server for all the commands received.

▲ **Maximum Limit** The maximum limit depends on the NumCommandBuffers. If the NumCommandBuffers is set to 64, then the CommandAckThresh should not be set more than 64, as the client does not acknowledge more than 64 commands. The best practice is to set the CommandAckThresh to 1 for the best performance of the client and server.

DataAckThresh = 1

▼ **Description** This setting defines that the client will wait for 1 sound packets/data to be sent by the server before it sends an acknowledgment to the server for all the sound packets/data received.

▲ **Maximum Limit** The maximum limit depends on the NumDataBuffers. If the NumDataBuffers is set to 32, then the DataAckThresh should not be set higher than 32, as the client does not acknowledge more than 32 sound data/packets. The best practice is to set the DataAckThresh to 1 for the best performance of the client and server.

AckDelayThresh = 50

▼ **Description** This setting defines that the client will wait for 50 milliseconds before it sends an acknowledgment to the server for all the commands received from the server.

■ **Maximum Limit** 350. AckDelayThresh and CommandAckThresh are not interdependent. Say, for example, CommandAckThresh is set to 10 and AckDelayThresh = 350. If 350 milliseconds have not yet passed since the client last sent an acknowledgment, but 10 commands have been sent by the server to the client, the client will still send the acknowledgment. The same holds true if the 350 milliseconds have passed, but the server has not sent 10 commands. The client sends the acknowledgment to the server without waiting for 10 commands.

▲ **Minimum Limit** 50. Anything less than 50 milliseconds might degrade the performance of the client, as it will start acknowledging to the servers regularly, which will interfere with executions of the commands from the server.

PlaybackDelayThresh = 50

▼ **Description** This setting defines that the client will wait for 50 milliseconds before it sends an acknowledgment to the server for all the sound data/packets received from the server.

■ **Maximum Limit** 250. PlaybackDelayThresh and DataAckThresh are not interdependent. For example, if DataAckThresh is set to 10 and PlaybackDelayThresh = 250, if 250 milliseconds have passed after the client has sent an acknowledgment, but 10 sound data/packets have not been sent by the server to the client, the client will still send the acknowledgment. The same holds true if the 250 milliseconds have not yet passed, but the server has already sent 10 sound data/packets. The client will send the acknowledgment to the server without waiting for 250 milliseconds.

▲ **Minimum Limit** 50. Anything less than 50 milliseconds might degrade the performance of the client, as it will send acknowledgments to the servers too often, which will interfere with the playing of the sound data/packets from the server.

PDA SYNCHRONIZATION

Presentation Server now supports the synchronization of USB-tethered and Microsoft Windows-powered PDAs that use ActiveSync as a synchronization agent. The following section addresses important considerations when incorporating this feature into your environment.

IMPORTANT PDA synchronization is available by default in the Enterprise edition of Presentation Server. To enable support for PDA Synchronization in the Advanced edition, apply hotfix PSE400W2K3002 for Windows 2003 or PSE400W2K002 for Windows 2000.

Using ActiveSync in an ICA Session

A long-standing obstacle to successfully making ActiveSync available to users via Presentation Server is that ActiveSync is not a Terminal Services-aware application. Even though ActiveSync is not a multiuser or Terminal Services-aware application, Presentation Server 4.0 utilizes the new virtual IP feature, as well as other techniques, to create Terminal Services compatibility. Although virtual IP is used to enable PDA synchronization with ActiveSync, no explicit virtual IP configurations are required by an administrator for PDA synchronization to work properly.

To enable PDA Synchronization:

1. Open the properties of a policy in which you want to enable PDA synchronization.

2. Enable the rule **Client Devices | Resources | PDA Devices | Turn on automatic virtual COM port mapping**.

3. Disable the rule **Client Devices | Resources | Ports | Turn off COM ports** (or set it to **Not Configured**).

NOTE Do not plug PDAs into the server console while ICA sessions are connected. If you do so, although PDA users in ICA sessions are isolated from each other, they might have access to the PDA on the server console. In addition, if you then unplug the PDA from the server console, all the PDAs in ICA sessions are disconnected.

Publishing ActiveSync

To properly make ActiveSync available as a published application, it is important to specify WCESMGR.EXE as the application to be launched, not WCESCOMM.EXE. WCESCOMM.EXE is the system tray process. While both executables can start each other once a PDA is detected, if WCESCOMM.EXE is the only application in a session and no PDA is present at ICA session startup, the ICA session may log off before a user can insert a PDA.

If you connect to a published desktop as any user after ActiveSync has been installed, you may see the ActiveSync icon in the system tray. Also, if you have a PDA plugged into the USB port on the client, ActiveSync may attempt to synchronize to the device. The administrator can do the following to prevent this from occurring:

1. Using the System Configuration Utility (MSCONFIG), remove the ActiveSync options from the Startup tab.

2. Even if ActiveSync is removed from the startup options, it still runs on the console and re-creates the startup entries the next time it is launched. To prevent ActiveSync from re-creating the startup entries, delete the following registry value:

```
HKCU\Software\Microsoft\Windows\CurrentVersion\Run: H/PC Connection Agent
```

Additional Considerations

The following are additional considerations to keep in mind when using the PDA synchronization feature:

▼   Symbian OS-based and Blackberry PDAs are not supported.

■   ActiveSync does not need to be installed on every client.

▲   A device driver for the PDA must be installed on the local client workstation, so the client's operating system (OS) can recognize the PDA device.

VIRTUAL IP

Some applications use the machine IP address for addressing, licensing, identification, or other purposes. This means to use these applications in a Citrix Presentation Server environment, a unique IP addresses for each user is required for these applications to function properly. Other applications may also simply try to bind to a static port that causes multiple attempts to launch the application in a multiuser environment to fail because the port is already in use.

The Virtual IP feature enables you to assign a static range of IP addresses to a server and have these addresses individually allocated to each session, so configured applications that run within that session appear to have a unique address. Also, applications that depend on communications with localhost (127.0.0.1 by default) can be configured to use a unique address in the localhost range (127.*).

How to Use Virtual IP

To use Virtual IP effectively, it may be helpful to have a better understanding of how the feature is implemented and how it should be configured. First, you need to configure ranges of IP addresses that are excluded from any DHCP servers. These ranges should share the same subnets as the assigned IP addresses of the Presentation Servers that will be configured for Virtual IP. The pool of IP addresses assigned to the Presentation Server Farm needs to be large enough to include all user sessions on every server to be configured, not just the sessions running the application(s) that require Virtual IP Address functionality. These ranges are added to the Citrix Presentation Server Farm in the Farm Properties | Virtual IP Addresses page and the servers that require Virtual IP functionality that share the same subnet as the address range should be added to the range.

At this time, the addresses in the range are divided equally (by default) among the selected servers and assigned. You can then change the number of addresses assigned to each server. The recommendation is that you configure a Load Management Server User Load rule that is equal to or less than the total number of addresses assigned to the server.

How Virtual IP Works

During IMA startup, the Virtual IP Address Assigner binds the assigned IP addresses to the NIC that matches the same subnet as the virtual addresses. When Virtual IP is enabled on the server, the Virtual IP address allocator will allocate an address from the pool of available addresses, which were assigned by the Virtual IP address assigner, to all new sessions connecting to the server. This allocated address is assigned to the new session and removed from the pool of available addresses. This assigned address can be seen in the Presentation Server Console Servers node in the sessions tab or via MFCOM calls. When the session logs off, the allocated address is returned to the available address pool.

Once an address is allocated to a session, any application configured for Virtual IP uses the allocated virtual address, rather than the system's primary IP address, whenever the following calls are made:

Bind	Closesocket	Connect	WSAConnect	WSAAccept
Getpeername	Getsockname	Sendto	WSASendTo	WSASocketW
Gethostbyname	Gethostbyaddr	Getnameinfo	Getaddrinfo	

Remember, all processes that require this feature must be individually added to the Virtual IP Process list in the Presentation Server Console Farm properties Virtual IP Processes section. Child processes do not automatically inherit this functionality. Processes can be configured with full paths or just the executable name. For security reasons, the recommendation is to use full paths.

The Virtual Loopback functionality is simply either enabled or disabled, and other than specifying which processes use the feature, it does not require any additional configuration. When an application uses the localhost address (127.0.0.1) in a Winsock call, the Virtual Loopback feature simply replaces 127.0.0.1 with 127.X.X.X, where X.X.X is a representation of the session ID + 1. For example, a session ID of 7 would be 127.0.0.8. If the session ID exceeds the fourth octet (more than 255), it rolls over to the next octet (127.0.1.0), all the way to the maximum of 127.255.255.255 (it is highly unlikely to ever get that high).

The Virtual Loopback functionality allows multiple published applications that depend on the localhost interface for interprocess communication to function properly within the session. A good example of such an application is Microsoft ActiveSync. In fact, to provide the PDA synchronization feature, Presentation Server 4.0 utilizes the virtual IP feature, in addition to other techniques, to create Terminal Services compatibility for ActiveSync.

"Binding" applications to specific IP addresses is achieved by inserting a "filter" component between the application and winsock function calls, so out of all IP addresses allocated to the Presentation Server, the application sees only the IP address it is supposed to use. Any attempt by the application to listen (for TCP or UDP) is automatically bound to the Virtual IP address (or loopback address) it is supposed to use. And, any originating connections opened by the application are originated from the IP address this particular app/user is supposed to use.

In functions that return an address, such as gethostbyname() and GetAddrInfo(), if the local host's IP address is being asked for, Virtual IP looks at the returned IP address and changes it to the session's virtual IP address. Thus, applications that try to get the local server's IP address through such name functions only see the unique virtual IP address assigned to that session. This IP address is often used in subsequent socket calls (such as bind or connect).

Often, an application requests to bind to a port for listening on the address "0.0.0.0" (INADDR_ANY, which means all interfaces). When an application does this and uses a static port, you cannot launch more than one instance of the application. The Virtual IP feature changes also looks for 0.0.0.0 in these types of calls and changes the call to listen on the specific Virtual IP address. This allows more than one application to listen on the same port on the same machine as they are all listening on different addresses. (Note, this is changed only if it's in an ICA session and the Virtual IP feature is turned on.) For example, if two instances of an application running in different sessions both try to bind to all interfaces (0.0.0.0) and a specific port, say 9000, they would be bound to VIPAddress1:9000 and VIPAddress2:9000. There would no longer be a conflict.

Configuring Virtual IP for Applications

When attempting to configure Virtual IP for a particular application, the first step should be to load a tool such as the TCPView tool from Sysinternals (http://www.sysinternals.com). This tool lists all applications that attempt to bind specific IP addresses and ports. The recommendation is to disable the Resolve Addresses feature, so you see the IP addresses instead of hostnames. Launch the application and take note of which IP addresses and ports are opened by the application. Also, take note of which process names are opening these ports. Any processes that attempt to open either the server's IP address or 0.0.0.0 should be configured in the Virtual IP Process section in Farm Properties. Any processes that attempt to open 127.0.0.1 should be specified in the Virtual Loopback process section in Farm Properties. You may also want to attempt to launch an additional instance of the application to be sure it does not attempt to open the same IP address(es) on a different port. If that is the case, Virtual IP may be unnecessary for this application.

Client IP Address Feature

If an application is only failing because it requires a unique address strictly for identification or licensing purposes, but does not require a virtual address for actual communication, you may want to explore the Client IP Address feature. This feature only calls that return the host's IP address, such as GetHostByName. This should only be used by an application that takes the value in this type of call and sends the value to the server application for identification or licensing.

This feature is currently only enabled by changing several registry settings on the server. To configure this feature, two new registry entries can be added on the server where the application is deployed:

```
HKEY_LOCAL_MACHINE\Software\Citrix\VIP\
UseClientIP: REG_DWORD: 1 (enable) or 0 (disable, default)
HookProcessesClientIP: REG_MULTI_SZ
```

where:

UseClientIP is a DWORD value that should be set to either 1 or 0 (enable/disable this feature). The disabled state is the default if the registry value is not present.

HookProcessesClientIP is a multistring of process names from the application (the executable names) that are to use the Client IP address feature, rather than normal Virtual IP.

Once these values are configured, you must also configure either the Virtual IP Processes or the Virtual Loopback Processes with the same process names. The reason is this function creates and manages the following registry entry, which is still required for the ClientIP feature to work:

```
HKEY_LOCAL_MACHINE\Software\Citrix\CtxHook\AppInit_Dlls\VIPHook\<Processname>
```

NOTE   The Virtual IP address features (including Virtual Loopback and Client IP) only functions with applications that load the user32.dll system dynamic library.

CPU UTILIZATION MANAGEMENT

The CPU utilization management feature introduced in Citrix Presentation Server 4.0 ensures that the CPU resources are equitably shared among users. This is accomplished by providing CPU reservation and CPU shares.

- ▼ **CPU Reservation**   A defined percentage of CPU is guaranteed to be available to a user. If all the allocated reservation is not being used, other users or processes can use the available resource as needed.

- ▲ **CPU Shares**   A share is a relative percentage of the CPU time. By default, CPU utilization management allocates eight shares for each user. If two users are logged into a server (and no console session), each of the users gets 50% of the CPU. If there are four users with eight shares each, each user receives 25% of the CPU time.

NOTE   The range for CPU share is 1–64. For CPU reservation, the total cannot be more than 100%, which represents the entire CPU resource on the machine.

License Requirement for CPU Utilization

CPU utilization management requires an Enterprise edition license for Presentation Server 4.0.

Changing the Default Values for CPU Utilization via the Registry

By default, each user receives eight CPU shares. A *share* is a relative percentage of CPU time. If two users have eight shares each, they get 50% of CPU time. Similarly, if three users have eight shares each, they get one-third of the CPU time each. It is expected that the default values can accommodate most users' needs. However, it is possible to change the default values in the registry. If two users are present and the first user has a need for 16 shares (assuming he needs more CPU time) and the second user receives eight shares, then the first user gets 66% of the CPU time and the second user gets the remaining 33%.

Changing the CPU Share Allotment for a User

1. Go to HKLM\Software\Citrix\CTXCPU.

2. In the right pane, double-click the "Policy" Multi-String value.

3. In the Edit Multi-String window, you can see the default data for the NT AUTHORITY\SYSTEM context, which is 20000, meaning 20% of CPU Reservation.

4. Go to the end of the line and press ENTER to go to the next line.

5. To set CPU shares for a local user named "u1" on a Presentation Server named "Server1", type the following:

    Server1\u1,cpu.shares=16

    Note, 16 is the number of shares you want to assign to a user. This can be a number between 1 and 64.

6. Exit from registry editor to save the settings.

7. Restart the services "CTXCPUUtilMgmt User/Session Synchronization" and "CTXCPUUtilMgmt Resource Management".

Changing the CPU Reservation for Users

1. Open the registry by typing **regedt32** from Start...Run.

2. Go to HKLM\Software\Citrix\CTXCPU.

3. In the right pane, double-click the Policy Multi-String.

4. In the Edit Multi-String window, you see the default data for the NT AUTHORITY\ SYSTEM context, which is 20000. This represents the desired percentage of reservation multiplied by 1000, in this example, 20% of CPU Reservation.

5. Go to the end of line and press ENTER to go to the next line.

6. To set CPU shares for u1, u2, u3, and u3 on MPS server Server1, type the following:

   Server1\u1,cpu.reservation=20000

   Server1\u2,cpu.reservation=20000

   Server1\u3,cpu.reservation=20000

   Server1\u4,cpu.reservation=20000

7. Exit from registry editor to save the setting.

8. Restart the services "CTXCPUUtilMgmt User/Session Synchronization" and "CTXCPUUtilMgmt Resource Management".

NOTE   CPU share/reservation can only be assigned toward individual users, not toward user groups or applications. Also, CPU time sharing within a session is done by the OS, *not* by CPU utilization management.

Services Required for CPU Utilization

The services used for CPU Utilization are "CTXCPUUtilMgmt User/Session Synchronization" and "CTXCPUUtilMgmt Resource Management". In addition to these two services, "Citrix CPU Utilization Mgmt/CPU Rebalancer" service is installed on Windows Server 2003 multiprocessor systems.

Citrix CPU Utilization Mgmt/CPU Rebalancer Service

By design, the CPU rebalancer service is only installed on multiprocessor servers running Windows Server 2003. The service is not installed on Windows 2000 server or servers with only one processor. The CPU rebalancer service is used to alleviate a Microsoft issue that demonstrates itself under stress environments where a lot of short-lived processes are started and stopped. Because of the performance impact this service can cause, by default, the service is set to Manual.

The recommendation is to consider starting the CPU rebalancer service and setting the service to Automatic if your environment is running a lot of short-lived applications that all appear to be running on the same CPU (for example, if you see one CPU is running at 100% and another CPU is at 20% utilization). The CPU rebalancer service attempts to correct this by balancing the load equally across processors.

Performance Counters to Monitor CPU Utilization

Five Performance Counters are available for CPU Utilization. The counters are listed under the "CTXCPUUtilMgmtUser" object on the Presentation Server. They are

▼ CPU Entitlement

■ CPU Reservations

■ CPU Share

- ■ CPU Usage
- ▲ Long-term CPU Usage

> **NOTE**   The CPU Utilization management services must be running to add the performance counters into Performance Monitor.

Report Generation for CPU Utilization

A CPU Utilization report can be generated by using the Report Center feature in the Access Suite Console. Generating CPU Utilization reports requires RM Summary Database.

For more information about the CPU utilization management feature, refer to the Citrix knowledgebase article CTX106021.

VIRTUAL MEMORY OPTIMIZATION

The *virtual memory optimization* feature reduces the amount of virtual memory usage by rebasing DLLs to an optimized virtual address to avoid relocation of DLLs. The rebasing of the DLLs prevents performance impact caused by relocating. The rebasing performed by the virtual memory optimization feature modifies a copy of a DLL, so it loads at an optimal base memory address to avoid collisions and relocations.

License Requirement for Virtual Memory Optimization

Virtual memory optimization requires an Enterprise edition license for Presentation Server 4.0.

Exclusion List

The following applications are excluded from being rebased by virtual memory optimization:

- ▼ Applications that have digitally signed components.
- ■ Applications whose DLLs are protected by Windows Rights Management (WRM). Applications such as Office 2003 do not benefit from this feature because it uses WRM.
- ▲ Applications whose executable programmatically checks the DLL after it has been loaded.

The digitally signed files and the components protected by WRM are detected by the system automatically and are excluded from rebasing. The excluded DLLs and executables can be found in the registry at the following locations:

```
HKEY_LOCAL_MACHINE\SOFTWARE\Citrix\SFO\ComponentExclusionList
HKEY_LOCAL_MACHINE\SOFTWARE\Citrix\SFO\ProcessExclusionList
```

Services Required for Virtual Memory Optimization

Citrix Virtual Memory Optimization service is responsible for the virtual memory optimization feature. The scheduling of memory optimization is done using the Windows Task Scheduler.

Scheduling of Memory Optimization

By default, rebasing is scheduled to occur daily at 3 A.M. You can use the options in the Memory Optimization node under Farm Properties in the Presentation Server Console to change the default scheduling. Also, an alternate user account can be selected to run the scheduled task instead of using the "local system" account.

Troubleshooting Tips

The following session will provide troubleshooting guidelines for the most common issues around memory optimization.

Using Process Explorer to View Relocated DLLs

Sometimes, it becomes difficult to ascertain if the feature is truly rebasing DLLs or not. You can use "Process Explorer" from http://www.sysinternals.com to verify this. The goal of *Process Explorer* is to reduce the relocation of DLLs for applications. Process Explorer shows the relocated DLLs and, if the feature is working properly, the number of relocated DLLs should be minimal.

To use Process Explorer:

1. Install "Process Explorer" on all servers running Presentation Server.

2. Launch Process Explorer. Select the "View DLLs" button (the fifth button from the left on the tool bar, or press CTRL-D to view DLLs in a selected process).

3. In the Options menu, choose to configure highlighting. Check "Relocated DLLs" and change the highlight color to one you can easily spot.

4. Once Process Explorer is configured, if a running process (such as Visio32.exe) is selected from the upper panel, the DLLs/components loaded by that process are shown in the lower panel. The relocated DLLs should be highlighted.

Using the Repair.sfo File to View Rebased DLLs and DLLs That Are Pending Rebasing

Repair.sfo is located in Program Files\Citrix\Server Resource Management\Memory Optimization Management\Data and contains the list of DLLs that have been rebased. Repair.sfo also lists the DLLs that are in "pending" status. To troubleshoot virtual memory optimization, you can view this XML file. The file is created by the Citrix Virtual Memory Optimization Service (CtxSFOSvc.exe).

> **NOTE**   It takes time to fully rebase all the dlls for a system. Virtual memory optimization is a gradual process. For various reasons—such as files being used—sometimes all the DLLs cannot be optimized in a short period of time, but they are eventually rebased over a longer period of time.

Report Generation for Memory Optimization

The Report Center in the Access Suite Console contains reporting for virtual memory optimization. The report lists the virtual memory savings received when virtual memory optimization is being used.

Additional Information

For more information about the virtual memory optimization feature, refer to the Citrix knowledgebase article CTX106023. For a list of applications that show positive results in virtual memory savings when using the virtual memory optimization feature, see the Citrix knowledgebase article CTX106022

MULTIPLE-MONITOR ENHANCEMENTS

Presentation Server 4.0 and the 9.*x* version of the Presentation Server client for 32-bit Windows include improvements for using client workstations with multiple-monitor displays. This section includes information about establishing seamless ICA connections when operating a multiple-monitor environment. Complete the following tasks to configure the environment to provide the new multiple-monitor enhancements.

Issues Resolved

One goal of the Presentation server 4.0 and 32-bit Windows client version 9.*x* releases was to resolve issues that users with multiple monitors encountered. The following lists these enhancements. The list is separated into issues that are resolved by upgrading the client only, and issues that require both the upgraded client and Presentation Server 4.0.

Issues Resolved by Upgrading to the 9.*x* Client

▼   When locking and unlocking the workstation, the seamless application no longer jumps to another location or offscreen.

▲   Users can now connect in seamless mode, regardless of which monitor is set as the primary monitor.

Issues Resolved by Using the 9.*x* Client and Presentation Server 4.0

▼ When maximizing an application running in seamless mode, the application will no longer maximize to the top left-most monitor. Instead, the application will behave as if the application is running locally.

■ In previous versions, when roaming from a multiple-monitor machine to a single monitor machine, upon reconnecting the session, applications might be opened offscreen, representing portions of the desktop that were present on the multiple monitor machine but not present on the single monitor machine. These applications will no longer be created offscreen on reconnect and, instead, they will be moved onscreen.

▲ Application menus will no longer be drawn on the top left-most monitor. They will be drawn in the correct location.

Client Configuration

The client device requires a video card, or cards, to allow more than one display to be connected to a single machine. Furthermore, if a single video card is used, but supports more than one monitor, the client's OS must be able to distinguish that more than one monitor exists. Figure 12-1 is an example of the Settings tab of the Display Properties dialog on a triple-monitor machine where the OS has properly detected all the monitors.

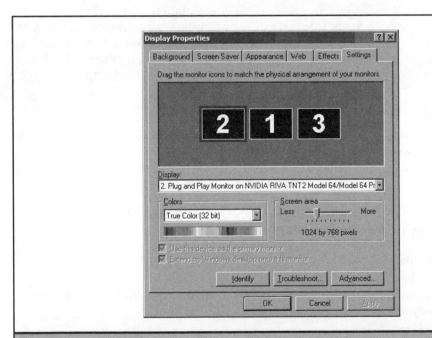

Figure 12-1. Multimonitor support

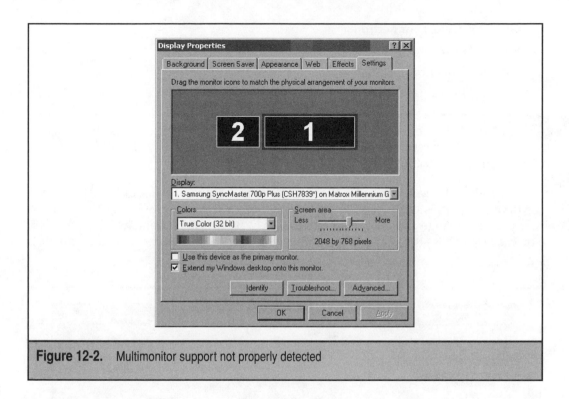

Figure 12-2.   Multimonitor support not properly detected

Figure 12-2 is an example of the Settings tab of the Display Properties dialog on a triple-monitor machine, in which the OS has not properly detected all the monitors. Notice only two monitors are shown, but one of the monitors has a resolution of 2048*768. The OS is viewing two monitors as a single monitor with a large desktop. In this scenario, the ICA client cannot distinguish between the two displays and, as such, the enhancements function as if the two monitors are one.

Server Configuration

The *server configuration* consists of defining the maximum amount of memory that can be allocated for the server LVB (Local Video Buffer), and choosing as to whether to degrade color or resolution when the client requires more LVB than is available on the server. To determine the size of the LVB required for a connection, use these formulas:

24-Bit (True Color) connections:

Virtual[1] Horizontal Resolution * Virtual Vertical Resolution * 3;

16-Bit (High Color) connections:

Virtual[1] Horizontal Resolution * Virtual Vertical Resolution * 2;

8-Bit (256 Color) connections:

Virtual[1] Horizontal Resolution * Virtual Vertical Resolution;

4-Bit (16 Color) connections:

(Virtual Horizontal Resolution * Virtual Vertical Resolution)/2;

> **NOTE**   *"Virtual"* represents the sum of the resolution of all the monitors combined. For example, a multiple-monitor setup with two monitors each with a resolution of 1024*768 in a horizontal layout would have a virtual resolution of 2048*768.

To modify the settings, open the Presentation Server Console and, on the server (or farm) properties under ICA Settings, you see the screenshot in Figure 12-3. On this tab, you can change the maximum amount of LVB anywhere from 150KB to 8192KB. You can also choose the fallback mechanism when the client requires more memory than

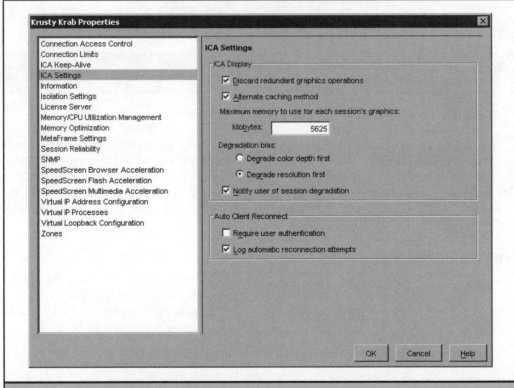

Figure 12-3.   ICA display settings for the farm

is available. The choices are either to degrade color depth or resolution. If color depth is selected, then the connection color depth is reduced to fit the user's requirement, based on the virtual resolution of the connecting machine. If resolution is selected, then the color depth is unchanged, but the user can only move the application to a subset of the client monitors, based on the color depth and largest resolution that can be supported by the server's LVB. If there is not enough LVB to support even one display, then the connection reverts to nonseamless mode.

Additional Information

▼   If the user wants to disable the capability to maximize the application to the proper screen, they can use the INI setting DisableMMMaximizeSupport. Supported values for this setting are TRUE and FALSE. Specifying this setting to FALSE reverts functionality back to pre-Presentation Server 4.0 behavior.

▲   The recommendation is to set all monitors to the same resolution and color depth, and then choose a standard rectangular layout for the monitors.

TWAIN REDIRECTION SUPPORT

Citrix Presentation Server 4.0 can now redirect client-connected TWAIN imaging devices—notably document scanners—from the client to the server, regardless of connection type. This enables users to control client-attached imaging devices from applications that run on the server; the redirection is transparent.

To capture an image, users connect to a server from a client machine that has an imaging device and the associated vendor-supplied TWAIN driver installed locally. When the TWAIN application is run from within this session, the application detects and interacts with the client-side device. The server-based application that is accessed runs in the same way as a client-based application.

Redirection support for TWAIN devices is available in the Advanced and Enterprise Editions of Citrix Presentation Server.

By default, users can use published applications to process data acquired by locally connected TWAIN devices. You can control the redirection of TWAIN devices by enabling the policy rule Configure TWAIN redirection.

1. Open the properties of a policy in which you want to control TWAIN redirection.

2. Enable the rule Client Devices | Resources | Other | Configure TWAIN redirection.

3. Use the options to allow and disallow TWAIN redirection, as well as to control the level of data compression.

TWAIN Additional Considerations

The following are additional considerations to be aware of when using TWAIN redirection.

1. The Imaging/Scanner software must be installed on the Presentation Server. Examples of supported applications include the following:

   ▼ Microsoft's PictureIT

   ■ OmniPage

   ■ PaperPort

   ■ Photoshop

   ■ Paint Shop Pro

   ▲ IrFanView

NOTE 16-bit TWAIN drivers are not supported.

2. You need scanner software on the client OS that can provide the USB device drivers. If available, the recommendation is also to install a test utility for the scanner on the client workstation to ensure functionality.

3. For TWAIN Redirection, some applications are not Terminal Services-aware and look for TWAIN32.DLL in the \WINDOWS directory of the User's profile (that is, C:\Documents and Settings\UserName\WINDOWS, unless otherwise changed). One resolution is to copy TWAIN32.DLL into the \WINDOWS directory of each user's profile. Referring to Microsoft knowledgebase article 186499, it is also possible to fix this by adding the application to the Terminal Services application compatibility list with the following two flags specified:

   ▼ Windows 32-bit application: 0x00000008

   ▲ Do not substitute user Windows directory: 0x00000400

Sample .REG file

The following is an example of a simple file that can be copied to notepad and saved as a .reg file to automate enabling these flags on your Presentation Server.

```
Windows Registry Editor Version 5.00
[HKEY_LOCAL_MACHINE\SOFTWARE\Microsoft\Windows NT\CurrentVersion\
Terminal Server\Compatibility\Applications\Photoshop]
"Flags"=dword:00000408
```

NOTE You may need to combine these flags with any other compatibility flags needed for the application.

Support for TWAIN Modes of Information Transfer

There are three modes of information transfer:

▼ Native

■ Disk file

▲ Buffered Memory

Most scanning software works by default in Buffered Memory mode. Disk file transfer is not supported. Native and Buffered Memory modes are supported.

Supported Devices

For a list of devices used during the testing of the TWAIN Redirection feature, refer to the Tested Hardware list found in Volume 2 of the Internal Advanced Concepts Guide.

Supported Presentation Server Clients

Version 9.x or later of the Presentation Server client for 32-bit Windows is supported.

CHAPTER 13

Printer Management

S ince the inception of networking, printing has been a primary concern during the design and implementation phases of building a network. Whether the issue is the quality of the print job, bandwidth needs, performance requirements, paper tray demystification, or simply determining where a print job went, administrators have struggled with providing secure, fast, and simple printing solutions to their users.

Because we covered, in detail, Windows printer management, configuration, troubleshooting, and the use of third-party tools in *Citrix Access Suite for Windows Server 2003: The Official Guide,* we focus in this chapter on the centralized printer management features in the Citrix Presentation Server Console of Citrix Presentation Server. We start with an overview of Presentation Server print architecture. Print Driver replication is discussed at length, along with optimizing Printer Creation and a review of the Presentation Server 4.0 client enhancements. We also cover the new Session Printers Policy features built into Citrix Presentation Server 4.0.

THE PRESENTATION SERVER PRINT ARCHITECTURE

Users connecting to a Presentation Server environment can print to the following types of printers:

▼ Printers connected to ports on the user's client device on Windows, Windows CE, DOS, Linux, UNIX, or Mac OS platforms

■ Virtual printers created for tasks such as printing from a PostScript driver to a file on a Windows client device

■ Shared printers connected to print servers on a Windows network

▲ Printers connected directly to Presentation Servers

The printer objects that Presentation Server clients use can be categorized by connection types. Three kinds of printer connections are in a Presentation Server farm: client connections, network connections, and local connections. This chapter refers to printers in a server farm as client printers, network printers, or local printers, depending on the type of connection they have in the farm.

Client Printers

Client printers are defined differently, depending on the Presentation Server Client platform:

▼ On DOS-based and Windows CE client devices, a client printer is physically connected to a port on the client device by a cable.

■ On UNIX and Macintosh client devices, a PC or PostScript printer connected to a serial port (or a USB port for newer Macintoshes) is considered a client printer.

▲   On 32-bit Windows platforms (Windows 9*x*, Windows NT, Windows 2000, and Windows XP), any printer that is set up in Windows is a *client printer* (these printers appear in the Printers folder on the client device). Locally connected printers, printers that are connected on a network, and virtual printers are all considered client printers.

Network Printers

Printers that are connected to print servers and shared on a Windows network are referred to as *network printers*. In Windows network environments, users can set up a network printer on their computers if they have permission to connect to the print server. In a Presentation Server environment, administrators can import network printers and assign them to users based on group membership. When a network printer is set up for use on an individual Windows computer, the printer is a client printer on the client device.

Local Printers

A *local printer* is created by an administrator on the Presentation Server using the Add Printer Wizard from within the Printers applet in the Control Panel. As with a network printer, print jobs printed to a local printer bypass the client device and can be sent either to a Windows print server or directly to a printer, depending on how the printer has been created on the server. If the printer is added to the Presentation Server with the port pointing to a share such as *printserver**sharename*, the print job is sent to the print server before heading to the printer.

The print queue can be Windows-, NetWare-, or UNIX-based. If the printer is added and the port specifies the actual printer itself (such as an lpr queue to the printer's IP address), the Presentation Server is essentially the print server, and the job is sent directly to the printer. Local printers are not typically utilized in an enterprise Presentation Server environment because of the need for the MetaFrame administrator to set up every printer in the environment on each Presentation Server. However, local printers can be utilized successfully in smaller Presentation Server farms (three or fewer servers).

PRINTER DRIVER REPLICATION

Printer driver replication was introduced in Presentation Server to reduce the management nightmare of ensuring that all Presentation Servers in the farm have the required printer drivers for an environment.

Printer driver replication is designed to copy printer driver files and registry settings across the server farm. You can install all required printer drivers on one Presentation Server in the farm, and then replicate the files and registry settings to all other servers in the farm. Management of printer driver replication is performed through the Presentation Server Console. Printer driver replication does not replicate printer properties, such as paper size and print quality.

TIP   Printer driver replication can be CPU-intensive on the source server. To improve performance, avoid replicating drivers while the farm is under heavy load, such as when many users are logging on.

Managing the Printer Driver Replication Queue

Each printer driver/server combination creates an item in the printer replication queue. For best performance, this queue should not exceed 1500 entries in length. To determine the queue size, use the following formula:

QueueSize = *Drivers* ∗ *Servers*

where *Drivers* is the number of printer drivers and *Servers* is the number of servers to which the printer drivers are being replicated.

Using this formula, the queue can include 30 drivers for replication to 50 servers (30 ∗ 50 = 1,500) or three drivers for replication to 500 servers (3 ∗ 500 = 1,500) without exceeding the queue size recommendation.

The replication queue items can be monitored with the qprinter/replica command. For more information on the qprinter command, see the next section, "qprinter Command."

qprinter Command

The *qprinter command* is a utility designed to enable administrators to monitor the progress of the printer driver replication queue and import printer name–mapping parameters into the data store. The syntax of the qprinter command is

```
qprinter [/replica]
qprinter [/imprmapping mappingfilename]
```

where *mappingfilename* specifies the full path to the text file containing the printermapping parameters to import. The filename cannot have more than 256 characters and cannot contain quotation marks.

Here are the options for the qprinter command:

▼   **/replica**   Displays all the replication entries queued for distribution, but not yet completed. The /replica switch displays all events in the queue, including broken or failed events.

▲   **/imprmapping** *mappingfilename*   Imports printer mappings from the file specified by *mappingfilename* into the data store. The file format can be in either the *Wtsprnt.inf* format or the *Wtsuprn.txt* format. The /imprmapping switch allows central administration of all printer name mappings. The file can be imported once from any server in the farm and is available for all servers in the farm. The /imprmapping switch does not process an improperly formatted file and does not return an error when provided with an invalid file format. To verify that the information is correctly imported into the data store, use the Citrix Management Console.

NOTE   Only MetaFrame administrators can execute this command.

The Presentation Server installation first attempts to import the *Wtsuprn.txt* file, followed by the *Wtsprnt.inf* file. If the two files fail to import, no error is returned. Use the /imprmapping switch to manually import either file.

Qprinter is not installed by default. It is in the \support\debug\W2K folder (for Windows 2000 Servers) or the \support\debug\W2K3 folder (for Windows 2003 Servers) on the Presentation Server CD.

TIP   You can determine the success or failure of printer driver replication by checking the Application log in Event Viewer on the target servers.

Driver Replication and Performance Issues

The number of printer drivers installed on or replicated to each server in the farm can affect server performance and the IMA service response time. The following sections provide recommendations for minimizing potential performance issues when installing or replicating printer drivers.

Driver Replication and Server Performance

The time required to complete printer driver replications depends on network traffic and server load. The replication distribution queue is handled by the IMA service.

The printer driver replication subsystem can process an average of 50 entries a minute in a 50-server farm under a light user and network load. A 500-server farm under the same conditions can process an average of 20 entries a minute.

The distribution subsystem monitors the load on the Presentation Server that is replicating the print drivers while they are distributed across the server farm.

To complete printer driver replication as quickly as possible, Citrix recommends that it be executed during off-peak hours, when higher-priority network traffic is at a minimum.

TIP   The progress of the replication jobs can be monitored by running qprinter/replica.

Driver Replication and IMA Performance

The data store holds one record for each printer driver, one record for each farm server, and one record for each printer driver/server combination. The more printer drivers installed on farm servers, the larger the printer driver tables in the data store, thus requiring more time to query information from the data store at startup. Introducing a large number of printer drivers to Presentation Server—whether they are manually installed or replicated—slows IMA response time.

The best practice is to limit the number of printer drivers in the farm using the following guidelines:

▼ Install printer drivers only for printers to be used by Presentation Server Clients in the farm.

■ Install printer drivers only on servers that will host users who need access to the printers.

■ Install printer drivers that work for multiple printer types, if possible.

■ Remove unnecessary printer drivers from cloned images.

■ In WAN environments where a large number of printer drivers are installed, use a replicated data store if better performance is necessary.

▲ Use the Citrix Universal Print Driver instead of the native Windows drivers, if possible.

Using Auto-replication

Every Presentation Server maintains a list of drivers that it received through autoreplication under HKLM\SOFTWARE\Citrix\IMAPrinter:AutoReplicate. This registry value contains IMA UIDs for each driver configured for autoreplication. During IMA service startup, the IMA service's Printer subsystem checks if a driver's UID is already present in the registry. If a driver is already registered as being replicated to a server, that driver is not reinstalled, even if the "overwrite" option is checked.

For "regular" replication (when auto-replication is not selected), when the replication job is started, if "overwrite" is not selected, the target server is checked to verify whether the server already contains the necessary files needed to install the driver. If the files exist, the server is told to install the driver. If the driver files are not already available on the target server, they are sent from the source server to the target server and installed. If "overwrite" is selected, the drivers are always sent from the source server to the targets.

This behavior ensures every server has the same version of the driver installed.

When an auto-replication job is scheduled, if the driver is not already detected as replicated in the aforementioned registry key, the IMA service attempts to download it during IMA service startup. If several printer replication jobs are destined for a server, the IMA service may take an extended period of time to start. If auto-replication must be used, keep the number of printer drivers to be replicated to a minimum.

OPTIMIZING PRINTER CREATION

Network printer shares that reside on the client system can cause an increase in client login times because the printers are created and deleted during each logon and logoff. Using autocreated network printers, instead of client network printer shares, can reduce login times because the connections to the network printers remain persistent. If the network printer is on the Presentation Server, no other action is required; otherwise, you need to perform the following steps to import the required network print servers into the farm.

To add network printers to a Presentation Server farm, follow these steps:

1. Open the Presentation Server Console and select the Printer Management node.

2. Right-click Printer Management and select Import Network Print Server.

3. Specify the network print server to import and add any necessary authentication credentials.

4. When the operation finishes, the print server appears on the Network Print Servers tab.

5. Install the printer drivers for your network printers on a Presentation Server in the server farm.

6. Within the Presentation Server Console, expand the Printer Management node, right-click Drivers, and select Auto-Replication to distribute the drivers to all Presentation Servers in the farm. This also maintains the replication job in the data store, so these drivers can be added to any new servers added to the farm in the future. Use the guidelines outlined previously in the section "Using Auto-replication" when performing replication.

To allocate network printers to users, follow these steps:

1. Within the Presentation Server Console, expand the Printer Management node.

2. Select the Printers node, and then select a printer.

3. Right-click on a printer and select Auto-Creation.

4. Specify a domain, and then select the groups and users who need to use the printer.

When a specified user logs onto a Presentation Server in the farm, the printer becomes available in the user's ICA session as if the printer were installed on the user's client device.

Controlling the Behavior of Autocreated Network Printers

By default, if a client machine's network printers are allowed to be autocreated in a session, during client logon the Presentation Server determines if it can contact the print server directly. If the Presentation Server can contact the print server directly, then it creates the user's network printer as if the network printer were configured on the Presentation Server. When a print job is sent to this printer, instead of being sent back to the client through the ICA printer virtual channel, the print job is sent directly from the Presentation Server to the print server.

In certain scenarios (such as when the print server is located across the WAN) or if you want to control client printing bandwidth, this can cause performance issues.

With previous versions of Presentation Server, a registry modification was required to control whether network printers were created with a direct connection from the server to the printer or as client printers that print through the ICA client device. With Presentation Server 4.0, you can configure a print job routing policy to control how printing requests to network printers are processed. For more information about using policies, see *Presentation Server Administrator's Guide* and the Presentation Server Console online help.

PRESENTATION SERVER CLIENT PRINTING ENHANCEMENTS

The Presentation Server Client for 32-bit Windows version 8.*x* and higher contains improvements in the PCL renderer that reduce the size of the spool files compared to earlier versions of the MetaFrame Access Client.

Enforce Printer Compatibility

This feature lets administrators disallow certain printer drivers from being used. During login, the autocreated client printers are checked against a banned list of printers restricted by the administrator. This enables the administrator to enforce banning print drivers, which may cause issues on a Presentation Server.

The administrator is able to configure drivers that are either allowed or banned using the Presentation Server Console. This is done by logging into the Presentation Server Console, expanding Printer Management plug-in, clicking on Drivers, and then by either clicking on the Compatibility icon on the tool bar or by right-clicking on Drivers, and then selecting the Compatibility option. In the Driver Compatibility window, the administrator has two options to select from: "Allow only drivers in the list" or "Allow all drivers except those in the list". There, the administrator makes their desired choice.

During logon time, the client printers are automatically mapped into the session and verified that they are allowed to be created by comparing against this print driver list. An event is generated for the banned client printer in the event log on the server.

NOTE   Once a driver is autoinstalled on the server, the driver remains on the server, unless it is removed from Start\Settings\Printers folder. Therefore, for the functionality of the check box of "Automatically install native drivers for auto-created client and network printers" to work properly, use a printer whose drivers are already not installed on the server. One way to check for the installed drivers on the server is to go to Start\Settings\Printers and ensure that nothing is highlighted in the printer's window, then go to File\Server Properties and click on Drivers. The drivers installed on the server are listed here.

If you want to revert to the behavior of previous Universal Printer drivers and print in black-and-white using the Presentation Server client for Windows version 7.*x* or later, you can edit the registry key: \HKLM\Software\Citrix\UniversalPrintDrivers by double-clicking the Driver List key and deleting "PCL5c".

SESSION PRINTERS POLICY

Citrix MetaFrame Presentation Server 3.0 included a more powerful and flexible policy engine that allowed many of the settings in Presentation Server to be centralized. The network printer autocreation facility, however, was unable to use this engine, printer connections could only be configured by user/group, and administrators resorted to complicated login scripts or third-party utilities to accomplish per-session customization of printer connections. They lacked the capability to build up customized printing workspaces based on any policy criteria via a simple UI. They also lacked the capability to designate which printer should be the user's default printer for those situations where they need to establish overrides for the default printer settings.

Citrix Presentation Server 4.0 has incorporated printer connections into the policy engine. This new policy setting lets Presentation Server administrators create customized printing workspaces based on any policy criteria. The administrator now has the ability to define a default printer without having to resort to login scripts.

The New Session Printers Policy

The *session printers policy feature* represents an extension of the current autocreated network printer functionality. By using the policy engine, administrators can now customize a client printer workspace based on criteria such as client name, client IP address, server, user, or group.

The session printers policy enables administrators to designate the following:

1. Which network printer(s) to connect within the session.

2. If a particular printer should be the user's default printer.

3. The ability to override default values of common printer settings for network printers.

These new options extend the flexibility of policies to allow customized printer workspaces to be constructed for specific sites, groups, users, servers, clients, and so forth. These new policy options also add the long sought-after capability to explicitly set the default printer for a user without resorting to login scripts and preserves the printer properties' overrides available with autocreated network printer support.

Creating and Applying Policies for Session Printing

Three aspects are involved in the creation and application of a policy configuration:

▼ The creation of a policy, its settings, and its resolution.

■ How Presentation Server determines which settings in a policy to apply.

▲ Policy enforcement.

Configuration   To create a policy that uses the new session printers rule, the administrator first creates a new policy object in the Presentation Server Management Console. The session printers rule is not configured by default. Next, the administrator modifies the session printers rule by either enabling or disabling it. If the rule is enabled, the administrator can then modify its settings. After the rule is configured, the administrator can update the policy's filter and priority.

Resolution   Resolution of the session printers policy rule occurs when a user creates a new session. Typically for every rule, the policy engine examines each policy in order of priority. For the majority of the policy rules, if the state of the highest priority policy is enabled, then the settings from this policy are used. The policy engine ignores any other rule defined in any of the other lower priority policies. In contrast to this behavior, the session printers rule has the capability to merge with lower priority policies. This allows for more flexible printer workspace configurations based on different filtering criteria. Presentation Server reflects the resultant policy into the system registry, including the list of configured printers and the default printer.

Enforcement   The enforcement code for printer connections are executed during the logon process. The Presentation Server gets the printer connection settings from the registry, and then interacts with the IMA printer subsystem to create the printers specified by the policy and, possibly, override their settings.

Important Considerations

Some situations must be taken into consideration when introducing the new session printers policy into your environment:

▼   The session printers policy rule merges its properties with lower priority policies. This is a new behavior introduced in the policy engine for Presentation Server 4.0.

■   Note, in Presentation Server 4.0, printer autocreation functionality in the Printer node has been removed from the Presentation Server Console. This means the session printers policy is now the only mechanism for adjusting printer settings on a network printer. Given that the session printers policy is only available as part of Presentation Server 4.0, you will be unable to administer previous versions of Presentation Servers' printer autocreation settings with the new version of the Presentation Server Console. Instead, use a previous version of the Presentation Server Console to access the autocreate objects.

▲   Session printers policies do not affect the functionality of older servers. The IMA service continues to hold autoconnect network printer objects and is still able to create, delete, and manage them separately from session printers policies. The Presentation Server Console UI for this functionality has been removed, so administrators need to use a previous version of the Presentation Server Console to administer autoconnect printer objects for Presentation Server 3.0 and earlier.

Troubleshooting

The following scenarios may arise when using the new session printers policy rules. At the end of each scenario's description, a possible resolution is provided.

Scenario 1: A New Printer Fails to Autocreate An administrator has created a session printers policy and assigned it to users of the Education Department. The administrator has defined two network printers—Printer1 and Printer2—to users of the Education Department. Now the department gets a new printer named Printer3. The administrator adds Printer3 to the policy, which is assigned to users of the Education Department.

When the users of the Education department login to the Presentation Server through an ICA session, they only see Printer1 and Printer2, but Printer3 is not getting autocreated.

Resolution: The administrator should install the driver for Printer3 on the Presentation Server. If the driver for the network printer is unavailable, the printer will not be autocreated.

Scenario 2: Session Network Printers Are Not Autocreated The administrator has a policy defined to autocreate printers using Universal Printer Driver only, but the Session Network Printers defined through a session printers policy are not autocreated using the Universal Printer Driver.

Resolution: Session Network printers are never autocreated using the Universal Printer Driver; they are always autocreated using the native drivers. In fact, none of the other printer policies affect the session printers policy.

Scenario 3: Users Working in Multiple Groups Want a Different Default Printer An administrator has two session printers policies—Policy1 and Policy2—and these are assigned to users of the Education Department and users of the Support Department, respectively. Policy1 has Printer1 and Printer2 defined to it, and Printer2 is further defined as the default printer. Policy2 has Printer3 and Printer4 defined to it, and Printer4 is defined as the default printer. Two users—User21 and User23—are members of both departments\ groups, but they are currently working in the Education Department. When User21 and User23 connect to the server through an ICA session, Printer1, Printer2, Printer3, and Printer4 are all autocreated, but Printer4 is set as the default printer. But, because User21 and User23 are currently working for the Education Department, they want their default printer to be Printer2.

Resolution: Policy2 has been set to a higher priority than Policy1. Set Policy1 to a higher priority than Policy2.

Session Printing Registry Settings

Presentation Server 4.0 provides registry settings that can be used to change the behavior of session printing. These settings are used to track the various printing-related settings on a per-session basis.

During login, the actual session settings for printing are derived from a combination of Presentation Server policies, base Terminal Server defaults, and an optional "DefaultPrnFlags" value in the Presentation Server's registry. In the absence of a configured policy or modifications to base Terminal Server defaults, default values for all bit flags listed in the following are initially zero. Setting a bit to 1 enables one of the following documented functions. As you can see from the names, enabling the bit flag is often used to disable or turn off default behavior.

To modify the system default values:

1. Navigate to HKLM\Software\Citrix\Print.
2. Add a REG_DWORD value named "DefaultPrnFlags" to the registry key.

For some settings, default values (before policy application) are taken from settings managed by the Terminal Server base functionality, instead of the DefaultPrnFlags value. All settings with an initial default provided by Terminal Server are highlighted in the following. These defaults apply, unless the CTXPRN_OVERRIDE_TS_DEFAULTS bit is set in the DefaultPrnFLags value.

NOTE Configured and enabled Presentation Server policy rules always override default settings whether they are read from the registry or provided by Terminal Server. However, policies do not exist for many of these settings as they may either not be of general interest or intended only as a failsafe to disable certain features for troubleshooting.

CTXPRN_OVERRIDE_TS_DEFAULTS (0x00000080)

Windows manages several printing-related session settings, which it derives from group policies, user settings, or the connection type defaults. Unless overridden, we use these settings as intended defaults. Settings that favor a Terminal Server-provided default are highlighted. To override Terminal Server default for any of the identified settings, this flag must be set in the DefaultPrnFlags registry value read from HKLM\Software\Citrix\Print in the system registry. If this flag is not set, then the normal Terminal Server defaults apply.

Client Printer Autocreation Flags

▼ CTXPRN_CLNTPRN_AUTOCREATE_NONE (0x00000004)

■ CTXPRN_CLNTPRN_AUTOCREATE_LOCAL_ONLY (0x00000002)

▲ CTXPRN_CLNTPRN_AUTOCREATE_DEFAULT_ONLY (0x00000001)

By default, all discovered client printers are autocreated. However, if any of these flags are set, only a subset of discovered client printers will be autocreated. If CTXPRN_CLNTPRN_AUTOCREATE_NONE is set, then none of the discovered client printers are autocreated. If AUTOCREATE_NONE is not set and CTXPRN_CLNTPRN_AUTOCREATE_LOCAL_ONLY is set, then only printers that appear to be local to the client are autocreated. If AUOTCREATE_NONE & AUTOCREATE_LOCAL_ONLY are not set, but CTXPRN_CLNTPRN_AUTOCREATE_DEFAULT_ONLY is set, then only the default client printer will be autocreated.

Default Value

Unless overridden, Terminal Server defaults for these settings are used. If CTXPRN_ OVERRIDE_TS_DEFAULTS flag is set in the "DefaultPrnFlags" value at HKLM\ Software\Citrix\Print\, then the Terminal Server defaults are ignored and default bit values are taken from this REG_DWORD value.

Overriding Presentation Server Policy Rule

Printing | Client Printers | Auto-Creation

CTXPRN_DISABLE_DIRECT_CONNECT_FOR_CLNTPRNS (0x00200000)

When autocreating a client printer that is a connection to a shared network printer, the system first attempts to establish a direct connection from the server session to the network print server using the login credentials of the server session. Failing this, the printer is still connected as a client printer. If this flag is set, the attempt to establish a direct printer connection from the presentation server to the print server is avoided, thereby forcing all client printers to be connected indirectly through the client.

Default Value

The default value is zero, unless the appropriate bit value is set in the REG_DWORD registry value "DefaultPrnFlags" at HKLM\Software\Citrix\Print\.

Overriding Presentation Server Policy Rule

Printing | Client Printers | Print Job Routing

CTXPRN_DONT_SET_DEFAULT_CLIENT_PRINTER (0x00000800)

By default, the system sets the session user's default printer to the client's default printer. If this flag is set, the client's default printer will not be set as the session user's default.

Default Value

Unless overridden, the Terminal Server default for this setting is used. If CTXPRN_ OVERRIDE_TS_DEFAULTS flag is set in the "DefaultPrnFlags" value at HKLM\ Software\Citrix\Print\, then the Terminal Server default is ignored and the default bit value is taken from this REG_DWORD value.

Overriding Presentation Server Policy Rule

Printing | Session Printers

CTXPRN_CREATE_LEGACY_CLIENT_PRINTERS (0x00000010)

By default, the system uses printer names and ports that are qualified by the session ID, so they will be unique to a particular session. If set, this flag causes old-style printer and port names derived only from the client name to be used. Although less secure, this setting is useful for applications that expect the old-style printer names to be used.

Default Value

The default value is zero, unless the appropriate bit value is set in the REG_DWORD registry value "DefaultPrnFlags" at HKLM\Software\Citrix\Print\.

Overriding Presentation Server Policy Rule

Printing | Client Printers | Legacy Client Printers

CTXPRN_AUTO_CREATE_GENERIC_UPD_PRINTER (0x00000020)

The latest 32-bit Windows clients are capable of receiving and displaying print jobs in a viewer application on the client. For such a client, it is possible to create a single generic universal printer within the session that is not bound to any of the underlying client printers. This printer is generic in the sense that it does not know about, or manage, any device-specific settings. As such, it is also more efficient to use because there is no need for capabilities or document settings exchanges with the client when printing. Because creating any additional printer within a session incurs overhead, by default, the creation of the generic UPD printer is OFF. If this flag is set, then the system will autocreate the generic "Citrix UNIVERSAL Printer" in addition to the other printers dictated by other autocreation flags. For customers that do not require special printer capabilities, creating only a single generic UPD printer within the session—instead of one printer for each underlying client printer—can provide a scalability savings. To see this savings, not only must this flag be enabled, but default autocreation polices also need to be overridden or assigned via policies.

Default Value

The default value is zero, unless the appropriate bit value is set in the REG_DWORD registry value "DefaultPrnFlags" at HKLM\Software\Citrix\Print\.

Overriding Presentation Server Policy Rule

None

Printer Driver Flags

▼ CTXPRN_DRIVERS_AVOID_REGULAR_DRIVERS (0x00000100)

■ CTXPRN_DRIVERS_NO_UPD_FALLBACK (0x00000200)

▲ CTXPRN_DRIVERS_ENABLE_UPD (0x00000400)

By default, the system attempts to use standard printer drivers as requested by the client if they are available. If the specific driver is unavailable and the client supports a UPD, then the printer will be autocreated using the universal driver as a fallback. The default behavior is modified by setting any of the following combinations:

▼ CTXPRN_DRIVERS_AVOID_REGULAR_DRIVERS and CTXPRN_DRIVERS_ ENABLE_UPD   Use universal driver only

▲ CTXPRN_DRIVERS_NO_UPD_FALLBACK set, others 0   Use model specific drivers only

Default Value

Default values are all zero, unless one or more of the appropriate bit values are set in the REG_DWORD registry value "DefaultPrnFlags" at HKLM\Software\Citrix\Print\.

Overriding Presentation Server Policy Rule

Printing | Drivers | Universal Driver

CTXPRN_DRIVERS_DISABLE_AUTO_INSTALL (0x00100000)

By default, both the network printer and client printer autocreation processes attempt to install needed drivers from the native set of printer drivers that ships with Windows (for example, Driver.cab/ntprint.inf). If set, this flag disables all such automatic driver installations, implying all drivers must be preinstalled or replicated to all required Presentation Servers.

Default Value

The default value is zero, unless the appropriate bit value is set in the REG_DWORD registry value "DefaultPrnFlags" at HKLM\Software\Citrix\Print\.

Overriding Presentation Server Policy Rule

Printing | Drivers | Native Printer Driver Autoinstall

CTXPRN_NO_UPD_FALLBACK_FOR_DISALLOWED_DRIVER (0x10000000)

When a driver name presented from the client fails the compatibility test (for example, the driver name is present in an exclude list or not present in an allow-only list), assuming UPD fallback is enabled, the normal behavior is to try to create the printer using the UPD. If set, this flag changes the default and avoids UPD creation for printers whose drivers fail the compatibility test.

Default Value

The default value is zero, unless the appropriate bit value is set in the REG_DWORD registry value "DefaultPrnFlags" at HKLM\Software\Citrix\Print\.

Overriding Presentation Server Policy Rule

None

Client Printer Properties Retention Flags

▼ CTXPRN_DISABLE_CLNTPRN_PROPS_EXCHANGE_WITH_CLIENT (0x00001000)

▲ CTXPRN_DISABLE_CLNTPRN_PROPS_PROFILE_SAVE_RESTORE (0x00002000)

By default, the system first attempts to save modified printer properties by sending them back to the client (if supported). Failing that, the system tries to save them in the user profile on the server. Setting either flag has the effect of disabling the printer properties save/restore to either (or both) the client exchange and/or the user profile.

Default Value

The default value is zero, unless the appropriate bit value is set in the REG_DWORD registry value "DefaultPrnFlags" at HKLM\Software\Citrix\Print\.

Overriding Presentation Server Policy Rule

Printing | Drivers | Printer Properties Retention

Client Printer Port Management

▼ CTXPRN_CREATE_BOTH_STD_AND_LEGACY_CLNTPRN_PORTS (0x01000000)

■ CTXPRN_CREATE_PORTS_FOR_AUTOCREATED_CLNTPRNS_ONLY (0x02000000)

▲ CTXPRN_DONT_DELETE_CLNTPRN_PORTS (0x04000000)

By default, the system creates ports for all discovered client printers during login or reconnects and deletes them at logout. The style of port created depends on the state of the CTXPRN_CREATE_LEGACY_CLIENT_PRINTERS flag. If any of these flags are set, the default port creation and deletion behavior is modified as follows:

▼ CTXPRN_CREATE_BOTH_STD_AND_LEGACY_CLNTPRN_PORTS Instead of creating either legacy style or standard port names, both types of ports are created.

■ CTXPRN_CREATE_PORTS_FOR_AUTOCREATED_CLNTPRNS_ONLY Creates ports only as needed for autocreated printers, rather than for every discovered client printer.

▲   CTXPRN_DONT_DELETE_CLNTPRN_PORTS   Does not delete ports at log-out. This works around a Windows 2000 spooler issue (see Microsoft knowledgebase article 893691) that can trap the spooler service. However, enabling this setting can lead to substantial port and handle accumulations in the spooler service that eventually require the service to be restarted.

Default Value

All default values are zero, unless one or more of the appropriate bit values is set in the REG_DWORD registry value "DefaultPrnFlags" at HKLM\Software\Citrix\Print\.

Overriding Presentation Server Policy Rule

None

Network Printer Connection Flags

▼   CTXPRN_DISABLE_NETWORK_PRINTER_AUTOCONNECT (0x00400000)

▲   CTXPRN_DISABLE_NETWORK_PRINTER_DISCONNECT (0x00800000)

The Presentation Server policies evaluated at login and reconnect include a special policy rule called "Session Printers," which can be used to add and delete network printer connections on behalf of the login user based on various policy criteria. Normally, these network printer connections are added during logins/reconnects, and then deleted during logout. The two flags listed previously are fail-safes that allow the administrator to temporarily disable all printer connection additions and deletions all at once, without having to disable many different policies. Of course, this is mostly useful in certain troubleshooting scenarios. That said, turning off only the disconnection of network printers can improve server scalability at the expense of allowing printer connections made by the Session Printers policy rule to accumulate in user profiles.

Default Value

The default values are all zero, unless one or more of the appropriate bit values is set in the REG_DWORD registry value "DefaultPrnFlags" at HKLM\Software\Citrix\Print\.

Overriding Presentation Server Policy Rule

None

Miscellaneous Printer Flags

▼   CTXPRN_DISABLE_CLIENT_PRINTER_MAPPING (0x00000008)

By default, the SPL virtual channel is initialized and client printer mapping is enabled. If set, this flag disables the SPL virtual channel, thereby disabling the client-printer mapping functionality of the system.

Default Value

Unless overridden, Terminal Server default for this setting is used. If CTXPRN_ OVERRIDE_TS_DEFAULTS flag is set in the "DefaultPrnFlags" value at HKLM \Software\Citrix\Print\, then the Terminal Server defaults are ignored and the default flag value is taken from this REG_DWORD value.

Overriding Presentation Server Policy Rule

Printing | Client Printers | Client Printer Mapping

CTXPRN_DONT_AUTO_CONNECT_LPTS (0x00000040)

For compatibility reasons, LPT ports discovered on the client are automatically mapped in client sessions. If the remapped LPT port is never used, then there is no good reason to have mapped it. If this flag is set, LPT ports can still be mapped in a client session, but they will not be automatically mapped. Instead, a net use command or the equivalent WNet* API must be used to establish any mapping, just as one would do for a redirected COM port.

Default Value

Default values are all zero, unless one or more of the appropriate bit values is set in the REG_DWORD registry value "DefaultPrnFlags" at HKLM\Software\Citrix\Print\.

Overriding Presentation Server Policy Rule

None

CTXPRN_ADMINS_CAN_MANAGE (0x00004000)

To preclude the possibility of an administrative user inadvertently printing to a printer in someone else's Terminal Services session, the default security descriptor used to autocreate client printers no longer includes any rights for the administrator's group. Only the user executing in the proper session context has rights to the autocreated printers for the session. Administrators may still grant themselves rights to any client printer by taking ownership of the print queue and adding the desired rights. Because this is a cumbersome process, administrators not requiring the level of security provided may opt to set this flag and the system then automatically adds usage rights to all autocreated client printers for members of the administrator's group.

Default Value

The default value is zero, unless the appropriate bit value is set in the REG_DWORD registry value "DefaultPrnFlags" at HKLM\Software\Citrix\Print\.

Overriding Presentation Server Policy Rule

None

CTXPRN_DONT_LOG_AUTOCREATE_FAILURE (0x08000000)

By default, printer autocreation failures cause events to be logged in the event viewer's application log. Even printers created by UPD result in an event because this is one of the few ways administrators can find out precisely which printer models are in use by the client population. Because this can result in a flood of events in the event viewer, this flag provides the means to avoid generating event log entries for autocreation failures.

Default Value

The default value is zero, unless the appropriate bit value is set in the REG_DWORD registry value "DefaultPrnFlags" at HKLM\Software\Citrix\Print\.

Overriding Presentation Server Policy Rule

None

CHAPTER 14

Farm Maintenance

This chapter covers best pracices, recommendations, and maintenance issues that might be encountered while administering a Citrix Presentation Server farm.

CONSOLIDATING MULTIPLE LICENSE FILES

If you have multiple Citrix license files installed on one license server, you can combine the files into one file.

IMPORTANT You can only combine license files containing the same HOSTNAME value. Consolidating license files from multiple servers or combining Citrix license files with another company's license files is not supported.

To Combine License Files

If your license files are compatible, you can use any text editor to combine them. The basic concept of creating a *single* license file is a process of empty text-file creation, where you copy appropriate sections into the file, save the file, and then force the Citrix License Server to reread the file. Think of the individual license files as INI files (with multiple sections). Follow this example:

1. Because all license files being combined are from the same HOSTNAME server, the following section only needs to occur once at the top of the file. Take this section from your existing license files and paste it into your new "empty" one.

    ```
    # This file is in UTF-8 format.
    #
    SERVER this_host HOSTNAME=domain
    VENDOR CITRIX
    USE_SERVER
    ```

2. Combine all of the following lines from each license file into one contiguous list.

    ```
    INCREMENT MPS_ENT_CCU CITRIX 2004.1027 27-oct-2004 99 \
    VENDOR_STRING=;LT=NFR;GP=96;CL=ENT,ADV,STD;SA=0;ODP=0;AP=ADMIN/LOGON/ALW:NONADMIN/
    LOGON/ALW \
        DUP_GROUP=V ISSUED=30-Apr-2004 NOTICE="Citrix Systems France" \
        SN=OR867:1265 START=30-apr-2004 SIGN="XXXX XXXX XXXX XXXX XXXX \
        XXXX XXXX XXXX XXXX XXXX XXXX XXXX XXXX XXXX XXXX XXXX   \
        XXXX XXXX XXXX XXXX XXXX XXXX XXXX XXXX XXXX XXXX XXXX XXXX   \
        XXXX "
    ```

3. Append the *CITRIXTERMs* at the end of the license file (especially if you have different edition licenses).

```
#[English]
#CITRIXTERM      FEATURE      1.0      MPS_STD_CCU      EN      MetaFrame Presentation
Server, Standard Edition|Concurrent User
#CITRIXTERM      FEATURE      1.0      MPS_ADV_CCU      EN      MetaFrame Presentation
Server, Advanced Edition|Concurrent User
#CITRIXTERM      FEATURE      1.0      MPS_ENT_CCU      EN      MetaFrame Presentation
Server, Enterprise Edition|Concurrent User

#[German]
#CITRIXTERM      FEATURE      1.0      MPS_STD_CCU      DE      MetaFrame Presentation
Server, Standard Edition|Gleichzeitige Benutzer
#CITRIXTERM      FEATURE      1.0      MPS_ADV_CCU      DE      MetaFrame Presentation
Server, Advanced Edition|Gleichzeitige Benutzer
#CITRIXTERM      FEATURE      1.0      MPS_ENT_CCU      DE      MetaFrame Presentation
Server, Enterprise Edition|Gleichzeitige Benutzer

#[French]
#CITRIXTERM      FEATURE      1.0      MPS_STD_CCU      FR      MetaFrame Presentation
Server, édition Standard|Utilisateurs simultanés
#CITRIXTERM      FEATURE      1.0      MPS_ADV_CCU      FR      MetaFrame Presentation
Server, édition Advanced|Utilisateurs simultanés
#CITRIXTERM      FEATURE      1.0      MPS_ENT_CCU      FR      MetaFrame Presentation
Server, édition Enterprise|Utilisateurs simultanés

#[Spanish]
#CITRIXTERM      FEATURE      1.0      MPS_STD_CCU      ES      MetaFrame Presentation
Server, Standard Edition|Usuario concurrente
#CITRIXTERM      FEATURE      1.0      MPS_ADV_CCU      ES      MetaFrame Presentation
Server, Advanced Edition|Usuario concurrente
#CITRIXTERM      FEATURE      1.0      MPS_ENT_CCU      ES      MetaFrame Presentation
Server, Enterprise Edition|Usuario concurrente

#[Japanese]
#CITRIXTERM      FEATURE      1.0      MPS_STD_CCU      JA      MetaFrame Presentation
Server, Standard Edition|\u540c\u6642\u4f7f\u7528\u30e6\u30fc\u30b6\u30fc
#CITRIXTERM      FEATURE      1.0      MPS_ADV_CCU      JA      MetaFrame Presentation
Server, Advanced Edition|\u540c\u6642\u4f7f\u7528\u30e6\u30fc\u30b6\u30fc
#CITRIXTERM      FEATURE      1.0      MPS_ENT_CCU      JA      MetaFrame Presentation
Server, Enterprise Edition|\u540c\u6642\u4f7f\u7528\u30e6\u30fc\u30b6\u30fc
#
```

4. Force the license server to reread the license file for changes to take effect. See "Updating License File Data on the License Server" in *MetaFrame Access Suite License Server Customizations*.

For more information about license files, see the *MetaFrame Access Suite Licensing Guide* and *MetaFrame Access Suite License Server Customizations*. These documents can be found in the Citrix Support Knowledgebase.

CYCLE BOOTING CITRIX PRESENTATION SERVERS

Citrix Presentation Servers do not require a regular restart cycle to run effectively. However, if cycle booting is desired, follow these guidelines.

When the IMA service starts after a restart, it establishes a connection to the data store and performs various reads to update the local host cache. These reads can vary from a few hundred kilobytes of data to several megabytes of data, depending on the size and configuration of the server farm.

To reduce the load on the data store and to reduce the IMA service start time, Citrix recommends maintaining cycle boot groups of no more than 100 servers. In large server farms with hundreds of servers, or when the database hardware is insufficient, restart servers in groups of approximately 50, with at least ten-minute intervals between groups.

TIP   If the Service Control Manager reports that the IMA service could not be started after a restart of a Citrix Presentation Server, but the service eventually starts, ignore this message. The Service Control Manager has a timeout of six minutes. The IMA service can take longer than six minutes to start because the load on the database exceeds the capabilities of the database hardware. To eliminate this message, try restarting fewer servers at the same time.

CHANGING FARM MEMBERSHIP OF SERVERS

Citrix Presentation Servers require the use of the chfarm command to change farm membership. The following discusses the correct use of the chfarm command that ships.

CAUTION   Misuse of chfarm can corrupt the data store. Before running the chfarm command on any server in the farm, back up the data store.

Using chfarm

Chfarm can be executed from %ProgramFiles%\Citrix\system32\citrix\ima, the installation CD, or a network image of the CD.

CAUTION   If chfarm reports any error, continuing the process can corrupt the data store. Instead, click Cancel and use the process for restoring an unresponsive server. See the section "Recovering an Unresponsive Server" in Chapter 17.

Executing chfarm

Executing chfarm does the following on the host server:

1. Attempts to remove the server from the farm.
2. Stops the IMA service.

3. Configures the data store.

4. Restarts the IMA service.

Important chfarm Considerations

Consider the following when using chfarm:

▼ Running chfarm on a server hosting the data store (MS Access, MSDE) deletes the current data store database. Do not use chfarm on the server hosting the MS Access or MSDE database until all other servers in that farm are moved to a new server farm. Failure to follow this process causes errors when chfarm is executed on those servers that no longer have a valid data store.

■ When creating a MS Access data store on a new server farm:

   ▼ Run chfarm first on the server hosting the new data store

   ■ Execute chfarm on other servers to be added to the new server farm

   ▲ Run chfarm on any servers that hosted an old data store last

■ Close all connections to the Presentation Server Console on the local server before executing the chfarm command.

▲ Execute chfarm only on a functioning Citrix Presentation Server. Do not execute chfarm on a server that was removed from a server farm.

IMPORTANT   Using chfarm does not migrate published applications or any server settings to the new server farm.

Using chfarm with MSDE

When using the chfarm utility to change a Citrix Presentation Server's farm membership or create a new farm that will use Microsoft SQL Server 2000 Database Engine Desktop Edition (MSDE) for the server farm's data store, a named instance of MSDE must be installed on the server on which you run chfarm.

The default named instance that chfarm uses is CITRIX_METAFRAME. Running chfarm does not automatically install MSDE; chfarm must be installed manually using the MSDE Windows Installer installation package included on the MetaFrame XP server CD located in the Support\MSDE\MSDE folder. To create and install a named instance of MSDE, complete the following steps:

1. Insert the Presentation Server CD in your computer's CD-ROM drive. Do not use the autorun feature.

2. Open a command prompt and change directories to the CD-ROM drive.

3. Navigate to Support\MSDE\MSDE.

4. Type the following at the command prompt:

```
msiexec -i "MSDE For MetaFrame.msi" INSTANCENAME=<name>
where <name> is the name you want to give the MSDE installation.
```

Optionally, you can run SetupMsdeForMetaFrame.cmd, which automatically creates the named instance and configures it properly.

Chfarm Options When Using MSDE

Use these options when running chfarm to create a new farm with MSDE as the data store:

/instancename:<*name*>
This is the name of the MSDE instance to which to migrate. The default value is CITRIX_METAFRAME.
/database:<*name*>
This is the name of the MSDE database to which to migrate. The default value is MF20.

NOTE You cannot migrate a database to the same named instance of MSDE already in use. If you are already using MSDE and you want to migrate to a new farm using MSDE, you must do one of the following: migrate to another database (Access or a third-party database), and then migrate back to MSDE, or install another named instance of MSDE, and then launch chfarm with the /instancename option.

To move a server to a new server farm using MSDE as the data store, complete the following steps:

1. Create a named instance of MSDE by installing MSDE on the first server in the new farm.

2. Run chfarm on the server you want to use to create the new farm using the /instancename:<*name*> option, where <*name*> is the name of the instance of MSDE created in step 1.

NOTE If a named instance of MSDE "CITRIX_METAFRAME" already exists, it is unnecessary to use the /instancename option.

BACKUP/RESTORE OF THE MSDE DATABASE

Use DSMAINT BACKUP to back up the MSDE database. Specify a local path for the location of the database backup files. Essentially, this command uses a default OSQL script to back up the database. Use DSMAINT RECOVER to restore a previously backed up copy of the MSDE database for use as the IMA data store.

If you want to create customized OSQL scripts for backup, please refer to the following Microsoft article for further details: http://support.microsoft.com/default .aspx?scid=241397.

NOTE   If you are moving the MSDE database to a different server in the farm, you need to perform DSMAINT FAILOVER on all indirect servers to point them to the new database server. This action is similar to "To move or restore an Access data store" found in the Citrix knowledgebase article CTX677542.

RENAMING A CITRIX PRESENTATION SERVER

The name and Security ID given to a server when it is installed and added to a server farm generally remains unchanged, but the server can be renamed, if necessary. To rename a server in a farm, complete the following steps:

1. In the Presentation Server Console, select the check box in the Add Administrators Wizard to add local administrators to the Citrix Administrator node and select Full Administration from the Select Tasks screen.

2. Use chglogon/disable to prevent users from logging into the server.

3. Remove the server to be renamed from published applications assigned to that server.

4. Stop the IMA service.

5. Change the name of the server.

6. Restart the server.

7. Log on to Presentation Server Console using the local administrator account.

8. Expand the Servers folder.

9. Remove the old server name from the Presentation Server Console's list of servers.

10. Add the new server name to the list of configured servers for published applications.

UNINSTALLING CITRIX PRESENTATION SERVERS IN INDIRECT MODE

If Citrix Presentation Server is removed from the server with a direct connection to the data store, indirect servers will no longer be able to access the data store. Information such as applications, MetaFrame Administrators, and so on will be lost. Citrix recommends uninstalling the indirect servers first and uninstalling the direct server last. Uninstalling the direct server first prevents any other servers from being uninstalled from the data store.

To force an uninstall of a Citrix Presentation Server when the data store cannot be accessed, use the following command:

```
msiexec /x mps.msi CTX_MF_FORCE_SUBSYSTEM_UNINSTALL=YES
```

Note, `mps.msi` is the name and location of the MSI package of Presentation Server. For more on how to pass properties to the Windows Installer, refer to the *MetaFrame Presentation Administrator's Guide*.

THE CITRIX PRESENTATION SERVER CONSOLE

This section offers recommendations for using the Presentation Server Console in an enterprise environment.

Configuring Data Refresh

By default, automatic refresh of data is disabled in the Presentation Server Console. Enabling automatic refresh increases CPU utilization by the Console and increases TCP traffic on the network. Opening multiple Presentation Server Console instances in the same farm with automatic refresh enabled increases network congestion.

In some cases, you might want to enable automatic refresh. For example, you can enable automatic refresh to view real-time data on Citrix Access Client connections and disconnections.

To enable automatic data refresh in the Presentation Server Console:

1. Launch the Presentation Server Console and log in to the farm.
2. Choose View | Preferences | User Data tab.
3. Select the automatic refresh options and enter the refresh rate. You can specify automatic refresh for server data, server folders, and application user data.
4. Click OK to apply the settings.

Auto Refresh settings are saved on the server on which the Presentation Server Console is running.

Performance Considerations

The Presentation Server Console queries the data collector and the member servers for information such as running processes, connected users, and server loads. Depending on the size of the server farm, the Presentation Server Console might affect performance in the server farm. The following are recommendations for managing performance issues with the Presentation Server Console:

▼ In Citrix Presentation Server deployments with hundreds of servers and thousands of users, connect only one instance of the Presentation Server Console to the farm for each zone.

- Connect the Presentation Server Console to a data collector, so the Presentation Server Console can query data directly, rather than through an intermediate Citrix Presentation Server.

- In large farms, the Presentation Server Console can take a long time to refresh. The refresh time depends on the number of servers in the zone, the number of Citrix Access Clients requesting connections, and the number of Presentation Server Console instances requesting information. If the refresh query takes longer to complete than the specified automatic refresh interval, the data collector becomes overloaded. Set the automatic refresh interval for users and applications as long as is practical. Using the minimum refresh interval of ten seconds is not recommended. For best performance, disable automatic refresh and manually refresh the data as needed.

- ▲ When managing a farm across a congested wide area network (WAN), run the Presentation Server Console within an ICA session to a remote server, rather than running it locally. Running the Presentation Server Console from within an ICA session reduces the amount of bandwidth consumed across the WAN and provides better performance from the Presentation Server Console.

Adding a Server to Multiple Published Applications

In customer environments with hundreds or thousands of published applications, adding a new server to all the published applications can be cumbersome. To add multiple applications to a server, you can launch the Presentation Server Console and select the existing published applications you want to publish to the new server. Drag the selected applications to the server you want to publish them in to the left-hand side of the console. This automatically adds all the selected applications to the server.

CAUTION   Make sure the new server has access to the user accounts the applications are published for. If the machine does not have permissions for the existing user accounts, the accounts will be reset and replaced with the Built-in User accounts.

Using Server and Application Folders

The Presentation Server Console provides the capability to group servers and applications into folders. No correlation exists between the Presentation Server Console folders and Program Neighborhood folders that appear in application sets.

The Presentation Server Console folders help to manage a large number of servers and applications. They also increase performance because the Presentation Server Console queries for data only for the servers or applications in the current folder view. One way to increase response time is to divide the list of servers into folders based on their zones.

TIP   Viewing server details on large groups of servers may result in incomplete information being gathered for all the servers. To reduce this occurrence, group servers in folders under the Servers node of the Presentation Server Console.

PRESENTATION SERVER EXTENSION AND CITRIX ACCESS SUITE CONSOLE

The Citrix Access Suite Console extends the capability to manage your Citrix Access Suite deployment by integrating consoles with the Microsoft Management Console (MMC). The Access Suite Console provides a central location for managing your Citrix Access Suite deployment. The following section provides some tips while using the Presentation Server Extension and Citrix Access Suite Console.

Citrix Access Suite Console is supported on the following platforms:

▼   Windows 2000 Server, Windows 2000 Professional, Windows XP, and Windows Server 2003.

■   Microsoft .NET Framework version 1.1, available in the Support folder of the server CD, is required to install Citrix Access Suite Console.

■   The Access Suite Console uses "pass-through" authentication. Ensure you are logged on to the client machine (where the Citrix Access Suite Console is installed) as a MetaFrame Administrator for the farm. To avoid issues with credentials, it's advisable to ensure that the console machine belongs to the same domain as the Presentation Server farm member machines.

■   While running discovery, only one server name is required for the farm.

■   Once the discovery is run for a certain farm, the discovered objects can be saved by saving the ".msc" (Microsoft Management Console) file. When the .msc file is launched again, it will know about the discovered objects. When launching the Citrix Access Suite Console from the ICA tool bar or from the Start menu, the choice to save the .msc file is unavailable because the console is saved automatically every time you close it.

■   Different web-based tools, such as Web Interface Console and Program Neighborhood Agent Console, can be launched from the Access Suite Console. To launch each tool using a separate Internet Explorer (IE) window, change the following parameter in IE.

    ○   Choose Tools | Internet Options | Advanced.

    ○   Under Browsing section, uncheck "Reuse windows for launching shortcuts."

■   Update of published applications doesn't happen automatically for the Applications node in the Presentation Server Extension (PSE). The discovery process needs to be rerun for the update to take effect.

■   If the Presentation Server Client for 32-bit Windows is not installed on the machine, the option to shadow from PSE is unavailable.

■   Use My Views to create custom views of frequently used applications and servers. This can save you time in the future.

- The Access Suite Console communicates with the server farm using the MetaFrame COM server service. When troubleshooting, ensure this service is running on the Presentation Server.

▲ A known issue after upgrade from MetaFrame XP Feature Release 1 to MetaFrame Presentation Server 3.0, is that the MetaFrame COM server service fails to start. The workaround is to unregister, and then reregister MFCOM service. From the command line, execute the following:

```
mfcom /unregserver
mfcom /regserver
```

LOAD MANAGEMENT TIPS

When selecting servers to participate in Load Management or when attaching load evaluators in large farms, a delay of several minutes can occur for population of the Available Servers and Selected Servers lists in the Management Console. During this retrieval, the Management Console does not always indicate it is still retrieving information.

Tuning the Load Bias Level

Prior to MetaFrame Presentation Server 3.0, the data collector temporarily increased the load of a server for each connection by 200 until it received a load update from the server. This increase is known as the *load bias*. In MetaFrame Presentation Server 3.0, this was changed to calculate the load-bias level based on the load-evaluator settings. For example, if a Server User Load evaluator was configured to report a full load at 40 users, the new bias level would be 250, not 200. To manually set the load-bias level, the following registry key needs to be added to the farm's data collectors and potential data collectors:

```
HKLM\Software\Citrix\IMA\LMS\ForceRegLoadBias
```

By default, this value is set to 0 (off). To force the load bias to the one configured in the registry, this value should be set to 1. While it is not generally recommended or necessary to modify the load bias specified in the registry, this setting can be changed by editing the value of:

```
HKLM\Software\Citrix\IMA\LMS\LoadBias
```

The default value is 200.

Performance Counters Utilized by Load Management

Some of the Load Evaluator rules that can be used by Load Management to calculate a server's load utilize Performance Monitor counters to obtain their values. Table 14-1 outlines these Load Evaluator rules and the associated Performance Monitor counters:

LE Rule	Description	Performance Monitor Value	Task Manager Value
CPU Utilization	Calculates load based on a moving average of total CPU utilization across all processors in the server.	TSE: System\ % Total Processor Time W2K: Processor\(_Total)\ % Processor Time	Performance\CPU Utilization
Memory Usage	Calculates load based on virtual and physical memory currently in use.	Memory\ % Committed Bytes In Use	Performance \ Memory Usage
Context Switches	Calculates load based on CPU Context switches.	System\Context Switches/sec	A context switch occurs every time the operating system (OS) switches from one executing process to another.
Disk Data I/O	Calculates a load based on the disk I/O throughput in kilobytes.	PhysicalDisk(_Total)\ Disk Bytes/sec	The value used by Disk Data I/O is the total for all disks on the machine.
Disk Operations	Calculates a load based on the number of disk operations per second.	PhysicalDisk(_Total)\ Disk Writes/sec + PhysicalDisk(_Total)\ Disk Reads/sec	The value used by Disk Operations is the total for all disks on the machine.
Page Faults	Calculates a load based on the number of page faults per second.	Memory\Page Faults/sec	A page fault occurs every time the OS accesses physical memory that has been flushed to disk.
Page Swap	Calculates a load based on the number of page swaps per second.	Memory\Pages/sec	A page swap occurs every time the OS swaps physical memory to virtual memory on disk.

Table 14-1. Load Evaluator Rules

NOTE The defaults for these rules are based on a single CPU Pentium 400 MHz machine with 192MB of RAM and a SCSI Ultra Wide Controller. Servers with multiple processors or disk controllers should change these default values. To determine the best values, use Performance Monitor to track the counters listed in the following table. Use values obtained during idle and full load conditions to set the appropriate thresholds.

INSTALLATION MANAGEMENT FOR CITRIX PRESENTATION SERVER

This section covers design and architecture topics that need to be understood before using Installation Manager to deploy applications to a Citrix Presentation Server farm in the enterprise environment. Concepts discussed include data store usage, group size considerations, WAN recommendations, and application deployment recommendations.

Group Size Considerations

Installation Manager permits the installation of applications to predefined groups of servers. A group allows a MetaFrame Administrator to install applications to a specific set of servers quickly and efficiently, so individual servers do not have to be selected with every installation, for example, Accounting dept.

When creating a server group for application deployment:

▼ Plan how you want to use and create your server groups.

▲ Keep your group size reasonable.

Installation Manager deploys applications to servers simultaneously, but it does not use multicasting. Each target server reads the data from the location where the installation package is stored. Large installation packages, such as Microsoft Office XP, copy more than 200 megabytes of data from the package server to the target server. The amount of data transferred across the network is

$$D = I \times N$$

where:

D = the amount of data
I = the size of the installation
N = the number of target servers

Smaller group sizes are needed when installing applications that require a server to restart. Installations occur simultaneously, and the Presentation Servers can be forced to restart at nearly the same time. Because of this, a transient load is placed on the data store. The data store server, the internetworking infrastructure, and the performance of the network can be greatly affected during application deployment and server restarting. The following table contains suggestions based on a 100 Mbps switched Ethernet infrastructure.

	Small	Medium	Large
Application size	<5MB	5–20MB	>20MB
Recommended group size	<100	<80	<50

Cluster groups logically. Deployment is more efficient if several logical groups are created that match the schema of the overall enterprise. One group might contain servers that host standard business applications; another group can host engineering applications, and so on.

Network Setup Recommendations

The network setup recommendations for Presentation Server also apply to Installation Manager. The more efficient and capable the network, the quicker and easier applications are to install. The use of switches, high-speed backbones, and high-speed disk drives greatly enhance the capability of Installation Manager to install applications to large server farms efficiently.

WAN Recommendations

Do not install applications to target servers across a WAN. The amount of bandwidth and time required to install an application over a WAN can congest the network for extended periods of time, which can result in networking timeouts. To avoid this situation, do the following:

▼ Create a new application package at the remote site where the application is to be deployed.

▲ If there is more than one remote target server, copy the package and the associated installation files over the WAN once, and then deploy it on that segment.

Installation Manager Application Deployment Recommendations

This section contains application deployment considerations when using Installation Manager in conjunction with Presentation Server. Concepts discussed include package server recommendations, deployment server recommendations, the network share account, job scheduling and staggered install, package group deployment, user specified restart, and recording applications requiring restarts during installation.

Package Server

The package server is used to record an application's installation. The package server can be used to generate packages for applications that do not have MSI installations. The generated package is then deployed to the Presentation Servers. The following package server recommendations help ensure a clean package file.

▼ Keep the package server as similar in configuration (both hardware and software) as possible to the target server.

■ Make the package server as "clean" as possible. Previously installed applications should be rolled back or uninstalled before recording. For additional information, see the *Installation Manager Administrator's Guide*.

■ Do not run other applications while an image is recording.

■ Any unnecessary background processes should be stopped before recording an installation using Packager, including the IMA Service, especially if a manual install needs to be performed. Background processes and file changes may be recorded by Packager and could overwrite important files, such as the local access database files used by the IMA Service.

▲ Do not package applications through an ICA session.

Deployment Server

The *deployment server* is the server where the package and installation files reside. All target servers communicate with this server to get the files and information they need to install the application. The following recommendations offer helpful information about deploying packages:

▼ Put the deployment server on a server grade machine. Each target server requests the same file set from the deployment server. The load on the deployment server can be high. The deployment server must be capable of handling the combined load of the servers connecting and requesting information simultaneously in a deployment group.

▲ Put the deployment server on a 100 Mbps-switched Ethernet port. Running the deployment server in a shared collision domain increases latency. Connections can be refused due to timeout or server overload. This problem increases on a busy network and when many servers are targeted for a single installation.

Network Share Account

The network share account allows the target server to have access rights to the network share point where the package is located. To set up a network share account, complete the following steps:

1. Right-click the Installation Manager node in the Presentation Server Console.
2. Select Properties.
3. Enter the domain account and password to be used to access network shares.

When performing an unattended install, the network share account must have administrator privileges on the target server.

IMPORTANT Installation Manager only supports Window Domain authentication models, not Workgroups.

Job Scheduling and Staggered Install

The following recommendations can lower bandwidth consumption, allowing the farm to function without a loss of performance.

▼ Schedule the installation of packages during times of low network usage.

▲ Avoid installations during scheduled server backups or restorations.

IMPORTANT While an application is being deployed to a server, all ICA connections are terminated until the installation is completed.

Installation Manager for Citrix Presentation Server supports staggered installations of package groups. Installation window options and multiple dates can be used for package groups to schedule the installation job during a certain time period within specific days. Options include:

▼ Scheduling the installation window during times of low network usage.

▲ Selecting multiple dates if the installation of the packages in a package group requires multiple dates for installation. The packages that haven't been installed begin installation in the same installation window on the selected dates.

IMPORTANT A staggered installation of a single package is not supported.

Package Group Deployment

Package groups are used to deploy multiple packages to the same target server or server groups in one schedule. The following are recommendations and best practices:

▼ Create package groups with similar packages to simplify deployment.

■ After the package groups have been deployed, do not make changes to the package group (that is, do not add or delete packages to/from the package group) because this causes unnecessary uninstall errors. If you need to deploy new packages, create a new package group, and then deploy it.

■ If changes are made to a deployed package group, the Job status tab of the Job properties window will not report installation status for the deleted or newly added package.

▲ After scheduling an installation of a package group, do not make changes to the package group contents because this may result in temporary inaccurate Job Result information. Refresh the Presentation Server Console to correct this behavior.

User Specified Reboot

The server restart behavior during package deployment is affected by three options:

1. If you set the option "Do not reboot servers if any user sessions are open" before deploying packages, the target server will not restart if a user connection to the target server is detected, even though the package deployment requires a restart. The target server will be restarted after the user logs off, to finish the deployment. This can be overwritten if the "Force reboot after job" option is selected during the scheduling of the installation of a package.

2. If you deploy a package group and one or more of the applications require a restart at the end of the deployment, you can set the "Delay reboot until the end of Job" option during scheduling the installation to postpone the restart until the end of the entire package group deployment.

3. If you set "Force reboot after job", the server will restart after the package has been deployed. Any active user sessions will receive a message from the server, asking them to log off. The messages will be sent in 5-minute intervals for 15 minutes (this is the default setting and can be changed). Any active sessions will be terminated, and then the server will restart.

Recording Applications Requiring Reboot During Installation

The Installation Manager Packager cannot resume package recording after a reboot during an application's installation. Please note the following:

1. When recording an application that prompts the user for a restart, cancel the restart and stop the recording on the Packager.

2. Installation Manager Packager cannot record an application that forces a restart that cannot be canceled by the user.

3. Installation Manager Packager cannot record an application that requires multiple server restarts during installation.

If an application has an unattended installation program, the Installation Manager Packager will create a package from the unattended installation program only. The Installation Manager Packager will not record the actual installation. When using the Installation Manager Packager to package the application, select "Package an **Unattended Program**" option to package the unattended install program and any other necessary files. This method allows applications that require one or more restarts during installation to be packaged.

Description of a Package Deployment Process

Table 14-2 describes the details of what happens when a package is deployed to Citrix Presentation Servers using Installation Manager. The process of adding a package to the Presentation Server Console has been omitted. For further details about adding packages to the Presentation Server Console, please see the *Installation Manager Administrator's Guide*.

Step	Area Involved	Description
1	Presentation Server Console	Administrator chooses to install a package within the Presentation Server Console: Right-click package Select servers to deploy package to Select package installation schedule
2	IMA	Presentation Server Console makes a call to the Installation Manager subsystem to schedule an install.
3	IMA	The Installation Manager subsystem adds entries to the Data Store based on the Administrator's selected options (which servers are to be rebooted and the list of servers to be deployed to).
4	Presentation Server Console	The Presentation Server Console receives notification that a job has been scheduled and the status of the job changes to "Pending."
5	IMA	A notification is sent to all servers of a Data Store change and the LHC of each server is updated.
6	IMA	The Installation Manager subsystem on each server checks to see if it is a "target server." If so, an installation job is added to the installer queue.
7	Target server	Logons are disabled.
8	IMA	The appropriate installer (MSI, ADF, or MSP) is run.
9	IMA	The Installation Manager subsystem reads the properties from the LHC to see where to get the package.
10	Presentation Server Console	The Presentation Server Console receives notification that the installation has started.

Table 14-2.   Package Deployment Sequence of Events

Step	Area Involved	Description
11	IMA	Once installation is complete, the Installation Manager subsystem adds a log entry to the data store under InstallationManagement | EventLog. In addition, an entry is added to the registry of the server under HKLM\SOFTWARE\Citrix\IMS\2.0\ Jobs\<jobid>, which describes the job status.
12	Presentation Server Console	The Presentation Server Console receives notification that the installation has completed.
13	IMA	An entry is written to the data store under InstallationManagement | Installations for the newly installed application.
14	Target server	A reboot is performed, if required, or the next package is installed.
15	Target server	Logons are reenabled.

Table 14-2.   Package Deployment Sequence of Events (*Continued*)

USER POLICIES BEST PRACTICES

With User Policies, you can apply select Presentation Server settings, including shadowing permission settings, printer autocreation settings, and client device mapping settings, to specific users or user groups. Using policies, you can tailor your environment at the user level.

This section contains tips and troubleshooting guidelines for working with user policies in Presentation Server.

▼ Assign user policies to user groups, rather than individual users. If you assign user policies to user groups, assignments are updated automatically when you add or remove users from the group.

■ Disable unused policies. Policies with all the rules set to Not Configured create unnecessary processing.

■ Avoid conflicting settings in Citrix Connection Configuration or in the farm-wide settings of the Presentation Server Console. Several policy rules can also be set in Citrix Connection Configuration and/or the farm-wide settings in the Presentation Server Console. When possible, keep all settings consistent (enabled or disabled) for ease of troubleshooting.

■ Use the search functionality to see which policy rules are being applied to users or user groups. Also use the Search function to determine the effective policy being applied to users. The resultant policy returned from a search enables you to determine which rules are in effect for users.

▲ Use the drag-and-drop feature of user policies to quickly assign the correct priority to a user policy. If you want to move a policy up or down in priority, you can drag the policy above or below the policy that currently has the rank you want to achieve.

USER-TO-USER SHADOWING BEST PRACTICES

Users can shadow other users without requiring administrator rights. Similar to Citrix Conferencing Manager, multiple users from different locations can view presentations and training sessions, allowing one-to-many, many-to-one, and many-to-many online collaboration.

NOTE   Although it is possible for users to shadow each other for collaboration, training, and other tasks, Conferencing Manager is a more suitable solution for performing these tasks.

▼ Do not assume that members of the administrators group have shadow rights by default. Although local administrators may have shadowing rights enabled in Citrix Connection Configuration, they are unable to shadow users who have been assigned to the policy by default. You must add the members of the local administrators group to the list of people with shadow rights in the user policy.

■ Although in general, user policies take precedence over settings configured in other Presentation Server utilities, shadowing is an exception. If shadowing was disabled during Presentation Server setup or disabled in Citrix Connection Configuration for a particular connection, then user policies with shadowing enabled have no effect.

■ At a minimum, apply Service Pack 3 for Windows 2000 or apply Microsoft Hotfix 281951 to disallow unwanted cross-server shadowing after configuring shadow policies in the Management Console for Presentation Server.

▲ Because the most restrictive of the three shadow settings—settings in the Citrix Connection Configuration, settings specified during the Presentation Server installation, and settings in shadow policies—go into effect, avoid unnecessary administration headache by using shadow policies as the central control to control shadow settings. Exceptions to this rule include the need to adhere to local governmental laws that stipulate certain privacy requirements.

ENHANCED DELEGATED ADMINISTRATION

Citrix Presentation Server delegated administration lets you assign custom roles to individual users or groups to facilitate management of your Presentation Server environment. In MetaFrame Presentation Server 3.0, this support was enhanced to include the capability to delegate permissions on Server and Application folders, thus enabling you to delegate administrative abilities at a much more granular level.

It is highly recommended to create NT, Active Directory, or NDS groups to assign these custom privileges to. When you create your custom MetaFrame Administrators, simply select the group instead of the user(s). This lets you add and remove users to these preconfigured groups without having to reconfigure all the permissions.

One new capability to the delegated administration feature of MetaFrame Presentation Server 3.0 is the capability to assign a server to a published application. This means, without any view or edit permissions to the server and without edit permissions to a published application, a user can still be granted rights to manage the addition and removal of the servers assigned to run this published application.

NOTE For the assign servers published application feature to function, you must grant the Assign Applications to Servers permission on the server folder that contains the servers the custom administrator will be allowed to assign. You also must grant at least view permissions on the application folder(s) that contains the application(s) for which the custom administrator is allowed to manage the server list.

IMPORTANT Proper design can be important when dealing with this feature. If an application is published on a server, but the custom administrator has not been granted the Assign Applications to Servers permission on the folder containing the server, they will be unable to see these servers in the published application properties. This could potentially lead to confusion for the administrator, as well as to complexities if servers are assigned that have different domain trust relationships.

Another new capability for MetaFrame Presentation Server 3.0 is the capability to assign permissions to a custom administrator to manage sessions at the Application level only. This means they would only be able to see and manage the users that are using a particular published application and not all users logged onto the server.

IMPORTANT Multiple published applications may be launched within the same session using the session sharing feature of Presentation Server. This means if a custom administrator attempts to use the logoff, disconnect, or reset session management options on a user running a particular published application, they will affect all other session-shared applications running within that session. Again, proper design can be important because, if a custom administrator has the rights to reset one published application that a user is running, but does not have any rights over another published application, they will still implicitly have rights over the other application if they both run in the same session.

Delegated Administrator Tips

▼ In MetaFrame Presentation Server 3.0, to assign the right to edit the farm's license server to a custom administrator, you must assign the *Edit License Server* privilege to at least one server folder.

▲ To let a user shadow through the Presentation Server Console, enable the following permissions at a minimum:

   ▼ **MetaFrame Administrators**   Log on to Presentation Server Console

   ■ **Servers**   View Server Information

   ▲ **Sessions**   View Session Management

You must also grant shadowing permissions in the Citrix Connection Configuration tool or configure a Presentation Server policy to enable shadowing for the user.

CITRIX RESOURCE MANAGEMENT

Resource Manager is a component of Presentation Server Enterprise edition and is not available in Presentation Server's Advanced or Standard editions.

The version of Resource Manager included with FR2 and later is improved in the areas of performance, usability, stability, and scalability. Resource Manager also includes the Summary Database, which allows historical data to be stored on metrics and servers and reports to be produced on the stored data.

Resource Manager Database and Metric Server

Resource Manager stores all its configurations, settings, thresholds, and metrics in the data store and in the local host cache. Previous versions of Resource Manager contained a local Resource Manager database and a Farm Metric Server. Feature Release 2 introduced a Database Connection Server used with Summary Database.

Local Resource Manager Database

Each Presentation Server with Resource Manager installed has a local database in which it stores the individual server's metric information. It is important to note the following:

▼ The *local Resource Manager database* is a Microsoft Access Jet Database called RMLocalDatabase.mdb that is located in %ProgramFiles%\Citrix\Citrix Resource Manager\LocalDB folder by default.

■ The local Resource Manager database is accessed when creating real-time graphs, displaying system snapshots, running reports on that specific server, and writing server metrics. You have the capability of real-time graphs, server snapshots, and current reports.

- Server metric and process data is written to the local Resource Manager database.

- The local Resource Manager database holds metric values and application information for the previous 96 hours.

▲ This database is compacted when the IMA service is started and once a day while the IMA service is running.

Farm Metric Server

The *Farm Metric Server* is used for application and server monitoring. The Farm Metric Server gathers its information from the data collector. Because the Farm Metric Server accesses the data collector every 15 seconds to obtain published application counters and every 30 seconds to determine if machines are offline, configuring data collectors to also perform the role of Farm Metric Servers and the backup Farm Metric Servers can improve performance. The Farm Metric Server may also perform the role of the Database Connection Server.

TIP   Although Resource Manager can track any Performance Monitor counter as a server metric, Citrix recommends you limit the total number of metrics tracked on a server to fewer than 50.

IMPORTANT   In a farm that contains servers with different feature release levels, if the primary Farm Metric server is not the server with the highest Feature Release level (FR2 or higher), an error with the Summary Database will occur.

Alerts

Resource Manager has the capability to send alerts to users or groups of users using either e-mail or SMS. It can also send alerts to a Single Network Management Protocol (SNMP) management console.

TIP   If the e-mail service will not send alerts, the MetaFrame Administrator should confirm that they are able to access the mail server using the configured account. Also, verify the mail client being used (for example, Microsoft Outlook) is the default mail client for the server and that no additional password is required to connect to the mail server.

TIP   To enable Resource Manager to send SNMP traps for Application Alerts, SNMP must be set up on the Primary and Backup Farm Metric Servers.

Summary Database

The *Summary Database* is used for storing historical data from servers in the farm. MetaFrame Administrators may produce reports, such as billing, based on the stored data. These can be based on several criteria, such as CPU usage or application usage.

▼   Each farm that requires the Summary Database must have a Database Connection Server (DCS), which writes the metric information from other farm servers to the Summary Database.

■   A System Data Source Name (DSN) called RMSummaryDatabase defines the connection between the DCS and the database where the metric information is stored.

■   Data is stored on each individual server in summary files. Summary files are updated whenever a session or process terminates or an event occurs, and once an hour for metrics.

■   Each Resource Manager server in the farm records its own summary data locally for 24 hours, and then transmits it to the Database Connection Server at a configurable time of day.

▲   Reports on data in the summary database can be generated via the Presentation Server Console in a manner similar to those available for the local database for each server.

In MetaFrame XP for Windows, with Feature Release 3, the following additional functionality was added:

▼   Folder and Zone Support

■   Oracle 7 and 8 seamless support without the need for a hotfix

■   Improved efficiency for some stored procedures

▲   Additional process information for processes taking more than 5% memory or CPU

TIP   Report templates for the popular Crystal Reports™ tool are available from the Citrix web site. Visit http://www.citrix.com.

TIP   By default, metrics are stored in the Summary Database. This can be changed on the Threshold Configuration screen. It is also possible to specify the time of day or week that metrics are recorded in the Summary Database on a per server basis.

Folders and Zones

Feature Release 3 and later now has the capability to record which folders and zone a server is in at the time of writing data to the summary file. This information can be used to group servers when creating reports outside of the Presentation Server Console. In Feature Release 3 and later, by default, the summary period for server metrics is one hour.

If either the folder or zone has changed for a server, just before writing the next set of server metric records to the Summary File, a new Folder and Zone record will be written. All following server metric records are then associated with this new Folder and Zone record. This means if the folder or zone changes multiple times within the summary period, only the one record will be written prior to writing the new server metric records to the summary file. All other folder and zone changes will go unnoticed.

SDB_Scratch Table

The *sdb_scratch table* is used with the generation of billing reports to store information about the reports currently opened, so the records being displayed in the report can be marked as billed. A record exists in the SDB_Scratch table per open billing report in the farm. On closing a report, the record is deleted from the table.

Data Purging

The Summary Database enables administrators to control how long data is stored by purging the database at set periods. It is also possible to turn purging off, in which case all data is kept for an indefinite period. If a purge is missed, for example, if the DCS is not online at the purge time, a purge is initiated when the DCS next starts up.

NOTE   Active sessions, and the processes associated with them, will not be purged from the database whether they are or are not billed.

NOTE   Processes are purged only if their "parent" session record is purged (that is, to maintain data integrity, it is not desirable to purge only process records).

Uploads to the Database Connection Server

Uploads to the DCS are initiated by the individual servers in the farm based on the Upload time.

The following sequence of events occurs for each Presentation Server with Resource Manager enabled when the Upload time is met each day.

1. Presentation Server closes the current summary file and begins a new file.

2. Presentation Server sends a notification to the DCS stating it has a summary file to be uploaded. One notification per summary file is ready to be uploaded.

3. DCS maintains a list of all notifications.

4. DCS requests files to be copied to it. The number of concurrent uploads is limited to reduce congestion.

5. When files are available on the DCS, the import starts. Imports are limited to a maximum concurrent amount.

6. For each file being imported, a new file is uploaded, so ten files are either copying or ready to be imported.

7. When the import succeeds, a message is sent to the originating host, informing it that the summary file can be safely deleted. The file is also deleted from the DCS.

8. This continues until there are no further summary files to be uploaded or imported.

Considerations

▼ Only Summary files that are not currently active will be uploaded to the DCS.

■ If the DCS receives another request to upload a summary file, it logs a Duplicate Request and the old request is deleted from the list. This can occur if updates are taking longer than 24 hours.

■ The default setting for concurrent uploads is 10. The default setting for concurrent imports is 1. The reason for this is to reduce the requirement on database connection licenses.

■ Importing a record into the Summary Database twice will not cause duplicate entries.

■ If a summary file takes longer than 30 minutes to transfer, the DCS assumes it has timed out and deletes any record of requesting it. This file is not retransmitted until the next update period, 24 hours later, unless a manual update is invoked. If the uploaded summary file eventually reaches the DCS after it has timed out, it is ignored and deleted.

■ Upload time is compared to the server time. The server's time zone is used to determine if uploads should begin. For example, a Presentation Server farm has the majority of the machines in the East Coast of the USA and a smaller zone in the UK with the upload time set to 1 A.M. The servers in the USA begin to upload files at 1 A.M. EST, while machines in the UK start their uploads at 1 A.M. UK time, which is 8 P.M. EST.

▲ A "Duplicate upload request" message in the DCS Server log is an indicator of problems in the system, but it is not an error. The duplicate request does not cause any invalid or duplicate data in the Summary Database and should be treated as an informational message. An example that could result in a "duplicate upload request" would be a manual upload requested when an upload is already under way—either a timed update or an previously requested manual request—or uploads taking more than 24 hours to complete, resulting in the next daily upload beginning before the previous one has completed.

Summary Files

Summary files are only written when the Summary Database has been enabled in the Presentation Server farm. Each file is given a random name when it is created. At creation time, a header is written to the file. This header contains the following fields: Schema Version, Server's Name, Server's Domain, and Farm Name.

Additional records are written to the file based on these events:

▼ When a process terminates, a process record is written to the file

■ Every 60 minutes, a metric record is written for each metric configured to store summary data

■ When a session is started, a session record is written

■ When a session ends, a session record is written

▲ When an event is generated, an event record is written

The following information is stored for each of the record types Metric records:

```
Object Name, Counter Name, Instance Name, Update Time, Server UTC Bias
(in minutes), Sample Period (in seconds), Data Count, Min Value, Max Value,
Mean Value, Std Dev value
```

Application Metric records:

```
Application Name, Application Type, Farm Name, Object name, Update time, Sample
period (in seconds), Data Count, Min Value, Max Value, Mean Value, Std Dev value
```

Process records:

```
User Name, Client Name, Client Address Family, Client Address, App name, App
Type, Path Name, Process Name, Version, Product Date, Type, PID, Exit Code,
Affinity, Start Time, End Time, Total Time, Active Time, Kernel Used, User Used,
User Active, Kernel Active, Memory, Memory Active, Working Set, Page File, Page
Faults, Paged Pool, Non Paged Pool,  SessionID, Server UTC Bias (in minutes),
User Domain, Session Start time
```

Session records:

```
User Name, Client Name, Client Address Family, Client Address, App Name,
App Type, Winstation, Protocol, Session Start, Session End, Duration
(in milliseconds), Server UTC bias (in minutes), Session UTC bias (in minutes),
Session ID, User Domain
```

Event records:

```
Server Name, NetDomain Name, Farm Name, Event Time, Server UTC Bias
(in minutes), Event Code
```

Folder records:

```
Folder Name
```

Zone records:

```
Zone Name
```

NOTE Only Server Up and Server Down events are stored. The *Server Down event* is generated by the Farm Metric server on detecting a server is no longer contactable. The *Server Up event* is generated by the server as the IMA Service is restarted.

NOTE Summary files can be manually copied to the DCS or other servers before the daily update is started. The header information in the summary file ensures the records are associated with the correct server.

SDB_Heuristics Table

With large amounts of data in a Summary Database (for example, of the gigabyte order), an administrator generating reports may encounter the situation whereby the Management Console is unable to display reports that are many megabytes in size. The sdb_heuristics table in the Summary Database is used by the Resource Manager to ensure that any summary report to be generated can be displayed within the Management Console. By default, it will contain the following entries and values:

PK_HEURISTIC	HEURVALUE
BILL_HTML_MAX (characters)	72500
MAXIMUM_PRACTICAL_HTML_BYTES (bytes)	1048576
PROCESSES_PER_SESSION	10
SESSIONS_PER_USER_PER_DAY	5
USERSUM_HTML_BYTES_PER_PROCESS	128

When the Administrator specifies various report options in the summary report generation dialog boxes, Resource Manager does calculations based on these options and the entries in the SDB_HEURISTICS table to estimate the size of the report to be returned. If this estimated value is greater than MAXIMUM_PRACTICAL_HTML_BYTES in the case of Process, User, and Server Summary reports, and BILL_HTML_MAX in the case of Billing reports, a warning message is displayed, stating that the report may be too large to be displayed within the Management Console. In such a case, the Administrator has the option to cancel the report generation or continue. If the Administrator continues and the report is too large to be displayed, an error message is displayed within the report window. The Administrator then has the option of saving the report directly to disk for viewing in another application that can display HTML (for example, Internet Explorer).

Depending on the usage of servers in the farm, an Administrator may want to configure the values in this table to more accurately reflect the amount of data that may be displayed in reports.

NOTE The capability of the Presentation Server Console to display reports is dependent on the number of report windows currently open. Each time a report is returned to the Presentation Server Console, a calculation is performed that subtracts the size of the report (in bytes for Summary Reports and characters for Billing reports) from the respective maximum values in the table producing an "available size" figure for subsequent reports. Accordingly, an Administrator is more likely to receive a warning in the report windows that the report cannot be displayed if they have multiple reports open. Once a report is closed, its "size" is returned to the "available size" figure for future reports.

NOTE If the Summary Database is unavailable, all reports (Current Process, Current User, and Server Snapshot) make use of a hard-coded default value of 1048576 bytes (= 524288 characters).

REPORT CENTER IN THE CITRIX ACCESS SUITE CONSOLE

The *Report Center* in the Citrix Access Suite Console extends the reporting capabilities in Resource Manager and lets you easily generate reports from a variety of real-time and historic data sources. A wizard helps you select the type of report, the data to be displayed, and the schedule for running the report. You can view the status of your scheduled reports and adjust the report parameters.

This section provides information about the different reports available, the data sources for these reports, and how to copy reports and report specifications to other servers.

Copying Report Center Reports and Specifications to a Different Console

The Citrix Access Suite Console provides a Report Center extension that enables MetaFrame Administrators to generate HTML and CSV reports from a variety of real-time and historic data sources. Commands are available to view the reports from within the console and to make the reports more widely available by copying them to other locations or e-mailing them to selected recipients.

Each successful report, and a copy of the specification used to generate it, is stored locally on the machine running the Access Suite Console. For reports that administrators plan to run regularly, they can also generate named specifications recording report formats, farm information, data source details, required time period, and other report parameters. These can then be run manually or scheduled to run when required.

Thus, if an administrator wants to generate reports from an Access Suite Console on a different machine, neither previous reports and their associated specifications nor any named specification will be available from the new console. However, it is possible to copy the necessary files across to the machine running the new console and use them from there, without editing anything, as long as the second machine has access to the same farm and Resource Manager Summary Database as the first one.

Understanding Where User-configured Report and Specification Files are Kept

Report Center stores its user-configurable data on the machine running the Access Suite Console. So, a Citrix administrator logged on to a Windows 2003 server can find their report and specification files in:

```
%APPDATA%\Citrix\ReportCenter
```

Specifications are stored as .spec files in appropriately named folders within:

`%APPDATA%\Citrix\ReportCenter\CustomSettings\Specifications`

Generated reports (and their associated unique specifications) are stored underneath:

`%APPDATA%\Citrix\ReportCenter\DataSets`

with each set of related files in a folder with a unique system-generated name (such as 4C7F885E0EF72F30).

NOTE Each report folder's set of files always includes a Results.xml file containing the raw data used to generate the necessary HTML reports, graphs, and CSV files when the user requests them. As the HTML and CSV folders and their contents are only generated when required, they may not be present when you examine the folders within DataSets. This is by design, and both types of reports can always be generated when required.

To move previously created specifications and reports to the new console, the administrator should copy all the relevant folders to their corresponding position on the new machine. Once Discovery has been run, and the Specifications and Jobs displays refreshed, all the transferred items should be listed as before. Administrators can then view previous reports and generate new ones as required.

Known Issues

In the Jobs display, the Elapsed Time values for the copied reports will be incorrect. (This is because of the way Report Center calculates Elapsed Time; it uses the creation time of the files and this time changed when the reports were copied across to the new machine.)

Available Report Center Reports and Their Data Sources

This section illustrates the various Report Center reports that can be created and provides information as to where the data for these reports exists.

Application Availability

Data Source: Summary Database
Table: SDB_APPHISTORY
Purpose: Determining if applications were always available for clients to connect.
Details: The *Application Availability report* displays the percentage of time the application was available in the farm during the reporting time period.

This report determines when the application was available for connection across any of the servers onto which it was published. *Unavailable* is defined as no servers online to be able to service the application to clients.

Application

Data Source: MFCOM via servers selected at the time of specification
Purpose: Listing settings for selected applications in the farm. This is a way to get all application settings quickly in one view.
Details: The *Application report* displays the settings for each published application selected. It details the configured users, servers, application location, working directory, appearance, client options, and current status in the farm, that is, whether it is enabled or disabled.

This report only provides information for applications published to clients, which includes published desktops and published content. It also provides information regarding the unused applications in the farm.

Application Usage

Data Source: Summary Database
Table: SDB_SESSION
Purpose: Viewing the usage of applications across selected servers over a period of time.
Details: The *Application Usage report* displays the total number of sessions and the maximum concurrent number of sessions for each application selected.

This report displays a table of the most heavily used applications out of the list of selected applications. *Heavily used* is defined by the highest values for maximum concurrent users. The total number of applications to display is configurable.

Optionally, the Application Usage report displays a table of unused applications. These are applications that have no sessions during the reporting period.

In addition, the Application Usage report optionally displays a graph of time vs. concurrent sessions for each application selected.

Client Type

Data Source: Summary Database
Tables: SDB_SESSION, SDB_CLIENTHISTORY
Purpose: Viewing different types of clients that have connected to the servers.
Details: The *Client Type report* displays the client type and version for connections made to the selected servers.

This report also includes a graph of the different client types and the percentage of connections made to each.

Disconnected Sessions

Data Source: Summary Database
Table: SDB_CONNECTIONHISTORY
Purpose: Displaying the number of disconnected sessions across a selection of servers over a period of time.

Details: The *Disconnected Sessions report* shows a graph displaying the number of disconnected sessions across the specified servers over the period of time being reported. It also displays a trend line of these disconnected sessions.

Policy

Data Source: MFCOM
Purpose: Displaying a list of policies in the farm.
Details: The *Policy report* lists all policies defined in the farm and displays the details of the policies. Policy settings that are not set to either enabled or disabled can be excluded from the report using the Hide Unconfigured Policies check box. Unchecking this box will include all details of the policies, even if they are set to "unconfigured".

Server Availability

Data Source: Summary Database
Table: SDB_EVENTLOG
Purpose: Determining the percentage of time the selected servers were available to service connections. This report determines the period of time for which servers were down due to scheduled reboots. It also determines the period of time for which servers were down due to unexpected reboots.
Details: The *Server Availability report* displays a table with the percentages of uptime, unscheduled downtime, and scheduled downtime.

A graph is also displayed with a separate bar for each server selected. The bar is color coded to show the uptime, the scheduled downtime, and the unscheduled downtime during the reported time period.

Server Performance

Data Source: Summary Database
Tables: SDB_METRICS, SDB_CONNECTIONHISTORY
Purpose: Determining the most heavily used server across a selection of servers based on CPU load, available memory, or maximum concurrent sessions.
Details: The *Server Performance report* displays load information for all the selected servers.

This report also shows three separate tables detailing the servers that had the highest load. These tables only show servers selected for inclusion in the report.

The number of servers listed in these tables can be configured using the "Number of servers to display" setting.

The tables contain data based on the report period for the following three criteria:

▼ Highest CPU load

■ Lowest available memory

▲ Highest maximum concurrent sessions

Server Reboot

Data Source: Summary Database
Table: SDB_EVENTLOG
Purpose: Determining when servers have been rebooted. This determines which servers shut down, but were not restarted.
Details: The *Server Reboot report* shows, in table format, the times at which servers started up, the times at which they were available to handle client connections, and the times at which they were rebooted.

Server Utilization (CPU)

Data Source: Summary Database
Tables: SDB_PROCESS, SDB_METRICS
Purpose: Listing processes across servers that take more than a defined average percentage of the CPU. This report displays the average percentage of the server's CPU for the reported time period.
Details: The *Server Utilization* (CPU) *report* displays the servers in the selection that have the highest average CPU during the reported time period. The number of servers to be displayed is configurable, allowing the server selection to be the entire farm, but only allowing the heaviest used servers to be displayed in the table.

A separate table for each server is in the list to show all the processes with high CPU usage during the reported time period. The criterion for "high CPU usage" is configurable.

Server Utilization (Memory)

Data Source: Summary Database
Tables: SDB_PROCESS, SDB_METRICS
Purpose: Displaying the servers with the least available memory. This report displays the processes consuming the most memory on individual servers.
Details: The *Server Utilization* (Mcmory) *report* displays servers that have had the least available memory within the server selection and reported time period. For each server listed, there is a separate table to show the processes that consumed the most memory during the reported time period. The number of servers and processes to be displayed is configurable.

Session Statistics

Data Source: Summary Database
Table: SDB_SESSION
Purpose: Displaying the number of concurrent sessions made to a selection of servers. This report displays the servers that have received the most concurrent sessions.
Details: The *Session Statistics report* lists, in table format, the servers that have the highest number of concurrent sessions during the reported time period. The number of servers to be included in this table is configurable.

A scatter graph showing the highest number of concurrent sessions across the server selection based on time is also displayed.

CONSIDERATIONS WITH NETWORK MANAGER FOR CITRIX PRESENTATION SERVER

Network Manager is a component of Presentation Server Enterprise edition and is not available in Presentation Server's Advanced or Standard editions. The following are some known issues with Network Manager.

▼ In *Tivoli NetView,* sometimes the server icon is green, while the subsystem icons are light blue. In this case, highlight the green server icon and perform a Status Update to update the status of the subsystem icons. This is a Tivoli NetView IP Map issue that occurs while running over long periods of time.

■ When using Tivoli NetView, if the Trapd.exe process is killed while the Metadis.exe and Metalan.exe services are running, each service acquires 50% CPU utilization. The services do not return to normal CPU levels until Trapd.exe is restarted. This is a known issue with Tivoli NetView.

■ In *HP Network Node Manager,* a link-down status is represented by a blue icon. This happens only if the server cannot be contacted by the console when the Status Update is performed. In Tivoli NetView, a link-down status is displayed in red.

■ When Network Manager is uninstalled from one of the SNMP management consoles, by default, the Network Management icons stay in the IP Map until they are deleted and the nodes are rediscovered. The icons can be deleted prior to uninstalling in NetView, by going to properties under the Edit pull-down menu and selecting the application Network Manager, and then clicking the Properties button. These icons can also be deleted in Openview by selecting properties under the Map pull-down menu, clicking the Application tab, selecting Network Manager, and then pressing the Configure for this map button.

▲ For Unicenter to be able to reclass Windows servers as Presentation Servers, Security Management (secadmin) must be configured and enabled. Otherwise, a message similar to "Security authorization failure. The action has been denied" appears in the Unicenter event log (conlog).

Network Manager SNMP Agent Issues

The following are known issues and recommendations for the SNMP Agent:

▼ In Windows 2000, the default security for the SNMP service is Read Only. Network administrators cannot perform SET operations (Logoff, Disconnect, Send Message, and Terminate Process) from Network Management consoles unless security is Read/Create.

Action: Change security to Read/Create.

■ For Windows 2003 Server, the SNMP service, by default, only accepts SNMP messages from Local Host. Windows 2000 and previous OSs allowed any SNMP messages from any host from the start.

Action: Add more servers to the list of allowed hosts (recommended) or allow messages from any host (not secure)

■ Older versions of Network Manager had the capability to shut down or restart a Presentation Server. To comply with Microsoft SNMP security, these options have been removed in newer versions of the plug-ins. Any attempt to reboot a Presentation Server with an older version of a Network Manager plug-in is denied.

▲ Microsoft has released security bulletins for SNMP security risks. The following bulletins should be applied to all Presentation Servers and Management Consoles:

▼ MS00-095: Windows NT 4.0

■ MS00-096: Windows 2000

▲ MS02-006: Windows NT4, TSE, Windows 2000, and Windows XP

TIP   Enable or disable the SNMP Agent when farm activity is low.

USING VBSCRIPT AND METAFRAMECOM TO ADD OR REMOVE A USER FROM A PUBLISHED APPLICATION

MetaFrameCOM (MFCOM) is a Component Object Model (COM) server that exposes some of the Presentation Server control and monitoring functions through the objects and interfaces defined in this COM server.

MFCOM is a programming interface to the functions provided by the Presentation Server Console. MFCOM is a COM object that meets the requirements defined in the Microsoft Component Object Model Specification. MFCOM is a COM server, not a COM client. MFCOM exposes objects that can be accessed from a COM client. It is a free-threading COM server and supports automation. MFCOM is also a DCOM server; that is, a COM client that can remotely connect to a Presentation Server.

Using MFCOM

In most cases, MFCOM can be used on Presentation Servers with no additional configuration. MFCOM is installed and registered by the installation of Presentation Server. The C:\program files\citrix\system32\mfreg.exe program can be used to register or unregister MFCOM manually on the server.

To use MFCOM remotely, a utility program—c:\program files\citrix\mpssdk\utils\ mfreg.exe—must be used to register MFCOM as a remote server. To obtain the mfreg .exe program, download the Presentation Server SDK (MPSSDK) from the downloads section on http://www.citrix.com. Installing the MPSSDK package provides a prompt to register the Presentation Server. To register or unregister the DCOM client, manually use the c:\Program files\citrix\mpssdk\utils\mfreg.exe program. Additionally, you may have to use the Microsoft tool DCOMCNFG.EXE to change the default impersonation to "impersonate." This change requires a reboot. For additional information, please visit the Citrix Developer Network at http://apps.citrix.com/cdn/.

Presentation Server COM VBScripting

Although MFCOM can be used with any COM-compliant programming language, such as Visual Basic 6.0, Visual C++, Perl, VB.Net, C#.Net, and C++.net, it is convenient to use VBScript. This is because VBScript is included in most versions of Microsoft Windows. *VBScript* is a perfect programming tool for Presentation Server administrators who want to take advantage of scripting to overcome the difficult tasks of server maintenance. The following example can be used to add or remove an Active Directory Services (ADS) domain user or group to or from a published application. It demonstrates how a simple VBScript can be created. With modification to the script, you can do other tasks applicable to your published applications, as well.

The Purpose of the Following Script (Addacct.wsf or Rmacct.wsf)

Using the Presentation Server Console to add or remove domain users and groups can be a tedious task for an administrator of published applications. If your farms have just a few published applications, using a script to add or remove a couple of user accounts may not seem beneficial. If you have a large number of published applications, though, you'll save yourself a lot of time. Scripts can be used to batch the process of adding or removing accounts from published applications.

To run the following script, you can execute the command,

```
d:>cscript  addacct.wsf
```

from a CMD window, where d: is the drive where the script is located.

```
<package>
  <job id="AddAcct">
    <comment>
    File:          addacct.wsf
    Description:    Example of how to add a ADS user or group to a published
application.
    Requirements:   WSH 5.5 or higher.

        Copyright (c) 2004 Citrix Systems, Inc.

    </comment>
    <runtime>
        <description>
            Add a user or group to an application.
        </description>
```

```
            <example>
                CScript //nologo USAGE: Addacct.wsf  DOMAIN NAME, USER|GROUP NAME

                    Example: Addacct.wsf  MYADS  Domain Users
                        Use Double Quotes for names such as Domain Users
                    Example: Addacct.wsf  MYADS  JONDOE
            </example>

        </runtime>
        <reference object="MetaFrameCOM.MetaFrameFarm"/>
        <script language="VBScript">

     Option Explicit

     Dim  AAName, AcctName, theFarm, anApp, MFUser, aWinApp

            if  WScript.Arguments.Count <> 2 Then
                   WScript.Echo "USAGE: Addacct.wsf  DOMAIN NAME, USER|GROUP NAME"
                   WScript.Echo ""
                   WScript.Echo "Example: Addacct.wsf  MYADS  Domain Users"
                   WScript.Echo " Use Double Quotes for names such as Domain Users"
                   WScript.Echo "Example: Addacct.wsf  MYADS  JONDOE"
                   WScript.Quit 0
            Else
        AAName = WScript.Arguments(0)
               AcctName  = WScript.Arguments(1)
wscript.echo AAName, ACCTNAME
            End If

'
'
'


            Set theFarm = CreateObject("MetaFrameCOM.MetaFrameFarm")
             if Err.Number <> 0 Then
                 WScript.Echo "Can't create MetaFrameFarm object"
                 WScript.Echo "(" & Err.Number & ") " & Err.Description
                 WScript.Echo ""
                 WScript.Quit Err.Number
             End if


' Initialize the farm object.
'
            theFarm.Initialize(MetaFrameWinFarmObject)
            if Err.Number <> 0 Then
                WScript.Echo "Can't  Initialize MetaFrameFarm object"
                WScript.Echo "(" & Err.Number & ") " & Err.Description
                WScript.Echo "quiting "
                WScript.Quit Err.Number
```

```
              End if
'
'
'          Are you Citrix Administrator?
'
'
           if theFarm.WinFarmObject.IsCitrixAdministrator = 0 then
               WScript.Echo "You must be a Citrix admin to run this script"
               WScript.Echo ""
               WScript.Quit 0
           End If

'
'      Display all applications in the farm.
'
'

           For Each anApp In theFarm.Applications
               if Err.Number <> 0 Then
                   WScript.Echo "Can't enumerate applications"
                   WScript.Echo "(" & Err.Number & ") " & Err.Description
                   WScript.Echo ""
                   WScript.Quit Err.Number
               End if

'
'    Create the user object
'

           Set MFUser = CreateObject("MetaFrameCOM.MetaFrameUser")

           MFUser.initialize MFAccountAuthorityADS, AAName,MFAccountDomainUser,
AcctName

'
'        Add the user or group to all published applications
'

               anApp.LoadData(TRUE)
               if anApp.AppType = MetaFrameWinAppObject Then
                   ' MetaFrameWinApp object.
                   Set aWinApp = anApp.WinAppObject
                   anApp.Adduser MFAccountAuthorityADS, AAName, MFAccountDomainUser,
AcctName
        anApp.SaveData
               end if
           Next

    </script>
    </job>
</package>
```

Modifying one line of code in the previous Windows Script File can produce an entirely different result. For example, replacing the line,

```
anApp.Adduser MFAccountAuthorityADS, AAName, MFAccountDomainUser, AcctName
```

with

```
anApp.removeuser MFAccountAuthorityADS, AAName, MFAccountDomainUser, AcctName
```

can remove an ADS user or group from all the published applications.

In this simple functional VB script, the MFAccountAuthorityADS and MFAccount-DomainUser enumerations are coded into the calls to add and remove ADS users and groups. If you are adding or removing users and groups from other account authorities, such as NDS, NT, or a local machine, you need to change these parameters (enumerations) at a minimum. For additional information, please visit the Citrix Developer Network at http://apps.citrix.com/cdn/.

CHAPTER 15

Password Manager Administration

In this chapter, we explore Password Manager Administration. We also look at several security-related topics around the Password Manager Agent, Hot Desktop configurations, backing up the credential store and managing multiple domains.

ACCESSING LOGON MANAGER WITH A DISABLED TRAY ICON

In Citrix Password Manager 4.*x*, the administrator can choose whether to display the agent's tray icon on a per deployment basis. This setting can be deployed as a registry setting or as an Agent Setting using the Password Manager Console.

The default installation configures the agent to be run with the "/background" flag, which does not invoke the logon manager on startup, but only starts the background process. Terminal Servers start the agent during a logon via the registry entry HKLM\ Software\Microsoft\Windows NT\Current Version\winlogon\appsetup. Desktop operating systems (OSs) start the agent via the Start menu's startup folder. Once the user has logged in and the agent is running, users can invoke logon manager by double-clicking the tray icon. If the tray icon is disabled, you can still invoke logon manager, by running ssoshell.exe without the "/background" flag.

NOTE The shortcut installed in the Start menu contains the "/background" flag and will not invoke logon manager if the tray icon is disabled. In a Presentation Server environment, you can choose to publish ssoshell.exe with no arguments to allow users to access the logon manager.

To disable the tray icon:
Set "ShowTrayIcon" = "Do not show the tray icon" under Shell\Agent Settings in the console.

NOTE Changing the tray icon display behavior does not affect the agent until the agent is restarted by either logging out or shutting down the agent manually.

AUTOMATIC KEY RECOVERY

This section covers advanced concepts of Citrix Password Manager's Automatic Key Recovery. Topics include

▼ Migrating the V4 Secret from one Password Manager Service machine to another. This covers how to migrate the important V4 Secret in case a server is to be decommissioned and replaced by another.

▲ A comparison between Automatic Key Recovery feature offered with Citrix Password Manager. This is an overview of how key recovery is handled without Automatic Key Recovery and how Automatic Key Recovery handles this differently.

Migrating the V4 Secret from One Citrix Password Manager Service Machine to Another

The encryption mechanism uses a master secret named V4. *V4* is one of a set of four random numbers used by the Automatic Key Recovery Service to generate a key that encrypts and decrypts the Primary Authentication Key. The *V4 secret* is a cryptographically strong random number that is encrypted using machine-level DPAPI and stored on the local hard drive of the machine running the Citrix Password Manager Service. Only code running on the Citrix Password Manager Service machine can decrypt V4. V4 is the only one of the four random numbers that remains static throughout the course of a deployment. If this number changes and Agent users have already registered with Automatic Key Recovery with a previous V4, their credentials are lost.

If multiple instances of the Citrix Password Manager Service are installed in a deployment and load balanced using a third-party load-balancing mechanism, it is necessary to copy V4 (as well as the Data Integrity certificate and private key data) to these other machines.

To facilitate this activity, a command-line tool named CtxMoveKeyRecoveryData is installed with the Citrix Password Manager Service and enables the administrator to copy the secret data from one machine to another. CtxMoveKeyRecoveryData can be found in the following location:

```
C:\Program Files\Citrix\MetaFrame Password
Manager\Service\Tools>CtxMoveKeyRecoveryData
```

Usage:

```
CtxMoveKeyRecoveryData [option] [filename]
```

Options:

 ▼ -generation   Generates new key recovery data for the Automatic Key Recovery function.

 ■ -export [filename] Exports the key recovery data, encrypts it with a user-supplied password, and writes it to the specified file.

 ▲ -import [filename]   Reads the key recovery data from the specified file, decrypts it with a user-supplied password, and imports it.

On export, the tool creates a 3-DES encrypted file of the V4 secret, using the password to compose the key. On the migrated system when an import is done, the password is used to 3-DES decrypt the V4 secret, which then is encrypted automatically using DPAPI.

Comparison Between Automatic Key Recovery and Existing Question-based Key Recovery Methods

Automatic key recovery is an alternative to the use of Security Questions (Question-based Authentication) or Previous Password mechanisms for recovering the Authentication key. Automatic key recovery, unlike the other methods, does not require any interaction from the user.

Figure 15-1 illustrates the steps when Security Questions or Previous Password is used.

1. The end user enters primary logon credentials and answers user questions during setup if Security Questions is used.

2. The Crypto API generates a unique Primary Authentication Key during setup (first-time-use).

3. The Primary Authentication Key is encrypted with the password of the primary logon credentials and the resulting key is stored in MS CAPI.

   If Security Questions is being used, the Primary Authentication Key is encrypted with the user question, and the resulting key is stored in MS CAPI.

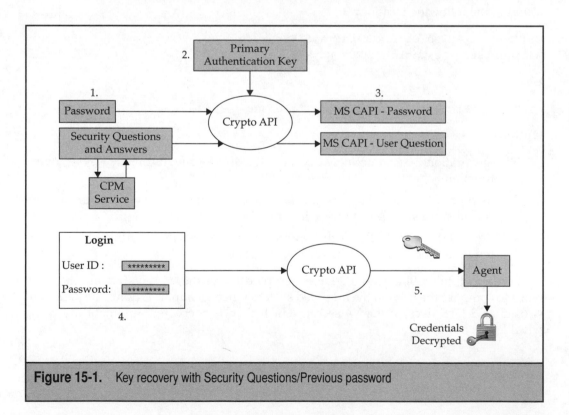

Figure 15-1. Key recovery with Security Questions/Previous password

4. When subsequent logons occur, successful authentication unlocks MS CAPI, and the Primary Authentication Key is unlocked and becomes available to the Crypto API.

5. Crypto API passes the key to the Shell (agent), which uses it to decrypt end-user credentials.

The main difference between Automatic Key Recovery and other methods is how the Authentication key is encrypted. This involves the use of the Citrix Password Manager Service.

Enrollment for Automatic Key Recovery

At a high level, the sequence in Figure 15-2 occurs when a user first uses the Password Manager Agent.

1. The Agent executes an algorithm, which results in deriving a 3DES key, called the Automatic Key Recovery encryption key (AKRKey). (The Agent uses the AKRKey in a similar manner as it ordinarily uses the key derived from the user's Security Questions or Password information.)

2. The Agent conceptually breaks the key into two parts. The Agent stores one part of the data in the user's object on the synchronization point. The Agent transmits the second part of the data to the Citrix Password Manager Service.

3. The Citrix Password Manager Service encrypts its portion of the key derivation data and stores the resulting encrypted data in the user's folder or under the user's AD object on the synchronization point.

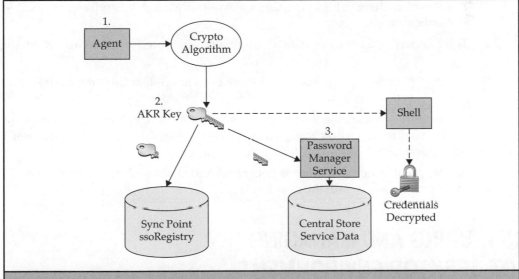

Figure 15-2. Automatic Key Recovery enrollment process

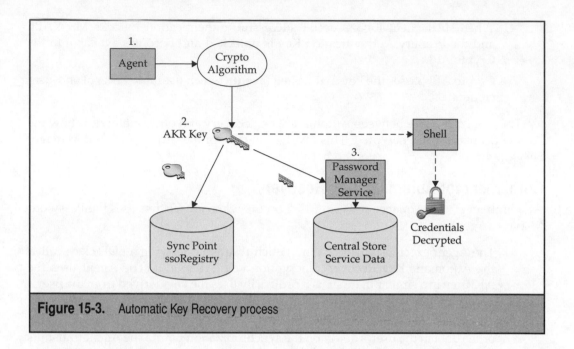

Figure 15-3. Automatic Key Recovery process

Key Recovery

After a password change initiated by the Administrator or a Self-service Password Reset, the sequence in Figure 15-3 occurs to recover the key.

1. The Agent authenticates to the Citrix Password Manager Service using NTLM authentication.

2. The Service decrypts the data it originally encrypted and returns it to the Agent.

3. The Agent retrieves its portion of the key derivation data from the central store and uses both parts of the data to reconstitute the AKRKey.

4. The Agent then uses the AKRKey in a similar fashion as it ordinarily uses the key derived from the user's Security Questions information to recover the user's encryption key(s). No user interaction is required.

5. At this point, a new AKRKey is generated and the Agent performs the Enrollment process again with the new key data.

CONFIGURING AND MANAGING A HOT DESKTOP ENVIRONMENT

The following section covers configuring and managing Hot Desktop.

Bypassing Hot Desktop Mode

All administrative maintenance to a Hot Desktop environment must be performed after bypassing the automatic logon process of the Hot Desktop Shared Account. To bypass the automatic logon process, hold the SHIFT key during the Windows logon process. For more information on bypassing the automatic logon process please see Microsoft knowledgebase articles 310584 and 324737.

Hot Desktop Shared Account Automatic Logon

This section lists the Microsoft AutoAdminLogon registry keys used by the Hot Desktop Shared Account automatic logon process The following describes the registry keys used:

```
[HKEY_LOCAL_MACHINE\SOFTWARE\Microsoft\Windows NT\CurrentVersion\WinLogon]
AutoAdminLogon=dword:00000001
```

▼ **AutoAdminLogon** is used to enable or disable the automatic logon process used by the Hot Desktop Shared Account. A value of 0 disables the process, while a value of 1 enables it. If this key gets altered and the automatic logon process fails, use regedit to reenable the key to 1. This key is set to 1 to enable the AutoAdmin logon process during the agent installation:

```
[HKEY_LOCAL_MACHINE\SOFTWARE\Microsoft\Windows NT\CurrentVersion\WinLogon]
DefaultUserName="Hot Desktop Shared Account name"
```

■ **DefaultUserName** is the account name used in the automatic logon process triggered by the AutoAdminLogon key. If this key gets altered and the automatic logon process fails, use regedit to reenter your Hot Desktop Shared Account name. This key stores the name of the Hot Desktop Shared Account entered during agent installation:

```
[HKEY_LOCAL_MACHINE\SOFTWARE\Microsoft\Windows NT\CurrentVersion\WinLogon]
DefaultDomainName ="Domain of Hot Desktop Shared Account"
```

■ **DefaultDomainName** is the domain that the HotDesktop Shared Account specified in the DefaultUserName belongs to. If this key gets altered and the automatic logon process fails, use regedit to reenter your Hot Desktop Shared Account name. This key is set to the domain of the Hot Desktop Shared Account entered during agent installation:

```
[HKEY_LOCAL_MACHINE\SOFTWARE\Microsoft\Windows NT\CurrentVersion\WinLogon]
DefaultPassword ="Hot Desktop Shared Account password"
```

▲ This optional key is not recommended for security reasons because it exposes a clear text password in the registry. Normally, the password is stored in an encrypted format inside the NTSecret object. This key enables an administrator to hardcode a password for the Hot Desktop Shared Account to be used in the automatic logon process. This key is not created or set during the agent installation process because the agent stores the password in the NTSecret object.

> ***NOTE***   If the Hot Desktop Shared Account password is changed or becomes corrupted in the registry, log on to Hot Desktop like a regular Hot Desktop User, but use the Hot Desktop Shared Account. Once logged in interactively, press CTRL-ALT-DEL keys and perform a normal password change. This process reencrypts the Hot Desktop Shared Account password and stores it in the NTSecret object used in the automatic logon process.

ShellExecute—Identifying Application Executables

Once you identify the applications you want to run in the context of the current Hot Desktop User, you must add the executable names to the ShellExecute section of the process.xml file. (This section of the process.xml file is referred to as ShellExecute for the remainder of this document.) Two variables are considered when adding executables to ShellExecute.

1. How will users launch applications (Start | Run, File Type Association, command prompt)?
2. What is the correct executable to define in ShellExecute?

Notes:

▼ The following ShellExecute example entries are not case-sensitive

■ The XML syntax is case-sensitive

▲ Applications launched with additional parameters are not supported in Shell-Execute

Start | Run   If the administrator allows the Run option to be accessible on the Start menu, all forms of the executable should be listed in the ShellExecute section. Executables may require multiple entries in ShellExecute because the Run dialog box does not require file extensions. For example, the administrator wants calc.exe to run as the current Hot Desktop User each time it is executed. The following entry is made to the ShellExecute section.

```
<process>
    <name>calc.exe</name>
</process>
```

If a user entered "**calc**" (note the missing file extension) in the Run dialog box, it would be run in the context of the Hot Desktop Shared Account, not the Hot Desktop User account. Specify the executable name without the file extension to allow ShellExecute to launch the application as the Hot Desktop User account. For example, the following two entries would be required for the calc.exe application to run as the Hot Desktop User account:

```
<process>
      <name>Calc.exe</name>
</process>
<process>
      <name>Calc</name>
</process>
```

File Type Association   Launching an application by file type association provides another situation that ShellExecute must support. In this situation, use wildcards associated with the file type extension in the ShellExecute section to allow ShellExecute to match on the document type and launch the application as the Hot Desktop User account. For example, the administrator wants notepad.exe, as well as all text (txt) files opened, to be launched as the current Hot Desktop User account. To complete this requirement, add the following lines to the ShellExecute section:

```
<process>
      <name>notepad.exe</name>
</process>
<process>
      <name>notepad</name>
</process>
<process>
      <name>*.txt</name>
</process>
```

Command Prompt   All applications launched from within a command prompt are launched in the same user account context as the command prompt. By default, the command prompt is launched in the context of the Hot Desktop Shared Account, so any application launched from the command prompt is run as the Hot Desktop Shared Account. To cause all applications launched from the command prompt to run in the context of the Hot Desktop User account, add "**cmd.exe**" to ShellExecute section, as shown here:

```
<process>
      <name>cmd.exe</name>
</process>
<process>
      <name>cmd</name>
</process>
```

Defining the Correct Executable Name   Occasionally, the process defined in ShellExecute may have been launched by another executable and, thus, ends up in the context of the user account that launched the calling executable. In this case, tools such as SysInternal's

Process Explorer (http://www.sysinternals.com/), allow you to monitor the processes as they launch and determine the correct executable name to place in the ShellExecute section of process.xml.

For example, NetManage Rumba's AS400 display is launched via wddsppag.bin, which is the running process once the AS400 display is started. However, the wddsppag .bin process is launched by rumbawsf.exe, which is the executable that should be defined in ShellExecute, as shown here:

```
<process>
    <name>Rumbawsf.exe</name>
</process>
<process>
    <name>Rumbawsf</name>
</process>
```

To identify the correct executable names, you may use the following steps:

1. In a Hot Desktop environment, login as a Hot Desktop User account.

2. Run "procxp.exe" (SysInternals Process Explorer) as an administrator (administrative permissions are required to see all the process information), by right-clicking (hold down SHIFT as well on a Windows 2000 machine) on the procxp .exe and selecting "Run as..." from the Context menu. Enter the administrative credentials.

3. Edit the process explorer view to show the user column.

4. Launch the executable in question and use Process Explorer to identify the correct executable to include in the ShellExecute section.

Citrix Presentation Server Clients—Configuring in Hot Desktop

Using Citrix Presentation Server clients with Hot Desktop may require some additional configuration. This section is organized by client type and each section details the required configuration changes for that client.

Single Sign-on (SSO) Service (Citrix Presentation Server Clients)   The SSO Service provides pass-through authentication to Presentation Server Clients. In a Hot Desktop environment, the Hot Desktop GINA provides the service with up-to-date user information for the current Hot DesktopUser account. No additional configuration is required.

Program Neighborhood Agent   If you are not using the SSO Service, additional configuration is needed for Program Neighborhood Agent to function properly. When Program Neighborhood Agent is installed, a shortcut is placed in the All Users Startup folder and launched automatically at startup. To configure Program Neighborhood Agent to run in the context of the Hot Desktop User account, complete the following steps.

1. Remove the shortcut to Program Neighborhood Agent from the All Users Startup folder to prevent the agent from being launched in the Hot Desktop Shared Account context.

2. Add Program Neighborhood Agent to your HotDesktop start-up script to run as the current Hot Desktop User. (For additional instructions, see the following section, "Logon scripts and Network Shares," as well as the samples provided on the Password Manager CD in the \SUPPORT\HOTDESKTOP folder.)

3. Add PNAgent.exe to the transient process section of the process.xml file. This change causes the Program Neighborhood Agent to be terminated on user logoff or user switch events. The following is an example of a transient process entry for Program Neighborhood Agent. (For additional information, please see the *Password Manager Administrator's Guide*.)

```
<transient_processes>
        <process>
            <name>PNAgent.exe</name>
        </process>
</transient_processes>
```

Program Neighborhood Classic   Program Neighborhood Classic does not rely on user profiles and can be configured to request authentication from the Hot Desktop User, so no special configuration is required. As the following notes, however, Citrix recommends all Presentation Server clients be run in the context of the Hot Desktop User account for security reasons.

Web Interface   When connecting to a Presentation Server via Web Interface, the Internet Explorer (IE) process must be launched in the context of the current Hot Desktop User account, rather than the Hot Desktop Shared Account. Control this behavior by adding the following entry to the ShellExecute section of the process.xml file.

```
<process>
     <name>IExplore.exe</name>
</process>
<process>
     <name>IExplore</name>
</process>
<process>
     <name>*.html</name>
</process>
<process>
     <name>*.htm</name>
</process>
```

NOTE For security reasons, Citrix recommends all Presentation Server clients be run as the current Hot Desktop User, rather than the Hot Desktop Shared Account, to prevent sensitive data from being left behind in the shared profile.

Profiles When roaming profile users log on to a computer, the user's roaming profile is copied to the local computer and is referred to as the *local profile*. If the user has previously logged on to this computer, the roaming profile is merged with the local profile. Similarly, when the user logs off from this computer, the local copy of the profile, including any changes the user made, is merged with the server copy of the profile.

If you enable the Microsoft policy setting "Only allow local user profiles," the default roaming profile behavior just described changes. When the user first logs on, the user receives a new local profile instead of the roaming profile. At logoff, changes are saved to the local profile and not updated to the roaming profile. All subsequent logons use the local profile.

The following registry key controls the profile policy in use on the local machine:

```
[HKEY_LOCAL_MACHINE\SOFTWARE\Policies\Microsoft\Windows\System]
LocalProfile=dword:00000001
```

If this value does not exist, the Hot Desktop GINA creates the value and sets it to zero. Then, it is set to one during logon, the profile is loaded, and the value is set back to its original value.

The profile handling behavior can be controlled further within the Hot Desktop environment. To change the default behavior, the Administrator may create the following registry key:

```
[HKEY_LOCAL_MACHINE\SOFTWARE\Citrix\MetaFrame Password Manager\HotDesktop]
LoadLocalUserProfile=dword:00000001
```

▼ **Zero** No profile is loaded or unloaded. When using this option, remember, some applications might require the presence of a user profile to function properly, for example, Program Neighborhood Agent and Web Interface. This setting provides the fastest user-switching time, but at the expense of not supporting some applications requiring access to the Hot Desktop User's user profile.

■ **One** A local profile is loaded and unloaded (This is the default value if the previous registry value is not present). When using this option, the local user profile is created, but Roaming or Mandatory profiles are not loaded. This setting provides compatibility for the widest range of applications (flexibility), while minimizing the profile load time (speed).

▲ **Two** No restrictions on which profile is loaded or unloaded. The standard Windows algorithm is used to locate and load the user's profile. This setting is slower when switching users, but it provides compatibility with all applications using profiles.

Additional information regarding User Profiles can be found in the Microsoft article "User Data and Settings Management" located at the URL http://www.microsoft.com/technet/prodtechnol/winxppro/maintain/xpusrdat.mspx.

Logon Scripts and Network Shares

Hot Desktop does not support logon scripts or home folders assigned to a user through Active Directory or NT Domain policies. However, an Administrator can use the following alternatives to accomplish the same functionality.

▼ Logon scripts can be executed through the start script portion of the Session .xml file. Use this section to locate and launch the logon script. Use the account setting to control whether the script is launched as the Hot Desktop User or the Hot Desktop Shared Account. Here is an example of a start script setting in the Session.xml file:

```
<startup_scripts>
    <script>
        <account>HDU</account>
        <working_directory>c:\script path</working_directory>
        <path>c:\script path\scriptname.bat</path>
    </script>
</startup_scripts>
```

■ The start script can also be used to access logon scripts on network shares. Before a network share can be accessed, however, you first need to create a logon script that contains the drive letters and network shares you want to assign to the Hot Desktop User account. Verify the script is launched as the Hot Desktop User and not the Hot Desktop Shared Account. In addition, you can also specify the application run as the Hot Desktop User through settings in the Process.xml file. When the Hot Desktop User launches the application, the user is able to access the network shares assigned to them using the start script/logon script solution. Processes that are not running in the context of the Hot Desktop User do not have access to the network shares.

▲ If logon scripts and network shares are common to all users, they can be assigned to the Hot Desktop Shared Account. In this scenario, the logon script is only launched once during startup of the Hot Desktop environment. The network shares are accessed as the Hot Desktop Shared Account, therefore, access cannot be restricted to a specific user. Also, all Hot Desktop User accounts have access to the all Hot Desktop Shared Account network shares, unlike the previous alternatives.

Because the console allows user configurations to be set at the user level, the Administrator can assign different logon scripts and/or network shares to different users via the Session.xml setting in the user configuration. For more information regarding Process.xml and Session.xml, please reference the *Password Manager Administrator's Guide*.

Stop Script Impacts Session Termination   Occasionally, a misbehaving session stop script might impact the session termination process and leave the Hot Desktop User's desktop open. As a preventative measure, if the stop script is still running after a 60-second (default) interval, then Hot Desktop agent terminates the process and allows the session to end. The timeout interval can be controlled through the following registry key:

```
[HKEY_LOCAL_MACHINE/SOFTWARE/Citrix/MetaFrame Password Manager/GINA/HotDesktop
ScriptLaunchWaitSecs=dword:0000003C
```

▼ Specifies the number of seconds to wait on a session stop script before terminating the script and allowing the session to end. Default is 60 seconds.

Unload User Profile Impacts Session Termination   If Windows cannot unload a profile, by default it retries 60 times, at 1 retry per second. This slows session termination substantially and cannot be controlled using the standard Microsoft group policy setting "Maximum retries to unload and update user profile." When Hot Desktop is installed and it cannot unload a profile, it retries 15 times at 1 retry per second. The Hot Desktop setting can be configured through the following registry key:

```
[HKEY_LOCAL_MACHINE\Software\Citrix\HotDesktop]
UnloadUserProfileRetries=dword:000000F
```

▼ Specifies the number of retry attempts to unload a user profile before ending the session without unloading the profile. Each attempt occurs at one-second intervals. This setting impacts user switching if the user profile cannot be unloaded.

Storage Location for User Profile Data and HKCU   Normally, the user's local data is stored and protected by the user's profile. All the files are located in the user profile's application data folder (C:\Documents and Settings\ <username>\Application Data\Citrix\ MetaFrame Password Manager) and access to this folder is controlled by access rights inherited from the user profile. Similarly, the HKEY_CURRENT_USER hive is loaded from and protected by the user profile.

In a Hot Desktop environment, the agent is running in a shell that has the Hot Desktop Shared Account as the interactive user. In some use cases, the profile of the currently logged on Hot Desktop User does not exist on the workstation. So, the user's profile folder (C:\Documents and Settings\<username>\Application Data\Citrix\ MetaFrame Password Manager) is unavailable for the agents to access.

To work around these restrictions, the Hot Desktop installer creates the Citrix\ MetaFrame Password Manager subfolder under the All Users\Application Data folder. It adjusts the ACLs on Citrix\MetaFrame Password Manager folder, so the agent can create a subfolder for a user when executing as that user. The ACLs match those of the People folder created by the File Share Synchronization Point Preparation tool, CtxFileSyncPrep.exe.

The user's Password Manager registry data resides in the [HKEY_CURRENT_USER] portion of the registry. During normal agent operation, this data is duplicated on the central store's synchronization point and updated in the registry at each synchronization event. In the Hot Desktop environment, the [HKEY_CURRENT_USER] hive belongs to the Hot Desktop Shared Account, so the Hot Desktop User account does not typically have access to this registry hive. With a Hot Desktop installation, the user's Password Manager registry data instead resides in a new file—Registry.MMF—that is located in the same folder as the user's local data.

CONFIGURING AND MANAGING SELF-SERVICE (PASSWORD RESET AND ACCOUNT UNLOCK)

This section covers the following topics:

▼   A sequence flow of the Question-based Authentication (Security Questions) Registration process. This covers the various stages that take place during Security Questions registration.

■   A sequence flow of the Self-service process. This covers the various stages that take place during Password Reset and Account Unlock.

■   Special privileges required to restrict the Self-service account. The requirements to limit the Domain user to an account with the minimum privileges to carry out this sensitive function.

■   Factors influencing registration and reregistration—what causes a user or users to be forced to reregister.

▲   Lockout policies and how they affect authentication for Self-service and the capability to do Account Unlocks.

A Sequence Flow of the Question-based Authentication (Security Questions) Registration Process

The registration process involves the use of the Password Manager Service. Figure 15-4 illustrates the sequence of steps that occur when the user is enrolled for Self-service Password Reset.

1. The administrator configures Self-service Password Reset and/or Account Unlock for a User Configuration.

2. On Initial Credential Setup (First-Time-User), the agent reads the user's Self-service configuration status from the central store.

3. The user is prompted to register for Self-service and initiates a registration request.

4. The Service reads the set of questions from the central store and forwards them to the Agent.

5. The user responds to the set of questions.

6. The Service saves the user responses on the central store.

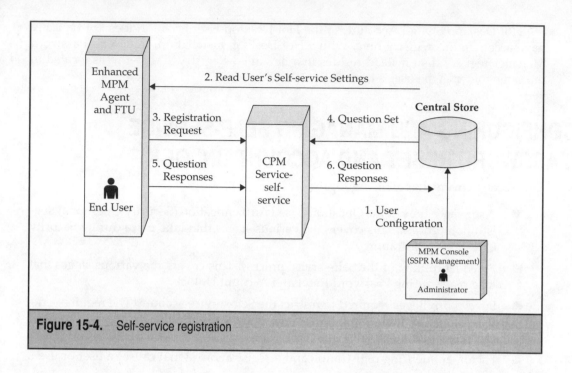

Figure 15-4.   Self-service registration

A Sequence Flow of the Self-service Process

The reset/unlock process, shown in Figure 15-5, also involves the use of the Password Manager Service. The user is authenticated by supplying the answers given to the questions during the time of enrollment.

1. To do a reset, the user requires an authentication, by submitting their User name.

2. The service does a proxy read to determine if the user has registered.

3. A series of questions is sent to the user.

4. The user supplies the response and it is compared with what is read from the central store. If a match occurs, the user gets presented with the next question.

5. Once all questions are answered correctly, the user is allowed to proceed with Account Self-service.

6. The service attempts a password reset or account unlock on the Authentication Authority.

7. The user is informed of the result: success or failure.

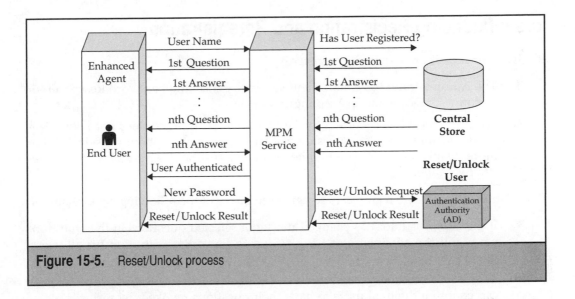

Figure 15-5. Reset/Unlock process

Special Privileges Required to Restrict the Self-service Account

To maximize security, the Self-service account should be a domain user with the minimum privileges required to carry out this sensitive function.

▼ The Self-service Account must be a local Administrator on the Password Manager Service machine.

▲ The Self-service Account must have the following Active Directory Permissions on the Organizational Unit (OU) where the Password Manager Users are located:

Reset Password	User Objects
Read pwdLastSet	User Objects
Write PwdLastSet	User Objects
Read LockoutTime	User Objects
Write LockoutTime	User Objects

Using ADSI edit, apply the permissions by choosing the Self-service account and select the respective check boxes for the remaining privileges.

Factors Influencing Registration and Reregistration

Registration: Users are required to register if:

▼ The Administrator has enabled Self-service by checking Password Reset and/or Account Unlock in the User configuration.

▲ Security Questions is chosen for key recovery. This alone does not allow Self-service actions, however, unless one of the previous two options are selected. For more details on Question-based key recovery, see the *Password Manager Administrator's Guide*.

Reregistration: Users are required to reregister in either of the following circumstances:

▼ If the Administrator has changed the set of selected questions in the Questionnaire and the administrator has decided to Force Reregistration for all users, when prompted to do so.

■ The user's questions have been revoked by the Administrator. Administrators can choose individual users to have their questions revoked, requiring a reregistration. (See the *Password Manager Administrator's Guide,* available in the Console, for details on this task.)

▲ The Administrator has decided to force reregistration for all users, using the task of this name in the Console.

Lockout Policies

The following section details lockout policies and their effect on users' sessions.

Authentication

This affects the capability to do Self-service. If a user exceeds the number of chances given to respond to any question, that user is locked out for a period of Y minutes from using the Self-service features.

▼ The number of valid chances available to be authenticated to do Self-service is done on a per-question basis: the user gets X chances (default of 4 on install) to answer each question, after which the user gets locked out.

■ Once locked out, the user must wait Y minutes (default of 60 on install) before again attempting to do Self-service.

▲ The count for attempts on a question is reset to the full amount after Z minutes. That is, the user gets X chances renewed for that question, Z minutes (default of 60 on install) after the last attempt to answer that question.

To summarize the Policy variables,

▼ X is the Lockout Threshold

■ Y is the Lockout Duration

▲ Z is the ResetAttemptsDuration

These variables are editable in the QBAuthConfig section of the C:\Program Files\ Citrix\Metaframe Password Manager\Service\WebService\web.config file, on the Service machine.

The number of chances shown in the following example indicate what is available to the user for each question, prior to that attempt. The example assumes a default of four chances, with just four Security questions (as in a new installation).

Remaining Chances Before Each Answer

	4	3	2	1
Question 1	Wrong	Wrong	Wrong	Correct
Question 2	Correct	-	-	-
Question 3	Wrong	Wrong	Correct	-
Question 4	Wrong	Correct	-	-

Whenever a question is answered correctly, the number of chances is reset to the original amount of X, and the user is presented with the next question. If the user successfully answers the final question, the user is informed that all the answers were correct and is prompted to enter a new password or gets their account unlocked.

Account Unlock

This affects the frequency with which Account Unlocks can occur. If a user exceeds the number of times to do an Account Unlock, that user is disallowed for a period of Y minutes from doing Account Unlocks with Password Manager.

▼ The number of valid chances available to do an Account Unlock is set as a variable on the Service machine. The user gets X chances (default of 4 on install) to do Account unlocks, after which the user can no longer unlock this function with Password Manager.

■ Once the user is barred from doing Account unlocks, the user must wait Y minutes (default of 60 on install) before again attempting to do Account unlocks.

▲ The count for attempts on a question is reset to the full amount after Z minutes. That is, the user gets their original X chances renewed for that question, Z minutes (default of 60 on install) after the last time an Account unlock was attempted.

The following table summarizes the Policy variables:

	CPM Service Variable	Default	Range
X	Lockout Threshold	4	1–999
Y	Lockout Duration	60 Minutes	1–99,999
Z	ResetAttemptsDuration	60 Minutes	1–99,999

These variables are editable in the SSAULockOut section of the C:\Program Files\ Citrix\Metaframe Password Manager\Service\WebService\web.config file, on the Service machine.

HOW TO BACK UP AND RESTORE THE CITRIX PASSWORD MANAGER SERVICE

Before reading this section, you should be familiar with installing and configuring the Citrix Password Manager Service. To find more information, please refer to the following sections and pages in the *Password Manager Administrator's Guide*:

▼ "Installing and Configuring Automatic Key Recovery," pp. 99–103.

■ "Installing, Configuring, and Enabling the Account Self-Service Features," pp. 107–111.

▲ "Installing the Citrix Password Manager Service," pp. 140–148.

To back up the Service:

1. Take note of the settings you make when you run the Service Configuration tool to set up your Service.

2. Export the service data to a secure share or floppy disk using CtxMoveService-Data.exe:

   a. Open a command prompt and go to C:\Program Files\Citrix\MetaFrame Password Manager\Service\Tools.

   b. Type **CtxMoveServiceData.exe –export <\\server\share\backupfile>**.

NOTE   Do not use environment variables in your path.

   c. You will be asked for a password. Enter a password of your choice. Make note of the password.

IMPORTANT The service data you save to your backup file will be encrypted using your password—do not lose your password.

    d. You will be asked to confirm your password. Enter your password again.

    e. Verify your backup file was created.

 NOTE For security purposes, store the backup file in a secure place.

To restore the Service:

1. Install the Service from the installation media.

 NOTE If you are restoring data you backed up using Citrix Password Manager 4.0, please skip to the next section.

2. Configure the Service with the proper settings, using the notes you made when you backed up the service. If you are using Data Integrity, make sure you configure the Data Integrity server location properly, whether the Data Integrity server location has changed or stayed the same. Finish the configuration and allow the Service to start. After the Service starts, you can immediately stop the Service if you choose.

3. Import the service data from a secure share, or floppy disk, using CtxMoveServiceData.exe:

    a. Open a command prompt and go to C:\Program Files\Citrix\MetaFrame Password Manager\Service\Tools.

    b. Type **CtxMoveServiceData.exe –import <\\server\share\backupfile>**.

    c. Enter the correct password when prompted.

    d. The system will ask if you want to overwrite AKR.DAT. Select Yes.

4. Restart the service. The service should now be ready for use.

To restore the service using data you backed up using Citrix Password Manager 4.0:

Password Manager 4.0 used a different procedure to back up the service. If you backed up your service while you were running Password Manager 4.0, you can restore your data directly into Password Manager 4.1. You should have three files containing your data:

▼ PrivateKeyCert.cert

■ PublicKeyCert.cert

▲ Your exported V4 secret

> *NOTE*   You will not be restoring Provisioning data because provisioning was not supported in Password Manager 4.0.

Use the following procedure to restore your data:

1. Install the service from the installation media.

2. Configure the service with the proper settings, using the notes you made when you backed up the service. If you are using Data Integrity, make sure you configure the Data Integrity server location properly, whether the Data Integrity server location has changed or stayed the same. Finish the configuration and allow the Service to start. After the Service starts, you can immediately stop the service if you choose.

3. Take note of the NTFS permissions on the following files:

   ▼ C:\Program Files\Citrix\MetaFrame Password Manager\Service\Certificates\PrivateKeyCert.cert

   ▲ C:\Program Files\Citrix\MetaFrame Password Manager\Service\Certificates\PublicKeyCert.cert

4. Copy the Certificates from the secure share or floppy disk:

   a. Replace C:\Program Files\Citrix\MetaFrame Password Manager\Service\Certificates\PrivateKeyCert.cert with the PrivateKeyCert.cert file stored on the secure share or floppy disk.

   b. Replace C:\Program Files\Citrix\MetaFrame Password Manager\Service\Certificates\ PublicKeyCert.cert with the PublicKeyCert.cert stored on the secure share or floppy disk.

5. Verify that the NTFS permissions of the Certificates you copied over in step 4 match the permissions you took note of in step 3. Set the permissions manually, if necessary.

6. Import the V4 Secret from the shared drive using ctxmovekeyrecoverydata .exe –import (this step is only necessary if you have the Key Recovery module installed):

   a. Open a command prompt and go to C:\Program Files\Citrix\MetaFrame Password Manager\Service\Tools.

   b. Type **ctxmovekeyrecoverydata.exe –import <shared drive file name>**.

   c. Enter the correct password when prompted.

7. Restart the service. The service now should be ready for use.

CITRIX PASSWORD MANAGER—HOW TO MIGRATE USER CONFIGURATIONS FROM A CHILD DOMAIN TO A PARENT DOMAIN IN AN ACTIVE DIRECTORY FOREST

This section describes the steps and the tools available to migrate Citrix Password Manager from a child to a parent domain. These steps can be followed to move Password Manager from a pilot into production or from a parent to a child domain. This section discusses the assumption about the forests and the procedure for the migration.

Assumptions

The procedure assumes the schema in the forest has been upgraded with the CtxSchemaPrep.exe utility from Citrix.

This utility is available on the Password Manager CD in the Tools directory or from the Autorun in the Prerequisites, Create Your Central Store Active Directory.

Using Autorun to create the central store will need to be executed with an account that is part of the Schema Admin Group.

NOTE For more information about Flexible Single Master Operation (FSMO) roles in Active Directory and how to determine which Domain Controller in the Active Directory Forest is the owner of the Schema Master role, please refer to the Microsoft knowledgebase article 324801, "How to View and Transfer FSMO Roles in Windows Server 2003,"
http://support.microsoft.com/default.aspx?scid=kb;en-us;324801.

Warnings

Migrating a user configuration from a Child Domain to a Parent Domain or vice versa uses the memory mapped file (MMF) saved locally on the computer where the agent is installed. During the procedure, "Delete user's data folder and registry keys" (DeleteOnShutdown) is disabled and the data saved in the local profile is used by Password Manager to point the users to the new synchronization point. During the procedure, a Microsoft tool provided in the Microsoft Windows 2003 Distribution Media is used. The Active Directory Migration tool must initiate the move on the Domain Controller acting as the RID master of the domain that currently contains the object.

Procedure

Follow this procedure to migrate user configurations from a child domain to a parent domain in an Active Directory Forest.

Step 1: Create a Synchronization Point on the Child Domain

In a typical migration scenario, the synchronization point is created on a child domain.

▼ **Create Synchronization Point** The Password Manager CtxDomainPrep.exe utility prepares the domain creating the required objects and attributes, and applying the necessary permissions. The Citrix Utility is available on the Password Manager CD in the \Tools Folder.

▲ **Verify Synchronization Point** In the Active Directory Users and Computers, a new object is created under the domain\Program Data. The object can be seen interactively with specialized tools, such as ADSIEDIT (available in the Windows 2003 Distribution Media—SUPPORT\TOOLS\SUPPORT.CAB) or selecting View—Advanced Features in the Active Directory Users and Computers Management Console.

Step 2: Create a User Configuration on the Child Domain

Deploy the Citrix Access Suite Console on a workstation that is part of the child domain. Administrative Rights to the domain are required to be able to perform a successful discovery. To successfully migrate the user configuration, Data Integrity and Retrieve Key Automatically should be disabled. You can enable these settings after migration.

▼ Using the Password Manager Distribution Media, choose Installation Menu | Install Citrix Password Manager Console.

■ Create a new user configuration for the child domain launching the Access Suite Console from Programs | Citrix | Management Consoles.

■ Configure and run Discovery. Press Next.

■ In the Identify Central Store Screen, select Active Directory, and then press Next. In the following screen, do not select Data Integrity. If Data Integrity is part of the pilot or proof of concept, it needs to be deactivated before the migration. After the migration is completed, it may be reactivated.

■ Press Next and complete the discovery process.

■ Create or Import Applications and Policies, and Create a new User Configuration.

▲ In the new user configuration, do not use Retrieve Key automatically for the Identity Verification Method. You need to disable it before the migration.

Step 3: Deploy Citrix Password Manager Agent on a Workstation in the Child Domain

After the creation of the new user configuration, at least one workstation should have the Password Manager Agent installed:

▼ Using the Password Manager distribution media, choose Installation Menu | Install MetaFrame Password Manager Agent—Confirm the EULA.

■ Do not choose Data Integrity. If Data Integrity is a requirement, it can be reactivated afterward.

■ Specify Active Directory as the Synchronization Point.

■ Reboot the Workstation and log on.

▲ The Agent either asks for the Identity Verification Question or uses the current password as the Identity Verification Question, depending on how the user configuration has been created.

Step 4: Create a Synchronization Point in the Parent Domain

Each Password Manager Synchronization Point contains specific information relating to the domain it was originally created in. In the case of multiple domains within the same forest, each of those domains needs to run the CtxDomainPrep utility.

Step 5: Export Administrative Data Using Access Console on the Child Domain

Export the Applications, Application Templates, User Verification Questions, and Password Policies.

▼ Using Access Suite Console, launch the Citrix Access Suite Console from Programs | Citrix | Management Consoles.

■ Select the Password Manager Node by right-clicking or pressing TAB until you get to the Export administrative data task.

▲ Export the Administrative Data and save the XML file to a diskette or to a secured network location accessible from the parent domain.

Step 6: Import Administrative Data Using the Access Console on the Parent Domain

Deploy the Access Suite Console in a workstation that is part of the parent domain. To perform a successful discovery, Administrative Rights to the domain are required.

▼ Using the Password Manager CD, choose Installation Menu | Install Citrix Password Manager Console.

■ Configure and run Discovery. Press Next.

■ In the Identify Central Store screen, select Active Directory, and then press Next.

■ Press Next and complete the discovery process.

■ Launch the Citrix Access Suite Console from Programs | Citrix | Management Consoles.

■ Select the Password Manager Node by right-clicking or pressing TAB until you get to the Import administrative data task.

▲ Import the Administrative Data from the XML file saved in step 5.

Step 7: Create a User Configuration on the Parent Domain

Create a new user configuration for the parent domain by launching the Access Suite Console from Programs | Citrix | Management Consoles.

Step 8: Redirect User Configuration on the Child Domain

Follow these steps:

1. Select the Password Manager Node.
2. Select the User Configuration that you need to migrate.
3. Right-click and select Redirect Users.
4. On the redirect users, leave Active Directory selected.

NOTE   *The Password Manager Administrator's Guide* explains in detail what happens when the user configuration is redirected.

Step 9: Use the Active Directory Migration Tool to Move the Users from Child Domain to Parent Domain

Use the Active Directory Migration tool to move users from child to the parent domain in an Active Directory Forest.

NOTE   The tool is included in the Windows 2003 distribution CD or is available for download from the Microsoft web site for the Windows 2000 Distribution at http://www.microsoft.com/windows2000/downloads/tools/admt/default.asp. The tool needs to be executed pointing to the RID Masters of each domain.

Step 10: Move Workstations from Child to Parent Domain

Follow these steps:

1. Disjoin all user workstations from the child domain.
2. Restart the user workstation.
3. Rejoin all user workstations to the parent domain.
4. The first time the user logs on after migration, the verification of the last password or Identity Verification Question is prompted to verify the user.

HOW TO USE A SINGLE SYNCHRONIZATION POINT FOR MULTIPLE DOMAINS THAT HAVE AN ESTABLISHED TRUST BETWEEN THEM

As enterprises expand, companies often create multiple trusted domains within their forests, yet administrators require centralized administration of products, such as Citrix Password Manager. This section addresses a solution for administrators who have more than one domain for their users to authenticate to, but who do not want to administer multiple synchronization points. This is achieved through the creation of shortcuts and permissions. The following example is the best way to explain the process.

In this example, Robert logs in to three domains within his enterprise: Domain *A*, Domain *B*, and Domain *C*. Robert has three separate user IDs for each of these domains: DomainA\Robert, DomainB\Bob, and DomainC\RobertK.

Robert is a domain administrator in Domain *A* and already has a file synchronization point located there. He would like to have his credentials stored at the same file synchronization point when he logs in to Domain *B* and Domain *C*.

These are the steps Robert can use to solve his problem:

1. Open the synchronization point in Domain *A* and go into the People folder.

2. Create a new shortcut to identify Robert in Domain *B* (DomainB\Bob) and Domain *C* (DomainC\RobertK). Have these new shortcuts point to the DomainA\Robert folder.

3. Add permissions to the DomainA\Robert folder for his two other accounts in the other domains (see the section in the *Password Manager Administrator's Guide* that details the required security settings).

After completing the previous steps, Robert can log in from any of the three domains and still maintain his credentials from a single synchronization point.

PREVENTING USERS FROM DISABLING THE CITRIX PASSWORD MANAGER AGENT

As a Citrix Administrator, you may want to force all users to use the Citrix Password Manager Agent. To accomplish this, you must prevent users from disabling the agent by all possible means. The following is a list of steps to accomplish your goal:

1. Prevent the user from being a member of the computer's administrative groups.

    The user should not have administrative privileges and should not be part of the Administrators, Power Users, Server Operators, Domain Administrators, or any other group that gives the user administrative rights. Without these privileges, the user cannot alter any program files, system files, or registry keys that may affect the behavior of the agent.

2. Disable Access to the Add/Remove Control Panel Applet, the Command Prompt, Task Manager, Run, and ability to create/modify shortcuts.

   It would be efficient to create a Group Policy with the following settings and apply it to the OU or group that contains the user accounts.

   ▼ **Add/Remove Control Panel**   By disabling access to this applet, the user is prevented from being able to remove the agent or other components the agent may rely on to operate. To apply this setting, open the group policy and enable the following policy:

   User Configuration | Administrative Templates | Control Panel | Add/Remove Programs | Disable Add/Remove Programs

   ■ **Command Prompt**   Prohibiting a user to have access to the command prompt prevents the execution of any commands that may delete or alter files, shutdown programs, or cause other results that would disable the agent. To apply this setting, open the group policy and enable the following policy:

   User Configuration | Administrative Templates | System | Disable the command prompt

   The previous policy, however, only disables the CMD.exe file. In the WINNT\System32 folder, there is another command line utility—command.com—that a user can still run and disable the agent. To avoid this, you must restrict a user from running the command.com file. To do this, enable and edit the following policy:

   User Configuration | Administrative Templates | System | Don't run specified Windows applications.

   Click the Show button and add command.com,

   or

   Computer Configuration | Windows Settings | Security Settings | Software Restriction Policies | Additional Rules

   Create a new Hash Policy to prohibit the execution of command.com.

   ■ **Run**   Similar to the command prompt, removing the run command prevents the execution of any commands that may delete or alter files, shut down programs, or cause other results that would disable the agent. To apply this setting, open the group policy and enable the following policy:

   User Configuration | Administrative Templates | Start Menu & Taskbar | Remove Run menu from Start Menu

- **Task Manager** If a user can access the task manager, they have the capability to end processes and tasks relevant to the agent, thus causing the agent to stop. You can enforce a policy that prohibits the user from accessing the task manager. To apply this setting, open the group policy and enable the following policy:

  User Configuration | Administrative Templates | System | Logon/Logoff | Disable Task Manager

- ▲ **Ability to Create/Modify Shortcuts** Although we have restricted the user from being able to execute any command-line commands, he is still able to create a shortcut and modify the properties of that shortcut to add the switch "/shutdown" that would disable the agent. To prevent this, you should disable the user's ability to create and modify shortcuts. To make this secure, you must modify two policies. To apply these settings, open the group policy and enable the following policies:

  1. *UserConfiguration | AdministrativeTemplates | WindowsComponents | Windows Explorer | Disable Windows Explorer's default Context menu.*

  2. *User Configuration | Start Menu & Taskbar | Disable drag-and-drop Context menus on the Start Menu.*

3. Hide the Citrix Password Manager Agent tray icon.
   If the user has access to the Password Manager Agent tray icon, he can easily right-click the icon and choose to shut down the agent. As a Password Manager administrator, you can configure the agent to hide the tray icon while the agent still functions normally. To configure this setting, edit your User Configuration, and under Agent User Interface, disable the setting "Show notification icon."

4. Force credential storage.
   By default, if a user opens an application requiring authentication, the agent asks if they would like to store their credentials in logon manager. The user could simply press "No" without storing their credentials in logon manager. When this dialog box is disabled, users are not prompted with the question to store credentials but, rather, are directly prompted to store their credentials in logon manager. To configure this behavior, edit your user configuration and, under Client-side Interaction, disable the setting "Enable users to cancel credential storage when a new application is detected."

SETTING THE CITRIX PASSWORD MANAGER AGENT LAUNCHER DELAY

Occasionally, the Citrix Password Manager Agent may not recognize or submit credentials to web applications. This issue stems from Password Manager initializing before the web page is ready for input. To alleviate this issue, Password Manager now has incorporated an "Agent Launcher Delay." This section discusses how this delay can be manually set by using the registry on a per-agent basis.

Technical Background

When launching published applications, occasionally the SSOLauncher will prematurely determine that SSOShell and SSOBHO are ready. The SSOLauncher makes this determination using the FindWindow() function on SZ_WND_TRAY + SZ_WND_BHO_HOOK. In some cases, this prevents the Password Manager Agent from submitting credentials to the published web applications launched by the user.

Configuring the Citrix Password Manager Agent Launcher Delay

To alleviate this issue, Password Manger has incorporated a registry setting that can be implemented manually. After setting the registry entry, the SSOLauncher sleeps a predetermined amount of time after detecting SZ_WND_TRAY and SZ_WND_BHO_HOOK. The default setting for this sleep interval is 0, but the interval can be customized with a new registry value LauncherDelay. This value is a DWORD expressed in milliseconds.

To manually add LauncherDelay to the registry:

1. As an administrator, launch regedit.exe and browse to

   `HKEY_LOCAL_MACHINE\SOFTWARE\Citrix\MetaFrame Password Manager\Shell\`

2. If the entry LauncherDelay does not exist, create a new DWORD Value named LauncherDelay and set it to 1 or higher.

NOTE   Some experimenting will need to be performed by the administrator until a proper timing is achieved.

CHAPTER 16

Tuning and Optimizations

This section suggests optimizations that can increase the performance of Presentation Server. Many of the recommendations are from Microsoft knowledgebase articles. Make sure you read the articles from Microsoft to better understand ramifications and expected results from any tuning you perform on the systems.

PROCESSOR SCHEDULING

Microsoft has published knowledgebase article 259025, which discusses how the Processor Scheduling setting affects processor operation for machines running Windows 2000.

Presentation Servers that are hosting published applications should be configured with the Programs setting to enhance the end-user ICA session experience, as each process will wait less time for processor attention and input/output will appear more fluid. However, "infrastructure" machines, such as zone data collectors and especially dedicated database servers, should use the Background Services setting, as the processes running on these machines require more CPU cycles. This recommendation relies on the assumption that background services are assumed to benefit from more CPU time and applications require shorter time slices, so they can be more responsive to keyboard input and to more threads, as in Terminal Services in Application Server mode.

DISK OPTIMIZATIONS

Several registry settings can be modified to increase disk performance and throughput. Enhancements include disabling disk caching, increasing I/O locks, and disabling last file access updates.

I/O Locks

The registry setting *IoPageLockLimit* specifies the limit of the number of bytes that can be locked for I/O operations. Because random access memory (RAM) is being sacrificed for increased disk performance, determine the optimal setting for this value through pilot tests. Changing this setting from the default can speed file system activity. Use Table 16-1 as a guide for changing the registry setting.

Modify the registry setting as follows:

```
HKEY_LOCAL_MACHINE\SYSTEM\CurrentControlSet\Control\Session Manager\
Memory Management
Value: IoPageLockLimit (REG_DWORD): 0 (512 KB is used)
```

For additional information on the IoPageLockLimit registry setting, see Microsoft knowledgebase articles 121965 and 102985.

Server RAM (MB)	IoPageLockLimit (decimal)	IoPageLockLimit (hex)
64–128	4096	1000
256	8192	2000
512	16384	4000
1024+	65536	10000

Table 16-1. IoPageLockLimit Settings

Last Access Update

The NTFS file system stores the last time a file is accessed, whether it is viewed in a directory listing, searched, or opened. In a multiuser environment, this updating can cause a small performance decrease. Modifying the following registry setting and adding the following value disables this feature:

```
HKEY_LOCAL_MACHINE\SYSTEM\CurrentControlSet\Control\FileSystem
Value: NtfsDisableLastAccessUpdate (REG_DWORD): 1
```

MEMORY OPTIMIZATIONS

This section describes configurations for the direct-mapped level 2 (L2) cache, the system paging file, and system page table entries.

Level 2 Cache

For processors that use a direct-mapped L2 cache, configuring the value manually can yield a performance improvement. Direct-mapped L2 cache does not provide performance gains on Pentium II and later processors. For more information, see Microsoft knowledgebase support articles 228766 and 183063. The following registry setting can be used to modify the direct-mapped L2 cache:

```
HKEY_LOCAL_MACHINE\SYSTEM\CurrentControlSet\Control\Session Manager\
Memory Management
Value: SecondLevelDataCache (REG_DWORD): x, where x is the L2 size in
decimal (default: 0, which sets the cache to 256KB)
```

NOTE   Example—If the CPU has a 512KB cache, set the entry to 512 (in decimal).

Paging File

The paging file is temporary storage used by the operating system (OS) to hold program data that does not fit into the physical RAM of the server. The ratio of physical memory to paged memory is the most important factor when determining the size of a paging file. When configuring the paging file, follow these guidelines:

▼ A proper balance between physical memory and paged memory prevents thrashing. Verify that more memory is in physical RAM than paged to disk. For optimal performance, this ratio should be approximately 3:1.

■ Place the paging file on its own disk controller or on a partition that is separate from the OS, application, and user data files. If the paging file must share a partition or disk, place it on the partition or disk with the least amount of activity.

■ To prevent disk fragmentation of the paging file, always set the paging file initial size as the same as the maximum size.

■ The optimal size of a paging file is best determined by monitoring the server under a peak load. Set the paging file as three to five times the size of the physical RAM, and then stress the server while observing the size of the paging file. To conserve resources, set the paging file to a value slightly larger than the maximum utilized while under stress.

▲ If the server is short on physical RAM, use the paging file to provide additional memory at the expense of performance.

NOTE For debugging purposes, create a paging file on the root partition that is slightly larger than the amount of RAM installed.

Page Table Entries

You can improve single-server scalability (number of users on a server) by manually adjusting the page table entries (PTE) in the registry. The Windows NT kernel uses PTE values to allocate physical RAM between two pools of memory. By manually setting the maximum space allocated to the system PTE, the remaining space can be used to increase the number of users supported on the server.

Determining the optimal configuration for PTE values is a complex task. For detailed information, see the Microsoft knowledgebase article 247904. A Kernel Tuning Assistant for Windows 2000 server is also available from Microsoft.

Client Drive Mapping Accelerator and Paged Pool Memory on Windows Server 2000

Client Drive Mapping (CDM) Accelerator is a new feature included in Citrix Presentation Server 4.0. *CDM* dramatically speeds file operations and directory listings within an ICA session. To accomplish this increase in disk access performance, the CDM Accelerator feature uses more paged pool kernel memory than MetaFrame Presentation Server 3.0. It also has the potential to cause kernel memory to become a single server scalability bottleneck in 32-bit OSs.

> **NOTE**   Because of the redesigned memory management system of Windows Server 2003, the OS is less likely to be bound by paged pool kernel memory.

If this bottleneck is encountered, the default size of the paged pool can be increased by modifying the following registry key for Windows 2000:

```
HKEY_LOCAL_MACHINE \SYSTEM\CurrentControlSet\Control\Session Manager\
Memory Management\.
PagedPoolSize to value -1 (xFFFFFFFF)
```

If the cost of this feature outweighs the benefits, the following registry key can be set on the Citrix Presentation Server to disable it:

```
HKEY_LOCAL_MACHINE \System\CurrentControlSet\Control\Terminal Server\Wds\icawd\
DriveOptimizeDisable key to 0x00000007
```

Microsoft link for setting PagedPoolSize:
http://www.microsoft.com/resources/documentation/Windows/2000/server/reskit/en-us/Default.asp?url=/resources/documentation/Windows/2000/server/reskit/en-us/regentry/29937.asp

Microsoft link for setting NonPagedPoolSize:
http://www.microsoft.com/resources/documentation/Windows/2000/server/reskit/en-us/Default.asp?url=/resources/documentation/Windows/2000/server/reskit/en-us/regentry/29935.asp

NETWORK OPTIMIZATIONS

Some simple changes to network settings can often improve network performance. This section covers a few common issues that can be remedied by adjusting the default Windows NT network configuration.

Network Cards

Most 10/100-based network cards autosense the network speed by default. Manually setting these cards prevents the autosensing process from interfering with communication and forces the desired speed. If the server is connected to an autosensing device, apply these settings to this device as well.

Verify that only the necessary protocols are installed and the binding order of those protocols to the network interface card lists the most commonly used protocol first.

Refused Connections

The server can refuse connections due to self-imposed limits specified by the MaxMpxCt and MaxWorkItem registry values. If this happens, users see the following errors:

```
"System could not log you on because domain <domainname> is not available."
"You do not have access to logon to this session."
```

Before adding these values, read the Microsoft knowledgebase article Q232476. When modifying these registry settings, be sure the MaxWorkItems value is always four times the MaxMpxCt value. Suggested new values for MaxMpxCt and MaxWorkItems are 1024 and 4096, respectively.

```
HKEY_LOCAL_MACHINE\SYSTEM\CurrentControlSet\Services\LanmanServer\Parameters
Value: MaxMpxCt (REG_DWORD): 1024
Value: MaxWorkItems (REG_DWORD): 4096
```

SERVER OPTIMIZATIONS

Correctly configuring Windows services and applications for use in a multiuser environment improves performance and prevents system problems.

Auto-End Tasks

If an application does not properly exit when closed or on server shutdown, the OS can be configured to terminate the application using Auto-End Tasks. *Auto-End Tasks* terminates any task that does not respond to a shutdown notice within the default timeout period.

Enabling Auto-End Tasks affects all applications on the server and can cause issues with some applications that require a shut-down time period that is longer than the default timeout period. Therefore, the default timeout period must be greater than the time required for the longest successful shutdown for any server application. To enable Auto-End Tasks and set the default timeout period, modify the following registry settings:

```
HKEY_USERS\.DEFAULT\Control Panel\Desktop
Value: AutoEndTasks (REG_SZ): 1
Value: WaitToKillAppTimeout (REG_SZ): x, where x is the interval in
milliseconds (default is 20000)
```

For more information, see the Microsoft knowledgebase articles Q123058 and Q191805.

Processes Preventing a Graceful Logoff

When a process does not terminate within a MetaFrame Presentation Server session, it may prevent the session from logging off gracefully, and the session still appears active in the Presentation Server Console. In the Presentation Server Console, you can see the processes running in the session and killing the responsible process allows the logoff to complete. One example of such a process is Wisptis.exe. *Wisptis* is an acronym for Windows Ink Services Platform Tablet Input Subsystem. This is a pen-input device tool for the Microsoft Tablet PC platform and, sometimes, it can be observed in a session running Windows Office 2003. The registry can be modified to allow the logoff process to ignore such processes and successfully complete a graceful logoff. To add a process to the ignore list, follow these steps:

1. Open the registry and navigate to

   `HKEY_LOCAL_MACHINE\SYSTEM\CurrentControlSet\Control\Citrix\wfshell\TWI`

2. From the Edit menu, choose Add Value if no **LogoffCheckSysModules** value exists.

   a. Type **LogoffCheckSysModules** in the Value Name box.

   b. Select REG_SZ in the Data Type box. Click OK.

   c. Type the name of the processes' executable in the Data box. Click OK.

   d. Enter the list of executable names with a comma and no spaces between them.

For more information about LogOffCheckSysModules, see Citrix knowledgebase article CTX891671.

System Hard Error Messages

Messages generated by system hard errors appear on the server console. If left unanswered on an unattended console, messages can cause ICA sessions to hang. You can configure system hard errors to create an entry in the system log, instead of displaying a message on the console.

Disabling the display of messages to the console decreases the likelihood of hung ICA sessions, but it increases the need to monitor the event log for these types of errors. For more information, see Microsoft knowledgebase articles Q124873 and Q229012.

The following registry change disables system hard error messages on the console:

```
HKEY_LOCAL_MACHINE\SYSTEM\CurrentControlSet\Control\Windows
Value: ErrorMode (REG_DWORD): 00000002
```

Dr. Watson

If using Dr. Watson, run the Dr. Watson Application Compatibility script to prevent stability problems. Citrix recommends you disable the Visual Notification option, available on the main screen of Drwtsn32.exe.

Dr. Watson can be disabled completely by clearing the following registry key value:

```
HKEY_LOCAL_MACHINE\SOFTWARE\Microsoft\Windows NT\CurrentVersion\AeDebug
Value: Debugger REG_SZ: (blank)
```

You can restore Dr. Watson as the default debugger by executing this command: **drwtsn32.exe –i**.

Configuring the Event Log

Change the default event log configuration to prevent log files from running out of space, which generates errors.

1. Launch Event Viewer.
2. Right-click system log and choose Properties.
3. Set the Maximum Log Size to at least 1024KB.
4. Choose Overwrite events as needed.
5. Click OK to save the settings.
6. Repeat steps 3–5 for the Application Log.

Configuring Print Job Logging

By default, each print job logs two informational messages to the system log. On Presentation Servers with many users, this feature generates numerous events and fills the log faster. If these messages are not wanted, disable them by changing the following registry setting:

```
HKEY_LOCAL_MACHINE\SYSTEM\CurrentControlSet\Control\Print\Providers
Value: EventLog (REG_DWORD): 0
```

Removing the EventLog value from the registry and restarting the server reenables the logging of all print events.

RPC Services

When opening remote procedure call (RPC)-aware applications, such as Windows Explorer and Control Panel, delays of several minutes can be the result of incorrect service startup settings. Verify the RPC service Startup type is set to Automatic and the RPC Locator service Startup type is set to Manual.

Server Service

Configure the server service to represent the server role more appropriately. The performance boost realized from this server optimization setting depends on the function of the server.

For example, if the server has available RAM, select the Maximize Throughput for Network Applications. Otherwise, select Minimize Memory Used. To configure the Server service on Windows 2000 servers:

1. Open the Network and Dial-up Connections Control Panel.

2. Right-click Local Area Connection and choose Properties from the Context menu.

3. Select File and Printer Sharing for Microsoft Networks.

4. Click the Properties button.

For more information, see the Microsoft knowledgebase article Q154075.

USER OPTIMIZATIONS

Correctly setting up users can provide additional performance gains. Where possible, modify the Default User profile to include the following recommendations.

TIP   When making changes to the Default User profile, restarting the server might be necessary before the changes take effect because the Ntuser.dat file is in use and unavailable to new users.

Windows NT Policies

Use system and group policies where possible, especially in an Active Directory environment. For more information about configuring policies, see Microsoft knowledgebase articles 161334 and 260370.

Profiles

Users require an initial setup when logging on for the first time. This setup time is minimized by the use of roaming profiles. For more information about configuring roaming profiles, see Microsoft knowledgebase articles 142682 and 154120.

Observe the following when you set up roaming profiles:

▼   Configure a dedicated server to host the profiles. If placing the profiles on a dedicated server is impossible, place them on an isolated disk or partition.

▲   When using a server or drive dedicated to profiles and temp files, change the users' profile and temp directories to point to the dedicated location.

Cached Profiles

Disable locally cached profiles by changing the access of the following registry key and all subkeys to Read access only for everyone except SYSTEM (which should have Full Control):

```
HKEY_LOCAL_MACHINE\SOFTWARE\Microsoft\WindowsNT\CurrentVersion\ProfileList
```

Menu Refresh

You can change the menu refresh rate to expedite menu response time by modifying the following registry key:

```
HKEY_USERS\.DEFAULT\Control Panel\Desktop
Value: MenuShowDelay (REG_SZ): 10
```

REMOVING UNNECESSARY FEATURES

To conserve ICA bandwidth, remove any unnecessary drive mappings, printers, or ports. Unless any of the following features are needed for specific applications, disable them:

▼   Active Desktop

■   Disable Active Desktop through Terminal Services Configuration.

■   Desktop Wallpaper (In addition, remove any bmp files found in the %systemroot% directory to prevent users from selecting them.)

■   Screen savers

■   Microsoft Office FindFast

▲   Microsoft Office Assistants

Smooth Scrolling

Many applications have smooth scrolling or other features that increase the frequency of updates sent to the client workstation. If applications exhibit poor performance, disable these features to improve performance. Two common settings are in Microsoft Excel and Microsoft Internet Explorer:

▼   Microsoft Excel 97/2000

    ▼   Choose Tools | Options.

    ■   Select the Edit tab.

    ▲   Clear the Provide feedback with Animation option.

▲   Microsoft Internet Explorer 5

    ▼   Choose Tools | Internet Options.

    ■   Select the Advanced tab.

    ▲   Clear the Use Smooth Scrolling option in the Browsing section.

TIP   While the server is in install mode (change user /install), changing application settings applies the changes to all future users. When finished, place the server back into execute mode (change user/execute).

Microsoft Internet Explorer Wizard

On the first launch of Microsoft Internet Explorer, the Internet Connection Wizard requests the connection type. If the connection type is a local area network (LAN) connection, this dialog box can be bypassed by editing the default user's registry settings as follows:

```
HKEY_USERS\.DEFAULT\Software\Microsoft\Internet Connection Wizard
Value: Completed (REG_DWORD): 0x1
```

Explorer Tips

Modifying the following registry settings disables the tips displayed at server startup:

```
HKEY_CURRENT_USER\Software\Microsoft\Windows\CurrentVersion
\Explorer\Tips
Value: DisplayInitialTipWindow (REG_DWORD): 0x0
Value: Next (REG_DWORD): 0x100
Value: ShowIE4 (REG_DWORD): 0x0
```

Reduce ICA Traffic by Disabling the Windows Network Status Icon

In Windows 2000 Server and Windows 2003 Server, an available option shows the network icon in the system tray. When this option is selected, a network icon is displayed in the system tray within the session, and this network icon blinks each time network traffic occurs. Because the network icon blinks for each update, an infinite feedback loop occurs. When the network icon in the system tray blinks, it causes the ICA session to update and, because the ICA session is being updated, network traffic occurs that causes the network icon to blink, thus causing the infinite loop.

1. Go to Start | Settings | Control Panel | Network and Dial-up Connections | Local Area Connection.

2. Right-click Local Area Connection and select Properties.

3. Uncheck "Show Icon in notification area when connected." In Windows 2000 Server, the option states, "Show Icon in taskbar when connected."

4. Repeat these steps for each network adapter or connection on every server in your farm.

ICA PRIORITY PACKET TAGGING

The Citrix ICA protocol includes a feature that identifies and tags ICA data based on the virtual channel from which the data originated. This feature, referred to as ICA Priority Packet Tagging, lays the foundation for a more granular Quality of Service (QoS) solution by providing the capability to prioritize ICA sessions, based on the virtual channel data being transmitted. This section describes virtual channel priorities and how ICA data is tagged with these priorities when sent over an Ethernet network using TCP/IP. This white paper also discusses important considerations to be addressed by QoS solutions when implementing ICA Priority Packet Tagging.

This section assumes the reader is generally familiar with ICA virtual channels, the TCP/IP protocol, and QoS solutions.

VIRTUAL CHANNEL PRIORITIES

ICA Priority Packet Tagging provides the capability to prioritize ICA sessions based on the virtual channel data being transmitted. TCP/IP must be the protocol used. This is accomplished by associating each virtual channel with a two-bit priority. This two-bit priority is included as part of each ICA framing header (the ICA framing header is described in more detail in the section "Quality of Service Solutions"). The two priority bits combine to form four priority values:

- ▼ 00 (0)—High Priority
- ◼ 01 (1)—Medium Priority
- ◼ 10 (2)—Low Priority
- ▲ 11 (3)—Background Priority

Each virtual channel is assigned one of these priority values. The default virtual channel priorities are described in Table 16-2.

The priority settings for all virtual channels are stored in the following Registry key:

```
[HKLM\System\CurrentControlSet\Control\Terminal Server\Wds\icawd\Priority]
(REG_MULTI_SZ)
This key contains one line for each virtual channel in the format:
VirtualChannelName,Priority
VirtualChannelName is the standard virtual channel abbreviation as specified in
the above table.
VirtualChannelName must be 7 characters, so trailing spaces must be added before
the comma when necessary.  Priority is one of the following numeric priority
values: 0, 1, 2, 3.
```

The ThinWire virtual channels (CTXTW and CTXTWI) are the only high-priority virtual channels by default, thus ensuring that time-sensitive user interface data is sent ahead of all other data.

Virtual Channel	Default Priority	Description
CTXTW	0	Remote windows screen update data (ThinWire)
CTXTWI	0	Seamless windows screen update data (ThinWire)
CTXCLIP	1	Clipboard
CTXCAM	1	Client audio mapping
CTXLIC	1	License management
CTXVFM	1	Video server video (that is, not ThinWire video)
CTXPN	1	Program Neighborhood
CTXCCM	2	Client COM port mapping
CTXCDM	2	Client drive mapping
CTXCM	3	Client management (Auto Client Update)
CTXLPT1	3	Printer mapping for nonspooling clients (that is, WinTerms)
CTXLPT2	3	Printer mapping for nonspooling clients (that is, WinTerms)
CTXCOM1	3	Printer mapping for nonspooling clients (that is, WinTerms)
CTXCOM2	3	Printer mapping for nonspooling clients (that is, WinTerms)
CTXCPM	3	Printer mapping for spooling clients
OEMOEM	3	Used by OEMs
OEMOEM2	3	Used by OEMs

Table 16-2. Virtual Channel Descriptions and Priorities

ICA DATA TRANSMISSION

The implementation details of ICA Priority Packet Tagging are better understood by examining the different layers of the ICA protocol and how the ICA protocol interacts with TCP/IP to send ICA data over an Ethernet network. The priority bits used for ICA Priority Packet Tagging are determined and set within this data transmission process.

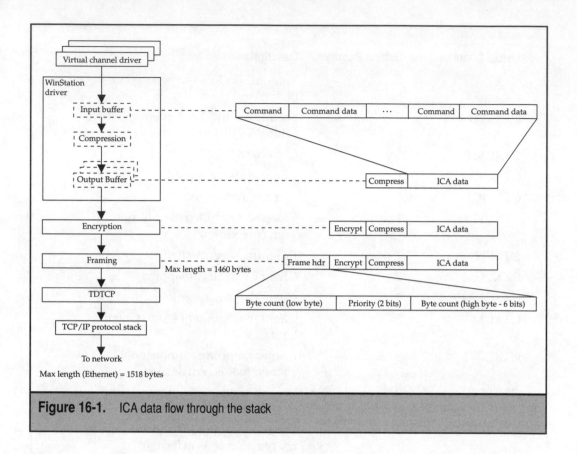

Figure 16-1.   ICA data flow through the stack

Figure 16-1 depicts the flow of ICA data through each protocol layer as it is generated by the client application (or server) and packaged for delivery to a server (or client application) over a TCP/IP network.

ICA data travels through the same protocol layers, but in the reverse direction when received at the destination (client or server). All ICA protocol layers reside at the Presentation layer of the OSI networking model. The ICA protocol layers depicted in the previous diagram are described further in the following sections.

Virtual Channel Drivers

Each virtual channel has its own virtual channel driver that sends virtual channel data to the WinStation driver (described in the following section). The format of the virtual channel data is not standardized as it depends completely on the virtual channel implementation.

WinStation Driver

The WinStation driver receives ICA virtual channel data from multiple virtual channel drivers and packages the data for receipt by lower network layers. The WinStation driver works at the Application, Presentation, and Session layers of the OSI networking model. The WinStation driver performs the following functions:

▼ Establishes the ICA session between the client and the server, and maintains session information, such as whether compression and encryption are turned on, and whether ICA Priority Packet Tagging are to be used.

▲ Encodes ICA command information and transforms input virtual channel data into ICA packets, which are placed in the WinStation driver's input buffer. An ICA packet consists of a single command byte, followed by optional command data, as shown here:

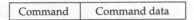

Command	Command data

An ICA packet is not required to contain command data and, therefore, may only contain a single command byte. An ICA packet contains data from only one virtual channel. The maximum length of a single ICA packet cannot exceed 2048 bytes (2KB).

▼ Compresses the ICA packets (when compression is turned on).

■ Combines or separates compressed ICA packets (or uncompressed ICA packets if compression is not being used) into an available output buffer. The WinStation driver determines the amount of data to include in each output buffer, so the length of the ICA data when leaving the framing protocol driver does not exceed 1460 bytes (to keep ICA data from being broken up when transmitted by TCP/IP).

■ Appends a compression header to the beginning of the output buffer (when compression is turned on).

■ Determines the priority of each output buffer based on the virtual channel from where the data originated and passes this information to the framing protocol driver. When multiple ICA packets are combined into one output buffer, the WinStation driver determines the priority of the output buffer based on the highest priority ICA packet included. For example, if the output buffer contains ThinWire (priority 0) and printing (priority 3) ICA packets, the output buffer is given a priority of 0 based on the included ThinWire data.

▲ Forwards the output buffer to the encryption protocol driver (when encryption is turned on).

Encryption Protocol Driver

When encryption is turned on, the encryption protocol driver adds an encryption header to the output buffer data passed from the WinStation driver. All data after the encryption header is encrypted, including the compression header (if included).

Framing Protocol Driver

The framing protocol driver calculates the byte count of the output buffer and adds a framing header. In addition to the byte count, the framing header includes a two-bit priority value, as determined by the WinStation driver. For example, if the total byte count of the output buffer is 1320 bytes and the packet is high priority, the binary value of the framing header is as follows:

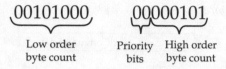

00101000	00000101
Low order byte count	Priority bits High order byte count

The low-order and high-order bytes are reversed for network transmission, and the framing header is created as follows:

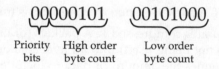

00000101	00101000
Priority bits High order byte count	Low order byte count

TCP Transport Driver (TDTCP)

The ICA protocol transfers control to the TCP/IP protocol stack through TDTCP, the TCP transport driver. TDTCP is the interface of ICA (and RDP) to the TCP/IP protocol stack. TDTCP does not append any additional header or trailer information to the ICA data.

TCP/IP

Once TDTCP transfers control to the TCP/IP protocol stack, the TCP/IP protocol drivers prepare the ICA data for network transmission. Detailed information on the TCP/IP standards and how TCP/IP encapsulates data for network transmission can be found in the Request for Comments (RFC) and Standards (STD) documents available on the Internet (http://www.faqs.org/).

QUALITY OF SERVICE SOLUTIONS

Quality of Service (QoS) solutions are designed to prioritize ICA traffic against all other traffic on the network. These solutions are able to identify network traffic as ICA traffic either based on the TCP port (1494 by default) or by identifying the ICA initialization handshake that occurs when a new session is established (this is safer than using the TCP port because the TCP port number is configurable). Some QoS solutions can also identify ICA traffic based on other information, such as published application or source IP address. This identification allows ICA sessions to be prioritized against each other across the entire network. For example, all ICA sessions where users are running a business-critical application, such as PeopleSoft, can be given a higher priority than sessions performing functions that are not as business critical.

ICA Priority Packet Tagging provides QoS solutions with the opportunity to identify virtual channel priorities within an ICA session, so ICA sessions transmitting higher priority data are delivered first. ICA Priority Packet Tagging requires that the following considerations be addressed when used in combination with a QoS solution:

▼ TCP and IP are stream-oriented protocols. When ICA data is received by TCP, and then by IP, it may be combined or broken up differently than how it was packaged by the ICA protocol drivers. The ICA output buffers are specifically limited to 1460 bytes, so they remain intact when delivered to the TCP/IP protocol stack. However, the output buffers are not guaranteed to remain intact. Therefore, the priority bits in the ICA framing header may not always be in the same place in the TCP segment or IP packet. This prevents QoS solutions from relying on a data offset to identify the priority bits at the TCP or IP layers. To circumvent this potential issue, QoS solutions must verify that the byte count in the header information of the TCP and IP layers matches the byte count in the first two bytes of the ICA data (when aligned correctly, these first two bytes include the priority bits and the byte count of the ICA framing header). When the byte counts do not match, the ICA output buffers are most likely not intact within the TCP segments, so the first two bits of ICA data in the IP packet should not be interpreted as priority bits.

■ ICA Priority Packet Tagging is implemented at the Presentation layer (the sixth layer of the OSI networking model). Most routers read data at lower layers (layers two through four). Therefore, routers don't have access to the ICA Priority Packet Tagging information. When IP packets are sent through a router, the packets may be fragmented. If this is the case, the first packet contains the framing header, including the priority bits and a now incorrect byte count (because the packet has been fragmented). Subsequent packet fragments do not have a framing header and, thus, do not include the priority bits (or a byte count). Therefore, if QoS solutions receive the ICA traffic after fragmentation by a router, not all IP packets will have the priority bits. Verifying the byte counts between the IP layer and the ICA framing header as previously described ensures that the priority bits are interpreted correctly.

■ TCP requires an acknowledgment of receipt for each TCP segment in the TCP buffer before sending additional segments. This prevents QoS solutions from being able to implement functionality that holds back printing ICA data and forward on ThinWire ICA data within a single ICA stream (which is also a single TCP stream). TCP would report a failure of receipt for the TCP segments being held because they were not received by the destination in a timely manner. QoS solutions must implement ICA Priority Packet Tagging in such a way that the transmission speed of each TCP stream is dynamically altered based on the priority bits of the ICA data being transmitted, instead of attempting to hold back individual pieces of data within the stream.

▲   Program Neighborhood clients and Presentation Servers running a software version prior to MetaFrame 1.8 Feature Release 1 can establish ICA sessions without ICA Priority Packet Tagging. Unless QoS solutions detect the Citrix software version in use by the ICA session, all ICA traffic in these sessions are treated as high priority (priority 0) because the two bits that are now used for ICA Priority Packet Tagging were not used (and, thus, set to 0) in previous versions of Presentation Server.

SUMMARY

ICA Priority Packet Tagging provides a mechanism for prioritizing ICA sessions based on the virtual channel from which the data originated. The implementation of ICA Priority Packet Tagging is best understood after examining how ICA data is packaged for transmission across an Ethernet network using TCP/IP. QoS solutions that take advantage of ICA Priority Packet Tagging provide QoS benefits that are more granular than prioritizing ICA traffic based only on application name or user name.

CHAPTER 17

Presentation Server Troubleshooting

This section describes troubleshooting techniques for Presentation Server. It includes sections on troubleshooting the Independent Management Architecture (IMA) service, collecting Citrix technical support information, frequently encountered obstacles, troubleshooting dropped sessions, and known issues.

TROUBLESHOOTING IMA

The IMA service is the core of Presentation Server and runs on all farm servers. The solutions presented in this section can help resolve most production IMA issues.

IMA Service Fails to Start

The following guidelines and hints can be useful when the IMA service fails to start:

▼ If the Service Control Manager reports that the IMA service could not be started, but the service eventually starts, ignore this message. The Service Control Manager has a timeout of six minutes. The IMA service can take longer than six minutes to start because the load on the database exceeds the capabilities of the database hardware or because the network has high latency.

1. Go to HKEY_LOCAL_MACHINE\SYSTEM\CurrentControlSet\Control and, if it does not already exist, create a new DWORD value, ServicesPipe-Timeout.

2. Right-click the ServicesPipeTimeout DWORD value, and then click Modify.

3. Click Decimal and type a value of **600000**, and then click OK. This value is in milliseconds and is equivalent to ten minutes. This change will not take effect until the server is restarted. The value can be adjusted to suit your needs.

NOTE   You can increase the default timeout value for the Service Control Manager in the registry.

■ Examine the following registry setting:

    HKEY_LOCAL_MACHINE\SOFTWARE\Citrix\IMA\Runtime\CurrentlyLoadingPlugin

■ If the IMA service fails to start and this value is blank, the IMA service could not connect to the data store or the local host cache is missing or corrupt.

■ If a value exists, the IMA service made a connection to the data store. The value displayed is the name of the subsystem that failed to load.

NOTE   During the normal start-up process of the IMA service, this value cycles through the names of the subsystems as the subsystems are loaded. Once the IMA service has started successfully, the value will be blank.

- If a direct connection to the data store is being used, verify that ODBC connectivity exists. For more information, see the section "ODBC Connection Fails" in this chapter.

- If an indirect connection to the data store is being used, verify that the IMA service is running on the direct server.

- Review the entries in the event log for the IMA service error code that is returned. See "IMA Error Codes" for more information on why the IMA service fails to start.

- Verify that the Spooler service is started in the context of system rather than a user.

- If you get an "IMA Service Failed" message when restarting a server, with error code 2147483649, the local system account can be missing a temp directory. Change the IMA Service startup account to the local administrator. If the IMA service starts under the local administrator's account, check for a missing temp directory.

Switch the service back to the local system account and try manually to create the temp directory `%systemroot%\temp`. Verify that both the TMP and TEMP environment variables point to this directory. For more information, see Microsoft article 251254.

IMA Service Fails to Stop

The SMS Netmon2 client utility is not supported on Presentation Servers. IMA Service fails to stop when running on a server with this utility installed. Uninstall the Netmon2 client when installing Presentation Server on servers that have this utility already installed.

ODBC Connection Fails

If using direct mode connections to the data store, ODBC connectivity is required for proper operation of the IMA service. If ODBC issues are suspected, try the following:

- ▼ Verify that the database server is online.
- Verify the name of the DSN file the IMA service is using by looking in the registry at:

  HKEY_LOCAL_MACHINE\SOFTWARE\Citrix\IMA\DataSourceName.

- ▲ Attempt to connect to the database using the DSN file with an ODBC Test Utility (such as Oracle ODBC Test, DB2 Client Configuration Assistant test, or SQL Server ODBC Test).

Verify that the correct user name and password are being used for database connectivity. The user name and password can be changed using the dsmaint config command. For more information, see the *MetaFrame Presentation Server Administrator's Guide.*

▼ Reinstall MDAC 2.6 SP1 or later to verify that the correct ODBC files are installed.

▲ Enable ODBC Tracing for further troubleshooting. For more information, see the section "ODBC Tracing."

Presentation Server Fails to Connect to the Data Store

This error can indicate a corrupt Local Host Cache (LHC). Before attempting these steps, verify ODBC connectivity to the database, as in the previous section.

▼ Copy imalhc.mdb to another directory for backup purposes.

■ Stop the IMA service. This can be accomplished from the Services control panel or from a command prompt by typing **net stop imaservice**.

■ From the command prompt, re-create the local host cache using the dsmaint recreatelhc command.

▲ Start the IMA service. This can be accomplished from the Services control panel or from a command prompt by typing **net start imaservice**.

Failed to Initialize Permanent Storage During Installation

This error usually indicates that the IMA service is unable to create objects in the data store. Before attempting these steps, verify ODBC connectivity to the database.

▼ Verify that the user account for the database has permissions to create tables, stored procedures, and index objects. For Microsoft SQL Server, the permission is db_owner. For Oracle, the permission is resource. For DB2, the permission is database administrator authority or the list of permissions set in the Citrix Presentation Server Administrator's Guide.

▲ Verify that the system tablespace is not full on the Oracle server.

RECOVERING FROM A FAILED INSTALLATION

If installation fails, there is a possibility that the data collector will continually attempt to contact the failed server that was uninstalled.

After a failed installation, the list of servers in the Management Console should be compared to the list of servers returned by queryhr. Use the command queryhr -d *hostID* to remove any servers listed in the queryhr results that are not listed in the Management Console.

CAUTION   Do not use the –d switch on farm servers that are functioning properly. This switch removes the server from the farm. The server must be reinstalled into the farm to regain functionality.

Recovering an Unresponsive Server

If a member server is no longer responding to IMA requests and the IMA service cannot be started, the server is considered unresponsive. The chfarm command cannot be used with an unresponsive server because the command requires connectivity to the data store.

CAUTION   The original state of the server cannot be recovered after performing the next procedure. Before using this technique, first attempt all other solutions presented in the previous section, "Troubleshooting IMA."

To rejoin an unresponsive server to the farm, perform the following steps:

1. Uninstall Presentation Server on the unresponsive server.

2. Remove the unresponsive server from the farm using Citrix Management Console.

3. Reinstall Presentation Server on the unresponsive server and rejoin the farm during installation.

RESOURCE MANAGER TROUBLESHOOTING QUESTIONS AND ANSWERS

The following questions and answers apply to Resource Manager for Presentation Server regarding the Database Data Source Name, alerts for high-context switches, the zone elections counter, certain error messages when using Oracle, and multiple duplicate import request messages.

Resource Manager Summary Database Data Source Name

The *RMSummaRyDataBASE* DSN (Data Source Name) is *not* case-sensitive for FR-2, FR-3, or MetaFrame Presentation Server 3.0. Any case can be used for the Summary Database DSN.

Resource Manager Node Still Shows in Management Console After Uninstalling Resource Manager

This is because at least one server in the farm is set to Feature Release 3 and the resource manager node is available to service that server.

NOTE The resource manager node can be removed from a Presentation Server Console by removing or renaming the C:\Program Files\Citrix\Administration\Plugins\ResourceManager.jar and restarting the console.

Alerts Regarding High-context Switches/Second

The default metric threshold values are a *baseline configuration* for an administrator to tune. The default metric threshold values are determined for a minimal server configuration and, although most metric defaults will be suitable as a "one size fits all" solution, such as Processor—%Processor Time defaults, some metrics such as System—Context Switches / Sec need to be tuned for the environment for which they are intended.

Administrators can achieve more realistic threshold values for their environment by utilizing the Visual Threshold Configuration graph in a test-bed or production environment. Here, an administrator can see where the peaks and troughs exist for up to 96 hours worth of sampled data and estimate based on this real data what the threshold value should be for the environment.

Zone Elections Counter

Data Collectors store dynamic data about the Zone. This can be a considerable amount of data if you have many active connections, users, published applications, servers, and so on.

Monitoring this metric can be useful to determine whether excessive Data Collector elections are taking place, because of intermittent networking, IMA Service restarts, Data Collector failures, or when another Presentation Server requests an election. This can happen when a communication failure occurs between any Presentation Servers in any Zone.

Proactive monitoring can help prevent excessive amounts of data from transmitting between Zones as elections are won. This can also be tracked with the Citrix MetaFrame Presentation Server—Zone Elections Won metric.

Resource Manager Error Message: "[Oracle][ODBC][Ora]ORA-02074: Cannot ROLLBACK in a Distributed Transaction"

When using Resource Manager with Oracle, the system may continually generate messages about ROLLBACK of distributed transactions. This can occur if the Disable Microsoft Transaction Server (MTS) support in the Oracle ODBC driver workarounds configuration is set.

If the workaround is not enabled (by default on most Oracle ODBC configurations), this leads to a unique key violation that terminates the SQL transaction and the following resource manager server log entry: [Oracle][ODBC][Ora]ORA-02074: cannot ROLLBACK in a distributed transaction.

Error Message: "Must Reparse Cursor to Change Bind Variable Datatype"

After you reboot the Resource Manager Database Connection Server, the system may generate an Oracle ODBC error in the resource manager server log, such as this:

```
14 June 2003 11:32:26 - System - [Oracle][ODBC][Ora]ORA-01475: must
reparse cursor to change bind variable datatype
```

To resolve this, set the Oracle ODBC workaround for Enable Closing.

Resource Manager Error Message: "Failed to Create Summary Database"

If summary database creation fails, the system may generate an error indicating schema deployment problems for the summary database. Here's a typical "Failed to create summary database" error in the Resource Manager server log:

```
July 2002 12:26:02 - System - Failed to create summary database.
```

The most common causes for resource manager to produce this error are

▼ A database problem has been creating the SDB schema initially. For example, an Oracle database configuration, such as the rollback segment is too small and non-autoextending. This can prevent successful deployment of the resource manager schema when resource manager is creating some of the packages.

▲ The database user has insufficient privileges to create the schema. For example, resource manager may be unable to insert data into tables or create packages.

Solutions

▼ Check the Oracle or SQL Server configuration settings to ensure enough space is in the database to create the schema. Several megabytes should be enough space to create the schema.

■ Check that all rollback segments are autoextending. These can be tuned after the database is created.

▲ Ensure that the user has rights to the database and can successfully communicate with the database server.

Resource Manager Error Message: Multiple Duplicate Import Request Messages

The resource manager server log is showing multiple duplicate import request messages. These informational messages appear in the Resource Manager server log when multiple duplicate import requests occur. The following message is usually observed many times in the server log file:

```
22 November 1978 00:02:10 - System - Ignoring duplicate import request for file
"C:\Program Files\Citrix Resource Manager\SummaryFiles\1C2865FABC926CA" from
host "XXXXXXX".
```

This usually occurs because the Update Now button has been activated multiple times or spurious network conditions cause the server to request an import more than once. In these conditions, this message is quite normal and summary file imports will complete unaffected.

TROUBLESHOOTING NOVELL DIRECTORY SERVICES INTEGRATION

This section lists troubleshooting tips and known issues that can occur when using Presentation Server in an NDS environment.

Novell Troubleshooting Tips

If you are unable to log on or to assign rights to published applications using NDS credentials, try the following troubleshooting tips to correct the problem:

▼ Verify that NDS is enabled for the farm. Right-click the farm name in the CMC and choose Properties. Then, navigate to the MetaFrame Settings tab and verify the Novell Directory Services Preferred Tree is set correctly.

■ Verify you are using a valid user name, password, context, and tree name during logon by logging on from another computer using the same information.

■ Verify that the Novell Client is configured correctly by browsing the tree and logging on from the console of the server.

▲ If the ZENworks Dynamic Local User policies are not being applied on some Presentation Servers, check the Novell Workstation Manager component of the Novell Client.

To check the Novell Workstation Manager component in Windows 2000, complete the following tasks:

1. Right-click the My Network Places icon on the server's desktop and select Properties.

2. In the Network and Dial-up Connections window, right-click Local Area Connection and select Properties.

3. Select Novell Workstation Manager from the components list and click the Properties button.

4. Verify the following settings:

   ▼ Workstation Manager is enabled

   ■ The tree name is set to the tree that has the DLU policies applied

   ▲ All other options have the default settings applied

If you set the Dynamic Local User policy in NDS to delete users after they log out (Volatile User option) and the volatile user accounts are not being deleted, make sure the Enable Volatile User Caching option is disabled.

If you are experiencing autologon problems with or without the ZENworks Dynamic Local User (DLU) feature as the Windows authentication method, try the following:

1. Make a desktop connection using a ICA Custom Connection with the Autologon feature enabled.

2. Specify the following User Credentials:

   ▼ **Username** A valid Distinguished Name, such as .SampleUser.company

   ■ **Password** A valid password

   ▲ **Domain** The NDS tree name is contained

IMPORTANT The following "If" statements are not always true if the custom connection is not created exactly like the previous one.

3. Launch the connection and based on the result, troubleshoot using these guidelines:

   ▼ Novell Client displays an error message about an invalid user name, server, or tree.

   Action: Log on to the console as the same user. If the logon is not successful, then the Novell Client is not configured properly.

   ■ Microsoft Client prompts you to reenter your credentials or displays an error message.

   Action: Click cancel to return to the Novell logon dialog box. On the NT/2000 tab, view the user information.

   ■ If the User name field in the NT/2000 tab field contains a Distiguished Name (.username.context.)

   Action: Upgrade to Novell Client 4.81 or later. (Older Novell Clients do not parse the user name from the Distiguished Name.)

   ■ If the Domain name is blank or set to the local machine name and ZENworks DLU feature is being used

   Action: Troubleshoot Dynamic Local User policies. (DLU is not functioning properly.)

- If the Domain name is blank or is set to the local machine name and ZENworks DLU feature is not being used

  Action: Locate or create the following the registry key HKEY_LOCAL_MACHINE\Software\Citrix\ NDS\SyncedDomainName, and set the registry key value to the name of the NT domain that is synchronized with the NDS tree.

- If the Domain field contains the name of the NDS tree

  Action: Enable NDS integration.

▲ If the Domain field contains the name of an NT domain and you are not using ZENworks DLU functionality for Windows authentication

  Action: Verify the server has a valid trust relationship between the server's domain and the user's domain.

Known Issues and Workarounds

ZENworks for Desktops 3 does not distinguish between users with the same user name, even if they are in different contexts. If the first user is still logged in when the second user logs on, the profile of the first user is utilized by the second user. Because of this, be sure to use unique names in the tree. If your tree already includes users with the same user name, you can work around this by creating aliases. See "Creating Alias" in this guide.

CAUTION   Logging on to a Presentation Server can fail if you uninstall the Novell Client from the server after Presentation Server is installed. If this occurs, do not restart the Presentation Server until you follow these instructions:

▼ To add the registry keys after uninstalling the Novell Client on Presentation Server, you need to reapply the proper settings to the registry after removing the Novell Client. The following registry key contains the GINA values:

```
HKEY_LOCAL_MACHINE\Software\Microsoft\Windows NT\CurrentVersion\Winlogon
```

The registry values for the default Presentation Server logon screen (without the Novell Client) are

```
GinaDLL Data: Ctxgina.dll
CtxGinaDLL Data: Msgina.dll
```

- If you designate an NDS preferred tree, but none of the servers have been set to MetaFrame XP Feature Release 1 or later, Presentation Server prompts your users for NDS credentials, but it does not accept them.

  Workaround: Set the feature release level to Feature Release 1 or later on at least one sever in the farm, remove the NDS tree name in the NDS Preferred Tree field Farm Properties | MetaFrame Settings, and then reset the Feature Release level to None.

- The session-sharing feature is not supported for ICA Win32 Client custom ICA connections that are configured for NDS user credentials.

  Workaround: To use session sharing for custom ICA connections in Program Neighborhood, do not specify user credentials on the Login Information tab in the Properties dialog box.

- ▲ If connecting by dial-up ICA to a MetaFrame XP Feature Release 2 server that has the Novell Client installed, the server returns the Microsoft logon dialog box, instead of the Novell logon dialog box. This occurs because the Use Default NT Authentication option (under Advanced Connection Settings in Citrix Connection Configuration) is selected by default on Windows 2000 servers.

  Workaround: If you want to use Novell authentication on a server under these circumstances, deselect the Use Default NT Authentication option in Citrix Connection Configuration, Advanced Connection Settings. If a Windows 2000 server without Service Pack 2 is set up to use the default Windows NT authentication and a third-party authentication software, such as the Novell Client is installed, the third-party logon dialog box appears instead of the default Windows logon dialog box. Installing Service Pack 2 for Windows 2000 resolves the problem.

IMPORTANT   When using the Management Console to remove a server from a farm that has NDS enabled, connect the Management Console to a server that has Feature Release 2 or later installed.

NOTE   The Novell Client does not set the APPDATA environment variables.

COLLECTING CITRIX TECHNICAL SUPPORT INFORMATION

This section discusses methods for collecting information that Citrix Technical Support can use for debugging purposes. Before contacting Citrix Technical Support, try the solutions in the previous section "Troubleshooting IMA."

Obtaining Installation/Uninstallation Logs

If the Presentation Server installation fails to complete, Citrix Technical Support requires an installation log file to troubleshoot the problem. Because the Presentation Server installation is a Windows Installer package (.msi file), the Windows Installer must be invoked with the /l command line option to create an installation log file. Citrix recommends that if the installation fails, a second installation be attempted, using the following command line to create a log file:

Msiexec /i <*CD*>\MF\MPS.msi /l*v %SystemDrive%\msi.log

Replace *<CD>* with the CD drive letter (for example, D:) containing the installation CD. If the installation CD was copied to a hard drive or network share, *<CD>* could also be replaced with the full path to the installation CD image. This command line creates a log file named msi.log in the root of the system drive.

Please refer to the following URL for additional information about the Windows Installer:

http://www.microsoft.com/windows2000/docs/wininstaller.doc

Capturing Presentation Server Console Debug Output

To capture debug output from the Presentation Server Console, the Presentation Server Console must be launched with the –debugFile command line option. The recommendation is that a shortcut be created using the following process:

1. Right-click on the desktop and select New | Shortcut from the Context menu.

2. The Create Shortcut Wizard starts. In the "Type the location of the item" field, enter: %SystemRoot%\system32\java.exe. When prompted to "Type a name for this shortcut:", enter descriptive text, such as MC Debugging. The shortcut is then created.

3. Right-click the new shortcut and select Properties from the Context menu.

4. In the Shortcut tab, enter the following text in the Target field (the following text is word wrapped, but it must be entered as one line):

   java.exe -Djava.ext.dirs="ext;%ProgramFiles%\Java\jre1.4.1\lib\ext" -jar Tool .jar -debugFile:output.log

5. Change the Start in field to: %ProgramFiles%\Citrix\Administration.

6. Click the Change Icon button and enter: %ProgramFiles%\Citrix\Administration\ctxload.exe.

7. In the Layout tab, configure the Screen buffer size properties to 9999 lines.

8. Click OK to save the shortcut.

When the shortcut is launched, two windows are displayed. The first is a command window containing the debug messages output by java.exe. The second is the Presentation Server Console user interface. If the Presentation Server Console hangs or otherwise fails, press CTRL+ BREAK in the command window to view the stack trace.

NOTE   This may fail if another Java application is installed that loads the Java Access Bridge screen reader. If this software is installed, you may need to modify the path before launching the Presentation Server Console in this manner. Before launching the Java command, strip the path down to only the essentials, similar to the following:
\path=c:\winnt\system32; c:\winnt\java -Djava.ext.dirs=Ext -jar tool.jar

Obtaining System Information

Citrix Technical Support may also request information about the state of the system when troubleshooting an issue. The easiest way to obtain such information is to execute winmsd, which launches the System Information tool on Windows 2000. From the MMC Action menu, select "Save as System Information File." The file may then be sent to Citrix Technical support, if necessary.

ODBC Tracing

Additional ODBC tracing information might be requested by Citrix Technical Support or the database vendor support team. The procedure to enable ODBC tracing depends on the database server software being used.

▼ To activate Microsoft SQL Server ODBC tracing:

1.   Launch the ODBC Data Source Administrator.

2.   Select the Tracing tab.

3.   Enter a path for the log file in the Log File Path box.

4.   Click Start Tracing Now to begin tracing. Click Stop Tracing Now to end tracing.

■ To activate Oracle ODBC Tracing:

1.   Launch the Net8 Assistant.

2.   Select Configuration | Local | Profile.

3.   Select General from the drop-down box on the right pane.

4.   Use the Tracing and Logging tabs to configure ODBC tracing, as needed.

▲ To activate IBM DB2 ODBC Tracing:

1.   Launch the DB2 Client Configuration Assistant.

2.   Select Client Settings… | Diagnostics.

3.   Set the "Diagnostic error capture level" to 4 (all errors, warnings, and information messages).

Installation Manager Debug Files

Obtain the relevant Installation Manager files before calling Citrix Technical Support for Installation Manager troubleshooting questions:

▼   wfs (the package script)

■   ael (the recorder log file)

■   aep (the packager project file)

▲   log (the windows installer log file)

TROUBLESHOOTING FREQUENTLY ENCOUNTERED OBSTACLES

The following is a list of frequently encountered obstacles that are a result of misconfiguration or misconception.

Program Neighborhood Agent Cannot Connect Through Secure Gateway for Citrix Presentation Server

If a client receives the message "Cannot connect to the Citrix server: Protocol driver error" popup message when attempting to connect to Secure Gateway for MetaFrame from Program Neighborhood Agent, the cause is most likely that the client machine does not have the proper encryption level installed. The client needs to have 128-bit encryption installed.

Cannot Launch Secure Web Interface for Citrix Presentation Server Application Through Internet Explorer

If you have users connecting through a secure web Interface site (HTTPS), and they receive an error message of "ICA file not found," ensure the security settings within Internet Explorer are not set to "Do not save encrypted pages to disk." To check security settings in Internet Explorer:

▼   Open Internet Explorer.

■   Click on Tools | Internet Options.

■   Click the Advanced tab.

■   Scroll all the way down to Security.

■   Ensure there is no check in the box next to Do not save encrypted pages to disk.

▲   Click OK to close this process.

Folders Do Not Appear in Program Neighborhood

Folders that you create to organize applications in the Presentation Server Console are not related to application folders that appear in Program Neighborhood. To specify application folders for Program Neighborhood, use the Program Neighborhood Settings tab in the Properties dialog box for the published application.

1. Right-click the published application in the Presentation Server Console, and then choose Properties.

2. On the Program Neighborhood Settings tab, type the folder name in the Program Neighborhood Folder box.

Importing Network Printers from Other Domains

Printers cannot be imported from a Network Print Server when:

▼   The print server resides in a workgroup

▲   The printer is in a different domain from any servers in the server farm

To enable the printer to be imported:

1. Do one of the following:

    ▼   Add the Network Print Server to the same domain as the Presentation Servers.

    ▲   Add one of the Presentation Servers to the same domain as the Network Print Server.

2. Assign the printers to the Everyone group instead of to groups or users. Authenticate without credentials to receive the list of printers assigned to everyone.

3. To let Novell users access Microsoft Print Servers, you must enable the Guest account and assign Everyone or Guest access.

USB Redirection Does Not Work

MetaFrame Presentation Server XP 1.0 with Feature Release 3 and later supports USB printers installed on the server.

▼   Win32 ICA Clients support installed USB printers when the client platform is Windows 98, Windows 2000, or Windows Me.

■   Other USB devices, including scanners and cameras, are not currently supported by MetaFrame Presentation Server 3.0 and older. Presentation Server 4.0 now offers support for Activesync via USB devices and support for TWAIN-compliant scanners through the newly added feature of TWAIN redirection.

▲   For more information about USB support, refer to Citrix knowledgebase article CTX816193, "USB Support in MetaFrame Products."

Content Redirection Issues

If you install and then publish applications after installing MetaFrame XP Feature Release 3 or later, you must update the file type associations in each server's registry. To update file type associations in a server farm:

1. Open the Presentation Server Console.

2. Expand the Servers node in the left window pane.

3. Right-click a server and select "Update File Types from Registry."

Once the file type updates have taken place, go back to the properties of the published application. The content redirection options should no longer be disabled.

Windows Server 2003 Issues, Recommendations, and Workarounds

This section illustrates the most common issues, recommendations, and workarounds for Forest Trusts and multidomain environments.

Forest Trusts

With Windows Server 2003 Active Directory forests, you can create a two-way forest trust that allows a transitive trust between all child domains in the trusted forests. Citrix Presentation Server does not support the use of this type of trust between child domains. If you require a trust between two child domains in separate forests, then creating an explicit trust between domains is necessary.

Another workaround for trusts is to place all Citrix Presentation Servers in the same domain. Create a Local Group in this domain. Populate this Domain Local Group with Global Groups from other domains.

User Access to Terminal Servers

By default on Windows Server 2003, members of the Administrators and Remote Desktop Users groups can connect via Terminal Services. The Remote Desktop Users group contains no users when it is initially created. You must manually add any users or groups that require Terminal Services access. If the users are not already members of the computer's local group, it is also necessary to add them. Unlike Windows 2000 Server policies, the Computer Local Policy under User Rights, "Allow log on locally" no longer provides access to Terminal Service connections. For additional information, please refer to Windows Server 2003 online documentation.

TROUBLESHOOTING TIPS, ERROR MESSAGES, AND CONDITIONS

This section will help troubleshoot issues with Presentation Server Console launch failures, PDA synchronization, the Citrix XTE service, and disconnected sessions.

Presentation Server Console Fails to Launch

If the Sun JRE 1_5_0_02 is installed prior to installing the Presentation Server 4.0 Console, logins to the console may fail. When JRE 1.5 is already present, the JRE 1.4.2_06 installer doesn't add a registry key that is needed by the console. This is resolved by manually adding one key and one value to the registry:

1. Create the following registry key:

    HKEY_LOCAL_MACHINE\Software\JavaSoft\Java Runtime Environment\1.4

2. Create a string value "JavaHome."

3. Locate the following key in the registry:

    HKEY_LOCAL_MACHINE\Software\JavaSoft\Java Runtime
    Environment\1.4.2_06

4. Copy the data from the "JavaHome" value in that key to the "JavaHome" value in the key you created.

PDA Synchronization Potential Issues and Workarounds

The following is a list of issues encountered during the testing of the PDA synchronization feature.

▼ **PDA synchronization does not work as expected when Presentation Server is set to Advanced edition.** To enable support for PDA synchronization in the Advanced edition, apply hotfix PSE400W2K3002 for Windows 2003 or PSE400W2K002 for Windows 2000.

■ **PDA synchronization/ActiveSync does not function properly within a Conferencing Manager session.** This is as designed.

■ **Launching a published instance of ActiveSync opens, but then closes before you can insert the PDA into the USB cradle.** Check the command line for the published application. To properly make ActiveSync available as a published application, it is important to specify WCESMGR.EXE as the application to be launched, not WCESCOMM.EXE. WCESCOMM.EXE is the system tray process. While both executables can start each other once a PDA is detected, if WCESCOMM.EXE is the only application in a session and no PDA is present at ICA session startup, the ICA session may log off before a user can insert a PDA. This is as designed.

■ **Nonseamless ICA sessions to ActiveSync as a published application do not log off completely.** When running ActiveSync as a nonseamless published application, you do not see the ActiveSync connection icon in the system tray. If you close the main ActiveSync window, you are unable to completely log off the ICA session until the PDA is removed. Because the PDA remains in the USB cradle, the WCESCOMM.EXE process is still active and, although you may not see the system tray icon, you cannot close the session until this process is closed.

■ **Using the default ActiveSync driver that ships with Windows XP can cause issues.** For example, the PDA may not disconnect when the ICA session closes. The next ICA session attempting to connect to the PDA will be unable to do so unless the PDA is removed and replaced in the USB cradle. For optimal performance, install the most recent version of ActiveSync. The latest version of ActiveSync can be downloaded from Microsoft's web site.

■ **Application isolation environments and PDA synchronization.** ActiveSync does not require an application isolation environment for Terminal Services compatibility. Because ActiveSync installs a service and isolation environments do not isolate services, if ActiveSync is installed into an isolation environment, it will fail. Isolation environments can be configured on a Presentation Server to isolate other applications without impact on ActiveSync.

▲ **Allowing COM port connections within ActiveSync.** If you modify the connection settings within ActiveSync to allow COM port connections, and then disconnect and reconnect the PDA in rapid succession, the PDA connects, but you cannot start WCESMGR.EXE until the currently running WCESMGR.EXE is killed or a one-minute timeout occurs. This is a third-party issue with Active-Sync and can occur on a console outside of an ICA session as well. The easiest way to avoid this issue is to disable COM port connections through ActiveSync. If you manually disable COM port connections in the GUI, you must log off and log back on to resolve the issue. To disable COM port connections for all users, modify the following registry key:

```
Key: HKLM\Software\Microsoft\Windows CE Services
Value: REG_DWORD:ConnectTypesAllowed

Settings:
Allow serial cable or infrared connection to a COM port:
0x00000002

Allow network (Ethernet) and Remote Access Service (RAS) server
connection with the desktop computer:
0x00000004

Allow USB connection with the desktop computer:
0x00000008
```

The per-user key gets created the first time AS is used by the respective user, at which point all key values are populated using the defaults in HKLM.

NOTE   Users can reenable ActiveSync COM port connections by modifying the options in Connection Settings.

Citrix XTE Service MaxThreads and Session Reliability

When *Session Reliability* is enabled for client connections, the number of connections is limited to 150 users on a server powerful enough to accept more. This is due to the ThreadsPerChild value of 150 in the httpd.conf configuration file located in the `%Program Files%\Citrix\XTE\conf` folder. The value is persistent, but it can be changed by editing the Registry. In `HKLM\Software\Citrix\XTEConfig`, add a DWord Value called MaxThreads. Modify the value of `MaxThreads` to be a decimal value equal to or greater than the number of users you expect to get on the machine.

After the value is set, stop and restart the IMA service or reboot the machine, so your changes take effect.

Troubleshooting Disconnected Sessions

With MetaFrame XP Server for Windows—with Feature Release 3 and later—there is the capability to log TD Errors to a log file. This can track any kind of Winsock errors the client receives. This is useful in troubleshooting why sessions may be getting disconnected. To enable the logging, the following parameters must be added when launching the ICA connection via wfcrun32. The command is

```
Wfcrun32 /c:0x00000040 /e:0x00100000 /logfile:<log file path> <connection name>
```

The 0x00000040 tells to log in Transport Driver. The 0x00100000 tells to log any Auto Client Reconnect related information.

If an error is encountered, it is contained within the log file along with an error code. The error code may be a Winsock error code. Check MSDN site for the code: http://msdn.microsoft.com/library/default.asp?url=/library/en-us/winsock/winsock/windows_sockets_error_codes_2.asp.

CHAPTER 18

Troubleshooting the Other Access Suite Products

This chapter presents an overview of Citrix policies, tips for using GoToMeeting, and Troubleshooting Access Gateway with Advanced Access Control. Additionally, we review troubleshooting and issue resolution scenarios for Password Manager.

CITRIX POLICIES OVERVIEW

The following section provides information regarding the Citrix policies available in the Presentation Server Console. While the policies are configured in the Presentation Server Console, the MetaFrame Component Object Model Software Development Kit (MFCOM SDK) can also be used to facilitate the process. Utilizing the MFCOM SDK is beyond the scope of this chapter. For information about using the MFCOM SDK, see the Citrix Developer Network: http://apps.citrix.com/cdn/Default.asp.

Citrix policies are not the same as the Microsoft policies. They are applied on a per-ICA session, not tied to a specific user account, and can be prioritized to customize which configured policies take precedence when applying configured settings.

Presentation Server 4.0 contains 44 specific Citrix policy rules that govern the user experience in the following areas:

▼ Bandwidth

■ Client Devices

■ Printing

■ User Workspace

▲ Security

To determine the scenario under which a policy is applied, you can choose a filter from the following options:

▼ **Access Control**   The policy is applied based on connections made through MetaFrame Secure Access Manager or Access Gateway

■ **Client IP Address**   The policy is applied based on the actual client IP address or range of addresses

■ **Client Name**   A policy can be applied to the name of a client device

■ **Servers**   A policy can be applied to a specified Presentation Server

▲ **Users**   A policy can be applied to specified local server accounts, Windows NT Domain accounts, Active Directory accounts, and Novell NDS trees

NOTE   The name of the client device is a string value that can be manually configured on the client host. As the client device name can be set to an arbitrary value by the client, it may not always be appropriate to base-policy filtering decisions on this value. In cases where the client should not be permitted to influence the policy filtering, then it may not be appropriate to make use of the client device name. See CTX107705 for more information.

Architecture Details

The Policy subsystem receives requests from the IMA Policy Subsystem SAL and returns responses. The Policy subsystem SAL makes calls to the LHC, which, in turn, makes calls to the DataStore. When an ICA connection is established and a Citrix policy is applied to the session, policy information is stored in the registry under HKLM\Software\Citrix\ Policies\LogonID. This information is deleted at session logoff.

Citrix policies are IMA-related and information regarding Citrix policies is also stored in the farm's DataStore. Figure 18-1 outlines the Citrix policies architecture.

Hierarchy

Citrix policies override settings contained in Citrix Connection Configuration, MFCFG .exe, or TSCC.msc. They also override Microsoft policies, those related to typical RDP client connection settings, such as:

▼ Desktop wallpaper

■ Menu animations

▲ Windows contents while dragging

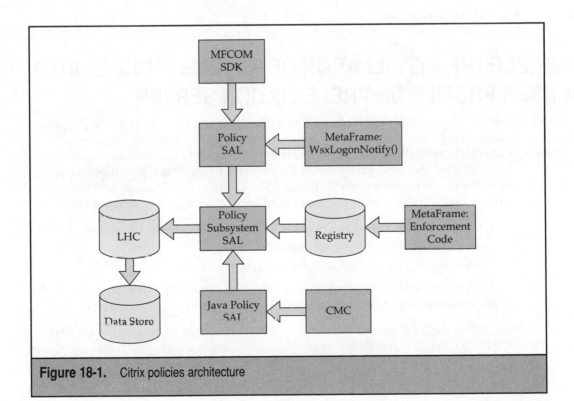

Figure 18-1.   Citrix policies architecture

Scalability

Scalability may be impacted by an increase in logon time. The increase is proportional to the number of policies and the complexity of the policies used (that is, the number of filters, number of rules, and so forth). When policies are not used, there should be no impact to logon time. If logon time performance is a concern for your environment, perform tests to determine an acceptable level of performance for your environment and adjust the Citrix policies accordingly.

Troubleshooting Policies

If policies are not being applied or working properly, tracing can be performed to troubleshoot all Citrix policies. Using CDF tracing, specify the following modules:

▼ IMA_Library_ImaRpc

■ IMA_Sals_ImaRpcClient

■ IMA_Subsystems_Policy

■ IMA_Subsystems_PolicyApi

■ MF_DLL_Wsxica (This is the WsxLogonNotify MetaFrame function in wsxica.dll)

▲ MF_Session_Wfshell

DISABLE THE INSTALLATION OF GOTOMEETING 2.0 INTO A USER PROFILE ON PRESENTATION SERVER

GoToMeeting 2.0 provides for integration with Presentation Server for 32-bit Windows. Using the GoToMeeting Installation Wizard to install GoToMeeting on Presentation Server allows Presentation Server Administrators to install GoToMeeting on the server. GoToMeeting also redirects all meetings to the local client desktop, while still allowing integration with published applications, such as Microsoft Outlook and IBM Lotus Notes. Running GoToMeeting on the client device provides the following benefits:

1. Allows a GoToMeeting Organizer or Attendee to present both published applications and locally installed applications

2. Avoids any impact to the Presentation Server resources

3. Allows Presentation Server Administrators the capability to configure the GoToMeeting installment to best suit the specific server/client environment.

For additional information see the Citrix Support knowledgebase article "CTX107190—Citrix Presentation Server Administrator's Guide for Installing Citrix GoToMeeting 2.0" and the GoToMeeting online help articles "Set Up GoToMeeting for

Use with Citrix Presentation Server" and "GoToMeeting for Citrix Presentation Server FAQs," located at https://www.gotomeeting.com.

To prevent users from being able to install GoToMeeting into their profile during a session on either a 32-bit or 64-bit Presentation Server, a registry key can be created:

```
HKLM\Software\Citrix
Under this key add DWORD: AdminBlockGoToMeeting
Set the value to 1.
```

This blocks users from installing GoToMeeting into their local profile on the Presentation Server. This is especially important on Presentation Server for 64-bit Windows as GoToMeeting is not currently supported on a 64-bit Presentation Server platform.

When the previous key is added to the server's registry, if a user attempts to run either the ActiveX or a downloaded installation of GoToMeeting, they receive an error message and, instead, the local client machine's browser is redirected to https://www.gotomeeting.com/.

TROUBLESHOOTING ACCESS GATEWAY WITH ADVANCED ACCESS CONTROL

The following provides troubleshooting information for Access Gateway with Advanced Access Control. Topics covered are how to enable verbose scan results for the Citrix Advanced Access Control 4.2 End Point Analysis scans and Registering .NET Framework if Internet Information Server (IIS) is not installed first.

REGISTERING .NET FRAMEWORK IF IIS IS NOT INSTALLED FIRST

If you have a problem accessing the Authentication Service test page, it may be because the .asmx, .aspx, or .config extensions are not correctly registered in IIS. This may happen if the .NET Framework was installed before IIS. You can either uninstall and reinstall the .NET Framework, or register the appropriate extensions in IIS, by doing the following:

1. Open the IIS Manager (Windows 2003) or Internet Service Manager (Windows 2000).
2. Right-click the AuthService virtual directory (located underneath the access center virtual directory) and select properties.
3. On the Virtual Directory tab, select the Configuration button.
4. Under Application Mappings, select Add.

5. For the executable, enter the location of the .NET Framework aspnet_isapi.dll. This is generally located under WINNT\Microsoft.NET\FrameWork\v1.1.*xxx.*

6. For the extension, enter .asmx.

7. Limit verbs to GET,HEAD,POST,DEBUG.

8. Check the box for the script engine.

9. Repeat, adding the same entry for the .aspx and .config extensions.

NOTE   Lack of proper registration may cause problems with other file extensions.

VERBOSE SCAN RESULTS FOR CITRIX ADVANCED ACCESS CONTROL 4.2

When using Citrix Advanced Access Control 4.2 in an environment with multiple End Point Analysis scans applied to a logon point, troubleshooting client access issues may be confusing for administrators. Using this diagnostic procedure can be helpful in identifying denied client criteria as configured in the admin console.

To use this troubleshooting capability, find the following file on the Advanced Access Control server:

Path:

```
C:\inetpub\wwwroot\citrixlogonpoint\samplelogonpoint (or appropriate logon point
directory)
```

File:

```
disallowed.ascx
```

Open this file with a text editor. Toward the bottom of the file, you see the following section, commented out with apostrophes. Uncomment this section and save the file.

```
if(hash.Count > count)
        scanFailure2.InnerHtml = "<table border=2><tr><th>" & Citrix.LogonAgent
.Util.Localization.ResourceManager.GetString( "EPARULE" )
        scanFailure2.InnerHtml = scanFailure2.InnerHtml & "</th><th>" &
Citrix.LogonAgent.Util.Localization.ResourceManager.GetString( "EPAVALUE" )
        scanFailure2.InnerHtml = scanFailure2.InnerHtml & "</th></tr>"
        Dim keys(hash.Count) as String
        hash.keys.CopyTo(keys, 0)
        Dim n as Integer
```

```
            n = 0
            Do
                if(keys(n) <> "EPAReferenceID")
                ' This adds one line of text for each EPA output variable giving its
                ' name and value; but other HTML could be added as desired
                ' such as making it a table
                Dim line as String
                line = "<tr><td>"&keys(n)&"</td><td>"& hash.item(keys(n))&"</td></tr>"
                scanFailure2.InnerHtml = scanFailure2.InnerHtml + line
            end if
            n = n+1
            Loop Until n = hash.Count
              scanFailure2.InnerHtml = scanFailure2.InnerHtml + "</table>"
            else
                  scanFailure2.InnerText =
Citrix.LogonAgent.UserInterface.DisallowedPage.GetEmptyResultString()
            end if '(hash.Count > count)
              end if
```

Doing so enables verbose results, which do not pass all End Point Analysis scans as configured in the console, to be displayed to clients attempting to connect to the logon point. Table 18-1 shows an example of the output shown to the client:

NOTE   Once the administrator has finished troubleshooting, it is highly suggested that the previous mentioned section of code in disallowed.ascx be commented out.

Rule	Output Value
Citrix Scans for Internet Explorer. IE Scan. Verified-Internet-Explorer-Installed.	true
Citrix Scans for Windows Service Pack. Windows Service Pack Scan. Verified-Windows-Service-Pack.	true
Citrix Scans for Domain Membership. Domain Scan. Verified-domain.	false
Citrix Scans for Internet Explorer. IE Scan. Verified-Internet-Explorer-Connecting.	true

Table 18-1.   Verbose Scan Results for Citrix Advanced Access Control 4.2

TROUBLESHOOTING THE CITRIX PASSWORD MANAGER SERVICE

The best troubleshooting resources for Citrix Password Manager Service are the error messages encountered in the console, agent, and XTE Service Error logs. The most-common error messages have been typed in this chapter to allow for quick location and resolution. This section is organized into seven parts to provide easy access to the most common errors encountered.

A. **Password Manager Service Frequently Asked Questions**

   a. What is the XTE Service?

   b. Are the signing and validation certificates related to the SSL certificate?

   c. Do I have to use CtxCreateSigningCert?

   d. How do I enable Data Integrity on an environment that already has been established as a "non-Data Integrity" deployment?

B. **Issues and Errors Encountered on the Service Machine**

   a. Service Configuration tool does not start

   b. Service Configuration tool does not complete its configuration

   c. Shutting down/restarting the Citrix XTE Service

   d. Using the Data Signing tool

C. **Issues and Errors Encountered on the Console Machine**

   a. Configure and run discovery (Data Integrity)

   b. Console error messages—Data Integrity

   c. Console error messages—Provisioning

D. **Issues and Errors Encountered on the Agent Machine**

   a. Data Integrity-related errors

   b. Automatic Key Recovery authentication failed, module could not be contacted

   c. Automatic Key Recovery post-password change

   d. Self-Service Password Reset registration failed

   e. Provisioning: Failure to consume queued commands

E. **Troubleshooting the Connection**

   a. Testing the connection

   b. Repairing the connection

  F. **Data Integrity—Recovering from Data Corruption**

  G. **XTE Service Error Log**

    a. SSL certificate/machine name mismatch

    b. SSL handshake failure

    c. User not authorized to access the page

    d. Require user/group line is invalid

    e. File not found or unable to stat

    f. Attempt to serve directory

Password Manager Service Frequently Asked Questions

What is the XTE Service? Is it the same as the Access Suite's XTE Service?

XTE stands for eXtensible Transformation Engine. *XTE* is a common infrastructure component used in multiple Citrix products. The XTE Service hosts the Password Manager web services.

This service is the same XTE Service that Citrix Access Suite uses, however, it uses added modules with a different configuration. The added modules and configurations prevent the Password Manager Service from being installed on a machine with other Citrix applications that use the XTE Service. In addition, the security model recommends the Password Manager Service server be placed in a physically secure location with limited access.

Are the signing/validation certificates related to the SSL certificate?

No, the SSL certificate (supplied from your certificate authority) is a totally separate entity from the signing/validation certificates created by the Password Manager Service.

What is the purpose of the SSL certificate?

An *SSL certificate* is necessary to ensure encrypted communication from the Service to the agents and console, and to guarantee that the agent and console are talking to the correct Service machine. The SSL certificate name must exactly match the fully qualified name of the Password Manager Service machine to verify that the Password Manager Service machine is, indeed, the correct machine.

What is the purpose of the signing/validation certificates?

The signing and validation certificates are created by the Password Manager Service and have no relation to the SSL certificate. They are used by the Data Integrity Service to authenticate the information stored in the central store. Automatic Key Recovery and Self-Service Password Request also use the signing certificate to verify the user identity token. The signing certificate absolutely does not encrypt any data. It takes the data from the console and generates a cryptographic signature, which is appended to the data. If the data is changed without using the signing service to append a new signature, the agent displays a validation error when attempting to use the data and discards the data.

Do I have to use CtxCreateSigningCert to create the signing/validation certificates?

In most cases, no. After a successful configuration of the Password Manager Service using the Service Configuration tool, the signing and validation certificates are created automatically. The only case where you would create a new signing/validation certificate pair is when you want to sign the data using a new certificate pair. You would need a new certificate pair if the certificate expires or is compromised.

How do I enable Data Integrity on an environment that already has been established as a "non-Data Integrity" deployment?

Follow these steps:

1. Sign the data with the Signing tool from the Password Manager Service machine. More information on using the Signing tool can be found in the *Password Manager Administrator's Guide*.

2. Configure and run discovery on the console. The console should automatically recognize that the data on the central store is signed and prompts the user to enter the Password Manager Service URI.

3. Modify the installation of the agent to enable Data Integrity by selecting the Data Integrity feature and entering the URI of the Password Manager Service machine.

Service-side Issues and Resolutions

The following section can be used to help troubleshoot service-related issues.

Service Configuration Tool Will Not Start

Here are the two most common reasons why the Service Configuration tool does not start:

▼ **The Service cannot find a valid SSL Web Server Certificate installed on the Password Manager Service machine.**

An SSL web server certificate from your certificate authority (CA) is required. Also, the root CA must be trusted on every machine that contacts the Service: the agent, console, and Service.

▲ **The user running the Service Configuration tool must be a member of the Domain and a member of the local machine administrators group.**

Service Configuration Tool Does Not Complete Its Configuration

Depending on where it stops, the Applying [Configuration] Settings status dialog window can give clues as to what function of the Service Configuration failed.

A. **Failure to configure the Data Proxy account:**

   Error: The account credentials provided for the application are invalid.

   Issue: This usually occurs because the user credentials configured to run the Data Proxy were entered incorrectly. Go back to the "Configure data proxy" page of the Service Configuration tool, and reenter the credentials.

B. **Failure to configure the Self-Service Password Reset account:**

   Error: The account credentials provided for the application are invalid.

   Issue: This usually occurs because the user credentials configured to run the Self-Service Password Reset account were entered incorrectly. Go back to the "Provide password reset credentials" page of the Service Configuration tool and reenter the credentials.

C. **Failure to start the XTE Service:**
   Several issues can cause this failure:

   a. **The SSL Certificate name does not exactly match the fully qualified domain name (FQDN) of the Password Manager Service machine.**

      Error: The server process could not be started. Make sure the port is not in use. Refer to the Windows event log and Citrix XTE Server error log for more information.

      Issue: The only way to verify this is the problem is to look at the Citrix XTE Service error logs. Refer to the "XTE Service Error Log" section for more details on a resolution to an SSL server certificate/machine name mismatch.

   b. **The Port is in use by another service (that is, IIS Admin Service).**

      Error: The server process could not be started. Make sure the port is not in use. Refer to the Windows event log and Citrix XTE Server error log for more information.

      Issue: If you are unsure which program is occupying the Password Manager Service default port 443, run port monitoring software to determine what is running on the port. The typical culprit is IIS. Uninstall the IIS Service (or other web service running on 443), or choose to run the Password Manager Service on a different port.

   c. **Credentials are incorrect.**

      Error: The server process could not be started because the account name is invalid or does not exist, or the password is invalid for the account name specified.

      Issue: Go back to the "Configure service" page of the Service Configuration tool and reenter the account credentials for the Citrix XTE Service.

Shutting Down, Restarting the Citrix XTE Service

Refer to the "Resolution 1.3: Restart the XTE Service and COM+ Objects" section for steps to shut down and start the Citrix XTE Service.

Using the Data Signing Tool

The *Data Signing tool* is a command line utility located on the Password Manager Service machine at C:\Program Files\Citrix\MetaFrame Password Manager\Service\ SigningTool\. The Data Signing tool (CtxSignData.exe) should be used in the following situations:

▼ Enable/Disable Data Integrity in an existing deployment of Password Manager.

■ Verify all the signatures on a central store that has Data Integrity enabled.

▲ Resign all the data on the central store with a newly created signing certificate after data corruption or after signing/validation certificate expiration.

Details and examples on using the data signing tool are located in the *Password Manager Administrator's Guide*.

Console-side Issues and Resolutions

This section deals with console-related issues and troubleshooting.

Impact of Data Integrity on Configure and Run Discovery

When running "Configure and run discovery" on the console with a central store that has never been configured, the administrator is provided a choice to enable Data Integrity. When "Configure and run discovery" is activated on a central store that has previously been configured—either with Data Integrity on or off—the administrator is not allowed to change the Data Integrity setting from the console. Please see the *Password Manager Administrator's Guide* for more on disabling or enabling Data Integrity in an existing deployment.

When running "Configure and run discovery," if Data Integrity is enabled, the user must fill in the Service URI and port number for the Citrix Password Manager Service machine. The following issues may be encountered:

▼ The Service URI is typed incorrectly or the console is unable to contact the Service

■ The Service port is typed incorrectly

■ SSL certificate trust failed

▲ An unexpected error occurred

Each of the specific errors is explained here:

▼ **Service URI Error: The underlying connection was closed: The remote host-name could not be resolved.**

The Service URI is typed incorrectly or the console is unable to contact the Password Manager Service machine.

■ **Service Port Error: The remote service point could not be contacted at the transport level.**

The Password Manager Service port is typed incorrectly or the Citrix XTE Service is not running on the Password Manager Service machine.

■ **SSL Trust Error: SSL server certificate could not be validated.**

The SSL server certificate is not trusted and a connection will not be made.

The XTE Service error log also prints the following if the SSL handshake failed (that is, when the SSL certificate is not trusted): "SSL handshake from client failed." Please see the "XTE Service Error Log" section for more details on how to avoid this error.

■ **An exception of unknown type has occurred during connection to the service host. Service may have encountered internal error or misconfiguration.**

Issue: This error typically appears when an unauthorized user is trying to configure and run discovery on a central store that has Data Integrity enabled. Not only will the console user require read/write access to the central store, but in the case of Data Integrity, the console user also needs access to the PrivateKeyCert .cert file on the Password Manager Service machine. If not activating Configure and run discovery as a Domain Administrator, special access must be granted to the user or group of users that use the signing (PrivateKeyCert.cert) certificate on the Password Manager Service machine.

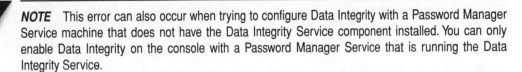

NOTE   This error can also occur when trying to configure Data Integrity with a Password Manager Service machine that does not have the Data Integrity Service component installed. You can only enable Data Integrity on the console with a Password Manager Service that is running the Data Integrity Service.

Resolution: Read the Citrix XTE Service error log in C:\Program Files\ Common Files\Citrix\XTE\logs\ to verify that the issue is a "user not authorized" error. Proceed to the "XTE Service Error Log" section for more information to resolve this issue.

■ **Console error messages—Data Integrity**

Error: One or more <CentralStoreRoot objects> could not be read from the central store. Your Windows Event Log contains additional error information.

Issue: Check which object has been corrupted using the Event viewer. Refer to the *MetaFrame Password Manager Administrator's Guide* and the "Data Integrity— Recovering from Data Corruption" section for more information.

■ **Console error messages—Provisioning**

Error: Provisioning is disabled. Enable provisioning and provide the address to the Citrix Password Manager Service.

Issue: This error is received after selecting a user configuration and attempting to run either "Generate provisioning template" or "Run Provisioning" tasks from the console. This is because the selected user configuration does not have the provisioning module enabled or configured.

Resolution: To resolve this issue, edit the user configuration and, on the provisioning module, enable the feature by checking the "Use Provisioning" option, and then enter the service URL and port.

Error: Batch, Failure, "The name resolver service could not resolve the host name."

Issue: This error is received when running the "Run Provision" task from the console. This is because the service URL specified in the selected user configuration is unable to be resolved.

Resolution: To resolve this issue, edit the user configuration and, on the provisioning module, use the validate button to verify the service URL and port. Refer to the "Troubleshooting the Connection" section for more information on how to resolve this issue.

Error: "Data Integrity Status Mismatch"

Issue: This error is received when running the "Run Provision" task from the console. If Data Integrity is enabled or disabled, it must have the same on/off setting throughout the CPM environment

Resolution: Verify Data Integrity is consistently enabled or disabled in the following places.

■ **The central store**   The data must be signed or unsigned

■ **The Service Configuration tool**   Data Integrity must be on or off

▲ **The agent**   Data Integrity must be on or off

Agent-side Issues and Resolutions

This section addresses the most common Agent-related issues for Password Manager.

Data Integrity Errors

The agent's most common Data Integrity error, "Data integrity failed...," occurs on agent startup. When using the agent, if a Data Integrity failure occurs, the agent is unable to grab any settings applied with the console. On First Time Use of the agent, you will be unable to get a license. When you receive this error, verify the following:

▼   The root CA is trusted on the certificate *physical store* of the agent machine.

■   The Password Manager Service URI and port have been typed correctly on the agent installation. The registry key that holds this information is HKLM\ Software\Citrix\Metaframe Password Manager\Extensions\Server\BaseURL.

▲   Connect via Internet Explorer (IE) to the Password Manager Service machine from the agent machine. Refer to the "Troubleshooting the Connection" section for details on contacting the Password Manager Service via IE.

All the necessary checks can be performed by following the instructions in the "Troubleshooting the Connection" section.

Automatic Key Recovery: Authentication Failed or Key Management Module Could Not Be Contacted

The following errors may occur if authentication fails or the key management module cannot be contacted:

Error: Password Manager authentication failed.

Error: The Password Manager Service Key Management Module could not be contacted. Contact your administrator. Password Manager agent will now shut down.

Issue: The most common Automatic Key Recovery error, "Password Manager authentication failed…," occurs on agent startup. When using the agent for the first time, the Automatic Key Recovery Service is called immediately to generate a key used to decrypt credentials in case of a future password change.

Several possible issues can cause these errors:

▼   The Central Store Proxy account does not have adequate permissions. Try making the Central Store Proxy account a Domain Administrator, to verify this is not the case. Also, the Central Store Proxy account must have access to AuthenticatedWS web service—refer to the "XTE Service Error Log" section for more information. Regarding Central Store Proxy account permissions, please see the Advanced Concepts Guide article "Configuring Citrix Password Manager 4.0 Administrative Access without being a Domain Administrator" in Volume 3.

▲   Data Integrity status mismatch: If Data Integrity is enabled or disabled, it must have the same on/off setting throughout the Password Manager environment. If Data Integrity is disabled, this setting must be present in three places:

   ▼   The administrator must verify the central store remains unsigned.

   ■   The Service Configuration tool must have Data Integrity disabled.

   ▲   The agent must have Data Integrity disabled.

The console must also remain consistent and the console administrator is automatically prompted to Configure and run discovery if the central store Data Integrity setting has changed.

Automatic Key Recovery: Post-password Change

The following error may occur after a password change occurs:

Error: The Password Manager Service Key Management Module could not locate your keys. Contact your administrator. Password Manager agent will now shut down.

Issue: Three possible causes for this error exist:

▼ The Central Store Proxy account does not have adequate permissions. Try making the Central Store Proxy account a Domain Administrator, to verify this is not the case. Also, the Central Store Proxy account must have access to AuthenticatedWS web service—refer to the "XTE Service Error Log" section for more information. Regarding Central Store Proxy account permissions, please see the Advanced Concepts Guide article "Configuring Citrix Password Manager 4.0 Administrative Access without being a Domain Administrator" in Volume 3.

■ The AKR.dat Service key (V4) has changed on the Password Manager Service machine. This can occur if the Password Manager Service machine was moved without exporting AKR.dat using the CtxMoveKeyRecoveryData tool. The V4 (AKR.dat) must remain static throughout a deployment when users have configured application credentials. For more information on migrating AKR.dat, see the Advanced Concepts Guide article "Advanced Concepts in Automatic Key Recovery" in Volume 4.

▲ The user's data has not replicated across multiple domain controllers.

First-time Use: Self-service Password Reset Registration Failed

The following errors may occur during first time use of the Self-service Password Reset:

Error: You cannot register for the password reset feature. Please contact your administrator.

Issue: This error can appear both before and after a user encounters any Self-Service Password Reset questions.

The following lists reasons that the error appears both before and after Self-Service Password Reset questions are encountered:

▼ Check that the Password Manager Service URI is correctly configured on the agent machine. The registry key that holds this information is HKLM\Software\Citrix\MetaFrame Password Manager\Extensions\Server\BaseURL. Copy this URI from the key and paste it into IE, and then add the required .asmx filename to the end of it. The .asmx files associated with this error are NTLMAuthSvc .asmx, EnrollmentSvc.asmx, and AuthSvc.asmx, in the order they are called. Refer to the "Troubleshooting the Connection" section for more information on testing the connection to these component service pages.

- If using a central store proxy account that is not a Domain Administrator, check that the account has adequate permissions on the central store. Also, the central store proxy user, when not in the Domain Administrators group, must be added to the "require group" line of the XTE Service httpd.conf file. Refer to the "XTE Service Error Log" section for more information to resolve this issue. Also, to verify this is, indeed, a permissions issue, try configuring the Password Manager Service with a Domain Administrator as the central store proxy account (using the Service Configuration tool).

- Check that the root CA is trusted in the certificates' *physical store* of the agent machine. Refer to the "Troubleshooting the Connection" section for more information on how to resolve this issue.

- ▲ Data Integrity status mismatch: if Data Integrity is enabled or disabled, it must have the same on/off setting throughout the Password Manager environment. If Data Integrity is disabled, this setting must be present in three places:

   - ▼ The administrator must verify that the central store remains unsigned.
   - The Service Configuration tool must have Data Integrity disabled.
   - ▲ The agent must have Data Integrity disabled.

The console must also remain consistent and the console administrator is automatically prompted to Configure and run discovery if the central store Data Integrity setting has changed.

Provisioning: Failure to Consume Queued Commands

The following error may occur during provisioning:

Error: The agent does not consume a provisioning command for a user that has a provisioning command in their queue.

Issue: If the agent fails during the provisioning operation that occurs each time the agent is launched (when provisioning is enabled), the user does not receive an error but, rather, the agent silently fails and continues with normal operations. To determine what is causing the provisioning operation to fail, you should enable the agent's advanced logging capabilities (see the ACG article "Enabling Advanced Logging for the Password Manager 4.1 Agent"). Once the logging has been enabled, restart the agent to reproduce the failure. In the generated agent log, find the following line:

```
ProvisionAgent(), GetProvisioned() returned: X
```

In this example the X at the end of the line refers to the failure status code that can be determined from most commonly found codes in the following list. Once you determine the reason for the failure, refer to the "Troubleshooting the Connection" and "XTE Service Error Log" sections for more information on how to resolve this issue.

1—Not Authorized	7— Success
2—Deprovisioned	8—Completed
3—Refused Auth	9—Nothing To Do
4—Failure	10—Timed Out
5—Auth Failure	

Troubleshooting the Connection

The two most common issues related to Password Manager Service configurations are SSL certificate and DNS issues. In the situation where the console or agent is unable to connect or interact with the Password Manager Service, the following series of steps may help determine whether the issue is related to DNS Configuration, SSL certificates, or both.

Testing the Connection

The following describes how to test the connection for the Password Manager Service:

Check 1: Contact the Password Manager Service Through Internet Explorer   With a failure to connect to the Password Manager Service, the first, and most important, step is to check whether it is accessible through the network. The Password Manager Service is a web service, therefore, each of the web services is accessible through IE. Seven component service pages are associated with the Automatic Key Recovery, Self-Service Password Request, and Data Integrity modules of the Password Manager Service. Listed next to each component service are the services that use it. Any service that fails should be tested by visiting its corresponding component pages.

▼ /MPMService/AuthenticatedWS.asmx
   ▼ Data Integrity, Automatic Key Recovery, Self-Service Password Reset (Only accessible to users in the "require group" line in httpd.conf)
■ /MPMService/AuthSvc.asmx
   ▼ Self-Service Password Request
■ /MPMService/DataIntegritySvc.asmx
   ▼ Data Integrity
■ /MPMService/EnrollmentSvc.asmx
   ▼ Automatic Key Recovery, Self-Service Password Request
■ /MPMService/KeyRecoverySvc.asmx
   ▼ Automatic Key Recovery
■ /MPMService/NTLMAuthSvc.asmx
   ▼ Automatic Key Recovery, Self-Service Password Request
▲ /MPMService/PwdResetSvc.asmx
   ▼ Self-Service Password Request

Each of these individual web services is accessible as a web page through IE. The format to view these pages when the Password Manager Service is running is https://<FQDN of Service Machine>:<Port>/MPMService/<webservice>.asmx. For example, to test that the Data Integrity Service is running, go to https://<FQDN of Service Machine>:<port>/MPMService/DataIntegritySvc.asmx. Based on the possible results listed here, proceed to the next check or resolution indicated.

▼ **Result 1.1: You were unable to reach the Password Manager Service page through IE:**

(Proceed to Check 2)

If you are unable to connect to the Password Manager Service through IE, check that you typed the correct web address, including HTTPS and the port. Proceed to Check 2.

■ **Result 1.2: You were able to reach the Password Manager Service page, but IE asked you if you trust the SSL certificate:**

(Proceed to Resolution 1.1)

If you were able to view the Password Manager Service page, but only after you answered yes to trust the SSL certificate, proceed to Resolution 1.1.

▲ **Result 1.3: The Password Manager Service page reports an "Error in Application":**

(Proceed to Resolution 1.3)

If an "Error in Application" page is displayed when contacting one of the Password Manager Service component pages in IE, go to "Resolution 1.3: Restart the XTE Service and COM+ Objects."

Check 2: Ping the Fully Qualified Domain Name of Password Manager Service Machine   If you were unable to view the Password Manager Service page, the next step is to see if you are able to ping the FQDN of the Service. Ping the fully qualified (as opposed to NetBIOS) name of the Password Manager Service machine from the client machine.

▼ **Result 2.1: FQDN ping request fails:**

Now, ping the NetBIOS name of the service from the client machine. If you receive a reply, then do an NSLOOKUP of the service machine from the client machine. If you receive a different FQDN than expected, check that the Password Manager Service machine and the client machine have the DNS settings set up correctly. The Password Manager Service machine name should exactly match NSLOOKUP's reply of the fully qualified name of the Password Manager Service machine. If a mismatch exists between the NSLOOKUP reply and the actual FQDN of the Password Manager Service machine, proceed to Resolution 1.2—Fix the DNS settings of the Password Manager environment.

▲ **Result 2.2: FQDN ping succeeds:**

Go to the Service machine and check that the Citrix XTE Service is running. On the Service machine, use IE to contact the web services (the previous Check 1). Verify that you tried contacting the service machine on the correct port.

Repairing the Connection

The following describes how to repair the connection for the Password Manager Service:

Resolution 1.1: Add the Certificate to the Trusted Root Certificates This step is encountered when you are able to view the Password Manager Service page, but you are unable to proceed without first trusting the SSL certificate. If your CA is located within the same domain that uses the Password Manager Service, then you should automatically have trust established. To check that your root CA is trusted, you must open the certificates component of the Windows Management console (Run: mmc). Choose the certificates (Local Computer) snap-in and view Trusted Root Certificates. The root CA must be trusted on the Physical Store of each of the client machines (not the registry per user).

Resolution 1.2: Fix the DNS Settings of the Password Manager Environment DNS settings can cause some machines to "resolve" differently within different places in an environment. DNS must be set up consistently throughout an environment. The DNS configuration is especially important regarding connections to the Password Manager Service. This is because of the SSL security involved with verifying the identity of the Password Manager Service machine.

Resolution 1.3: Restart the XTE Service and COM+ Objects The Citrix XTE Service runs in the Services console in Windows. To shut down the XTE Service, go to Administrative Tools\Services (or Run: Services.msc) and look for Citrix XTE Server. Use the Services console GUI to restart the service.

NOTE When changes are applied with the Service Configuration tool, the XTE Service and COM+ objects are restarted.

If you go to the Properties page for the Citrix XTE Server, you see the user that was entered in the Service Configuration tool.

CAUTION Do not "manually" change users here! Use the Service Configuration tool, because several directories are in the Password Manager Service machine where permissions are set for the XTE Service user account, in addition to the various other hidden configurations made by the Service Configuration tool.

Data Integrity—Recovering from Data Corruption

If the Data Integrity service detects an inconsistency between data on the central store and its associated signature, an error is thrown in the console when trying to make changes to the central store. These errors prevent the console administrator from making changes to a central store deployment. To recover, unsign the data on the central store, and then sign the data with a new signing certificate (for maximum security). The re-sign option from the signing tool cannot be used because the re-sign operation verifies the data first and, in the case of corrupted data, re-sign fails.

Because you want to ensure that you do not sign bad data, you should first get an idea of which data is corrupted. Five basic areas exist where data corruption could occur: CentralStoreRoot, ADMINOVERRIDES, ENTLIST, FTULIST, SYNCSTATE. If data corruption occurs on an object within the CentralStoreRoot, the console administrator is notified of it when a change is attempted on the object. The exact object can be manually deleted using Explorer or ADSIEdit on the central store. If data corruption occurs on one of the ADMINOVERRIDES, ENTLIST, FTULIST, or SYNCSTATE objects, the following steps must be performed to ensure proper security.

1. For maximum security, close access to the central store.

2. Using the signing tool, unsign all the data on the central store.

3. Use the signing certificate creation tool, CtxCreateSigningCert.exe, to create a new signing certificate.

4. Sign the central store with the new signing certificate.

5. Open the console.

6. At this point, all settings in ADMINOVERRIDES, ENTLIST, FTULIST, and SYNCSTATE must be reset for all deployments. The only way to guarantee an update of these four objects is to make changes to the CentralStoreRoot that will force the objects to be redeployed to all user configurations.

    ▼ ADMINOVERRIDES   A change in client settings, such as "show computer name," forces an update of ADMINOVERRIDES on a "per User Configuration" basis.

    ■ ENTLIST   A change in policies, applications, and sharing groups forces an update of ENTLIST on a "per User Configuration" basis.

    ■ FTULIST   A change in Identity Verification Questions, initial credential setup applications, or key recovery type forces an update of FTULIST on a "per User Configuration" basis.

    ▲ SYNCSTATE   This object is updated for all deployments when any change is made to the CentralStoreRoot.

7. Reopen access to the central store.

All future agent logins following these changes receive the new settings and verify the integrity of the information on the central store using the new validation certificate (PublicKeyCert.cert).

XTE Service Error Log

The following is a list of possible errors encountered in the Citrix XTE Service error logs, ranked in order from most common to least common. The XTE Service error log is located at C:\Program Files\Common Files\Citrix\XTE\logs\error.log.

SSL Certificate/Machine Name Mismatch

The following error may occur if a mismatch exists between the SSL Certificate and the machine name:

Error: The certificate with identifier <ID> for virtual server <FQDN of Service Machine>:<Port> has subject common name (CN) <Not FQDN>. The subject common name must match the server name of the virtual host.

Issue: Although the Service Configuration tool starts when it finds an SSL server certificate, the XTE Service is later unable to start unless the name on the SSL server certificate exactly matches the name of the Service machine.

Resolution: The Service machine name must be referred to by its FQDN, therefore, when creating the SSL server certificate, the name on the certificate must be the FQDN of the service machine.

SSL Handshake Failure

The following error may occur if an SSL handshake fails:

Error: SSL handshake from client failed.

Issue: Handshake errors usually occur when the client does not have the root CA in the "Trusted Root Certificates" bin in its physical computer certificate store (as opposed to registry store).

Resolution: The root CA must be trusted in the physical certificate store of the Service machine and all clients (agent and console).

User Not Authorized to Access the Page

The following error may occur if a user is not authorized to access the page:

Error: [client x.x.x.x] Overlapped I/O operation is in progress. : mod_auth_ntlm: User is not authorized to access the page.

Issue: The user on machine with IP Address x.x.x.x was unable to use AuthenticatedWS web service. This issue typically appears when using Data Integrity with a Password Manager console administrator account that has not been added to the Citrix XTE Service configuration file (httpd.conf). Also, it can occur if the central store proxy account has not been added to the XTE configuration file.

The AuthenticatedWS web service provides access to the PrivateKeyCert.cert file, which is needed by the console to sign and verify data (and is also used by the C.S. proxy to encrypt the AKR data on the central store). This error is received when a user tries to access this web service, but is not permitted to use the key. Typically, a Password Manager Administrator running the console receives this error because they have not been added to the group that is allowed to use the PrivateKeyCert .cert file to sign data. This error also occurs when the C.S. proxy account has not been added to the group. By default, the group permitted to use this signing service is the Domain Admins group.

Resolution: To remedy this issue and add a user or group of users to those permitted to use the signing certificate, the XTE Service configuration file—httpd.conf—must be modified. The configuration file is found at C:\Program Files\Common Files\ Citrix\XTE\conf\. Open it in a text editor and add the following lines for each user or group within the AuthenticatedWS tag:

```
require user "<Domain>\\<User>"
require group "<Domain>\\<Group>"
```

The line, require group "<Domain>\\Domain Admins," has been added inside the AuthenticatedWS tag and can be used as an example for syntax.

The Required User/Group Line (in httpd.conf file) Is Invalid

The following error may occur if the user/group line in the httpd.conf file is invalid:

Error received: No mapping between account names and security IDs was done: mod_auth_ntlm: Failed to lookup for a group name - <BadDomain>\\<Group> or <Domain>\\<BadGroupName>.

Issue: This error occurs on more rare occasions, but it occurs when the Password Manager Administrator modifies the httpd.conf file by adding an invalid "require user/group" line.

Resolution: To remedy this issue, open the httpd.conf file and modify the require user/group line that was in the error log: <BadDomain>\\<Group> [or <Domain>\\ <BadGroupName>].

File Not Found or Unable to Start

The following error may occur if a file is not found or is unable to start:

Error received: Mod_aspdotnet: File not found or unable to start: …/Service/ WebService/DataIntegritySvc.asmx.

Issue: If running Configure and run discovery on the console, you point to a Password Manager Service machine that does not have Data Integrity installed, and this error is received.

NOTE   This error is also received when trying to contact the Password Manager Service via IE, and the filename is typed incorrectly.

Resolution: Install Data Integrity on the service machine you are pointing to, or point to a Password Manager Service machine that has Data Integrity service installed.

Attempt to Serve Directory

The following error may occur if the index file cannot be found:

Error received: Attempt to serve directory …/Service/WebService/.

Issue: When trying to connect to the Password Manager Service machine using the address "https://<FQDNofServiceMachine>:<Port>/MPMService/," the index file will not be found.

Resolution: There is not an index page for the Password Manager web services. To contact each individual web service, refer to Check 1 in the "Troubleshooting the Connection" section.

CHAPTER 19

Disaster Recovery Planning and Configuration

In preparing for disasters, whether natural or man-made, today's Information Technology (IT) management must maintain nothing less than uninterrupted service for employees, customers, suppliers, and business partners. Citrix access infrastructure solutions enable this level of continued operation by protecting critical information and applications, providing secure web access to essential business resources, and enabling users to continue working from anywhere, with any device, over any connection.

The *Citrix Access Suite* provides the capability to:

▼ Resume customer access quickly without waiting to rebuild the network.

■ Empower employees to continue working from alternative locations, including their homes—even if the company's main physical location is down. Displaced workers can securely access their key applications and data remotely over the Internet.

▲ Provide application redundancy by supporting seamless access through remote data centers.

The Citrix Access Suite provides a critical component to an efficient and cost-effective business continuity solution by enabling users to continue working after an unplanned disruption. From events such as losing the local network or power to the loss of the entire workplace due to fire or flood, employees and business partners can connect securely to critical applications and information from any remote workplace, on any network and device. Citrix solutions assure rapid, secure access to, and restoration of, business-critical data and applications.

OVERVIEW

This chapter describes a simulated business faced with constructing a disaster recovery plan utilizing the Citrix Access Suite. The business planning team will decide on a disaster recovery site and recovery model. They provide component redundancy against hardware failure by following Citrix recommendations. In addition, they formulate a deployment architecture and plan for implementation within their sites. Finally, they create a backup plan for all components of the Access Suite to prevent against logical and configuration errors that may occur in their environment.

This chapter can help you to successfully create and implement a disaster recovery plan for your organization. All recommendations in the chapter focus strictly on the configuration and redundancy of the Access Suite. Recommendations for the individual products are clearly separated, so documents can be used for disaster recovery planning of individual products, as well as the entire suite.

In addition to what is provided in this chapter, the redundancy and disaster recovery plans must also be created for the following components. This type of planning is outside the scope of this chapter:

▼   Physical network infrastructure (routers, switches, and so on)

■   Directory services (Active Directory, Novell eDirectory, LDAP)

■   Network services (DNS, DHCP, and so on)

▲   Data storage and replication

Definitions

Before reading this chapter, it is important to understand the following terms:

▼   **Fault Tolerance** means having a backup system to activate during a primary system failure. An example of fault tolerance with regard to Presentation Server is using database clustering for the data store.

■   **Disaster Recovery** is the capability of an organization to provide business-critical information in the event of a disaster. Disaster recovery consists of activities and processes designed to return the business to an acceptable service level after an unplanned event.

■   **Disaster Recovery Plan** is having a management-approved document that defines the resources, tasks, and data required to manage the technical recovery effort.

▲   **Business Continuity** is the capability of an organization to ensure continuity of service and support for its customers after an unplanned event. Also, business continuity represents the capability of an organization to maintain viability before, after, and during an event.

Figure 19-1 is a diagram of how these concepts relate to each other.

Introducing XYZ Corp

XYZ Corp is a national healthcare organization. XYZ headquarters and its main data center are located in Fort Lauderdale, Florida. XYZ has a second office and smaller data center in Redmond, Washington. XYZ also has a third office in Tampa Bay, Florida. Operations are divided between the two data centers, although both of the data centers operate independently of each other. XYZ is currently using the Citrix Access Suite as its access solution.

The data centers are responsible for serving the following business functions:

▼   Access to mission-critical applications for 60,000 corporate users

　　▼   40,000 in Fort Lauderdale and Tampa Bay

　　▲   20,000 in Redmond

■   Access to applications for 1,000 remote and traveling users

▲   Access to partner applications for business partners

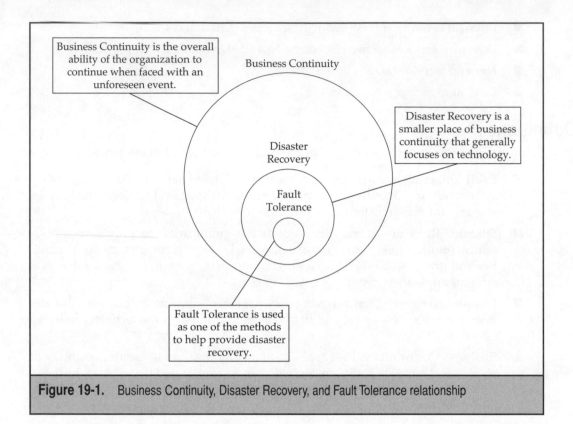

Figure 19-1.   Business Continuity, Disaster Recovery, and Fault Tolerance relationship

In addition to providing access for all its corporate users, XYZ must give its partners secure access to data and proprietary applications. XYZ uses Access Gateway–Advanced Access Control to grant access to the specific information and data required by the partners, while preventing unwanted access to the XYZ corporate network.

XYZ Corp employs a hybrid administration model. The architecture group is based in the Fort Lauderdale office and is responsible for farm-wide deployment decisions, driving the overall design of the farm. Their tasks include administering the license server, zone configuration, and other farm-wide settings.

Within the two data centers, XYZ has separate local administrators responsible for maintaining the servers in their respective sites. The administrators are responsible for tasks such as managing applications, restarting servers, and monitoring resources at their sites.

Everything was running smoothly for XYZ Corp until a recent corporate audit identified that XYZ is lacking a documented and tested disaster recovery plan. The auditors explain to XYZ that HIPAA and the Joint Commission on Accreditation of Healthcare Organizations (JCAHO) require a well-documented and tested disaster recovery plan.

Identifying the Recovery Objectives

XYZ Corp immediately begins to formulate its disaster recovery plan and concludes that two questions need to be answered:

▼ What is the acceptable amount of time the business can be down? This is commonly referred to as the recovery time objective (RTO).

▲ How much data will be lost after recovery? This is defined as the recovery point objective (RPO).

Recovery Time Objective

As a health care organization, XYZ cannot afford any downtime for its mission-critical applications. Should these mission-critical applications fail, patients' lives could be endangered. To facilitate this requirement, XYZ hosts all mission-critical applications on computers running Presentation Server.

XYZ also has less-critical applications that reside on individual users' desktop machines. These applications are not critical to XYZ's business, so they are not included in disaster recovery planning. Access for remote users does not have the same strict requirements as the mission-critical applications, therefore, XYZ decides its remote users and partners can go without access for up to one business day.

After analyzing the user-facing aspects of the business, XYZ directs its focus to tasks the IT staff performs. XYZ needs to determine how long the IT department can go without being able to make changes to their environment in a failure situation. The changes XYZ is evaluating include tasks such as:

▼ Deploying new applications

■ Adding new users to the environment

■ Monitoring the health of the environment

▲ Maintaining the Access Suite infrastructure

The disaster recovery team concludes these activities cannot be down longer than five business days.

Recovery Point Objective

How much data can XYZ afford to lose? After some deliberation, the team decides XYZ cannot afford to lose any data that is relevant to the everyday business processes. The data used by the IT staff to manage and monitor their farms is the only data not required to be protected because it is not relevant to sustaining the business and is deemed less critical.

Planning for Recovery

With the RTO and RPO identified, XYZ can now plan the details of its recovery. The XYZ disaster recovery plan is broken into three distinct categories:

▼ **Configuring for component redundancy** Prevents component outage caused by downed servers due to equipment failure, such as failed power supplies, network cards, and so on.

■ **Planning for site failover** Enables users to be routed from one site to another when a disaster such as fire, flood, hurricane, earthquake, or power loss occurs.

▲ **Defining a component backup plan** Prevents logical error and user error due to viruses, database corruption, or an administrator accidentally deleting configurations.

The following sections of this chapter outline all the configuration options for each of the previous categories. After solutions in all three categories are planned, the final cost of recovery can be calculated.

CONFIGURING FOR COMPONENT REDUNDANCY

The key to creating a solid plan is understanding exactly what is affected when certain components within the Access Suite fail. To provide guaranteed service levels, the following points should be considered for each component of the Access Suite:

▼ What is the minimum acceptable downtime a user can experience?

■ How often are changes made to the environment?

■ What is the acceptable amount of time before changes must be made to the environment?

▲ Is loss of monitoring data during an outage acceptable?

After these points are evaluated, XYZ can begin its redundancy planning. When planning for redundancy, two aspects should be considered:

The first aspect is the redundancy of the physical server components. The following lists a few recommendations for redundant components.

▼ Redundant power supplies

■ Fault-tolerant RAID setup depending on business requirements (for example: RAID 1, 5, 1+0)

▲ Fault-tolerant network interface card (NIC) teaming

The second aspect is the redundancy of the services the physical server provides.

After the physical server components are addressed, the focus can shift to creating redundant solutions for the services provided by the servers, such as the data collector for Presentation Server or the central store for Password Manager.

Included in the following sections are redundancy recommendations for each product in the Citrix Access Suite.

Citrix Presentation Server 4.0

Citrix Presentation Server is the industry-standard way to virtualize the delivery of business applications through a centralized and secure architecture. Presentation Server enables IT to centrally deploy and manage business applications providing secure, on-demand access to these resources for users anywhere, on any device and any network. Running on Microsoft Windows Server and UNIX operating systems (OSs), Presentation Server supports virtually any custom or commercially packaged Windows, UNIX, Java, and web application, regardless of the infrastructure diversity. Presentation Server delivers the best access experience for everyone: instant return on investment for the business, improved productivity for users, and enhanced administrative efficiency, system control, and security for IT.

The following sections provide a breakdown of the redundancy recommendations for each component of Presentation Server.

Data Store

The *data store* provides a central repository of persistent information for the farm. Data that resides in the data store includes

▼ Farm configuration information

■ Published applications

■ Server configuration

▲ Static policy configuration

When an administrator makes a change to this persistent information through the Presentation Server Console, the server to which the console is connected contacts the data store. For most changes, only the server that is running the Presentation Server Console contacts the data store.

Servers in the farm also access the data store to check the coherency of the Local Host Cache (LHC) each time the IMA service is started. The *LHC* is a database containing a subset of the data from the data store that resides on each of the computers running Presentation Server. The LHC is a mechanism built into IMA that provides a level of redundancy if communication with the data store fails. To ensure the LHC is up-to-date, the servers synchronize their LHC with the data store every 30 minutes.

When a Failure Occurs　In Presentation Server 3.0 and 4.0, the state of the data store has no impact on users connecting to the farm. Prior to Presentation Server 3.0, when licensing was included in the data store, users were impacted after the expiration of the 96-hour grace period. This is no longer a concern because licensing is removed from the data store.

In Presentation Server 3.0 and 4.0, the data store can be down indefinitely and connected users or new users connecting to the farm are not impacted. Users can still connect to the farm and the member servers can be restarted as necessary, but no configuration changes are possible when the data store is unreachable.

Detecting When a Failure Occurs   Presentation Server includes many useful performance counters that can be used to monitor the health of the server farm. The *Data Store Connection Failure counter,* which is located under the Citrix MetaFrame Presentation Server performance object, can monitor the connection to the data store. Under normal operating conditions, this counter is always zero.

Resource Manager's server metrics can be used to monitor the data store connection as well. Resource Manager provides additional capability over performance monitor to allow alerting through e-mail, short message service (SMS), or Simple Network Management Protocol (SNMP) when the data store is down. In addition to the alerts, scripts can be written that dynamically reassign the server to a warm data-store backup.

Selecting a Redundancy Solution   Table 19-1 illustrates the recommended redundancy solutions based on the business needs for an acceptable restoration time. The times given are specific to XYZ Corp and may not apply to all deployment situations. They are provided as a general guideline for weighing the benefits and costs of each solution.

Clustered Database   Database clustering provides the highest level of fault tolerance for the data store. The clustering capability provided by Microsoft Clustering Services (MSCS) and Oracle Real Application Clusters meet even the most-stringent business requirements.

Microsoft Clustering Services provides the capability to failover the data store to a functioning server in the event of a catastrophic failure. MSCS is available on Windows 2000 Server Advanced Server and Datacenter editions, as well as Windows Server 2003 Enterprise and Datacenter editions.

When using Oracle Real Application Clusters, all Oracle server nodes actively process requests against the same backend database. In addition to the fault-tolerance benefits, using an Oracle Real Application Clusters for the data store provides improved IMA service start times, as well as performance improvements during read-intensive operations, such as Installation Manager package deployment.

Acceptable Down Time	User Impact	Supported Databases	Recommended Solution
None	None	Oracle and SQL	Clustered database
Hours	None	Oracle and SQL	Database replication
Days	None	Oracle, SQL, DB2, MSDE, and Access	Restore from backup

Table 19-1.   Data Store Redundancy Options

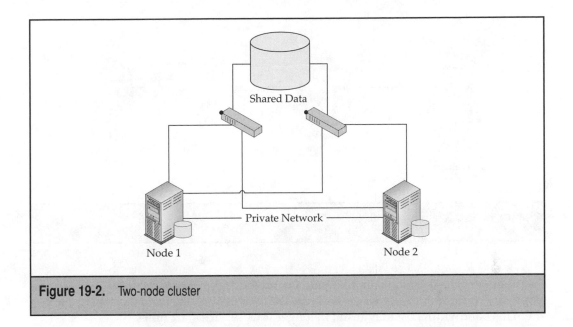

Figure 19-2.   Two-node cluster

Figure 19-2 depicts a standard two-node cluster setup on a storage area network. A storage area network is not required for clustering, however, it provides the greatest redundancy against any hardware failures. In an active/passive clustering setup, such as Microsoft Clustering Services, the active node (Node 1) is responsible for handling all the database operations for the farm running Presentation Server. If a failure occurs, the passive node (Node 2) takes over. This process is seamless to IMA and requires no administrator interaction.

Consult the Microsoft MSCS and Oracle Real Application Clusters documentation for details about implementing clustering with each of these database products.

Database Replication   Database replication is another method of providing fault tolerance. *Database replication* can be used as a hot standby when an unexpected outage occurs with the primary database. This type of setup is shown in Figure 19-3.

In this scenario, all servers contact the primary data store. If the primary data store fails, the replica data store can be promoted to become the new primary. This promotion is necessary because the replica remains in read-only mode until a new primary is selected. After the replica is promoted, all servers in the farm can be pointed to the new data store. To point the computers running Presentation Server to the new data store, see the next section, "Database Restoration."

Database replication can also be used as a redundancy solution in a multisite environment, as shown in Figure 19-4.

In this type of multisite environment, during a data store failure, computers running Presentation Server from the site with the offline database are configured to connect to

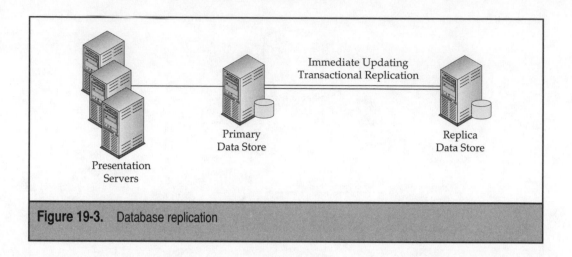

Figure 19-3. Database replication

the other site. During failover situations, a bandwidth cost exists for having the servers at one site communicate across the wide area network (WAN) to the data store in another site. This bandwidth cost may result in longer IMA service start times.

Database Restoration Database backup and restoration can be used to avoid data store failure. The following steps describe how to restore the data store, depending on the database type.

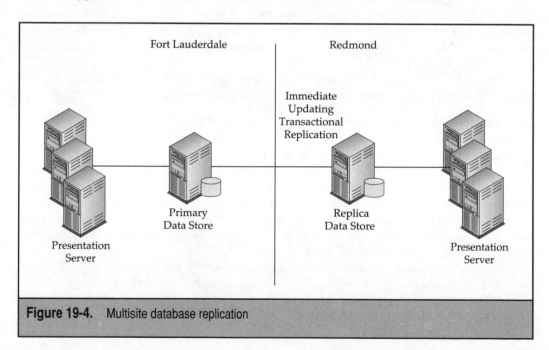

Figure 19-4. Multisite database replication

Microsoft Access or MSDE   Follow this procedure to install a backup of the data store or to move an original data store to a new host server in the event of hardware failure:

1. Copy the backup database or the original database to the server that is to become the new host server.

2. On the new host server, create a new "File DSN" pointing to the new local database from step 1.

3. On all servers in the farm, execute

   ```
   dsmaint failover Direct Server
   ```

   to point to the new host server.

NOTE   The IMA service must be running on these servers for the command to execute properly. This must be done before executing dsmaint config on the new host server as specified in the next step. Otherwise, the other servers in the farm cannot write to the database.

4. On the new host server, execute the dsmaint config command to point the IMA service to the newly created DSN file from step 2.

   ```
   DSMAINT CONFIG  [/user:<username>] [/pwd:<password>] [/dsn:<filename>]
   ```

IMPORTANT   For Microsoft Access, if no security is set on the Access database, use the default user account and password information (citrix/citrix).

NOTE   Include the full path (in quotes) in the /dsn: switch to the file dsn. For example:

   ```
   /dsn:"C:\Program Files\Citrix\Independent Management Architecture\MF20.dsn"
   ```

5. Stop and restart the IMA service on the new host server.

6. When the IMA service on the new host server is running, stop and restart the IMA service on all the other servers in the farm.

Microsoft SQL, Oracle, or IBM DB2   In a situation where a backup must be restored to a new database server, each farm server requires a new DSN file and updated registry information for the new database.

For the best performance, execute this procedure on the data collectors after all other servers are reconfigured:

1. Restore the database.

2. Create a new DSN file that points to the restored database.

3. Execute the dsmaint config command on the server with the new DSN file.

   ```
   DSMAINT CONFIG  [/user:<username>] [/pwd:<password>] [/dsn:<filename>]
   ```

4. Stop and restart the IMA service.

5. Verify the server is using the correct DSN by checking the following registry setting:

   `HKEY_LOCAL_MACHINE\SOFTWARE\Citrix\IMA\DataSourceName`

6. After the IMA service starts successfully, copy the DSN file created in step 2 to all servers in the farm.

7. Execute the dsmaint config command to change the configuration on all servers in the farm.

8. Stop and restart the IMA service on all servers in the farm.

Data Collector

Zones are logical groupings of servers that allow efficient collection of dynamic farm information. Each server in the farm has at least one Zone. Zones are somewhat like Active Directory sites in that they are designed around areas of high bandwidth. Each Zone in the farm has exactly one data collector. All the member servers in a particular Zone communicate their dynamic information to the data collector for their Zone. The data collector then shares this information with all other data collectors in the farm.

The data collector has two main responsibilities. The first is to manage all dynamic information in the farm. *Dynamic information* is the data in the farm that changes frequently. Examples of dynamic information include the following:

▼ Online servers

■ Connected sessions

■ Disconnected sessions

▲ Load-balancing information

The second main responsibility of the data collector is to handle client resolution requests. A *resolution request* is the process by which the data collector determines to which server to load balance a connection. When a user connects to an application, the client contacts the data collector and requests the least-loaded server that is hosting the target application. The data collector then looks through its load list, selects the least-loaded server, and then sends that server address to the client. This entire process is called a *resolution*.

When a Failure Occurs During normal farm operation, every server in the farm communicates with its respective data collector as events are generated. When a user logs on or off from the farm, the member server updates the data collector with its new user session information and server load count. Through this process, every server in a zone monitors the health of its respective data collector. In addition to the event-driven communication, IMA also pings among the member servers of a zone and the data collector, as well as among the data collectors in all zones.

If, at any time, the communication to the data collector fails, the election process is immediately initiated by the first server to identify the failed data collector. The server that detected the fault looks through its local host cache to find the server in the zone with the highest data-collector preference level. If multiple servers exist with the same preference level, the server with the highest IMA host ID is used to break the tie. When the new data collector is identified, a message is sent directing that server to become the data collector. When that message is received, the new data collector informs all servers in the zone and all other zone data collectors that it is the new data collector. After receiving this message, all member servers in the zone send their user session data and server load to the new data collector. All data collectors in the other zones also send their user session information to the new data collector. If load sharing among data collectors is enabled, load information from the other data collectors is sent as well.

IMPORTANT   No data is lost during this failover process. Each member server retains in memory all data that it sends to the data collector. When a failure occurs, the servers send their locally stored data to the new data collector. This operation has no impact on currently connected users.

In the Citrix *e*Labs, a 1,000-server farm with 500 servers in a single zone completes the election process and all data transfers to the new data collector within approximately 40 seconds. During this time period, clients cannot resolve because the new data collector is being elected. After the election completes, clients can connect again. Users currently connected to the farm are completely unaffected by the data-collector election process.

NOTE   In a smaller farm with a dedicated data collector, this operation takes only a few seconds.

Selecting a Redundancy Solution   Because the data collector plays such a vital role in a server farm, data collector redundancy is highly integrated into its architecture. When a data collector fails, the election process is started automatically. A new data collector is elected according to the preference levels set for each server. Data collector preference for servers can be set as Most Preferred, Preferred, Default Preference, and Not Preferred. These preference levels are then stored by all servers in the farm in their local host cache.

Each zone, regardless of size, should have a preconfigured default data collector and backup data collector. This task can be completed by setting the server preference for the computer identified as the default data collector to Most Preferred. The computer identified as the backup is configured as Preferred. All other servers in the farm are set to No Preference. In larger farms, dedicated servers are configured as data collectors and are configured so they do not accept user connections.

Farm Metric Server

The farm metric server is a component of Resource Manager. The primary job of the *farm metric server* is to track the state of all servers in the farm and report that state to the administrator through the Presentation Server Console or the Access Suite Console.

The state of the individual servers is monitored using metrics assigned to each server. These metrics contain thresholds defined by the administrator that are based on Microsoft Performance Monitor objects or Resource Manager application counters. As specific thresholds are crossed, green, yellow, or red alerts are sent from the member servers to their data collector. The data collector then forwards this information to the farm metric server. In addition to monitoring and alerting, the farm metric server reports whether or not any servers in the farm are offline.

When a Failure Occurs   User logons are not impacted in any way during a farm metric server failure and the administrator can still make configuration changes to the farm. When a farm metric server fails, the only thing affected is the real-time monitoring of Resource Manager metrics and server states. Alerts are no longer generated in the Resource Manager watcher window for metrics or applications counts. Server metrics can still be monitored, but no alerts appear in the watcher window and no notifications are sent through SMS, SNMP, and Messaging Application Programming Interface (MAPI).

Selecting a Redundancy Solution   As with the data collector, the farm metric server also has built-in redundancy. The Presentation Server Console enables the configuration of a primary and backup farm metric server. When the primary farm metric server fails, the backup takes over. The failover process takes a maximum of 60 seconds to start. As with the data collector, the failover time is dependent on the events taking place in a farm. The more active the server farm, the faster the failover occurs.

In tests conducted at the Citrix *e*Labs on a 1,000-server farm, it took around 90 seconds for the watcher window to become fully populated after the primary farm metric server failed. Approximately 100 alerts appeared in the farm watcher window.

When the backup farm metric server takes over as the primary, it remains in that role until the administrator manually changes the settings. For example, in a farm where the primary farm metric server is Server *A* and the backup is Server *B,* if Server *A* fails, Server *B* takes over as the primary farm metric server automatically. When the problem with Server *A* is resolved and that server is brought back online, Server *A* does not resume its old role as the primary farm metric server. Rather, Server *A* remains as the backup farm metric server. To promote Server *A* back to the primary role, it must be manually configured in the Presentation Server Console.

Citrix best practices recommend placing the primary farm metric server on a data collector for maximum uptime. The backup farm metric server should be placed on the backup data collector.

Database Connection Server

The database connection server is a component of Resource Manager that provides the communication link to the summary database. With the summary database enabled, each server in the farm sends its Resource Manager data to the database connection server at an administrator-specified time of day. This setting is configurable in the Presentation Server Console and is set to midnight by default.

When the summary database is enabled in a server farm, all servers in the farm immediately start to collect summary data based on the configuration specified by the administrator. Each server in the farm keeps track of its data in an Access database. Once a day, the database connection server downloads the summary data from all the servers in the farm. These files are temporarily stored in two locations: one copy remains on each of the member servers in the farm and another copy exists in the temp directory on the database connection server. After all summary files are downloaded, the database connection server attempts to commit these files to the summary database. Neither copy of the summary file is deleted until all data in the file is committed to the database.

When a Failure Occurs As with the farm metric server, users are not impacted in any way if a database connection server failure occurs. Administrators can still make configuration changes in the farm as normal. If the database connection server fails, no summary data is lost because all the data is stored on the member servers until it is transferred into the summary database. This design ensures no data is lost in the event of a database connection server failure.

If the database connection server fails while the member servers in the farm are sending their daily update, no data is lost. Each member server retains its summary data until a new database connection server is brought online. When a new database connection server is brought online, the new server downloads data files from all the member servers. If the database connection server has any problems connecting to one of the member servers, it retries the connection seven times. If it fails on the seventh time, the database connection server moves on to the next server. During the next update interval, the database connection server attempts again to contact the failed server.

If, for any reason, the database connection server cannot write the summary data to the database, the database connection server deletes its copy of the summary data. No data loss occurs because the data is still stored on the individual member servers. During the next update interval, the database connection server downloads all the data again from the member servers and it attempts to upload the data into the database.

Selecting a Redundancy Solution Because no data is lost during a database connection server failure, no need exists to have redundant hardware. However, in cases where the summary database is used for critical operations such as billing, a cold standby database connection server can be created on another server in the farm.

To create a cold standby server:

1. Select a server in the farm that has high availability. Remember, this server is busy during the update interval if it needs to take over as a database connection server.

2. Create a system DSN on the standby server and name it **RMSummaryDatabase**. Configure this system DSN to point at the Resource Manager summary database.

When a failure occurs, run the Presentation Server Console and configure Resource Manager to use the cold standby database connection server.

Acceptable Downtime	User Impact	Recommended Solution
None	None	Clustered database
Days	None	Restore from backup

Table 19-2. Summary Database Redundancy Options

Summary Database

The *summary database* is a component of Resource Manager that stores all the historical Resource Manager information. The summary database is the actual SQL or Oracle database that the database connection server uses.

Selecting a Redundancy Solution Table 19-2 illustrates the recommended redundancy solutions based on the business needs for an acceptable restoration time. The times given are generic and may not apply to all deployment situations. They are provided as a general guideline for weighing the benefits and costs of each solution.

Clustered Database As with the data store, the best redundancy solution for the summary database is clustering. MSCS and Oracle Real Application Clusters can be used in this scenario.

Consult MSCS and Oracle Real Application Clusters documentation for details about implementing clustering with each of these database products.

Restoring from Backup Consult the Oracle and Microsoft SQL Server documentation for details about restoring a backup database to a new database server.

After the database is restored, the database connection server must be reconfigured to point at the new database. This is done by using the Microsoft Open Database Connectivity (ODBC) Data Source Administration tool on the server to reconfigure the RMSummaryDatabase system DSN. If the user information to connect to the database changed, you must use the Presentation Server Console to configure a new user name and password for the summary database connection.

Web Interface

Web Interface provides users with access to Citrix Presentation Server applications and content through a standard web browser or through Program Neighborhood Agent. This functionality is provided using Java and .Net running on a standard web server.

Web Interface provides the functionality to create three different types of sites:

▼ Citrix Presentation Server

■ Program Neighborhood Agent Services

▲ Conferencing Manager Guest Attendee

Acceptable Downtime	User Impact	Recommended Solution
None	No impact	Hardware load balancer
Minutes	DNS time-out delays	DNS multiple host (A) records
Days	Down until Web Interface is restored.	Restore from backup

Table 19-3. Web Interface Redundancy Options

Selecting a Redundancy Solution   Web Interface is a vital component of a farm running Presentation Server. Clients using Web Interface or Program Neighborhood Agent can no longer connect to the farm if a Web Interface server failure occurs. For this reason, Web Interface is one of the most important components to protect from failure.

Table 19-3 illustrates the recommended redundancy solutions based on the business needs for an acceptable restoration time. The times given are specific to XYZ Corp and may not apply to all deployment situations. These times are provided as a general guideline for weighing the benefits and costs of each solution.

Network Load Balancer   Citrix recommends using the Citrix NetScaler Application Switch to load balance multiple Web Interface servers. (See Figure 19-5.) When using a hardware load balancer, remember that the load balancers are not monopolized by Web Interface. They can be used for multiple components and services throughout the organization.

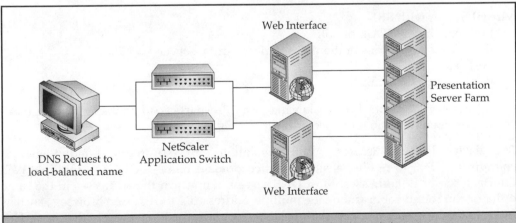

Figure 19-5.   Load-balancing Web Interface with NetScaler application switches

When using the Citrix NetScaler Application Switch, the client connects to the fully qualified domain name the switch is using for the Web Interface servers. The load balancer then directs the connection to one of the Web Interface servers based on the load-balancing method. If one of the Web Interface servers goes down, the load balancer automatically bypasses that server. In Figure 19-5, the NetScaler Application Switches are shown in high-availability mode to avoid a single point of failure. This configuration is not required, but it is recommended for maximum availability.

When configuring the NetScaler Application Switch for Web Interface, create a virtual server along with a service for each of the Web Interface servers. For a default Web Interface server, use the following settings for the services and virtual server:

Services Without SSL
Protocol: HTTP
IP Address: IP address of the Web Interface server
Port: 80
Monitor: HTTP

Virtual Server Without SSL
Protocol: HTTP
IP Address: IP address of the Web Interface virtual server
Port: 80
Persistence: COOKIEINSERT
Backup Persistence: SOURCEIP

Services with SSL
Protocol: SSL_BRIDGE or SSL
IP Address: IP address of the Web Interface server
Port: 443
Monitor: HTTPS

Virtual Server with SSL
Protocol: SSL_BRIDGE or SSL
IP Address: IP address of the Web Interface virtual server
Port: 443
Persistence: SOURCEIP

If Microsoft Network Load Balancing or a third-party load balancer is being used, consult its documentation for specific setup details.

DNS Multiple Host (A) Records Another solution for Web Interface redundancy is configuring DNS to resolve a fully qualified domain name (FQDN) to multiple Web Interface server IP addresses. Most DNS servers can return the addresses in the same order or can round-robin among the multiple addresses. Modern Web browsers, such as Internet Explorer (IE), use the multiple DNS records that are returned to the client. This solution works for redundancy, however, it is not ideal because the end user is subject to DNS time-outs when failures occur.

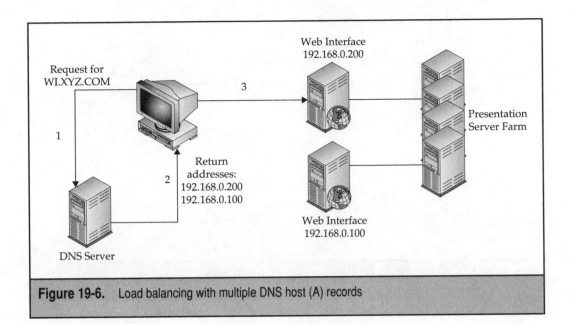

Figure 19-6. Load balancing with multiple DNS host (A) records

Figure 19-6 shows this solution during normal operation:

1. The browser running on the client device requests the IP address for WI.XYZ.COM.

2. The DNS server returns multiple IP addresses for the name and those IP addresses are cached on the client device. The DNS server can be set to return these addresses in static order or round-robin.

3. The client then selects the first IP address from the list and attempts a connection. In this example, it connects to 192.168.0.200.

Figure 19-7 illustrates what happens during a failure scenario.

1. The browser running on the client device requests the IP address for WI.XYZ.COM.

2. The DNS server returns multiple IP addresses for the name and those IP addresses are cached on the client device.

3. The client selects the first IP address from the list and attempts a connection. In this example, it attempts to connect to 192.168.0.200. This attempt fails because the server is down.

IMPORTANT In this example, the 192.168.0.200 server is down. When this occurs, IE has to wait for the first IP address entry to time-out before moving on to the second. While it is performing this process, the end user has to wait for IE and is not presented with any error messages.

4. After the attempt to the first address times out, IE automatically attempts the second address and connects successfully in this scenario.

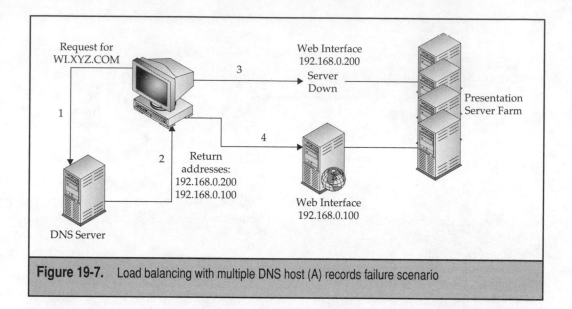

Figure 19-7.   Load balancing with multiple DNS host (A) records failure scenario

Restoring from Backup   If the Access Suite Console is used to export the Web Interface configuration information, the generated backup file can be used to restore the Web Interface settings on a new server. The process to restore the file is outlined here:

1. Install Web Interface on a new server.

2. Using the Access Suite Console, connect to the newly created Web Interface server and create a new site.

3. When the site is created, select the site under the Web Interface node, and then select the Import Configuration option in the Access Suite Console.

4. Select the exported configuration file and click OK.

5. The new Web Interface server now contains all the settings of the old server.

After restoring the configuration information, it is important to restore any third-party software or settings to the Web Interface server.

Licensing: Presentation Server

Reference the Access Suite licensing section for full details about the redundancy solutions for the license server. The following describes some specifics about how Presentation Server uses the licensing service.

The licensing process begins when the computer running Presentation Server starts up and checks out a start-up license. When a user logs on to that computer, the license server is contacted to verify if the user on the connecting client device already has a license. If the user does not already have a license, one is checked out for the client device. If licenses are available, the user is allowed to logon. This license check executes in parallel with the other logon processes, so logon time is not affected. If the computer running Presentation

Server has a connection to the license server, but cannot check out a license in five seconds, Presentation Server grants a temporary grace-period license to the user. After granting the license, the server attempts to check out the license in the background. If the connection to the license server is lost, the computer enters into the licensing grace period. This process is seamless to the user, but the administrator is notified by an event log message.

> **IMPORTANT**   All computers running Presentation Servers must contact the license server at least once to obtain a start-up license. This process gives the servers the capability to issue grace period licenses.

While in the grace period, each server is licensed for the entire farm license count. For example, if the license server is configured with a 1,000 concurrent user license, when the computer running Presentation Server enters the grace period, each server could grant up to 1,000 licenses.

When the license server comes back up, Presentation Server checks out the necessary licenses for the number of users currently logged on. In an overcommitted situation, existing users are not forced to log off, although no new users can log on until the concurrent connected user count moves back under the license limit.

Detecting a Failure   The most efficient way to verify that the computer running Presentation Server is connected to the license server is to use the License Server Connection Failure Microsoft Perfmon counter installed by default with Presentation Server. This counter is located under the Citrix MetaFrame Presentation Server performance object.

In addition to the perfmon counter, messages are written to the event log when entering and exiting the license grace period.

Citrix Access Gateway 4.1

The Citrix Access Gateway is a universal SSL virtual private network (VPN) that provides secure, always on, single-point-of-access to any information resource. It combines the best features of IP Security (IPSec) and typical SSL VPNs without the costly and cumbersome implementation and management. The Access Gateway makes access easy for users, is secure for the company, and is low cost for IT administrators.

The Citrix Secure Access Gateway supports all applications and protocols, including voice over IP (VoIP). The Access Gateway also provides industry standard encryption that secures and protects information and includes seamless support for secure access to applications on computers running Presentation Server.

The Access Gateway provides multiple methods for accessing secure data from the internal network. When connecting to the web address of the Advanced Gateway device, the user is prompted to select one of two connection types to initiate.

Securing Desktop Access

When selecting the Secure Desktop Access option, the user downloads the Secure Access Client. After downloading the Secure Access Client and authenticating, the Access Gateway establishes a secure tunnel to the internal network.

Acceptable Downtime	User Impact	Recommended Solution
None	No impact	Hardware load balancer
None	No impact	Built-in failover
Minutes	DNS time-out delays	DNS multiple host (A) records
Days	Down until restored	Restore from backup

Table 19-4. Secure Desktop Access Clients Only

NOTE   Administrative access to the user's computer is required to install the full client. If administrative access is not available, though, the client runs with reduced functionality.

Securing Application Access

When selecting the Secure Application Access option, the user connects to a secure web page configured by the administrator. In Access Suite deployments, this web page is typically configured to connect to a Web Interface server on the internal network.

Selecting a Redundancy Solution   Access Gateway is a key component for accessing a server farm from outside the corporate network. If an Access Gateway failure occurs, external users can no longer connect to the internal network. For this reason, make sure the Access Gateway is protected from failure.

Tables 19-4 and 19-5 illustrate the recommended redundancy solutions based on the business needs for an acceptable restoration time. The times given are specific to XYZ Corp and may not apply to all deployment situations. These times are provided as a general guideline for weighing the benefits and costs of each solution.

Acceptable Downtime	User Impact	Recommended Solution
None	No impact	Hardware load balancer
Minutes	DNS time-out delays	DNS multiple host (A) records
Hours	Reconnect with new URL	Multiple URLs
Days	Down until restored	Restore from backup

Table 19-5.   Mixed Secure Desktop Access Clients and Secure Application Access Connections

Because of the different methods of connecting to the Access Gateway server, different redundancy guidelines are provided, depending on the type of client connection.

Hardware Load Balancer

Citrix recommends using the Citrix NetScaler Application Switch for load balancing multiple Access Gateway appliances. (See Figure 19-8.) Remember, when using a hardware load balancer, the load balancers are not monopolized by Access Gateway. They can be used for multiple components and services throughout the organization.

When using a hardware load balancer, the user connects to the DNS load-balanced address for the Access Gateway servers. The load balancer then directs the connection to one of the Access Gateway servers, based on the load-balancing method. If one of the Access Gateway servers goes down at any point, the load balancer automatically bypasses the server. In Figure 19-8, the NetScaler Application Switches are shown in high-availability mode to avoid a single point of failure. This configuration is not required, but it is recommended for maximum availability.

When configuring the hardware load balancer, remember to properly configure how the load balancer distributes requests from the same client. The Access Gateway modifies all packets to include the external public IP address of the Access Gateway server. The external public address ensures that the redirected client returns to the Access Gateway it first encountered, providing session continuity.

The most important thing to remember when using a load-balancing solution is this: the load balancer's FQDN must be used for all components that need to reference Access Gateway.

IMPORTANT The security certificates on all the Access Gateway servers must be identical and be configured for the load-balanced FQDN.

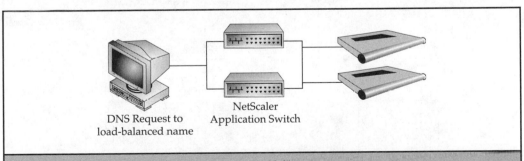

DNS Request to load-balanced name

NetScaler Application Switch

Figure 19-8. Load balancing Access Gateways with NetScaler Application Switches

When configuring the NetScaler Application Switch for the Access Gateway, create a virtual server along with a service for each of the Access Gateway appliances. For a default Access Gateway deployment, use the following settings for the services and virtual server:

Services
   Protocol: SSL_BRIDGE
   IP Address: IP address of the Web Interface server
   Port: 443
   Monitor: tcps

Virtual Server
   Protocol: SSL_BRIDGE
   IP Address: IP address of the Web Interface virtual server
   Port: 443
   Persistence: SOURCEIP

If a third-party load balancer is being used, consult its documentation for specific setup details.

Access Gateway Client Built-in Failover

The Access Gateway has a built-in failover mechanism that allows failover to multiple Access Gateway servers. (See Figure 19-9.) Because the Access Gateway failover works in

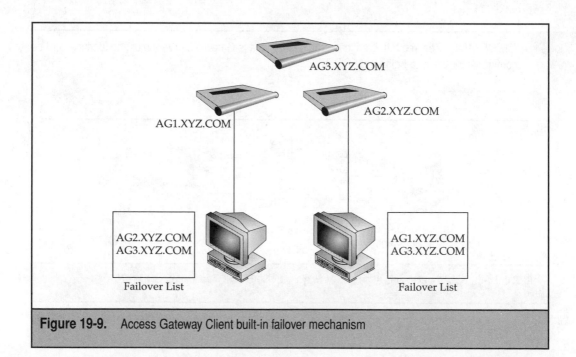

Figure 19-9.   Access Gateway Client built-in failover mechanism

an active/passive fashion, provide multiple URLs to the users to load-balance connections between multiple Access Gateway servers. When using this method of redundancy, remember the Access Gateway Client is required. This does not work with the Secure Access Application connection method. Also, the Access Gateway Client must make at least one successful connection to an Access Gateway server to obtain the list of failover servers.

During the initial connection, the Access Gateway provides the failover list to the Secure Access Client. If the client loses the connection to the primary Access Gateway, it iterates through the list of Access Gateways in the failover list. If the primary Access Gateway fails, it waits for 20 seconds, and then goes to the failover list to attempt a new connection. The client performs a DNS lookup for the first failover Access Gateway and tries to connect to that server. If the first failover Access Gateway is unavailable, the client tries the next failover server. When the client successfully connects to a failover Access Gateway, the client is prompted to log on.

In this scenario, the security certificates on all the Access Gateway servers must be unique and configured for each Access Gateway server's FQDN.

To configure Access Gateway failover:

1. Click the Access Gateway Cluster tab, and then click the Failover Servers tab.

2. In Failover Server 1, Failover Server 2, and/or Failover Server 3, type the external IP address or the FQDN of the Access Gateway(s) to be used for failover operation. The Access Gateways are used for failover in the order listed.

3. In Port, type the port number. The default is 443.

4. Click Submit.

DNS Multiple Host (A) Records   Another solution for redundancy is to configure DNS to resolve a specific name to multiple Access Gateway servers. Most DNS servers can be configured to return the addresses in the same order or configured to round-robin the addresses.

Modern web browsers, such as IE, attempt to use the multiple DNS records returned to the client when the first one in the list fails. This solution works for redundancy, but it is not ideal because the user is subject to DNS time-outs when failures occur.

Multiple URLs

Multiple URLs for different Access Gateway servers can be given to provide a rudimentary form of redundancy when using the Secure Application Access connection method. This method is used in conjunction with built-in failover for the Access Gateway Client users. The administrator provides users multiple URLs to the Access Gateway servers. If one of the servers goes offline, the users try different URLs until a connection is successful.

This solution applies only to the users using the Secure Application Access connection method because the built-in failover mechanism provides redundancy for the users connecting with the Access Gateway Client.

Restoring from Backup   In the event of a hardware failure, the saved configuration file can be used to restore all settings on a new Access Gateway server.

To restore a saved configuration:

1. In the Administration Tool, click the Access Gateway Cluster tab.

2. On the Administration tab, by "Upload a Server Upgrade or saved Config," click Browse.

3. Locate the file named config.restore and click Open. After the configuration file is uploaded, the Access Gateway restarts. All the configuration settings, licenses, and certificates are restored.

Citrix Password Manager 4.0

Citrix Password Manager provides password security and single sign-on access to Windows, web, proprietary, and host-based applications. Users authenticate once with a single password and Citrix Password Manager authenticates the users to all other password-protected applications—providing one, easy-to-remember, secure way to log on everywhere.

The following sections provide a breakdown of the redundancy recommendations for each component of Password Manager.

Central Store

The *central store* is a repository for the data Citrix Password Manager needs to function, including user credentials, agent settings, application policies, and more. Credentials are also stored in the user's local credential store. The data in the local credential store is collected in an encrypted file located in the user's profile on the client device. The central store can be integrated with the network directory service you employ. Also, the central store can be a network share on a Windows server, a container in an Active Directory schema, or a shared folder in a Novell NetWare environment.

When a Failure Occurs   Regardless of the network services hosting the central store (Active Directory or file share), the loss of the central store has the effect of preventing new settings from being distributed to users and the users from accessing their credentials. When the central store is unavailable, the agent can continue to run using the current set of user configuration settings and encrypted credentials located in the local credential store of the user's profile. When planning for a potential central store failure, several specific settings control how the agent behaves when it is unable to access the central store.

▼   *Delete user's data folder and registry key when the agent is shut down.* This is formally known as DeleteOnShutdown in Version 2.5. It controls whether or not the local credential store is removed on agent shutdown. When this setting is enabled, the local credential store is not cached on the client after shutdown and a connection to the central store is required for the agent to start the next time. The default for this setting is DISABLED. *Enabling this setting prevents fault tolerance of the Password Manager agent when the central store is unavailable.*

▲ *Allow agent to operate when unable to reconnect to central store.* This is formally known as WorkDisconnected in Version 2.5, and it controls whether or not the agent software continues to operate if unable to contact the central store. The default setting is ENABLED. Disabling this setting prevents the Password Manager Agent from operating when it cannot contact the central store for synchronization.

Both of these settings are included for organizations that have strict security requirements. By default, these settings are configured so the agent still functions properly even when the central store is down or unavailable. If the agent cannot contact the central store, the user receives an error message, but the agent continues to log the user on to all the applications. The agent can function because it stores a 3DES encrypted copy of the user's logon and password information in a local file with an .mmf extension. By default, this file is located in the user's APPDATA folder, which is normally *C:\Documents and Settings\User Name\Application Data*.

When the central store is down, the Password Manager Console and the Application Definition Tool cannot function. The administrator cannot make any changes to the Password Manager administrative data or user configurations until the central store is online.

Providing a fault-tolerant solution for the central store is a paramount concern because some of the Password Manager optional features rely on being able to access the central store. These service-dependent features include Self-Service Password Reset and Automatic Key Recovery. The following sections describe the end-user impact if these optional features are installed and the central store is unavailable.

Self-service Password Reset

During an outage, users cannot change their passwords using the Self-Service Password Reset functionality provided by Password Manager. The Password Manager service stores the questions and personalized answers for the users in the central store, and, even though the service may be available, if the central store is unavailable, the service cannot retrieve the users' answers. If a password reset is necessary, users need to contact the administrator or Help desk to reset their passwords.

Automatic Key Recovery

When choosing a key recovery option, consider fault tolerance with your organization's security and usability requirements. A new feature of Password Manager 4.0 is Automatic Key Recovery. *Automatic Key Recovery* allows Password Manager to function after the user's primary password change, without the user needing to answer a verification question or provide a previous password. For this feature to work, however, both the agent and the service must be able to contact the central store.

This normally is not a problem because the central store should be deployed in a redundant manner. In the unlikely event where the central store cannot be relied on, select different key recovery methods, such as Identify Verification and/or Previous Password, in place of Automatic Key Recovery. When these methods are chosen, Password Manager functions similarly to the previous released Version 2.5 and key recovery functions without the need for the service.

Key recovery is used only when the agent is unaware of a user's password change event, such as when an administrator changes the user's primary domain password or if the Self-Service Password Reset feature is used to change the user's primary password. If this event occurs when the central store is down, the agent cannot unencrypt a user's credentials until the central store and service are back online. If the reliability of the central store is in question or no high-availability alternatives are implemented, do not use Automatic Key Recovery. Citrix recommends using Identify Verification and Previous Password or previous Password only as the key recovery methods.

Another scenario to be aware of with Automatic Key Recovery is when the central store is down and users change their primary domain password. If the users are required to change their password and the agent is loaded on the machine they are using, the agent continues to work properly and handles the password change because the Automatic Key Recovery service is unnecessary. If a user moves to another machine that may be using a different .mmf file, though, the agent fails to start and cannot access the credentials because the synchronization process fails when the central store is unavailable. This situation is resolved by bringing the central store back online.

Selecting a Redundancy Solution Using Active Directory　The redundancy solution that should be chosen depends greatly on the business requirements. Table 19-6 illustrates the recommended redundancy solutions based on the business needs for an acceptable restoration time. The times given are specific to XYZ Corp and may not apply to all deployment situations. They are provided as a general guideline for weighing the benefits and costs of each solution.

Multiple Domain Controllers

When using Active Directory for the central store, having more than one domain controller at each site is important because Password Manager relies on Active Directory for redundancy. If only a single domain controller exists and it fails, the central store will be unavailable to the agents, unless the agent can contact a different site's domain controller. Reference Microsoft's recommendations for how to install multiple domain controllers at each site.

Acceptable Downtime	Recommended Solution
None	Multiple domain controllers
Days	Restore domain controller data

Table 19-6.　Password Manager Redundancy Options with Active Directory

Acceptable Downtime	Recommended Solution
None	Clustered file server
None	Distributed file system
Days	Restore from backup

Table 19-7.   Password Manager Redundancy Options with Shared Folders

Restoring Domain Controller Data

All Password Manager data is stored in the NTDS domain partition. Regular backups of the Active Directory database help to recover the Password Manager data, if necessary. To restore the Password Manager data, follow Microsoft's best practices for restoring Active Directory from backup.

Selecting a Redundancy Solution Using Shared Folder   The redundancy solution that should be chosen depends greatly on the business requirements. Table 19-7 illustrates the recommended redundancy solutions based on the business needs for an acceptable restoration time. The times given are specific to XYZ Corp and may not apply to all deployment situations. These times are provided as a general guideline for weighing the benefits and costs of each solution.

Clustered File Server

For the greatest level of redundancy, Citrix recommends a clustered file server with a network area storage backend to store the Password Manager central store data. A diagram of this type of setup is shown in Figure 19-10.

Clustering solutions, like the one shown in Figure 19-10, are offered by many different vendors. In this area, Microsoft offers Clustering Services (MSCS). MSCS is available on Windows 2000 Advanced Server and Datacenter products, as well as on Windows Server 2003.

Distributed File System

A Citrix Password Manager file synchronization point can be implemented using Windows 2000 or Windows 2003 distributed file system (DFS). Consider using DFS as an alternative to a single synchronization point when fault tolerance and distributed work loads are required.

Restoring from Backup Using Active Directory as Central Store

Follow Microsoft's recommendations for restoring Active Directory. When the Active Directory domain controllers are restored, no additional steps are necessary.

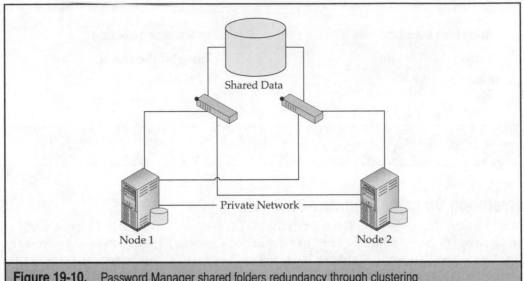

Figure 19-10. Password Manager shared folders redundancy through clustering

Restoring from Backup Using Shared Folder as Central Store

Citrix recommends that the Password Manager central store data be restored to a server with the same name. When restoring to a server with the same name, no configuration changes are necessary on the Password Manager agents or on the Password Manager service.

NOTE If the central store must be migrated to another location after restoration, follow the instructions in the MetaFrame_Password_Manager_Guide.pdf under the section "Migrating MetaFrame Password Manager Administrative Data." If Presentation Server is being used to host applications and the Password Manager agent, the Password Manager policy can be used to redirect users on the computer running Presentation Server to a new file share central store location. Also, in an emergency situation, you can use a HKEY_CURRENT_USER registry key to redirect the agents to a new location. For more information about these alternatives, reference the Citrix knowledgebase article CTX103564 at http://support.citrix.com/article/CTX103564.

Password Manager Service

The Citrix Password Manager Service is a new enhancement to Citrix Password Manager's architecture. The Citrix Password Manager Service runs on a web server that provides the foundation for optional features included in this release. Install the Citrix Password Manager Service if at least one of the following modules is being implemented:

▼ **Self-Service Password Reset**   Enables users to reset their passwords by answering a set of questions based on personal information.

■ **Data Integrity**   This feature protects data from being compromised while in transit from the central store to the agent. The service signs the data in the central store. The agent downloads a public key, so it can read and verify data from the central store.

▲ **Automatic Key Recovery**   Lets users log on to the network and have immediate access to applications managed by Citrix Password Manager. This feature eliminates the need for users to provide identity verification upon a password change.

CAUTION   Password Manager 4.0 does not currently support Data Integrity and Automatic Key Recovery at the same time. For more information, reference the Citrix knowledgebase article CTX106759 at http://support.citrix.com/article/CTX106759.

When a Failure Occurs   When a failure occurs with the server hosting the Password Manager Service, the following features may be impacted:

▼ Self-Service Password Reset

■ Data Integrity

▲ Automatic Key Recovery

Following is a description of the impact of the service being down for each of the features that may be in use.

Self-service Password Reset

When the service is down, Self-Service Password Reset is unavailable. The failed service has no impact on users, unless they forgot their primary passwords. If users attempt to use Self-Service Password Reset when the service is down, an error message appears. Optionally, users can contact the administrator or Help desk to reset their passwords.

Data Integrity

If the service fails for any reason and data integrity is being used for the central store, users receive an error message. In most cases, however, the agent continues to function. In most scenarios, the service is not needed after the agent downloads the public key from the Password Manager Service. In several instances, the agent needs to contact the service for data integrity verification.

When the agent is first installed, the agent is required to contact the service to get the public key. If the service is down, newly deployed agents cannot obtain a copy of the public key, thus, cannot verify whether or not the configurations are valid, which prevents the agent from functioning. The agent also needs to contact the service for data integrity when the public key expires. By default, the public key expires every 12 months and the agent is required to contact the service to download the new public key. If the service is unavailable, the agent runs with the current configuration settings until the service is available and new settings can be obtained. If the agent is starting for the first time, it terminates if the service is unavailable.

Automatic Key Recovery

Reference the section "When there is a failure" of the central store component. The behavior of the Automatic Key Recovery feature is the same in both instances.

Selecting a Redundancy Solution   The redundancy solution you choose depends greatly on your business requirements. Table 19-8 illustrates the recommended redundancy solutions based on the business needs for an acceptable restoration time. The times given are specific to XYZ Corp and may not apply to all deployment situations. These times are provided as a general guideline for weighing the benefits and costs of each solution.

Hardware Load Balancer

Citrix recommends using the Citrix NetScaler Application Switch for optimal Password Manager Service redundancy solution. (See Figure 19-11.) Remember, when using a hardware load balancer, the load balancers are not monopolized by Web Interface. The hardware load balancers can be used for multiple components and services throughout the organization.

When using the Citrix NetScaler Application Switch, the client connects to the fully qualified domain name the switch is using for the computers running the Password Manager Service. The load balancer directs the connection to one of the computers running the Password Manager Service based on the configured load-balancing method. If one of the computers goes down, the load balancer automatically bypasses that server. In Figure 19-11, the NetScaler Application Switches are shown in high-availability mode to avoid a single point of failure. This configuration is not required, but it is recommended for maximum availability.

Acceptable Downtime	Recommended Solution
None	Hardware load balancer
Hours	Cold standby
Days	Restore from backup

Table 19-8.   Password Manager Service Redundancy Options

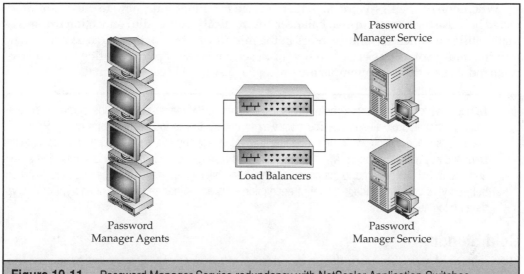

Figure 19-11.   Password Manager Service redundancy with NetScaler Application Switches

When configuring the hardware load balancer, it is important to properly configure how the load balancer distributes multiple requests from the same client. For the Password Manager agent, the load balancer must be configured so multiple requests from the same client device get redirected to the same Password Manager server.

When configuring the NetScaler Application Switch for the Password Manager Service, you need to create a virtual server, along with a service for each of the Password Manager servers. For a default Password Manager Service install, use the following settings for the services and virtual server:

Services
    Protocol: SSL_BRIDGE
    IP Address: IP address of the Web Interface server
    Port: 443
    Monitor: tcps

Virtual Server
    Protocol: SSL_BRIDGE
    IP Address: IP address of the Web Interface virtual server
    Port: 443
    Persistence: SOURCEIP

If a third-party load balancer is being used, consult the load-balancer documentation for specific configuration information.

When one of the Password Manager Service machines fails, new requests are unaffected because the hardware load balancer automatically routes the connection to a server that is still available. If a failure occurs in the middle of a transaction, such as a user who is in the middle of a Self-Service Password Reset, a message appears stating that an error occurred. When the user attempts the process again, it succeeds as normal.

NOTE When load balancing between multiple Password Manager servers, the same certificates must be installed on all servers. The best way to ensure this is to configure one of the Password Manager service machines. When everything is working properly, follow the procedure to back up the keys and key recovery secret. When a new Password Manager service machine is installed, the keys and secret can be restored to the new machine. If the backup and restore procedures are followed, both servers contain an identical set of encryption keys and either server can unencrypt or encrypt data on the central store.

Cold Standby

Having a cold standby is another redundancy solution for the Password Manager Service. You can create a cold standby server by cloning the Password Manager Service machine on to another machine. Keep this cold standby off the network and activated only when the primary server fails.

You can create the cold standby server by following the recommendations for Password Manager Service backup and restore.

IMPORTANT Remember, the cold standby must have the same public and private keys, as well as the same key recovery secret.

Restoring from Backup The following procedure can be used to restore the backed-up Password Manager service data on to a new replacement server.

1. Install the service from the installation media on to the new server.

IMPORTANT This server should have the same name as the original server that hosted the Password Manager Service.

2. Configure the service with the proper settings and allow the service to start. Verify that the service starts up properly. If any errors exist at this point, consult the Password Manager Administrator's Guide for troubleshooting tips.

3. Stop the Password Manager Service.

4. Record the NTFS permissions on the following files:
   a. Backed up copy of PrivateKeyCert.cert
   b. Backed up copy of PublicKeyCert.cert

NOTE   Record the permissions on the newly created files. The service configuration tool assigns the appropriate permissions to the files. Remember, the same permissions must be in place when the files are restored.

5. Copy the backed-up certificates to the following default locations:

    a. Copy PrivateKeyCert.cert to C:\Program Files\Citrix\MetaFrame Password Manager\Service\Certificates\.

    b. Copy PublicKeyCert.cert to C:\Program Files\Citrix\MetaFrame Password Manager\Service\Certificates\.

6. Verify that the NTFS permissions of the certificates copied over in step 5 match the permissions noted in step 4. Set the permissions manually, if necessary.

7. Import the key recovery secret (only if the AKR module is installed):

    a. From a command prompt, go to the default location: C:\Program Files\ Citrix\MetaFrame Password Manager\Service\Tools.

    b. Type ctxmovekeyrecoverydata.exe –import file name.

8. Enter the correct password when prompted. This is the password that was given when the key recovery secret was originally backed up.

9. Restart the service. The service is now ready for use. Verify connectivity from an agent.

Licensing: Password Manager

Reference the Access Suite Licensing section for full details about the redundancy solutions for the license server. The following describes some specifics about how Password Manager uses the licensing service.

Like all other products in the Citrix Access Suite, Password Manager has support for the 30-day grace period. No matter what type of license is selected, the grace period allows users an additional 30 days of functionality if they cannot contact the license server. Each Password Manager agent must connect to the license server at least once to have the capability to enter the grace period. If a new agent is installed and the license server is unavailable, the agent stops functioning after 96 hours and the agent will not get the full 30-day licensing grace period.

Depending on the licensing method selected, Password Manager supports three different types of licensing configurations. The selected licensing method determines when the grace period starts.

Concurrent Connected User

The concurrent connected user model is recommended for users who are on the corporate network. With the *concurrent connected user* model, the agent checks out a license when it initially starts up and it returns the license at logoff. By default, the agent checks out the license for 90 minutes. Every 60 minutes, the agent attempts to check out the license for another 90 minutes. If the agent fails to contact the license server for any reason during this process, the client goes into a grace period. This process is completely seamless to the user.

Named User

The *named user* model is recommended for environments where users are taking their machines off the network frequently. Roaming corporate laptops are a good example of the user who would benefit from a named user license. By default, with named user licensing, the agent checks out a license for 21 days. This lease period is configurable through the Password Manager Console. With this model, licenses are never checked back into the license server. When the lease expires, the license server checks in the license. When using named user, the Password Manager agent attempts to renew its lease every six hours. If the agent cannot contact the license server, it does not immediately go into a grace period. The agent continues to use the leased license until it expires. At license-expiration time, if the agent still cannot contact the license server, it enters the 30-day grace period. In this example, with a default lease of 21 days, the agent can run for 51 days before both the lease period and the grace period expire.

Concurrent Connected User with Disconnect Mode Period Enabled

The last type of license is a hybrid of both the concurrent user and named user licenses. In the *concurrent connected user with disconnect mode period enabled* model, a concurrent connected user license is used, but the administrator has the option to set lease periods on a per-user basis. When this model is used, the grace period behaves identically to the named user license.

Citrix Access Gateway–Advanced Access Control 4.0

Access Gateway–Advanced Access Control is the new name for the product formerly known as Citrix Secure Access Manager. *Access Gateway–Advanced Access Control* offers the following new features to increase security while increasing access options:

▼ **SmartAccess** Citrix *SmartAccess* provides identity-driven access tailored to any user environment, improving productivity, while ensuring a highly secure access environment. SmartAccess analyzes the access scenario, and then delivers the appropriate level of access without compromising security. Depending on where users are, and what device and network they are using, users are granted different levels of access, such as the ability to preview, but not edit, documents.

▲ **SmoothRoaming** Access Gateway–Advanced Access Control supports *SmoothRoaming* by ensuring that as users move between devices, networks, and locations, the appropriate level of access is automatically configured for each new access scenario.

The following outlines all the different components and server roles necessary for an Access Gateway–Advanced Access Control deployment. Depending on the size of the deployment, many of these components can run on the same server.

Database Server

Access Gateway–Advanced Access Control uses a Microsoft SQL server to store all the state information for the entire access farm. In previous releases, this task was performed by the state server. In this latest version, the state server is replaced by the database. All components in the access farm communicate with the database to keep their state information current. The database performs some of the following operations:

▼ Maintains the state of all users who are currently using the access farm

■ Keeps the dynamic load data on the agent servers for load balancing

▲ Holds all machine and user configuration information for the access farm

Selecting a Redundancy Solution   Because the database contains all the static and dynamic information for the access farm, the database server should always remain online. The entire access farm fails if the database server goes down. For this reason, be sure to have scheduled backups, as well as a fault-tolerance solution, that fit your organization's business requirements.

The redundancy solution you choose depends greatly on the business requirements. Table 19-9 illustrates the recommended redundancy solutions based on the business needs for an acceptable restoration time. The times given are specific to XYZ Corp and may not apply to all deployment situations. These times are provided as a general guideline for weighing the benefits and costs of each solution.

Clustered Microsoft SQL Server

The highest level of fault tolerance for the database server is achieved through database clustering. The clustering capability provided by MSCS meets the most-stringent business requirements.

Acceptable Downtime	User Impact	Recommended Solution
None	None	Clustered SQL Server
Days	No access until database is restored	Restore from backup

Table 19-9.   Advanced Access Control 4.0 Redundancy Options

MSCS provides the capability to failover the Access Gateway–Advanced Access Control database server to a functioning server in the event of a catastrophic server failure. MSCS is available on Windows 2000 Advanced Server and Datacenter products, and Windows Server 2003.

Consult Microsoft MSCS documentation for details about implementing clustering with Microsoft SQL Server.

Restoring from Backup   Follow normal database restore procedures when restoring a backed-up database. Consult the Microsoft SQL Server documentation for details about restoring a backup database to a new database server.

Web Server

The Access Gateway–Advanced Access Control Web Server component is responsible for processing the access center HTTP requests. The web servers act as an entry point for the access farm. The web server is also responsible for forwarding requests to appropriate agent servers for processing when the Access Center user interface is being used. After the request is processed by the agent server, the response is returned to the web server and forwarded to the client browser.

Selecting a Redundancy Solution   As a vital component of the access farm, it is important that at least one web server is online at all times. If all the web servers in the access farm fail, no functionality is available for the users.

To prevent this from happening, Citrix recommends that multiple web servers be configured in the access farm. As with any other standard web server, a hardware load balancer or Microsoft's network load balancing should be used to load balance connections to the web servers. In addition to providing load balancing, this configuration permits redundancy if one of the web servers fails. When using a hardware load balancer with multiple web servers, the user is unaffected during a failure, primarily because the web servers do not hold any state information and any requests from currently connected users can be routed seamlessly to another web server.

The most important thing to remember when using a load-balanced solution is that the load-balanced FQDN must be used for all components that need to reference the web server.

IMPORTANT   The security certificates on all the web servers must be identical. In addition, the security certificates must be configured for the load-balanced FQDN.

Logon Agent

The main task of the *logon agent* is to provide the user interface for authenticating to the access server farm. Some of the logon agent's other responsibilities include

▼   Forwarding the authentication request to the authentication service

■   Redirecting users to their target home page

▲   Reporting the endpoint security evidence to the authentication service

Selecting a Redundancy Solution   The redundancy recommendations and requirements for the logon agent are identical to that of the web server. As with the web server, use Microsoft Network load balancing or a hardware load balancer.

The logon agent is also completely stateless. When using multiple logon agents with a hardware load balancer, new users, as well as currently logged-on users, are unaffected if a logon agent fails.

HTML Preview Server

The *HTML preview server* is responsible for converting Microsoft Office and Adobe PDF documents to HTML when the HTML Preview activation option is enabled.

Selecting a Redundancy Solution   Because the load balancing and fault tolerance for the HTML preview server is built in, Citrix recommends having at least two HTML preview servers for a redundant deployment.

Access Gateway–Advanced Access Control has a built-in mechanism to load balance against multiple HTML preview servers. This load-balancing functionality also provides redundancy for the HTML preview server. The load-balancing mechanism is based on server load, as well as document cache. The first time a document is previewed, it is put into cache. The server with the lowest load is chosen by the load-balancing algorithm. However, in cases where the loads are close, the web server selects the HTML preview server that has the requested document cached.

To provide failover capability, the web servers poll the HTML preview servers every three to five seconds. If one of the HTML preview servers does not respond to the polling request, that server is not used by the web servers. The web servers do not maintain a list of downed HTML preview servers. All HTML preview servers continue to be polled, no matter how long they are offline.

Agent Server

This service is used only in conjunction with access centers. The agent server processes incoming requests received from the web server and sends responses back to the web server for CDA delivery to the client browser.

Selecting a Redundancy Solution   The agent server plays a vital role in delivering access-center content to the user. When one of the agent servers fails, users receive an error message and cannot navigate to the access center. Note, the navigation user interface (UI) is unaffected by any agent server failures; only the access center UI is affected. Citrix recommends more than one agent server be in the access farm to prevent failure of the access center UI. With multiple agent servers in the access farm, the user is unaffected by an agent server failure. Existing users are routed to the agent server that is still online. This redirection occurs transparently in the middle of the user's session. This redirection is possible because all the state information is stored on the database server, not on the individual agent servers.

Redundancy for the agent servers is built into the product. When multiple agent servers are in the same farm, requests to those servers are load balanced to the least-loaded server, based on the CPU usage. If a web server fails to communicate with an agent server for any reason, the agent server is marked as offline in the database. Every five minutes, the web server attempts to contact the offline agent server to determine if it is back online.

Licensing: Access Gateway—Advanced Access Control

Reference the Access Suite Licensing section for full details about the redundancy solutions for the license server. The following describes some specifics regarding how the Access Gateway–Advanced Access Control uses the licensing service.

As with the other products in the Access Suite, Access Gateway–Advanced Access Control has support built in for a 30-day grace period. This 30-day grace period takes effect if communication with the license server is lost. During the grace period, users connecting to the access farm are unaffected. No notifications or error messages appear.

Citrix Secure Gateway 4.0

Secure Gateway is a Citrix Access Suite infrastructure component used to securely access resources and applications hosted inside the corporate network. The Secure Gateway transparently encrypts and authenticates all user connections to protect against eavesdropping, data tampering, and theft.

Secure Gateway eases firewall traversal and provides a secure Internet gateway between internal applications and resources, as well as external client devices. All data traversing the Internet between a remote workstation and the Secure Gateway is encrypted using Secure Sockets Layer (SSL) or Transport Layer Security (TLS) security protocols.

Following are recommended topologies in which Secure Gateway can be deployed with Web Interface and Citrix Access Gateway—Advanced Access Control.

Presentation Server

Figure 19-12 shows a Secure Gateway deployment used to secure a server farm. The unsecured network contains a client device running a web browser and Citrix Presentation Server Client. The demilitarized zone (DMZ) contains the Secure Gateway and Web Interface components installed on the same server. The secure network contains a server farm with Citrix Presentation Server with one computer running the Secure Ticket Authority (STA). The Secure Gateway needs to connect to only one server running the STA. A server within the server farm runs the Citrix XML Service. A firewall separates the unsecured network from the demilitarized zone and a second firewall separates the demilitarized zone from the secure network. Root and server certificates are installed on the appropriate machines to enable secure communications.

Figure 19-13 shows a Secure Gateway deployment used to secure a server farm in a double-hop DMZ environment. The secure enterprise network is separated from the Internet by a double-hop DMZ. The enterprise network contains a server farm including

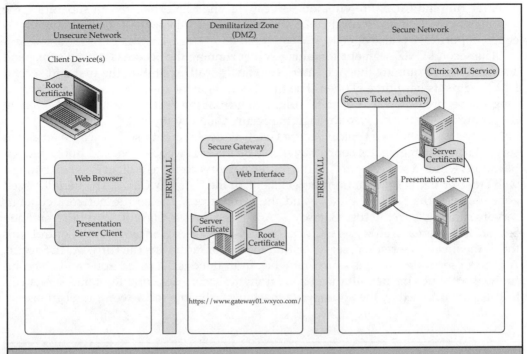

Figure 19-12. Presentation Server single-hop DMZ

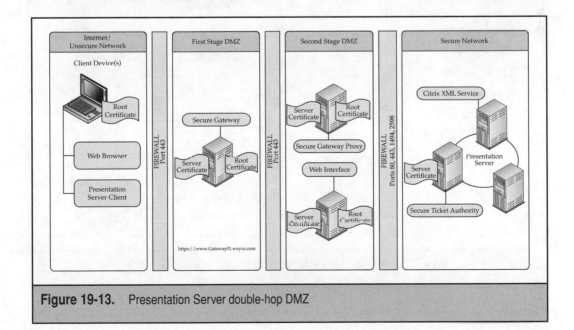

Figure 19-13. Presentation Server double-hop DMZ

a server running Citrix Presentation Server with the STA. The firewall separating the secure network from the second DMZ segment has port 443 open. If session reliability is enabled, port 2598 is also open.

The second DMZ segment contains a server running the Secure Gateway proxy and a second server running the Web Interface. The firewall separating the first and second DMZ segments has port 443 open. The first DMZ segment contains a single server running the Secure Gateway. All traffic originating from the Secure Gateway to servers in the secure network is proxied through the Secure Gateway proxy.

Figure 19-14 shows a typical Secure Gateway deployment used to secure an access server farm that aggregates content available on internal web servers and published applications within a server farm. The unsecured network contains a client device running a web browser, Citrix Presentation Server Client, or the Gateway Client. The demilitarized zone contains the Secure Gateway and the logon agent. The secure network contains servers running Citrix Access Gateway—Advanced Access Control, Citrix Presentation Server, and internal web servers. Citrix Access Gateway–Advanced Access Control runs the authentication service. A server within the server farm runs the Citrix XML Service. A firewall separates the unsecured network from the demilitarized zone and a second firewall separates the demilitarized zone from the secure network. Root and server certificates are installed on the appropriate machines to enable secure communications.

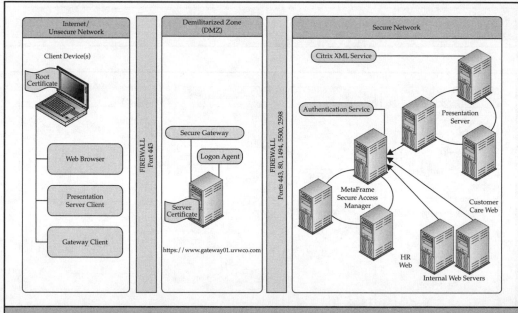

Figure 19-14. Access Gateway–Advanced Access Control single-hop DMZ

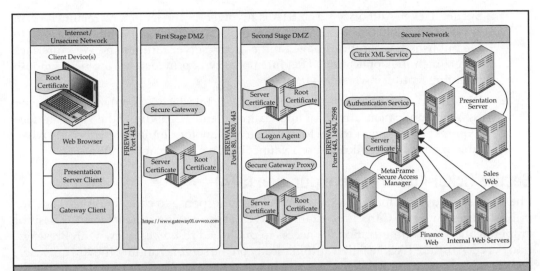

Figure 19-15. Access Gateway–Advanced Access Control double-hop DMZ

Figure 19-15 shows a typical double-hop Secure Gateway deployment used to secure an access server farm that aggregates content available on internal web servers and published applications within a server farm. The unsecured network contains a client device running a web browser and Citrix Presentation Server Client. The first stage of the demilitarized zone contains the Secure Gateway. The second stage of the DMZ contains the Secure Gateway proxy and logon agent.

The secure network contains servers running Citrix Access Gateway—Advanced Access Control, Citrix Presentation Server, and internal web servers. The authentication service runs on Citrix Access Gateway—Advanced Access Control. A server within the server farm runs the Citrix XML Service. The content from the internal web servers and server farm is aggregated by Citrix Access Gateway—Advanced Access Control.

A firewall separates the unsecured network from the first stage of the demilitarized zone, a second firewall separates the first stage of the demilitarized zone from the second stage of the demilitarized zone, and a third firewall separates the second stage of the demilitarized zone from the secure network. Root and server certificates are installed on the appropriate computers to enable secure communications.

When a Failure Occurs The client response to a failure depends on which component fails in the Secure Gateway deployment and at what point in the session the server fails. Types of server failure include:

▼ **Secure Gateway** The Secure Gateway is involved during application launch and the time an application remains active. If a server fails, the client connection goes to another server and the session reconnects automatically without the user having to log on again.

- ■ **Secure Ticket Authority**   The STA is involved in the launch or relaunch of an application. Failure of the STA during application launch requires returning to the published applications page on the access server farm or the Web Interface to relaunch the application. This functionality is provided by the new Smooth Roaming feature in Version 4.0.

- ▲ **Web Interface**   The server running the Web Interface is involved during user sign-on, application launch, or application relaunch. Failure of the Web Interface requires reconnection to the logon page and another input of credentials when launching a new application or relaunching an existing application.

Secure Ticket Authority Configuration (STA)

The STA is responsible for issuing session tickets in response to connection requests for published resources on Citrix Presentation Server. These session tickets form the basis of authentication and authorization for access to published resources. New with Presentation Server 4.0, the STA is installed automatically on the servers running the XML Service, so it is no longer necessary to reserve a separate server for the STA when using Secure Gateway with Presentation Server. For maximum availability, Citrix recommends that all Secure Gateway and Web Interface servers point to multiple secure ticket authorities.

Secure Gateway Server

The Secure Gateway is a MetaFrame Access Suite component you can use to secure access to Citrix Presentation Server, Advanced Access Controls, and MetaFrame Secure Access Manager. The Secure Gateway transparently encrypts and authenticates all user connections to protect against data tampering and theft.

Selecting a Redundancy Solution   Secure Gateway is a key component for accessing a server farm and Access Gateway Advanced access farm from outside the corporate network. If a Secure Gateway failure occurs, external users can no longer connect to the internal network and access their information. For this reason, Secure Gateway should be protected from failure.

Table 19-10 illustrates the recommended redundancy solutions for both the single-hop and double-hop DMZ deployment methods; these recommendations are based on

Acceptable Downtime	User Impact	Recommended Solution
None	No impact	Hardware load balancer
Minutes	Reconnect with new URL	Multiple URLs
Days	Down until restored	Restore from backup

Table 19-10.   Secure Gateway Server Redundancy Options

the business needs for an acceptable restoration time. The times given apply to XYZ Corp and may not apply to all deployment situations. These times are provided as a general guideline for weighing the benefits and costs of each solution.

Hardware Load Balancer

Citrix recommends using the Citrix NetScaler Application Switch for load balancing multiple Secure Gateway servers. When using a hardware load balancer, remember the load balancers are not monopolized by Secure Gateway. Rather, they can be used for multiple components and services throughout the organization.

When using a hardware load balancer, the user connects to the DNS load-balanced address for the Secure Gateway servers. The load balancer then directs the connection to one of the Secure Gateway servers based on the load-balancing method. If one of the Secure Gateway servers goes down at any point in time, the load balancer automatically bypasses the server. The NetScaler Application Switches are recommended to be deployed in high-availability mode to avoid a single point of failure. This configuration is not required, but it is recommended for maximum availability.

When setting up the hardware load balancer, remember to properly configure how the load balancer distributes multiple requests from the same client. It is crucial that you install the same server certificate on all load-balanced Secure Gateway servers. Use this name when configuring client access.

When configuring the NetScaler Application Switch for Secure Gateway, create a virtual server along with a service for each of the Secure Gateway servers. For a default Secure Gateway deployment with no SSL acceleration on the NetScaler switch, use the following settings for the services and virtual server:

Services
> Protocol: SSL_BRIDGE
> IP Address: IP address of the Web Interface server
> Port: 443
> Monitor: tcps

Virtual Server
> Protocol: SSL_BRIDGE
> IP Address: IP address of the Web Interface virtual server
> Port: 443
> Persistence: SOURCEIP

If the HTTPS or HTTPS-ecv monitors are used, disable the virtual server IP address from logging, so each HTTPS ping is not logged as a connection attempt. If they are not excluded, the logs are likely to fill quickly.

If a third-party load balancer is being used, consult the load balancer documentation for specific configuration information.

Multiple URLs

Multiple URLs for different Secure Gateway servers can be given out to provide a rudimentary form of redundancy. In this scenario, each Secure Gateway server points to multiple STAs and, in the double-hop DMZ scenario, multiple Secure Gateway proxies. Multiple Web Interface servers are needed and each server points to a Secure Gateway server.

The administrator provides users multiple URLs to the Secure Gateway servers. If one of the servers goes offline, the users would try different URLs until a connection is successful.

Restoring from Backup

The following steps are required to restore a Secure Gateway server:

1. Import the certificate.

2. Install Secure Gateway on the new server.

3. Copy the configuration file back.

4. Restart the Secure Gateway server.

Each of the previous steps is described in the following sections.

Importing the Certificate

1. Copy the PKCS #12 file, *filename.pfx*, to the server running the SecureGateway.

2. Open an MMC console that contains the certificate snap-in.

3. The Certificates Snap-In dialog box appears. Select Computer Account and click Next.

4. The Select Computer dialog box appears. Select Local Computer and click Finish.

5. Click Close, and then OK.

6. In the console tree, click Certificates, and then click Personal.

7. On the Action menu, click All Tasks, and then click Import.

8. In the Certificate Import Wizard, do the following to import the PFX file:

    a. Browse to and select the file containing the certificate being imported.

    b. Type the password used to encrypt the private key.

    c. Select whether the certificate is placed automatically in a certificate store (based on the type of certificate) or if it should be user-specified.

9. The certificate, filename.pfx, is now imported and stored in the local certificate store.

Installing Secure Gateway   After copying the certificate, install Secure Gateway on the new server.

Restoring the Configuration File   Restore the backup copy of the httpd.conf file to the "%Program Files%\Citrix\Secure Gateway\conf\" directory. Restart the Secure Gateway service after restoring the certificate and configuration file.

Secure Gateway Proxy

The Secure Gateway Proxy is a special mode of Secure Gateway that "proxies" communication through a multiple-hop DMZ.

Selecting a Redundancy Solution   Unique to the double-hop DMZ deployment scenario is the Secure Gateway proxy. The Secure Gateway is installed in the first DMZ and the Secure Gateway proxy is installed in the second DMZ. The Secure Gateway proxy acts as a conduit for traffic originating from the Secure Gateway to servers in the secure network, and from servers in the secure network to the Secure Gateway. Secure Gateway proxy servers are load balanced in the same way as the Secure Gateway. However, instead of requiring an external load balancer, the Secure Gateway proxy has built-in support for load balancing. Please see Figure 19-16 for Secure Gateway redundancy options.

Configure each Secure Gateway server to point to multiple Secure Gateway proxy servers. The Secure Gateway servers round-robin connections between the Secure Gateway Proxy servers in the list. If one of the Secure Gateway proxy servers goes offline, existing and new users connecting are not impacted. After five minutes, the Secure Gateway servers remove the offline Secure Gateway proxy server from the list. When the Secure Gateway Proxy server comes back online, the server is added back.

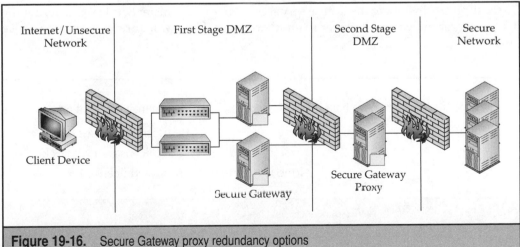

Figure 19-16.   Secure Gateway proxy redundancy options

Citrix License Server

Each Citrix Access Suite deployment must have at least one license server. The license server is the component that allows licenses to be shared across the network for different Citrix products. For users to connect to Access Suite products, they must first obtain a license from the license server. This process is accomplished in a couple of different ways, depending on the specific product being used.

In conjunction with the license server are the license file and the License Management Console. The *license file* is stored on the license server and it contains the purchased licenses. The *License Management Console* is a web-based administration interface used to manage the license server.

Licensing Grace Period   By default, all Citrix Access Suite products ship with a 30-day grace period. If the license server cannot be contacted for any reason, the Citrix Access Suite products immediately go into a 30-day grace period, provided the Citrix product successfully contacted the license server at least once. This process is seamless to the user.

Selecting a Redundancy Solution   If a license server fails, the grace period allows full functionality up to 30 days. During this period, users are not affected in any way. However, based on the redundancy needs of different organizations, a few other options exist that can be used to supplement the 30-day grace period. The following outlines the recommendations for license-server fault tolerance based on business need.

Table 19-11 illustrates the recommended redundancy solutions based on the business needs for an acceptable restoration time. The times given are specific to XYZ Corp and may not apply to all deployment situations. These times are provided as a general guideline for weighing the benefits and costs of each solution.

Clustered License Server

Citrix supports installing the license server in a Microsoft Cluster Service. Clustering the license server allows it to failover to another server if hardware or the licensing service fails.

Acceptable Hardware Downtime	User Impact	Recommended Solution
None	None	Clustered license server
Hours	None for 30 days	Cold license server backup
Days	None for 30 days	Archived license file

Table 19-11.   License Server Redundancy Options

NOTE   Clustering the license server does not protect against network connectivity failure. Network connectivity failure does not initiate failover to the passive node of the cluster.

When installing Citrix Access Suite licensing on a cluster-enabled server, Citrix recommends specifying the name of the cluster when configuring product-side licensing settings during product setup. In addition, a cluster name must be specified when generating license files from MyCitrix.com. For more information, reference the Licensing Guide PDF provided on the installation CD, as well as Citrix knowledgebase article CTX107213 located at http://support.citrix.com/article/CTX107213.

Cold Backup License Server

Creating a redundant license server is not required in most environments because of the long licensing grace period. The long licensing grace period makes network connectivity problems that result in license logon rejections unlikely. However, a backup license server can be created in case of long-term hardware failure. Follow these steps to back up the license server:

1. Duplicate the license server and its contents. Give the backup machine the same name as the active license server and store it off the network.

2. Store an additional license server on the network with a different server name. In this case, when the active license server fails, the Access Suite product is reconfigured to point to the new license server.

Remember these two key points:

▼ Because license files reference the server specified during allocation, the backup server must have the same name as the original license server

▲ Two license servers with the same name cannot be active on the network at the same time

IMPORTANT   The name of the server being used as the cold backup cannot be changed after installing the license server. Remember to rename the server first, and then install the license server components.

NOTE   The server name used for the license file is *case-sensitive*.

Archived License File

At a minimum, the license file should be archived to provide a basic level of redundancy. Archiving the license file provides the capability to recover from logical disasters, such as viruses or user error.

In the case of a license server failure, a new server can be provisioned within days. After installing the license server software and giving the backup server the same name as the original license server, the archived file can be placed on the scrver.

PLANNING FOR SITE FAILOVER

Site failure is the most costly and damaging failure XYZ can experience, but the Citrix access infrastructure that XYZ uses allows them to create a solution at a fraction of the cost when compared to other options.

Identifying a Backup Site and Recovery Model

XYZ's initial task is to select a disaster recovery site. One of the existing sites in Tampa Bay or Redmond could be selected because each has sufficient infrastructure to host a recovery site. The decision would be based solely on the potential disasters each site faced.

The analysis pointed out that Tampa Bay has a high likelihood of a single hurricane affecting both itself and Fort Lauderdale. The remaining location (Redmond, Washington) is a good choice for XYZ because it is relatively free from natural disaster. Also, a single disaster is not likely to affect both Fort Lauderdale and Redmond.

XYZ has the benefit of selecting a disaster recovery site from one of their corporate locations. If XYZ did not have a suitable existing location, they could consider using a third-party data center hosting facility.

If a failure occurred, Redmond needs the capacity to support the additional users from Fort Lauderdale and Tampa. The reverse is true as well. Fort Lauderdale needs enough capacity to host additional Redmond users in the case of a Redmond site failure.

For the recovery model, the disaster recovery team has to select between active-passive or active-active.

The *active-passive model* is one in which the disaster recovery data center is in a warm-standby mode until required. All users connect to one of the data centers. The remaining data center is unused until a failure occurs.

Active-active describes a disaster recovery environment in which the site designated as the disaster recovery data center is online and functions in conjunction with the primary data center. In this model, users connect locally to the site with the least latency.

XYZ selects the active-active recovery model based on the improved user experience due to reduced connection latency. The business requires a full disaster recovery plan that provides access to all corporate users even when one site is offline. Each site is fully redundant and has the capacity to service all users in the entire organization.

The Citrix Access Suite is only one piece of the redundancy and disaster recovery puzzle. The Access Suite helps make the planning easier. To have a complete solution, however, plans must be created for the following infrastructure components:

▼ Physical network infrastructure (routers, switches, and so on)

■ Directory Services (Active Directory, Novell eDirectory, LDAP)

■ Network services (DNS, DHCP, and so on)

■ Data storage and replication

■ Application access and management

▲ User access points

As you can see from this list, the Citrix Access Suite helps only with the last two items. For the purposes of this chapter, the assumption is that the XYZ Corp planning team already created well-defined plans for the first four items on the list given an active-active deployment. The following sections outline the decision-making process that XYZ goes through to deploy its Access Suite.

Citrix Presentation Server 4.0

As the foundation of the Access Suite, XYZ Corp must select a Presentation Server architecture that would stand up to a site failure and, at the same time, meet all of XYZ's disaster recovery requirements. With an active-active recovery model, Citrix recommends that a single farm be used to span the primary and disaster recovery site. XYZ has a redundant 100 Mbps connection between the two sites, so network connectivity is not an issue.

The first question to be answered when planning a multisite farm is this: How many servers does XYZ need to support all of its users? Based on server scalability tests, XYZ determines that each of their servers could support 125 users. Using this value, along with the requirement to support 60,000 users at each site, XYZ determines that it needs 480 servers in both Fort Lauderdale and Redmond.

Zone Design

The next task to complete is the creation of the zone structure. Citrix best practices dictate that XYZ should have two zones, one at each site. Two zones are used to reduce the amount of traffic going between each site. All IMA traffic between the two sites is communicated by the data collector in each zone. The zone names are FTL and RED to represent the Fort Lauderdale and Redmond sites.

Data Store

To provide support for site failover, XYZ has to choose a database that Presentation Server supports for replication. This means XYZ has the option of using either Microsoft SQL Server or Oracle 8*i* or greater. Because Microsoft SQL Server 2000 is the XYZ Corp standard, they select it as the database platform for the Data Store.

Database replication allows XYZ Corp to host a database server at each site, providing improved performance for most operations. The primary database resides in Fort Lauderdale and the replica in Redmond. In Fort Lauderdale, XYZ chooses to implement database clustering as an additional fault-tolerant solution to replication, thus providing confidence that their primary database server in Fort Lauderdale would only go down in the case of a network or site failure.

Replication allows two copies of the data store to be available—one at each site. Reads performed to the data store occur local to the site hosting the computers running Presentation Server. Because the IMA Service primarily performs read operations to the data store, this greatly improves performance, while decreasing network traffic across the WAN. For the data store, immediate updating transactional replication must be used. With the immediate-updating model of replication, only the publisher can write information directly to the data store. If a configuration setting is modified on one of the servers pointing to the subscriber, the change is first sent to the publisher. Using the two-phase commit model, the publisher locks the associated records and writes the change, and at the same time, notifies the subscriber to complete the transaction.

If the primary data store in Fort Lauderdale fails, the replica data store in Redmond has all the static farm information. This data store remains in read-only mode until it is promoted to become the new primary. While in read-only mode, no configuration changes can be made to the farm. Promoting the replica is necessary so the administrator can make changes to the farm again. Users are unaffected in a data store failure because the local host cache provides enough information for user connections to continue.

User Connections

Because the two sites are so geographically distant, XYZ users prefer to connect to the nearest site to maintain the highest performance standards for their users. The Zone Preference and Failover policy on Presentation Server enables them to meet that user expectation. Zone Preference and Failover gives administrators the capability to publish a single application on the farm that provides seamless failover to other zones in the case of disaster.

The Zone Preference and Failover policy sets an affinity based on user name, client name, or client IP address to determine the zone that is optimal for the user to connect to as defined by the administrator. During application resolution time, the data collector filters the list of available servers hosting the published application based on the client's preference setting and performs the resolution only in the primary zone. If the primary zone is unavailable, the client fails over to the next preferred zone.

NOTE Zone Preference and Failover is available only with Web Interface and Program Neighborhood Agent. Program Neighborhood Classic is not supported.

All internal corporate users are directed either to Redmond or Fort Lauderdale, depending on the IP address of their client device. All roaming corporate users are directed to a specific site based on their user name. The user-name policy filter is used for roaming users because it is difficult for the administrators to predict what the IP address will be for the roaming clients.

IMPORTANT The load management IP rule and Scheduler rule conflict with the Zone Preference and Failover policy. When using these rules, zone preference does not allow for failover because these rules take precedence.

Configuring Server Location

Another important design consideration is the server location options set in Program Neighborhood, Web Interface, and Program Neighborhood Agent clients. These settings are what ultimately give the users the ability to connect when the most preferred data collector fails. The following includes recommendations and guidelines for configuring the server location for the different clients.

Web Interface and Program Neighborhood Agent Client   The Web Interface and Program Neighborhood Agent configuration is the same when it comes to setting the server location. When configuring the Presentation Server list, the two most important settings are "Use the server list for load balancing" and "Bypass any failed server for." When "Use the server list for load balancing" is selected, Web Interface randomly selects a server from the list each time it attempts to contact the server farm. If communication with any of the servers fails, the failed server is removed from the list for the period of time specified in the "Bypass any failed server for" setting. When "Use server list for load balancing" is not selected, Web Interface always contacts the first server in the list. The only time it moves on to other servers in the list is when a failure occurs.

If business needs dictate that the Web Interface server should fail over to multiple sites, turn off "Use the server list for load balancing," so strict control can be maintained over which server site is contacted. If this setting is enabled, the Web Interface server can contact servers at other sites, which, in turn, has an adverse effect on resolution performance depending on the connection speed between sites. In this scenario, configure the server list in the following order:

▼   Data collector for closest zone

■   Backup data collector for closest zone

■   Second backup data collector in closest zone

■   Data collector in another zone/site

▲   Backup data collector in another zone/site

This approach balances redundancy requirements with performance requirements. For the best resolution performance, Web Interface first tries to contact the zone with which it has the best connectivity. After specifying a few servers in the local zone, servers in other zones and other sites can then be specified.

NOTE   When using the server location for fault tolerance, round-robin is not a recommended solution if the only address specified is the server list in the round-robin FQDN. This is primarily because the client may get directed to a server that is down.

Program Neighborhood Client

To understand how to correctly configure the Program Neighborhood client, an understanding of server location is necessary. The Program Neighborhood classic client has three different server location groups to configure (primary, backup1, and backup2) and two important settings in the user's Appsrv.ini file. The following settings are in the Appsrv.ini file located on the client:

```
BrowserRetry = 3
BrowserTimeout = 1000 (milliseconds)
```

When a client attempts to perform an application resolution, it first contacts all servers in the primary group. Then, it waits the amount of time specified by BrowserTimeout for one of the servers in the list to respond. Each server in the list is contacted three times. If the client fails to get a response, it moves to the backup1 group and tries all the servers in that group. Again, the client waits for the amount of time specified by the BrowserTimeout value. If no response occurs, the same process continues with the backup2 group. This entire iteration from primary to backup1 to backup2 is considered one resolution attempt. If no response is received, the client repeats this entire process for the number of retries specified in the BrowserRetry value. Based on the default settings previously shown, the client iterates through all the server groups three times.

In large environments, where resolution performance is of concern, list only one server per server location group when using the TCP/IP server location network protocol. This recommendation is made because all servers in a given group are contacted at the same time. If the client is configured with both server *A* and server *B* in the primary group, the client attempts a resolution by contacting both servers simultaneously. The client then takes the first response it gets back, thereby creating unnecessary network traffic.

For best performance, list the data collector in the primary group. The backup1 group should contain the address of the backup data collector and the backup2 group should be used as the "catch all" list with multiple servers that are unlikely to be offline, such as member servers in the closest zone or data collectors in other zones. Configuring the client in this manner provides the best response time and the least network traffic, and it still provides a fault-tolerant solution if an entire zone fails.

When using TCP+HTTP, this is not a concern because the client attempts to contact only one address at a time when multiple addresses are specified in the same group. The client does iterate through the list sequentially, however.

Client Connection Configuration

Figure 19-17 illustrates the architecture XYZ chooses to implement for its server farm. This can be used to help understand how the client behaves under normal circumstances and during a failure.

IMPORTANT   The load balancer being used for Web Interface is not explicitly shown in the picture.

The process varies, depending on the connection method being used. Several connection methods are discussed next.

Web Interface   The Web Interface server location list is configured based on the recommendations in the previous section and the server-list load balancing is turned off.
The server list is configured in the following order:

A.   Fort Lauderdale data collector

B.   Fort Lauderdale backup data collector

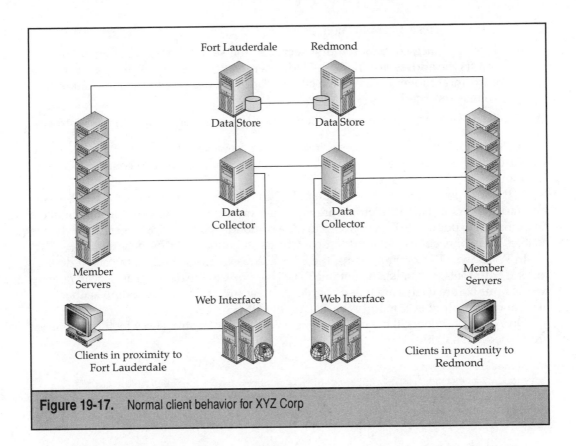

Figure 19-17.   Normal client behavior for XYZ Corp

C. Fort Lauderdale member server

D. Redmond data collector

E. Redmond backup data collector

The normal connection process for a user in proximity to Fort Lauderdale when using Web Interface is as follows:

1. The user opens a browser on a client device and enters the FQDN for the Fort Lauderdale Web Interface server, WIFTL.XYZ.COM.

2. The client authenticates to Web Interface.

3. Web Interface contacts the first server in the server location settings for Web Interface. In this case, the first server in the list is the local data collector in Fort Lauderdale.

4. The data collector returns a list of applications to which the user has access and displays it in the browser.

5. The user clicks an application.

6. Web Interface contacts the first server in the server location list again and requests the address for the least-loaded server. Because XYZ is using zone preference and failover based on the client IP address, a server in the Fort Lauderdale zone is returned.

7. The client now initiates an ICA connection to the server address that is returned.

A similar process applies to users in Redmond, however, they contact the Redmond Web Interface server using WIRED.XYZ.COM. All of their users also connect locally in Redmond.

In the situation where the Fort Lauderdale site is obliterated by a hurricane and the Web Interface servers in Fort Lauderdale are no longer online, the administrator must make a DNS change to point WIFTL.XYZ.COM to the Redmond Web Interface servers. This change enables user connectivity, but it may impact the users until their DNS cache expires.

In Windows DNS environments, the DNS addresses are cached on the client devices for one hour (3600 seconds), the default TTL. Therefore, in the default case, it can take up to one hour before clients are failed over to the new site. If this failover time is unacceptable, another option is to modify the TTL on the DNS server.

On Windows clients, there is also a registry value that controls how long DNS entries are cached. This value is

```
MaxCacheEntryTtlLimit
HKEY_LOCAL_MACHINE\SYSTEM\CurrentControlSet\Services\DNScache\Parameters
Default Value = 0x15180 (86400 seconds or 1 Day)
Data Type = REG_DWORD
Range = 0x1-0xFFFFFFFF (seconds)
```

IMPORTANT   Modifying this value affects the DNS cache for the entire client device. Consult Microsoft documentation before modifying this value to understand all the possible side effects.

Please see Figure 19-18 for an example of this DNSCache change and the impact this change has.

If the Fort Lauderdale site is down, the connection process works as follows:

1. The user opens a browser on the client device and enters the FQDN for the Fort Lauderdale Web Interface server, WIFTL.XYZ.COM.

2. The DNS server returns the IP address of the Web Interface server in Redmond.

3. The client connects to the Redmond Web Interface server.

4. Web Interface contacts the first server in the server location settings for Web Interface. In this case, the first server in the list is the local data collector in Redmond.

5. The data collector returns a list of applications to which the user has access and displays it in the browser.

6. The user clicks an application.

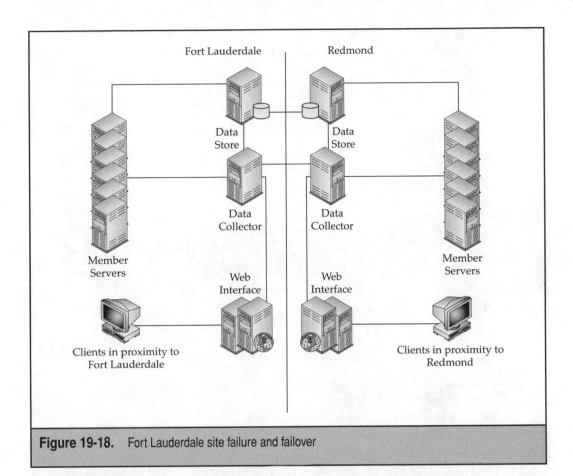

Figure 19-18.   Fort Lauderdale site failure and failover

7. Web Interface contacts the first server in the server location list and requests the address for the least-loaded server. Because XYZ is using zone preference and failover based on the client IP address, the data collector attempts to connect the user to Fort Lauderdale. Because all Fort Lauderdale servers are offline, the data collector uses Redmond, which is the backup site.

8. The ICA connection now launches to the server address that is returned.

Client Connections with Global Server Load Balancing

XYZ is using the two fully qualified domain names to point to each site because its load balancers do not support global server load balancing. If XYZ purchases a load balancer with the capabilities of a Citrix NetScaler Application Switch, they could use a single Web Interface fully qualified domain name for all users in the organization. The global server load-balancing option on the Citrix NetScaler Application Switch allows user

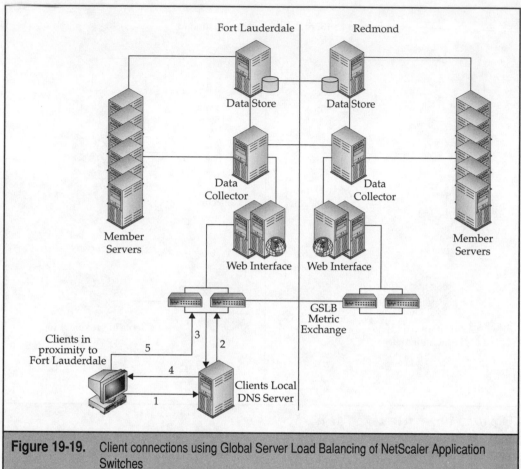

Figure 19-19.   Client connections using Global Server Load Balancing of NetScaler Application Switches

traffic to be distributed automatically among the sites. Users can be directed statically to a specific site or they can be directed dynamically to the closest site, based on the round-trip time. When a site failure occurs, all traffic is routed from the failed site to the site that is still online. Figure 19-19 is an example of a client connecting through NetScaler Application Switches using the Global Server Load-Balancing option.

The connection process using global server load balancing works as follows:

1. The user opens a browser on the client device and enters the FQDN for the Web Interface Server, WI.XYZ.COM. This request is sent to the local DNS server.

2. The client's local DNS server gets the IP address of the XYZ corporate DNS server from a root DNS server. The client's local DNS server contacts the IP address returned by the root DNS server. This returned address is the address of the NetScaler DNS proxy.

3. Before resolving the name request, the NetScaler machine has to calculate the closest site. It does this either statically with a predefined lookup table or dynamically based on the round-trip time between the sites and the client's local DNS server. Based on the NetScaler measurements, the Fort Lauderdale site has the shortest round-trip time. The IP address of the Fort Lauderdale Web Interface server is returned to the client's local DNS server.

4. The client's local DNS server returns the IP address to the client.

5. The client now connects to the Web Interface server. The NetScaler Application Switch selects the particular Web Interface server, based on the configured load-balancing method.

6. Web Interface contacts the first server in the server location settings for Web Interface. In this case, the first server in the list is the local data collector in Fort Lauderdale.

7. The data collector returns a list of applications to which the user has access and displays it in the browser.

8. The user clicks an application.

9. Web Interface contacts the first server in the server location list again and requests the address for the least-loaded server. Because XYZ is using zone preference and failover, the data collector attempts to connect the user to Fort Lauderdale

10. The ICA connection now launches to the returned server address.

Figure 19-20 is similar to Figure 19-19 but is an example of an actual "outage." If the Fort Lauderdale site is down, the connection process works as follows:

1. The user opens a browser on the client device and enters the FQDN for the Web Interface Server, WI.XYZ.COM. This request is sent to the local DNS server.

2. The client's local DNS server gets the IP address of the XYZ corporate DNS server from a root DNS server. The client's local DNS server contacts the IP address returned by the root DNS server. This returned address is the address of the NetScaler DNS proxy in Fort Lauderdale.

3. Because the Fort Lauderdale NetScaler switch is offline, the client's local DNS server tries the backup XYZ DNS server, which is the Redmond NetScaler switch.

4. Before resolving the name request, the NetScaler machine has to calculate the closest site. It does this either statically with a predefined lookup table or dynamically, based on the round-trip time between the sites and the client's local DNS server. Based on the NetScaler measurements, the Fort Lauderdale site has the shortest round-trip time, but the Fort Lauderdale site is offline. Because Fort Lauderdale is offline, NetScaler returns the IP address of the Redmond Web Interface server to the client's local DNS server.

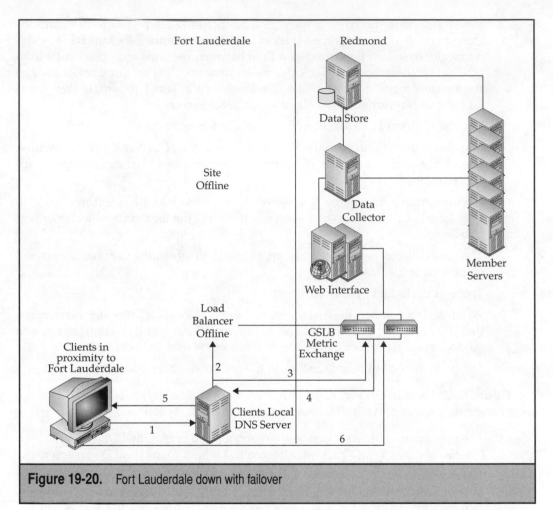

Figure 19-20.   Fort Lauderdale down with failover

5. The client's local DNS server returns the IP address to the client.

6. The client now connects to the Web Interface server. The NetScaler Application Switch selects the particular Web Interface server based on the configured load-balancing method.

7. Web Interface contacts the first server in the server location settings for Web Interface. In this case, the first server in the list is the local data collector in Redmond.

8. The data collector returns a list of applications to which the user has access and displays it in the browser.

9. The user clicks an application.

10. Web Interface contacts the first server in the server location list again and requests the address for the least-loaded server. Because XYZ is using zone preference and failover, the data collector attempts to connect the user to Fort Lauderdale. Because the Fort Lauderdale site is offline, the data collector chooses the backup zone, which is Redmond.

11. The ICA connection now launches the returned address to the Redmond server.

Program Neighborhood Agent   The connection process for the Program Neighborhood Agent is similar to the process described for Web Interface. If a failure occurs with the Web Interface server, the previously outlined process also works for Program Neighborhood Agent.

Program Neighborhood Classic   XYZ Corp does not use the Program Neighborhood Classic client in its environment because it has no support for Zone Preference and Failover. User connections cannot be routed to specific sites using Program Neighborhood Classic.

Resource Manager Configuration

One final point of planning for the XYZ team is deciding how to implement Resource Manager. (See Figure 19-21.) Resource Manager is used primarily by the IT staff to monitor and troubleshoot their Presentation Server environment. Based on the planning meetings, no additional requirements are placed on Resource Manager, primarily because the Resource Manager data is not being used for anything critical.

As you can see in Figure 19-21, all Resource Manager components reside in the Fort Lauderdale data center. In this type of deployment, the member servers from Redmond communicate with the database connection server. Both the primary and backup farm metric servers are located in Fort Lauderdale. If the Fort Lauderdale site fails, XYZ has to reconfigure both the primary and backup farm metric servers to the Redmond datacenter. This task is accomplished using the Presentation Server Console in Redmond. Of course, before this is done, personnel must first promote the data store in Redmond to primary, so changes can be made to the farm.

Other Options

In situations where multiple farms in each site are required for redundancy, the Presentation Server configuration is straightforward. Create a single server farm at each of the sites following Citrix's best practices for farm creation. To ease failover, each of these farms can be configured identically, including applications, application users, and all other resources required by the server farm. Connections are routed to each farm by using a separate Web Interface server for each farm. Any of the Web Interface redundancy solutions can be used to split users between the two farms. Follow the Web Interface redundancy recommendations in case of a failure where all users need to be routed from one site to the other.

This type of setup can be run as either active-active or active-passive. The main difference between the two is this: the active-passive setup has all Web Interface servers pointing to a single site until a failure occurs.

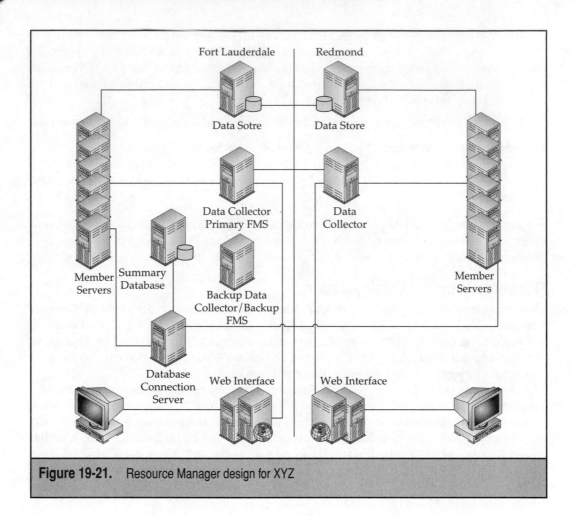

Figure 19-21.   Resource Manager design for XYZ

Citrix Password Manager 4.0

To alleviate a large number of Help desk calls, XYZ Corp uses Password Manager to simplify user password management. For the Password Manager implementation, XYZ decides to use the shared folder method for the central store. XYZ has strict rules for its Active Directory deployment and cannot modify the Active Directory schema to store the Password Manager data.

Central Store

XYZ decides to host a central store at each of the sites. XYZ has a fast stable link between the two sites and users generally connect to either Fort Lauderdale or Redmond. If XYZ had a large number of users who needed to connect to both sites simultaneously, while running the same application at each site, a single central store would be chosen. Because of DFS conflict-resolution rules, in scenarios where the same user is connected to multiple central stores and changes the same data simultaneously, data corruption can occur.

To provide redundancy if the site fails, XYZ is using Microsoft's DFS, which fits in well with its corporate infrastructure. XYZ is already using DFS for existing data replication needs, so the additional configuration is limited to the creation of another share point. The Password Manager agents are all configured to point to the DFS share located at \\XYZ.COM\citrixsync$. The DFS logic connects clients to the closest available central store point. When a failure occurs, all users are directed to one of the redundant DFS servers.

Password Manager Service

To ensure availability of the Password Manager service, XYZ is using load-balanced servers at each of the sites. The fully qualified domain names of the load balancers set up at Fort Lauderdale and Redmond are MPMSFTL.XYZ.COM and MPMSRED.XYZ.COM, respectively. The Password Manager agent on each user's device is configured to point to the closest Password Manager server. This is provided during the Password Manager agent installation.

Because XYZ has configured multiple Password Manager servers, it is important that all servers have the same public and private keys, as well as the same key recovery secret. XYZ accomplishes this by installing a single server, configuring it correctly, documenting the settings, and testing the server. After successfully testing the service, XYZ follows the backup procedure documented in the Password Manager component redundancy section to export the signing keys and key recovery secret. Additional Password Manager servers are then installed and configured with the same settings as the first one. Per Citrix's documentation, the key restoration process is then used on the new servers, allowing the servers to encrypt and unencrypt the service data.

If one of the sites fails, the administrator has to reconfigure the FQDN for the failed server to the service running in the other site. For example, if the Password Manager servers are destroyed in Fort Lauderdale, the administrator needs to reconfigure MPMSFTL .XYZ.COM to point to the IP address of the Password Manager server in Redmond. As with other types of DNS changes, the administrator has to wait for the DNS cache on the client devices to time-out. When the cache times out, the Password Manager agents automatically connect to the service running at the other site.

NOTE Attention must be paid to the DNS time-to-live values. Even though the IP address for the DNS name is changed on the server side, the locally cached client values must first expire before the client can use the new address.

IMPORTANT If XYZ is using the global server load-balancing options provided by the Citrix NetScaler Application Switch, the fully qualified domain names on the DNS servers do not need to be reconfigured.

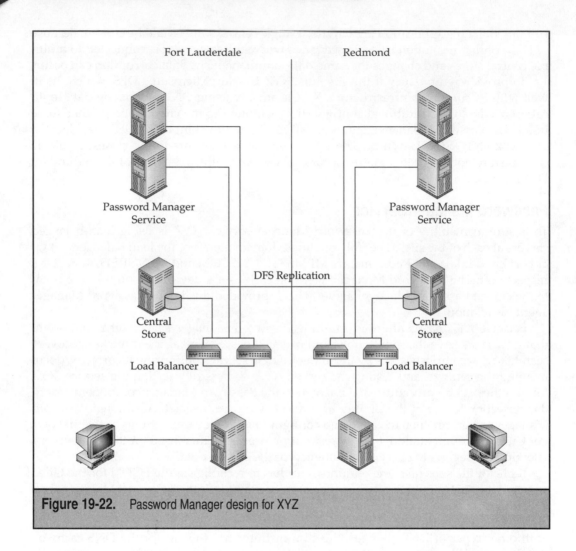

Figure 19-22. Password Manager design for XYZ

Figure 19-22 illustrates the way in which XYZ architected its Password Manager setup.

Remote Presentation Server Users Through Access Gateway 4.1

To deploy corporate applications to remote employees, XYZ uses the Access Gateway to control access into the corporate network. XYZ ensures Access Gateway redundancy by using a hardware load balancer at each site. The load balancer is not represented in Figure 19-23, but it is being used to load balance the Access Gateway and Web Interface servers at each site. For more details about setup recommendations for the load balancer, see the section on Access Gateway redundancy recommendations.

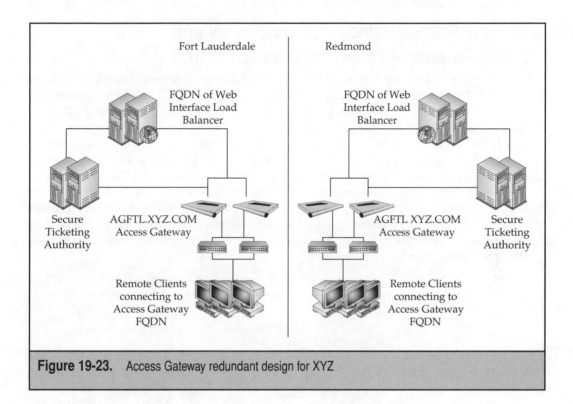

Figure 19-23. Access Gateway redundant design for XYZ

XYZ distributes the load between the two sites by training users to connect to their closest site. The FQDN of the load-balanced Access Gateway machine in Fort Lauderdale is AGFTL.XYZ.COM and the FQDN in Redmond is AGRED.XYZ.COM. For the site failure to be seamless, the certificates on the Access Gateway machines must be configured correctly. XYZ wants to support failover from one site to the other using the same name, so *.XYZ.COM is used for the Access Gateway certificate names.

If a site failure occurs, a DNS change is required for the FQDN of the Access Gateway machine in the failed site. For example, if an earthquake obliterated the Redmond data center, the administrator needs to change the AGRED.XYZ.COM DNS entry to point to the Access Gateway servers in Fort Lauderdale. This change has no impact on users beyond waiting for their DNS cache to expire.

NOTE Attention must be paid to the DNS time-to-live values. Even though the IP address for the DNS name is changed on the server-side, the locally cached client values must first expire before the client can use the new address.

IMPORTANT If XYZ is using the global server load-balancing options provided by the Citrix NetScaler Application Switch, the fully qualified domain names on the DNS servers do not need to be reconfigured.

Remote User Access Using Secure Gateway and Access Gateway—Advanced Access Control

XYZ uses Secure Gateway and Access Gateway–Advanced Access Control to provide secure clientless access to internal applications and web content for all their partners and suppliers. To meet the defined recovery objective, the site failover plan that XYZ chose requires them to have identical Secure Gateway and Access Gateway–Advanced Access Control environments at each site. At each site, the access farm should point only to resources at the specific site. For example, the Fort Lauderdale access farm should point only to computers running Presentation Server, Active Directory, and Exchange servers in Fort Lauderdale. This configuration step is important, so the access farm does not rely on any resources at the other site. If a site failure occurs, everything is contained to one site. This approach also requires the XYZ administrators configure each access farm to be identical, including creation of identical roles for all users at both sites. Figure 19-24 outlines the setup that XYZ implemented.

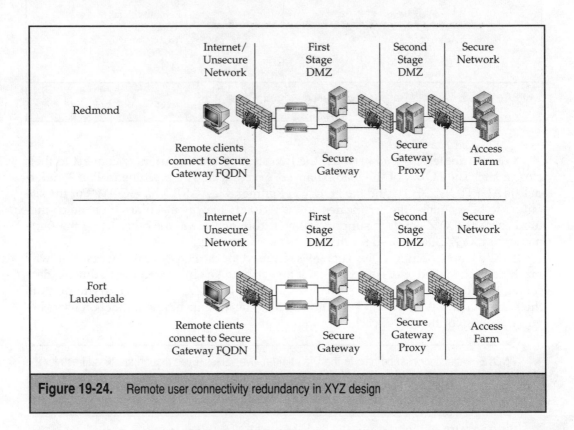

Figure 19-24.   Remote user connectivity redundancy in XYZ design

XYZ uses redundant hardware load balancers at each site. For more details about the setup recommendations for the load balancer, reference the section on component redundancy recommendations.

XYZ distributes the load between the two sites by having users connect to their local site. The Secure Gateway FQDN in Fort Lauderdale is SGFTL.XYZ.COM, while the Redmond one is SGRED.XYZ.COM. The XYZ user population is trained to connect to the site closest to them.

When setting up the Secure Gateway servers with load balancers, remember to use the proper certificate names. All Secure Gateway servers in the Fort Lauderdale site are using a certificate with the same FQDN as the load balancer. This configuration is true also for the Redmond site.

If a site failure occurs, the administrator has to change the FQDN for one site to point to the other. If the Fort Lauderdale data center goes down, the administrator has to change the SGFTL.XYZ.COM DNS entry to the IP address of the load-balanced Secure Gateway servers in Redmond. Because XYZ is using only the Navigation User interface on the Access Gateway–Advanced Access Control farm, users are not impacted. This user interface has no user-specific settings, so users are presented with the same UI, regardless of which side hosts the connection. If XYZ was using the Access Center interface, users would notice some changes because their user-specific customizations would not be on the new access farm. Users would still have access to all the same information and business tasks, but their background or CDA order might look different.

NOTE   Attention must be paid to the DNS time-to-live values. Even though the IP address for the DNS name is changed on the server side, the locally cached client values must first expire before the client uses the new address.

IMPORTANT   If XYZ was using the global server load-balancing options provided by the Citrix NetScaler Application Switch, the fully qualified domain names on the DNS servers do not need to be reconfigured.

Citrix License Server

XYZ hosts their corporate license server in the Fort Lauderdale data center. All their Access Suite products at both sites connect to this license server. The license server name is LICSERVER.XYZ.COM. With the licensing grace period, all the Access Suite products have full functionality for 30 days. (See Figure 19-25.)

For license server redundancy, XYZ created a cold backup of the license server at the Redmond site. This *cold backup* is created by cloning the original license server to another server. This server is offline at the Redmond site. In the event of a Fort Lauderdale site

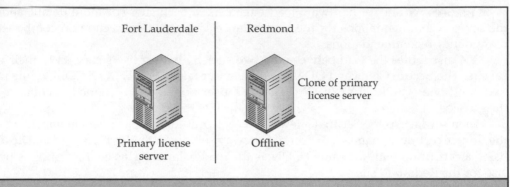

Figure 19-25.   Redundant license server design for XYZ

failure, the cold backup is put on the network and brought online. LICSERVER.XYZ
.COM is modified to point to the license server now online in Redmond. As the DNS
entries time-out, all the Access Suite products connect to the license server in Redmond.
Because the same name is used, no reconfiguration is necessary on any of the Access
Suite products.

IMPORTANT   The name of the server being used as the cold backup cannot be changed after
installing the license server. Remember to rename the server first, and then install the license server
components.

Complete Design

Figure 19-26 shows the complete XYZ Access suite architecture. To simplify the diagram,
the firewalls and network load balancers are not shown.

During normal operation, four different types of communication occur cross-site.

▼   **Presentation Server**   IMA data collector communication and member server to
database connection server traffic

■   **Presentation Server**   Data store transactional replication traffic associated with
the SQL Server or Oracle data being replicated across the network

■   **Password Manager**   Central store distributed file-system replication traffic

▲   **License Server**   Access Suite products communicate with the license server for
license check-outs and heartbeats

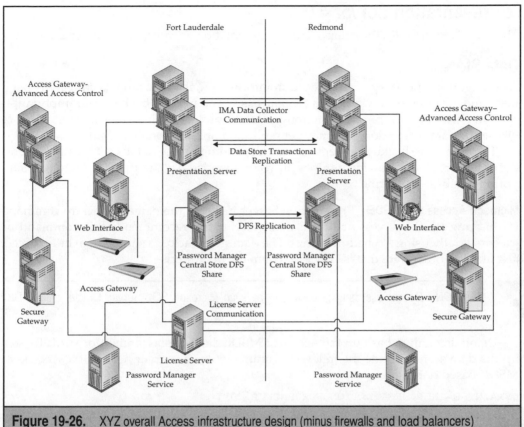

Figure 19-26. XYZ overall Access infrastructure design (minus firewalls and load balancers)

DEFINING A COMPONENT BACKUP PLAN

The modern computing world has many logical errors that can cause potential downtime. XYZ immediately identifies threats from viruses, hackers, and disgruntled employees. It also understands that logic errors can come in the form of data corruption, such as a database that includes corrupted data.

In addition to these logic errors, the possibility exists of a user error causing failure. User errors can take many different forms, such as an administrator who accidentally deletes vital information.

XYZ concludes that these logical and user errors are easy to prevent with a well-thought-out backup plan that includes regularly scheduled backups, along with offsite backup archival.

Included in the following sections are the Citrix recommended backup guidelines for the Access Suite that XYZ used to create their plan.

Citrix Presentation Server 4.0

The following includes the components of Presentation Server that should be backed up.

Data Store

As the central repository of all static farm information, the data store is crucial to operations and must be backed up on a regular basis. The regular backups are important—even in clustered or replicated environments—to protect against logical errors, such as viruses or data corruption, that may get replicated unintentionally.

The data-store backup procedures vary depending on the database type used to host the data store. The following outlines the recommended backup procedures for the supported database platforms.

Microsoft Access and MSDE   Presentation Server includes the dsmaint backup command for backing up the Access or MSDE data store. Citrix recommends this command be executed daily using a scheduler script. The data store backups should then be archived, just like any other data that is critical to company operations.

> *CAUTION*   Do not use dsmaint backup to back up Microsoft SQL Server, Oracle, or IBM DB2 databases.

Using dsmaint to back up the Access or MSDE data store is straightforward. To back up the data store, execute the following command on the server hosting the Access- or MSDE-based data store:

```
DSMAINT BACKUP DESTINATION FOR BACKUP COPY
```

> *NOTE*   When using MSDE, this command uses a default OSQL script to back up the database. If creating customized OSQL scripts for backup of the MSDE-based data store, refer to the following Microsoft article for further details: http://support.microsoft.com/default.aspx?scid=241397.

Microsoft SQL, Oracle, or IBM DB2   These third-party databases do not require any special commands to be executed on the computers running Presentation Server. When using a Microsoft SQL Server, Oracle, or IBM DB2 data store consult the database documentation for scheduling automated backups of the data store. In most cases, daily backup is sufficient to prevent loss of farm data.

Summary Database

The backup schedule for the Resource Manager summary database is highly dependent on how the data in the summary database is being used. In most instances, the summary database is used only to look back in time a few weeks. In these types of instances, it may not be cost-effective to back up the summary database. In other situations, where the summary database is used for billing customers based on farm usage, backing up the database is of great importance.

Consult the Oracle and Microsoft SQL Server documentation for details about implementing a scheduled backup routine.

Web Interface

With Web Interface 4.0, several different options exist for saving the configuration information for Web Interface. Before discussing the backup procedures, understanding the differences between these two options is necessary. The two configuration methods offered when creating a new site are local configuration files and centralized configuration.

The *local configuration option* is similar to previous versions of Web Interface and it stores the configuration information directly on the Web Interface server. Local configuration allows the editing of the configuration information through the Access Suite Console or by manually editing the configuration files on the Web Interface server.

Centralized configuration is new for Web Interface 4.0. The *centralized configuration option* stores all the Web Interface configuration information in the farm data store. Some benefits of this new configuration method are

▼ Administration of UNIX Web Interface servers using the Access Suite console

▲ Capability to group Web Interface sites together, so multiple sites can be kept synchronized, which is especially useful when using hardware load balancers to keep each Web Interface site identical

To transfer the information to the data store, Web Interface must point at a configuration server. This *configuration server* is any server in the farm that is running the XML Service. Citrix recommends that multiple configuration servers be specified for each site that is created. Good candidates for configuration servers are backup data collectors, farm metric servers, and data collectors or other highly available farm servers.

Local Configuration

To back up the local configuration information, the Access Suite Console provides a method to export the site configuration for Web Interface, which can be completed by following these steps.

1. Load the Access Suite Console and run discovery for the Web Interface server.

2. Expand the Web Interface node and select the site to back up.

3. In Other Tasks, select the Export Configuration option.

4. Select Export Configuration and specify a location for the file.

Centralized Configuration

When using this method, all configuration information is stored in the data store. Because everything is in the data store, regular backups of the data store are important. Reference the section on data-store backup for recommendations about backup procedures.

In addition, for additional redundancy, the site information can be exported to a file using the Access Suite Console. To complete this task, follow the instructions provided in the previous section, "Local Configuration."

In addition to saving the Web Interface configuration information, be sure to back up all non-Citrix information as well. This information includes, but is not limited to:

▼ SSL Certificates

■ Third-party software, such as RSA SecureID or SafeWord

▲ Web Interface customizations

Citrix Access Gateway 4.1

The backup process for the Access Gateway saves all the configuration settings, including uploaded certificates, licenses, and portal pages.

To back up the Access Gateway configuration, perform the following steps:

1. In the Access Gateway Administration Tool, click the Access Gateway Cluster tab.

2. On the Administration tab, by "Save the current configuration," click Save Configuration.

3. Save the file, named config.restore, to the computer.

The entire Access Gateway configuration—including system files, uploaded licenses, and uploaded server certificates—is saved.

Citrix Password Manager 4.0

Included here are the components of Password Manager that should be backed up.

Central Store Active Directory   When using Active Directory as the central store, all Password Manager data is stored within the Active Directory database itself. To back up the Password Manager data, follow Microsoft's best practices for backing up Active Directory data.

Central Store Shared Folder   When using a shared folder as the central store for Password Manager, the backup procedures are the same as with normal files and data. Remember to use a software backup package that stores the NTFS permissions, as well as the data, to the subfolders.

Password Manager Service

When using Data Integrity and Automatic Key Recovery, the Password Manager certificates and key recovery secrets must be properly backed up. Use the following procedure to back up the necessary data from the Password Manager service.

▼ Record all settings made when the Service Configuration Tool is run to set up the service. These settings are necessary when configuring the Password Manager service on a replacement server.

■ Copy the certificates to a secure location by following these steps:

  ▼ Copy C:\Program Files\Citrix\MetaFrame Password Manager\Service\ Certificates\PrivateKeyCert.cert to a shared drive.

  ▲ Copy C:\Program Files\Citrix\MetaFrame Password Manager\Service\ Certificates\PublicKeyCert.cert to a shared drive.

▲ If the Automatic Key Recovery module is being used, export the key recovery secret to a secure location by following these steps:

  1. From a command prompt, go to the default location for the back tool: C:\Program Files\Citrix\MetaFrame Password Manager\Service\Tools.

  2. Type **ctxmovekeyrecoverydata.exe –export** *shared drive file name*.

  3. Enter a password of your choice when prompted. Make note of the password.

NOTE   For security purposes, store the certificates and the exported key recovery secret in a secure place.

Setting Up a Distributed File System for Citrix Password Manager

Citrix recommends creating a DFS structure for Citrix Password Manager before you deploy Password Manager to your environment. Follow these steps to create a domain DFS root on Windows Server 2003:

1. Create a file synchronization point in the designated servers. Select a server to be used as Password Manager's file synchronization point and run the ctxfilesyncprep.exe utility. By default, this utility creates the directory c:\ citrixsync on drive *C* and shares it as \\%servername%\citrixsync$. Assign the proper permissions. You can use the /Path and /share command-line parameter to set your own directory and name your own share. Citrix recommends creating an administrative share to which nonadministrators do not have direct access.

2. Select another server also to be used as file synchronization point and repeat step 1. Make sure the share name is the same on all the servers.

3. After you configure all the servers to be used as file synchronization points, create the DFS structure.

4. Open the MMC snap-in for the DFS on a Windows Server 2003, typically located in Start|Programs|Administrative Tools|Distributed File System. Make sure you launch the MMC snap-in under the security environment of Domain Administrator.

5. Right-click the Distributed File System icon, select New Root, and click Next.

6. Select Domain Root and click Next.

7. Select the host domain of the DFS root and click Next.

8. Select the name of the server where you created the file share for the DFS root and click Next.

9. Enter the share name exactly like the name you created in step 1. If the share name you enter is different from the one you created in step 1, the DFS creates a new share on the existing share that will not have the necessary permissions set. Click Next.

10. In the shared folder, browse to the folder you used to create the share in step 1. Click Next, and then click Finish.

11. Right-click the DFS root you just created and select New Root Target.

12. Type the server name where you already created the file synchronization point share and click Next. Click Finish.

13. Repeat steps 11 and 12 if you want to add more root replicas.

14. Right-click the DFS root name and select Start Replication.

15. Select the necessary replication topology, and then click Next. For the appropriate replication topology, refer to the Microsoft DFS documents.

16. Click Finish.

Additional Information About Distributed File System and File Replication Services

Replica Synchronization is managed by the File Replication Service (FRS), which operates on Windows Active Directory domain controllers and member servers. *FRS* is a multithreaded, multimaster replication engine that replicates system policies, logon scripts, fault-tolerant DFS root, and child node replicas.

In Active Directory deployments, the *Knowledge Consistency Checker* is responsible for building NTDS connection objects to form a well-connected topology between domain controllers in the domain and the forest.

RepAdmin.exe is a utility available in the support.cab archive of the Windows 2000 Servers' installation CD. *RepAdmin.exe* can be used to check if replication is taking place using the default intervals for intersite replication: once every three hours between domain controllers in different sites (the minimum is 15 minutes).

FRS replicates entire files in sequential order, according to when files are closed, so the entire file is replicated even if you change only a single byte in the file. Changes for intersite replication are set using a three-second aging cache, so only the last iteration of a file that is constantly modified is sent to the replica members. Five minutes is the maximum replication value for servers hosting replicas, but it can be seconds if the server is not overwhelmed.

The following articles about setting up and tuning FRS may be useful for administrators:

▼   "Description of the FRS Replication Protocol, Notification, and Schedule for DFS Content"

http://support.microsoft.com/default.aspx?scid=kb;en-us;220938&Product= win2000

▲   "FRS Builds Full-Mesh Replication Topology for Replicated DFS ROOT and Child Replicas"

http://support.microsoft.com/default.aspx?scid=kb;en-us;224512&Product= win2000

Citrix Access Gateway–Advanced Access Control 4.0

All configuration data for Access Gateway–Advanced Access Control is stored in the database server. Consult the Microsoft SQL Server documentation for scheduling automated backups of the database server. In most cases, daily backup is sufficient to prevent loss of farm data.

Citrix Secure Gateway

The Secure Gateway server is backed up by archiving the configuration file and the server certification.

To back up Secure Gateway server configuration, back up the httpd.conf file located in the %Program Files%\Citrix\Secure Gateway\conf\ directory to a safe location.

To back up Secure Gateway server certificate, follow these steps:

1.   Log on to the system as an administrator.

2.   Click Start, and then click Run.

3.   In Open, type **mmc**, and then click OK.

4.   From the File menu, select Add/Remove Snap-in, and then click Add.

5.   Under Snap-in, double-click Certificates.

6.   Select Computer Account, and then click Next. The Select Computer dialog box appears.

7.   Select Local Computer and click Finish.

8.   Click Close, and then click OK.

9.   In the console tree, click Certificates, click Personal, and then click Certificates. A list of available certificates appears in the right pane.

10.   In the Details pane, click the certificate for export.

11.   From the Action menu, click All Tasks, and then click Export. The Certificate Export Wizard screen appears. Click Next.

12. Select "Yes, export the private key."

13. When prompted, provide a password for the private key. This password is necessary to restore the key on a new server.

IMPORTANT The server certificate should be exported in PKCS #12 (Personal Information Exchange Syntax Standard) format. This standard specifies a portable format for storing or transporting a user's private keys and certificates.

14. Follow the instructions in the Certificate Export Wizard to export the certificate.

With the configuration file and server certificate backed up, a new server can be brought online quickly in the event of server failure.

Citrix License Server

The license file must be archived to provide redundancy. Archiving the license file provides the capability to recover from logical disasters, such as viruses or user error.

If a license server fails, a new server can be provisioned within days. After renaming the server to the original license server name and installing the license server software, place the archived file on the server.

IMPORTANT The name of the server being used as the cold backup cannot be changed after installing the license server. Remember to rename the server first, and then install the license server components.

CONCLUSION

Citrix Access infrastructure should be a critical part of any institution's Business Continuity/Disaster Recovery solution. The Citrix Access infrastructure addresses multiple facets of business continuity, ranging from simple interruptions due to system upgrades, local power outage, or data corruption to more dramatic outages due to natural or man-made disasters. With Citrix Access infrastructure, server processing and utilization can be easily balanced across multiple server farms or even data centers.

Displaced workers can continue operating from another backup location or from their homes. Access to applications and information can be redirected instantaneously to backup or alternate server farms. IT staff can focus on restoring the core business, versus configuring networks, PCs, and applications across a geographically dispersed workplace.

By following the guidelines and recommendations in this chapter, XYZ's Access Suite implementation is now in place and protected against hardware failures, data corruption, user error, and site failure.

PART III

Appendices

APPENDIX A

Error Messages

This section provides a listing of IMA error codes and event log (*imamsgs.dll*) error messages intended to help in troubleshooting and resolving problems with Presentation Server.

IMA ERROR CODES

Table A-1 lists the IMA service error codes that might appear in the Event Viewer.

Hex Value	Signed Value	Unsigned Value	Mnemonic
00000000h	0	0	IMA_RESULT_SUCCESS
00000001h	1	1	IMA_RESULT_OPERATION_INCOMPLETE
00000002h	2	2	IMA_RESULT_CALL_NEXT_HOOK
00000003h	3	3	IMA_RESULT_DISCARD_MESSAGE
00000004h	4	4	IMA_RESULT_CREATED_NEW
00000005h	5	5	IMA_RESULT_FOUND_EXISTING
00000009h	9	9	IMA_RESULT_CONNECTION_IDLE
00130001h	1245185	1245185	IMA_RESULT_DS_NOT_INSTALLED
00130002h	1245186	1245186	IMA_RESULT_SECURITY_INFO_INCOMPLETE
002D0001h	2949121	2949121	IMA_RESULT_ALREADY_MASTER
80000001h	−2147483647	2147483649	IMA_RESULT_FAILURE
80000002h	−2147483646	2147483650	IMA_RESULT_NO_MEMORY
80000003h	−2147483645	2147483651	IMA_RESULT_INVALID_ARG
80000004h	−2147483644	2147483652	IMA_RESULT_UNKNOWN_MESSAGE
80000005h	−2147483643	2147483653	IMA_RESULT_DESTINATION_UNREACHABLE

Table A-1.   IMA Error Codes

Hex Value	Signed Value	Unsigned Value	Mnemonic
80000006h	−2147483642	2147483654	IMA_RESULT_REFERENCE_COUNT_NOT_ZERO
80000007h	−2147483641	2147483655	IMA_RESULT_ENTRY_NOT_FOUND
80000008h	−2147483640	2147483656	IMA_RESULT_NETWORK_FAILURE
80000009h	−2147483639	2147483657	IMA_RESULT_NOT_IMPLEMENTED
8000000Ah	−2147483638	2147483658	IMA_RESULT_INVALID_MESSAGE
8000000Bh	−2147483637	2147483659	IMA_RESULT_TIMEOUT
8000000Ch	−2147483636	2147483660	IMA_RESULT_POINTER_IS_NULL
8000000Dh	−2147483635	2147483661	IMA_RESULT_UNINITIALIZED
8000000Eh	−2147483634	2147483662	IMA_RESULT_FINDITEM_FAILURE
8000000Fh	−2147483633	2147483663	IMA_RESULT_CREATEPOOL_FAILURE
80000010h	−2147483632	2147483664	IMA_RESULT_SUBSYS_NOT_FOUND
80000013h	−2147483629	2147483667	IMA_RESULT_PS_UNINITIALIZED
80000014h	−2147483628	2147483668	IMA_RESULT_REGMAPFAIL
80000015h	−2147483627	2147483669	IMA_RESULT_DEST_TOO_SMALL
80000016h	−2147483626	2147483670	IMA_RESULT_ACCESS_DENIED
80000017h	−2147483625	2147483671	IMA_RESULT_NOT_SHUTTING_DOWN
80000018h	−2147483624	2147483672	IMA_RESULT_MUSTLOAD_FAILURE
80000019h	−2147483623	2147483673	IMA_RESULT_CREATELOCK_FAILURE
8000001Ah	−2147483622	2147483674	IMA_RESULT_SHUTDOWN_FAILURE
8000001Ch	−2147483620	2147483676	IMA_RESULT_SENDWAIT_FAILURE

Table A-1.   IMA Error Codes (*Continued*)

Hex Value	Signed Value	Unsigned Value	Mnemonic
8000001Dh	−2147483619	2147483677	IMA_RESULT_NO_COLLECTORS
8000001Eh	−2147483618	2147483678	IMA_RESULT_UPDATED
8000001Fh	−2147483617	2147483679	IMA_RESULT_NO_CHANGE
80000020h	−2147483616	2147483680	IMA_RESULT_LEGACY_NOT_ENABLED
80000021h	−2147483615	2147483681	IMA_RESULT_VALUE_ALREADY_CREATED
80000022h	−2147483614	2147483682	IMA_RESULT_UID_EXCEEDED_BOUNDS
80000023h	−2147483613	2147483683	IMA_RESULT_NO_EVENTS
80000024h	−2147483612	2147483684	IMA_RESULT_NOT_FOUND
80000025h	−2147483611	2147483685	IMA_RESULT_ALREADY_EXISTS
80000026h	−2147483610	2147483686	IMA_RESULT_GROUP_ALREADY_EXISTS
80000027h	−2147483609	2147483687	IMA_RESULT_NOT_A_GROUP
80000028h	−2147483608	2147483688	IMA_RESULT_GROUP_DIR_ACCESS_FAILURE
80000029h	−2147483607	2147483689	IMA_RESULT_EOF
8000002Ah	−2147483606	2147483690	IMA_RESULT_REGISTRY_ERROR
8000002Bh	−2147483605	2147483691	IMA_RESULT_DSN_OPEN_FAILURE
8000002Ch	−2147483604	2147483692	IMA_RESULT_REMOVING_PSSERVER
8000002Dh	−2147483603	2147483693	IMA_RESULT_NO_REPLY_SENT
8000002Eh	−2147483602	2147483694	IMA_RESULT_PLUGIN_FAILED_VERIFY
8000002Fh	−2147483601	2147483695	IMA_RESULT_FILE_NOT_FOUND
80000030h	−2147483600	2147483696	IMA_RESULT_PLUGIN_ENTRY_NOT_FOUND
80000031h	−2147483599	2147483697	IMA_RESULT_CLOSED

Table A-1.   IMA Error Codes (*Continued*)

Hex Value	Signed Value	Unsigned Value	Mnemonic
80000032h	−2147483598	2147483698	IMA_RESULT_PATH_NAME_TOO_LONG
80000033h	−2147483597	2147483699	IMA_RESULT_CREATEMESSAGEPORT_FAILED
80000034h	−2147483596	2147483700	IMA_RESULT_ALTADDRESS_NOT_DEFINED
80000035h	−2147483595	2147483701	IMA_RESULT_WOULD_BLOCK
80000036h	−2147483594	2147483702	IMA_RESULT_ALREADY_CLOSED
80000037h	−2147483593	2147483703	IMA_RESULT_TOO_BUSY
80000038h	−2147483592	2147483704	IMA_RESULT_HOST_SHUTTING_DOWN
80000039h	−2147483591	2147483705	IMA_RESULT_PORT_IN_USE
8000003Ah	−2147483590	2147483706	IMA_RESULT_NOT_SUPPORTED
80040001h	−2147221503	2147745793	IMA_RESULT_FILE_OPEN_FAILURE
80040002h	−2147221502	2147745794	IMA_RESULT_SESSION_REQUEST_DENIED
80040003h	−2147221501	2147745795	IMA_RESULT_JOB_NOT_FOUND
80040004h	−2147221500	2147745796	IMA_RESULT_SESSION_NOT_FOUND
80040005h	−2147221499	2147745797	IMA_RESULT_FILE_SEEK_FAILURE
80040006h	−2147221498	2147745798	IMA_RESULT_FILE_READ_FAILURE
80040007h	−2147221497	2147745799	IMA_RESULT_FILE_WRITE_FAILURE
80040008h	−2147221496	2147745800	IMA_RESULT_JOB_CANNOT_BE_UPDATED
80040009h	−2147221495	2147745801	IMA_RESULT_NO_TARGET_HOSTS
8004000Ah	−2147221494	2147745802	IMA_RESULT_NO_SOURCE_FILES
80060001h	−2147090431	2147876865	IMA_RESULT_ATTR_NOT_FOUND

Table A-1.   IMA Error Codes (*Continued*)

Hex Value	Signed Value	Unsigned Value	Mnemonic
80060002h	−2147090430	2147876866	IMA_RESULT_CONTEXT_NOT_FOUND
80060003h	−2147090429	2147876867	IMA_RESULT_VALUE_NOT_FOUND
80060004h	−2147090428	2147876868	IMA_RESULT_DATA_NOT_FOUND
80060005h	−2147090427	2147876869	IMA_RESULT_ENTRY_LOCKED
80060006h	−2147090426	2147876870	IMA_RESULT_SEARCH_HASMORE
80060007h	−2147090425	2147876871	IMA_RESULT_INCOMPLETE
80060008h	−2147090424	2147876872	IMA_RESULT_READEXCEPTION
80060009h	−2147090423	2147876873	IMA_RESULT_WRITEEXCEPTION
8006000Ah	−2147090422	2147876874	IMA_RESULT_LDAP_PARTIALINSTALL
8006000Bh	−2147090421	2147876875	IMA_RESULT_LDAP_NOTREADY
8006000Ch	−2147090420	2147876876	IMA_RESULT_BUFFER_TOO_SMALL
8006000Dh	−2147090419	2147876877	IMA_RESULT_CONTAINER_NOT_EMPTY
8006000Eh	−2147090418	2147876878	IMA_RESULT_CONFIGURATION_ERROR
8006000Fh	−2147090417	2147876879	IMA_RESULT_GET_BASEOBJECT
80060010h	−2147090416	2147876880	IMA_RESULT_GET_DERIVEDOBJECT
80060011h	−2147090415	2147876881	IMA_RESULT_OBJECTCLASS_NOTMATCH
80060012h	−2147090414	2147876882	IMA_RESULT_ATTRIBUTE_NOTINDEXED
80060013h	−2147090413	2147876883	IMA_RESULT_OBJECTCLASS_VIOLATION
80060014h	−2147090412	2147876884	IMA_RESULT_ENUMFAIL

Table A-1. IMA Error Codes (*Continued*)

Hex Value	Signed Value	Unsigned Value	Mnemonic
80060015h	−2147090411	2147876885	IMA_RESULT_ENUMNODATA
80060016h	−2147090410	2147876886	IMA_RESULT_DBCONNECT_FAILURE
80060017h	−2147090409	2147876887	IMA_RESULT_TRUNCATE
80060018h	−2147090408	2147876888	IMA_RESULT_DUPLICATE
80060019h	−2147090407	2147876889	IMA_RESULT_PS_NOTINITIALIZED
8006001Ah	−2147090406	2147876890	IMA_RESULT_USING_ORACLE_7
8006001Bh	−2147090405	2147876891	IMA_RESULT_USING_ORACLE_8
8006001Ch	−2147090404	2147876892	IMA_RESULT_USING_ORACLE_UNKNOWN
8006001Dh	−2147090403	2147876893	IMA_RESULT_LOAD_DAO_ENGINE_FAILED
8006001Eh	−2147090402	2147876894	IMA_RESULT_COMPACT_DB_FAILED
80060033h	−2147090381	2147876915	IMA_RESULT_ODBC_NO_CONNECTIONS_AVAILABLE
80060034h	−2147090380	2147876916	IMA_RESULT_CREATE_SQL_ENVIRONMENT_FAILED
80060035h	−2147090379	2147876917	IMA_RESULT_SQL_EXECUTE_FAILED
80060036h	−2147090378	2147876918	IMA_RESULT_SQL_FETCH_FAILED
80060037h	−2147090377	2147876919	IMA_RESULT_SQL_BIND_PARAM_FAILED
80060038h	−2147090376	2147876920	IMA_RESULT_SQL_GET_COLUMN_DATA_FAILED
80060039h	−2147090375	2147876921	IMA_RESULT_REPLICATED_DATA_CONTENTION

Table A-1. IMA Error Codes (*Continued*)

Hex Value	Signed Value	Unsigned Value	Mnemonic
8006003Ah	−2147090374	2147876922	IMA_RESULT_DB_TABLE_NOT_FOUND
8006003Bh	−2147090373	2147876923	IMA_RESULT_CONNECTION_EXIST
8006003Ch	−2147090372	2147876924	IMA_RESULT_QUERY_MAX_NODEID_FAILED
8006003Dh	−2147090371	2147876925	IMA_RESULT_SQL_FUNCTION_SEQUENCE_ERROR
8006003Eh	−2147090370	2147876926	IMA_RESULT_DB_CONNECTION_TIMEOUT
8006003Fh	−2147090369	2147876927	IMA_RESULT_SQL_INVALID_TRANSACTION_STATE
80060040h	−2147090368	2147876928	IMA_RESULT_DB_NO_DISK_SPACE
80110104h	−2146369276	2148598020	LMS_RESULT_NO_SERVER_AVAILABLE
80110105h	−2146369024	2148598272	IMA_RESULT_FULL_SERVER_OR_APP_LOAD_REACHED
80130001h	−2146238463	2148728833	IMA_RESULT_MORE_ITEMS
80130002h	−2146238462	2148728834	IMA_RESULT_INVALID_ACCOUNT
80130003h	−2146238461	2148728835	IMA_RESULT_INVALID_PASSWORD
80130004h	−2146238460	2148728836	IMA_RESULT_EXPIRED_PASSWORD
80130005h	−2146238459	2148728837	IMA_RESULT_GROUP_IGNORED
80130006h	−2146238458	2148728838	IMA_RESULT_BUILTIN_GROUP
80130007h	−2146238457	2148728839	IMA_RESULT_DC_NOT_AVAILABLE
80130008h	−2146238456	2148728840	IMA_RESULT_NW_CLIENT_NOT_INSTALLED

Table A-1. IMA Error Codes (*Continued*)

Hex Value	Signed Value	Unsigned Value	Mnemonic
80130009h	−2146238455	2148728841	IMA_RESULT_ACCOUNT_LOCKED_OUT
8013000Ah	−2146238454	2148728842	IMA_RESULT_INVALID_LOGON_HOURS
8013000Bh	−2146238453	2148728843	IMA_RESULT_ACCOUNT_DISABLED
8013000Ch	−2146238452	2148728844	IMA_RESULT_PREFERRED_TREE_NOT_SET
80160001h	−2146041855	2148925441	IMA_RESULT_NODE_NOT_FOUND
80160002h	−2146041854	2148925442	IMA_RESULT_NODE_NAME_INVALID
80160003h	−2146041853	2148925443	IMA_RESULT_NODE_NOT_EMPTY
80160004h	−2146041852	2148925444	IMA_RESULT_NODE_MOVE_DENIED
80160005h	−2146041851	2148925445	IMA_RESULT_NODE_NAME_NOT_UNIQUE
80160006h	−2146041850	2148925446	IMA_RESULT_NODE_RENAME_DENIED
80160007h	−2146041849	2148925447	IMA_RESULT_CONSTRAINT_VIOLATION
80160008h	−2146041848	2148925448	IMA_RESULT_LDAP_PROTOCOL_ERROR
80160009h	−2146041847	2148925449	IMA_RESULT_LDAP_SERVER_DOWN
8016000Ch	−2146041844	2148925452	IMA_RESULT_NODE_DELETE_DENIED
8016000Fh	−2146041841	2148925455	IMA_RESULT_CANNOTCHANGE_PASSWORD
80160010h	−2146041840	2148925456	IMA_RESULT_CANNOTCHANGE_LAST_RW

Table A-1.   IMA Error Codes (*Continued*)

Hex Value	Signed Value	Unsigned Value	Mnemonic
80160011h	−2146041839	2148925457	IMA_RESULT_LOGON_USER_DISABLED
80160012h	−2146041838	2148925458	IMA_RESULT_CMC_CONNECTION_DISABLED
80160013h	−2146041837	2148925459	IMA_RESULT_INSUFFICIENT_SERVER_SEC_FOR_USER
80160014h	−2146041836	2148925460	IMA_RESULT_FEATURE_LICENSE_NOT_FOUND
80160015h	−2146041835	2148925461	IMA_RESULT_DISALLOW_CMC_LOGON
80260001h	−2144993279	2149974017	IMA_RESULT_NW_PRINT_SERVER_ALREADY_PRESENT
80260002h	−2144993278	2149974018	IMA_RESULT_SERVER_ALREADY_PRESENT
802D0001h	−2144534527	2150432769	IMA_RESULT_TABLE_NOT_FOUND
802D0002h	−2144534526	2150432770	IMA_RESULT_NOT_TABLE_OWNER
802D0003h	−2144534525	2150432771	IMA_RESULT_INVALID_QUERY
802D0004h	−2144534524	2150432772	IMA_RESULT_TABLE_OWNER_HAS_CHANGED
802D0005h	−2144534523	2150432773	IMA_RESULT_SERVICE_NOT_AVAILABLE
802D0006h	−2144534522	2150432774	IMA_RESULT_ZONE_MASTER_UNKNOWN
802D0007h	−2144534521	2150432775	IMA_RESULT_NON_UNIQUE_HOSTID
802D0008h	−2144534520	2150432776	IMA_RESULT_REG_VALUE_NOT_FOUND
802D0009h	−2144534519	2150432777	IMA_RESULT_PARTIAL_LOAD

Table A-1.   IMA Error Codes (*Continued*)

Hex Value	Signed Value	Unsigned Value	Mnemonic
802D000Ah	−2144534518	2150432778	IMA_RESULT_GATEWAY_NOT_ ESTABLISHED
802D000Bh	−2144534517	2150432779	IMA_RESULT_INVALID_ GATEWAY
802D000Ch	−2144534516	2150432780	IMA_RESULT_SERVER_NOT_ AVAILABLE
80300001h	−2144337919	2150629377	IMA_RESULT_SERVICE_NOT_ SUPPORTED
80300002h	−2144337920	2150629378	IMA_RESULT_BUILD_SD_FAILED
80300003h	−2144337921	2150629379	IMA_RESULT_RPC_USE_ ENDPOINT_FAILED
80300004h	−2144337922	2150629380	IMA_RESULT_RPC_REG_ INTERFACE_FAILED
80300005h	−2144337923	2150629381	IMA_RESULT_RPC_LISTEN_ FAILED
80300006h	−2144337924	2150629382	IMA_RESULT_BUILD_FILTER_ FAILED
80300007h	−2144337925	2150629383	IMA_RESULT_RPC_BUFFER_ TOO_SMALL
80300008h	−2144337926	2150629384	IMA_RESULT_REQUEST_TICKET_ FAILED
80300009h	−2144337927	2150629385	IMA_RESULT_INVALID_TICKET
8030000Ah	−2144337928	2150629386	IMA_RESULT_LOAD_ TICKETDLL_FAILED

Table A-1.   IMA Error Codes (*Continued*)

PRESENTATION SERVER EVENT LOG ERROR MESSAGES

Table A-2 lists the Event log error messages created in the Windows Server 2000 or Windows 2003 Server Event Viewer by Presentation Server.

Message ID	Message Text
3584	Failed to open system registry key with error %1
3585	Failed to initialize registrar component with error %1
3586	Failed to prepare the transport system for operation with error %1
3587	Incompatible WinSock version
3588	Failed to prepare the messaging system for operation with error %1
3589	Invalid FailedComponentId (%1)
3590	Failed to prepare the plugin system with error %1
3591	Failed to initialize all components with error %1
3592	Failed to start transport with error %1
3593	Failed to create a new message port with error %1
3600	Failed to create an event queue with error %1
3601	Failed to load initial plugins with error %1
3602	Failed to unload initial plugin with error %1
3603	Failed to unload subsystems with error %2
3604	Failed to destroy system event queue with error %1
3605	Failed to stop transport with error %1
3606	Failed to stop system with error %1
3607	Failed to uninitialize system with error %1
3608	Failed to start system with error %1
3609	Failed to load plugin %1 with error %2
3610	Failed to initiate RPC for Remote Access Subsystem with error %1
3611	Failed to connect to the database. Error – %1 Increase the number of processes available to the database. See MetaFrame XP documentation for details.
3612	The server running MetaFrame Presentation Server failed to connect to the Data Store %1. Invalid database user name or password. Please make sure they are correct. If not, use DSMAINT CONFIG to change them.
3613	Failed to connect to the database with error. Error – %1. The ACCESS .mdb file is missing.

Table A-2. Event Log Error Messages

Message ID	Message Text
3614	The server running MetaFrame Presentation Server failed to connect to the Data Store. Error – %1. The database is down or a network failure occurred.
3615	The server running MetaFrame Presentation Server failed to connect to the Data Store. Error – %1. An unknown failure occurred while connecting to the database.
3616	Configuration error: Failed to read the farm name out of the registry on a server configured to access the Data Store directly.
3617	Configuration error: Failed to get the farm name from the Data Store proxy server with Error – %1. This server is configured to access the Data Store indirectly. The server specified as the Data Store proxy is unavailable. Verify that the Data Store proxy server is accessible and the IMA Service is started on it.
3618	Configuration error: Failed to open IMA registry key.
3619	Since last successful connection to the Data Store, 96 hours have passed. This server will no longer accept connections until successful connection to the Data Store is established.
3840	Unable to bind to group context in data store. Group consistency check will not run. (Result: %1)
3841	Unable to locate groups in data store at DN %1. Group consistency check will not run. (Result: %2)
3842	Group Consistency Check: Group at DN %1 is missing the GroupMember Attribute.
3843	Group Consistency Check: Group at DN %1 contains reference to an unknown object with type %3 and UID %2.
3844	Group Consistency Check: Group at DN %3 contains an object with UID %1 and type %2. This object is missing the %4 attribute.
3845	Group Consistency Check: Group at DN %3 contains an object with UID %1 and type %2. This object is missing the value for the %4 attribute.
3872	Unable to bind to server contexts in data store. Server consistency check will not run. (Result: %1)

Table A-2.   Event Log Error Messages (*Continued*)

Message ID	Message Text
3873	Server Consistency Check: Unable to locate host records in data store. The server host record consistency check will not run. (Result: %1)
3874	Server Consistency Check: Unable to locate common server records in data store. The common server consistency check will not run. (Result: %1)
3875	Server Consistency Check: Unable to locate MetaFrame server records in data store. The MetaFrame server consistency check will not run. (Result: %1)
3876	Server Consistency Check: Host record for HostName %2 at DN %1 references a Common Server record that cannot be found in the data store.
3877	Server Consistency Check: Host record for HostName %2 at DN %1 references a Common Server record that has a HostName of %3. This mismatch is an error.
3878	Server Consistency Check: Host record for HostName %2 at DN %1 references a Common Server record that cannot be found in the data store. (Result: %3)
3879	Server Consistency Check: Common Server record for HostName %2 at DN %1 references a Host record that cannot be found in the data store.
3880	Server Consistency Check: Common Server record for HostName %2 at DN %1 has a HostID of %3. The corresponding Host record has a HostID of %4. This mismatch is an error.
3881	Server Consistency Check: Common Server record for HostName %2 at DN %1 references a Host record that cannot be found in the data store. (Result: %3)
3882	Server Consistency Check: The Common Server record with HostName %1 at DN %2 is invalid. There is no registered server product for this record.
3883	Server Consistency Check: The Common Server record with HostName %1 at DN %2 is invalid. The corresponding MetaFrame Server record cannot be accessed.

Table A-2.   Event Log Error Messages (*Continued*)

Message ID	Message Text
3884	Server Consistency Check: The MetaFrame Server record with HostName %1 at DN %2 is invalid. The associated Common Server UID is not set.
3885	Server Consistency Check: The MetaFrame Server record with HostName %1 at DN %2 is invalid. The associated Common Server record cannot be accessed.
3886	Server Consistency Check: The MetaFrame Server record with HostName %1 at DN %2 may be invalid. The MetaFrame Server record HostID of %3 does not match the Common Server record HostID of %4.
3887	Server Consistency Check: The MetaFrame Server record with HostName %1 at DN %2 is invalid. The associated Common Server record has a different HostName (%3).
3888	Server Consistency Check: Unable to locate Load Manager for MetaFrame XP(TM) Server entry for HostName %1. (Result: %2)
3889	Server Consistency Check: The MetaFrame Server record with HostName %1 at DN %2 may be invalid. The Load Manager for MetaFrame XP(TM) Server entry was not found.
3890	Server Consistency Check: The MetaFrame Server record with HostName %1 at DN %2 is invalid. The associated Account Authority Server record was not found.
3904	Unable to bind to application contexts in data store. Application consistency check will not run. (Result: %1)
3905	Application Consistency Check: Unable to locate Common Application records in the data store. Common application consistency check will not run. (Result: %1)
3906	Application Consistency Check: Unable to locate MetaFrame Application records in the data store. MetaFrame application consistency check will not run. (Result: %1)
3907	Application Consistency Check: The Common Application record at DN %1 does not have a Friendly Name. (Result: %2)
3908	Application Consistency Check: The Common Application record at DN %1 does not have a Browser Name. (Result: %2)

Table A-2.   Event Log Error Messages (*Continued*)

Message ID	Message Text
3909	Application Consistency Check: The Common Application record with Friendly Name %1 at DN %2 does not have a specialized application UID. (Result: %3)
3910	Application Consistency Check: The Common Application record with Friendly Name %1 at DN %2 references a MetaFrame Application record that cannot be accessed. (Result: %3)
3911	Application Consistency Check: The Common Application record with Friendly Name %1 at DN %2 references a MetaFrame Application record. This record does not have a Friendly Name. (Result: %3)
3912	Application Consistency Check: The Common Application record with Friendly Name %1 at DN %2 references a MetaFrame Application record. This record does not have a Browser Name. (Result: %3)
3913	Application Consistency Check: The Common Application record at DN %2 has a Friendly Name of %1. The corresponding MetaFrame Application record has a Friendly Name of %3. This mismatch is an error.
3914	Application Consistency Check: The Common Application record at DN %2 has a Browser Name of %1. The corresponding MetaFrame Application record has a Browser Name of %3. This mismatch is an error.
3915	Application Consistency Check: The MetaFrame Application record at DN %1 does not have a Friendly Name. (Result: %2)
3916	Application Consistency Check: The MetaFrame Application record at DN %1 does not have a Browser Name. (Result: %2)
3917	Application Consistency Check: The MetaFrame Application record with Friendly Name %1 at DN %2 does not have a common application UID. (Result: %3)
3918	Application Consistency Check: The MetaFrame Application record with Friendly Name %1 at DN %2 references a Common Application record (UID %3) that cannot be accessed. (Result: %4)

Table A-2. Event Log Error Messages (*Continued*)

Message ID	Message Text
3919	Application Consistency Check: The MetaFrame Application record with Friendly Name %1 at DN %2 references a Common Application record. This record does not have a Friendly Name. (Result: %3)
3920	Application Consistency Check: The MetaFrame Application record with Friendly Name %1 at DN %2 references a Common Application record. This record does not have a Browser Name. (Result: %3)
3921	Application Consistency Check: The MetaFrame Application record at DN %2 has a Friendly Name of %1. The corresponding Common Application record has a Friendly Name of %3. This mismatch is an error.
3922	Application Consistency Check: The MetaFrame Application record at DN %2 has a Browser Name of %1. The corresponding Common Application record has a Browser Name of %3. This mismatch is an error.
3936	Common Application cleanup, deleting record at DN <%1>
3937	MetaFrame Application cleanup, deleting record at DN <%1>
3938	MetaFrame Server cleanup, deleting record at DN <%1>
3939	Common Server cleanup, deleting record at DN <%1>
3940	Server Host Record cleanup, deleting record at DN <%1>
3952	Unable to open Citrix Runtime registry key. Application terminated. (Status: %1)
3953	Unable to read Neighborhood name from registry. Application terminated. (Status: %1)
3954	Unable to initialize Data Store connection. This server must have a direct connection to the data store. Application terminated. (Result: %1)
3956	Data Store Validation Utility. Version: %1
3957	Unable to initialize event log. Messages will be displayed on console only.

Table A-2. Event Log Error Messages (*Continued*)

Message ID	Message Text
3958	%1 [/Clean] Perform validation checks on a MetaFrame Farm's data store. Results will be displayed on the console and also entered into the Event Log. The /Clean option will delete records that are inconsistent. The data store should be backed up prior to using the /Clean option.
3959	All consistency checks were successful.
3960	Some consistency checks were unsuccessful. The following results indicate the number of errors or −1 for test not run: Server Errors = %1, Application Errors = %2, Group Errors = %3.
3961	The Data Collector is out of memory, and the Dynamic Store data might be out of sync. Please elect a new Data Collector and make sure you have enough memory on the new Data Collector.
3968	Buffer overrun detected.
3969	Error occurred during uninstall. Some objects may not have been removed from the data store properly. Subsystem id = %1, error = %2. Please verify data store consistency.

Table A-2.   Event Log Error Messages (*Continued*)

APPENDIX B

Registered Citrix Ports

Table B-1 provides a complete listing of the various registered ports and private enterprise numbers (SNMP MIB) for Presentation Server.

REGISTERED CITRIX PORTS

NOTE The Access Management Console uses MSRPC on port 135 for communications.

Name	Number	Protocol	Description
ica	1494	TCP	ICA
ica	1494	UDP	<not used>
ica	0x85BB	IPX	ICA
ica	0x9010	SPX	ICA
icabrowser	1604	TCP	<not used>
icabrowser	1604	UDP	ICA Browser
icabrowser	0x85BA	IPX	ICA Browser
citrixima	2512	TCP	IMA (server to server)
citrixima	2512	UDP	<not used>
citrixadmin	2513	TCP	IMA (Presentation Server Console to server)
citrixadmin	2513	UDP	<not used>
citriximaclient	2598	TCP	Session Reliability
citriximaclient	2598	UDP	<not used>
citrix-rtmp	2897	TCP	Rtmp (Control) Video Frame
citrix-rtmp	2897	UDP	Rtmp (Streaming Data) Video Frame
Citrix Systems	3845	MIB	Private Enterprise Number. Used for SNMP MIB Object ID and Active Directory Schema Object IDs (OID).

Table B-1. Registered Citrix Ports

APPENDIX C

Files, Folder Locations, and Registry Entries for the Presentation Server Client for 32-bit Windows

The purpose of this appendix is to outline the various files, locations, and registry entries that are added to a system when Presentation Server Client for 32-bit Windows (Program Neighborhood Client), Web Client, and Program Neighborhood Agent are installed onto a client machine. This information is relevant only to a PC client (as apposed to a thin-client device).

PROGRAM NEIGHBORHOOD CLIENT FILES

The purpose of this section is to outline the various files, locations, and registry entries that are added when installing the Presentation Server Client for 32-bit Windows onto client machines. This section assumes a PC rather than a thin-client device.

The Full Program Neighborhood Client may be installed using one of the following packages:

▼ **ica32.exe**   A self-extracting executable, approximately 4.0MB in size compressed.

▲ **ica32pkg.msi**   A Windows Installer package for use with Windows 2000 Active Directory Services or Microsoft Systems Management Server, approximately 3.1MB in size compressed.

For more information on the Program Neighborhood Client software, see the *Client for 32-bit Windows Administrator's Guide* and the *MetaFrame Presentation Server Administrator's Guide* included in your Presentation Server CD.

Regardless of which package is used, they both install the same files and registry entries.

NOTE   Some files and registry entries that are added/modified are specific to the installer program used. These files and registry entries are not covered in this appendix.

Installed Folders and Files

This section lists the folders, files, and other details added when the Program Neighborhood Client is installed (the locations provided are for a default installation).

New Folders Created

The following new folders are created on installation of the Program Neighborhood Client:

```
%ProgramFiles%\Citrix\
%ProgramFiles%\Program Files\Citrix\ICA Client
%ProgramFiles%\Program Files\Citrix\ICA Client\Cache
%ProgramFiles%\Program Files\Citrix\ICA Client\Resource
%ProgramFiles%\Program Files\Citrix\ICA Client\Resource\EN
```

New Files Added into the Folder

Table C-1 shows the files are created on installation of the Program Neighborhood Client in the following path:

```
Location = %ProgramFiles%\Citrix\ICA Client
```

%ProgramFiles%\Citrix			
ICA CLIENT	DIR	%DATE%	6:06:15 P.M.
%ProgramFiles%\Citrix\ICA CLIENT			
CACHE	DIR	%DATE%	6:06:08 P.M.
RESOURCE	DIR	%DATE%	6:06:08 P.M.
acrdlg.dll	28.3KB (28,944 bytes)	2/21/2004	12:17:20 A.M.
adpcm.dll	32.3KB (33,040 bytes)	2/21/2004	12:17:20 A.M.
appsrv.ini	1.8KB (1871 bytes)	%DATE%	6:06:20 P.M.
appsrv.src	1.7KB (1738 bytes)	12/1/2003	10:40:04 P.M.
audcvtN.dll	32.3KB (33,040 bytes)	2/21/2004	12:17:20 A.M.
cgpcfg.dll	20.3KB (20,752 bytes)	2/21/2004	12:17:20 A.M.
CgpCore.dll	68.3KB (69,904 bytes)	2/21/2004	12:17:20 A.M.
concentr.cnt	0.0KB (43 bytes)	1/12/2004	6:07:28 P.M.
concentr.dll	104.3KB (106,768 bytes)	2/21/2004	12:17:22 A.M.
CONCENTR.hlp	8.8KB (9005 bytes)	1/15/2004	10:53:48 A.M.
ICAClObj.class	4.0KB (4075 bytes)	2/21/2004	12:11:28 A.M.
icadlgn.dll	36.3KB (37,136 bytes)	2/21/2004	12:17:22 A.M.
icalogon.dll	44.3KB (45,328 bytes)	2/21/2004	12:17:22 A.M.
IICAClient.xpt	3.1KB (3169 bytes)	2/21/2004	12:11:30 A.M.
License.txt	20.6KB (21,072 bytes)	1/14/2004	12:02:22 P.M.
Mfc30.dll	315.3KB (322,832 bytes)	10/23/2001	11:48:40 A.M.
migrateN.exe	52.3KB (53,520 bytes)	2/21/2004	12:16:10 A.M.
modem.ini	684.7 KB (701,103 bytes)	12/1/2003	10:39:58 P.M.
modem.src	684.7KB (701,103 bytes)	12/1/2003	10:39:58 P.M.

Table C-1.   File and Folder Structure of the Program Neighborhood Client Installation

modemN.dll	28.3KB (28,944 bytes)	2/21/2004	12:17:22 A.M.
module.ini	38.1KB (38,993 bytes)	%DATE%	6:06:21 P.M.
module.src	38.1KB (38,981 bytes)	12/1/2003	10:40:04 P.M.
msvcrt.dll	288.1KB (295,000 bytes)	2/7/2002	8:42:50 P.M.
neHttpN.dll	44.3KB (45,328 bytes)	2/21/2004	12:17:22 A.M.
neipxn.dll	28.3 KB (28,944 bytes)	2/21/2004	12:17:22 A.M.
nenetbn.dll	28.3KB (28,944 bytes)	2/21/2004	12:17:22 A.M.
nenumn.dll	24.3KB (24,848 bytes)	2/21/2004	12:17:22 A.M.
netcpN.dll	32.3KB (33,040 bytes)	2/21/2004	12:17:22 A.M.
npicaN.dll	304.3KB (311,568 bytes)	2/21/2004	12:17:22 A.M.
nrhttpn.dll	44.3KB (45,328 bytes)	2/21/2004	12:17:22 A.M.
nripxN.dll	40.3KB (41,232 bytes)	2/21/2004	12:17:22 A.M.
nrnetbN.dll	40.3KB (41,232 bytes)	2/21/2004	12:17:22 A.M.
nrnetwN.dll	32.3KB (33,040 bytes)	2/21/2004	12:17:22 A.M.
nrtcpn.dll	40.3KB (41,232 bytes)	2/21/2004	12:17:22 A.M.
pcl4rast.dll	1.28MB (1,339,664 bytes)	2/21/2004	12:17:22 A.M.
pdc128N.dll	76.3KB (78,096 bytes)	2/21/2004	12:17:22 A.M.
pdcompN.dll	28.3KB (28,944 bytes)	2/21/2004	12:17:22 A.M.
pdframeN.dll	28.3KB (28,944 bytes)	2/21/2004	12:17:22 A.M.
pdmodemN.dll	28.3KB (28,944 bytes)	2/21/2004	12:17:22 A.M.
pdreliN.dll	28.3KB (28,944 bytes)	2/21/2004	12:17:22 A.M.
pdtapiN.dll	52.3KB (53,520 bytes)	2/21/2004	12:17:22 A.M.
pn.exe	428.3KB (438,544 bytes)	2/21/2004	12:14:48 A.M.
pn.ini	0.4KB (428 bytes)	12/1/2003	10:40:04 P.M.
pn.src	0.4KB (428 bytes)	12/1/2003	10:40:04 P.M.
pnapin.dll	52.3KB (53520 bytes)	2/21/2004	12:17:22 A.M.
pncachen.dll	108.3KB (110,864 bytes)	2/21/2004	12:17:22 A.M.
pndskint.dll	32.3KB (33,040 bytes)	2/21/2004	12:17:22 A.M.
pnipcn.dll	20.3KB (20,752 bytes)	2/21/2004	12:17:22 A.M.
pnsson.dll	36.3KB (37,136 bytes)	2/21/2004	12:17:22 A.M.

Table C-1.   File and Folder Structure of the Program Neighborhood Client Installation (*Continued*)

pnstub.exe	24.3KB (24,848 bytes)	2/21/2004	12:08:34 A.M.
progn.cnt	2.9KB (3,013 bytes)	1/22/2004	4:18:50 P.M.
PROGN.hlp	118.0KB (120,804 bytes)	1/30/2004	2:46:18 P.M.
ProxySup.ocx	72.3KB (74,000 bytes)	2/20/2004	11:56:42 P.M.
PScript.dll	24.3KB (24,848 bytes)	2/21/2004	12:17:22 A.M.
scriptN.dll	36.3KB (37,136 bytes)	2/21/2004	12:17:22 A.M.
srcflter.dll	80.3KB (82,192 bytes)	2/21/2004	12:17:22 A.M.
sslsdk_b.dll	56.3KB (57,616 bytes)	2/21/2004	12:17:22 A.M.
ssoncom.exe	20.3KB (20,752 bytes)	2/21/2004	12:08:48 A.M.
ssonstub.dll	24.3KB (24,848 bytes)	2/21/2004	12:17:22 A.M.
ssonsvr.exe	16.3KB (16,656 bytes)	2/21/2004	12:08:54 A.M.
statuin.dll	32.3KB (33,040 bytes)	2/21/2004	12:17:22 A.M.
TcpPServ.dll	24.3KB (24,848 bytes)	2/21/2004	12:17:22 A.M.
tdcommN.dll	40.3KB (41,232 bytes)	2/21/2004	12:17:22 A.M.
tdnetbN.dll	40.3KB (41,232 bytes)	2/21/2004	12:17:22 A.M.
tdwsipxN.dll	44.3KB (45,328 bytes)	2/21/2004	12:17:22 A.M.
tdwsspxN.dll	44.3KB (45,328 bytes)	2/21/2004	12:17:22 A.M.
vdcamN.dll	36.3KB (37,136 bytes)	2/21/2004	12:17:22 A.M.
vdcmN.dll	40.3KB (41,232 bytes)	2/21/2004	12:17:22 A.M.
vdcom30N.dll	48.3KB (49,424 bytes)	2/21/2004	12:17:22 A.M.
vdcpm30N.dll	32.3KB (33,040 bytes)	2/21/2004	12:17:22 A.M.
vdfon30n.dll	48.3KB (49,424 bytes)	2/21/2004	12:17:22 A.M.
vdmmn.dll	40.3KB (41,232 bytes)	2/21/2004	12:17:22 A.M.
vdpnn.dll	24.3KB (24,848 bytes)	2/21/2004	12:17:22 A.M.
vdscardn.dll	36.3KB (37,136 bytes)	2/21/2004	12:17:22 A.M.
vdspmike.dll	24.3KB (24,848 bytes)	2/21/2004	12:17:22 A.M.
vdsspin.dll	28.3KB (28,944 bytes)	2/21/2004	12:17:22 A.M.
vdtw30n.dll	136.3KB (139,536 bytes)	2/21/2004	12:17:22 A.M.
vdzlcn.dll	88.3KB (90,384 bytes)	2/21/2004	12:17:22 A.M.
version.dat	0.0KB (12 bytes)	2/21/2004	12:17:10 A.M.

Table C-1.   File and Folder Structure of the Program Neighborhood Client Installation (*Continued*)

wfclient.ini	0.5KB (553 bytes)	%DATE%	6:06:20 P.M.
wfclient.src	0.5KB (553 bytes)	2/20/2004	10:16:14 P.M.
wfcmoveN.exe	100.3KB (102,672 bytes)	2/21/2004	12:13:38 A.M.
wfcrun32.exe	236.3KB (241,936 bytes)	2/21/2004	12:13:34 A.M.
wfcwin32.log	0.1KB (53 bytes)	%DATE%	6:06:23 P.M.
wfcwinn.dll	32.3KB (33,040 bytes)	2/21/2004	12:17:22 A.M.
Wfica.ocx	400.3KB (409,872 bytes)	2/21/2004	12:11:26 A.M.
wfica32.exe	756.3KB (774,416 bytes)	2/21/2004	12:12:44 A.M.

%ProgramFiles%\Citrix\ICA CLIENT\CACHE

%ProgramFiles%\Citrix\ICA CLIENT\RESOURCE

EN	DIR	3/16/2004	6:06:11 P.M.

%ProgramFiles%\Citrix\ICA CLIENT\RESOURCE\EN

acrdlgUI.dll	44.3KB (45,328 bytes)	2/20/2004	11:53:28 P.M.
concenUI.dll	100.3KB (102,672 bytes)	2/20/2004	11:53:34 P.M.
icadlgUI.dll	36.3KB (37,136 bytes)	2/20/2004	11:53:36 P.M.
icalogUI.dll	32.3KB (33,040 bytes)	2/20/2004	11:53:30 P.M.
migratUI.dll	20.3KB (20752 bytes)	2/20/2004	11:53:22 P.M.
npicanUI.dll	40.3KB (41,232 bytes)	2/20/2004	11:52:52 P.M.
nrhttpUI.dll	44.3KB (45,328 bytes)	2/20/2004	11:52:40 P.M.
nripxnUI.dll	44.3KB (45,328 bytes)	2/20/2004	11:52:44 P.M.
nrnetbUI.dll	44.3KB (45,328 bytes)	2/20/2004	11:52:46 P.M.
nrnetwUI.dll	20.3KB (20,752 bytes)	2/20/2004	11:52:46 P.M.
nrtcpnUI.dll	44.3KB (45,328 bytes)	2/20/2004	11:52:48 P.M.
pnapinUI.dll	92.3KB (94,480 bytes)	2/20/2004	11:53:10 P.M.
pndskiUI.dll	20.3KB (20,752 bytes)	2/20/2004	11:53:08 P.M.
pnstubUI.dll	20.3KB (20,752 bytes)	2/20/2004	11:53:12 P.M.
pnUI.dll	644.3KB (659,728 bytes)	2/20/2004	11:53:42 P.M.
scriptUI.dll	20.3KB (20,752 bytes)	2/20/2004	11:52:56 P.M.

Table C-1.   File and Folder Structure of the Program Neighborhood Client Installation (*Continued*)

sslsdkUI.dll	24.3KB (24,848 bytes)	2/20/2004	11:53:32 P.M.
statuiUI.dll	24.3KB (24,848 bytes)	2/20/2004	11:54:04 P.M.
tdcommUI.dll	20.3KB (20,752 bytes)	2/20/2004	11:52:58 P.M.
tdnetbUI.dll	20.3KB (20,752 bytes)	2/20/2004	11:53:00 P.M.
tdwsipUI.dll	40.3KB (41,232 bytes)	2/20/2004	11:53:02 P.M.
tdwsspUI.dll	40.3KB (41,232 bytes)	2/20/2004	11:53:04 P.M.
vdcmnUI.dll	20.3KB (20,752 bytes)	2/20/2004	11:53:06 P.M.
vdzlcnUI.dll	20.3KB (20,752 bytes)	2/20/2004	11:53:14 P.M.
wfcmovUI.dll	20.3KB (20,752 bytes)	2/20/2004	11:53:44 P.M.
wfcrunUI.dll	76.3KB (78,096 bytes)	2/20/2004	11:53:46 P.M.
wfica3UI.dll	84.3KB (86,288 bytes)	2/20/2004	11:53:16 P.M.
wficaUI.dll	44.3KB (45,328 bytes)	2/20/2004	11:52:50 P.M.

%DATE% = Current Installation Date

Table C-1.   File and Folder Structure of the Program Neighborhood Client Installation (*Continued*)

First-time Started Application Files

This section lists the file and folder directory structure created in the user profile after the application is started for the first time.

New Folder Locations

The following folders are created in the user profile after the client is run for the first time:

%USERPROFILE%\Application Data\ICAClient
%USERPROFILE%\Application Data\ICAClient\Cache
%USERPROFILE%\Application Data\ICAClient\Cache\ZLCache

Additional Files

The default base folder location for the Program Neighborhood Client user profile installation is %USERPROFILE%\Application Data\ICAClient. Table C-2 lists the file and directory structure.

%USERPROFILE%\Application Data\ICAClient

CACHE	DIR	%DATE%	11:15:35 A.M.
APPSRV.INI	3.3KB (3401 bytes)	%DATE%	11:20:19 A.M.
PN.INI	0.5KB (513 bytes)	%DATE%	11:08:02 A.M.
UISTATE.INI	0.1KB (109 bytes)	%DATE%	11:15:56 A.M.
WFCLIENT.INI	0.6KB (577 bytes)	%DATE%	11:20:19 A.M.
WFCWIN32.LOG	0.2KB (159 bytes)	%DATE%	11:15:56 A.M.

%USERPROFILE%\Application Data\ICAClient\CACHE

ZLCACHE	DIR	%DATE%	11:15:35 A.M.

%USERPROFILE%\Application Data\ICAClient\CACHE\ZLCACHE

%DATE% = Current Installation Date

Table C-2. User Profile File and Directory Structure

Registry Entries for Program Neighborhood Client

This section lists the registry keys added for the Program Neighborhood Client. These registry keys assume a default installation of the client.

```
Key Name:          SOFTWARE\Citrix
Class Name:        <NO CLASS>
Last Write Time:   3/16/2004 - 3:51 P.M.

Key Name:          SOFTWARE\Citrix\CitrixCAB
Class Name:        <NO CLASS>
Last Write Time:   3/16/2004 - 3:51 P.M.
Value 0
  Name:            <NO NAME>
  Type:            REG_SZ
  Data:            1


Key Name:          SOFTWARE\Citrix\ICA Client
Class Name:        <NO CLASS>
Last Write Time:   3/16/2004 - 3:51 P.M.
Value 0
```

```
       Name:              MsiInstallDir
       Type:              REG_SZ
       Data:              C:\Program Files\Citrix\ICA Client\

Value 1
       Name:              ProgramFolderName
       Type:              REG_SZ
       Data:              Citrix\MetaFrame Access Clients


Key Name:             SOFTWARE\Citrix\Install
Class Name:           <NO CLASS>
Last Write Time:      3/16/2004 - 3:51 P.M.

Key Name:             SOFTWARE\Citrix\Install\MUI
Class Name:           <NO CLASS>
Last Write Time:      3/16/2004 - 3:51 P.M.

Key Name:             SOFTWARE\Citrix\Install\MUI\Modules
Class Name:           <NO CLASS>
Last Write Time:      3/16/2004 - 3:51 P.M.
Value 0
       Name:              Module.1F7C76CE_0458_4E22_A908_E3F38F4E31BA
       Type:              REG_SZ
       Data:              en

Value 1
       Name:              Module.4788A191_9E75_405B_866C_7B2FA459A38F
       Type:              REG_SZ
       Data:              en


Key Name:             SOFTWARE\Citrix\Install\{94F321B9-45B0-4125-970D-DE3D98CBCA1C}
Class Name:           <NO CLASS>
Last Write Time:      3/16/2004 - 3:51 P.M.
Value 0
       Name:              InstallLocation
       Type:              REG_SZ
       Data:              C:\Program Files\Citrix\ICA Client\


Key Name:             SOFTWARE\Citrix\MUI
Class Name:           <NO CLASS>
Last Write Time:      3/16/2004 - 3:51 P.M.
Value 0
       Name:              ICA_DefaultLanguage
       Type:              REG_SZ
       Data:              en
```

WEB CLIENT PACKAGE

The Web Client can be installed using one of the following packages:

▼ **ica32t.exe**   A self-extracting executable, approximately 2.5MB in size, this package is significantly smaller than the other clients. The smaller size allows quicker downloads and installation. You can configure the Web Client for silent user installation.

■ **Wficat.cab**   A Windows cab file, approximately 2.2MB in size compressed.

■ **Wficac.cab**   A Windows cab file, approximately 1.3MB in size compressed.

▲ **Wfica.cab**   A Windows cab file, approximately 3.9MB in size compressed.

For more information on the client software, see the *Client for 32-bit Windows Administrator's Guide* and the *MetaFrame Presentation Server Administrator's Guide*.

Both *Ica32t.exe* and *Wficat.cab* install the same files and registry entries. The *Wfica.cab* file is the full Program Neighborhood Client. The *Wficac.cab* file installs a smaller client without encryption and UPD support.

NOTE   Some files and registry entries added/modified are specific to the installer program used. These files and registry entries are beyond the scope of this document.

Installed Folders and Files

This section lists the folders, files, and other details added when the Web Client is installed. The locations provided are for a default installation.

New Folders Created

%ProgramFiles%\Citrix\
%ProgramFiles%\Citrix\icaweb32

New Files Added into Folder

Table C-3 lists the files and folders added to the base installation folder, %ProgramFiles%\Citrix\icaweb32, for the Web Client location.

First-time Started Application Files

This section lists the files and folders added to the user profile directory after the Web Client is started for the first time.

%ProgramFiles%\Citrix\icaweb32

acrdlg.dll	28.3KB (28,944 bytes)	2/21/2004	12:17:20 A.M.
adpcm.dll	32.3KB (33,040 bytes)	2/21/2004	12:17:20 A.M.
APPSRV.INI	1.7KB (1738 bytes)	12/1/2003	10:40:04 P.M.
APPSRV.SRC	1.7KB (1738 bytes)	12/1/2003	10:40:04 P.M.
audcvtn.dll	32.3KB (33,040 bytes)	2/21/2004	12:17:20 A.M.
cgpcfg.dll	20.3KB (20,752 bytes)	2/21/2004	12:17:20 A.M.
cgpcore.dll	68.3KB (69904 bytes)	2/21/2004	12:17:20 A.M.
concentr.cnt	0.0KB (43 bytes)	1/12/2004	6:07:28 P.M.
concentr.dll	104.3KB (106,768 bytes)	2/21/2004	12:17:22 A.M.
concentr.hlp	8.8KB (9005 bytes)	1/15/2004	10:53:48 A.M.
ICAClobj.class	4.0KB (4075 bytes)	2/21/2004	12:11:28 A.M.
icadlgn.dll	36.3KB (37,136 bytes)	2/21/2004	12:17:22 A.M.
icalogon.dll	44.3KB (45,328 bytes)	2/21/2004	12:17:22 A.M.
IICAClient.xpt	3.1KB (3169 bytes)	2/21/2004	12:11:30 A.M.
mfc30.dll	315.3KB (322,832 bytes)	10/23/2001	11:48:40 A.M.
migraten.exe	52.3KB (53,520 bytes)	2/21/2004	12:16:10 A.M.
MODULE.INI	38.1KB (39,001 bytes)	2/21/2004	12:22:28 A.M.
MODULE.SRC	38.1KB (39,001 bytes)	2/21/2004	12:22:28 A.M.
msvcrt.dll	288.1KB (295,000 bytes)	2/7/2002	8:42:50 P.M.
netcpn.dll	32.3KB (33,040 bytes)	2/21/2004	12:17:22 A.M.
npican.dll	304.3KB (311,568 bytes)	2/21/2004	12:17:22 A.M.
nrhttpn.dll	44.3KB (45,328 bytes)	2/21/2004	12:17:22 A.M.
nrtcpn.dll	40.3KB (41232 bytes)	2/21/2004	12:17:22 A.M.
pcl4rast.dll	1.28MB (1,339,664 bytes)	2/21/2004	12:17:22 A.M.
pdc128N.dll	76.3KB (78,096 bytes)	2/21/2004	12:17:22 A.M.
pdcompN.dll	28.3KB (28,944 bytes)	2/21/2004	12:17:22 A.M.
ProxySup.ocx	72.3KB (74,000 bytes)	2/20/2004	11:56:42 P.M.
pscript.dll	24.3KB (24,848 bytes)	2/21/2004	12:17:22 A.M.
srcflter.dll	80.3KB (82,192 bytes)	2/21/2004	12:17:22 A.M.
sslsdk_b.dll	56.3KB (57,616 bytes)	2/21/2004	12:17:22 A.M.

Table C-3.   File and Directory Structure of the Citrix Presentation Server Web Client

statuin.dll	32.3KB (33,040 bytes)	2/21/2004	12:17:22 A.M.
tcppserv.dll	24.3KB (24,848 bytes)	2/21/2004	12:17:22 A.M.
uninst.inf	3.9KB (3972 bytes)	%DATE%	4:19:49 P.M.
vdcamN.dll	36.3KB (37,136 bytes)	2/21/2004	12:17:22 A.M.
vdcmN.dll	40.3KB (41,232 bytes)	2/21/2004	12:17:22 A.M.
vdcom30n.dll	48.3KB (49,424 bytes)	2/21/2004	12:17:22 A.M.
vdcpm30n.dll	32.3KB (33,040 bytes)	2/21/2004	12:17:22 A.M.
vdfon30n.dll	48.3KB (49,424 bytes)	2/21/2004	12:17:22 A.M.
vdmmn.dll	40.3KB (41,232 bytes)	2/21/2004	12:17:22 A.M.
vdscardn.dll	36.3KB (37,136 bytes)	2/21/2004	12:17:22 A.M.
VDSSPIN.dll	28.3KB (28,944 bytes)	2/21/2004	12:17:22 A.M.
vdtw30n.dll	136.3KB (139,536 bytes)	2/21/2004	12:17:22 A.M.
vdzlcn.dll	88.3KB (90,384 bytes)	2/21/2004	12:17:22 A.M.
VERSION.DAT	0.0KB (12 bytes)	2/21/2004	12:17:10 A.M.
WFCLIENT.INI	0.5KB (553 bytes)	2/20/2004	10:16:14 P.M.
WFCLIENT.SRC	0.5KB (553 bytes)	2/20/2004	10:16:14 P.M.
wfcmoven.exe	100.3KB (102,672 bytes)	2/21/2004	12:13:38 A.M.
wfcrun32.exe	236.3KB (241,936 bytes)	2/21/2004	12:13:34 A.M.
WFCSETUP.INI	0.1KB (88 bytes)	12/1/2003	10:38:58 P.M.
wfcwinN.dll	32.3KB (33,040 bytes)	2/21/2004	12:17:22 A.M.
wfica.ocx	400.3KB (409,872 bytes)	2/21/2004	12:11:26 A.M.
wfica32.exe	756.3KB (774,416 bytes)	2/21/2004	12:12:44 A.M.

%DATE% = Current Installation Date

Table C-3.   File and Directory Structure of the Citrix Presentation Server Web Client (*Continued*)

New Folder Locations

The Web Client creates the following directories after it is run for the first time:

> %USERPROFILE%\Application Data\ICAClient
> %USERPROFILE%\Application Data\ICAClient\Cache
> %USERPROFILE%\Application Data\ICAClient\Cache\ZLCache

%USERPROFILE%\Application Data\ICAClient			
CACHE	DIR	%DATE%	11:50:17 A.M.
APPSRV.INI	1.9KB (1957 bytes)	%DATE%	11:50:14 A.M.
UISTATE.INI	0.1KB (109 bytes)	%DATE%	11:50:32 A.M.
WFCLIENT.INI	0.5KB (553 bytes)	2/20/2004	10:16:14 P.M.
wfcwin32.log	0.2KB (159 bytes)	%DATE%	11:50:32 A.M.
%USERPROFILE%\Application Data\ICAClient\CACHE			
ZLCACHE	DIR	%DATE%	11:50:17 A.M.
%USERPROFILE%\Application Data\ICAClient\CACHE\ZLCACHE			

%DATE% = Current Installation Date

Table C-4.   User Profile and Directory Structure for Installation of Web Client

Additional Files

The default base folder location for the Web Client user profile installation is %USERPRO-FILE%\Application Data\ICAClient. Table C-4 lists the file and directory structure.

Registry Entries for the Web Client

This section lists the registry changes created from the installation of the Web Client. The following registry keys assume a default installation of the client.

```
Key Name:           SOFTWARE\Citrix
Class Name:         <NO CLASS>
Last Write Time:    3/16/2004 - 4:30 P.M.

Key Name:           SOFTWARE\Citrix\CitrixCAB
Class Name:         <NO CLASS>
Last Write Time:    3/16/2004 - 4:30 P.M.
Value 0
  Name:             <NO NAME>
  Type:             REG_SZ
  Data:             1


Key Name:           SOFTWARE\Citrix\MUI
Class Name:         <NO CLASS>
```

```
Last Write Time:    3/16/2004 - 4:30 P.M.
Value 0
  Name:             ICA_DefaultLanguage
  Type:             REG_SZ
  Data:             en
```

PROGRAM NEIGHBORHOOD AGENT PACKAGE

The Program Neighborhood Agent can be installed using the following package:

▼ **ica32a.exe** A self-extracting executable, approximately 3.6MB in size. You can configure the Program Neighborhood Agent for silent user installation.

For more information on the client software, see the *Client for 32-bit Windows Administrator's Guide* and the *MetaFrame Presentation Server Administrator's Guide*.

Installed Folders and Files

This section lists the folders and files added when the Program Neighborhood Agent is installed. The locations provided are based on a default installation.

New Folders Created

The following folders are created on installation of the Program Neighborhood Agent Client:

%ProgramFiles%\Citrix\
%ProgramFiles%\Citrix\PNAgent
%ProgramFiles%\Citrix\PNAgent\Cache
%ProgramFiles%\Citrix\PNAgent\Resource
%ProgramFiles%\Citrix\PNAgent\Resource\EN

New Files Added into the Folders

Table C-5 lists the file and directory structure created by the Program Neighborhood Agent in the base installation point, %ProgramFiles%\Citrix\PNAgent.

First-time Started Application Files

This section lists the files and folders added to the user profile directory after the application is started for the first time.

%ProgramFiles%\Citrix\PNAgent			
CACHE	DIR	%DATE%	5:18:37 P.M.
RESOURCE	DIR	%DATE%	5:18:23 P.M.
acrdlg.dll	28.3KB (28,944 bytes)	2/21/2004	12:17:20 A.M.
adpcm.dll	32.3KB (33,040 bytes)	2/21/2004	12:17:20 A.M.
appsrv.ini	1.9KB (1937 bytes)	%DATE%	5:18:37 P.M.
audcvtN.dll	32.3KB (33,040 bytes)	2/21/2004	12:17:20 A.M.
cgpcfg.dll	20.3KB (20,752 bytes)	2/21/2004	12:17:20 A.M.
cgpcore.dll	68.3KB (69,904 bytes)	2/21/2004	12:17:20 A.M.
changeno.dat	0.0KB (19 bytes)	2/20/2004	11:52:38 P.M.
concentr.cnt	0.0KB (43 bytes)	1/12/2004	6:07:28 P.M.
concentr.dll	104.3KB (106,768 bytes)	2/21/2004	12:17:22 A.M.
CONCENTR.hlp	8.8KB (9,005 bytes)	1/15/2004	10:53:48 A.M.
dpihand.dll	32.3KB (33,040 bytes)	2/21/2004	12:17:22 A.M.
ICAClObj.class	4.0KB (4075 bytes)	2/21/2004	12:11:28 A.M.
icadlgn.dll	36.3KB (37,136 bytes)	2/21/2004	12:17:22 A.M.
icalogon.dll	44.3KB (45,328 bytes)	2/21/2004	12:17:22 A.M.
IICAClient.xpt	3.1KB (3169 bytes)	2/21/2004	12:11:30 A.M.
license.txt	20.6KB (21,072 bytes)	1/14/2004	12:02:22 P.M.
mfc30.dll	315.3KB (322,832 bytes)	10/23/2001	11:48:40 A.M.
migrateN.exe	52.3 KB (53520 bytes)	2/21/2004	12:16:10 A.M.
module.INI	38.1KB (39,002 bytes)	2/21/2004	12:27:20 A.M.
module.src	38.1KB (38,981 bytes)	12/1/2003	10:40:04 P.M.
msvcrt.dll	288.1KB (295,000 bytes)	2/7/2002	8:42:50 P.M.
npicaN.dll	304.3KB (311568 bytes)	2/21/2004	12:17:22 A.M.
nrhttpn.dll	44.3KB (45,328 bytes)	2/21/2004	12:17:22 A.M.

Table C-5.   Program Neighborhood Agent File and Directory Structure

nrtcpn.dll	40.3KB (41,232 bytes)	2/21/2004	12:17:22 A.M.
pcl4rast.dll	1.28MB (1,339,664 bytes)	2/21/2004	12:17:22 A.M.
pdc128N.dll	76.3KB (78,096 bytes)	2/21/2004	12:17:22 A.M.
pdcompN.dll	28.3KB (28,944 bytes)	2/21/2004	12:17:22 A.M.
pnagent.cnt	0.7KB (722 bytes)	1/21/2004	11:15:08 A.M.
pnagent.exe	208.3KB (213,264 bytes)	2/21/2004	12:16:02 A.M.
pnagent.hlp	14.0 KB (14307 bytes)	2/10/2004	4:45:44 P.M.
ProxySup.ocx	72.3KB (74,000 bytes)	2/20/2004	11:56:42 P.M.
pscript.dll	24.3KB (24,848 bytes)	2/21/2004	12:17:22 A.M.
srcflter.dll	80.3KB (82,192 bytes)	2/21/2004	12:17:22 A.M.
sslpdo.dll	20.3KB (20,752 bytes)	2/21/2004	12:17:22 A.M.
sslsdk_b.dll	56.3KB (57,616 bytes)	2/21/2004	12:17:22 A.M.
statuin.dll	32.3KB (33040 bytes)	2/21/2004	12:17:22 A.M.
tcppserv.dll	24.3KB (24,848 bytes)	2/21/2004	12:17:22 A.M.
vdcamN.dll	36.3KB (37,136 bytes)	2/21/2004	12:17:22 A.M.
vdcmN.dll	40.3KB (41,232 bytes)	2/21/2004	12:17:22 A.M.
vdcom30N.dll	48.3KB (49,424 bytes)	2/21/2004	12:17:22 A.M.
vdcpm30N.dll	32.3KB (33040 bytes)	2/21/2004	12:17:22 A.M.
vdfon30n.dll	48.3KB (49,424 bytes)	2/21/2004	12:17:22 A.M.
vdmmn.dll	40.3KB (41,232 bytes)	2/21/2004	12:17:22 A.M.
vdscardn.dll	36.3KB (37,136 bytes)	2/21/2004	12:17:22 A.M.
vdspmike.dll	24.3KB (24848 bytes)	2/21/2004	12:17:22 A.M.
VDSSPIN.dll	28.3KB (28,944 bytes)	2/21/2004	12:17:22 A.M.
vdtw30n.dll	136.3KB (139,536 bytes)	2/21/2004	12:17:22 A.M.
vdzlcn.dll	88.3KB (90,384 bytes)	2/21/2004	12:17:22 A.M.
version.dat	0.0KB (12 bytes)	2/21/2004	12:17:10 A.M.
wfclient.ini	0.5KB (553 bytes)	%DATE%	5:18:37 P.M.
wfclient.src	0.5KB (553 bytes)	2/20/2004	10:16:14 P.M.
wfcmoveN.exe	100.3KB (102,672 bytes)	2/21/2004	12:13:38 A.M.

Table C-5.   Program Neighborhood Agent File and Directory Structure (*Continued*)

wfcrun32.exe	236.3KB (241,936 bytes)	2/21/2004	12:13:34 A.M.
wfcwinn.dll	32.3KB (33,040 bytes)	2/21/2004	12:17:22 A.M.
wfica.ocx	400.3KB (409,872 bytes)	2/21/2004	12:11:26 A.M.
wfica32.exe	756.3KB (774,416 bytes)	2/21/2004	12:23:34 A.M.
winsock1.dll	24.3KB (24,848 bytes)	2/21/2004	12:17:22 A.M.
winsock2.dll	24.3KB (24,848 bytes)	2/21/2004	12:17:22 A.M.

%ProgramFiles%\Citrix\PNAgent\CACHE
%ProgramFiles%\Citrix\PNAgent\RESOURCE

EN	DIR	%DATE%	5:18:24 P.M.

%ProgramFiles%\Citrix\PNAgent\RESOURCE\EN

acrdlgUI.dll	44.3KB (45,328 bytes)	2/20/2004	11:53:28 P.M.
concenUI.dll	100.3KB (102,672 bytes)	2/20/2004	11:53:34 P.M.
icadlgUI.dll	36.3KB (37,136 bytes)	2/20/2004	11:53:36 P.M.
icalogUI.dll	32.3KB (33,040 bytes)	2/20/2004	11:53:30 P.M.
migratUI.dll	20.3KB (20,752 bytes)	2/20/2004	11:53:22 P.M.
npicaNUI.dll	40.3KB (41,232 bytes)	2/20/2004	11:52:52 P.M.
nrhttpUI.dll	44.3KB (45,328 bytes)	2/20/2004	11:52:40 P.M.
nrtcpnUI.dll	44.3KB (45,328 bytes)	2/20/2004	11:52:48 P.M.
pnagenUI.dll	128.3KB (131,344 bytes)	2/20/2004	11:52:54 P.M.
sslsdkUI.dll	24.3KB (24,848 bytes)	2/20/2004	11:53:32 P.M.
statuiUI.dll	24.3KB (24,848 bytes)	2/20/2004	11:54:04 P.M.
vdcmNUI.dll	20.3KB (20,752 bytes)	2/20/2004	11:53:06 P.M.
vdzlcnUI.dll	20.3KB (20,752 bytes)	2/20/2004	11:53:14 P.M.
wfcmovUI.dll	20.3KB (20,752 bytes)	2/20/2004	11:53:44 P.M.
wfcrunUI.dll	76.3KB (78,096 bytes)	2/20/2004	11:53:46 P.M.
wfica3UI.dll	84.3KB (86,288 bytes)	2/20/2004	11:53:16 P.M.
WficaUI.dll	44.3KB (45,328 bytes)	2/20/2004	11:52:50 P.M.

%DATE% = Current Installation Date

Table C-5.   Program Neighborhood Agent File and Directory Structure (*Continued*)

%USERPROFILE%\Application Data\Citrix			
PNAGENT	DIR	%DATE%	11:33:51 A.M.
%USERPROFILE%\Application Data\Citrix\PNAGENT			
APPCACHE	DIR	%DATE%	11:33:45 A.M.
RESOURCECACHE	DIR	%DATE%	11:34:12 A.M.
%USERPROFILE%\Application Data\Citrix\PNAGENT\APPCACHE			
appdata.xml	2.8KB (2844 bytes)	%DATE%	11:33:45 A.M.
%USERPROFILE%\Application Data\Citrix\PNAGENT\ RESOURCECACHE			

%DATE% = Curent Installation Date

Table C-6.   Program Neighborhood Agent Default User Profile File and Directory Structure

New Folder Locations

Table C-6 lists the file and directory structure for the Program Neighborhood Agent. The default base folder locations are

%USERPROFILE%\Application Data\Citrix
%USERPROFILE%\Application Data\ Citrix\PNAgent
%USERPROFILE%\Application Data\ Citrix\PNAgent\AppCache
%USERPROFILE%\Application Data\ Citrix\PNAgent\ResourceCache

Registry Entries for the ICA Win32 Program Neighborhood Agent

This section lists the registry entries for the Program Neighborhood Agent installation. These registry keys assume a default installation of the client.

```
Key Name:        SOFTWARE\Citrix
Class Name:      <NO CLASS>
Last Write Time: 3/16/2004 - 5:17 P.M.

Key Name:        SOFTWARE\Citrix\Citrix Program Neighborhood Agent
Class Name:      <NO CLASS>
Last Write Time: 3/16/2004 - 5:18 P.M.

Key Name:        SOFTWARE\Citrix\Citrix Program Neighborhood Agent\1.00.000
Class Name:      <NO CLASS>
Last Write Time: 3/16/2004 - 5:18 P.M.
```

```
Key Name:            SOFTWARE\Citrix\CitrixCAB
Class Name:          <NO CLASS>
Last Write Time:     3/16/2004 - 5:17 P.M.
Value 0
  Name:              <NO NAME>
  Type:              REG_SZ
  Data:              1


Key Name:            SOFTWARE\Citrix\MUI
Class Name:          <NO CLASS>
Last Write Time:     3/16/2004 - 5:18 P.M.
Value 0
  Name:              ICA_DefaultLanguage
  Type:              REG_SZ
  Data:              en


Key Name:            SOFTWARE\Citrix\Program Neighborhood Agent
Class Name:          <NO CLASS>
Last Write Time:     3/16/2004 - 5:18 P.M.
Value 0
  Name:              Config Url
  Type:              REG_SZ
  Data:              larryh2

Value 1
  Name:              DeleteBasedOnFilenamesOnly
  Type:              REG_DWORD
  Data:              0

Value 2
  Name:              DirectoryDepth
  Type:              REG_DWORD
  Data:              0

Value 3
  Name:              PersistentDesktopIcons
  Type:              REG_DWORD
  Data:              0x1

Value 4
  Name:              ProgramFolderName
  Type:              REG_SZ
  Data:              Citrix\MetaFrame Access Clients
```

```
Key Name:          SOFTWARE\Citrix\Program Neighborhood Agent\Uninstall
Class Name:        <NO CLASS>
Last Write Time:   3/16/2004 - 5:18 P.M.
Value 0
  Name:            0_desktop
  Type:            REG_SZ
  Data:            C:\Documents and Settings\Administrator\Desktop

Value 1
  Name:            0_IconName
  Type:            REG_SZ
  Data:            My Program Neighborhood Applications

Value 2
  Name:            0_programs
  Type:            REG_SZ
  Data:            C:\Documents and Settings\Administrator\Start Menu\Programs

Value 3
  Name:            0_RootFolder
  Type:            REG_SZ
  Data:

Value 4
  Name:            0_RootFolder_root
  Type:            REG_DWORD
  Data:            0x1

Value 5
  Name:            0_startmenu
  Type:            REG_SZ
  Data:            C:\Documents and Settings\Administrator\Start Menu

Value 6
  Name:            Cache
  Type:            REG_MULTI_SZ
  Data:            C:\Documents and Settings\Administrator\Application Data
```

APPENDIX D

Tested Hardware

The following hardware was used in the Citrix *e*Labs for testing Presentation Server.

SERVERS

Dell OptiPlex GX1	Dell OptiPlex Gxa	Dell PowerEdge 1400	Dell PowerEdge 1600SC
Dell PowerEdge 1655MC	Dell PowerEdge 1650	Dell PowerEdge 1750	Dell PowerEdge 1800
Dell PowerEdge 1850	Dell PowerEdge 1855	Dell PowerEdge 2650	Dell PowerEdge 2850
Dell PowerEdge 6650	Dell Precision 220 machines	Dell Precision 340	Dell Precision 360
Hewlett Packard NetServer E60	Hewlett Packard NetServer LXe Pro	Hewlett Packard TC4100	HP Aero
HP Deskpro DPENM	HP Deskpro DPEND	HP Deskpro EN SFF	HP Proliant DL320
HP Proliant DL360	HP Proliant DL380	HP Proliant DL580	HP EVO T20
HP Proliant 1850R	HP Proliant 800	HP Proliant 8500R	HP Proliant ML330
HP Proliant ML350	HP Proliant BL20p	HP Proliant BL25p	HP Proliant BL30p
HP Proliant BL35p	HP Proliant BL40p	HP Proliant ML150	HP Proliant DL360
HP Proliant DL585	IBM BladeCenter HS20	IBM IntelliStation APro	IBM IntelliStation EPro
IBM IntelliStation MPro	IBM NetFinity 3000	IBM NetFinity 3500 M10	IBM NetFinity 3500 M20
IBM NetFinity 5500	IBM xSeries 226	IBM xSeries 325	IBM xSeries 335
IBM xSeries 336	IBM xSeries 440		

CLIENT MACHINES

Acer Power Sd—PIV	Acer TravelMate C100	Acer TravelMate C110	Apple iMac
Apple Power MAC G4	Apple PowerBook G4	Fujitsu LifeBook P Series	Fujitsu Stylistic 4100
Fujitsu Stylistic ST4000 tablet PC	HP Jornada	HP TabletPC	IBM IntelliStation M-Series
IBM IntelliStation E-Series	IBM ThinkPad R32	Sun Blade 150	Sun Ultra 5
Toshiba Portege 3500	ViewSonic Airpanel 100	Wyse Winterms WT9450, WT1200LE	

TWAIN TESTING

Canon CanonScan 3200F	Epson Perfection 3170 Photo—USB	Hewlett Packard OfficeJet 7130 All-In-One
Hewlett Packard ScanJet 8290	Microtek ScanMaker 5950—USB	QuickCam Messenger Logitech
Visioneer OneTouch 9320	Xerox DocuMate 510	

CLIENT PERIPHERAL DEVICES

HHP USB Barcode Scanner

FOR PDA SYNCHRONIZATION

DELL AXIM X5   HP iPAQ h4350   HP iPAQ h4150

STRONG AUTHENTICATION

Identix Biometric Login
USB devices (fingerprint)

Panasonic PrivateID iris-scan

Precise Biometrics 100MC
fingerprint readers (USB)

Startek fingerprint reader (USB)

BI-DIRECTIONAL AUDIO DEVICES

Philips SpeechMike 6174

Philips SpeechMike 6184

Philips SpeechMike Classic 6164

Philips SpeechMike Pro 6284

WIRELESS NETWORK INTERFACE CARDS

Cisco Aircards (802.11b)   DLink DWL-650+ Wireless Card (22MB)   Sierra Wireless PCMCIA cards

PRINTERS

Dell Laser 1700n	Dell Laser 3100cn	Dell Workgroup Laser M5200	Dell Workgroup Laser W5300
Dell Laser 5100cn	HP Color LaserJet 4550DN	HP DesignJet 5000	HP DeskJet 5550
HP DeskJet 5700	HP DeskJet 5740	HP DeskJet 6540	HP DeskJet 5650
HP DeskJet 6122	HP LaserJet 4600	HP LaserJet 4200	HP Business InkJet 1100
HP Business InkJet 2300	Lexmark All-in-one X6170 Inkjet	Ricoh Afficio CL-7100 with 2-tray finisher and duplex unit	

NETWORKING DEVICES

Alteon 2424 Load Balancer

Checkpoint Firewall-1 Firewall

Cisco Wireless WAP

Cisco LocalDirector 416

Cisco PIX 515 Firewall Appliance

EMC Celerra SE

F5 BigIP 540 Load Balancer

Gateway ALR 7200

HP ProCurve Switches

HP StorageWorks FC-AL Switch

HP StorageWorks RA4100

HP StorageWorks MSA1000

HP StorageWorks MSA1500

HP TaskSmart N2400

Lucent NavisRadius

Lucent Pipeline ISDN Router

NCipher nForce SSL Accelerator Card

Net6 SSL VPN

Nortel Networks Alteon 184 hardware load balancer

Nortel Networks Alteon Application Switch 2424 Load Balancing Device

Packeteer AppVantage ASM-70

Packeteer PacketShaper 2500

Packeteer Packetshaper 4500

Rainbow CryptoSwift 200 SSL Accelerator Cards

Rainbow CryptoSwift 600 SSL Accelerator Cards

RSA SecurID

Secure Computing Gauntlet G2 Firewall

Secure Computing SafeWord

Shunra Storm

APPENDIX E

Citrix Presentation Server 4.0 for Microsoft Windows Server 2003 x64 Edition

With the introduction of support for Microsoft Windows Server 2003 x64 Edition, there are new technical items to consider. The following topics address load balancing published applications in a mixed environment, consisting of both 32-bit and 64-bit servers in a Presentation Server farm, and utilizing the PDA Synchronization feature with ActiveSync 4.0 on a 64-bit Presentation Server.

LOAD BALANCING PUBLISHED APPLICATIONS IN A MIXED ENVIRONMENT

By default, on a Presentation Server where drive letters are not remapped, most applications on 32-bit servers are installed in C:\program files\. On 64-bit servers, however, most 32-bit applications, by default, are installed in C:\program files (x86). If you want to load balance published applications in a mixed environment, you must ensure that the application path for the published application for each server correctly identifies its location.

To edit the path during the publishing process:

1. In the Management Console for Presentation Server, under the Applications node, right-click the application you want to load balance.

2. Click Properties.

3. From the left pane, click Servers. In the Configured Servers list, select a server, click Edit Configuration, and then verify the path.

NOTE   If the server is a 32-bit server and the path is correct, all the 32-bit servers in the list will be correct as well. Similarly, the same is true if you select a 64-bit server and the path is correct.

4. After you identify the servers with the incorrect paths, select all the servers with the incorrect paths and click Edit Configuration.

5. In the Command Line field, type the correct location of the published application.

6. Correct the Working Directory, if necessary.

7. Click OK. Then, click OK again to return to the Management Console.

Similarly, the installation paths you may choose to specify when installing applications may be different on 32-bit and 64-bit servers in your farm. The same procedure as the previous one can be used to specify your applications' customized locations.

USING ACTIVESYNC 4.0

To use ActiveSync on a 64-bit Presentation Server, you must install and publish ActiveSync 4.0 in a Citrix Application Isolation Environment (AIE). This involves the following actions:

▼ Creating an AIE using the Management Console for MetaFrame Presentation Server

■ Creating rules for the AIE

■ Installing ActiveSync 4.0 in the AIE

■ Publishing ActiveSync 4.0 in the AIE

▲ Associating other applications outside the AIE to ActiveSync 4.0

To Create an AIE Using the Presentation Server Console

1. Launch the Management Console.
2. Right-click the Isolation Environments node and click New isolation environment.
3. Name the isolation environment and click OK.

To Configure the First AIE Rule

1. In the Citrix Management Console, click the Isolation Environments node.
2. In the right pane, right-click the isolation environment that you created and click Properties.
3. In the left pane, click Rules, and then click Add.
4. In the Action group box, click Isolate. Then, in the Object group box, click Named Objects.
5. Click Next, and then click Add.
6. In the Named field, type **global\AS_ACCEPTANCE_SEMA**, and then click OK.
7. Click Add and, in the Named field, type **global\RAPIMgr8a0cc91f-759a-4b35-9906-d7e44ffc4d88**.
8. Click OK, and then Next.
9. Click "Per isolation environment," and then click Next.
10. Assign a name or accept the default name, and then click Finish.

To Configure the Second AIE Rule

1. Click Add.
2. In the Action group box, click Ignore. In the Object group box, click Registry Entries.

3. Click Next, and then click "Some registry entries."

4. Click Add. Then, in the Choose Registry Entry dialog box, from the Hive list, click HKEY_LOCAL_MACHINE.

5. In the Key field, type **Software\Citrix\IMA**, and then click OK.

6. Click Next, and then Finish.

7. Click OK to close the dialog box.

To Install ActiveSync 4.0 in the AIE

1. From a command prompt, change directory to the folder where the ActiveSync 4.0 install program is located.

2. At the command prompt, type **aiesetup** *<isolation environment name> <ActiveSync 4.0 install program name>*. For example, if the isolation environment name is AS-Isolation and the ActiveSync 4.0 installation program name is setup.exe, type the command **aiesetup AS-Isolation setup.exe**.

3. Press ENTER. The Microsoft ActiveSync 4.0 Installation dialog box appears.

4. Install ActiveSync 4.0.

5. After the installation is complete, click Finish. Then, press ENTER and proceed with the application discovery process.

6. When the process is complete, close the window.

To Publish ActiveSync 4.0 in the AIE

1. In the Management Console, right-click the Applications node, and then click Publish Application.

2. In the Display Name and Application Description fields, identify the application and click Next.

3. In the Specify What To Publish page, select the Isolate Application check box and click Settings.

4. In the Isolation environment list, click the isolation environment you created for ActiveSync.

5. Select the "Application was installed into environment" check box.

6. In the "Choose installed application" box, click Microsoft ActiveSync.

7. Click OK, and then click Next.

8. Follow the remaining wizard instructions to publish the application and assign users.

NOTE   You can install and publish Microsoft Outlook and Word applications normally (outside of AIE), but you must associate them with the same isolation environment that ActiveSync 4.0 is installed and published under.

To Associate Published Applications That Reside Outside the ActiveSync AIE

1. After you install and publish Microsoft Outlook or Word, in the Citrix Management Console, click the Isolation Environments node.

2. Right-click the isolation environment where you installed and published ActiveSync 4.0.

3. Click Properties.

4. In the left pane, click Applications, and then click Add.

5. From the list of applications, click the published application (for example, Outlook or Word), and then click OK. The application is associated with the isolation environment you created for ActiveSync.

Important Notes

▼ ActiveSync 4.0 is not supported on Citrix Presentation Server for 32-bit servers.

■ The PDA Synchronization feature of Citrix Presentation Server for Microsoft Windows Server 2003 x64 Edition does not support the Remote Application Programming Interface (RAPI).

■ The PDA Synchronization feature is supported only through ActiveSync 4.0 published application sessions (PDA Synchronization is not supported in a desktop session running an ActiveSync 4.0 application).

■ The PDA Synchronization feature is supported only on the Enterprise version of Citrix Presentation Server for Microsoft Windows Server 2003 x64 Edition.

▲ To enable the Explore functionality of ActiveSync 4.0 on 64-bit platforms, you must add the following Microsoft registry keys to the registry using regedit.exe:

```
[HKEY_LOCAL_MACHINE\SOFTWARE\Wow6432Node\Microsoft\WindowsNT\CurrentVersion\
Terminal Server\Compatibility\Applications\wcescomm]
"Flags"=dword:0x00000408

[HKEY_LOCAL_MACHINE\SOFTWARE\Wow6432Node\Microsoft\WindowsNT\CurrentVersion\
Terminal Server\Compatibility\Applications\wcesmgr]
"Flags"=dword:0x00000408
```

NOTE   16-bit TWAIN drivers are not supported. On Citrix Presentation Server 4.0 for Microsoft Windows Server 2003 x64 Edition, only 32-bit TWAIN applications are supported.

Sample .REG File

The following is an example of a simple file that can be copied to Notepad and saved as a .reg file to automate enabling these flags on your Presentation Server.

```
Windows Registry Editor Version 5.00
[HKEY_LOCAL_MACHINE\SOFTWARE\Microsoft\Windows NT\CurrentVersion\Terminal
Server\Compatibility\Applications\Photoshop]
"Flags"=dword:00000408
```

For Citrix Presentation Server 4.0 for Microsoft Windows Server 2003 x64 Edition, the registry location should be specified as:

```
[HKEY_LOCAL_MACHINE\SOFTWARE\Wow6432Node\Microsoft\Windows NT\CurrentVersion\Terminal
Server\Compatibility\Applications\Photoshop]

"Flags"=dword:00000408
```

ADVANTAGES OF WINDOWS SERVER 2003 x64 EDITION AND CITRIX PRESENTATION SERVER x64

The following sections discuss the performance and scalability improvements you may realize when using Citrix Presentation Server 4.0 for Microsoft Windows Server 2003 x64 Edition. Items discussed include performance improvements in the x64 operating system and results from scalability testing performed in Citrix' *e*labs.

Increased Kernel Memory Availability

In 32-bit Windows, memory is limited to the 32-bit address space, thus limiting the amount of virtual memory that can be directly addressed to 4GB (232). This 4GB of addressable memory is divided into two equal parts: 2GB allocated to processes and 2GB allocated to the operating system that is used for the kernel memory, system cache, and drivers.

The /PAE switch in the Boot.ini file can be enabled to increase the physical memory on the server. This switch allows Windows Server 2003 to take advantage of the Physical Address Extensions (PAE) of x86 processors. Using the /PAE switch can be beneficial in situations where servers are not kernel memory–bound and the published applications use large amounts of memory. The memory enabled with the /PAE switch is allocated to the user space while the kernel is still limited to 2GB. There is also a small kernel memory cost because the operating system needs to track this additional memory in the form of PTEs (Page Table Entries). Note that the /PAE switch requires programmers to use the Address Windows Extensions (AWE) application programming interface (API) to take advantage of the memory.

Physical Memory Limits	32-bit	64-bit
Windows Server 2003, Standard Edition	4GB	32GB
Windows Server 2003, Enterprise Edition	64GB	1TB
Windows Server 2003, Datacenter Edition	64GB	1TB
General Memory Limits	**32-bit**	**64-bit**
Total virtual address space (based on a single process)	4GB	16TB
Virtual address space per 32-bit process	2GB*	4GB*
Virtual address space per 64-bit process	Not applicable	8TB
Paged pool	470MB	128GB
Nonpaged pool	256MB	128GB
System Page Table Entry (PTE)	660MB to 900MB	128GB

*   Higher if compiled with /LARGEADDRESSAWARE

Table E-1.   Limitations of Windows Server 2003 Running on a 32-bit Platform Versus Windows Server 2003 Running on a 64-bit Platform

One of the most obvious advantages of using Presentation Server x64 with Windows Server 2003 x64 Edition is the increased virtual address space. Windows Server 2003 x64 Edition can address 16TB of virtual memory. This 16TB is divided into equal parts of 8TB of virtual address space for applications and 8TB for the operating system. Based on this increase in available user and kernel memory, Presentation Server can be expected to reach new scalability plateaus without architectural limitations getting in the way. Table E-1 compares the limitations of Windows Server 2003 running on a 32-bit platform to Windows Server 2003 running on a 64-bit platform.

Server Consolidation by Scaling Up

32-bit Windows servers are limited in their ability to scale up. This limitation is based on the kernel memory constraint. Now that 64-bit has eliminated the kernel memory constraint, Presentation Server x64 has the ability to scale up to unprecedented levels.

The advantages of scaling up with larger, more powerful servers revolve around the lower cost associated with managing fewer servers. Server consolidation leads to cost savings by:

▼ Allowing for fewer administrators to maintain physical servers

■ Reducing overhead in managing hotfixes, service packs, and other updates

■ Utilizing a smaller footprint in the data center, which lowers power and space consumption

■ Lowering software costs due to reduced server-based licensing

▲ Saving on infrastructure costs

For example, a company that needs to support 10,000 users on Presentation Server would need to purchase and maintain 50 dual- or quad-processor 32-bit servers to service the population, while they would need only 32 quad-processor 64-bit servers.

Compatibility with Existing Applications and Easy Migration from 32-bit

Windows Server 2003 x64 Edition can execute 64-bit and 32-bit applications. This is accomplished by running 32-bit applications inside the WoW64 (Windows on Windows 64) execution layer. WoW64 isolates 32-bit applications from 64-bit applications while providing interoperability and data exchange through COM and remote procedure calls (RPC). It also prevents file and registry collisions between 32-bit and 64-bit versions of the same application. 64-bit applications that are written to run natively in Windows Server 2003 x64 Edition have full access to the large virtual memory address space (16TB).

There are some limitations when running 32-bit applications inside WoW64. These include the inability to directly access the operating system's 64-bit DLLs and the inability to address the larger memory pool that Windows Server 2003 x64 Edition offers. WoW64 does not support most 16-bit applications and all kernel mode drivers must be 64-bit. From a performance perspective, 32-bit applications running through WoW64 can cause a small degradation in performance when compared to a native 32-bit system.

Another important compatibility feature of Windows Server 2003 x64 Edition is the binary compatibility between the AMD64 and Intel EM64T processors that support the x64 extensions.

This allows administrators to purchase the latest hardware on the market and reap the benefits of the faster processor and bus speeds running their 32-bit applications, while waiting for their applications to be ported to 64-bit.

Increased Hardware Capability and Performance

A major area of improved efficiency in the 64-bit architecture is the increased number of registers available. All 32-bit x86 processors are limited to eight 32-bit general-purpose registers, eight floating-point registers, and eight SSE/SSE2 registers. The 64-bit architecture uses twice as many general-purpose registers, each a full 64-bits wide, and doubles the number of 128-bit wide SSE/SSE2 registers to 16.

Another performance improvement with the 64-bit architecture is the gain in overall I/O efficiency and throughput. With support for greater physical memory and memory address space, caches can be substantially larger than in 32-bit Windows, enabling the Windows x64 Editions to fully utilize the improved I/O hardware available, such as PCI Express, to improve overall I/O performance. The larger address space allows more I/O to be in progress simultaneously.

CITRIX PRESENTATION SERVER x64 SCALABILITY AND PERFORMANCE

This section contains the results of scalability and performance tests run against Citrix Presentation Server x64 in Citrix' *e*labs.

Test Methodology

For Citrix Presentation Server x64 deployments, many hardware and software choices must be made. The largest of these choices is the decision to scale up by adding more powerful servers or scale out by adding more servers to the farm. While there is no substitute for in-house scalability testing based on a planned deployment, this section helps in the decision-making process by illustrating the capabilities of Presentation Server x64 running on Windows Server 2003 Enterprise x64 Edition.

Several important factors need to be taken into consideration when determining the number of users that a server can support. Sizing the Presentation Server deployment depends on the following criteria:

▼ Hardware specifications of the Presentation Server (CPU, memory, and disk)

■ Application requirements

■ User activity

▲ Maximum desired resource usage on the server, for example:

    ▼ 80% CPU usage

    ■ 70% memory usage

    ▲ User response times

Citrix ICAMark 3.0 was used for all Presentation Server user capacity measurements in this chapter.

User Load Simulation

Citrix ICAMark 3.0 is an internal tool that is based on the Citrix Server Test Kit (CSTK). This tool is used by Citrix Product Development for benchmarking purposes to simulate the number of client sessions that can be connected to a computer running Presentation Server with acceptable performance.

ICAMark measures the user capacity based on the session response time for a particular iteration. As part of these measurements, it calculates a score that is used to determine the server scalability. All tests are run until the resource thresholds are met or the end-user experience degrades below the defined threshold.

The test simulates users performing various actions in Microsoft Excel 2003, Microsoft Access 2003, and Microsoft PowerPoint 2003. For this paper, all applications run with ICAMark 3.0 are 32-bit applications. It is important to remember when comparing the results from this paper with another environment that different applications will utilize more or less memory and CPU than Microsoft Office 2003, producing different results.

Test Profiles

The ICAMark test has different user profiles that determine which applications are launched and what actions are performed in the applications. All tests are verified not to be bound by disk or network resources.

Light User   The light user is considered a data entry worker; these users employ the basic functionality within a single application. The light user works at a slower pace with occasional pauses. This test is indicative of environments where applications or kernel memory tend to be the limiting factor on single server scalability.

The Light User script opens Microsoft Excel and simulates the input of data in a spreadsheet. The simulated users in this test are constantly typing in Microsoft Excel 2003 at around 20 words per minute. The ICAMark score is calculated by comparing a calibration value of the script run time with the time gathered during the iteration. The calibration value was determined by running the scripts as one user. Each script was run locally and the data was recorded.

Heavy User   The heavy user is a user that utilizes the many functions available for applications he or she launches. These users consistently work at an accelerated pace moving from one application to the next. The Heavy User test is indicative of environments where CPU tends to be the bottleneck in single server scalability.

In the Heavy User test, after the first 10 users are logged on, ICAMark launches simulated user scripts on all 10 sessions. Each script opens Microsoft Excel and creates a spreadsheet with formulas and graphs. The script then simulates the creation of an Access database, including a table, query, and form, with data manipulation. When the Access phase is complete, a Microsoft PowerPoint presentation is created of six slides, including spell checking, font changes, slide copies, and deletions. The simulated users are constantly typing in these applications at an average of 40 words per minute and can be considered more "rigorous" than normal users.

When a script is finished, it remains idle until the scripts on all sessions are complete. The next iteration is then launched, adding 10 more sessions to the test. Iterations are continued to a predetermined maximum number of users. The ICAMark score is calculated by comparing a calibration value of the script time with the time gathered during the iteration. The calibration value was determined by running the scripts with a single user.

Typical results for the Heavy User profile show that session response time drops due to a lack of CPU resources.

PTE Limited Test

The PTE Limited test is designed to measure the maximum number of lightly loaded client sessions that can be connected to Presentation Server. Lightly loaded sessions can be equated to a user logging on the server and using minimal CPU when using applications.

The test begins by connecting a set number of users to the Presentation Server. Once the users are connected, the three applications (Access, Excel, and PowerPoint) are launched and verified to be functional. Then the next set of users is connected and the process repeats until a session connection or application launch failure occurs.

The typical bottleneck for this test is Page Table Entry exhausting in kernel memory.

CPU Utilization Test

The CPU utilization test uses the standard ICAMark Heavy User test with the addition of a CPU consumer application. The CPU consumer application uses a constant 20% of the server's CPU while running in a user session. This control session runs in parallel to all other sessions and is not running any scripts.

By increasing the CPU usage through the control session, users begin to compete for the remaining CPU cycles in order to complete the scripted tasks inside their applications. This is where the CPU utilization feature reduces the CPU usage of the control session in order to match up with the rest of the sessions running on the system.

Typical results for the CPU utilization test show that the fail point is reached and session response time drops due to the lack of CPU resources.

Virtual Memory Optimization Test

The virtual memory optimization test is designed to measure the maximum number of users that can be supported through the memory savings of the Virtual Memory Optimization feature. Each test iteration begins by launching ten ICA sessions to Presentation Server. Once each session is connected, a script is run that launches Microsoft Visio 2000 SR1. This script then opens two Visio drawings, each about 7MB in size. After each iteration is complete, the memory usage of the system is recorded. This process is continued until the system is out of memory. The number of users on the system at that time is the baseline. The system is then rebooted and the Virtual Memory Optimization feature is enabled. The process begins again until the system is out of memory. This second step is necessary because the Virtual Memory Optimization feature needs to detect the DLL conflicts before it can rebase them. After the system is rebooted a second time, all DLL conflicts will be rebased. The process starts a third time to realize the user scalability benefits of the Virtual Memory Optimization feature.

Operating System's Effect on Citrix Presentation Server Scalability

Presentation Server scalability is dependent on the underlying Windows operating system architecture. Since Windows 2000, each subsequent Windows release has increased the scalability of Presentation Server. The next section illustrates how user scalability is affected when the server hardware remains the same and the operating system is upgraded.

The operating system scalability enhancements when upgrading Windows versions is due in large part to kernel memory enhancements. When moving from Windows 2000 to Windows 2003, the scalability increase is attributed to substantial memory manager changes that allow the operating system to use kernel memory more efficiently when compared to Windows 2000 Server. These changes include an increased number of System PTEs and dynamic allocation of kernel memory. When moving from the 32-bit Windows 2000 and Windows 2003, the scalability increase is due to the increase of kernel memory size from 2GB to 8TB.

Table E-2 shows the difference in user scalability across Windows 2000 Server, Windows Server 2003 32-bit, and Windows Server 2003 x64 running Presentation Server. For this test, the Light User test profile was used, since it is indicative of kernel memory–bound environments.

All measurements for this test scenario were gathered on a server with four AMD 848 Opteron processors running at 2.2 GHz with 1MB L2 cache.

NOTE For specific server details, please refer to the "Hardware" section at the end of this chapter.

Test Results

A paged pool kernel memory bottleneck is encountered at 108 users on Windows 2000 Server and 201 users on Windows Server 2003. Presentation Server 4.0 scales 86% higher when moving from Windows 2000 Server to Windows Server 2003 32-bit.

Test Profile	Presentation Server 4.0 (Windows 2000)	Presentation Server 4.0 (Windows 2003)	Presentation Server x64 (Windows 2003 x64)
Light User	108 ± 1	201 ± 1 (86% improvement over Windows 2000)	327 ± 1 (203% improvement over Windows 2000)

Table E-2. Difference in Presentation Server 4.0 User Scalability Across Different Operating Systems

The kernel memory bottlenecks on the Windows 2000 Server and Windows Server 2003 32-bit platforms do not exist on Presentation Server x64 and Windows Server 2003 x64 Edition. The increased kernel memory capacity of 64-bit Windows leads to a 203% scalability increase over Presentation Server 4.0 on Windows 2000 Server with the same hardware and applications. If upgrading from Windows 2000 Server to Windows Server 2003 x64 as part of a Presentation Server deployment or upgrade, organizations can realize over three times more users per server.

Test Profile Effects on Presentation Server Scalability

User capacity is highly dependent on the application type and application usage in Presentation Server environments. In this section, the scalability benefits of Presentation Server 4.0 x64 are compared against the Presentation Server 4.0 for the Heavy and Light User test profiles.

The Light User profile simulates users that perform tasks such as data entry. The Light User test is less strenuous than the Heavy User test, allowing Presentation Server to exploit the larger memory pool offered by 64-bit Windows. The Light User profile hits kernel memory bottlenecks in 32-bit Windows well before a CPU bottleneck occurs.

The Heavy User profile simulates users that put higher demands on the CPU. Environments with users that closely match the Heavy User profile may see different scalability results when moving to Presentation Server 4.0 x64. This occurs as CPU intensive applications consume much more CPU before hitting a kernel memory bottleneck in 32-bit Windows.

The PTE Limited test simulates the lightest user profile. The PTE Limited test has very minimal CPU utilization and is indicative of environments were applications are loaded in the background and rarely used. Table E-3 shows the maximum number of sessions that can be connected before running out of all kernel memory on the server.

Test Profile	Citrix Presentation Server 4.0	Citrix Presentation Server x64	Difference
Light User	201 ± 1	327 ± 1	+63%
Heavy User	201 ± 1	255 ± 1	+27%
PTE Limited	235 ± 1	1000+	N/A

Table E-3.   Maximum Number of Sessions That Can Be Connected Before Running Out of All Kernel Memory

All measurements were gathered on a server with four AMD 848 Opteron processors running at 2.2 GHz with 1MB L2 cache. In both 32-bit and 64-bit mode, the server was configured with 32GB of memory. The /PAE switch was enabled for all 32-bit scalability tests.

NOTE   For specific server details, please refer to the "Hardware" section at the end of this chapter.

Light User Results

On a 32-bit system, even though the Light User script is less CPU intensive, the test fails at the same point as the Heavy User script. Kernel memory limitations prevent the 32-bit system from scaling higher regardless of the memory resources and processing power available to the server. On a 64-bit system with Presentation Server x64, quad processor servers show a 63% increase in scalability over Presentation Server 4.0 and Windows Server 2003.

Heavy User Profile Results

The Heavy User test is designed to represent environments where computers running Presentation Server are CPU bound. The 27% improvement is much lower than the 63% seen using the Light User profile because the 32-bit results already realize performance gains in moving from a dual-processor to a quad-processor server. The Light User test has the same scalability results on a dual- and quad-processor system due to kernel memory limitations being realized on a dual system. Even though this test is designed to hit a CPU bottleneck, it can become kernel memory–bound as the number of processors is scaled in the system, especially on 32-bit operating systems.

PTE (Page Table Entries) Limited User Profile

PTEs play an important role in Presentation Server scalability. A Presentation Server could potentially have thousands of processes running simultaneously. Each process requires memory, which in turn requires PTEs. When PTEs are depleted, the operating system is unable to allocate memory and the system will fail. This section discusses the difference in user capacity between Citrix Presentation Server 4.0 and Citrix Presentation Server x64 when faced with a Page Table Entry kernel memory bottleneck.

A PTE is used to associate a process with a memory page. The operating system must keep track of the memory usage for each process and decipher the process's actual memory usage to physical memory or page file locations. In order to accomplish this, the system creates a memory page table for each process within the nonpaged pool section of kernel memory. This page table is an index that keeps track of the actual locations of a process's memory pages. Each entry in this table tracks a different memory page and is called a *Page Table Entry*.

A PTE bottleneck is defined as having fewer than 3000 PTEs available to the operating system. If a low PTE situation occurs, scalability can be increased by modifying the System Pages registry key. However, increasing the number of PTEs will reduce the amount of Paged Pool available to the operating system.

Processor Type	Configuration	Presentation Server 4.0	Presentation Server x64	Difference
AMD64 Opteron	Quad Processor	201 ± 1	255 ± 1	+27%
Intel EM64T Xeon	Quad Processor (HT enabled)	201 ± 1	265 ± 1	+31%

Table E-4.   Similar Performance Between AMD64 Opteron and Intel EM64T Xeon in Quad-processor Configurations

By increasing the kernel memory from 2GB in 32-bit Windows to 8TB in 64-bit Windows, PTE bottlenecks are eliminated. Presentation Server x64 scales well beyond 1,000 users without encountering any PTE bottlenecks, while 32-bit Presentation Server runs out of PTEs at 235 users.

Processor Type Compatibility

The AMD64 Opteron and Intel EM64T Xeon architectures provide a smooth migration path from 32-bit systems to 64-bit systems by running 32-bit applications inside the WoW64 execution layer. This allows administrators to purchase the latest x64 hardware on the market and reap the benefits of the faster processor and bus speeds running their 32-bit applications, while waiting for their applications to be ported to 64-bit.

Although the underlying architectures are different, both the AMD64 Opteron and Intel EM64T processors exhibit similar scalability trends, as shown in Table E-4. Both systems reached failure points due to CPU bottlenecks, showing that their bus and memory subsystems are capable of supporting four processors and can maximize the benefits of Presentation Server x64. These numbers are not meant for comparison but to show that both platforms are equally capable in quad-processor configurations.

HARDWARE

The following sections list the hardware used in the performance tests mentioned in this chapter.

Servers

The following are the hardware specifications for the machines used as servers in the tests mentioned in this chapter.

HP Proliant DL585	AMD Opteron 848 Quad Processor Server
CPU	4 x 2.2 GHz AMD 848 Opteron, 2.2 GHz, 1MB L2 Cache, 1 GHz HT
Memory	32GB PC2100 DDR SDRAM, 266 MHz
Hard Drive	4 x Hot Plug SCSI 36GB Ultra320 RAID 1
Network Adapter	Embedded NC7782 Dual Port PCI-X 10/100/1000T Gigabit
HP Proliant DL585	AMD Opteron 850 Quad Processor Dual-Core Server
CPU	4 x 2.2 GHz AMD 850 Opteron, 1MB L2/Core Cache, 1 GHz HT
Memory	32GB PC2700 DDR SDRAM, 333 MHz
Hard Drive	2 x Hot Plug SCSI 36 GB Ultra320 RAID 1
Network Adapter	Embedded NC7782 Dual Port PCI-X 10/100/1000T Gigabit
HP Proliant DL580	Intel Xeon MP 3.3 GHz Quad Processor Server
CPU	4 x 3.3 GHz Intel Xeon MP, 8MB L3 Cache, 667 MHz FSB
Memory	32GB PC3200 DDR2 SDRAM, 400 MHz
Hard Drive	2 x SCSI 36GB Ultra320 RAID 1
Network Adapter	Broadcom Netxtreme Gigabit Dual Port PCI-X 10/100/1000T
Dell PowerEdge 6850	Intel Xeon MP 3.06 GHz Quad Processor Server
CPU	3.06 GHz Intel Xeon MP, 8MB L3 Cache, 667 MHz FSB
Memory	32GB PC3200 DDR2 SDRAM, 400 MHz
Hard Drive	2 x SCSI 36GB Ultra320 RAID 1
Network Adapter	Dual Embedded Broadcom Gigabit[2] 5704
Dell PowerEdge 2850	Intel Xeon 3.0 GHz Dual Processor Server
CPU	2 x 3.0 GHz Intel Xeon, 1MB L2 Cache, 800 MHz FSB
Memory	8GB Memory PC3200 DDR2 SDRAM, 400 MHz
Hard Drive	2 x Hot Plug SCSI 36 GB Ultra320 15K RAID 1
Network Adapter	Broadcom Netxtreme Gigabit Ethernet
Dell PowerEdge 1600SC	Intel Xeon 2.0 GHz Dual Processor Server
CPU	2 x 2.0 GHz Intel Xeon, 512KB L2 Cache, 533 MHz FSB
Memory	4GB Memory
Hard Drive	2 x Hot Plug SCSI 36 GB Ultra320 10K RAID 1
Network Adapter	Broadcom Netxtreme Gigabit Ethernet

Clients

The following are the hardware specifications for the client machines used for the tests mentioned in this chapter.

Dell PowerEdge 1750

CPU	Intel Xeon, 2.8 GHz, 512KB L2 Cache, 533 MHz FSB
Memory	1GB Memory
Hard Drive	MAXTOR 18GB, SCSI, U320, 15K
Network Adapter	Broadcom Netxtreme Gigabit Ethernet

Control System

IBM Netfinity 3000

CPU	Intel Pentium III 600 MHz, 512KB L2 Cache, 100 MHz FSB
Memory	768MB of SDRAM ECC
Hard Drive	Wide Ultra SCSI (PCI adapter), 9.1GB
Network Adapter	10/100 Network Adapter

INDEX

B

D

O

S

98% of the *Fortune* 500 use Citrix.

Obviously, there's room for improvement

When it comes to customers, we set the bar very high. Sure, 98% of the *Fortune* 500 use our software to deploy applications centrally so their workers have secure, easy, and instant access to business-critical information — anywhere, anytime, from any device, over any connection. But we won't be happy until the CIO of every company is running their organization as an on-demand enterprise — realizing the benefits of saving millions on their IT costs, ensuring secure access to information, improving employee productivity and increasing their business agility. As over 160,000 Citrix customers already do. To learn what we can do for your organization, visit **www.citrix.com**

Best Access Experience. Anytime. Anywhere.